THE LIFE OF
JESUS CHRIST
and
BIBLICAL REVELATIONS

Volume III

D1483296

Venerable Anne Catherine Emmerich
1774-1824
Mystic, Stigmatist, Visionary, and Prophet

THE LIFE OF JESUS CHRIST

and

BIBLICAL REVELATIONS

From the Visions of the Venerable
Anne Catherine Emmerich
as recorded in the journals of
Clemens Brentano

Arranged and edited by the Very Reverend
Carl E. Schmöger, C.SS.R.

Translated by an American Nun

Volume III

TAN BOOKS AND PUBLISHERS, INC.
Rockford, Illinois 61105

Nihil Obstat:
Em. DE JAEGHER
Can. lib. cens.
Brugis, 14 Februarii 1914

Imprimatur:
A. C. DE SCHREVEL
Vic. gen.
Brugis, 14 Februarii 1914

Originally published in 1914 by Desclée, De Brouwer & Co. of Lille, Paris, and Bruges, in conjunction with The Sentinel Press of New York. Reprinted by Academy Library Guild in 1954, and later by Apostolate of Christian Action, both of Fresno, California. Reprinted in 1979 by TAN Books and Publishers, Inc. Retypeset and published again in 1986 by TAN Books and Publishers, Inc.

Library of Congress Catalog Card No.: 86-50154

ISBN: Volume 1—0-89555-289-2
Volume 2—0-89555-290-6
Volume 3—0-89555-291-4
Volume 4—0-89555-292-2
The Set—0-89555-293-0

Printed and bound in the United States of America.

TAN BOOKS AND PUBLISHERS, INC.
P.O. Box 424
Rockford, Illinois 61105

1986

"But there are also many other things which Jesus did; which, if they were written every one, the world itself, I think, would not be able to contain the books that should be written."

—St. John the Evangelist
(*John* 21:25)

Ephesus

Tarsus

Antioch

Salamis
CYPRUS

Mt. Libanus
Damascus
Ornithopolis
Tyre   *Mt. Hermon*
Haifa   GESSUR

KED

Jerusalem
Ascalon   *Madian? (Madaba*
Gaza
Bersabee

Alexandria
Sais
Rameses
GOSHEN
Petra
EGYPT   SINAI
Heliopolis
Memphis

ARABIA

Mt. Sinai

Thebes

Miles
25   50   100   200
10   25   50   100
"Hours" or Leagues

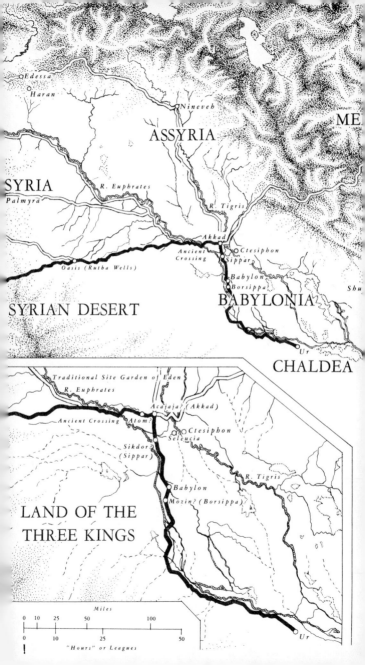

Edessa
Haran
Nineveh
ASSYRIA
ME
SYRIA
R. Euphrates
Palmyra
R. Tigris
Akkad
Ancient
Crossing
Ctesiphon
Sippar
Oasis (Rutba Wells)
Babylon
Borsippa
Shu
SYRIAN DESERT
BABYLONIA
Ur
CHALDEA

Traditional Site Garden of Eden
R. Euphrates
Acajaja? (Akkad)
Ancient Crossing Atom?
Ctesiphon
Sikdor?
Seleucia
(Sippar)
R. Tigris
Babylon
LAND OF THE
THREE KINGS
Mozin? (Borsippa)

Miles
0   10   25   50   100
0   10   25   50
"Hours" or Leagues
Ur

ANNE CATHERINE EMMERICH

ANNE CATHERINE EMMERICH was born on September 8th, 1774, at Flamske, near Koesfeld, Westphalia, in West Germany, and became a nun of the Augustinian Order on November 13th, 1803, in the Convent of Agnetenberg at Dülmen (also in Westphalia). She died on February 9th, 1824. Although of simple education, she had perfect consciousness of her earliest days and could understand the liturgical Latin from her first time at Mass.

During most of her later years she would vomit up even the simplest food or drink, subsisting for long periods almost entirely on water and the Holy Eucharist. She was told in mystic vision that her gift of seeing past, present and future was greater than that possessed by anyone·else in history.

From the year 1812 until her death, she bore the stigmata of Our Lord, including a cross over her heart and wounds from the crown of thorns. Though Anne Catherine Emmerich was an invalid confined to bed during her later years, her funeral was nevertheless attended by a greater concourse of mourners than any other remembered by the oldest inhabitants of Dülmen.

Her mission in life seems to have been to suffer in expiation for the godlessness that darkened the "Age of Enlightenment" and the era of the Napoleonic wars, a time during which she saw her convent closed and her order suppressed by Napoleon.

During the last five years of her life the day-by-day transcription of her visions and mystical experiences was recorded by Clemens Brentano, poet, literary leader,

friend of Goethe and Görres, who, from the time he met
her, abandoned his distinguished career and devoted the
rest of his life to this work. The immense mass of notes
preserved in his journals forms one of the most extensive
case histories of a mystic ever kept and provides the
source for the material found in this book, plus much of
what is found in her two-volume definitive biography
written by V. Rev. Carl E. Schmöger, C.SS.R.

PREFACE

This book is the first and only English version of the combined Biblical visions of the Venerable Servant of God, Anne Catherine Emmerich. The original was published in 1914 by Desclée, de Brouwer (Bruges, Belgium) as *The Lowly Life and Bitter Passion of Our Lord and Saviour Jesus Christ and His Blessed Mother, together with the Mysteries of the Old Testament.*

The text is that of the 4th German edition of the 1881 version of the Very Rev. Carl E. Schmöger, C.SS.R., a compilation of the three classic works: *The Life of Our Lord and Saviour Jesus Christ, The Bitter Passion of Our Lord Jesus Christ,* and *The Life of Mary.* The translation was made by an American nun, since deceased, who wished to remain anonymous.

The first edition was issued with the approval and warm recommendation of the following members of the American hierarchy: Cardinal Gibbons, Archbishops Gross, Feehan and Elder, and Bishop Toebbe. It also included testimonials from Michael Wittman, Bishop of Ratisbon, Dean Overberg, Sister Emmerich's spiritual director, Count Leopold von Stolberg, J. J. Goerres, Dom Prosper Guéranger and several others less well known in our day. To this list might be added the names of Claudel, the Maritains, Huysmans, Father Gerard Manley Hopkins, Leon Bloy . . . to name but a few who have written in glowing terms of the saintly "Bride of the Passion" who was privileged to bear the wounds of Him whose life she beheld in the prophetic eye of her spirit.

The publishers, in reprinting these volumes, do so in complete and willing conformity to the decrees of Pope

Urban VIII respecting private revelations, persons not as yet canonized, and the prudence with which all alleged supernatural phenomena not attested to by the Church must properly be regarded. The final decision in all such matters rests with the See of Rome, to which the publishers humbly submit.

Like other private revelations, Sister Emmerich's accounts of the life of Our Lord, His Blessed Mother, and other biblical personages should be treated with that respect and that degree of faith which they seem to merit when compared with the holy dogmas of our Faith as derived from Scripture and Tradition, as well as when compared with our knowledge of history, geography, and science. These revelations are not, of course, guaranteed free from all error, as are the Sacred Scriptures. The *Imprimatur* which these books bear simply means they have been judged by ecclesiastical authority to be free of error in matters of faith and morals. Nevertheless, these revelations show a remarkable harmony with what is known about the history, geography, and customs of the ancient world.

The visions of Anne Catherine Emmerich provide a wealth of information not found in the Bible. In these times of disbelief, when the Sacred Scriptures are so often regarded as symbolical narratives with little historical value, the visions of this privileged soul providentially confirm the Christian's faith in the rock-solid reality of the life of Our Lord Jesus Christ, of His words, His deeds, and His miracles.

In addition, Sister Emmerich's visions show how our sacred religious heritage goes back in an unbroken line all the way to the time of Adam, to the very beginning of the world—a line which no other religion but the Roman Catholic can claim. These revelations show how the Roman Catholic Church faithfully follows the teachings, and administers the Sacraments, of Jesus Christ Himself—

which teachings and Sacraments are in turn the perfect fulfillment of the Old Testament religion.

This crucial fact, which has been almost totally forgotten in our day, is nevertheless all-important in proving which is the one true religion established by Almighty God. The unbroken line of the Roman Catholic Church becomes obvious to all who read these accounts of the marvelous events which Anne Catherine Emmerich was privileged to behold. For this reason alone, they are priceless—a gift of Divine Providence to an unbelieving world.

May God guide these revelations into the hands of those who need them most. May they do immense good for souls, both in time and for eternity.

—The Publishers
January 31, 1986
Feast of St. John Bosco

CONTENTS OF VOLUME III

PREACHING AND MIRACLES OF JESUS IN CAPHARNAUM AND THE SURROUNDING DISTRICTS

FROM THE SECOND CONVERSION OF MAGDALEN TO THE DELIVERY OF THE KEYS TO PETER

FROM THE SECOND PASCH TO THE RETURN FROM CYPRUS

THE RAISING OF LAZARUS. JESUS IN THE LAND OF THE THREE HOLY KINGS

THE LIFE OF
JESUS CHRIST
and
BIBLICAL REVELATIONS

Volume III

PREACHING AND MIRACLES OF JESUS IN CAPHARNAUM AND THE SURROUNDING DISTRICTS

1. CORNELIUS THE CENTURION

From Gabara Jesus went to the estate of the officer Zorobabel near Capharnaum. The two lepers whom at His last visit to Capharnaum He had healed, here presented themselves to return Him thanks. The steward, the domestics, and the cured son of Zorobabel also were here. They had already been baptized. Jesus taught and cured many sick. In the dusk of the evening, after His disciples had separated and gone to their respective families, Jesus proceeded along the valley of Capharnaum to the house of His Mother. All the holy women were here assembled, and there was great joy. Mary and the women renewed their petition to Jesus that He would cross to the other side of the lake early next morning because the committee of the Pharisees was so irritated against Him. Jesus calmed their fears. Mary interceded for the sick slave of the Centurion Cornelius, who was, she said, a very good man. Although a pagan, he had, through affection for the Jews, built them a synagogue. She begged Him likewise to cure the sick daughter of Jairus, the Elder of the synagogue, who lived in a little village not far from Capharnaum.

When Jesus next morning, with some of the disciples, was going to the residence of the pagan officer Cornelius, which stood on a height to the north of Capharnaum, He was met in the neighborhood of Peter's house by the two

Jews whom Cornelius had once before sent to Him. They again begged Him to have pity on his servant, for Cornelius, they said, deserved the favor. He was a friend of the Jews and had built them a synagogue, reckoning it at the same time an honor to be allowed to do so. Jesus responded that He was even then on His way to Cornelius's, and He directed them to dispatch a messenger in haste to announce His coming. Before reaching Capharnaum, Jesus took, just to the right of the gate, the road running between the city and the ramparts and passed the hovel of a leper living in the city wall. A short distance farther on brought Cornelius's house in sight. Upon receiving the message sent by Jesus, Cornelius had left it as if to get a glimpse of Him. He knelt down and, esteeming himself unworthy to approach Him or to speak with Him personally, hurried off a messenger with these words: "The Centurion bids me say to Thee, 'Lord, I am not worthy that Thou shouldst enter under my roof! Speak but one word, and my servant shall be healed. For if I, who am only a humble man dependent upon my superior, say to my servant: Do this! Do that! and he does it, how much easier will it be for Thee to command Thy servant to be healed and that he should be so!'" When these words were delivered to Jesus by Cornelius's messenger, He turned to those standing around and said: "Verily, I say unto ye, I have not found such faith in Israel! Know ye then! Many shall come from the east and the west and shall take place with Abraham, Isaac, and Jacob in Heaven; and many of the children of God's kingdom, the Israelites, shall be cast out into exterior darkness where there shall be weeping and gnashing of teeth!" Then, turning to the servant of the Centurion, He said: "Go, and as thou hast believed, so be it done to thee!" The messenger bore the words to the kneeling Centurion, who inclined to the earth, arose, and has-

tened back to the house. As he entered, he encountered
his servant, who was coming to meet him, enveloped in a
mantle, his head bound in a scarf. He was not a native of
the country, as was indicated by his yellowish-brown
complexion.

Jesus immediately turned back to Capharnaum. As He
was again passing the leper's hut, the leper himself came
out and threw himself down before Him. "Lord," he said,
"if Thou wilt, Thou canst make me clean." Jesus replied:
"Stretch forth thy hands!" He touched them and said: "I
do will it. Be thou clean!" and the leprosy fell from the
man. Jesus commanded him to present himself to the
priests for inspection, to make the offering prescribed by
the Law, and to speak to none other of his cure. The
man went to the pharisaical priests and submitted himself
to their examination as to whether he was cured or not.
They became enraged, examined him rigorously, but
were forced to acknowledge him cured. They had so
lively a dispute with him that they almost drove him from
their presence.

Jesus turned off into the street that led into the heart of
the city, and for about an hour cured numbers of sick
that had been brought together, also some possessed.
Most of the sick were lying near a well, around which
stood little huts. After that Jesus, with several of the disciples, left the city and went to a little vale beyond Magdalum not far from Damma. There they found a public
inn, at which were Maroni, the widow of Naim, and the
pagan Lais of Naim and her two daughters, Sabia and
Athalia, both of whom Jesus, when at Meroz, had from a
distance delivered from the devil. Maroni, the widow of
Naim, now came beseeching Jesus to go to her son Martial, a boy of twelve years, who was so ill that she feared
to find him dead on her return. Jesus told her to go home
in peace, that He would follow her—but when, He did
not say. Maroni had brought with her presents for the

inn. She immediately hurried back home with her servant. She had about nine hours to travel. She was a wealthy woman and very good, a mother to all the poor children in Naim.

Bartholomew also had arrived bringing with him Joses, the little son of his widowed sister, perhaps to be baptized. Thomas too was there and with him Jephte, the little cured son of Achias, the Centurion of Giskala. Achias himself was not present, but Judas Iscariot had come from Meroz. Lais and her two daughters had already embraced Judaism in Naim and renounced idolatry before the Jewish priests. At this ceremony a kind of baptism was performed by the priests which, however, consisted only of a sprinkling with water and other purifications. In such cases, the Jews baptized women, but the Baptism of Jesus and of John was not conferred upon females before Pentecost.

All the future Apostles were now in Capharnaum, with the exception of Matthias. A great many of Jesus' disciples and relatives, among the latter many women related to Him by blood, were present. Of the number was Mary Heli, Mary's elder sister. She was now perhaps seventy years old, and together with her second husband, Obed, had come bringing an ass laden with presents to Mary. She dwelt at Japha, a little place an hour at most from Nazareth, where Zebedee once lived and where his sons were born. She was greatly rejoiced at seeing again her three sons, James, Sadoch, and Heliacim, all disciples of John. This James was as old as Andrew. He is the same that with two other disciples, Cephas and John, once disputed with Paul on the subject of Jewish circumcision. After Jesus' death he became a priest, and was one of the oldest and most distinguished of the seventy disciples. Later he accompanied James the Greater to Spain, to the islands, into Cyprus, and into the idolatrous countries bordering the confines of Judea. Not this James, but

James the Lesser, the son of Alpheus and Mary Cleophas, became the first Bishop of Jerusalem.[1]

1. This remark of Sister Emmerich throws light upon the second chapter of the *Epistle to the Galatians,* and agrees with the tradition related by Eusebius. According to this tradition the *Cephas* of whom St. Paul speaks in this place was not *St. Peter,* but one of the seventy-two disciples. *(Note taken from the first edition of the* Life of Our Lord *according to Sister Emmerich.)*

2. MIRACULOUS CURES WROUGHT BY JESUS. HIS REASONS FOR TEACHING IN PARABLES

The Pharisees and Sadducees determined to oppose Jesus today in the synagogue. They had laid their plans and bribed the people to raise a tumult in which Jesus was to be formally thrust out of the edifice or taken prisoner. But the affair turned out quite differently. Jesus commenced His teaching in the synagogue by a very vigorous address, like one having power and authority to speak. The rage of the exasperated Pharisees increased at each moment. It was about to be let loose upon Him when suddenly a great disturbance arose in the synagogue. A man belonging to the city and possessed by the devil, and who on account of his madness had been fast bound, had while his keepers were in the synagogue broken his bonds. He came plunging like a fury into the synagogue, and with frightful cries pressed his way through the people, whom he tossed right and left, and who also began to utter screams of terror. He ran straight to the spot where Jesus was teaching, crying out: "Jesus of Nazareth! What have we to do with Thee? Thou hast come to drive us out! I know who Thou art! Thou art the Holy One of God!" But Jesus remained quite unmoved. He scarcely turned from His elevated position toward him, made only a menacing gesture sideways with His hand, and said quietly: "Be still, and go out of him!" Thereupon the man, becoming silent, sank down, still tossed to and fro on the ground, and Satan departed from him under the form of a thick, black vapor. The man now grew pale and calm, prostrated on the ground, and wept. All present were witness to this awful and wonderful spectacle of Jesus' power. Their terror was changed into a murmur of admiration. The courage of the Pharisees forsook them, and they huddled together, saying to one another: "What manner of man is this? He commands the spirits, and they go out of the possessed!" Jesus went on quietly with His discourse. The man that had been freed from the devil, weak and emaciated, was conducted home by his wife and relatives, who had been in the synagogue. When the sermon was over, he met Jesus and asked for some advice. Jesus warned him to refrain from his evil habits lest something worse might befall him, and exhorted him to penance and Baptism. The man was a cloth weaver. He made cotton scarfs, narrow and light, such as were worn around the neck. He returned to his work perfectly cured in mind and body. Such unclean spirits often domineer over men that freely give themselves up to their passions.

After this scene, the Pharisees were afraid to assault Jesus that day, and so they remained quiet while He went on with His teaching. The lessons for the Sabbath were taken from Moses and Osee. There were no more interruptions, though Jesus spoke very forcibly and severely. His appearance and His words were much more impressive than usual. He spoke as One having authority. The instruction over, He went to Mary's, where were gathered the women with many relatives and disciples.

I counted all the holy women who were associated together till the death of Jesus to help the little Community. There were seventy. At this time there were already thirty-seven who took part in this duty. Sabia and Athalia also, the daughters of Lais of Naim, were toward the last admitted among the female followers. At the time of St. Stephen, they were among the Christians who settled in Jerusalem.

Next morning Jesus again taught unmolested in the synagogue. The Pharisees had said to one another: "We can do nothing with Him now, His adherents are too numerous. We shall contradict Him now and then, we shall report all at Jerusalem, and wait till He goes up to the Temple for the Pasch." The streets were again filled with the sick. Some had come before the Sabbath, and some till now had not believed, but on the report of the possessed man's cure, they had themselves transported thither from all quarters of the city. Many of them had been there before, but had not been cured. They were weak, tepid, slothful souls, more difficult to convert than great sinners of more ardent nature. Magdalen was converted only after many struggles and relapses, but her last efforts were generous and final. Dina the Samaritan turned at once from her evil ways, and the Suphanite, after sighing long for grace, was suddenly converted. All the great female sinners were very quickly and powerfully converted, as was also the sturdy Paul, to whom conversion came like a flash of lightning. Judas, on the contrary, was always vacillating, and at last fell into the abyss. It was the same with the great and most violent maladies which I saw Jesus, in His wisdom, cure at once. They that were afflicted with them, like the possessed, had no will whatever to remain in the state in which they were, or again, self-will was entirely overcome by the violence of the malady. But as to those that were less grievously affected, whose sufferings only opposed an obstacle to their sinning with more facility, and whose conversion was insincere, I saw that Jesus often sent them away with an admonition to reform their lives; or that He only alleviated without curing their bodily ills, that through their pressure the soul might be cured. Jesus could have cured all that came to Him, and that instantaneously, but He did so only for those that believed and did penance, and He frequently warned them against a relapse. Even those that were only slightly sick He sometimes cured at once, if such would prove beneficial to their soul. He was not come to cure the body that it might the more readily sin, but He cured the body in order to deliver and save the soul. In every malady, in every species of bodily infirmity, I see a special design of God. Sickness is the sign of some sin. It may be his own or another's, a sin of which he may be conscious or not, that the sufferer has to expiate, or it may be a trial expressly prepared for him, which by patience and submission to God's will he may change into capital that will yield a rich return. Properly speaking, no one suffers innocently, for who is innocent, since the Son of God had to take upon Himself the sins of the world that they might be blotted out? To follow Him, we are all obliged to bear our cross after Him.

Since joy and the highest degree of patience in suffering, since the union of pain with the Passion of Jesus Christ, belong to the perfect, it follows that a disinclination to suffer is in itself an imperfection. We are created perfect and we shall again be born to perfection, consequently the cure of sickness is an effect of pure love and mercy toward poor sinners, a favor wholly unmerited by them. They have deserved more than sickness, they have deserved death; but the Lord by His own death has delivered them that believe in Him and perform works in accordance with their faith.

And so I saw Jesus on this day cure many possessed, paralyzed, dropsical, gouty, dumb, blind, many afflicted with an issue of blood, in fine, violent maladies of all kinds. I saw Him several times pass by some that were able to stand. They were those who had frequently received slight relief from Him, but their conversion not being earnest, they had relapsed in body and soul. As Jesus was passing by them, they cried out: "Lord, Lord! Thou dost cure all that are grievously sick, and Thou dost not cure us! Lord, have pity on us! We are sick again!" Jesus responded: "Why do ye not stretch forth your hands to Me?" At these words, all stretched out their hands to Him, and said: "Lord, here are our hands!" Jesus replied: "Ye do indeed stretch forth these hands, but the hands of your heart I cannot seize. Ye withdraw them and lock them up, for ye are filled with darkness." Then He continued to admonish them, cured several, who were converted, slightly relieved others, and passed by some unnoticed.

That afternoon He went with all His disciples and relatives to the lake. There was on the south side of the valley a pleasure garden provided with conveniences for bathing, the water being furnished from the brook of Capharnaum. Here they paused, and administered Baptism in the garden.

The Blessed Virgin with several of the women, among them Dina, Mary, Lais, Athalia, Sabia, and Martha, went for a walk in the neighborhood of Bethsaida, a little beyond the lepers' asylum. A caravan of pagans was encamped thereabouts, and among them were several women from Upper Galilee. The Blessed Virgin consoled and instructed them. The women sat in a circle on a little eminence, and Mary sometimes sat, sometimes walked among them. They asked her questions which she answered clearly, and told them many things about the Patriarchs, the Prophets, and Jesus.

Jesus meantime was instructing a crowd in parables. The disciples did not understand Him. Later, when again alone with them, He explained the parable of the sower. He spoke of the tares among the wheat and of the danger of pulling up the wheat with them. It was principally James the Greater who told Jesus that he and his companions did not understand Him, and he asked Him why He did not speak more clearly. Jesus answered that He would make all intelligible to them, but that on account of the weak and the pagans, the mysteries of the Kingdom of God could not then be exposed more plainly. As even with such precautions, these mysteries alarmed His hearers, who in their state of depravity, esteemed them too sublime for them, they must at first be presented, as it were, under the cover of a similitude. They must fall into their hearts like the grain of seed. In the grain the whole ear is enclosed, but to produce it, the grain must be hidden in the earth. He explained to them likewise the parable referring to their own call to labor in the harvest. He insisted chiefly upon their following Him; they would soon be with Him always, and He would explain all things to them. James the Greater said also: "Master, why wilt Thou explain all to us who are so ignorant? Why must we publish these things to others? Tell them rather to the Baptist, who believes so firmly who Thou really art. He can publish them, he can make them known!"

That evening when Jesus was teaching again in the synagogue, the Pharisees, who could once more breathe somewhat freely, began to dispute with Him on the subject of His forgiving sins. They reproached Him with the fact of His having in Gabara said to Mary Magdalen that her sins were forgiven her, and they asked how He knew that. How could He do that? Such talk was blasphemy! Jesus silenced them. Then they tried to provoke Him to say that He was not a man, that He was God. But Jesus again confounded them in their words. This scene took place in the forecourt of the synagogue. At last the Pharisees raised a great cry and tumult. But Jesus slipped from their hands and into the crowd, so that they could not tell where He had gone. He went by the flowery dale back of the synagogue to the garden of Zorobabel and thence by roundabout ways to the house of His Mother. He tarried there a part of the night, and sent word to Peter and the other disciples to meet Him next morning at the opposite side of the valley beyond Peter's fishery, as He wished them to go with Him to Naim.

The Centurion Cornelius and his servant asked Jesus what they should do. He answered that they and all their family should receive Baptism.

3. THE RAISING OF THE YOUTH OF NAIM FROM THE DEAD

The road to Naim crossed the valley of Magdalum above Peter's fishery to the east of the mountain that looked down upon Gabara, and then ran into the valley eastward of Bethulia and Giskala. Jesus may have journeyed with the disciples nine to ten hours when they put up at a shepherd inn about three or four hours from Naim. They had crossed the brook Cison once. Jesus taught the whole way, explaining to His disciples in particular how they would be able to detect false teachers.

Naim was a beautiful little place with well-built houses, and was sometimes known also as Engannim. It lay upon a charming hill on the brook Cison to the south, about an hour from Mount Thabor, and facing Endor on the southwest. Jezrael was more to the south, but was hidden by intervening heights. The beautiful Plain of Esdrelon stretched out before Naim, which was almost three or four hours distant from Nazareth. The country here was uncommonly rich in grain, fruit, and wine. The widow Maroni owned a whole mountain covered with the most beautiful vineyards. Jesus had about thirty companions. The path over the hill was rather narrow, so some went on before Jesus, and others behind Him. It was almost nine in the morning when they drew near to Naim and encountered the funeral procession at the gate.

A crowd of Jews enveloped in mourning mantles passed out of the city gate with the corpse. Four men were carrying the coffin, in which reposed the remains upon a kind of frame made of crossed poles curved in the middle. The coffin was in shape something like the human form, light like a woven basket, with a cover fastened to the top. Jesus passed through the disciples who, formed into two rows on either side of the road, advanced to meet the coming procession, and said: "Stand still!" Then as He laid His hand upon the coffin, He said: "Set the coffin down." The bearers obeyed, the crowd fell back, and the disciples ranged on either side. The mother of the dead youth, with several of her female friends, was following the corpse. They too paused just as they were passing out of the gate a few feet from where Jesus was standing. They were veiled and showed every sign of grief. The mother stood in front shedding silent tears. She may indeed have been thinking: "Ah, He has come too late!" Jesus said to her most kindly and earnestly: "Woman, weep not!" The grief of all present touched Him, for the widow was much loved in the city, on account of her great charity to orphans and the poor. Still there were many wicked and malignant people around, and numbers of others came flocking from the city. Jesus called for water and a little branch. Someone brought to a disciple, who handed them to Jesus, a little vessel of water and a twig of hyssop. Jesus took the water and said to the bearers: "Open the coffin and loosen the bands!" While this command was being executed, Jesus raised His eyes to Heaven and said: "I confess to Thee, O Father, Lord of Heaven and earth, because Thou hast hidden these things from the wise and prudent, and hast revealed them to little ones. Yea, Father, for so it hath seemed good in Thy sight. All things are delivered to Me by My Father, and

not one knoweth the Son but the Father; neither doth anyone know the Father but the Son, and he to whom it shall
please the Son to reveal Him. Come to Me, all you that
labor and are burdened, and I will refresh you. Take up
My yoke upon you, and learn of Me, because I am meek
and humble of heart, and you shall find rest to your souls,
for My yoke is sweet and My burden light!" When the
bearers removed the cover, I saw the body wrapped like a
babe in swaddling clothes and lying in the coffin. Supporting it in their arms, they loosened the bands, drew
them off, uncovered the face, unbound the hands, and left
about it only one linen covering. Then Jesus blessed the
water, dipped the little branch into it, and sprinkled the
crowd. Thereupon I saw numbers of small, dark figures
like insects, beetles, toads, snakes, and little black birds
issuing from many of the bystanders. The crowd became
purer and brighter. Jesus then sprinkled the dead youth
with the little branch, and with His hand made the Sign of
the Cross over him, upon which I beheld a murky, black,
cloudlike figure issuing from the body. Jesus said to the
youth, "Arise!" He arose to a sitting posture, and gazed
around him in questioning astonishment. Then Jesus said:
"Give him some clothing!" and they threw round him a
mantle. The youth then rose to his feet and said: "What is
all this? How came I here?" The attendants put sandals
upon his feet and he stepped forth from the coffin. Jesus
took him by the hand and led him to the arms of his
mother, who was hastening toward him. As He restored
him to her, He said: "Here, thou hast thy son back, but I
shall demand him of thee when he shall have been
regenerated in Baptism." The mother was so transported
with joy, amazement, and awe, that she uttered no thanks
at the moment. Her feelings found vent only in tears and
embraces. The procession accompanied her to her home,
the people chanting a hymn of praise. Jesus followed with
the disciples. He entered the widow's house, which was

very large and surrounded by gardens and courts. Friends came crowding from all quarters, all pressing eagerly to see the youth. The attendants gave him a bath, and clothed him in a white tunic and girdle. They washed the feet of Jesus and the disciples, after which the customary refreshments were presented them. Now began at once a joyous and most abundant distribution of gifts to the poor, who had gathered around the house to offer congratulations. Clothing, linen, corn, bread, lambs, birds, and money were given out plentifully. Meantime Jesus instructed the crowds assembled in the courtyards of the widow.

Martial, in his white tunic, was radiant with joy. He ran here and there, showing himself to the eager throng, and helping in the distribution of gifts. He was full of childish gaiety. It was amusing to see school children brought by their teachers into the courtyard and approaching him. Many of them hung back quite timidly as if they thought Martial a spirit. He ran after them and they retreated before him. But others played the valiant and laughed at their companions' fears. They looked with disdain upon the cowardly and gave Martial their hand, just as a large boy touches with the tips of his fingers a horse or other animal of which the little ones are afraid.

Tables were spread both in the house and courts, and at them all were feasted. Peter, as the widow's relative, for she was the daughter of his father-in-law's brother, was especially happy and at home in the house. He discharged in a certain degree the office of father of the family. Jesus frequently addressed questions and words of instruction to the resuscitated boy. He did this in the hearing of those present, who all appeared to be touched by what He said. His words implied that death, which had entered the world by sin, had bound him, had enchained him, and would have dealt him the mortal blow in the tomb; furthermore, that Martial with eyes closed would have been cast into the darkness and later would have opened them where neither mercy nor help could be extended to him. But at the portals of the tomb the mercy of God, mindful of the piety of the boy's parents and of some of his ancestors, had broken his bonds. Now by Baptism he was to free himself from the sickness of sin, in order not to fall into a still more frightful imprisonment. Then Jesus dilated upon the virtues of parents.

Their virtues profit their children in after years. It was in consideration of the righteousness of the Patriarchs that Almighty God, down to the present day, had protected and spared Israel; but now, enchained in sin and covered with the veil of mental blindness, they had become like unto this youth. They were standing on the brink of the grave, and for the last time was mercy extended to them. John had prepared the way and with a powerful voice had called upon their hearts to arise from the slumber of death. The Heavenly Father had now, for the last time, pity upon them. He would open to life the eyes of those that did not obstinately keep them closed. Jesus compared the people in their blindness to the youth shut up in his coffin who, though near the tomb, though outside the gate of the city, had been met by salvation. "If," He said, "the bearers had not heeded My voice, if they had not set down the coffin, had not opened it, had not freed the body from its winding sheet, if they had obstinately hurried forward with their burden, the boy would have been buried—and how terrible that would have been!" Then Jesus likened to this picture He had drawn the false teachers, the Pharisees. They kept the poor people from the life of penance, they fettered them with the bonds of their arbitrary laws, they enclosed them in the coffin of their vain observances, and cast them thus into an eternal tomb. Jesus finished by imploring and conjuring His hearers to accept the proffered mercy of His Heavenly Father, and hasten to life, to penance, to Baptism!

It was remarkable that Jesus blessed on this occasion with holy water, in order to drive out the evil spirits that held sway over several of the bystanders. Some of the latter were scandalized, others were envious, and some again were full of a certain malicious joy at the thought that Jesus would certainly be unable to raise the youth from the dead. When Jesus blessed with the water, I saw a little cloud, composed of the figures or shadows of noxious vermin, arise from the youth's body and disappear in the earth. At the raising of others from the dead, Jesus called back the soul of the deceased, which was separated from the body and in the abode assigned it according to its deeds. It came at the call of Jesus, hovered over the dead body, finally sank into it, and the dead arose. But with the youth of Naim, it was as if death—like a suffocating weight—had been taken away from his body.

The meal over, Jesus went with the disciples to the beautiful garden of the widow Maroni at the southern end of the city. The maimed and sick lined His whole route, and He cured them all. The streets were alive with excitement. It was already growing dark when Jesus entered the garden where Maroni with her relatives and domestics, several Doctors of the Law, Martial, and some other boys were gathered. There were several summer houses in the garden. Before one more beautiful than the others, whose roof was supported on pillars, and which might be shut in by movable screens, was a flambeau placed high under the palm trees. Its flames lighted up the whole hall, and glistened beautifully on the long, green leaves. Near the trees on which fruit was still hanging, one could see as distinctly and clearly by the light of the flambeau as by day. At first Jesus taught and explained walking around; afterward, He entered the summer house. He often spoke to Martial in the hearing of others. It was a wonderfully beautiful evening in that garden. The night was advanced when Jesus and His followers returned to Maroni's house, in whose side buildings all found lodgings.

At the news of Jesus' presence in Naim and the resurrection of the boy, crowds of people, among them many sick, gathered into the city from the whole country around. They completely filled the street in front of Maroni's residence, where they stood in long rows. Jesus cured part of them the next morning, and established peace in several households. Several women had come to Him, asking whether He could not give them a bill of divorce. They complained of their husbands with whom, they said, they could no longer live. This was an artful device of the Pharisees. They were confounded by His miracles and could do nothing against Him; but yet being full of wrath, they resolved to tempt Him to say on the subject of divorce something against the Law, that they might be able to accuse Him as a teacher of false doctrine. But Jesus said to the discontented wives: "Bring me a vessel of milk and another of water. Then I shall answer ye." They went into a neighboring house and returned with a bowl of milk and one of water. Jesus poured one into the other and said: "Separate the two again, so that the milk shall be again by itself, and in like manner the water. Then I shall give you a bill of divorce." The women replied that they could not do that. Then Jesus spoke of the indissolubility of marriage, and that it was only on account of the obduracy of the Jews that Moses had allowed divorce. But perfectly disunited husband and wife never could be, since they are one in the flesh; and although they might not live together, yet must the husband support the wife and children, and neither could remarry. After that Jesus accompanied the wives to their homes, where He had a private interview with the husbands. Then He saw each couple together, reproached both parties, the wives coming in for the larger share, and ended by forgiving them. The delinquents shed tears and afterward lived happily together, more faithful to each other than they had ever before been. The Pharisees were furious on seeing that their design had completely failed.

That morning Jesus restored sight to many of the blind by mixing in His hand clay and saliva and smearing it to their eyes.

4. JESUS IN MAGEDDO. JOHN'S DISCIPLES

When Jesus was leaving Naim, Maroni, her boy and her domestics, all the cured, and many good people of the city accompanied Him, singing Psalms and bearing green branches before Him. He went with the disciples westward along the north bank of the Cison. The mountain that shut in the valley of Nazareth lay to the right. Toward evening He and the disciples arrived at the environs of Mageddo, which stood on the mountain chain whose eastern declivity leads down into the valley of Zabulon. Here He entered an inn, and soon afterward gave an instruction in front of it. When the laborers in the fields saw Jesus and His followers drawing near, they threw on the garments which at their work they had laid aside.

Mageddo stood on an eminence and was partly fallen to decay. In the very heart of the city there were ruins entirely overgrown with moss, while here and there arose a dilapidated arch. They must have belonged to a castle of the kings of Canaan.[1] I heard that Abraham also once sojourned in this region. The suburb in which Jesus put up was more modern and more full of life than the city itself. It consisted of a long row of houses at the base of the mountain, over which ran a great commercial highway from Ptolomais. There were numerous large inns in the neighborhood, and many publicans dwelt here. They had heard Jesus' teaching and had resolved to receive penance and Baptism. The Pharisees of the place were scandalized at these things. A great crowd of sick were already gathered and others were constantly coming. Jesus sent word to them by the disciples that He would go to them toward evening, and He directed how they should be arranged, which directions the disciples fulfilled. Outside the city of Mageddo was a large meadow surrounded by walls and porches wherein the sick were brought and laid in order.

Meanwhile Jesus, with the disciples, went through the fields outside the city instructing in parables the laborers there engaged in sowing. Some of the disciples taught those at a greater distance until Jesus came up; then they turned back to those that Jesus had already instructed, explained to them whatever they had not clearly understood, and told them about the Lord's miracles. Jesus and the disciples always taught the same things to the different sets of workmen, so that on comparing notes, they all found that they had heard the same. They who had understood better, could afterward explain to the others. They often discontinued their work in this hot country to rest, and it was of these intermissions, and the opportunity afforded by the time devoted to meals, that Jesus took advantage to teach.

While Jesus was thus traversing the fields with the disciples, four of John's followers arrived. They saluted the disciples and paid attention to their instructions. They had strips of fur around their necks, and leathern thongs bound their waists. They had not been sent by John, although they had constant intercourse with him and his disciples. They were degenerate followers of John, sworn to the Herodians, who had sent them to follow Jesus and hear what He taught concerning His Kingdom. They were more austere, though at the same time more polished in their manners, than Jesus' disciples. Some hours after, another troop of John's disciples made their appearance. They were twelve in number, only two of whom had been sent by John; the rest had come through curiosity. As they approached, Jesus was returning to the city, and they followed Him. Some of them had been present at the last miracles wrought by Jesus, and had hastened back to tell John what they had seen. When Jesus raised the youth of Naim, some of them were present, and they hurried off to Machaerus to inform John. They said to him: "What is it? What must we think? We have seen Him perform such and such miracles! We have heard such and such words from His lips! But His disciples are much less strict than we in the observance of the Law. Whom shall we follow? Who is Jesus? Why does He cure all that appeal to Him? Why does He console and help strangers, though He does not take a step toward freeing you?"

John always had trouble with his disciples, for they would not separate from him. It was for that reason that he sent them so often to Jesus, that they might learn to know Him and eventually follow Him. But they were so prejudiced in favor of John that what they saw and heard made little impression upon them. It was his desire that his disciples should follow Jesus that led John to urge Him so frequently to manifest Himself; he hoped that his followers would yield to the movement that converted the other Jews. He thought that, seeing them come again and again with their doubts, Jesus would be, as it were, necessitated to proclaim aloud that He was the Messiah, the Son of God; therefore it was that he sent those two with their usual questions to Him.

On entering the city with His disciples, Jesus went to the circular enclosure where the sick from the whole country around were encamped. Among them were some from Nazareth who knew Him. The lame, the blind, the dumb, the deaf, the sick of all kinds were here gathered, also several possessed. Making a turn around the circle, Jesus cured the last named, many of whom were suffering from different degrees of possession. They were indeed not so violent as such poor creatures had been at other times, but they were afflicted with convulsions and their limbs were distorted. Jesus cured them with a word of command uttered as He passed and at some distance. A dark vapor issued from them, they became somewhat faint and, when returned to full consciousness, they were quite changed. The vapors, on first issuing from their bodies, appeared quite subtle; but they soon condensed and united. Sometimes they sank into the earth, or again rose in the air; on this occasion they followed the former course. The evil spirit often departs like a dark shadow in human form. Instead of vanishing immediately, I have seen him wandering around among the bystanders before disappearing.

Jesus had scarcely begun to cure when John's disciples, with a certain air of importance—as if the bearers of a commission—stepped up to Him and gave signs of their desire to address Him. Jesus, however, paid no attention to them, but went on with the cures. Such treatment was greatly displeasing to them, and they could not understand it. Many of John's disciples were decidedly narrow-minded and jealous. Jesus wrought miracles, John did not. John spoke so highly of Jesus, and yet Jesus made no effort to free him from confinement. Although impressed by His miracles and doctrine, yet they soon allowed themselves to be influenced again by the public voice which was asking: "Who is He? Are not His poor relatives known by everyone?" Then again, they could not understand His words relative to His Kingdom. They saw no kingdom and no preparations for one. As John had been honored by so many and now lay proscribed in prison, they thought, among other things, that Jesus did not help him, that He allowed him to languish in captivity, in order to increase His own popularity. They were scandalized also at the liberty of His disciples. They esteemed it excessive humility in John to prize Jesus so highly and that he was constantly sending to implore Him to manifest Himself, to make an open declaration of who He was. As Jesus always spoke evasively on that point and as they had no idea that John sent them to Him in order that they might know Him, this knowledge was to them at the time, on account of their preconceived ideas, more difficult than it might have been to the most simple child.

As Jesus was making the circuit of the enclosure curing, He came to a sick man from Nazareth who began to speak of his acquaintance with Him. "Do You remember," he said, "that You lost Your grandfather when You were twenty-five years old? We were often together in those days." The man referred to the death of St. Anne's second or third husband. Jesus did not pause for many words. He answered merely: "Yes, yes, I remember," and turned at once to the man's sins and sufferings. When He found him penitent and believing, He cured him, addressed to him some words of admonition, and passed on to the next invalid.

When Jesus reached the opposite side of the enclosure, the disciples sent by John confronted Him. They had, from their stand in the center, watched with amazement the miracles wrought. They now addressed Him in these words: "John the Baptist has sent us to Thee to ask art Thou He who is to come or look we for another?" Jesus answered: "Go and relate to John what you have heard and seen. The blind see, the lame walk, the lepers are cleansed, the deaf hear, the dead rise again, widows are consoled, the poor have the Gospel preached to them. What is crooked is made straight. And blessed is he that shall not be scandalized in Me." After these words Jesus turned away, and John's disciples took their departure.

Jesus could not speak more plainly of Himself, for who would have understood Him? His disciples were good, simple-hearted, generous, and pious souls, but as yet quite incapable of comprehending such a mystery. Many of them were related to Him by ties of blood, consequently they would have been scandalized at more precise language on Jesus's part, or would have conceived erroneous ideas of Him. As for the multitude at large, they were altogether unprepared for such a truth, and besides, He was encompassed by spies. Even among John's disciples, the Pharisees and Herodians had their creatures.

When John's messengers had departed, Jesus began to teach. The cured, crowds of people, the Scribes of the place, His disciples, and the five publicans that dwelt here, formed the audience. The instruction was continued by the light of flambeaux, and the remaining sick were afterward cured. Jesus took for the subject of His discourse His own reply to John's disciples. He spoke of how they should use the benefits received from God, and exhorted to penance and a change of life. As He knew that some of the Pharisees present had taken occasion, from the brevity of His reply to John's messengers, to say to the people that He, Jesus, made little account of John and was willing enough to see him ruined in public estimation that He Himself might be exalted, He explained the answer He had given as well as what He had said on the score of penance. He also recalled to them what they themselves had heard John say of Him. Why, He asked, were they always doubting? What did they expect from John? He said: "What went ye out to see when ye went to John? Did ye go to see a reed shaken in the wind? Or a man effeminately and magnificently clothed? Listen! They that are clothed sumptuously and who live delicately are in the palaces of kings. But what did ye desire to see when ye went in quest of him? Was it to see a Prophet? Yea, I tell ye, ye saw more than a Prophet when ye saw him. This is he of whom it is written: *Behold, I send my angel before thy face, who shall prepare thy way before thee.* Amen, I say to you there hath not risen among them that are born of women a greater Prophet than John the Baptist, and yet he that is least in the Kingdom of Heaven is greater than he. And from the days of John the Baptist until now the Kingdom of Heaven suffereth violence, and the violent bear it away. For all the Prophets and the Law prophesied of it until John; and if ye will receive it, he is Elias that is to come. He that hath ears to hear, let him hear!"

All present were very much impressed by Jesus' words, and wanted to receive Baptism. The Scribes alone murmured. They were especially scandalized at Jesus because He accepted hospitality from the publicans, who also were present at this instruction. Jesus therefore profited by this opportunity to speak of all the reports they had set afloat concerning both John and Himself, particularly of the reproach made against Him of frequenting the company of publicans and sinners.

After that Jesus entered the house of one of the publicans, where He found the other four, and there He taught. Among His hearers on this occasion were some that had determined to amend their lives and to receive Baptism. This house was near the enclosure wherein Jesus had just cured the sick. There was another publican's house at the entrance of the city, and still some others beyond.

Debbaseth, where Bartholomew resided, could be seen from the road when first starting from Naim to Mageddo, but on a nearer approach the heights of the latter place concealed it from view. It was situated about an hour and a half to the west on the Cison, at the entrance of the valley of Zabulon.

1. *Jos.* 12:21; *3 Kgs.* 9:15.

5. JESUS LEAVES MAGEDDO. CURE OF A LEPER

As the Feast of the New Moon was beginning, Jesus took the return route from Mageddo to Capharnaum. He was accompanied by about twenty-four of His disciples, the four false disciples of John, and some of the publicans of Mageddo who wanted to be baptized in Capharnaum. They journeyed along slowly, sometimes pausing to stand or sit in the charming spots through which they passed, for Jesus taught the whole time. The way led from Mageddo northeastward, and off to the northwest side of Thabor. Jesus' teaching was a preparation for the definitive calling and sending of the Apostles, which was soon to take place. He earnestly exhorted them to lay aside all worldly cares and to abandon their possessions. His words were so touching and affectionate. Once He snapped off a flower that was growing by the wayside, and said: "These have no cares! Look at their beautiful colors, their delicate little stamens! Was Solomon the Wise in all his magnificence more beautifully clothed than they?" Jesus often made use of this similitude.

He continued His instruction in a series of parables so striking that each of the Apostles could recognize the one intended for himself. He spoke also of His Kingdom, telling them that they should not be so eager after high employments therein, should not picture it to themselves as something earthly. Jesus said this because John's four disciples, who were secret partisans of the Herodians, were especially interested in this part of His discourse. He warned the disciples of what people they should for the future beware, and described the Herodians in terms so exact that no one could fail to recognize them. Among other things, He said that they should beware of certain people in sheep's skins and long leathern straps!

"Beware," He said, "of the profane in sheepskins and long girdles!" By these words, Jesus signified the lurking Herodian disciples of John who, in imitation of John's true followers, wore a kind of sheepskin stole around the neck and crossed on the breast. They might know them, He said, by this, that they could not look one straight in the face; or again, if they (the disciples of Jesus), their hearts overflowing with joy and ardor, should impart something of their feelings to one of these false zealots in sheepskins and girdles, they might recognize him for what he was in reality by the agitation of his heart. It would turn this way and that way like a restless animal. Jesus named a beetle which, when confined, runs round and round, seeking some hole by which to escape. Once He bent back a thornbush, saying: "Look, and see whether you can find any fruit here or not." Some of the disciples had the simplicity to look into the bush. But Jesus said: "Do men seek figs upon thistles and grapes upon thorns?"

Toward evening they arrived at a row of houses, twenty in number, with a school on the northwestern side of the foot of Thabor. The place lay from one and a half to two hours eastward from Nazareth and one-half hour from the city of Thabor. The people here were a good-natured set. They had known Jesus in His early years when He used to wander around Nazareth with His young friends. They were for the most part shepherds. While guarding their flocks, they busied themselves in gathering cotton which, as soon as they spied Jesus coming, they packed up in their sacks and carried to their homes, after which they hurried forth to meet Him. I saw them with their rough fur caps in their hands, but in the school their heads were covered. They received Jesus at the spring, washed His feet and those of the disciples, and offered them some refreshment. There was no synagogue in the place, only a school with its resident teacher. Jesus went to it, and taught in parables.

This little village belonged to a distinguished man who lived with his wife in a large house at some distance. This man had fallen into sin and was now afflicted with leprosy; consequently, he lived apart from his wife. She occupied the upper stories of the house, while he lodged in one of the side buildings. In order to escape the grievous alternative of entire separation from his fellow-men, he had not made known his malady. His case was not, however, so secret that many were not aware of its existence, but they connived at it. It was well known in the little village, and although the ordinary route ran past his dwelling, the people always managed to take another way. They informed the disciples of the circumstance. The poor leper had for a long time sincerely bewailed his transgressions and longed for the coming of Jesus. And now he called a little boy of about eight years, his slave, who supplied him with necessaries, and said to him: "Go to Jesus of Nazareth and watch your chance. When you see Him at some distance from His disciples or walking apart from them, cast yourself at His feet and say: 'Rabbi, my master is sick. He thinks that Thou canst help him by merely passing before our house, a way that all others shun. He humbly beseeches Thee to have compassion on his misery and to walk along the street, for he is certain of being cured." The boy went to Jesus and very cleverly executed the commission. Jesus replied: "Tell your master that I shall go to him in the morning," and He took the boy by one hand, laying the other on his head with words of praise. This meeting took place as Jesus was leaving the school to go to the inn. Jesus knew that the boy was coming, and had designedly remained a little behind the disciples. The boy wore a yellow tunic.

Anne's property lay on a height to the west of Nazareth. It was distant about an hour, and was between the valley of Nazareth and that of Zabulon. A narrow

vale planted with trees ran from it to Nazareth, and by it
Anne could go to Mary's house without traversing the
city.

Next morning at early dawn Jesus left the inn with the
disciples. When He turned into the street that ran past
the leper's dwelling, they told Him that He ought not to
go that way. But He went on and commanded them to
follow. They did so, but timidly and apprehensively, for
they feared being reported at Capharnaum. John's disciples did not go with Him by this way.

The boy, who was on the watch, notified his master of
Jesus' approach. The sick man came down by a path
leading to the street, paused at some distance, and cried
out: "Lord, do not come nearer to me! If Thou dost
merely will me to be healed, I shall be saved." The disciples remained standing at a distance. Jesus replied: "I
will it!" went up to the man, touched him, and spoke to
him, as he lay prostrate on his face at His feet. He was
clean; his leprosy had fallen off. He related to Jesus all
the circumstances of his case, and received for reply that
he should return to his wife, and by degrees appear again
among the people. Jesus admonished him of his sins,
commanded him to receive the penance of Baptism, and
enjoined upon him a certain alms. He then went back to
His disciples and spoke to them of the cure just wrought.
He told them that whoever had faith and possessed a
pure heart might with impunity touch even the leprous.

When the cured man had bathed and dressed, he went
to his wife and told her of the miracle just effected in
him by Jesus. Some spiteful people of the place sent news
of the affair to the priests and Pharisees of the city of
Thabor, who immediately saw fit to institute a commission of investigation. They surprised the poor man by
submitting him to a close examination as to whether he
was really cured or not, and sharply called him to account for keeping his malady secret. They now made a

great noise over the affair which, though publicly known, they had long tolerated.

Jesus journeyed quickly with the disciples all the remainder of the day, pausing only now and again to rest a few moments and take some refreshment. He taught all along the way about the forsaking of temporal goods, and in parables instructed them upon the Kingdom of God. He told them that it was impossible to make all these things clear to them just then, but a time would come when they would comprehend all. He spoke of giving up earthly care of food and raiment. They would soon see a hungry multitude with provisions far from sufficient for their wants. They, the disciples, would say to Him: "Whence shall we get bread?" and a superabundance should be given unto them. They had to build houses and build them securely! Jesus said this in such a way as to intimate that it was by sacrifice and personal exertion that these houses, namely, employments and charges in His Kingdom, were to be obtained. The disciples, however, understood Him in a worldly sense. Judas was very much rejoiced. He gave noisy expression to his satisfaction and said aloud in the hearing of all that he would not shirk labor, that he would do his share of the work. On hearing this, Jesus stood still and said: "We are not yet at the end of our mission. It will not always be as it is now. Ye will not always be well received and entertained, ye will not always have things in abundance. The time will come when they will persecute you and thrust you out, when ye will have neither shelter, nor food, nor clothing, nor shoes." And He went on to tell them that they should think seriously of these things and hold themselves in readiness to renounce everything, also that He had something important to propose to them. He spoke likewise of two kingdoms opposed to each other. No one can serve two masters. Whoever desired to serve in His Kingdom must forsake the other. Then passing to the

Pharisees and their accomplices, He said something about the masks or disguises that they wore. They taught the dead form of the Law and sought to have it observed; but the best part of it, its purport—the charity, forgiveness, and mercy that it inculcates—they wholly neglected. But He, Jesus, taught just the contrary, namely that the rind without the kernel is dead and barren. First comes the essence of the Law, and then the Law itself; the kernel must increase with the growth of the shell. He gave them also some instructions on prayer. They should, He said, pray in secret and not ostentatiously before others. Many similar things He said on this occasion.

When journeying with His disciples, Jesus generally instructed them, thus preparing them to understand better what they would hear in His next public discourse and be able to make it clear to the people. He often repeated the same things, though in different words and order. Among the disciples who accompanied Jesus today, James the Greater and Judas Barsabas most frequently put questions to Him, though Peter did so sometimes. Judas often spoke in a loud voice. Andrew was already well acquainted with the teachings of his Master. Thomas was preoccupied, as if weighing consequences. John took everything simply and lovingly. The best instructed of the disciples were the most silent, partly through modesty, and partly because they were not always willing to show that they did not understand Jesus' words.

Thus journeying through the valleys, they arrived shortly before the beginning of the Sabbath at the valley east of Magdalum. Here they encountered the pagan Cyrinus of Dabereth, and the centurion Achias of Giskala, who were going to Capharnaum for Baptism.

When nearing Capharnaum, Jesus was instructing the disciples as to how they should exercise themselves in obedience as a preparation for their mission, and especially how they should conduct themselves when He should send them to teach the people. He gave them likewise some general rules for their deportment when in certain company. He did this in a few words before the departure of the four Herodians who had journeyed with His little party, and sufficiently loud for them to hear. He said: "If on your journeys worldly men join you—whom ye may recognize by their smooth speech and sly questions—who will not be shaken off, who always, half agreeing, half good-naturedly contradicting, question and discuss various subjects that agitate the heart, then should ye at any cost break away from them. And why? Because ye are still too weak, too simple-hearted. Ye might easily fall into the snares of such lurkers. I do not shun them, for I know them, and I wish them to hear My teaching."

6. JESUS TEACHES IN THE SYNAGOGUE OF CAPHARNAUM, AND HEALS TWO LEPERS

Jesus again passed by the estate of the Centurion Zorobabel as He and His disciples were hurrying along, for the Sabbath had already begun. In his charity, Zorobabel had permitted two young Scribes of about twenty-five years, who on account of their dissolute life had been stricken with leprosy, to take up their abode in his garden. They were perfectly loathsome to look upon, and in their misery subjected to the greatest contempt. The red mantles that enveloped them hid the ulcers with which they were covered. They had once formed a part of Magdalen's gay coterie at Magdalum, had afterward carried on their excesses in other places, and fell at last into the extreme misery in which they now were. At Jesus' recent visit to these parts, they were ashamed to present themselves before Him, but now, convinced by the news of His miracles and great mercy, they had allowed themselves to be dragged to a place near the road by which He would pass and where they could cry to Him for help. Jesus would not pause. He hurried on, but told two of Zorobabel's servants, who came running after Him pleading for the unfortunate creatures, to bring them to the synagogue in Capharnaum. When the people were assembled, they (the servants) were to conduct the lepers to the gallery one story high that had been built adjoining the synagogue, and from which the teaching going on inside could be heard by those from without. There they should pray and excite themselves to contrition until He should call them. The servants immediately hastened back, and took the poor men by a shortcut through the flowery ravine to Capharnaum. They dragged them, though not without difficulty, up the outside steps to the gallery where, leaning in at the windows of the synagogue, they could, apart from the throng and in the open air, listen to the teachings of Jesus and with penitent hearts await their Saviour's call.

Jesus soon arrived with the disciples. After they had washed their feet and ungirded their garments, they entered the synagogue. When Jesus approached the pulpit, He found it occupied by one who was reading aloud. The latter, however, at once arose and yielded his place to Jesus, who immediately took the roll of Scriptures and began to teach upon the passages referring to Jacob's being called to account by Laban, his struggle with the angel, his reconciliation with Esau, and the seduction of Dina, after which He turned to the Prophet Osee. When Jesus without the least hesitation took the rolls and began to read, the Pharisees smiled scornfully, as if to pronounce Him wanting in courtesy. They were exasperated at Jesus' reappearance, for the raising of the youth of Naim, as well as His numerous cures in Mageddo, were already noised throughout Capharnaum. They watched eagerly and with inquietude to see what new thing He was now going to undertake. Almost all of Jesus' relatives, including the women, were gathered today in the synagogue.

As the crowd was leaving the synagogue followed by Jesus, the disciples, and the Pharisees, these last thought they would still carry on the dispute with Jesus in the portico, but an unforeseen incident prevented their design. Jesus went to the door, looked up to the gallery where the two unclean men were still standing, and called to them to come down. But they were timid and ashamed. Through fear of the Pharisees, they did not venture to obey at once. Then Jesus commanded them, in a name that I cannot recall, to come down, and to their own great astonishment they found themselves able to descend the steps alone. The portico had been lighted up with torches for the convenience of the dispersing crowd. How furious were the Pharisees when they recognized by the dull glare of the torches the two poor, despised sinners in their red mantles! The lepers sank trembling on their knees before Jesus. He laid His hand on them, breathed into their faces, and said: "Your sins are forgiven you!" and admonished them to continence and the baptism of penance. He commanded them also to forsake their vain studies, for that He Himself would teach them the truth and the way. They rose up. Their disfigurement had visibly decreased, their ulcers had dried, and the scales had fallen off. With tears they thanked their Benefactor, and left the place with Zorobabel's servants. Many of the well-disposed among the bystanders pressed around the cured, celebrating in words of praise their penance and their healing.

The Pharisees, however, were mad with rage. They cried out to Jesus: "What! Healest Thou on the Sabbath! And dost Thou also forgive sins! How canst Thou forgive sins?" Then, turning to the people, they cried: "He has a devil who helps Him! He is a madman! That is easily seen in His wandering about. Scarcely had He begun to carry on His game here, when off He goes to Naim to raise the dead, then to Mageddo, and then back here again! No good man in his senses would carry on in that way! He has a powerful, wicked spirit who helps Him!" And they added: "When Herod finishes with John, this Man's turn will come, unless He takes Himself out of the way!" But Jesus went out through the midst of them. His female relatives, who had waited for Him in a neighboring house after leaving the synagogue, wept and lamented over the violent rage of the Pharisees.

Jesus left the city and, taking the road to the northeast, directed His steps to the hill beyond the valley where Mary's house stood. On the way thither were clumps of trees and grottos in which He stopped to pray. He arrived late at Mary's, where He consoled the women, after which He again went out and spent the whole night in prayer.

Next morning, Jesus repaired to the garden in the neighborhood of Peter's house. It was enclosed by a hedge, and in it all the preparations for Baptism had been made. There were several circular cisterns, formed in the ground and surrounded by a little channel, into which the water of a stream running nearby could be turned. A long arbor could, by hangings and screens, be divided into little compartments for the convenience of the neophytes when disrobing. An elevated stand had been erected for Jesus. The disciples were all present and about fifty aspirants to Baptism, among the latter some relatives of the Holy Family, an old man and three youths from Sephoris, the boy whom Jesus had healed at that same place, and the old woman from there, who had recently visited Jesus in Abez. There were present, moreover, Cyrinus from Cyprus; the Roman Centurion Achias and his little, miraculously cured son Jephte, of Giskala; the Centurion Cornelius, his yellow slave who had been cured by Jesus, and several of his domestics; many pagans from Upper Galilee; a dark-skinned slave of Zorobabel; the five publicans of Mageddo; some boys, among whom was Joses, the nephew of Bartholomew; likewise all the cured lepers and possessed of these parts, including the two young Scribes healed the preceding evening. The last mentioned were indeed free from ulcers, but their countenance was still disfigured and bore the marks of suffering.

All the neophytes were clothed in penitential robes of gray wool, a four-cornered kerchief over their heads. Jesus instructed and prepared them for Baptism, after which they retired into the arbor and put on their baptismal garments, white tunics, long and wide. Their heads were uncovered, the kerchief, now thrown round their shoulders, and they stood in the channel around the basins, their hands crossed on their breasts. Andrew and Saturnin baptized, while Thomas, Bartholomew, John and others imposed hands as sponsors. The neophytes, with bared shoulders, leaned over a railing around the edge of the basin. One of the disciples carried a vessel of water that had been blessed by Jesus, from which the baptizers scooped some with the hand and poured it thrice over the heads of those being baptized. Thomas was sponsor to Jephte, the son of Achias. Although several received Baptism at the same time, yet the ceremony lasted until nearly two o'clock in the afternoon.

7. THE RESURRECTION OF THE DAUGHTER OF JAIRUS, THE CHIEF OF THE SYNAGOGUE

Later on when Jesus was curing some of the sick in the square before the synagogue of Capharnaum, Jairus, the Chief of the synagogue, presented himself before Him. He cast himself at His feet and implored Him to visit and cure his sick daughter, who was then breathing her last. Jesus was on the point of starting with Jairus when messengers hastily arrived from the house of the latter

and thus addressed him: "Thy daughter has expired.
There is no need further to trouble the Master." On hearing these words, Jesus said to Jairus: "Fear not! Trust in
Me, and thou shalt receive help!" They directed their
steps to the northern quarter of the city where dwelt Cornelius, whose house was not far removed from that of
Jairus. As they drew near they saw a multitude of
minstrels and female mourners already assembled in the
courtyard and before the door. Jesus entered, taking with
Him only Peter, James the Greater, and John. In passing
through the court, He said to the mourners: "Why do ye
thus lament and weep? Go your way! The damsel is not
dead, but only sleeping." At this the crowd of mourners
began to laugh Him to scorn, for they knew that she was
dead. But Jesus insisted on their retiring even from the
court, which He ordered to be locked. Then He entered
the apartment in which the grief-stricken mother was
busied with her maid preparing the winding sheet;
thence, accompanied by the father, the mother, and the
three disciples, He passed on to the chamber in which the
girl lay. Jesus stepped toward the couch, the parents
standing behind Him, the disciples to the right at the foot
of the bed. The mother did not please me. She was cold
and wanting in confidence. The father, too, was not a
warm friend of Jesus. He would not willingly do anything
to displease the Pharisees. It was anxiety and necessity
alone that had driven him to Jesus. He was actuated by a
double motive. If Jesus cured his child, she would be
restored to him; if not, he would have prepared a
triumph for the Pharisees. Still, the cure of Cornelius's
servant had greatly impressed him and awakened in him
a feeling of confidence. The little daughter was not tall,
and she was very much wasted. At most, I should say she
was eleven years old, and even at that small for her age,
for the Jewish girls of twelve are usually full-grown. She
lay on the couch enveloped in a long garment. Jesus

raised her lightly in His arms, held her on His breast, and breathed upon her. Then I saw something wonderful. Near the right side of the corpse was a luminous figure in a sphere of light. When Jesus breathed upon the little girl, that figure entered her mouth as a tiny human form of light. Then He laid the body down upon the couch, grasped one of the wrists, and said: "Damsel, arise!" The girl sat up in her bed. Jesus still held her by the hand. Then she stood up, opened her eyes, and supported by the hand of Jesus, stepped from the couch to the floor. Jesus led her, weak and tremulous, to the arms of her parents. They had watched the progress of the event at first coldly, though anxiously, then trembling with agitation, and now they were out of themselves for very joy. Jesus bade them give the child to eat and to make no unnecessary noise over the affair. After receiving the thanks of the father, He went down to the city. The mother was confused and stupefied. Her words of thanks were few. The news soon spread through the mourners that the maiden was alive. They immediately returned, some confused at their former incredulity, others still uttering vulgar pleasantries, and went into the house, where they saw the damsel eating.

On the way back, Jesus spoke with His disciples on the subject of this miracle. He said that these people, namely, the father and mother, had had neither real faith nor an upright intention. If the daughter was raised from the dead, it was for her own sake and for the glory of God's Kingdom. The death from which she had just been roused, that is, the death of the body, was a guiltless one, but from the death of the soul she must now preserve herself. Jesus then went to the great square of the city, cured many sick there awaiting Him, and taught in the synagogue until the close of the Sabbath. The Pharisees were so agitated and incensed that it would not have taken much to make them lay hands on Jesus if He had trusted Himself among them. They began again to declare that He effected His miracles by the power of sorcery. Jesus, however, slipped out of the city through Zorobabel's garden, and the disciples also dispersed.

Jesus spent part of the night retired in prayer. He supplicated for the conversion of sinners and besought His Heavenly Father to confound and frustrate the designs of the Pharisees, for He acted in everything as man, in order that we should imitate Him. He also begged His Father to allow Him to perfect His work, since according to our way of thinking, the Pharisees were ready to tear Him to pieces. He withdrew from their presence, but on the following day, the Sabbath itself, He again cured at the door of the synagogue and taught inside. And why did not the Pharisees drive the sick away? Why did they not forbid Jesus to teach in the synagogue? It was because Prophets and Doctors had at all times the right to teach, to help, and to heal. They did indeed accuse Him of error and blasphemy, though they were unable to prove their accusations. As for the Baptism that He gave, they did not trouble themselves about it and went not to where it was administered. There was no public highway through the valley; only a road over the mountains led to Bethsaida. The valley was traversed by only the footpath taken by the fishermen and the peasants when on their way to the lake.

Martha and the holy women of Jerusalem, Dina and others, after Jesus' departure went back to Naim and thence to their own homes. Maroni and her son were so beset by people desirous of seeing one raised from the dead that they were obliged to conceal themselves.

Cornelius the Centurion gave a feast at his house in honor of his cured servant. Numbers of heathens were in attendance, also crowds of the poor. Immediately after the miracle, Cornelius informed Jesus of his intention to sacrifice burnt offerings of all kinds of animals. But Jesus replied that it would be better for him to invite his enemies in order to reconcile them one with another; his friends, that he might lead them to the truth; and the poor, that he might recreate and entertain them with the food he had destined for sacrifice, for God no longer delighted in burnt offerings. Multitudes of heathens went from beyond Bethsaida and the mountains to the house of Cornelius, where the feast was celebrated.

Jesus was again at the place of Baptism. Saturnin experienced great joy in baptizing his two younger brothers and an uncle, all of whom were heathens. Their mother also had come with them. She was already a Jewess. His father was dead. Saturnin was descended from a royal race. His parents dwelt in Patras. At the time of which I speak his father was dead, but his stepmother with two daughters and two sons still lived there. From a brown-skinned man, a relative and follower of the dark complexioned one of the Three Kings, and whom he had met on a journey, Saturnin heard the story of the star and the birth of Jesus. Thereupon he went to Jerusalem and, when John began his career, became one of his first disciples; but after Jesus' baptism, he went with Andrew to Jesus. His stepmother with her two little girls had removed to Jerusalem with him, while the boys remained behind with their uncle. They too were now come to their brother. They were rich.

There were about twelve other men baptized. When they stepped into the channel around the basin, they tucked up their long garments and leaned over the edge. After their Baptism they retired into the arbor and reclothed themselves, putting on a baptismal garment consisting of a long white mantle. The Jews did not trouble themselves about the baptized heathens. If the latter did not present themselves before the priests for circumcision, the former took no notice of it. They did not make much account of the heathens, for they themselves were quite lukewarm and they avoided whatever could give them trouble. Cornelius, who dwelt among them and had caused a synagogue to be built, would probably have to receive circumcision if he wished to continue his intercourse with them.

Jesus afterward taught on the borders of the lake, not far from Peter's fishery. He had journeyed with the disciples over the mountain back of Mary's and Peter's dwellings in the direction of Bethsaida, and thence had descended to the lake. The shore near Bethsaida was steep, but at the point to which I now allude it gently sloped and afforded an easy landing place. Peter's ship and Jesus' little barque lay here. The latter was small and could at most contain fifteen men.

8. JESUS INSTRUCTS FROM HIS BARQUE. CALL OF MATTHEW

A great crowd of pagans who had been at Cornelius's feast were here assembled. Jesus was instructing them and, as the throng became very great, He with some of His disciples went on board His little barque, while the rest of them and the publicans went on Peter's boat. And now from the barque He instructed the heathens on the strand, making use of the parables of the sower and the tares in the field. The instruction over, they struck out across the lake, the disciples in Peter's boat plying the oars. Jesus' barque was fastened to Peter's, and the disciples took turns to row. Jesus sat on a raised seat near the mast, the others around Him and on the edge of the boat. They interrogated Him upon the meaning of the parable and asked why He spoke in similitudes. Jesus gave them a satisfactory explanation. They landed at a point between the valley of Gerasa and Bethsaida-Julias. A road ran from the shore to the houses of the publicans, and into it the four who were with Jesus turned. Jesus meanwhile, with the disciples, continued along the shore to the right, thus passing Matthew's residence, though at a distance. A side path ran from this road to his custom office, and along it Jesus bent His steps, the disciples timidly remaining behind. Servants and publicans were out in front of the custom house, busied with all kinds of merchandise. When Matthew from the top of a little eminence beheld Jesus and the disciples coming toward him, he became confused and withdrew into his private office. But Jesus continued to approach, and from the opposite side of the road called him. Then came Matthew hurrying out, prostrated with his face on the ground before Jesus, protesting that he did not esteem himself worthy that Jesus should speak with him. But Jesus said: "Matthew, arise, and follow Me!" Then Matthew arose, saying that he would instantly and joyfully abandon all things and follow Him. He accompanied Jesus back to where the disciples were standing, who saluted him and extended to him their hands. Thaddeus, Simon, and James the Less were particularly rejoiced at his coming. They and Matthew were half brothers. Their father Alpheus, before his marriage with their mother Mary Cleophas, was a widower with one son, Matthew. Matthew insisted upon all being his guests. Jesus, however, assured him that they would return next morning, and then they continued their way.

Matthew hurried back to his house, which stood in a corner of the mountains about a quarter of an hour from the lake. The little stream that flows from Gerasa into the lake ran past it at no great distance, and the view extended over lake and field. Matthew at once procured a substitute in his business, an excellent man belonging to Peter's barque, who was to discharge his duties until further arrangements could be made. Matthew was a married man with four children. He joyfully imparted to his wife the good fortune that had fallen to him, as well as his intention to abandon all and follow Jesus, and she received the announcement with corresponding joy. Then he directed her to see to the preparing of an entertainment for the next morning, he himself taking charge of the invitations and other arrangements. Matthew was almost as old as Peter. One might easily have taken him for the father of his young half brother Joses Barsabas. He was a man of heavy, bony frame with black hair and beard. Since his acquaintance with Jesus on the way to Sidon, he had received John's baptism and regulated his whole life most conscientiously.

On leaving Matthew, Jesus crossed the mountain at the rear of his dwelling and proceeded northward into the valley of Bethsaida-Julias, where He found encamped caravans and travelling pagans, whom He instructed.

Toward noon the next day Jesus returned with the disciples to Matthew's, where many publicans who had been invited were already assembled. Some Pharisees and some of John's disciples had joined Jesus on the way, but they did not enter Matthew's. They stayed outdoors, sauntering around the garden with the disciples, to whom they put the question: "How can you tolerate your Master's making Himself so familiar with sinners and publicans?" They received for answer: "Ask Himself why He does so!" But the Pharisees responded: "One cannot speak with a man who always maintains that he is right."

Matthew received Jesus and His followers most lovingly and humbly, and washed their feet. His half brothers warmly embraced him, and then he presented his wife and children to Jesus. Jesus spoke to the mother and blessed the children, who then retired, to return no more. I have often wondered why the children whom Jesus blessed usually appeared no more. I saw Jesus seated, and Matthew on his knees before Him. Jesus laid His hand upon him, blessed him, and addressed to him some words of instruction. Matthew had formerly been called Levi, but now he received the name of Matthew. The feast was a magnificent one. The table, in the form of a cross, was set in an open hall. Jesus sat in the midst of the publicans. In the intervals between the different courses, the guests arose and engaged in conversation with one another. Poor travellers passing by were supplied with food by the disciples, for the street on which the house stood led down to the ferry. It was on the occasion of their leaving table that the Pharisees approached the disciples, and then occurred the speeches and objections narrated in the Gospel of *St. Luke* 5:30-39. The Pharisees insisted particularly on the subject of fasting, because among the strict Jews a fast day began that evening in expiation of the sacrilege King Joachim committed by burning the Books of the Prophet Jeremias. Among the Jews, especially in Judea, it was not customary to pluck fruit by the wayside. Now Jesus permitted it to His disciples, and this the Pharisees made a subject of reproach to Him. While giving His answers to the Pharisees, Jesus was reclining at table with the publicans, whereas the disciples to whom the questions of the Pharisees were addressed were standing or walking among them. Jesus turned His head from side to side in answering.

Capharnaum was much more lively now than formerly. Crowds of strangers were streaming in on account of Jesus, some of them His friends, others His enemies, and most of them pagans, the followers of Zorobabel and Cornelius.

9. THE FINAL CALL OF PETER, ANDREW, JAMES, AND JOHN. JESUS STILLS THE TEMPEST ON THE LAKE

Next morning when Jesus went to the lake, which was about a quarter of an hour distant from Matthew's dwelling, Peter and Andrew were upon the point of launching out on the deep to let down their nets. Jesus called to them: "Come and follow Me! I will make you fishers of men!" They instantly abandoned their work, hove to their boat, and came on shore. Jesus went on a little farther up the shore to the ship of Zebedee, who with his sons James and John was mending his nets on the ship. Jesus called the two sons to come to Him. They obeyed immediately and came to land, while Zebedee remained on the ship with his servants.

Then Jesus sent Peter and Andrew, James and John into the mountains where the heathens were encamped, with the order to baptize all that desired it. He Himself had prepared them for it during the two preceding days. With Saturnin and the other disciples, Jesus went in another direction. All were to meet again that evening at Matthew's, and I saw Jesus pointing out with His finger the way they were to take. While He was calling the four disciples, the others had waited for Him at a little distance up the road, but when He commissioned those four to go and baptize, they were all together.

Jesus had indeed, at an earlier period, formally called the fishermen from their occupations, but with His consent they had always returned to them. So long as they themselves were not engaged in teaching, it was not necessary for them to follow Him constantly. Their means of navigation and their intercourse with the pagan caravans were very advantageous, likewise, while He sojourned at Capharnaum. When, after the last Pasch, they had for a longer time been with Jesus, they had indeed taught here and there, and had even wrought some miraculous cures. In these latter, however, they were not always successful, on account of their want of faith. They had also suffered persecution at this early stage of their apostolic career. In Gennabris they were led bound before the Pharisees and cast into prison. They received at that time from Jesus the power to bless the water intended for Baptism. This power was not imparted to them by the imposition of hands, but with a blessing.

Peter was, besides his fishery, engaged also in agriculture and cattle raising; consequently it was harder for him than for the others to break away from his business affairs. To this was added the feeling of his own unworthiness and his fancied incapacity for teaching, which made separation from his surroundings still more difficult. His house outside Capharnaum was large and long, surrounded by a courtyard, side buildings, halls, and sheds. The waters of the brook of Capharnaum, flowing in front of it, were dammed nearby into a beautiful pond in which fish were kept. All around were grass plots, upon which bleaching was done and nets were spread.

Andrew had followed the Lord longer, and he was already more detached from worldly affairs than his brother. James and John up to this period were accustomed to return at intervals to their parents.

It is understood that the Gospels do not contain the details of Jesus' intercourse with the disciples, but only a short statement of it. This call of the fishermen from their boats to make them fishers of men is there set down as happening at the beginning of His public life, and as the only call that Saints Peter, Andrew, John, and James received. Many of the miracles, parables, and instructions of Jesus are afterward recorded as instance of His power and wisdom, without any reference whatever to their order of time.

Peter, Andrew, James and John went to the pagan encampment, and there Andrew baptized. Water was brought from the brook in a large basin. The neophytes knelt in a circle, their hands crossed upon their breasts. Among them stood boys from three to six years. Peter held the basin, and Andrew, scooping the water up with his hand three different times, sprinkled the heads of the neophytes three at a time and repeated the words of Baptism. The other disciples went around outside the circle laying their hands on the newly baptized. These latter then withdrew, and their places were immediately filled by others. The ceremony was discontinued at intervals, and then the disciples recounted the parables they had learned from their Master, spoke of Jesus, His doctrine, and His miracles, and explained to the pagans points of which they were still ignorant regarding the Law and the Promises of God. Peter was particularly animated in his delivery and accompanied his words with many gestures. John and James likewise spoke very beautifully. Jesus meantime was teaching in another valley, and with Him was Saturnin, baptizing.

That evening when all were again assembled at Matthew's, the crowd was very great and pressed around Jesus. On that account, with the twelve Apostles and Saturnin He went on board Peter's barque and commanded them to row toward Tiberias, which was on the opposite side of the lake in its greatest breadth. It looked as if Jesus wanted to escape from the crowd that pressed upon Him, for He was worn out with fatigue. Three platforms surrounded the lower part of the mast, like steps one above the other. In the middle one, in one of the apartments used by the sentry, Jesus lay down and fell asleep, for He was very tired. The rowers were above Him. From Jesus' resting place, although protected by a roof, there was an unobstructed view over the whole lake. When the party put out from shore, the weather was calm and beautiful, but they had scarcely reached the middle of the lake before a violent tempest arose. I thought it very strange that, although the sky was shrouded in darkness, the stars were to be seen. The wind blew in a hurricane and the waves dashed over the boat, the sails of which had been furled. I saw from time to time a brilliant light glancing over the troubled waters. It must have been lightning. The danger was imminent, and the disciples were in great anxiety when they awoke Jesus with the words: "Master! Hast Thou no care for us? We are sinking!" Jesus arose, looked out on the water, and said quietly and earnestly, as if speaking to the storm: "Peace! Be still!" and instantly all became calm. The disciples were struck with fear. They whispered to one another: "Who is this Man that can control the waves?" Jesus reproved them for their little faith and their fear. He ordered them to row back to Corozain, for so the place of Matthew's custom house was called, on account of the city of Corozain. The region on the other side of the lake between Capharnaum and Giskala was named Genesareth. Zebedee's barque also returned with them, and another filled with passengers went off to Capharnaum.

There were in all about fifteen men on the boat with Jesus. We must not be surprised at the rowers' position above the sleeping place of Jesus, nor at the fact of Jesus' being able, notwithstanding, to take in the whole view of the lake. The oars rested upon the high sides of the boat and struck far out into the water. They were provided with long handles and the rowers were obliged to stand high. It was about one hour from Corozain to the south-west and a little to the north of Gergesa, which occupied a less elevated position.

At the place where Jesus paused to address the multitude there was a stone seat intended for the teacher. The instruction had been announced two days before, and there were in all probability two thousand listeners in attendance. Jesus healed also a great crowd of people, the blind and lame, the dumb and leprous. As He began to teach, some of the possessed who had been led thither commenced to shout and to rave. Jesus commanded them to be silent and to lie down on the ground. Like frightened dogs they lay on the ground and moved not until, at the close of His discourse, He went to them and delivered them.

Among the numerous cures, I remember that of a man with an arm perfectly withered and a hand shrunken and crooked. Jesus stroked down the arm, took the hand in His own, and straightened out each finger one after the other, at the same time gently bending and pressing it. All this took place almost instantaneously, in a shorter time than one takes to say how it was done. The hand was restored to its proper shape, the blood began to circulate, and the man could move it although it was still wasted and weak. Its strength, however, momentarily increased.

There were in the crowd many women and children of all ages. Jesus had them brought to Him in bands, one after another. He walked about among them, gave them His blessing, and instructed them in tones loud enough to be heard by all. I saw Him during this instruction take a child by the hand and turn it here and there, to show how men, without complaint or resistance, should allow themselves to be conducted by God. He paid great attention to the children. Most of these people were heathens, others were Jews from Syria and Decapolis. At the spreading rumor of Jesus' doings, they had come in great caravans with their servants and children and sick to the teaching, healing, and Baptism. Jesus came to meet them here, that the crowd in Capharnaum might not become too great. Among them I saw the relatives of the woman mentioned in the Gospel, the woman afflicted with the issue of blood, who was then at Capharnaum. Those relatives were an uncle of her deceased husband from Paneas, in whose house she had been married; her grown daughter; and another woman. They spoke to the disciples, begging them to conduct them to Capharnaum that evening, and they inquired also after their sick relatives.

They heard Jesus' instructions.

Baptism was administered the whole day at this place. As on the preceding day, the neophytes knelt in circles. I saw again many little boys baptized. They stood in circles, their hands joined on their breasts. The water had been brought in leathern bottles from the valley of Corozain. Present among the crowd of hearers were some Pharisees from the surrounding districts and some of John's false disciples, who acted as spies upon Jesus. In the evening He returned to Matthew's with the disciples. He related another parable, that of the treasure which a man found hidden in his neighbor's field. Without disclosing the secret, he went and sold all that he owned in order to buy that field. This parable Jesus applied to the great desire of the Gentiles to seize upon the Kingdom of God. To escape the crowd that pressed upon Him, Jesus again went on board a barque and there taught. He did not, however, go far out on the water, but returned and spent the night in prayer.

Next morning the disciples brought Him the news that Mary Cleophas was lying very ill at Peter's near Capharnaum, that His Mother entreated Him to come to her soon, and that a great multitude of sick of whom many were from Nazareth, were awaiting His arrival. Jesus again taught and cured numbers on the shore of the lake. Many possessed were brought to Him, and He delivered them. The crowd of people and the pressure of the throng were constantly on the increase, and no words can say how unweariedly Jesus labored and helped all in need.

That afternoon He and all His Apostles rowed over to Bethsaida. Matthew had delivered the custom house to a man belonging to the fishery. Since his reception of John's baptism, he had carried on his business in an altogether blameless manner. The other publicans also were honest in their dealings and very liberal men, who

gave large alms to the poor. Judas is still good. He is uncommonly active and ready to render service, though in
his distribution of alms somewhat close and calculating.
A large number of Gentiles crossed the lake today. Those
that were not going on further, to Capharnaum for instance, left their camels and asses on rafts towed by the
boats, or led them over the bridge that crossed the Jordan
above the lake.

It was approaching four o'clock when Jesus reached
Bethsaida, where Mary with Maroni and her son, who
had been here for two days, were awaiting His coming
along with others. Jesus took some refreshments, while
Mary Cleophas's sons repaired at once to their sick
mother. A crowd of people was assembled in front of
Andrew's house, and Jesus taught and cured until after
night had closed.

The throng of strangers to Capharnaum at this time,
both Jews and Gentiles, surpassed anything that can be
imagined. Great caravans were encamped in all the country around. Very probably the number of strangers sojourning all around the country on Jesus' account
amounted to twelve thousand. The valleys and nooks of
the surrounding districts were alive with grazing camels
and asses. The fodder was put before them at a convenient height, and then they were tied to it. They browsed
also on the numerous buds of the hedges and thickets,
though to the great prejudice of the same. Tents were
pitched everywhere. Since Jesus' sojourn Capharnaum
had greatly increased in size, wealth, and importance.
Many families from afar had there taken up their abode,
and the throng of visitors brought money into the city.
Zorobabel's house, as well as that of Cornelius, were now
almost connected with the city proper.

Numerous sick were brought to Capharnaum from the
towns and villages lying around. All had been thrown
into excitement by the raising of the youth of Naim, and

the other astonishing miracles. Many sick from Nazareth, even those that were considered incurable and others nigh unto death, had been brought hither to Jesus in all confidence by their friends. Peter's house outside the city, its courtyard, outbuildings, and sheds were crowded with them. Tents and arbors of all kinds were hastily put up and provisions provided. The widow of Naim, who was related to Peter, and Mary Cleophas, likewise a connection of his through her third husband, were there. Mary Cleophas's usual residence was at Cana, but she had accompanied the widow of Naim to Capharnaum. She had with her Simeon, the son of her third marriage, a boy of eight years. She was already fever-stricken on her arrival, and her sickness was on the increase. Jesus had not yet gone to her. I remarked some people from Greece among the multitudes here awaiting Jesus, some from Patras, Saturnin's native city.

10. JOHN THE BAPTIST'S MESSAGE TO THE SYNAGOGUE. THE MIRACULOUS DRAUGHT OF FISHES

Several of John's disciples, sent by their master, came from Machaerus to Capharnaum before the Sabbath began. They were some of the oldest and most confidential of his disciples, and among them were the brothers of Mary Cleophas, James, Sadoch, and Heliachim. They called the Elders and the committee appointed by the Pharisees into the porch before the synagogue, and there presented to them a long, narrow, conical roll of parchment. It was a letter from John, and contained in strong and expressive terms his testimony of Jesus. While they were reading it and, somewhat perplexed, were discussing its contents among themselves, a numerous crowd assembled, to whom the messengers from John made known what their master had at Machaerus declared in a magnificent discourse before Herod, his own disciples, and a crowded audience. I saw the whole scene. When the disciples whom John had sent to Jesus at Mageddo had returned to their master, bringing with them the news of Jesus' miracles and teachings, as well as the persecution He endured from the Pharisees; when they repeated the various rumors afloat concerning Jesus and the complaints of many because He made no effort to release him (John), the Baptist felt himself urged once more to bear public witness to Him. This he did the more readily since all his efforts to induce Him to testify of Himself had been fruitless. Therefore he sent a request to Herod to allow him to address his disciples and all others who might desire to hear him. He brought forward as a plea in his own favor that he should soon be reduced to silence. Herod did not hesitate to grant the favor asked. John's disciples and a crowd of people were admitted to the open square of the castle in which the Precursor was confined. Herod and his wicked wife sat on elevated seats surrounded by a numerous guard of soldiers. Then John was led forth from his prison and he began his discourse. Herod was quite pleased that the affair should come off, as he was glad of the opportunity to appease the people by letting them see how light and easy was the imprisonment to which John was subjected. Under the powerful inspiration of the Holy Ghost, the Baptist spoke of Jesus. He himself, he said, was sent only to prepare the ways for Him. He had never announced another than Jesus; but, stubborn as they were, the people would not acknowledge Him. Had they then forgotten, he asked, what he had told them of Him? He would recall it to them clearly once more, for his own end was not far distant! At these last words, the whole assembly was moved, and many of John's disciples wept. Herod grew uneasy and embarrassed, for he had by no means resolved upon John's death, while his concubine dissembled her feelings as best she could. John continued zealously to speak. He recounted the wonders that took place at Jesus' baptism and declared Him the Beloved Son of God announced by the Prophets. His doctrine was the same as His Father's. What He did the Father also did, and no one can go to the Father excepting by Him, that is, by Jesus. And so he went on, refuting at length the reproaches of the Pharisees against Him, and especially that of His healing on the Sabbath day. Everyone, he said, should keep holy the Sabbath, but the Pharisees profaned it, since they did not follow the teachings of Jesus, the teachings of the Son of Him who had instituted the Sabbath. John said many things of a similar nature, and proclaimed Jesus the One outside of whom no salvation could be found. Whoever believed not in Him and followed not His doctrine, would be condemned. He exhorted his disciples to turn to Jesus, not to remain standing blindly near Him on the threshold, but to enter into the Temple itself.

After his discourse, John sent several of his disciples with a letter to the synagogue of Capharnaum. In it he repeated all that he had said in testimony of Jesus, namely, that He was the Son of God and the fulfillment of the Promise, and that all His acts and teachings were right and holy. He refuted their objections, threatened them with God's judgments, and earnestly entreated them not to turn away from salvation. He commanded the disciples to read to the people another letter containing the same things, and to repeat to them all that he had just said. And now I saw John's disciples doing in Capharnaum what had been commanded them. An unusually large crowd was assembled, for the city was actually swarming with people on this Sabbath. There were here Jews from all quarters, and they listened with great joy to John's testimony of Jesus. Many gave utterance to loud acclamations, and their faith gained new strength.

The Pharisees had to give way to the multitude; they

could not say a word. They shrugged their shoulders, shook their heads, and feigned to be well-disposed. They, however, asserted their own authority and told John's disciples that they would place no obstacle in Jesus' way if He refrained from violating the laws and disturbing the public peace. He was, it was true, very wonderfully endowed; but it was theirs to maintain order, and there should be moderation in all things. John too was a good man, but shut up as he was in prison, he might easily form a wrong estimate of things; besides, he had never been much with Jesus.

And now the hour for the Sabbath struck, and all betook themselves to the synagogue, among them Jesus and the disciples. All listened with the greatest admiration to Jesus' words. He spoke of Joseph, sold by his brethren, and explained some passages from Amos that contained the menaces of God against the prevarications of Israel.[1] No one interrupted Him. The Pharisees listened with secret envy and astonishment that they could not repress. John's testimony, proclaimed so boldly to the public, had somewhat intimidated them.

But suddenly there arose fearful cries in the synagogue. Some people had brought in a man, violently possessed, belonging to Capharnaum. All of a sudden he made an assault on those around him, and attempted to tear them with his teeth. Jesus turned to the side whence the noise proceeded and said: "Silence! Take him!" The man became perfectly calm. They led him out of the synagogue, and he threw himself on the ground, looking quite intimidated. When Jesus had finished the Sabbath instructions and was about to withdraw, He went to where the man was lying and delivered him from the devil. After that He repaired with the disciples to Peter's near the lake, because there He could be more at peace. That night He went off by Himself to pray. Among all those that Jesus cured, I never saw any such as we call insane. They were all demoniacs and possessed.

The Pharisees were still together. They ran through all kinds of ancient writings relative to the Prophets, their manner of life, their teachings, and their actions. They dwelt especially upon Malachias, of whom many traditions were still extant, and compared what they found with the doctrine of Jesus. They were obliged to give Jesus the preference and admire His gifts, though they continued to criticize His teachings.

Next morning Jesus again taught in the synagogue before an immense crowd. Meanwhile Mary Cleophas had become so sick that the Blessed Virgin sent to Jesus to implore His help. Jesus then went to Peter's near the city where Mary, the widow of Naim, and the sons and brothers of the sick woman were. The sorrow of little Simeon, then about eight years old, was quite remarkable. He was the youngest son of Mary Cleophas by her third husband, Jonas. Jonas was the young brother of Peter's father-in-law, who had been associated with him in the fishery, and who had died about half a year previously. Jesus went to the sick woman's bed, prayed, and laid His hands upon her. She was quite exhausted by fever. Then He grasped her by the hand and told her that she should no longer be sick. He directed them to give her to eat, and I saw them bringing her a cup of something, after which she had to eat a little. This He ordered to almost all the sick whom He cured, and I heard that it bore some signification to the Most Blessed Sacrament. As a general thing, Jesus blessed the food thus ordered. The joy of her sons, and especially that of little Simeon, was indescribable when their mother arose cured and began to serve the other sick. As for Jesus, He went out immediately and began to cure the crowds of sick awaiting His coming in the sheds and buildings around the house. The sick of all kinds were gathered here, some of long duration looked upon as incurable, others apparently at the point of death. They had been brought from far and wide; some were even from Nazareth and had known Jesus in His early youth. I saw some carried to Him on the shoulders of others, looking more like corpses than creatures with life.

Some of John's disciples, they that had brought the writings, came here to Jesus to amuse themselves and tell Him how indignant they were against Him because He made no effort to deliver their master from imprisonment. They told Him how rigorously they had fasted to obtain that God would move Him to free their master. Jesus comforted them and again praised John as the holiest of men. After that I heard them speaking with Jesus' disciples. They inquired why Jesus did not Himself baptize. Their master, as they said, labored so zealously in that way. The disciples of Jesus answered in words like these: "John baptized, because he is the Baptist; but Jesus heals, because He is the Saviour," adding that John had never effected a miraculous cure.

And now there came to Jesus some Scribes from Nazareth. They were very courteous, and besought Him once more to visit Nazareth. It looked as if they wanted to make Him forget what had happened there. But Jesus replied that no Prophet is esteemed in his own native city. He went then to the synagogue, where He delivered the Sabbath instructions till its close. On leaving the synagogue, He cured a blind man.

Peter's wife presided over the domestic affairs of his house outside the city, while those of the other near the lake were directed by his mother-in-law and step-daughter. Jesus went away to pray. Some of the disciples, they that had formerly been engaged in fishing, asked and obtained their Master's permission to go on board their barques and pass the night at their old occupation, since there was great need of fish to supply the stupendous multitude of strangers then present in Capharnaum.

There were also many desirous of crossing to the other side of the lake.

The disciples spent the whole night in fishing, and next morning rowed many passengers across. Jesus meanwhile, with the rest of the disciples, busied Himself in distributing alms to the poor, to the sick that had been cured, and to needy travellers. This distribution was accompanied by instruction. With His own hands Jesus presented to each one that of which he had need, giving him at the same time words of consolation and advice. The alms consisted of clothing, various materials and covers, bread, and money. The holy women also gave alms from their own stock of provisions, as well as from the gifts bestowed upon them by certain benevolent persons. The disciples carried the bread and clothing in baskets, and made the distribution of them according to Jesus' orders.

Later in the day Jesus gave at Peter's fishery a discourse, which was attended by an immense crowd. The boats of Peter and Zebedee were lying not far from the shore. The disciples who had been fishing the night before were on the shore a little distant from the crowd, busy cleaning their nets. Jesus' little barque was lying near the larger ones. When the press became too great—for the level shore was very narrow at this point, a rocky mountain wall rising in the rear—Jesus made a sign to the fishermen, and they rowed His barque to where He was standing. While it was approaching, a Scribe from Nazareth, who had come hither with some of the sick whom Jesus had cured yesterday, said: "Master, I will follow Thee whithersoever Thou goest!" Jesus replied: "The foxes have holes, and the birds of the air nests, but the Son of Man has not where to lay His head."

The little barque pushed up to the shore, and Jesus entered it with some of His disciples. They rowed out a short distance from the land and then up and down, pausing sometimes here, sometimes there, while Jesus instructed the crowd on the shore. He related to them several parables of the Kingdom of God, among them that in which the Kingdom of Heaven is compared to a net cast into the sea, and that of the enemy who sowed cockle among the wheat.

Evening was now closing. Jesus told Peter to row his boat out on the lake and to cast his nets to the fish. Peter, slightly vexed, replied: "We have labored all night and have taken nothing, but at Thy word I will let down the net," and he with the others entered their barques with their nets and rowed out on the lake. Jesus bade adieu to the crowd, and in His own little boat—wherein were Saturnin, Veronica's son, who had arrived the day before, and some of the other disciples—He followed after Peter's. He continued to instruct them, explaining similitudes, and when out on the deep water told them where to let down the nets. Then He left them and rowed over in His little boat to the landing place near Matthew's.

By this time it was night, and on the edge of the boats near the nets, torches were blazing. The fishers cast out the net, and rowed toward Chorozain, but soon they were unable to raise it. When at last, continuing to row eastward, they dragged it out of the deep into shallow water, it was so heavy that it gave way here and there. They inserted scoops formed like little boats into the net, seized the fish with their hands, and put them into smaller nets and into the casks that floated at the sides of their barques. Then they called to their companions on Zebedee's boat, who came and emptied a part of the net. They were actually terrified at the sight of the draught of fishes. Never before had such a thing happened to them. Peter was confounded. He felt how vain were all the cares they had hitherto bestowed upon their fishing, how fruitlessly they had labored, notwithstanding their trouble—and here, at a word from Him, they had caught at one draught more than they had ever done in months together.

When the net was relieved of part of its weight, they rowed to the shore, dragged it out of the water, and gazed awestruck at the multitude of fish it still contained. Jesus was standing on the shore. Peter, humbled and confused, fell at His feet and said: "Lord, depart from me, for I am a sinful man!" But Jesus said: "Fear not, Peter! From henceforth thou shalt catch men!" Peter, however, was quite overcome by sadness at the sight of his own unworthiness and vain solicitude for the things of this life. It was now between three and four in the morning, and it began to grow light.

The disciples, having put the fish into a place of safety, retired to their boats for a short sleep. Jesus, with Saturnin and Veronica's son, turned off to the east, and climbed the northern end of the mountain ridge upon whose southern extremity stood Gamala. Little hills and thickets were here scattered around. Jesus instructed Saturnin and Veronica's son how to pray and gave them several points upon which to reflect. Then He withdrew from them into solitude, while they rested, walked about, and prayed.

The disciples spent the next day in transporting their fish, a great portion of which was distributed to the poor, and to all they recounted the wonderful circumstances attending their labor. The pagans bought a great many, and many more were taken to Capharnaum and Bethsaida. All were now firmly convinced of the folly of solicitude for the nourishment of the body; for as the sea obeyed Jesus in the time of tempest, so did the fish obey Him. They were caught at His word.

Toward evening they went again to the landing place on the east side of the lake, and Jesus with the two disciples went with them toward Capharnaum. He repaired to Peter's house outside the city, and there until after night

He cured by the light of torches many sick, men and women, who were quite abandoned on account of their maladies, which were considered unclean. Their friends had not dared to bring them openly with the other sick. Jesus cured them secretly by night in Peter's yard. There were some among them who for years had been separated from their friends, and who were in a most pitiable condition. All the rest of the night Jesus spent in prayer.

1. *Gen.* 37:1-41; *Amos* 2:6, 3:9.

11. THE SERMON ON THE MOUNT. CURE OF A PARALYTIC

Jesus rowed with several of the disciples over the lake and landed one hour to the north of Matthew's. Already many pagans, as well as those whom Jesus had cured and the newly baptized, had repaired to the mountain east of Bethsaida-Julias where Jesus was to teach. All around stood the camps of the pagans. The disciples who had been fishing on the night of the miraculous draught asked Jesus whether they too should go with Him, for their recent success had freed them from anxiety upon the score of provisions, and they felt that all was in His hands. Jesus replied that they should baptize those that were still in Capharnaum, and after that employ their time at their accustomed occupations, as the immense number of strangers then in and around the city rendered extra supplies necessary.

Before crossing the lake, Jesus delivered to His disciples a comprehensive instruction. In it He gave them an idea of the whole plan of the discourses upon which He intended to dwell for a long time. He told them that they (the disciples) were the salt of the earth destined to vivify and preserve others, consequently that they themselves must not lose their savor. Jesus explained all this to them at full length, making use of numerous examples and parables. After that He rowed across the lake.

The disciples (the fishermen) and Saturnin began their work of baptizing in the valley of Capharnaum. The son of the widow of Naim was here baptized and named Martial, Saturnin imposing hands upon him. The holy women did not follow Jesus to the instructions, but remained behind to celebrate with the widow of Naim the baptismal feast of her son.

There were with Jesus, Joseph of Arimathea's nephews, who had come from Jerusalem; Nathanael; Manahem of Korah; and many other disciples. In these last days I saw about thirty of them gathered together in Capharnaum.

On landing at the east side of the lake just below the mouth of the Jordan, the traveller ascended the mountain to the east and then, turning westward, went on to the spot upon which the instruction was to be given. Another way could be taken, namely, that over the Jordan bridge to the north of the lake. But this latter way, on account of the wild character of the country and its numerous ravines, was rather a difficult road to the mountain. Bethsaida-Julias was situated on the eastern bank of the mouth of the Jordan, the river there forming a bend. The western shore was high, and to it ran a road.

There was no teacher's chair on the mountain, only an eminence surrounded by a mound of earth and covered by an awning. The view from the west and southwest extended over the lake and to the opposite mountains. One could even descry Mount Thabor. Crowds of people, most of them pagans that had received Baptism, were encamped around. There were Jews also present. Separation between them was not so rigorously observed here, since communication between the Jews and Gentiles was greater in these parts, and on this side of the lake the latter enjoyed certain privileges.

Jesus began by enumerating the Eight Beatitudes, and

then went on to explain the first: "Blessed are the poor in spirit, for theirs is the Kingdom of Heaven." He related examples and parables, spoke of the Messiah, and especially of the conversion of the Gentiles. Now was accomplished what the Prophet foretold of the Desired of Nations: "And I will move all nations. *And the Desired of all nations shall come,* and I will fill this house with glory, saith the Lord of hosts."[1] There was no curing on this day, for the sick had been healed on the preceding days. The Pharisees had come over in one of their own boats and they listened to Jesus' words with chagrin and jealousy. The people had brought with them food, which they ate during the pauses of the instruction. Jesus and the disciples had fish, bread, and honey, also little flasks of some kind of juice, or balm, a few drops of which were mixed with the water they drank.

Toward evening the people from Capharnaum, Bethsaida, and other neighboring places returned to their homes in the boats that awaited them on the lake. Jesus and His disciples went down toward the valley of the Jordan and into a shepherd inn, where they passed the night. Jesus still continued to teach the disciples, thus to prepare them for their future mission.

Jesus devoted fourteen days to instructions on the Eight Beatitudes, and spent the intervening Sabbath in Capharnaum.

On the following day He continued His preaching on the mountain. Mary, Mary Cleophas, Maroni of Naim, and two other women were present. When Jesus with the Apostles and disciples went back to the lake, He spoke of their vocation in these words: "Ye are the light of the world!" He illustrated by the similitude of the city seated on a mountain, the light on the candlestick, and the fulfilling of the Law. Then He rowed to Bethsaida, and put up at Andrew's.

Among the neophytes whom Saturnin baptized on those

days near Capharnaum were some Jews from Achaia whose ancestors had fled thither at the time of the Babylonian Captivity.

Bethsaida-Julias was a recently built city inhabited mostly by pagans. There were, however, some Jews, and the city possessed a famous school in which all kinds of knowledge were taught. Jesus had not yet visited it, but the inhabitants went out to the instruction and also to Capharnaum, where their sick were cured. Bethsaida-Julias was beautifully situated in the narrow valley of the Jordan, built a little up on the eastern side of the mountain, one-half hour from the point where the river flows into the lake. One hour northward, a stone bridge spanned the Jordan.

While going down from the mountain whereon He had been teaching, Jesus again instructed the disciples, and spoke of the sufferings and sharp persecutions in store for them. He slept that night in Peter's barque.

When Jesus next day went down from the mountain to Capharnaum, He found a crowd of people assembled to bid Him welcome. He repaired to Peter's house near the city. It stood outside the gate to the right on entering the city from the valley. When it was known that Jesus and the disciples were in the house, a crowd soon gathered around Him. The Scribes and Pharisees also hastened out to hear Him. The whole court around the open hall in which Jesus sat and taught with the disciples and Scribes was full. He spoke of the Ten Commandments and, coming to the words recorded in the Gospel of the Sermon on the Mount: "You have heard that it was said to them of old: Thou shalt not kill," He based upon them His instruction on the forgiveness of injuries and the love of one's enemies. Just at this moment a loud noise arose on the roof of the hall, and through the usual opening in the ceiling a paralytic on his bed was lowered by four men, who cried out: "Lord, have pity upon a poor sick man!"

He was let down by two cords into the midst of the assembly before Jesus. The friends of the sick man had tried in vain to carry him through the crowd into the courtyard, and had at last mounted the outside steps to the roof of the hall, whose trap door they opened. All eyes were fixed upon the invalid, and the Pharisees were vexed at what appeared to them a great misdemeanor, a piece of unheard-of impertinence. But Jesus, who was pleased at the faith of the poor people, stepped forward and addressed the paralytic, who lay there motionless: "Be of good heart, son, thy sins are forgiven thee!" words which were, as usual, particularly distasteful to the Pharisees. They thought within themselves: "That is blasphemy! Who but God can forgive sins?" Jesus saw their thoughts and said: "Wherefore have ye such thoughts of bitterness in your heart? Which is easier to say to the paralytic: Thy sins are forgiven thee; or to say: Arise, take up thy bed, and walk? But that you may know that the Son of Man has power on earth to forgive sins, I say to thee" (here Jesus turned to the paralytic): "Arise! Take up thy bed, and go into thy house!" And immediately the man arose cured, rolled up the coverlets of his bed, laid the laths of the frame together, took them under his arm and upon his shoulder, and accompanied by those that had brought him and some other friends went off singing canticles of praise while the whole multitude shouted for joy. The Pharisees, full of rage, slipped away, one by one. It was now the Sabbath, and Jesus, followed by the multitude, repaired to the synagogue.

1. *Aggeus* 2:8.

12. JAIRUS AND HIS DAUGHTER. HER RELAPSE. CURE OF A WOMAN AFFLICTED WITH AN ISSUE OF BLOOD, OF TWO BLIND MEN, AND OF A PHARISEE

Jairus, the Chief of the synagogue, was also present at that last miracle in the synagogue. He was very sad and full of remorse. His daughter was again near death, and truly a frightful death, as it had fallen upon her in punishment of her own and her parents' sins. Since the preceding Sabbath she had lain ill of a fever. The mother and her sister together with Jairus's mother, who all lived in the same house, had, along with the daughter herself, taken Jesus' miraculous healing in a very frivolous way, without gratitude and without in any way altering their life. Jairus, weak and yielding, entirely under the control of his vain and beautiful wife, had let the women have their own way. Their home was the theater of female vanity, and all the latest pagan styles of finery were brought into requisition for their adornment. When the little girl was well again, these women laughed among themselves at Jesus and turned Him into ridicule. The child followed their example. Until very recently she had retained her innocence, but now it was no longer so. A violent fever seized upon her. The burning and thirst that she had endured were something extraordinary; the last week was spent in a state of constant delirium, and she now lay near death. The parents suspected that it was a punishment of their frivolity, though they would not acknowledge it to themselves. At last the mother became so ashamed and so frightened that she said to Jairus: "Will Jesus again have pity on us?" and she commissioned her husband once more humbly to implore His assistance. But Jairus was ashamed to appear again before the Lord, so he waited till the Sabbath instructions were over. He had full faith that Jesus could help him at any time, if He would. He was too ashamed to be seen by the people again asking for help.

When Jesus was leaving the synagogue, a great crowd pressed around Him, for there were many, both sick and well, who wanted to speak to Him. Jairus approached with trouble on his countenance. He threw himself at Jesus' feet, and begged Him again to have pity on his daughter whom he had left in a dying state. Jesus promised that He would return with him. And now there came someone from Jairus's house looking for him, because he stayed so long, and the mother of the girl thought that Jesus would not come. The messenger told Jairus that his daughter was already dead. Jesus comforted the father and told him to have confidence. It was already dark, and the crowd around Jesus was very great. Just then a woman afflicted with an issue of blood, taking advantage of the darkness, made her way through the crowd, leaning on the arms of her nurses. She dwelt not far from the synagogue. The women afflicted with the same malady, though not so grievously as herself, had told her of their own cure some hours earlier. They had that day at noon, when Jesus was passing in the midst of the crowd, ventured to touch His garments, and were thereby instantly cured. Their words roused her faith. She hoped in the dusk of evening and in the throng that would gather round Jesus on leaving the synagogue, to be able to touch Him unnoticed. Jesus knew her thoughts and consequently slackened His pace. The nurses led her as close to Him as possible. Standing near her were her daughter, her husband's uncle, and Lea. The sufferer knelt down, leaned forward supporting herself on one hand, and with the other reaching through the crowd she touched the hem of Jesus' robe. Instantly she felt that she was healed. Jesus at the same moment halted, glanced around at the disciples, and inquired: "Who hath touched Me?" To which Peter answered: "Thou askest, 'Who touched Me?' The people throng and press upon Thee, as Thou seest!" But Jesus responded: "Someone hath touched Me, for I know that virtue is gone out from Me." Then He looked around and, as the crowd had fallen back a step, the woman could not longer remain hidden. Quite abashed, she approached Him timidly, fell on her knees before Him, and acknowledged in hearing of the whole crowd what she had done. Then she related how long she had suffered from the bloody flux, and that she believed herself healed by the touch of His garment. Turning to Jesus, she begged Him to forgive her. Then Jesus addressed to her these words: "Be comforted, My daughter, thy faith hath made thee whole! Go in peace, and remain free from thy infirmity!" and she departed with her friends.

She was thirty years old, very thin and pale, and was named Enue. Her deceased husband was a Jew. She had only one daughter, who had been taken charge of by her uncle. He had now come to the Baptism, accompanied by his niece and a sister-in-law named Lea. The husband of the latter was a Pharisee and an enemy of Jesus. Enue had, in her widowhood, wished to enter into a connection which to her rich relatives appeared far below her position; therefore they had opposed her.

Jesus with rapid steps accompanied Jairus to his house. Peter, James, John, Saturnin and Matthew were with Him. In the forecourt were again gathered the mourners and weepers, but this time they uttered no word of mockery, nor did Jesus say as He did before: "She is only sleeping," but passed on straight through the crowd. Jairus's mother, his wife, and her sister came timidly forth to meet Him. They were veiled and in tears; their robes, the garments of mourning. Jesus left Saturnin and Matthew with the people in the forecourt, while accompanied by Peter, James, and John, the father, the mother, and the grandmother, He entered the room in which the dead girl lay. It was a different room from the first time. Then she

lay in a little chamber; now she was in the room behind
the fireplace. Jesus called for a little branch from the
garden and a basin of water, which He blessed. The
corpse lay stiff and cold. It did not present so agreeable
an appearance as on the former occasion. Then I had
seen the soul hovering in a sphere of light close to the
body, but this time I did not see it at all. On the former
occasion, Jesus said: "She is sleeping," but now He said
nothing. She was dead. With the little branch Jesus
sprinkled her with the blessed water, prayed, took her by
the hand, and said: "Little maid, I say to thee, arise!" As
Jesus was praying, I saw the girl's soul in a dark globe approaching her mouth, into which it entered. She suddenly
opened her eyes, obeyed the touch of Jesus' hand, arose
and stepped from her couch. Jesus led her to her parents
who, receiving her with hot tears and choking sobs, sank
at Jesus' feet. He ordered them to give her something to
eat, some bread and grapes. His order was obeyed. The
girl ate and began to speak. Then Jesus earnestly exhorted
the parents to receive the mercy of God thankfully, to
turn away from vanity and worldly pleasure, to embrace
the penance preached to them, and to beware of again
compromising their daughter's life now restored for the
second time. He reproached them with their whole manner of living, with the levity they had exhibited at the
reception of the first favor bestowed upon them, and their
conduct afterward, by which in a short time they had exposed their child to a much more grievous death than that
of the body, namely, the death of the soul. The little girl
herself was very much affected and shed tears. Jesus
warned her against concupiscence of the eyes and sin.
While she partook of the grapes and the bread that He
had blessed, He told her that for the future she should no
longer live according to the flesh, but that she should eat
of the Bread of Life, the Word of God, should do penance, believe, pray, and perform works of mercy. The

parents were very much moved and completely transformed. The father promised to break the bonds that bound him to worldliness, and to obey Jesus' orders, while the mother and the rest of the family, who had now come in, expressed their determination to reform their lives. They shed tears and gave thanks to Jesus. Jairus, entirely changed, immediately made over a great part of his possessions to the poor. The daughter's name was Salome.

As a crowd had gathered before the house, Jesus told Jairus that they should make no unnecessary reports concerning what had just taken place. He often gave this command to those whom He cured, and that for various reasons. The chief was that the divulging and boasting of such favors troubles the recollection of the soul and prevents its reflection upon the mercy of God. Jesus desired that the cured should enter into themselves instead of running about enjoying the new life that had been given them, and thereby falling an easy prey to sin. Another reason for enjoining silence was that Jesus wanted to impress upon the disciples the necessity of avoiding vainglory and of performing the good they did through love and for God alone. Sometimes again, He made use of this prohibition in order not to increase the number of the inquisitive, the importunate, and the sick who came to Him not by the impulse of faith. Many indeed came merely to test His power, and then they fell back into their sins and infirmities, as Jairus's daughter had done.

Jesus and His five disciples left Jairus's house by the rear, in order to escape the crowd that pressed around the door. The first miracle here was performed in clear daylight; that of today was after the Sabbath and by the light of lamps. Jairus's house was in the northern part of the city. Jesus, on leaving it, turned to the northwest off toward the ramparts. Meanwhile two blind men with their guides were on the lookout for His coming. It seemed almost as if they scented His presence, for they followed after Him, crying: "Jesus, Thou Son of David, have pity on us!" At that moment Jesus went into the house of a good man who was devoted to Him. The house was built in the rampart and had on the other side a door opening into the country beyond the city precincts. The disciples sometimes stopped at this house. Its owner was one of the guards in this section of the city. The blind men, however, still followed Jesus, and even into the house, crying in beseeching tones: "Have mercy on us, Son of David!" At last Jesus turned to them and said: "Do you believe that I can do this unto you?" and they answered: "Yea, Lord!" Then He took from His pocket a little flask of oil, or balsam, and poured some into a small dish, brown and shallow. Holding it and the flask in His left hand, with the right He put into the dish a little earth, mixed it up with the thumb and forefinger of the right hand, touched the eyes of the blind men with the same, and said: "May it be done unto you according to your desire!" Their eyes were opened, they saw, they fell on their knees and gave thanks. To them also Jesus recommended silence as to what had just taken place. This He did to prevent the crowd from following Him and to avoid exasperating the Pharisees. The cries of the blind men as they followed Him had, however, already betrayed His presence in this part of the country, and besides this, the two men could not forbear imparting their happiness to all whom they met. A crowd was in consequence soon gathered around Jesus.

Some people from the region of Sephoris, distant relatives of Anne, brought hither a man possessed of a dumb devil. His hands were bound, and they led him and pulled him along by cords tied around his body, for he was perfectly furious and oftentimes scandalous in his behavior. He was one of those Pharisees that had formed a committee to spy the actions of Jesus. He was named Joas, and belonged to the number of those that had disputed with Jesus in an isolated school between Sephoris and Nazareth. When Jesus returned from Naim, that is about fourteen days before, the demon seized upon Joas, because, silencing his own interior convictions, he had, through sheer adulation of the other Pharisees, joined in the calumnious cry against Jesus: "He is possessed by the devil! He runs like a madman about the country!" It was on the subject of divorce that Jesus had disputed with him at Sephoris. The man was in grievous sin. As he was led up, he made an attempt to rush upon Jesus, but He, with a motion of the hand, commanded the devil to withdraw. The man shuddered, and a black vapor issued from his mouth. Then he sank on his knees before Jesus, confessed his sins, and begged forgiveness. Jesus pardoned him, and enjoined certain fasts and alms as a penance. He had likewise to abstain for a long time from several kinds of food of which the Jews were exceedingly fond, garlic for instance. The excitement produced by this cure was very great, for it was considered a most difficult thing to drive out dumb devils. The Pharisees had already put themselves to much trouble on Joas's account. Were it not that he was brought by his friends, he never would have appeared before Jesus, for the Pharisees would not have permitted it. Now indeed were they indignant that one of their own number had been helped by Jesus and had openly avowed his sins, in which they themselves had had a share. As the cured man was returning to his home, the news of his deliverance was spread throughout Capharnaum, and the people everywhere proclaimed that such wonders had never before been heard in Israel. But the Pharisees in their fury retorted: "By the prince of devils, He casteth out devils."

Jesus now left the house by the back door, and with Him the disciples. They went around to Peter's on the west side and a little distant from the city, and here Jesus spent the night.

During these days Jesus repeated to His disciples His testimony of John the Baptist. "He is," He said, "as pure as an angel. Nothing unclean has ever entered his mouth, nor has an untruth or anything sinful ever come forth from it." When the disciples asked Jesus whether John had long to live, Jesus answered that he would die when his time came, and that was not far off. This information made them very sad.

13. CURE OF A MAN WITH A WITHERED HAND. "BLESSED IS THE WOMB THAT BORE THEE!"

When Jesus went to the synagogue to teach, the Pharisees laid a snare for Him. In a corner of the synagogue was a poor creature with a withered hand. He had not ventured to appear before Jesus, and now held back, intimidated by the presence of the Pharisees. These latter were reproaching Jesus, asking Him how He could make His appearance with a publican like Matthew. To this Jesus responded that He had come to console and convert sinners, but that no Pharisee should ever be numbered among His disciples. The Pharisees mockingly retorted: "Master, here is one for whom Thou hast come. Perhaps, Thou wilt heal him also." Thereupon Jesus commanded the man with the withered hand to come forward and stand in the midst of the assembly. He did so, and Jesus said to him: "Thy sins are forgiven thee!" The Pharisees, who scorned the poor man—whose reputation was not of the best—cried out: "His withered hand has never hindered him from sinning." Then Jesus grasped the hand, straightened the fingers, and said: "Use thy hand!" The man stretched out his hand, found it cured, and went away giving thanks. Jesus justified him against the calumnies of the Pharisees, expressed compassion for

him, and declared him a good-hearted fellow. The
Pharisees were covered with confusion and filled with
wrath. They declared Jesus a Sabbath-breaker against
whom they would lodge an accusation, and then took
their departure. In the neighborhood of the synagogue
they met some Herodians with whom they consulted as to
how they should lie in wait for Jesus on the next feast in
Jerusalem.

When Jesus later on addressed the people in Peter's
house, among the other women present was Lea, the
sister-in-law of Enue, recently cured of the issue of
blood. Her husband was a Pharisee and a zealous oppo-
nent of Jesus, but Lea herself was profoundly impressed
by the instructions she had heard. I saw her at first, calm
and sorrowful, often changing her place among the
crowd, as if looking for someone, but I found out that
she was in this way obeying the impulse that prompted
her to proclaim aloud her reverence for Jesus. Then approached the Mother of Jesus accompanied by several
women, namely, Martha, Susanna of Jerusalem, Dina the
Samaritan, and Susanna Alpheus, a daughter of Mary
Cleophas and sister of the Apostles. She was about thirty
and had grown children. Her husband lived in Nazareth,
and it was there that she had joined the holy women.
Susanna Cleophas desired to be admitted among the
Community of women that rendered service to Jesus and
His disciples. Mary and her companions entered the
court that led to the hall in which Jesus was teaching. He
had been reproaching the Pharisees with their hypocrisy
and impurity and, because He always interwove some of
the Beatitudes with His other teachings, He just at that
moment exclaimed: "Blessed are the pure of heart, for
they shall see God!" Lea, meanwhile, seeing Mary coming in, could no longer restrain herself and, as if intoxicated with joy, she cried out from among the crowd:
"More blessed" (these are the exact words that I heard)

"more blessed the womb that bore Thee and the breasts that gave Thee suck!" To which I saw Jesus quietly replying: "And far more blessed are they that hear the word of God and keep it!" and He went on with His discourse. Lea went to Mary, saluted her, spoke of Enue's cure and of her own resolve to give her wealth to the Community, and requested Mary to intercede with her Son for her husband's conversion. He was a Pharisee of Paneas. Mary conversed with her in a low voice. She had not heard Lea's sudden exclamation nor Jesus' reply, and soon she withdrew with the women.

Mary was possessed of admirable simplicity. Jesus never showed her any marks of distinction before others, excepting that He treated her with reverence. She never had much to do with any, unless with the sick and the ignorant, and her demeanor was always marked by humility, recollection, and simplicity. All, even the enemies of Jesus, honored her; and yet she never sought after anyone, but was always quiet and alone.

Jesus went next to Peter's fishery where, before a great crowd of people, He taught in parables of the Kingdom of God. Then He mounted His little barque and taught from the lake. A Scribe from Nazareth named Saraseth proposed himself as a disciple, when Jesus repeated to him the words: "The foxes have their holes, etc." Saraseth afterward married Salome, the daughter of Jairus. After Jesus' death, both husband and wife joined the Community.

Besides this Scribe, there were two others who for some time followed Jesus as disciples. One of them asked Him whether He would not soon take possession of His Kingdom, for He had already sufficiently proved His mission. Would He not soon seat Himself upon the throne of David? Jesus having reprimanded him and ordered him to follow Him with docility, he replied that he would first go and take leave of his family. To this Jesus

responded: "Whoever puts his hands to the plough, etc."
A third, who had joined Jesus at Sephoris, expressed his
wish to go and bury his father. Jesus replied: "Let the
dead bury their dead." These words were not spoken
literally, for his father was not yet dead. It was an expression which meant receiving one's share of the
patrimony and providing for one's parents.

Jesus spent that night on the mountain near Corozain
with two of the disciples, under a tent and in prayer. The
other disciples came next morning to the sermon. Jesus
explained today the fourth Beatitude and this passage
from Isaias: "Behold My servant, I will uphold him: My
elect, My soul delighteth in him. I have given My Spirit
upon him, he shall bring forth judgment to the Gentiles."[1] The multitude was very great. There was present
a troop of Roman soldiers from the different garrisons
around the country. They had been sent to hear Jesus'
doctrines, to note His bearing, and to give information on
the same. From Gaul and other provinces of the Empire
they had written to Rome for news of the Prophet of
Judea, because this last named country was under the
Roman sway. Rome had in consequence made inquiries
of the officers of the different garrisons, and these latter
had now sent about a hundred of their trusty soldiers,
who stood where they could both see and hear well.

The instruction over, Jesus went with the disciples
down the mountain to the valley on the south. Here there
was a spring, and here too had bread and fish been prepared by the holy women who devoted themselves to
such services. The multitude had encamped on the mountainside. Many of them were without provisions, and they
sent some of their number to beg food of the disciples.
The bread and fish were arranged in baskets on a grassy
mound. Jesus blessed the baskets and helped the disciples
to distribute their contents to all that asked. It was apparently far from enough, and yet all received what they

needed. I heard the people saying: "It is multiplied in His hands." The Roman soldiers also asked for some of the blessed bread, for they wanted to send it to Rome as a testimony of what they had seen and heard. Jesus ordered what remained to be given to them, and there was still enough for all the leaders. They wrapped it up carefully and took it away with them.

1. *Is.* 42:11.

14. JESUS IN MAGDALA AND GERGESA. THE DEMON DRIVEN INTO THE SWINE

In the intervals of His public teaching and curing, Jesus, whenever He found Himself alone with His Apostles and disciples, prepared them for their mission. Today He led The Twelve to a retired spot near the lake, placed them in the order mentioned in the Gospel, and conferred upon them the power of healing and of casting out devils. To the other disciples, He gave only the power to baptize and impose hands. At the same time, He addressed to them a touching discourse in which He promised to be with them always and to share with them all that He possessed. The power to heal and to drive out the devil, Jesus bestowed in the form of a blessing. All wept, and Jesus Himself was very much moved. At the close He said that there was still much to be done and then they would go to Jerusalem, for the fullness of time was drawing near. The Apostles were glowing with enthusiasm. They expressed their readiness to do all that He would command and to remain true to Him. Jesus replied that there were afflictions and hardships in store for them, and that evil would glide in among them. By these words He alluded to Judas. With discourses such as the above, they reached their little barques. Jesus and The Twelve, with about five of the disciples, among them Saturnin, rowed to the east bank of the lake, down past Hippos, and landed near the little village of Magdala. This place lay close to the lake and north of the dark ravine into which flowed the waters from the pool near Gergesa, higher up the country. To the east of Magdala rose a mountain. The village was built so near to it that it enjoyed the benefit of only the midday and evening sun; it was consequently damp and foggy, especially in the neighborhood of the ravine.

Jesus and His disciples did not at once enter Magdala. Peter's barque was lying near a sandbank to which extended a bridge. As soon as Jesus stepped on shore, several possessed came running toward Him with loud cries. They asked what He wanted there, and cried out for Him to leave them in peace. This they did of their own accord. Jesus delivered them. They gave thanks, and went into the village. And now others came, bringing with them other possessed. Some of the disciples, Peter, Andrew, John, James and his cousins then went into Magdala, where they delivered the possessed and cured many sick, among others some women attacked by convulsions. They drove out devils and commanded sickness to disappear in the Name of Jesus of Nazareth. I heard some of them adding the words, "Whom the storm of the sea obeyed." Some of those that were cured by the disciples went to Jesus to hear His admonitions and instructions. He explained to them and to the disciples why the possessed were so very numerous in these parts. It was because the inhabitants were so intent upon the things of this world and so given up to the indulgence of their passions. Several of these possessed were from Gergesa, which lay up on the mountain about one hour to the east of Magdala. They infested the surrounding country, hiding in the caves and tombs. Jesus continued the cures until after twilight, and then spent the night on the barque with the disciples.

From the region of Gergesa, which had a circumference of about four hours, none had attended Jesus' instructions on the mountain.

On the following day Jesus climbed the mountain, and encountered two Jewish youths who had come from Gergesa to meet Him. They were possessed by the devil. They were not furious, though the attacks of the evil one were frequent, and they roved restlessly about. When Jesus some time before had crossed the Jordan from Tarichea and passed Gerasa, these young men were not yet possessed. They had then come out to meet Him and begged to be received among His disciples, but Jesus sent them away. Now again, after Jesus had delivered them, they desired to be received by Him. They told Him that the misfortune from which He had just freed them never would have overtaken them if He had yielded to their first request. Jesus exhorted them to amendment of life, and bade them return home and announce by what means their deliverance had been effected. The youths obeyed. As Jesus went along, pausing here and there to teach before the huts and homes of the shepherds, many possessed and simpletons ran hiding behind the hedges and hills, crying after Him and making signs for Him to keep off and not disturb their peace. But Jesus called them to Him, and delivered them. Many of those thus freed cried out, imploring Him not to drive them into the abyss! Some of the Apostles also performed cures by the imposition of hands, and engaged the people to repair to the mountain beyond Magdala to the south, where Jesus was going to deliver an instruction.

A great crowd assembled at the place designated. Jesus exhorted them to penance, spoke of the near approach of the Kingdom of God, and reproached them with clinging to the goods of this world. He spoke also of the value of the soul. They should know, He said, that God prizes the soul more highly than man's great, worldly possessions.

By these last words, Jesus made reference to the herd of swine which was soon to be precipitated into the lake, for the people had invited Jesus to go again to Gergesa. To this invitation Jesus replied that He would indeed accept it, but that His coming would be an untimely one for them, and that they would not give Him a very warm welcome. They begged Him not to traverse the ravine on His return to them, for there were two furious possessed roaming about in it who had broken their chains and had already strangled some people. But Jesus responded that on that very account He would, when it was time, go that way, for He had been sent upon earth for the sake of the miserable. It was at this conjuncture that He uttered the passage in which it is said, "If Sodom and Gomorrha had heard and seen the things that have taken place here in Galilee, they would have done penance."[1]

When Jesus was about to depart, the people prayed Him to tarry awhile longer, for never had they heard so pleasing a discourse. It was, they said, like the morning sunbeams shining upon their gloomy, foggy home. They begged Him to remain, for it was already dark. To this Jesus replied in a similitude on the darkness: He feared not this darkness, but they should dread remaining in eternal darkness, and that at a time in which the light of the Word of God had shone upon them. Then He retired to the ships with the disciples. They rowed at first as if directing their course across to Tiberias, but then turned again to the east, lay to about one hour south of the ravine, and spent the night on their ships.

Magdala was an unimportant place, smaller than Bethsaida. It was only a landing place for boats, and derived its subsistence from Hippos, which was largely engaged in trade and commerce. A highroad ran past Gerasa and down to Hippos, and was the scene of constant traffic. The country of Magdala was known also as the country of Dalmanutha, from the town that lay a couple of hours further to the south and on the other side of the ravine.

When Jesus landed next morning, several demoniacs were presented to Him, and He cured them by laying His hands upon them. The people of this region practiced sorcery. They ate of a certain herb that grew abundantly in the ravine and on the mountain, and thus became intoxicated and fell into convulsions. They had another plant of which they made use to counteract the effects of the first, but for some time past it had lost its virtue and now the poor creatures were left in their misery. The country of the Gergeseans was a tract of land from four to five hours in length, and about a half-hour in breadth. It was distinguished from the surrounding districts by its history and the character of its inhabitants, which latter was not of the best. It began with the ravine between Dalmanutha and Magdala, included the ravine, and on the south began with and comprised ten villages scattered in a row along the narrow strip of land, with Gergesa and Gerasa at either end. Beyond Gerasa it was bounded by the region of Corozain, the land of Zin, and a district containing many deserts. On the east it was bounded by the long mountain ridge on whose southern extremity stood the citadel of Gamala; on the south, by the ravine; and on the west, the valley on the shore of the lake. In this valley lay Dalmanutha, Magdala, and Hippos, which did not belong to the country of Gergesa, no more than the rest of the lakeshore, excepting the ravine to the south of Magdala. On the north it ended with Corozain. This district with its ten villages must not be confounded with the Decapolis, or that of the ten cities, which extended far around it and from which it was wholly distinct. In Gedeon's struggle against the Madianites, the inhabitants of the ten villages supported the pagans who since that time had acquired the upper hand and kept the Jews in great subjection. They raised in all these places, to the scandal of the Jews that dwelt there, immense numbers of swine, which in herds of several thousands were turned out to fatten in a great marsh on the northern height of the ravine. They were attended by a hundred heathen herdsmen and their boys. The marsh, which was about three quarters of an hour southeast of Gergesa, at the foot of the mountain of Gamala, discharged its boggy waters southward into the ravine over a dam of logs and heavy planks that changed the brook above it into a swamp. The superfluous waters flowed through the ravine into the Sea of Galilee. Numbers of huge oaks grew near the marsh and on the sides of the ravine. No part of this region was very fertile, and only in a few sunny places grew some vines. They had also a kind of reed from which sugar can be made, but they exported it in its crude state.

It was not so much their idolatrous worship that subjected the people of this region to the power of the devil, as the depth to which they were sunk in sorcery. Gergesa and the surrounding places were full of wizards and witches who carried on their disorders by means of cats, dogs, toads, snakes, and other animals. They conjured up these creatures, and even went around in their form injuring and killing men. They were like werewolves that can hurt people even at a distance, that take revenge after a long time upon those whom they hate, and that can raise storms at sea. The women used to brew some kind of a magical beverage. Satan had entirely conquered this region, which possessed innumerable demoniacs, raging lunatics, and victims of convulsions.

It was approaching ten in the morning when Jesus with some of the disciples mounted a little boat, crossed the brook some distance up to the stream, and rowed into the ravine. This was a shorter way than that by land. Jesus climbed the northern side of the ravine, and the disciples joined Him one after another. While He was ascending, two raging possessed higher up on the mountain were running about, darting in and out of the sepulchers, casting themselves on the ground, and beating themselves with the bones of the dead. They uttered horrible cries and appeared to be under the spell of some secret influence, for they could not flee. As Jesus drew nearer, they cried out from behind the bushes and rocks that lay a little higher up on the mountain: "Ye Powers! Ye Dominations! Come to our aid! Here comes One stronger than we!" Jesus raised His hand toward them and commanded them to lie down. They fell flat on their faces, but raising their heads again, cried out: "Jesus! Thou Son of God the Most High, what have we to do with Thee? Why art Thou come to torment us before the time? We conjure Thee in the name of God to leave us in peace!" By this time Jesus and the disciples had reached them as they lay trembling, their whole persons horribly agitated. Jesus ordered the disciples to give them some clothing, and commanded the possessed to cover themselves. The disciples threw to them the scarfs they wore around their necks and in which they were accustomed to muffle their heads. The possessed, trembling and writhing convulsively, covered themselves, as if constrained to do so against their will, arose, and cried out to Jesus not to torture them. Jesus asked: "How many are ye?" They answered, "Legion." The wicked spirits spoke always in the plural by the mouth of these two possessed. They said that the evil desires of these men were innumerable. This time the devil spoke the truth. For seventeen years these men had lived in communication with him, and in the practice of sorcery. Now and then they had suffered assaults like the present, but for the last two years they had been running, frantic, around the desert. They had been entangled in all the abominations of magic.

Nearby was a vineyard on a sunny slope, and in it an immense wooden vat formed of great beams. It was not quite the height of a man, but so broad that twenty men could stand in it. The Gergeseans used to press in it grapes mixed with the juice of that intoxicating herb of which I have spoken. The juice ran into little troughs and thence into large, earthen vessels with narrow necks which, when full, were buried underground in the vineyard. This was that intoxicating beverage which produced effects so fatal upon all that drank of it. The herb was about the length of one's arm, with numerous thick green leaves one above the other, and it terminated in a bud. The people of these parts used the juice in order to rouse in themselves diabolical ecstasies. On account of its inebriating vapors, the drink was prepared in the open air, though during the operation a tent was erected over the vat. The pressmen were just coming to their work when Jesus commanded the possessed, or rather the legion in them, to overturn the vat. The two men seized the great, full vat, turned it upside down without the least difficulty, the contents streamed around, and the workmen fled with cries of terror. The possessed, trembling and shuddering, returned to Jesus, and the disciples also were very much frightened. The devil now cried out by the mouth of the possessed, begging Jesus not yet to cast them into the abyss, not yet to drive them from this region, and ended by the request: "Let us go into yonder swine!" Jesus replied: "Ye may go!" At these words the two miserble possessed sank down in violent convulsions, and a whole cloud of vapors issued from their bodies in numberless forms of insects, toads, worms, and chiefly mole-crickets.

A few moments after, there arose from the herds of swine sounds of grunting and raging, and from the herdsmen shouts and cries. The swine, some thousands in number, came rushing from all quarters and plunged down through the bushes on the mountainside. It was like a furious tempest, mingled with the cries and bellowings of animals. This scene was not the work of a few minutes only. It lasted a couple of hours, for the swine rushed here and there, plunging headlong and biting one another. Numbers precipitated themselves into the marsh and were swept down over the waterfall, and all went raging toward the lake.

The disciples looked on disquieted, fearing lest the waters in which they fished, as well as the fish themselves, would be rendered impure. Jesus divined their thoughts, and told them not to fear, since the swine would all go down into the whirlpool at the end of the ravine. There was at this place a great pool of stagnant water completely separated from the lake by a sandbank, or strip of shore. It was overgrown with reeds and bushes, and at high water was frequently submerged. This pool was a deep abyss which, through the sandbank, had an inlet from the lake, but no outlet into the same, and in it was a whirlpool. It was into this caldron the swine plunged. The herdsmen who had, at first, run after the animals, now came back to Jesus, saw the possessed who had been delivered, heard all that had happened, and then began to complain loudly of the injury done them. But Jesus replied that the salvation of these two souls was worth more than all the swine in the world. Then He bade them go to the owners of the swine and say that the devil, whom the godlessness of the inhabitants of this country sent into men, had by Him been driven out of the men, and that they had gone into the swine! The possessed who had been delivered, Jesus sent to their homes to procure clothing, while He Himself with the disciples went up toward Gergesa. Several of the herdsmen had already run to the city and, in consequence of the reports they spread, people came pouring out from all sides. They that had been cured at Magdala, as well as the two Jewish youths cured the day before, and most of the Jews of the city, had assembled to wait for Jesus' coming. The two possessed, now cured, came back in a short time decently clothed, to hear Jesus' preaching. They were distinguished pagans belonging to the city, relatives of some of the pagan priests.

The people employed in preparing the wine mentioned above, and whose full vat had been overturned, were also running about the city, publishing everywhere the loss they had sustained at the hands of the possessed. This gave rise to great alarm and uproar. Many ran to see whether they could rescue some of the swine, while others hurried out to the wine cask. The confusion lasted until after nightfall.

Jesus meanwhile was instructing on a hill about one-half hour from Gergesa. But the chief men of the city and the pagan priests sought to keep the people from Him by telling them that Jesus was a mighty sorcerer through whom great evils would come upon them. When they had taken counsel together, they sent out a deputation to Jesus with instructions to hasten and beg Him not to tarry in those parts and not to do them still greater injury. The deputies added that they recognized in Him a great magician, but begged Him to withdraw from their boundaries. They sorely lamented their swine and the overturning of their brewing vat. Their fright and amazement were extreme when they beheld the two possessed, cured and clothed, sitting among the listeners at Jesus' feet. Jesus bade them dismiss their fears, because He would not trouble them long. He had come for the sake of the poor sick and possessed alone, since He knew well that the unclean swine and the infamous beverage were of more value to them than the salvation of their souls. But the Father in Heaven, who had given to Him the power to rescue the poor people before Him and to destroy the swine, judged otherwise. Then He held up to them all their infamy, their sinful dealing in sorcery, their dishonest gains, and their demonolatry. He called them to penance, to Baptism, and offered them salvation. But they had the injury done them, the loss of the swine, in their heads, and so persisted in their pressing, though half-frightened request, that He would go away. After that they returned to the city.

Judas Iscariot was particularly busy and active among the Gergeseans, for he was well-known in these parts. His mother had dwelt here with him for some time when he was still young, and just after he had run away from the family in which he had been secretly reared. The two possessed were acquaintances of his youth.

The Jews rejoiced in secret over the loss sustained by the Gentiles in their swine, for they were very much oppressed by them and greatly scandalized on account of the unclean animals. Still there were many among them who lived on easy terms with the pagans and defiled themselves with their superstitious practices.

All that had been cured on that day and the day before, as also the two possessed, were baptized by the disciples. They were very much impressed and thoroughly changed. The two possessed last delivered and the two Jewish youths entreated Jesus to allow them to remain with Him and be His disciples. To the two last delivered, Jesus replied that He would give them a commission, namely, they should go through the ten villages of the Gergeseans, show themselves everywhere, and everywhere relate what had happened to them, what they had heard and seen, call the inhabitants to penance and Baptism, and send them to Him. He added that they should not be troubled if they were greeted by a shower of stones from those whom they addressed. If they executed this commission properly, they should receive in recompense the spirit of prophecy. Then they would always know where to find Him, in order to send thither those that desired to hear His teachings, and they should impose hands on the sick, who would thereby be healed. Having thus spoken, Jesus blessed the two young men, who on the next day began their mission, and later on became disciples.

The Apostles in baptizing here used water that they had brought with them in leathern bottles. The people knelt in a circle around them, and they baptized three at a time out of the basin that one held, sprinkling each three times with water scooped up in the hand.

That evening Jesus and the disciples entered Gergesa, and went to the house of the ruler of the synagogue. Then came the magistrates of the city urging the ruler to make Jesus depart as soon as possible, and threatening to hold Him responsible for any further injury the city might sustain at His hands. Jesus told the disciples that He had permitted the demons to overturn the vat and to enter into the swine, that the proud pagans might see that He was the Prophet of the Jews whom they so shamefully despised and oppressed. He wished at the same time, as He said, by the loss of the swine, in which so many of them bore a share, to draw the attention of these people to the danger that threatened their souls, and to arouse them from the sleep of sin that they might hearken to His teaching. The beverage He had allowed to be wasted as it was the principal cause of their vices and demoniacal possession.

On the following day a great crowd again gathered around Jesus, for His miracles had become known throughout the whole country, and many Jews who had been converted left Gergesa at once.

The Apostles, who had been healing in the villages nearby, returned in time for Jesus' discourse, bringing with them those they had cured. There were some women among them carrying baskets of provisions, which they gave to the Apostles. Once when Jesus was closely pressed by the crowd, a woman from Magdala approached Him. She was afflicted with an issue of blood. Though long unable to walk, she had gathered up strength to slip alone through the crowd and to kiss His garment, whereupon she was healed. Jesus went on with His discourse, but after a little while He said: "I have healed someone. Who is it?" At these words, the woman drew near, giving thanks. She had heard of Enue's cure, and had imitated her example. That evening Jesus, the disciples, and the two Jewish youths lately delivered from demoniacal possession, left Gergesa, jour-

neyed around Magdala, and climbed the mountain north of
Hippos. This last named place was not situated on the lake,
but on a mountain some distance inland. Jesus and His
followers descended on the opposite side and put up at a
shepherd's house.

Here Jesus reminded the disciples that the birthday of
Herod would soon be celebrated, and told them that He intended going to Jerusalem. They tried to dissuade Him from
doing so, saying that the Pasch was now not far off, and
then they should be obliged to go. But Jesus replied in such
a way as to give them to understand that He did not intend
to show Himself openly at the feast. The two Gergesean disciples again begged to be allowed to accompany Him. Jesus
replied that He had another mission in reserve for them,
namely, to go around among the ten cities between Cedar
and Paneas, and announce to the Jews of those places all
that they had seen and heard. He gave them His benediction
and made them the same promises as to the other two. If
they fulfilled their commission well, the spirit of prophecy
should be given to them, they should always know His
whereabouts, and should be able to heal the sick in His
name. As with the others, so too with them, a certain time
had to elapse before these promises would be realized. The
two others had first to announce Him in the ten Gergesean
villages, and afterward to the heathens of the Decapolis.
The youths bade farewell to Jesus, who directed the disciples to go to Bethsaida and, in spite of their entreaties, He
Himself remained behind. He retired into a wilderness near
the shore to pray. I saw Him walking about among the
steep, rocky hills, some of which looked black and like
human figures amid the darkness of night.

It was already quite dark when I saw Jesus walking
straight over the waves. It was almost opposite Tiberias, a
little eastward of the middle of the lake. He appeared as if
intending to pass within a little distance of the disciples'
barque. The high wind was contrary, and the disciples

weary of rowing. When they saw the figure on the waves, they were affrighted, for they knew not whether it was Jesus or His spirit, and they cried aloud from fear. But Jesus called out: "Fear not! It is I!" Then Peter cried: "Lord, if it be Thou, bid me come to Thee upon the waters." And Jesus said: "Come!"

Peter, in his ardor, leaped on the little ladder and out of the boat. He hurried along for a short distance on the troubled waters toward Jesus, as if on level ground. It seemed to me that he hovered over the surface, for the ine-quality of the waves appeared to be no obstacle to his prog-ress. But when he began to wonder, and to think more of the sea, its winds and its waves, than of the words of Jesus, he grew frightened and commenced to sink. Crying out, "Lord, save me!" he sank up to the breast and stretched out his hand. Instantly Jesus was at his side. He seized his hand and said: "O thou of little faith, why didst thou doubt?" Then they entered the barque, and Jesus reproached Peter and the others for their fear. The wind lulled immediately and they steered toward Bethsaida. A ladder was always in readiness to be thrown over the side of the boat for the con-venience of those about to enter.

1. *Matt.* 11:20 etc.

15. JESUS CURES IN BETHSAIDA AND AGAIN RETURNS TO CAPHARNAUM

Two blind men came to meet Jesus on His arrival in Bethsaida, crying out to Him for help and, as if to disprove the old saying, they were leading each other. Jesus restored their sight, cured also the lame and gave speech to the dumb. Wherever He appeared, crowds pressed around Him bringing to Him their sick. Many touched Him, and were cured. The people were everywhere expecting Him, because they knew that He was coming again for the Sabbath. The story of the two possessed and of the swine was already well-known here, and had excited great comment and astonishment. Some of the disciples baptized the cured at Peter's house. But as Jesus continued His labors and took no time either to eat or to rest, the disciples sought Him out and tried to induce Him to take some repose and refreshment.

When He went back to Capharnaum, a man dumb, blind, and possessed by the demon came to meet Him, and Jesus cured him instantaneously. This miracle created intense astonishment, for even when approaching Jesus, the man had recovered his speech and cried out: "Jesus, Thou Son of David, have mercy on me!" Jesus touched his eyes, and he saw. He was possessed of many devils, having been wholly perverted by the heathens on the other side of the lake. The sorcerers and soothsayers of the land of Gergesa had seized upon him. They dragged him around with them by a cord and exhibited him in other places, where they showed off his strength in all kinds of skillful feats. They showed how he, though blind and dumb, still could accomplish everything, could know and understand all, could go everywhere, could bring everything and know everything by virtue of certain incantations, for all this the demon performed in him. These pagan sorcerers from Gergesa, who were ever wandering through the Decapolis and other cities, used the devil by means of that poor creature to help them earn their bread. If they journeyed over the sea, their miserable victim was not allowed to go on board a ship, but at the command of his masters, he was obliged to swim like a dog at its side. No one any longer troubled himself about him, for he was looked upon as forever lost. Most of the time he had no place of shelter. He lay in tombs and caves and endured all manner of ill-treatment from his cruel masters. The poor wretch had long been in Capharnaum, and yet no one had led him to Jesus. Now, however, he went to Him himself and was cured.

While Jesus was teaching in Peter's house near the city gate just before the Sabbath began, a great tumult arose in Capharnaum. The miracle of the swine and the deliverance of the dumb and blind possessed had created great excitement. Several boats of Jews from Gergesa had crossed the lake to spread far and wide the report that Jesus cast out devils by the power of the devil. This irritated the people, and they gathered in large numbers outside the synagogue. As Jesus drew near to the city, the man possessed of the devil, as well as blind and dumb, ran out through the streets to meet Him. He was without a keeper and was followed by a crowd of people who became witnesses of his miraculous cure. They were so transported by it that they gave loud expression to their indignation against the Pharisees, who never wearied inveighing against Jesus, repeating again as they were now doing that He healed through the power of the devil. Among the crowd here assembled were many armed with a crossbow. These men called out to the Pharisees to desist from slandering Jesus, to recognize His power and acknowledge that never before had such things been done in Israel, and that no Prophet before Him had ever wrought such wonders. If they did not cease from obstinately opposing Jesus, they might depart from Capharnaum, for that they (the people) could no longer support such abuse and ingratitude.

On hearing this, the Pharisees pretended to be quite subdued. One of them, a great, broad fellow, stepped out before the rest and craftily addressed the crowd. He said it was indeed true that never had such doctrines been heard, never had such doings, such wonders been seen in Israel, no Prophet had ever performed the like. But he begged them to consider the circumstances attending the driving out of the demon from the man of Gergesa, as also those connected with the similar wonders wrought among them that very day. The man whom they had just seen delivered from the power of the devil, owing to his relations with the Gergeseans, just as good as belonged to them. In the critical examination of such things, one could not be too circumspect, etc., etc. Then he went on to give them a lengthy description of the kingdom of darkness. He described its orders and hierarchies, and showed how one is subordinate to another. Jesus, he said, had now a powerful spirit in league with Him. If not, why had He not long ago delivered that furious demoniac? Why, if He were the Son of God, was He not able to banish the demons from the land of Gergesa, without going there in person? No! He was obliged first to go into that country, and conclude an agreement with the chief of the Gergesean demons. He had to make a bargain with that demon prince and give him the swine as his booty, for although inferior to Beelzebub, that prince was still of some consequence. And now since He had freed that man at Gergesa, He had, by virtue of the same agreement, delivered the one here in Capharnaum through the power of Beelzebub. With much cunning and eloquence the Pharisee advanced the above and similar stuff. Then he begged his hearers to be calm and attend to the conclusion, for their own doings would show forth the fruit of all this excitement. The laborer no longer performed his task on working days, but ran around after the new Teacher and His miracles, and the Sabbath was turned into a day of din and uproar. Then he exhorted them to reflect, to go home at once and take some rest in preparation for the coming feast. By such persuasions he succeeded in inducing the people to disperse, and many of the light-minded were half convinced by his empty babble.

It was the eve of the Feast of the Dedication of the Temple. In the houses and schools stood pyramids of lighted lamps, while in the gardens and courtyards and at the fountains were lights and torches arranged in all kinds of figures. Jesus, followed by His disciples, entered the synagogue and taught unmolested, for His enemies were afraid of Him. He knew their thoughts and in what terms they had addressed the people, and He made allusion to it in these words: "Every kingdom divided against itself shall not stand. And if Satan cast out Satan, he is divided against himself. How then shall his kingdom stand? And if I by Beelzebub cast out devils, by whom do your children cast them out?" With words like these Jesus silenced them and, without further contradiction, left the synagogue. He passed that night at Peter's.

The next day Jesus, accompanied by some of His disciples, visited Jairus's family, whom He consoled and exhorted to the practice of good. They were very humble and entirely changed. They had divided their wealth into three parts, one for the poor, one for the Community, and the third for themselves. Jairus's old mother was especially touched and thoroughly converted to good. The daughter did not make her appearance until called, and then came forward veiled, her whole deportment breathing humility. She had grown taller. She held herself erect, and presented the appearance of one in perfect health. Jesus visited likewise the pagan Centurion Cornelius, consoled and instructed his family, and then went with him to see Zorobabel, at whose house the conversation turned upon Herod's birthday and John. Both Zorobabel and Cornelius remarked that Herod had invited all the nobility, including themselves, to Machaerus for the celebration of his birthday, and they asked Jesus whether He would permit them to go. Jesus replied that if they dared to stand aloof from the evils that might there take place, it was not forbidden them to go, although it would be better if they could excuse themselves and remain at home. They expressed their indignation at Herod's adulterous life and John's imprisonment, and hoped confidently that Herod would set him at liberty on his birthday.

Jesus next visited His Mother, with whom were then stopping Susanna Alpheus, Mary, the daughter of Cleophas of Nazareth, Susanna of Jerusalem, Dina the Samaritan, and Martha. Jesus told them that He was going away the next morning. Martha was very sad on account of Magdalen's relapse into sin and the state of demoniacal possession in which she then was. She asked Jesus whether she should go to her, but He told her to wait awhile. Magdalen was now often like one beside herself. She yielded to fits of anger and pride, struck all that came in her way, tormented her maids, and was always arrayed in the most wanton attire. I saw her striking the man that lived as master in her house, and I beheld him returning her blows with ill-treatment. At times she fell into frightful sadness, she wept and lamented. She ran about the house seeking for Jesus and crying out: "Where is the Teacher? Where is He? He has abandoned me!" and then fell into convulsions like epileptic fits.

One may imagine the pain of her brother and sister at beholding one of a noble family, one so richly endowed by nature, given up to so frightful a state.

What a touching sight, that of Jesus traversing the streets of Capharnaum, His robe sometimes girded up, sometimes at full length; His motions so well regulated, and yet without stiffness; His step so gentle that He seemed rather to glide than to walk; His whole appearance, though breathing simplicity, so full of majesty that His like was never before seen! There was nothing strange in His look, no irresolution in His manner. He never took a false step, never a useless one. He cast no vain glance, made no aimless turn, and yet in all His bearing there was no trace of affectation or design.

Martha and Susanna had visited their inns on the way through Galilee to Samaria, for they exercised a kind of general superintendence, the other women seeing to those established in their own respective districts. They went together to the several inns, taking with them asses laden with all kinds of household necessaries. Once when Mary the Suphanite accompanied them, the report spread among the people that Mary Magdalen now went around with the women who provided for the needs of the Prophet of Nazareth and His party. The Suphanite was in figure very like Magdalen, and neither of them was very well-known on this side of the Jordan. Besides being called Mary and the ill repute her past life had gained for her, the Suphanite also had anointed Jesus at a feast given by one of the Pharisees. She was consequently, even at this early date, confounded with Magdalen, a mistake that only increased with time among those not well acquainted with the Community.

The holy women took care that their inns were well supplied with beds, coverlets, linen, woollen clothes, sandals, cups, jugs of balsam, oil, etc. Although Jesus had need of little, yet He was desirous that the disciples should not be a burden to others, and should find their necessary wants supplied. In this way He deprived the Pharisees of all reasonable cause of reproach.

16. THE MISSION OF THE APOSTLES AND DISCIPLES

At the close of the Sabbath, Jesus spoke again in the synagogue, inveighing in severe terms against the wickedness of the Pharisees in saying that He drove out devils through the power of the devil. He challenged them to say whether His actions and His teachings were not in perfect harmony, whether He did not practice what He preached. But they could allege nothing against Him.

In Peter's house outside the city gate, Jesus taught on the Beatitude: "Blessed are the poor in spirit," and made the application against the Pharisees. After that He prepared the disciples for their approaching mission.

Jesus would not longer remain in Capharnaum—the crowd was too great and too excited. Many Gergeseans also had come hither, and they wanted to follow Jesus. They were poor, were habituated to a wandering life, and thought it would be a good thing to be supported by Him. Besides this they were under the impression that Jesus would, like Saul or David, cause Himself to be anointed king and then establish His throne in Jerusalem. But Jesus told them to go back to their homes, to do penance, to keep the Commandments, and to practice the lessons they had heard from Him. His Kingdom, He said, was far different from what they imagined, and no sinner should have part therein.

Jesus afterward left Capharnaum, accompanied by The Twelve and by thirty disciples. They directed their steps northward. Crowds of people were journeying along the same way. Jesus frequently paused to instruct sometimes this, sometimes that crowd, who then turned off in the direction of their homes. In this way He arrived at about three in the afternoon at a beautiful mountain, three hours from Capharnaum and not quite so far from the Jordan. Five roads branched out from it, and about as many little towns lay around it. The people who had followed Jesus thus far now took their leave, while He with His own par-- ty, having first taken some refreshment at the foot of the mountain, began to ascend the height. There was a teacher's chair upon it, from which He again instructed the Apostles and disciples upon their vocation. He said that now they should show forth what they had learned. They should proclaim the advent of the Kingdom, that the last chance for doing penance had arrived, that the end of John's life was very near. They should baptize, impose hands, and expel demons. He taught them how they should conduct themselves in discussions, how to recognize true from false friends, and how to confound the latter. He told them that now none should be greater than the others. In the various places to which their mission called them, they should go among the pious, should live poorly and humbly, and be burdensome to none. He told them also how to separate and how again to unite. Two Apostles and some disciples should journey together, while some other disciples should go on ahead to gather together the people and announce the coming of the former. The Apostles, He said, should carry with them little flasks of oil, which He taught them how to consecrate and how to use in effecting cures.[1] Then He gave them all the other instructions recorded in the Gospels on the occasion of their mission. He made allusion to no special danger in store for them, but said only: "Today ye will everywhere be welcomed, but a time will come wherein they will persecute you!"

After that the Apostles knelt down in a circle around Jesus as He prayed and laid His hands upon the head of each; the disciples He only blessed. Then they embraced and separated.

Among the directions given to the Apostles, Jesus had indicated to them the place and time at which they should again join Him, in order to bring Him news and exchange places with the disciples that remained with Him. Six of the Apostles continued with Him: Peter, James the Less, John, Philip, Thomas and Judas, besides twelve of the disciples. Among the latter were the three brothers James, Sadoch, and Heliachim (Mary Heli's son), Manahem, Nathanael (also called Little Cleophas), and several others. The other six Apostles had with them eighteen disciples, among whom were Joses Barsabas, Judas Barsabas, Saturnin and Nathanael Chased. Nathanael, the bridegroom of Cana, did not travel around. He attended to other affairs for the Community, and like Lazarus rendered service in his own immediate circle. All shed tears on separating. The Apostles who were going forth on their mission descended the mountain by the eastern route leading to the Jordan, where I saw a place situated, Lecum by name, about a quarter of an hour from the river. When Jesus came down the mountain, He was again surrounded by a crowd returning home from Caphar-naum.

From the foot of the mountain Jesus started with the disciples southward from Saphet, which was situated on another high mountain, to a place called Hucuca. Before reaching this place, He was met by many people who received Him and the disciples with expressions of great joy.

At a fountain a blind man and several cripples were awaiting Jesus' coming, and they now implored Him for help. The blind man's eyes were infected with disease. Jesus ordered him to wash his face at the fountain. When he had done so, He anointed his eyes with oil, broke off a little twig from a bush nearby, held it before his eyes, and asked whether he saw it or not. The man answered: "Yes, I see a very tall tree." Jesus anointed his eyes once more and repeated His question, whereupon the man cast himself on his knees before Him, crying out joyfully: "Lord, I see mountains, trees, people! I see everything!" There was great jubilation among the people as they escorted the man back into the city. Jesus went on curing the lame and the palsied who were standing around on crutches made of light but very firm wood. Each had three feet, so that it could stand alone; and when the two were crossed together, the sick could rest the breast against them.

When the blind man and his escorts went shouting with joy into the city, many of the inhabitants, the Elders of the synagogue, and the school teachers with their scholars came flocking out to meet Jesus. They were full of joy. Jesus returned with them, went into the school and gave them some instructions in parables on the Eight Beatitudes. He exhorted all to penance, for the Kingdom was near. He explained the parables at great length. The disciples were present. Before beginning, Jesus had recommended to them strict attention, in order that they might repeat what they heard when they scattered around among the houses and villages in the environs. It was thus that they acquired in Jesus' public discourses what they, in their turn, had to teach in the country around; for the Apostles along with several of the disciples scattered as usual among the environs to cure and to teach. They met again in the evening at the place indicated by Jesus and to which He Himself had gone. Here they stopped with the Elder of the synagogue, who placed before them fish, honey, little rolls and fruit, of which they ate.

Hucuca was situated about five hours to the northwest of Capharnaum, five hours southwest of the mountain upon which Jesus had given the Apostles their mission, and about three hours south of Saphet. There were none but Jews in the place, and they were tolerably good people, for most of them had received John's baptism. They manufactured stuffs of fine texture, narrow scarfs of wool, tassels and fringes of silk; they knit sandals also, under which they placed two supports like heels. These sandals were flexible in the middle, and very comfortable, for they allowed the dust to fall through holes made for that purpose.

The Apostles and several of the disciples with them scattered, two by two, throughout the city and its environs. Hucuca must have once been a strong fortress, for it was surrounded by moats now dry, and its approach was over a bridge. One could look through the gate far into the city and see its beautiful synagogue. Hucuca was surrounded by verdant walks planted with trees so thick and high that, even at a short distance, its houses could not be seen. Its synagogue was extraordinarily beautiful. It was surrounded by a colonnade into which the main building could be opened for the accommodation of a

more considerable crowd; opposite the entrance the wall
was solid and formed a semicircle. It stood upon an open
square at the end of the street upon which was the
entrance. The whole city was well built and very clean.
The people gathered into the synagogue. Jesus went first
into two separate halls, in one healing many sick men, in
the other women sick of all kinds of maladies. Many sick
children were brought to Him, some young enough to be
carried in the arms, and He healed them. The healthy
children, He blessed.

In the synagogue Jesus taught of prayer and of the
Messiah. He said that the Messiah had already come
upon earth, that they (His hearers) were living in His
time, that they were listening to His teachings. He spoke
of the adoration of God in spirit and in truth, and I felt
that it meant the adoration of the Father in the Holy
Ghost and in Jesus Christ, for Jesus is the Truth. He is
the true, the living, the incarnate God, the Son conceived
of the Holy Spirit. At these words, the Doctors of the
synagogue humbly begged Him to say who He really was,
whence He came, whether they whom they looked upon
as His parents were not His parents, His relatives not His
relatives, whether He was really the Messiah, the Son of
God. It would be well, they said, for the Doctors of the
Law to know positively what to think. Being placed over
others, they before all others ought to know Him. But
Jesus answered them evasively. If He said, "I am He!"
they would not believe Him, but would say that He was
the Son of those people of whom they had spoken. They
should not inquire into His origin, but should hear His
doctrine and observe His actions. Whoever does the will
of the Father is the Son of the Father, for the Son is in
the Father and Father is in the Son, and whoever fulfills
the will of the Son fulfills the will of the Father. Jesus
spoke so beautifully on this subject and on that of prayer
that many cried out, "Lord, Thou art the Christ! Thou

art the Truth!" and falling down they wished to adore Him. But He repeated to them: "Adore the Father in spirit and in truth!" and He left the city with His disciples and the Elder of the synagogue, at whose house they passed the night. In this suburb there was a school very well attended, but no synagogue. The Feast of Lights was still being celebrated.

Next day Jesus taught again in Hucuca on the parable of the sower and the different ways in which the seed is received. Then He spoke of the Good Shepherd come to seek the lost sheep, and who would be happy to carry back even one on His shoulder. He said thus would the Good Shepherd do until His enemies put Him to death; and thus also should His servants and His servants' servant do until the end of time. If at the end only one sheep was saved, yet would His love rest satisfied. Jesus spoke most tenderly on this point.

1. *Mk.* 6:7-13; *Matt.* 10:1 *et seq.; Lk.* 9:1-6.

17. JESUS IN BETHANATH, GALGAL, ELCESE, AND SAPHET

The Apostles and several of the disciples went on ahead, while Jesus with some of the others returned by the way He had come; that is, He went back to Bethanath, one hour and a half to the south of Saphet.

When within about half an hour of Bethanath, He was met by a blind man, who was led by two lovely boys in short, yellow tunics and large chip hats that shaded them from the sun. They were the children of Levites. The man was old and of honorable standing; he had long hoped for Jesus' coming. Accompanied by the boys, who had seen Jesus approaching, he hurried forward to meet Him, crying out from a distance: "Jesus, Thou Son of David, help me! Have mercy on me!" When he came up with Him, he cast himself at His feet and said: "Lord, Thou wilt certainly give me light again! I have awaited Thee for so long, and for so long I have felt interiorly that Thou wouldst come and cure me!" Jesus replied: "As thou hast believed, so be it done unto thee according to thy faith," and taking him to a fountain in the grove, He commanded him to wash his eyes. The man's eyes, as well as his whole forehead, were ulcerated and covered with a crust. When he had washed, the scales fell from his eyes. Then Jesus anointed them with oil, as also his forehead and temples. Sight immediately returned, and the man gave thanks. Jesus blessed him and the two boys, and predicted that they should at some future day announce the word of God.

They now drew near the city, outside which the Apostles and other disciples again joined Jesus. Many of the citizens had here gathered, and when they saw the blind man coming back with his sight restored, their joy was quite extraordinary. The man's name was Ktesiphon. But he was not that blind Ktesiphon who likewise was cured, and who afterward became a disciple and went with Lazarus to Gaul.

Jesus, accompanied by the Levites and all the people, went to the synagogue in which He delivered an instruction. The Feast of the Dedication, or the Feast of Lights as it was sometimes called, was still being celebrated, so that it was a kind of holiday. Jesus again explained the parables of the sower and of the Good Shepherd. The people were good and quite joyous over Jesus' coming among them. He stopped in the Levites' house near the school. There were no Pharisees in Bethanath. The Levites lived together as in a monastery and sent people out to other places.

Bethanath was once a fortified city and full of pagans, for the tribe of Nephtali, instead of exterminating them, had long held them tributary. But at this time there were no pagans in the city. They had been expelled when the Temple was re-established, when Esdras and Nehemias had obliged the Jews to send away their heathen wives. The terrible threats that God made to His people by the Prophets if they persevered in such alliances and refused to drive the pagans from the country, thereby exposing themselves to ever-present temptation to contract marriages with heathens, were fully realized; for around Thabor and in the chain between Endor and Scythopolis, where the peaks are so irregularly piled one on another, and where I saw so much gold hidden in the earth, the heathens had never been driven out, and the country had therefore become a wilderness.

From Bethanath Jesus went with the Apostles and disciples northward around Saphet to Galgal, a large, beautiful place through which ran a great highway. He went with His followers to the synagogue. There were some Pharisees in this city. Jesus preached vehemently against them, explained all the passages of the Prophet Malachias that spoke of the Messiah, the Precursor John, and of the new, clean Sacrifice. He ended by announcing that the time for the fulfillment of these Prophecies had arrived.

From Galgal Jesus went eastward to Elcese, which lay to the north of Saphet, and where the Prophet Nahum was born. Here He taught for a short time and visited the leper hospital, where He cured about eight of the inmates and commanded them to show themselves to the priests in Saphet. He also taught the shepherds. I saw in the fields around Elcese grass of extraordinary height, and in it numbers of camels grazing. Jesus went likewise to a mountain containing many caves, in which dwelt heathens, whom He instructed. The whole day was spent in walking, instructing and curing, for everywhere on the roads the sick and suffering were brought to Jesus.

Toward evening He arrived at Bethan, which lay to the

west under the heights of Saphet and about one hour from Bethanath. It was a little place, a colony from Bethanath, and was situated so near to the steep, western heights of Saphet that from them they could look down upon the little town. Jesus and the disciples put up here with some relatives, for the daughter of Elizabeth's sister was married at Bethan. She had five children, of whom the youngest girl was about twelve years old. The sons were already from eighteen to twenty. This family, with some others disposed like themselves, lived apart in a row of houses built near the walls of the city. Some were built in the rocks, some in the walls themselves. All belonged to the married Essenians, and the husband of Elizabeth's niece was the Superior. The family owned here some property inherited from their forefathers. They were very pious people. They spoke to Jesus of John and asked Him with anxiety whether or not he would soon be set at liberty. Jesus replied in words that made them very grave and sad, though without disturbing their peace of mind.

John had visited them when he came first from the source of the Jordan in the wilderness, and they had been among the first to go to his baptism. They spoke to Jesus of their sons, whom they intended soon to send to the fishery at Capharnaum. Jesus replied that those fishermen, that is Peter and his companions, had begun another kind of fishing, and that their young sons also would follow Him in their own good time. They did indeed join The Seventy-Two. Jesus taught and cured here. I heard Him saying that the other disciples were then on the confines of Sidon and Tyre, and that He Himself would go back to Judea. I saw that Thomas showed great pleasure at the prospect of this journey, because he anticipated opposition on the part of the Pharisees and hoped to be able to dispute with them. He expressed his sentiments to the other disciples, but they did not appear to share his satisfaction. Jesus reproved his exaggerated zeal, and told him that a time would come when his own faith would waver. But Thomas could in nowise understand His words.

While Jesus was teaching on the Beatitudes in the school at Beten, the Pharisees of Saphet came down to invite Him to their city for the Sabbath. He explained before them the parable of the seed falling on different kinds of ground, but they would not understand the allusion contained in the rocky soil. They disputed the point with Him, but He soon reduced them to silence. When they invited Him for the Sabbath, He replied that He would go with them for the sake of the lost sheep, but that both they and the Sadducees (some of whom were at Saphet) would be scandalized on His account. They replied: "Rabbi, leave that to us." Jesus responded that He knew them well, and that their unrighteousness filled the land. He went up to Saphet, followed by many from Bethan. Saphet on this side was built on so steep a part of the mountain that frequently the roof of one house was on a level with the ground floor of another. The road lay far below the houses, to which one had to mount by steps hewn in the rock. It took half an hour to climb up to the synagogue, where the mountain assumed the form of a great plateau whose northeastern declivity was not so steep. Outside the city Jesus was received with solemn ceremony by many good people. They surrounded Him waving green branches and singing canticles. Then they washed His feet, as well as those of the disciples, and offered them the customary refreshments. Thus attended, Jesus reached the synagogue, where a great crowd was assembled. The Feast of the Dedication closed today, and they were celebrating that of the new moon as well as the Sabbath; besides all this, the desire to see Jesus and His disciples added to the numbers present.

Saphet could boast of many Pharisees, Sadducees,

Scribes, and simple Levites. There was a kind of religious school here, in which youths were educated in all the Jewish liberal arts and in theology. Thomas, a couple of years before, had been a student at this school. He went now to visit one of the head teachers, a Pharisee, who expressed his wonder at seeing him in such company. But Thomas silenced him by his zealous defence of Jesus' actions and teachings. Some Pharisees and Sadducees from Jerusalem had managed to insinuate themselves into this school, and their arbitrary dealings rendered them insupportable to even the Pharisees and teachers of the place. Among them were some of those who had sent for Jesus. They addressed Him in a very insinuating speech in which, alluding to His fame and His miracles, they suggested that He should raise no excitement or commotion in their city. They had been very much scandalized at the solemn reception tendered Him by the people. As the Sabbath had not yet begun, Jesus replied to them in the outer porch before all the people. He spoke in very strong language of the disturbance and scandal which, owing to their efforts, had been spread throughout the country. He, however, mentioned nothing in particular, though He challenged them to upbraid Him with anything wherein He had violated the Law, He who had been sent by His Father for its perfect accomplishment.

While thus disputing with them, the lepers whom He had healed the day before at Elcese presented themselves to fulfill His order to go to the priests for inspection. Jesus exclaimed: "Behold how I fulfill the Law! I ordered these men to appear before you, although they had no obligation to do so, since they were made clean instantaneously by the command of God, and not by the skill of man." This encounter greatly vexed the Pharisees, who went nevertheless to examine into the cure. It was usual in such cases merely to inspect the breast. If that was clean, the whole person was judged to be the same. The Pharisees, astounded and vexed, were forced to declare these men freed from the ban of leprosy.

Besides the passages of Scripture appointed for this particular Sabbath, Jesus taught from Genesis, from the First Book of Kings, and likewise upon the Ten Commandments. He dwelt upon several points deduced from His texts, which both Pharisees and Sadducees felt in their hearts were thrusts at themselves. He spoke of the fulfillment of the Promises and announced the chastisement of God upon all that would not profit by His exhortations to penance. He alluded to the destruction of the Temple and the ruin of many cities. He spoke of the true Law, which they did not comprehend, and of their own law of yesterday, as He denominated it, which He absolutely condemned. I understood that He meant by this latter something like the Jewish books of the present day, the Talmud, I think, because here at Saphet they were especially esteemed and studied.

The exercises of the synagogue over, Jesus and the disciples went to the house of one of the Pharisees to the place, who kept a public inn for teachers and rabbis. The other Pharisees also took part in the repast. During the meal, Jesus read the Pharisees a severe lecture, because they reproached the disciples for not washing their hands before coming to table and for neglecting other observances customary before eating. He likewise checked them for their ridiculous fastidiousness respecting the serving up of the food, for they were accustomed to reprehend the servers for the slightest stain upon the dishes or their contents.

Next morning numbers of very sick persons, some of them aged, were brought and ranged in the courtyard before the house in which Jesus was stopping. It had cost their friends no little trouble to bring them from the pathless, mountainous city. Jesus began to cure them one after another. Some were deaf; others blind, palsied, lame; in a word, there were sick of all kinds among them. Jesus made use of prayer, the imposition of hands, consecrated oil, and in general of more ceremonies than usual. He spoke with the disciples, taught them to make use of this manner of curing, and exhorted the sick according to their various needs.

The Pharisees and Sadducees from Jerusalem were very much scandalized at all that they saw. They wanted to send away some of the newly arrived sick, and they began to quarrel. They would by no means tolerate such disturbance on the Sabbath, and so great a tumult arose that Jesus, turning to them, inquired what they wanted. And now they began a dispute with Him on the subject of His teaching, especially of His constant reference to the Father and the Son. "But," they said, "we know well whose Son Thou art!" Jesus replied that whoever does the will of the Father is the son of the Father. But that he who does not keep the Commandments has no right to raise his voice in judgment upon others; he should rather rejoice at not being cast out of the house as an intruder. But they continued to allege all sorts of objections against His cures, to accuse Him of not having washed before the meal of the preceding evening, and to repudiate His charge against them of not keeping the Law. They went so far that Jesus, to their exceedingly great terror, began to write on the wall of the house, and in letters that they alone could decipher, their secret sins and transgressions. Then He asked them whether they wanted the writing to remain upon the wall and become publicly known, or whether, effacing it, they would permit Him to continue His work in peace. The Pharisees were thoroughly frightened. They rubbed out the writing and slunk away, leaving Jesus to continue His cures. These Pharisees had been guilty of embezzlement of the public funds. Legacies and donations intended for the foundation of homes for widows and orphans, they had used for the erection of all kinds of magnificent buildings. Saphet was rich in such establishments, and yet there were to be found in it numbers of poor, miserable creatures.

That evening Jesus closed the instructions in the synagogue, and passed the night in the same house. There was a fountain near the synagogue. The mountain of Saphet was beautiful and green, covered with numerous trees and gardens. The roads were bordered by sweet-scented myrtles. High up on the plateau were large, four-cornered houses and solid foundations around which could be erected tent habitations. This city was largely engaged in the manufacture of vestments for the priests, and it was full of students and learned men.

18. JESUS IN CARIATHAIM AND ABRAM

Jesus went with the disciples around the environs of Saphet and cured many sick who had been brought out of the houses and laid on the road by which He was to pass. Early in the morning He sent one of the nephews of Joseph of Arimathea, along with Seraphia's son, to the neighboring town of Cariathaim, about three hours from Saphet, with a commission to prepare the inn. He and the disciples left Saphet sometime after. The disciples scattered here and there on the road, while Jesus also went along teaching and healing. He went first westward between Bethan and Elcese, after which the road turned toward the south. Somewhat beyond Elcese—near which was a beautiful mountain—lay a little, oval lake as large as that near the Baths of Bethulia. It was the source of a stream that flowed down into the valley which, southeast of Cariathaim, declined into that of Capharnaum. This valley was narrow in some parts, wide in others, and extended seven hours before reaching Capharnaum.

On the way to Cariathaim, Jesus was met by some demoniacs who entreated Him to help them. They told

Him that the disciples had not been able to relieve them, and that they thought He could do better than they. Jesus replied that if the disciples had not relieved them, it was not the fault of the disciples but their own want of faith, and He commanded them to go to Cariathaim and remain fasting until He should deliver them. He let them wait awhile and do penance. Half an hour from Cariathaim, Jesus was received by the Levites of the place, the school teachers accompanied by their children, and many of the good inhabitants who had come out to meet Him. The two disciples who had gone on ahead to prepare the inn were also there. They received Jesus near a bathing garden, which was supplied with water conducted through a canal from that little stream of which I have spoken. The garden was full of beautiful trees, flowers, and covered walks, and enclosed by a rampart and an astonishingly dense hedge. They washed the feet of Jesus and His disciples and entertained them with the usual refreshments.

Jesus here instructed the children for a little while and gave them His blessing. It may have been nearly five o'clock when they started for the city, which lay upon a hill overlooking the valley. The whole way to the synagogue Jesus healed many sick of all kinds whom He met in the streets. In the synagogue He again taught on the Beatitudes, also of the punishment of those Levites that had dared to lay their hands upon the Ark of the Covenant. And yet greater chastisements, He said, would fall upon those that would lay hands on the Son of Man, of whom the Ark was only a symbol.

While in Cariathaim, Jesus put up at a hired inn which had been furnished with necessaries out of the common stock of the Community by the two disciples sent on ahead. The food was prepared at a house in the city, where also cooking for the sick was done. The Levites ate with Jesus and the disciples.

Cariathaim was a Levitical city, and in it were no Pharisees. A couple of its families were related to Zachary. Jesus visited them and found them very much troubled on John's account. He recalled to them the wonders that had preceded and accompanied John's birth, and spoke of his mission and wonderful life. He reminded them likewise of many circumstances attendant on the birth of Mary's Son, showed them that John's fate lay in the hands of God, and that he would die when he had fulfilled his mission. Jesus prepared them in this way for John's death.

The possessed whom He had sent to Cariathaim on the preceding day, and many other sick, accosted Him near the synagogue on the subject of their cure. He healed several, but others He sent away to fulfill certain prescriptions of fasting, alms-giving, and prayer. He did this here rather than elsewhere, because the people of this place were earnest in the keeping of the Law. After that He repaired with the disciples to the garden in which He had been received, where He taught and the disciples baptized. Encamped under tents in the neighborhood were pagans awaiting Jesus' coming. They had already been in Capharnaum, whence they had been ordered here. There were in all about a hundred baptized. They stood in the water around a basin. Peter and James the Less baptized, while the others laid their hands on the neophytes.

In the evening Jesus taught in the synagogue, His subject being the Eight Beatitudes. He spoke also of the false consolation of the false prophets who had rejected the menaces of the true whose prophecies had, nevertheless, been fulfilled. He repeated His threats against those who would not receive Him who was sent by God.

Leaving Cariathaim, Jesus went with the disciples toward the south. He was as solemnly escorted on His departure by the Levites and schoolchildren as He had been received on His entrance. The people of Cariathaim were engaged in the transportation of goods and the manufacture of vestments for priests out of the silk that they imported from afar. On the southern declivity of the opposite side of the valley, where lay a place called Naasson, there was a sugar cane plantation whose products formed a staple of trade. Jesus ascended that height, while the disciples scattered among some of the places more to the east of the valley. Jesus taught near Naasson those whom He met coming from Capharnaum, among them some idolaters. On such occasions, Jesus was frequently accompanied a part of His way by crowds. I saw Him curing several, among others two poor cripples who were lying on the roadside. He took them by the hand and commanded them to rise. They immediately wanted to follow Him, but He forbade them to do so. He traversed another valley, arrived at a height situated before the city of Abram in the tribe of Aser, and put up at an inn outside the city, where were found beautiful gardens and pleasure grounds. There were only two disciples with Jesus when He entered the inn, the others not having yet arrived. The country here on the eastern side of the high ridges that run from Libanus down to the valley of Zabulon was rich in meadow land and very charming. Herds of cattle and camels were grazing in the high grass. Westward toward the lake, orchards were more numerous.

Abram was situated about three hours south of Cariathaim. But Jesus, not having followed the direct route, was certainly five hours on His journey thither.

In the evening Thomas, John, and Nathanael joined Jesus in the inn. The others were still in the neighboring towns. The mountain upon which Abram was built formed in its length the boundary between Nephtali and Zabulon. The steward of the inn laid before Jesus a dispute, which he begged Him to decide. It had reference to the wells in the vicinity used for watering the cattle. As the two tribes were so near each other in this place and their pasturage so extensive, altercations on the subject of the wells were frequent. The host thus addressed Jesus: "Lord, we will not let Thee go until Thou dost decide our quarrel." Jesus' decision was something like this: They should from each side set free an equal number of cattle, and from whichever side the greater number went of their own accord to the wells, that side should have the greater right to the said wells. Jesus drew from this circumstance matter for a profoundly significant instruction on the living water that He Himself would give them, and which would belong to those that most earnestly desired it.

The next day Jesus went into Abram, which was in two sections and on two different roads. It was like two separate villages interspersed with numerous gardens. The teachers of the school came out of the city to meet Jesus, washed His feet, and escorted Him to the synagogue. On the way thither, He cured many sick and crippled whom He found lying on the street, also some old people languishing from weakness; and some demoniacs who, though not actually furious, were running about muttering to themselves like silly, vicious creatures. They came involuntarily to where Jesus was, again and again repeating the words: "Jesus of Nazareth! Jesus! Prophet! Thou Son of God! Jesus of Nazareth!" Jesus delivered them by a blessing. In the synagogue He taught of the Beatitudes and from some passages of the Prophet Malachias.

There were in Abram Sadducees, Pharisees, and Levites, also two synagogues, for each section of the city had its own. The Sadducees had their own special synagogue, but Jesus did not teach in it. The Pharisees conducted themselves very politely toward Jesus. His inn was distant, about a good quarter of an hour from the south-

ern end of the city, and was one of those established by
Lazarus for His convenience. The steward was a married
Essenian, a descendant of the family of that Zacharias
who was murdered between the Temple and the altar.
His wife was the granddaughter of one of Anne's sisters.
They had grown children, and possessed herds and
meadows near that field in which Joachim had tarried
before Mary's Conception. Having little occupation at
home, they had come hither to take charge of the inn;
later on they were relieved by others. Like all the others,
this inn was supplied with all kinds of necessaries, though
not with superfluities. It had also its garden, its field, and
its well.

There were no pagans in Abram, but down the mountain were some groups of houses inhabited by them.

The Apostles and disciples whom Jesus had left near
Cariathaim came back again to the inn, as did also
Andrew and Matthew. Thomas and James the Less went
instead of them to Achzib in the tribe of Aser, between
ten and twelve hours westward. Twenty men accompanied Andrew; some were strangers, and some had been
cured and wanted to hear Jesus' instructions. The two
Apostles related how things had gone with them, how all
had prospered with them, namely, healing, exorcising,
preaching, and baptizing. Many sick and many seeking
advice and consolation came to Jesus' inn. Most of them
were cripples with deformed limbs, old, emaciated people, demoniacs and infirm females, the latter of whom
were in a chamber apart. The paralytics whom Jesus had
healed the day before wanted to render assistance near
the other sick. But He refused their help, saying that He
was come to serve and not to be served.

Jesus taught and healed the whole morning, and had
besides to settle a dispute concerning the wells. As the
confines of Aser, Nephtali, and Zabulon here met, and
the people carried on cattle raising, there arose frequent

discussions on the subject of the wells. One man complained that another made use of the well that his ancestors had dug. He submitted the case to Jesus, saying that he would abide by His decision, though he did not wish to sacrifice lightly the rights of his children. Jesus decided that he should bore for a well in another field, which He pointed out to him. There he would find better and more abundant water. Between twenty and thirty Jews were baptized, among them those that had come hither with Andrew and Matthew. As there was here no brook in which they could stand, the neophytes knelt in a circle, and were baptized out of a basin with the hand. After that Jesus went into the city.

They whom Jesus cured in the city were for the most part affected with maladies similar to those already described. Their sufferings must have had some connection with the elevated situation of the city and the occupations in which they were engaged. Jesus took much notice of the children, who were standing in rows on the street corners and public squares, waiting for Him. He questioned them, instructed them, and gave them His blessing. The mothers brought to Him their sick little ones, and He healed them. Numbers of people from the country around had here assembled.

The Pharisees behaved most courteously to Jesus in the synagogue. They resigned the first place to Him, and gave the disciples seats around their Master, before whom they laid the rolls of Scripture. Jesus taught first on one of the Eight Beatitudes, then on the great persecutions that were to come upon Himself and His followers, and lastly, of the heavy chastisement, the destruction that was to befall Jerusalem and the whole country. The Pharisees, according to their custom, interrupted Him at times to ask for an explanation upon this or that point.

The people of Abram were very industrious. They prepared and sold cotton, of which wide strips moderately fine were made; they also wove something like flax. The thick stalk, after being split into fine strips, was passed over a sharp bone, or wooden instrument in order to detach the fine, long fibers. They were yellowish and shining, and were spun into the tunics worn when walking. It was neither flax nor hemp such as wĕ have. They were engaged also in the manufacture of covers for tents and light screens of wood and matting.

Jesus and the Apostles spent the whole of the following morning and a part of the afternoon among some of the houses in the southern quarter of the city, teaching, consoling, reconciling enemies and exhorting them to union, charity, and peace. When a family counted many members, Jesus taught them alone; but, as a general thing, the neighbors were called in. All disputes were adjusted, all differences arranged. These visits of Jesus were mostly made to those houses in which were old, bedridden people who could not be present at the instructions in the synagogue. Some very old men received Baptism in their beds. Two of them could sit upright only with support, and they were baptized out of a basin.

On the first day of His entrance into Abram, Jesus had instructed a couple for matrimony, and assisted at the nuptials. In another house there were three other couples in expectation of the same. When the parents, the nearest relatives, and some of the Pharisees were assembled for the ceremony, Jesus instructed them upon marriage. He spoke of the wife's submission in obedience to the Law, which followed the first sin as its consequence, though the husband should honor in his wife the Promise: "The seed of the woman shall crush the head of the serpent." But now that the time of fulfillment was drawing near, grace took the place of the Law. The wife should now obey through reverence and humility, and the husband command with love and moderation. In this instruction

Jesus said that the question as to how sin had entered the world was an unnecessary one. It had come from disobedience, but salvation was to spring from faith and obedience. He alluded also to divorce which, He said, could never take place, since husband and wife are one in the flesh. If, however, their living together was the occasion of great sins, then indeed they might separate, though without the liberty of marrying again. The Law had been made when the human race was in its infancy and in its early rude state; but now that they were no longer children and that the fullness of time had arrived, the remarrying of divorced spouses was a violation of the eternal law of nature. The privilege of separating was a concession granted when there was danger of offending God and only after a period of serious trial. Jesus delivered this instruction in the beautiful family mansion belonging to the parents of one of the bridal couples. All the young affianced were present, the brides separated from the grooms by a curtain, at one end of which Jesus stood. The parents also stood in order, the fathers on one side, the mothers on the other, while some of the disciples and Pharisees were grouped around Jesus.

This instruction on marriage gave rise to the first occasion for the Pharisees of this place to oppose Jesus. Nevertheless they did not begin their dispute at once, but waited till evening when Jesus was teaching in the synagogue upon the oppression of the Children of Israel in Egypt, and developing some passages from Isaiah. Here they attacked His doctrine on marriage. With regard to the wife's submission, they found Him too mild, and in respect to the divorce question, too severe. They had, they affirmed, previously consulted numerous writings on that subject, and in spite of His repeated explanations, they could not accept His teaching. Although the dispute was warmly maintained, yet were the limits of decorum never overstepped.

Next day Jesus assisted with two of the disciples at the marriage ceremony of the young couples. He even acted as witness. They were married facing the chest that contained the Law and under the open heavens, for they had opened the cupola of the synagogue. I saw that both parties allowed some drops of blood from the ring finger to fall into a glass of wine, which they then drank. They exchanged rings and went through other ceremonies. After the religious rites came the celebration of the nuptials beginning with dance and banquet and merry-making, to all of which Jesus and the disciples were invited. The festivities took place in the beautiful public hall, which was supported by a colonnade. The bridal couples were not all from the city, but from the neighboring localities. They celebrated their nuptials here together, according to an agreement they had made to that effect when the news of Jesus' coming was announced. Some of them, indeed, had been present with their parents at His instructions in Capharnaum. The people of this region were particularly good-natured and sociable. The weddings of the poorer were now celebrated with those of the rich, greatly to the advantage of the former.

I remarked that the guests brought certain presents, and that Jesus, in His own name and that of the disciples, made the young couples a gift in money. They, in their turn, sent back the money to His inn, and over and above as a present some baskets of nice wedding bread, all which Jesus caused to be distributed to the poor.

The feast began by a bridal dance in slow and measured step. The brides were veiled. The couples stood facing one another, and each bridegroom danced once with each bride. They never touched one another, but grasped the ends of the scarf that they held in their hands. The dance lasted one hour, because each groom danced once with all the brides separately, and then all danced together. Besides this, the step was very slow.

Then followed the banquet, at which the men and women were, as usual, separated. The musicians were children, little boys and girls, with crowns of wool on their heads and wreaths of the same on their arms. They played on flutes, little twisted horns, and other instruments. The banqueting tables were so placed that the guests could hear without seeing one another. Jesus went to that of the brides and related a parable, something in the style of that of the ten wise and the ten foolish virgins. He explained it in quite a homely way adapted to the occasion, though at the same time His words were full of spiritual signification. He told each how she should acquit herself of the duties of her new, domestic position and what provisions she should lay up for that. His instructions contained a spiritual sense, and were suited to the particular character and shortcomings of the one to whom they were addressed.

The banquet over, then came the game of riddles. The enigmas written on slips of paper were thrown on a board that was full of holes, through which they fell into bags. Everyone had to solve the particular enigma that had fallen into his or her bag, or else pay a forfeit. The unsolved riddles were again and again thrown on the board, and the one that was so fortunate as to solve them at last, could claim all that had been previously lost on their account. Jesus looked on during the game, making happy and instructive applications of all that took place.

At the close of the festivities, Jesus and the disciples returned to their inn outside the city, whither they were conducted with lighted torches.

After Jesus had again taught in the synagogue, He visited the school of the boys and youths, whom He questioned and instructed, and then took leave of several people. After the repast, at the time generally spent in promenading on the Sabbath, Jesus with two of His disciples visited a girls' school. It was, besides, a kind of em-

broidering establishment. The little girls were between
the ages of six and fourteen. There were a great many of
them, and today they were in their fine clothes. Two
Doctors of the Law were present, and they too were in
holiday attire, wearing broad girdles around their waists
and long maniples on their sleeves. Every day they explained to the children some part of the Law. About ten
widows superintended the affairs of the school. Besides
instruction in reading the Law, in writing and reckoning,
the girls worked at embroidery intended for sale.
Through a series of halls were extended long strips of
different materials, some an ell in width, some narrower,
of the breadth of a broad girdle. The finished end was always rolled up. The pattern from which the young embroiderers worked lay before them painted on a piece of
stuff. It was made up of flowers and leaves and little
branches and serpentine lines, all forming large figures.
The material upon which they worked was woven of very
fine wool, something like the light mantles worn by the
three Holy Kings, only it was rather stronger in texture
and of different colors. The children worked with fine,
colored wool, also with silk, yellow being one of the
principal colors. They did not use needles, but little
hooks. Some also worked on white strips that were narrower than the rest. Others were engaged on girdles,
upon which they embroidered certain letters. The little
girls stood at their work, one next the other. Their occupation was assigned them according to their age and
talent. I saw some of the little ones preparing the threads,
others smoothing the wool, and others spinning. All that
the embroiderers needed, such as thread and instruments,
was handed them by the younger ones. On this day they
were not working. While the children were showing their
work to Jesus as He passed through the halls with the
superintendents, the whole business of the institution was
shown me in a tableau. I saw also that some of the girls

embroidered figures, large and small, upon separate pieces of stuff which were private orders intended for sale, and these they showed to Jesus. The heathens exchanged all kinds of things for them.

Some of the girls lived in the house, of which two stories were given up to the business, and others came from the city. There was also a hall for instructions, and there Jesus taught and catechized the children, who held little rolls in their hands. The smallest stood in front, their mistresses behind them. The children advanced, one row at a time, to Jesus' chair. When He had blessed them and instructed them in familiar similitudes drawn from their work, He left the house, though not until they had presented Him with some strips of stuff and girdles, which they sent to His inn for Him. He afterward gave them to the different synagogues. Jesus then closed the exercises of the Sabbath in the synagogue. The whole country around had poured into the city, which was consequently crowded with people. Several of the disciples were still going around today among the houses outside the city. Jesus took leave of all present in the synagogue and made a brief recapitulation of what He had already taught them. All were very much touched and wanted Him to remain with them.

Before Jesus left Abram for Dothain, He despatched two disciples with a message to Capharnaum, and two others to Cydessa. Andrew and Matthias alone remained with their Master, the others having scattered to different places.

Dothain was built on the same mountain ridge as Abram, and may have been distant from it southward something like five hours. There was here a private inn established for Jesus and His disciples, and there He met Lazarus, who had come thither with two disciples from Jerusalem. The holy women also had journeyed with Lazarus to this inn from Jerusalem.

FROM THE SECOND
CONVERSION OF MAGDALEN
TO THE DELIVERY OF
THE KEYS TO PETER

1. JESUS TEACHING IN AZANOTH.
SECOND CONVERSION OF MAGDALEN

About an hour to the south of the inn at Dothain lay
the little town of Azanoth. It was built on an eminence
upon which was a teacher's chair and, in earlier times, it
had often been the scene of the Prophets' preaching.
Through the activity of the disciples, the report had been
spread throughout the whole region that Jesus was about
to deliver a great instruction in that place, and in consequence of this report, multitudes were gathered there
from all Galilee. Martha, attended by her maid, had journeyed to Magdalen in the hope of inducing her to be
present at the instruction, but she was received very
haughtily by her sister, with whom things had come to
the worst. She was, on Martha's arrival, engaged at her
toilet, and sent word that she could not speak to her then.
Martha awaited her sister's appearance with unspeakable
patience, occupying herself meanwhile in prayer. At last
the unhappy Magdalen presented herself, her manner
haughty, excited, and defiant. She was ashamed of
Martha's simple attire. She feared that some of her guests
might see her, consequently she requested her to go away
as soon as possible. But Martha begging to be allowed to
rest in some corner of the house, she and her maid were
conducted to a room in one of the side buildings where,
either through design or forgetfulness, they were allowed

to remain without food or drink. It was then afternoon. Meanwhile Magdalen adorned herself for the banquet, at which she was seated on a richly decorated chair, while Martha and her maid were in prayer. After the revelry, Magdalen went at last to Martha, taking with her something on a little blue-edged plate and something to drink. She addressed Martha angrily and disdainfully, her whole demeanor expressive of pride, insolence, uneasiness, and interior agitation. Martha, full of humility and affection, invited Magdalen to go with her once more to the great instruction Jesus was going to deliver in the neighborhood. All Magdalen's female friends, Martha urged, those whom she had lately met, would be there and very glad to see her. She herself (Magdalen) had already testified to the esteem in which she held Jesus, and she should now gratify Lazarus and herself (Martha) by going once more to hear Him preach. She would not soon again have the opportunity of hearing the wonderful Prophet and at the same time of seeing all her friends in her own neighborhood. She had shown by her anointing of Jesus at the banquet at Gabara that she knew how to honor greatness and majesty. She should now again salute Him whom she had once so nobly and fearlessly honored in public, etc., etc. It would be impossible to say how lovingly Martha spoke to her erring sister, or how patiently she endured her shamefully contemptuous manner. At last Magdalen replied: "I shall go, but not with you! You can go on ahead, for I will not be seen with one so miserably clothed. I shall dress according to my position, and I shall go with my own friends." At these words, the two sisters separated, for it was very late.

Next morning Magdalen sent for Martha to come to her room while she was making her toilet. Martha went, patient as usual and secretly praying that Magdalen might go with her and be converted. Magdalen, clothed in a fine woollen garment, was sitting on a low stool, while two of her maids were busily engaged washing her feet and arms and perfuming them with fragrant water. Her hair was divided into three parts above the ears and at the back of the head, after which it was combed, brushed, oiled, and braided. Over her fine woollen undergarment was put a green robe embroidered with large yellow flowers, and over that again a mantle with folds. Her headdress was a kind of crimped cap that rose high on the forehead. Both her hair and her cap were interwoven with numberless pearls, and in her ears were long pendants. Her sleeves were wide above the elbow, but narrow below and fastened with broad, glittering bracelets. Her robe was plaited. Her under-bodice was open on the breast and laced with shining cords. During the toilet, Magdalen held in her hand a round, polished mirror. She wore an ornament on her breast. It was covered with gold, and encrusted with cut stones and pearls. Over the narrow-sleeved underdress she wore an upper one with a long flowing train and short, wide sleeves. It was made of changeable violet silk, and embroidered with large flowers, some in gold, others in different colors. The braids of her hair were ornamented with roses made of raw silk, and strings of pearls, interwoven with some kind of stiff transparent stuff that stood out in points. Very little of the hair could be seen through its load of ornamentation. It was rolled high around the face. Over this headdress, Magdalen wore a rich hood of fine, transparent material. It fell on the high headdress in front, shaded the cheeks, and hung low on the shoulders behind.

Martha took leave of her sister, and went to the inn near Damna, in order to tell Mary and the holy women the success she had had in her efforts to persuade Magdalen to be present at the instruction about to be given in Azanoth. With the Blessed Virgin about a dozen women had come to Damna, among them Anna Cleophas,

Susanna Alpheus, Susanna of Jerusalem, Veronica, Johanna Chusa, Mary Marcus, Dina, Maroni, and the Suphanite.

Jesus, accompanied by six Apostles and a number of the disciples, started from the inn at Dothain for Azanoth. On the way, He met the holy women coming from Damna. Lazarus was among Jesus' companions on this occasion.

After Martha's departure, Magdalen was very much tormented by the devil, who wanted to prevent her going to Jesus' instruction. She would have followed his suggestions, were it not for some of her guests who had agreed to go with her to Azanoth, to witness what they called a great show. Magdalen and her frivolous, sinful companions rode on asses to the inn of the holy women near the Baths of Bethulia. Magdalen's splendid seat, along with cushions and rugs for the others, followed packed on asses.

Next morning Magdalen, again arrayed in her most wanton attire and surrounded by her companions, made her appearance at the place of instruction, which was about an hour from the inn at which she was stopping. With noise and bustle, loud talk and bold staring about, they took their places under an open tent far in front of the holy women. There were some men of their own stamp in their party. They sat upon cushions and rugs and upholstered chairs, all in full view, Magdalen in front. Their coming gave rise to general whispering and murmurs of disapprobation, for they were even more detested and despised in these quarters than in Gabara. The Pharisees especially, who knew of her first remarkable conversion at Gabara and of her subsequent relapse into her former disorders, were scandalized and expressed their indignation at her daring to appear in such an assembly.

Jesus, after healing many sick, began His long and severe discourse. The details of His sermon, I cannot now recall, but I know that He cried woe upon Capharnaum, Bethsaida, and Corozain. He said also that the Queen of Saba had come from the South to hear the wisdom of Solomon, but here was One greater than Solomon. And lo, the wonder! Children that had never yet spoken, babes in their mothers' arms, cried out from time to time during the instruction: "Jesus of Nazareth! Holiest of Prophets! Son of David! Son of God!" Which words caused many of the hearers, and among them Magdalen, to tremble with fear. Making allusion to Magdalen, Jesus said that when the devil has been driven out and the house has been swept, he returns with six other demons, and rages worse than before. These words terrified Magdalen. After Jesus had in this way touched the hearts of many, He turned successively to all sides and commanded the demon to go out of all that sighed for deliverance from his thralldom, but that those who wished to remain bound to the devil should depart and take him along with them. At this command, the possessed cried out from all parts of the circle: "Jesus, Thou Son of God!"—and here and there people sank to the ground unconscious.

Magdalen also, from her splendid seat upon which she had attracted all eyes, fell in violent convulsions. Her companions in sin applied perfumes as restoratives, and wanted to carry her away. Desiring to remain under the empire of the evil one, they were themselves glad to profit by the opportunity to retire from the scene. But just then some persons near her cried out: "Stop, Master! Stop! This woman is dying." Jesus interrupted His discourse to reply: "Place her on her chair! The death she is now dying is a good death, and one that will vivify her!" After some time another word of Jesus pierced her to the heart, and she again fell into convulsions, during which dark forms escaped from her. A crowd gathered round her in alarm, while her own immediate party tried once again to bring her to herself. She was soon able to resume her seat on her beautiful chair, and then she tried to look as if she had suffered only an ordinary fainting spell. She had now become the object of general attention, especially as many other possessed back in the crowd had, like her, fallen in convulsions, and afterward rose up freed from the evil one. But when for the third time Magdalen fell down in violent convulsions, the excitement increased, and Martha hurried forward to her. When she recovered consciousness, she acted like one bereft of her senses. She wept passionately, and wanted to go to where the holy women were sitting. The frivolous companions with whom she had come hither held her back forcibly, declaring that she should not play the fool, and they at last succeeded in getting her down the mountain. Lazarus, Martha, and others who had followed her, now went forward and led her to the inn of the holy women. The crowd of worldlings who had accompanied Magdalen had already made their way off.

Before going down to His inn, Jesus healed many blind and sick. Later on, He taught again in the school, and Magdalen was present. She was not yet quite cured, but profoundly impressed, and no longer so wantonly arrayed. She had laid aside her superfluous finery, some of which was made of a fine scalloped material like pointed lace, and so perishable that it could be worn only once. She was now veiled. Jesus in His instruction appeared again to speak for her special benefit and, when He fixed upon her His penetrating glance, she fell once more into unconsciousness and another evil spirit went out of her. Her maids bore her from the synagogue to where she was received by Martha and Mary, who took her back to the inn. She was now like one distracted. She cried and wept. She ran through the public streets saying to all she met that she was a wicked creature, a sinner, the refuse of humanity. The holy women had the greatest trouble to quiet her. She tore her garments, disarranged her hair, and hid her face in the folds of her veil. When Jesus returned to His inn with the disciples and some of the Pharisees, and while they were taking some refreshments standing, Magdalen escaped from the holy women, ran with streaming hair and uttering loud lamentations, made her way through the crowd, cast herself at Jesus' feet, weeping and moaning, and asked if she might still hope for salvation. The Pharisees and disciples, scandalized at the sight, said to Jesus that He should no longer suffer this reprobate woman to create disturbance everywhere, that He should send her away once for all. But Jesus replied: "Permit her to weep and lament! Ye know not what is passing in her"—and He turned to her with words of consolation. He told her to repent from her heart, to believe and to hope, for that she should soon find peace. Then He bade her depart with confidence. Martha, who had followed with her maids, took her again to her inn. Magdalen did nothing but wring her hands and lament. She was not yet quite freed from the power of the evil one, who tortured and tormented her with the most frightful remorse and despair. There was no rest for her—she thought herself forever lost.

Upon her request, Lazarus went to Magdalum in order to take charge of her property, and to dissolve the ties she had there formed. She owned near Azanoth and in the surrounding country fields and vineyards which Lazarus, on account of her extravagance, had previously sequestered.

To escape the great crowd that had gathered here, Jesus went that night with His disciples into the neighborhood of Damna, where there was an inn, as well as a lovely eminence upon which stood a chair for teaching. Next morning when the holy women came thither accompanied by Magdalen, they found Jesus already encompassed by people seeking His aid. When His departure became known, the crowds awaiting Him at Azanoth, as well as new visitors, came streaming to Damna, and fresh bands continued to arrive during the whole instruction.

Magdalen, crushed and miserable, now sat among the holy women. Jesus inveighed severely against the sin of impurity, and said that it was that vice that had called down fire upon Sodom and Gomorrha. But He spoke of the mercy of God also and of the present time of pardon, almost conjuring His hearers to accept the grace offered them. Thrice during this discourse did Jesus rest His glance upon Magdalen, and each time I saw her sinking down and dark vapors issuing from her. The third time, the holy women carried her away. She was pale, weak, annihilated as it were, and scarcely recognizable. Her tears flowed incessantly. She was completely transformed, and passionately sighed to confess her sins to Jesus and receive pardon. The instruction over, Jesus went to a retired place, whither Mary herself and Martha led Magdalen to Him. She fell on her face weeping at His feet, her hair flowing loosely around her. Jesus comforted her. When Mary and Martha had withdrawn, she cried for pardon, confessed her numerous transgressions, and asked over and over: "Lord, is there still salvation for me?" Jesus forgave her sins, and she implored Him to save her from another relapse. He promised so to do, gave her His blessing, and spoke to her of the virtue of purity, also of His Mother, who was pure without stain. He praised Mary highly in terms I had never before heard from His lips, and commanded Magdalen to unite herself closely to her and to seek from her advice and consolation. When Jesus and Magdalen rejoined the holy women, Jesus said to them: "She has been a great sinner, but for all future time, she will be the model of penitents."

Magdalen, through her passionate emotion, her grief and her tears, was no longer like a human being, but like a shadow tottering from weakness. She was, however, calm, though still weeping silent tears that exhausted her. The holy women comforted her with many marks of affection, while she in turn craved pardon of each. As they had to set out for Naim and Magdalen was too weak to accompany them, Martha, Anna Cleophas, and Mary the Suphanite went with her to Damna, in order to rest that night and follow the others next morning. The holy women went through Cana to Naim.

Jesus and the disciples went across through the valley of the Baths of Bethulia, four or five hours farther on, to Gathepher, a large city that lay on a height between Cana and Sephoris. They passed the night outside the city at an inn that was near a cave called "John's Cave."

2. JESUS IN GATHEPHER, KISLOTH, AND NAZARETH

Next morning Jesus approached Gathepher. The schoolmasters and Pharisees came out to meet Him and bid Him welcome, though making all kinds of remonstrances, and imploring Him not to disturb the peace of their city. They especially insisted upon His discountenancing the crowding around Him and clamoring of women and children. He might, they said, teach quietly in their synagogue, but public disturbance they did not want to see. Jesus replied in grave and severe words that it was precisely for those that cried after Him, longed for Him, that He had come, and He reproached them for their dissimulation. The Pharisees had, in fact, on hearing that Jesus was coming, issued an order that the women should not appear on the streets with their children nor should they go to meet the Nazarene with clamorous greeting. The cry of "Son of God," "Christ," was, they said, positively preposterous and scandalous, since everyone in this part of the country knew full well whence Jesus came, who were His parents, and who His brethren. The sick might assemble in front of the synagogue and allow themselves to be cured, but noise and excitement would not be tolerated. Such were the directions given by the Pharisees, who had likewise arranged the sick around the synagogue as they thought proper, just as if it were theirs by right to order Jesus' actions. When, however, they reached the city with Jesus, to their intense chagrin they beheld the streets filled with mothers surrounded by their little ones, and some with infants in their arms. The children were stretching out their hands to Jesus and crying: "Jesus of Nazareth! Son of David! Son of God! Holiest of Prophets!" The Pharisees tried to drive the women and children back, but all in vain. They came pouring out of the neighboring streets and houses, while the Pharisees, eaten with vexation, withdrew from Jesus' escort. The disciples too, who were surrounding Jesus, were somewhat timorous and frightened. They would have desired a less demonstrative entrance into the city, one attended by less danger, and so they remonstrated with Jesus while attempting to drive the children back. But Jesus reproached them with their faint-heartedness. He restrained them, allowed the children to press around Him, and showed Himself all love and affection for them. And thus they proceeded to the court before the synagogue amid the uninterrupted shouts of the little ones: "Jesus of Nazareth! Holiest of Prophets!" Even the sucklings that never yet had spoken, cried out after Him. They were witnesses to Jesus. They bore convincing testimony before all the people. In front of the synagogue the children halted, the boys on one side, the girls on the other, the mothers with their infants in the rear. Jesus blessed the children and addressed some words of instruction to the mothers and their domestics who likewise had made their way thither. He said to the mothers that they should regard these last as their children. He spoke to the disciples also of the high value God sets on the child. The Pharisees were annoyed at these delays, and the sick were impatient for their cure. At last Jesus went to the latter, cured many of them, and then entered the synagogue, where He taught about the Patriarch Joseph. During His discourse He took occasion to return to the dignity of children. Jesus did so because the Pharisees were complaining of what they called *the disturbance.*

When Jesus was leaving the synagogue, three women presented themselves before Him, requesting a private interview. When He withdrew with them from the crowd, they cast themselves on their knees before Him, and made their laments over their husbands, whom they begged Jesus to help. Their husbands, they said, were tormented by evil spirits, by whom they themselves were sometimes attacked. They had heard, they said, that He had helped Magdalen, and they hoped that He would likewise have pity on them. Jesus promised to visit their homes. He went first, however, with His disciples to the house of a certain Simeon, a simple-hearted man belonging to the married Essenians. He was of middle age and the son of a Pharisee of Dabereth on Thabor. Jesus and the disciples partook, in this house, of refreshments standing. Simeon was desirous of bestowing all his goods upon the Community, and he spoke with Jesus to that effect.

On leaving Simeon's Jesus went as He had promised to the homes of the women, and had an interview with them and their husbands. Affairs were not just as the wives had stated, for they had thrown upon their husbands the blame of which they were themselves deserving. Jesus exhorted both parties to live in harmony, to pray, to fast, and to give alms. After the Sabbath these infirm women followed Jesus to a mountain a little to the north of Thabor where He was going to deliver a discourse. He did not remain long there. He went southward toward Kisloth, which city the holy women passed on their road to Naim, Magdalen

also, when journeying with her party. On the way Jesus
again instructed the Apostles upon what was in store for
them. He told them how they should behave when they
arrived in Judea, where they would not be so well
received. He gave them new directions as to their conduct, also for the imposition of hands and the driving out
of the demon, and as an additional source of strength and
increase of grace, He again conferred upon them His
benediction.

Three youths from Egypt came to Jesus in this place.
He received them as disciples, though picturing to them at
the same time the hardships that awaited them. One was
named Cyrinus. They had been playmates of Jesus in
Egypt, and they were now about thirty years old. Their
parents had ever revered the dwelling and the fountain
used by the Holy Family as sacred memorials. The young
men had visited Bethlehem and Bethania, and had gone to
Dothain, to see Mary, to whom they delivered their
parents' greeting.

Some Pharisees of Nazareth came to Jesus at Kisloth to
invite Him to His native city. Those Pharisees who, on a
former occasion, wanted to hurl Him from the rock, were
no longer in Nazareth. The envoys told Jesus that He
ought to go to His native city and there exhibit some of
His signs and wonders. The people, they said, were eager
to hear His doctrine; then too He could cure His fellow
countrymen that were sick. But they laid down as a condition that He would not heal on the Sabbath day. Jesus replied that He would go and keep the Sabbath with them.
He warned them, however, that they would be scandalized
on His account, and as to the cures, He would condescend
to their desires even if it proved to their own detriment.
Upon receiving this answer, the Pharisees returned to
Nazareth, whither Jesus soon followed with His disciples,
whom He instructed on the way. It was noon when they
arrived. Many from curiosity, others really well inten-

tioned people, came forth from the city to meet Him. They washed the feet of the newcomers and offered them some refreshments. Jesus had two disciples from Nazareth, Parmenas and Jonadab. With the widowed mother of the latter, Jesus and His companions took up their quarters. These disciples had been friends of Jesus in early youth, and had accompanied Him on His first journey to Hebron after Joseph's death. He now employed them frequently in discharging commissions and errands of all kinds.

Jesus went to some sick who had implored His assistance. He knew that they believed in Him and had need of His aid. But He passed by many who wanted only to test His power or who, under the pretence of a cure, were desirous only of getting a sight of Him. An Essenian youth, paralyzed on one side from his birth, was brought to Him. He implored Jesus to cure him, and He did so on the street, as also two blind men. Then He entered certain houses wherein He cured many aged sick people, men and women. Some of them were afflicted with dropsy in its worst form; one woman in particular was frightfully swollen. Jesus cured, altogether, fifteen people.[1] After that He went to the synagogue where also some sick were gathered; but He passed without curing them, and celebrated the Sabbath without interruption. The reading for this Sabbath was about God's speaking to Moses in Egypt, also some chapters from Ezechiel.

Next morning Jesus again taught in the synagogue, but healed no one. At noon I saw Him walking with the disciples and some good people on the road between Nazareth and Sephoris. They entered one of the neighboring villages, as was usual on the Sabbath. The road from Nazareth to Sephoris extended toward the north and was tolerably level, but when within about a quarter of an hour from the latter place, it began to rise. I saw Jesus on this road instructing separate groups of people. The mem-

bers of some households in which reigned strife and dis-
union cast themselves at His feet. He made peace between
man and wife and reconciled neighbors, but performed no
cures. The two young men who had so often desired to be
received among the disciples met Jesus on this road. He
asked them again whether they were willing to forsake
home and parents, distribute their goods to the poor, obey
blindly, and suffer persecution for His sake. Their only
answer was a shrug of the shoulders as they turned away.

When returned to Nazareth, Jesus visited His parents'
house. It was in perfect order, but unoccupied. He visited
likewise Mary's elder sister, the mother of Mary
Cleophas, who took care of the house, though she did not
live in it. Jesus then went with the disciples to the synagogue, preached in sharp and severe terms, called God
His Heavenly Father, pronounced judgment upon
Jerusalem and upon all that would not follow Him, openly
addressed His disciples, alluded to the persecution that
awaited them, and exhorted them to fidelity and perseverance. When the Pharisees found that He did not intend to remain and that He would perform no more cures
in Nazareth, they began to give utterance to their vexation, and to ask, first this one, then that one: "Who is He,
then? Who does He pretend to be? Where did He get His
learning? Is He not of Nazareth? His father was the carpenter. His relatives, His brothers and sisters—all belong
here?" By these last words, they meant Anne's elder
daughter, Mary Heli and her sons James, Heliachim, and
Sadoch, all disciples of John, Mary Cleophas and her sons
and daughters. Jesus made them no answer, but went on
quietly instructing His disciples. Then another Pharisee, a
stranger from the region of Sephoris, more insolent than
the rest, cried out: "Who, then, art Thou? Hast Thou
forgotten that only some years before Thy father's death,
Thou didst help him to put up partitions in my house?"
Still Jesus deigned no answer. Then the Pharisees all

began to shout: "Answer! Is it good manners not to answer an honorable man?" At these words, Jesus addressed His bold questioner in terms like the following: "I did indeed work on wood belonging to thee. At the same time I cast a glance upon thee, and I grieved at not being able to free thee from the hard rind of thine own heart. Thou hast now proved thyself to be what I then suspected. Thou shalt have no part in My Kingdom, although I have helped thee to build up thy dwelling place upon earth." Jesus said likewise that nowhere was a Prophet without honor, excepting in his own city, in his own house, among his own relatives.

But what especially irritated the Pharisees were Jesus' words to His disciples; for instance, "I send ye as lambs among wolves"; "Sodom and Gomorrha will be less severely condemned on the last day than they that refuse to receive you"; "I am not come to bring peace, but the sword."

The close of the Sabbath found many waiting to be healed, but, to the great vexation of the Pharisees, Jesus cured none. Some of the people, imitating the insolence of the Pharisees in the synagogue, cried out to Jesus: "Don't you remember this? Don't you remember that?" And they recalled circumstances in which they had formerly seen Him. The Pharisees remarked to Him that this time He had come with fewer followers than on the preceding occasion, and they inquired whether He was not again going to take up His quarters among the Essenians. As a general thing, the Essenians did not much frequent Jesus' public instructions, and He rarely spoke of them. The enlightened among them at a later period joined the Community. They never opposed His doctrine, but looked upon Jesus as the Son of God.

Jesus did, in effect, again visit those Essenians with whom He had been the last time He was in Nazareth. He and the disciples took with them a light repast, after

which He taught during a part of the night. Toward ten
o'clock, Peter, Matthew and James the Greater returned
from the Apostles in Upper Galilee. They had left the rest
in the region around Seleucia to the east of Lake Merom.
Andrew, Thomas and Saturnin, who had lately arrived,
and another Apostle, immediately started to replace those
just come.

Jesus left Nazareth that night with His followers. He
journeyed about two hours toward Thabor to the little
place where recently, on His return to Capharnaum after
raising the youth of Naim, He had cured the leprous
property holder. An instruction had been announced for
the following day, which was to be delivered on a height
southwest of Thabor, about half an hour from the mountain itself. Jesus stopped again with the schoolmaster of
the place. The latter, counting upon Jesus' coming, had
received many sick into his house. Jesus restored speech
to one dumb. The boy that had so cleverly delivered to
Jesus the message sent by his leprous master was among
the schoolmaster's pupils. Jesus spoke to him. His name
was Samuel, and he afterward became a disciple.

1. Before giving this number, Sister Emmerich reflected a moment.
   Then counting on her fingers, she said: "So many lame, so many
   blind, so many dropsical; in all, fifteen." (From Father Schmöger's
   first edition of *Leben Jesus,* Vol. II).

3. JESUS' INSTRUCTION ON THE HEIGHT
NEAR THABOR, IN SUNEM

The lord of the place, he whom Jesus had healed of
leprosy, came to Him and renewed his acts of gratitude.
He pleaded for several other lepers for whom he had
caused a tent to be erected on the road by which Jesus
was to pass, and he likewise made overtures for applying
a part of his fortune to defraying the expenses of Jesus'

apostolic journeys.

It was still dawn when Jesus left the house and went out on the road where were awaiting Him about five men and women. From a retired spot, a little off from the road, they cried to Him for assistance. Jesus stepped to them, and they cast themselves at His feet. One of the women addressed Him: "Lord, we are from Tiberias, and until now we have hesitated to implore Thy help. The Pharisees told us that Thou art hard and pitiless toward sinners. But we have heard of Thy merciful compassion to Magdalen whom Thou didst free from her miseries, and whose sins Thou didst also forgive. All this gave us courage, and we have followed Thee thither. Lord, have mercy on us! Thou canst heal us and purify us. Thou canst likewise forgive us our sins." The men and women were standing apart from one another. They were afflicted with leprosy and other maladies. One woman was possessed by a wicked spirit who threw her into convulsions.

Jesus took them aside, one by one, to hear the particulars of their confession, inasmuch as the detailed account would serve to increase their sorrow and repentance. He did not exact this from all, unless it was necessary. He cured those of whom we are now speaking, and forgave them their sins. They melted into tears of gratitude, and begged Him to say what they should henceforth do. In reply, Jesus commanded them not to return to Tiberias, but to go to another place. I understood at that moment that Jesus Himself would not go to Tiberias, and indeed I never saw Him there. These people now went to the mountain to hear His instructions.

Jesus, however, turned off to the tent of the lepers, about four or five in number. He cured them, addressed to them words of admonition, commanded them to go to Nazareth and show themselves to the priests.

Jesus never lingered long over such cures, though there was never anything like precipitation in His manner. All was done with dignity and moderation, and especially without a superfluity of words. All was striking and appropriate whether He consoled or exhorted, whether He was gentle or severe. His manner was overflowing with patience and love. He went straight on with His work, but without the least hurry. Many of those that needed His help, Jesus went to meet; yes, even turning out of His way, He hastened to them, like a loving friend of men who sought to save them. From others, again, He turned away, permitting them to follow Him, to sigh after Him, a long time.

The spot upon which Jesus now taught was a beautiful plateau where, from the stone chair, the Prophets of bygone days had taught. From it one could see across the valley of Esdrelon and into the country around Mageddo. Crowds were gathered from the surrounding cities, and there were very many sick from Nazareth also, whom Jesus had not cured there, but who now were restored to health. There were some possessed, who testified to Him as usual and whom He delivered. He again taught upon the first four of the Eight Beatitudes, and related some parables referring to penance and the coming of the Kingdom. Then in most touching terms, He begged His hearers to profit by the grace offered them while still they had time. The Apostles listened attentively, because each in his own peculiar way was to repeat this instruction on his next mission.

Toward noon I saw Jesus gathering the Apostles and disciples around Him in a sequestered spot at the foot of the mountain. He sent them all out, two and two, with the exception of Peter, John, and some of the disciples who were to remain with Him. They were to go in three different directions: one set into the valley of the Jordan, another into that near Dothan, and a third to the west, into the country around Jerusalem. It was on this occasion that I heard Jesus telling the Apostles that they should go without purse, without scrip, girded with one garment only, and a staff in their hand. They were not to go to the heathens nor to the Samaritans, but to the lost sheep of Israel. He indicated to them how they might be received, told them where to shake the dust from their feet, and commanded them to preach penance.[1] Jesus thus particularized because He was sending the Apostles into a hostile part of the country, and because persecution threatened Himself after the death of John, which was now drawing nigh. Many of the private inns had been established in this part of the Holy Land, therefore it was that the Apostles had no need of money. But they that were sent to Upper Galilee and beyond the Jordan, had received some, though very little, money. And now began a new era in their apostolic career, and new regions were visited by them.

Jesus blessed them before their departure, and gave them some further instructions upon curing the sick and driving out demons. He blessed the oil also that was to be used for the sick. He notified some where they should again meet Him.

After healing many more sick, Jesus bade farewell to the multitude, and accompanied by Peter, John and the disciples, journeyed southward about three hours to Sunem. Many of the people followed Him, among others a man who, the last time that Jesus went from Samaria to Galilee, had entreated Him to visit his sick children who were at an inn not far from Endor. This man again proffered his request to Jesus, and now it was granted.

The two demoniacal women of Gathepher had followed Jesus to the instruction given on the mount, and had been delivered by the imposition of His hands. When He reached the brook Cison, before crossing He healed a poor leper whose condition was truly forlorn and despised. He had for twenty years been reduced to this pitiable state, and someone had built him a tent hut here on the roadside. Jesus hastened to him, healed him, and told him to join the others that were going to Jerusalem to show themselves to the priests.

It was dusk when Jesus arrived in Sunem. With Peter and John, He put up at the house of the man that had invited Him to visit his sick children, all of whom were in a most miserable state. One son, sixteen years old and very tall for his age, was deaf and dumb. He lay flat on the ground in convulsions with contortions of the body so frightful that his head and heels met. He was perfectly lame and unable to walk. Another son was a poor idiot afraid of everything, and his two daughters also were timorous and simple. Jesus cured the deaf mute that evening. Peter and John had gone into the city. Jesus with the parents went alone into the sick boy's chamber, knelt by his bed, prayed, and supporting Himself on His hands, inclined over the boy's face. He did this either to breathe into or to say something into his mouth. Then He took the boy by the hand and raised him up. The boy stood upright on his feet, and Jesus led him a few steps backward and forward. Then He took him alone into another room, made a salve out of His saliva and a little earth, took some upon His fingers and anointed his ears, and ran the first two fingers of His right hand under his tongue. Then began the boy in an unwonted, lively voice to cry: "I hear! I can speak!" The parents and servants rushed in at the sound and embraced him, weeping and shouting for joy. They cast themselves with their child on the ground before Jesus, sobbing and rocking to and fro for joy. During the evening Jesus had a private interview with the father, upon whom a great crime committed by *his own* father was still resting. The man asked Jesus whether the chastisement was to fall even to the fourth generation. Jesus answered that if he did penance and atoned for the crime, he might blot out its consequences.

In the morning Jesus cured the other son and the two

daughters of their idiocy. He performed the cure by the imposition of hands. When restored to sense, the children appeared to be perfectly amazed, and as if awaking from a dream. They had always thought that people wanted to kill them, and had in particular a great dread of fire. When on the day before Jesus healed the elder boy, He told (very unusual for Him) the father to go out and relate to all what had taken place. The consequence was a great concourse of people, among them numbers of sick, and that morning I saw Jesus instructing the people on the street, and curing and blessing many of the children.

After that I saw Him with Peter and John journeying rapidly the whole day and night through the plain of Esdrelon in the direction of Ginnim. They seldom paused to rest. I heard Jesus saying on the way that John's end was approaching, and after that, His enemies would begin their pursuit of Himself. But it was not lawful to expose one's self to one's enemies. I think I understood that they were going to Hebron, to console John's relatives and prevent any imprudent manifestation.

The holy women, Mary, Veronica, Susanna, Magdalen, and Mary the Suphanite, were now in Dothan near Samaria. They were stopping with Issachar, the sick husband, whom Jesus had lately healed. The holy women never went to the public inns. Martha, Dina, Johanna Chusa, Susanna Alpheus, Anna Cleophas, Mary Johanna Marcus, and Maroni went, two by two, to look after the inns and supply what was wanting. There were about twelve of these women.

Early the next morning, I saw Jesus and the two Apostles to the south of Samaria, where He met the two Egyptian disciples and the son of Johanna Chusa coming to Him from the East. These Egyptian disciples had already been over a year in Hebron, where they were studying. They had also been a long time in Bethlehem with Lazarus and other disciples that were on intimate terms with Jesus.

They were in consequence very well instructed.

Jesus and His companions some time afterward arrived at the shepherd houses where the holy women had met Him after His conversation with the Samaritan at Jacob's well, and where He had cured the landlord's sick son. They here partook of some refreshment and rested a little.

Some time after I had a vision of Jesus' instructing, near a well, the laborers gathered together from the neighboring fields. He was relating to them the parable of the treasure hidden in a field, also that of the lost drachma found again. Some of His hearers laughed at the latter, saying that they had often lost more than one drachma, but they had never taken the trouble to sweep the whole house on that account. But when Jesus reproached them for their levity, and explained to them what the drachma signified and the virtue implied by that general sweeping, they became confused and laughed no more.

These laborers were occupied in threshing the grain which was lying in heaps in the fields. This they did with wooden mallets which rose and fell by means of a cylinder. Several men were employed in pushing the grain under the mallets and in sweeping it away again. The operation was carried on in a pure rocky basin hewn out of solid stone, streaked with colored veinings. A large tree shaded the spot.

Jesus continued to teach here and there in the fields, and accompanied some of the laborers to their home in Thanath-Silo, which was not far off. The inhabitants received Him very cordially outside the city, presented refreshments, and washed His feet. They wanted to give Him also a change of raiment, but He declined. He related in their synagogue the parable of the king who made a great feast.

1. *Matt.* 10:9 *et seq.; Mk.* 6:10, 11; *Lk.* 9:1-5.

4. THE BEHEADING OF
ST. JOHN THE BAPTIST

For the last two weeks Herod's guests had been pouring into Machaerus, most of them from Tiberias. It was one succession of holidays and banqueting. Near the castle was an open circular building with many seats. In it gladiators struggled with wild animals for the amusement of Herod's guests, and dancers male and female performed all kinds of voluptuous dances. I saw Salome, the daughter of Herodias, practicing them before metallic mirrors in presence of her mother.

Zorobabel and Cornelius of Capharnaum were not among the guests. They had excused themselves.

For some time past, John had been allowed to go around at large within the castle precincts, and his disciples also could go and come as they pleased. Once or twice he gave a public discourse at which Herod himself was present. His release had been promised him if he would approve Herod's marriage, or, at least, never again inveigh against it. But John had always most forcibly denounced it. Herod, nevertheless, was thinking of setting him free on his own birthday, but his wife was secretly nourishing very different thoughts. Herod would have wished John to circulate freely during the festival, that the guests might see and admire the leniency of the prisoner's treatment. But scarcely had the games and banqueting begun, scarcely had vice commenced to run riot in Machaerus, when John shut himself up in his prison cell and bade his disciples retire from the city. They obeyed and withdrew to the region of Hebron, where already many were assembled.

The daughter of Herodias had been trained entirely by her mother, whose constant companion she had been from her earliest years. She was in the bloom of girlhood, her deportment bold, her attire shameless. For a long time Herod had looked upon her with lustful eyes. This the mother regarded with complacency, and laid her plans accordingly. Herodias herself had a very striking, very bold appearance, and she employed all her skill, made use of every means, to set off her charms. She was no longer young, and there was something sharp, cunning, and diabolical in her countenance that bad men love to see. In me, however, she excited disgust and aversion as would the beauty of a serpent. I can find no better comparison than this, that she reminded me of the old pagan goddesses. She occupied a wing of the castle near the grand courtyard, somewhat higher than the hall opposite in which the birthday feast was to be celebrated. From the gallery around her apartments, one could look down into that open, pillared hall. Before the latter and in Herod's courtyard, a magnificent triumphal arch had been raised. Steps led up to it, and it opened into the hall itself, which was so long that from the entrance the other end could not be descried. Mirrors and gold sparkled on all sides, flowers and green bushes everywhere met the eye. The splendor almost blinded one, for far, far back halls, and columns, and passages were blazing with flambeaux and lamps, with transparent glittering sentences, pictures, and vases.

Herodias and her female companions, arrayed in magnificence, stood in the high gallery of her apartments, gazing upon Herod's triumphal entrance into the banqueting hall. He came attended by his guests, all arrayed in pomp and splendor. The courtyard through which he passed to the triumphal arch was carpeted and lined with choirs of singers, who saluted him with songs of joy. Around the arch were ranged boys and girls waving garlands of flowers and playing upon all kinds of musical instruments. When Herod mounted the steps to the arch of triumph, he was met by a band of dancing boys and girls, Salome in their midst. She presented him with a crown

which rested on a cushion covered with sparkling ornamentation and carried by some of the children of her
suite under a transparent veil. These children were
clothed in thin, tightly fitting garments, and on their
shoulders were imitations of wings. Salome wore a long,
transparent robe, caught up here and there on the lower
limbs with glittering clasps. Her arms were ornamented
with gold bands, strings of pearls, and circlets of tiny
feathers; her neck and breast were covered with pearls
and delicate, sparkling chains. She danced for a while
before Herod who, quite dazzled and enchanted, gave expression to his admiration, in which all his guests
enthusiastically joined. She should, he said to her, renew
this pleasure for him on the next morning.

And now the procession entered the hall, and the banquet began. The women ate in the wing of the castle with
Herodias. Meantime I saw John in his prison cell kneeling in prayer, his arms outstretched, his eyes raised to
Heaven. The whole place around him was shining with
light, but it was a very different light from that which
glared in Herod's hall. The latter, compared with the
former, appeared like a flame from Hell. The whole city
of Machaerus was illuminated by torches and, as if on
fire, it cast a reflection far into the surrounding mountains.

Herod's banquet-hall opened toward that of Herodias
which, as I have said, was opposite, though a little more
elevated than the former. From this open side, the women
feasting and enjoying themselves were reflected in one of
the inclined mirrors of Herod's hall. Between pyramids of
flowers and fragrant green bushes, a playing fountain jet-
ted up in fine sprays. When all had eaten and wine had
flowed freely, the guests requested Herod to allow
Salome to dance again, and for this purpose, they cleared
sufficient space and ranged around the walls. Herod was
seated on his throne surrounded by some of his most inti-

mate associates, who were Herodians. Salome appeared with some of her dancing companions clothed in a light, transparent robe. Her hair was interwoven in part with pearls and precious stones, while another part floated around her in curls. She wore a crown and formed the central figure in the group of dancers. The dance consisted of a constant bowing, a gentle swaying and turning. The whole person seemed to be destitute of bones. Scarcely had one position been assumed when it glided into another. The dancers held wreaths and scarfs in their hands, which waved and twined around one another. The whole performance gave expression to the most shameful passions, and in it Salome excelled all her companions. I saw the devil at her side as if bending and twisting all her limbs in order to produce that abominable effect. Herod was perfectly ravished, perfectly entranced by the changing attitudes. When at the end of one of the figures Salome presented herself before the throne, the other dancers continued to engage the attention of the guests, so that only those in the immediate vicinity heard Herod saying to her: "Ask of me what thou wilt, and I will give it to thee. Yes, I swear to thee, though thou askest the half of my kingdom, yet will I give it to thee!" Salome left the hall, hurried to that of the women, and conferred with her mother. The latter directed her to ask for the head of John on a dish. Salome hastened back to Herod, and said: "I will that thou give to me at once the head of John on a dish!" Only a few of Herod's most confidential associates who were nearest the throne heard the request. Herod looked like one struck with apoplexy, but Salome reminded him of his oath. Then he commanded one of the Herodians to call his executioner, to whom he gave the command to behead John and give the head on a dish to Salome. The executioner withdrew, and in a few moments Salome followed him. Herod, as if suddenly indisposed, soon left the hall with his companions. He was very sad. I heard his followers saying to him that he was not bound to grant such a request; nevertheless they promised the greatest secrecy, in order not to interrupt the festivities. Herod, exceedingly troubled, paced like one demented the most remote apartments of his palace, but the feast went on undisturbed.

John was in prayer. The executioner and his servant took the two soldiers on guard at the entrance of John's prison in with them. The guards bore torches, but I saw the space around John so brilliantly illuminated that their flame became dull like a light in the daytime. Salome waited in the entrance hall of the vast and intricate dungeon house. With her was a maidservant who gave the executioner a dish wrapped in a red cloth. The latter addressed John: "Herod the King sends me to bring thy head on the dish to his daughter Salome." John allowed him little time to explain. He remained kneeling, and bowing his head toward him, he said: "I know why thou hast come. Thou art my guest, one for whom I have long waited. Didst thou know what thou art about to do, thou wouldst not do it. I am ready." Then he turned his head away and continued his prayer before the stone in front of which he always prayed kneeling. The executioner beheaded him with a machine which I can compare to nothing but a fox trap. An iron ring was laid on his shoulders. This ring was provided with two sharp blades, which, being closed around the throat with a sudden pressure given by the executioner, in the twinkling of an eye severed the head from the trunk. John still remained in a kneeling posture. The head bounded to the earth, and a triple stream of blood springing up from the body sprinkled both the head and body of the saint, as if baptizing him in his own blood. The executioner's servant raised the head by the hair, insulted it, and laid it on the dish which his master held. The latter presented it to the expectant Salome. She received it joyfully, yet not without secret horror and that effeminate loathing which those given to sin always have for blood and wounds. She carried the holy head covered by a red cloth on the dish. The maid went before, bearing a torch to light the way through the subterranean passages. Salome held the dish timidly at arm's length before her, her head still laden with its ornaments turned away in disgust. Thus she traversed the solitary passages that led up to a kind of vaulted kitchen under the castle of Herodias. Here she was met by her mother, who raised the cover from the holy head, which she loaded with insult and abuse. Then taking a sharp skewer from a certain part of the wall where many such instruments were sticking, with it she pierced the tongue, the cheeks, and the eyes. After that, looking more like a demon than a human being, she hurled it from her and kicked it with her foot through a round opening down into a pit into which the offal and refuse of the kitchen were swept. Then did that infamous woman together with her daughter return to the noise and wicked revelry of the feast, as if nothing had happened. I saw the holy body of the saint, covered with the skin that he usually wore, laid by the two soldiers upon his stone couch. The men were very much touched by what they had just witnessed. They were afterward discharged from duty and imprisoned that they might not disclose what they knew of John's murder. All that had any share in it were bound to the most rigorous secrecy. The guests, however, gave John no thought. Thus his death remained a long time concealed. The report was even spread that he had been set at liberty. The festivities went on. As soon as Herod ceased to take part in them, Herodias began to entertain. Five of those that knew of John's death were shut up in dungeons. They were the two guards, the executioner and his servant, and Salome's maid who had shown some compassion for the saint. Other guards were placed at the prison door, and they in turn were at regular intervals replaced by others. One of Herod's confidential followers regularly carried food to John's cell, consequently no one had any misgiving of what had taken place.

5. JESUS IN THANATH-SILO AND ANTIPATRIS

During the feast in Machaerus and the beheading of the Baptist, Jesus was in Thanath-Silo. There He heard from those that had returned from Jerusalem the catastrophe which had just occurred in the Holy City. A crowd of laborers lately engaged on a great building near the mount upon which stood the Temple, along with eighteen master workmen sent thither by Herod, had been buried under the falling walls. Jesus expressed compassion for the innocent sufferers, but said that the sin of the master workmen was not greater than that of the Pharisees, the Sadducees, and all those that labored against the Kingdom of God. These latter would likewise be one day buried under their own treacherous structures.

The aqueduct that had cost the lives of so many was probably a quarter of an hour in length. It was intended to conduct the water flowing from the Pool of Bethsaida up to the mount on which the Temple stood, thus to wash down from the court to the lower ravine the blood of the slaughtered animals. Higher up on the mountain was the Pool of Bethsaida, which discharged the waters received from its source, the Gehon. Three vaulted aqueducts ran far in under the Temple mount, and long arcades extended northward across the valley and up to the mount. Nearby stood a high tower in which, by means of wheelwork machinery, water was raised in great leathern vessels from the reservoir far below. The work had long been in progress. Being now in want of good building stone and master workmen, Pilate, acting on the advice of a member of the Sanhedrin, a Herodian in secret, had sought help from Herod. The master workmen sent by the latter were likewise Herodians. At Herod's instigation, they designedly carried on the building in such a way that the whole structure would necessarily fall at once. By this catastrophe, they intended to embitter the Jews still more against Pilate. The foundation was broad, but hollow, and the structure arose tapering, but heavy. When the disaster happened, the eighteen Herodians were standing upon a terrace opposite the building. They had commanded the wooden scaffolding over which it had been arched to be drawn out, for that now all was solid. The poor laborers were crowded on all parts of the high arches busily working. Suddenly all split asunder, the huge walls came toppling down, and cries went up on all sides. Crash after crash was heard, and clouds of dust swept over the whole region. Many little dwellings were crushed by the falling stones, as well as a number of laborers and others at the foot of the mount. The place on which the eighteen traitors were standing, loosened by the shock, slid down with the rest, and they too were buried in the ruins. This took place shortly before the festivities at Machaerus, consequently no Roman officer or civil functionary made his appearance at the feast. Pilate became very much enraged against Herod, and thought only of revenging himself. The building was an immense undertaking, and the loss very great. Enmity arose between Pilate and Herod on account of this affair; but by the death of Jesus, that is, by the demolition of the true Temple, they again became friends. The destruction of the first edifice buried the wily authors of it along with their innocent victims; that of the second brought judgment upon the whole nation.

The outlet of the Pool of Bethsaida was now entirely choked up, for the whole ravine was full of débris; in consequence of this, another pool was soon formed by the retarded waters.

When Pilate, greatly exasperated by what had taken place, sent some of his officers to Herod in Machaerus, the latter excused himself as absent from home.

Jesus restored sight to several blind persons in Thanath. After that He went with Peter and John through Sichem to Antipatris. Both of the Apostles inquired more than once on the way whether or not He intended to stop at Aruma and other places on their route. But Jesus answered that the people of those places would not receive Him, and He proceeded in the direction to Antipatris. During their journey, Jesus instructed His Apostles on prayer. He made use of the similitude of a man knocking at his friend's door during the night and begging the loan of three loaves. Toward evening Jesus and His companions reached the woody region outside Antipatris, and there took lodgings at an inn.

Antipatris was situated near a little river. It was a very beautiful city recently built by Herod in honor of his father, Antipater, on the site of a little place named Kaphar-Saba. During the war with the Machabees, General Lysias encamped at Kaphar-Saba, which even at that time was fortified with towers and walls. Being defeated by Judas Machabeus, he came to terms with him here, warded off from Judea the attacks of other nations, and gave large presents for the restoration of the Temple. Antipatris was six hours from the sea. It was Paul's halting place when being led a prisoner to Caesarea. The city was surrounded by uncommonly large trees, while throughout its interior were scattered gardens and magnificent walks. The whole city appeared to be clothed in verdure. The architecture was of pagan style; colonnades, under which one could walk, ran the entire length of the streets.

When Jesus with Peter and John left the inn and entered the city, He went to the house of the chief magistrate, who was named Ozias. It was principally on account of this man that He had come hither, for his trouble was well known to Jesus. Ozias had sent a messenger out to the inn to invite Jesus to visit him, for his daughter was very sick, and Jesus returned word that He would go that very day. Ozias received Him and the two Apostles very reverently, washed their feet, and wanted to offer refreshments. But Jesus went straight to the invalid, while the two Apostles proceeded through the city to announce the instruction about to be given in the synagogue. Ozias was a man of about forty years. His daughter was called Michol, and she may have been about fourteen. She lay stretched upon her couch, pale, wasted, and so paralyzed as to be unable to move any of her members. She could not raise or turn her head; her attendants had even to move her hands from one place to another. The mother was present and veiled. She bowed humbly before Jesus as He drew near to the maiden's couch, at one side of which she generally remained seated on a cushion in order to render assistance to her daughter. But when Jesus knelt down by the couch, for it was very low, the mother stood reverently on the opposite side, the father at the foot.

Jesus spoke with the invalid, prayed, breathed into her face, and motioned to the mother to kneel down opposite Him. She obeyed. Then Jesus poured some oil that He carried with Him upon the palm of His hand and, with the first two fingers of His right hand, anointed the sick maiden's forehead and temples, then the joints of both hands, allowing His own hand to rest for one moment upon them. Then He directed the mother to open Michol's long garment over the region of the stomach, which too He anointed with the oil. After that the mother raised the edge of the coverlet from her daughter's feet, and they also received the unction. Then Jesus said: "Michol, give Me thy right hand and thy mother thy left!" At this command, the maiden, for the first time, raised both hands and stretched them out. Jesus continued: "Stand up, Michol!" and the pale, haggard child arose to a sitting posture and then to her feet, tottering in the unaccustomed position. Jesus and the mother led her into the open arms of the father. The mother also embraced her. They wept for joy, and all three fell at Jesus' feet. And now came in the servant-men and maids of the house, praising the Lord in accents of joy. Jesus ordered bread and grapes to be brought, and the juice of the latter to be squeezed out. He blessed both, and commanded the maiden to eat and drink a little at a time. When Michol lay upon her couch, she was clothed in a long gown of fine white wool. The piece that covered the breast was fastened upon the shoulders so that it could easily be opened. Her arms were wrapped with broad strips of the same stuff which fastened to the back. Under this gown was a covering on the back and breast like a scapular. As she arose to stand, her mother threw around her a very large, light veil.

Michol's steps were at first tottering and uncertain. She was like one who had forgotten how to walk and stand upright, and she soon lay down again even while eating. But when her young friends and playmates came in, full of shy curiosity, to see with their own eyes the cure that was now noised about, Michol arose and, trembling with emotion, tottered to meet them. Her mother led her like a child. The girls were glad and joyous. They embraced Michol and led her around. Ozias asked Jesus whether his child's malady had come upon her on account of some sin of her parents. Jesus replied: "It came through a dispensation of God." Michol's young companions also thanked Jesus, who then proceeded to the forecourt of the house where He found numbers of people waiting for Him with their sick. Here too were Peter and John.

Jesus cured the sick of all kinds of maladies and, followed by a crowd, went to the synagogue where the Pharisees and a great multitude were awaiting His coming. He related the parable of the shepherd. He said that He was seeking the lost sheep, that He had sent His servants also to seek them, and that He would die for His sheep. He told them likewise that He had a flock upon His mountain, that they were more secure than some others, and that if the wolf devoured any one of them, it would be owing to its own imprudence. Speaking of His mission, He related another parable. He began: "My Father has a vineyard." At these words, the Pharisees smiled derisively and looked at one another. When He had finished the whole parable, in which He described the ill-treatment the servants of His Father had received from the wicked vinedressers, and said that His Father had now sent His Son whom they would cast out and murder, they laughed in scorn and asked one another: "Who is He? What is He about? Where has His Father that vineyard? He has lost His wits! He is a fool, that's plain to be seen!" And so they went on jeering and laughing. Jesus left the synagogue with Peter and John. The Pharisees continued their insults behind His back, ascribing His miracles to sorcery and the devil.

Jesus returned with Ozias to his house, and again cured many people who were waiting in the forecourt. He took a slight repast, and accepted some bread and balsam for the journey.

Jesus cured in various ways, each one having its own signification. I cannot now, however, repeat them as I saw them. Each had reference to the meaning and the secret cause of the malady, also to the spiritual needs of the invalid. In the anointing with oil, for instance, there was a certain spiritual strength and energy denoted by the signification of the oil itself. No one of these actions was without its own peculiar meaning. With these forms,

Jesus instituted all those ceremonies that the saints and priests who exercised their healing power would afterward make use of in His Name. They either received them from tradition, or were used in the Name of Jesus through an inspiration of the Holy Ghost. As the Son of God, in order to become man, chose the body of a most pure creature, thus to correspond to the requirements of man's nature, so did He frequently use in effecting His cures pure and simple creatures that had been blessed by His Spirit, as, for instance, oil. He afterward gave to the cured bread to eat with some juice of the grape. At other times He healed by a mere command uttered at a distance, for He had come upon earth to cure the most varied ills and that in the most varied ways. He had come to satisfy, for all that believed in Him, by His own great Sacrifice upon the Cross, in which Sacrifice were contained all pains and sorrows, all penances and satisfactions. With the various keys of His charity, He first opened the fetters and bonds of temporal misery and chastisement, instructed the ignorant in all things necessary for them to know, healed all kinds of maladies, and aided the needy in every way; then with that chief key of His love, the key of the Cross, He opened Heaven's expiatory door as well as the door of Limbo.

Michol, Ozias's daughter, had been paralyzed from her early years, and it was a special grace that she had for so long a time been unable to move. She had been chained down by sickness during the most perilous years of her childhood, years full of danger to innocence; and in consequence of the same, her parents had an opportunity for the exercise of charity and patience. Had she been well from infancy, what would perhaps have become of both her and her parents? Had the latter not sighed after Jesus, Michol never would have been so blessed. Had they not believed in Him, their daughter would never have been cured and anointed, which anointing had im-

parted wonderful strength and energy both to body and
soul. Her sickness was a trial, a consequence of inherited
sinfulness, but at the same time a loving discipline, a
means of spiritual progress for Michol's soul, as well as
for her parents. The patience and resignation of the
parents resulted from their cooperation with grace. It
brought to them the crown, the recompense of the struggle decreed for them by God, namely, the cure through
Jesus of soul and body. What a grace! To be bound down
by sufferings, and yet to have the spirit free for good until the Lord comes to deliver both body and soul!

Jesus conversed with Ozias, who told Him about the
fall of the tower of Siloe and of the unfortunate people
buried under its ruins. He spoke with horror of Herod,
whom some suspected of being at the bottom of the
affair. Jesus remarked that greater calamities would overtake the traitors and false architects than that which had
fallen upon the poor workmen. "If," He continued,
"Jerusalem does not embrace the salvation offered her,
the destruction of the Temple will follow that of the
tower." Ozias referred also to John's baptism, and expressed the hope that Herod would set him at liberty on
the occasion of his birthday festival. Jesus replied that
John would be freed when his time came. The Pharisees
said to Jesus in the synagogue that He should be on His
guard, lest Herod would imprison Him with John if He
went on as He was then doing. To this Jesus deigned no
reply.

About five o'clock in the afternoon, Jesus left Antipatris with Peter and John and went southward to Ozensara, from four to five hours distant. A Roman garrison
was stationed in Antipatris, and there were many large
trunks of trees brought hither for transportation to the
lake, where ship building was carried on. On their way to
Ozensara they encountered many such loads of timber
drawn by huge oxen and accompanied by Roman

soldiers. The trees of this region also were felled and hewed for the same purpose. Jesus instructed several workmen thus employed. It was late when they reached Ozensara, a town divided into two sections by a little river. Jesus put up here with some people whom He knew. He instructed and admonished a crowd that had collected near the inn. He had been here once before on His way to baptism. He cured and blessed the sick children.

6. JESUS IN BETHORON AND BETHANIA

It was about six hours from Ozensara to Bethoron. At some distance from the latter place, John and Peter went on ahead, leaving Jesus to follow alone. The Egyptian disciples, along with the son of Johanna Chusa, came to meet Jesus here. They brought news that the holy women were celebrating the Sabbath in Machmas, which was situated in a narrow defile four hours to the north of this place. Machmas was the place at which Jesus in His twelfth year withdrew from His parents and returned to the Temple. Here it was that Mary missed Him and thought that He had gone on to Gophna. Not finding Him at this latter place, she was filled with anxious solicitude, and made her way back to Jerusalem.

There was in Bethoron a Levitical school, with whose teacher the Holy Family was acquainted. Anne and Joachim had lodged with him on the occasion of their taking Mary to the Temple; and when returning to Nazareth as Joseph's bride, Mary had again stopped at his house. Several of the disciples from Jerusalem had come hither with Joseph of Arimathea's nephews at the time of Jesus' arrival. Jesus went to the synagogue where, amid the contradictions and objections of the Pharisees, He explained the Scripture appointed for that Sabbath. The instruction over, He cured the sick at the inn, among them several women afflicted with an issue of blood, and blessed some sick children. The Pharisees had invited Him to a dinner, and when they found Him so tardy in coming, they went to call Him. All things, they said, had their time and so had these cures. The Sabbath belonged to God, and He had now done enough. Jesus responded: "I have no other time and no other measure than the will of the Heavenly Father." When He had finished curing, He accompanied the disciples to the dinner.

During the meal, the Pharisees addressed to Him all kinds of reproaches; among others they alleged that He allowed women of bad repute to follow Him about. These men had heard of the conversion of Magdalen, of Mary Suphan, and of the Samaritan. Jesus replied: "If ye knew Me, ye would speak differently. I am come to have pity on sinners." He contrasted external ulcers, which carry off poisonous humors and are easily healed, with internal ones which, though full of loathsome matter, do not affect the appearance of the individual so afflicted. The Pharisees further alleged that His disciples had neglected to wash before the meal, which gave Jesus an opportunity for a timely and energetic protest against the hypocrisy and sanctimoniousness of the Pharisees themselves. When they spoke of the women of ill repute, Jesus related a parable. He asked which was the more praiseworthy, the debtor, who having a great debt, humbly implored indulgence until he could faithfully discharge it little by little; or another who, though deeply in debt, spent all he could lay his hands on in rioting and, far from thinking of paying what he owed, mocked at the conscientious debtor. Jesus related likewise the parables of the good shepherd and the vineyard, as He had done at Antipatris, but His hearers were indifferent; they did not seize the application.

Jesus and the disciples put up at the Levitical school.

Upper-Bethoron was so elevated that it could be descried from Jerusalem, but Lower-Bethoron lay at the foot of the mountain.

From Bethoron, which was six hours distant from Jerusalem, Jesus went straight on to Bethania, stopping at no place on the way excepting Athanot. Lazarus had already returned to Bethania from Magdalum, where he had put everything in order and engaged a steward for the castle and other property. To the man who had lived with Magdalen, he had assigned a dwelling situated on the heights near Ginnim and sufficient means for his support. The gift was gladly accepted.

As soon as she arrived in Bethania, Magdalen went straight to the dwelling of her deceased sister, Mary the Silent, by whom she had been very much beloved, and spent the whole night in tears. When Martha went to her in the morning, she found her weeping on the grave of her sister, her hair unbound and flowing around her.

The women of Jerusalem also had returned to their homes, all making the journey on foot. Magdalen, though exhausted by her malady and the shocks she had received, and wholly unaccustomed to such travelling, insisted upon walking like the others. Her feet bled more than once. The holy women who, since her conversion, showed her unspeakable affection, were often obliged to come to her assistance. She was pale and exhausted from weeping. She could not resist her desire to express her gratitude to Jesus, so she went over an hour's journey to meet Him, threw herself at His feet, and bedewed them with repentant and grateful tears. Jesus extended His hand to her, raised her, and addressed to her words of kindness. He spoke of her deceased sister, Mary the Silent. He said that she should tread in her footsteps and do penance as she had done, although she had never sinned. Magdalen then returned home with her maid by another way.

Jesus went with Peter and John into Lazarus's garden.

Lazarus came out to meet Him, conducted Him to the house and offered Him in the hall the customary attentions, namely, washing of feet and refreshments. Nicodemus was not there, but Joseph of Arimathea was present. Jesus stayed in the house and spoke with no one excepting the members of the family and the holy women. Only with Mary did He speak of John's death, for she knew of it by interior revelation. Jesus told her to return to Galilee within a week in order to escape the annoyances of a crowded road, for Herod's guests from that part of the country would a little later be going from Machaerus to their homes.

The disciples that were going to Judea at the same time as Jesus, though not with Him, stopped at the different places on the road, went into the huts on the wayside and to the shepherds in the fields, asking: "Are there any sick here whom we may cure in the Name of our Master, that we may freely give to them what He has freely given to us?" Then anointing the sick with oil, they were cured.

Jesus left Bethania the next morning. He crossed the Mount of Olives to teach and heal in a neighboring place where some masons and other mechanics were encamped. It was the camping ground of the day laborers and masons engaged on the interminable buildings of the Temple mount. There were some kitchens around the place in which poor women cooked the workmen's food for a trifle. There were many Galileans among the workmen, also some people who had been attracted thither by Jesus' teaching and miracles, some even whom He had cured. Some too were from Giskala, from Zorobabel the Centurion's estate, and many others from a little place near Tiberias on the northern height of the valley of Magdalum. Jesus cured many sick among these people. They bemoaned to Him the great misfortune that had happened about fourteen days before in the falling of that huge building, and begged Him to visit several of the wounded who had barely escaped with their lives. Ninety-three people, besides the eighteen treacherous architects, had been killed. Jesus went to the wounded, whom He consoled and healed. He healed several of contusions on the head by anointing the head with oil and pressing it between His hands; and crushed hands on which splinters of bones were projecting, He healed by fixing the pieces together, anointing them, and holding them in His own hands. Broken arms bound up in bandages Jesus anointed, then held the fractures in His hands, and they were made whole, so that the bandages could be removed and the arms used. The wounds of lost limbs, He closed.

I heard Jesus saying to the assembled multitude that they would have greater evils to bemoan when the sword would strike Galilee. He advised them to pay all taxes to the Emperor without murmuring, and if they had not the means to do so, they should apply to Lazarus in His name, and he would furnish what was necessary. Jesus spoke with touching kindness to these poor people. I heard them complaining that once they were able to obtain help at the Pool of Bethsaida, but now poor people could no longer look there for assistance—they had to languish unaided. For a long time past, they had heard of no cure at the pool.

Jesus wept as He crossed the Mount of Olives. He said, "If the city" (*Jerusalem*) "does not accept salvation, its Temple will be destroyed like this building that has tumbled down. A great number will be buried in the ruins." He called the catastrophe of the aqueduct an example that should serve to the people as a warning.

Jesus went afterward to the house outside the Bethlehem gate of Jerusalem at which Mary and Joseph had lodged with Him, a Babe of forty days, when they were going to present Him in the Temple. Anne also had spent a night here when journeying to the Crib, and Jesus had done the same when, in His twelfth year, He had at Machmas left His parents who were returning home and gone back to the Temple. This little inn was in the hands of very devout, simple-hearted people, and it was there that the Essenians and other pious souls took lodgings. The present proprietors were the children of those that had lived there thirty years before, and there was one old man who remembered perfectly all the circumstances of those visits. They did not, however, recognize Jesus, for He had not been there for a long time. They thought perhaps He was John the Baptist, of whom even here the report was current, that he had been set at liberty.

They showed Jesus in one corner of the house a doll in swaddling bands, clothed exactly as He Himself had been when Mary bore Him to the Temple. It was lying in a crib like His own, and around it burned lights and lamps that appeared to rise out of paper horns. They said to Jesus: "Jesus of Nazareth, the great Prophet, was born in Bethlehem three and thirty years ago, and was brought here by His Mother. What comes from God, one may honor, and why should we not celebrate His birthday for six weeks if similar honors are paid to Herod, who is no prophet?"

These people, through their intercourse with Anne and other intimate friends of the Holy Family, as well as through the accounts of the shepherds who put up at their inn when they visited Jerusalem, were reverential believers in Jesus, Mary, and Joseph. When Jesus now made Himself known to them their joy was beyond expression. They showed Him every place in the house and garden hallowed by the presence of Mary, Joseph, and Anne. Jesus instructed and consoled them, and they exchanged gifts. Jesus directed one of the disciples to give them some coins while at the same time He accepted from them some bread, fruit, and honey for His journey.

They accompanied Him quite a distance when, with the disciples, He left the inn and started for Hebron.

7. JESUS IN JUTTAH. HE MAKES KNOWN THE DEATH OF JOHN THE BAPTIST

Jesus went with His companions to Juttah, the Baptist's birthplace. It was five hours' distance from the inn outside Jerusalem and one hour from Hebron. Mary, Veronica, Susanna, Johanna Chusa, Johanna Marcus, Lazarus, Joseph of Arimathea, Nicodemus, and several of the disciples from Jerusalem were there awaiting Jesus. They had travelled in small parties and, having come by a shorter route from Jerusalem, had reached their destination several hours before Him.

Zachary's house was situated on a hill outside of Juttah. Both it and its surroundings, consisting of vineyards, were the inheritance of the Baptist. The son of his father's brother, likewise named Zachary, occupied the house at this time and managed affairs. He was a Levite and an intimate friend of Luke, by whom not long before he had been visited in Jerusalem, and had then heard many particulars of the Holy Family. He was younger than the Baptist, of the age of the Apostle John. From his early years he had been like an own child in Elizabeth's house. He belonged to that class of Levites who were most like the Essenians and who, having received from their ancestors the knowledge of certain mysteries, waited with earnest devotion for the coming of the Messiah. Zachary was enlightened and unmarried. He received Jesus and His companions with the customary marks of respect, washing of feet and refreshments. After that Jesus repaired to the synagogue in Hebron.

It was a fast day, and on that evening began a local celebration in Juttah and Hebron. It was in memory of David's victory over Absalom who had in Hebron, as being his birthplace, first raised the standard of revolt. Numerous lamps were lighted during this feast even in the daytime, both in the synagogue and private dwellings. The people gave thanks for the interior light which had at that time led their ancestors to choose the right, and implored a continuance of that heavenly illumination, to enable them always to make choice of the same. Jesus delivered an instruction to a very large audience. The Levites showed Him great esteem and affection, and He took a meal with them.

As Mary was making the journey with the women to this part of the country, she related to them many particulars connected with her former journey thither with Joseph on the occasion of her visit to Elizabeth. She showed them the spot on which Joseph had bade her farewell on his departure for home, and told them how uneasy she felt when she reflected upon what Joseph's thought would certainly be when on his return he would notice her changed condition. She visited likewise with the holy women all the places where mysteries connected with her Visitation and the birth of John had occurred. She told of John's leaping for joy in his mother's womb, of Elizabeth's salutation, and of the Magnificat which she had herself uttered under the inspiration of God, and which she afterward recited every evening with Elizabeth. She told of Zachary's being struck dumb and of God's restoring his speech at the moment in which he pronounced the name of John. All these mysteries, until now unknown to them, Mary, with tears started by tender recollections, related to the holy women. They too wept at the different places, but their tears were more joyful than those of Mary, who was at the same time mourning John's death, still unknown to them. She showed them also the fountain which at her prayer had sprung up near the house, and from it they all drank.

At the family meal Jesus taught. The women were

seated apart. After the meal, the Blessed Virgin went with Jesus, Peter, John, and the Baptist's three disciples, James, Heliacim, and Sadoc (the sons of her eldest sister Mary Heli) into the room in which John was born. They spread out a large rug, or carpet, on the floor and all knelt or sat around it. Jesus, however, remained standing. He spoke to them of John's holiness and of his career. Then the Blessed Virgin related to them the circumstances under which that rug had been made. At the time of her visit, she said, Elizabeth and herself had made it and on it John was born. It was Elizabeth's couch at the time of his birth. It was made of yellow wool, quilted and ornamented with flowers. On the upper border were embroidered in large letters passages from Elizabeth's salutation and the Magnificat. In the middle was fastened a kind of cover or pouch, into which the woman about to become a mother could have her feet buttoned up as in a sack. The upper part of this pouch formed a kind of hooded mantle that could be thrown around her. It was of yellow wool, with brown flowers, and was something like a dressing gown, the lower half being fastened to a quilted rug. I saw Mary raising the upper border before her while she read and explained the passages and prophecies embroidered on it. She told them also that she had prophesied to Elizabeth that John would see Jesus face to face only three times, and how this was verified: first, as a child in the desert when on their flight into Egypt, Jesus, Joseph, and herself had passed him, though at some distance; the second time, at Jesus' baptism; and the third, when at the Jordan he saw Jesus passing and bore witness to Him.

And now Jesus disclosed to them the fact that John had been put to death by Herod. Deep grief seized upon them all. They watered the rug with their tears, especially John, who threw himself weeping on the floor. It was heartrending to behold them prostrate on the floor, sob-

bing and lamenting, their faces pressed upon the rug.
Jesus and Mary alone were standing, one at each end.
Jesus consoled them with earnest words and prepared
them for still more cruel blows. He commanded silence
on the matter since, with the exception of themselves, it
was at present known only to its authors.

Southward from Hebron was the grove of Mambre and
the Cave of Machpelah, where Abraham and the other
Patriarchs were buried. Jesus gave an instruction and
cured some sick peasants who there lived isolated. The
forest of Mambre was a valley full of oaks, beeches, and
nut trees, that stood far apart. At the edge of the forest
was the vast Cave Machpelah, in which Abraham, Sara,
Jacob, Isaac, and others of the Patriarchs were en-
tombed. The cave was a double one like two cellars.
Some of the tombs were hewn out in the projecting rocks,
while others were formed in the rocky wall. This grotto is
still held in great veneration. A flower garden and place
for instruction guard its entrance. The rock was thickly
clothed with vines, and higher up grain was raised. Jesus
entered the grotto with the disciples, and several of the
tombs were opened. Some of the skeletons were fallen to
dust, but that of Abraham lay on its couch in a state of
preservation. From it they unrolled a brown cover woven
of camel's-hair cords thick as a man's finger. Jesus taught
here. He spoke of Abraham, of the Promise and its
fulfillment. Some of the sick whom Jesus cured were
paralyzed, others consumptive, others dropsical. I saw
here no possessed, though there were some simpletons
and lunatics. The country around was very fertile, and
the remarkably beautiful grain was already quite yellow.
The bread of these parts was excellent, and almost everyone had his own vine. The mountains terminated in
plateaus upon which grain was cultivated; their sides
were covered with vineyards, and in them extended wonderful caves.

When Jesus and the disciples went into the Cave Machpelah, they put off their shoes outside the entrance, walked in barefoot, and stood in reverential silence around Abraham's tomb. Jesus alone spoke. From there He went an hour southeast of Hebron into the little Levitical city of Bethain, which was reached by a very steep ascent. He wrought some cures and gave an instruction in which He spoke of the Ark of the Covenant and of David, for at Bethain, the Ark had once rested for fifteen days. David, on God's command, had caused the Ark to be secretly removed by night from the house of Obededon and brought hither, he himself preceding it barefoot. When he took it away again, the people were so exasperated that they almost stoned him.

There was up here near Bethain a very deep spring, from which the water was drawn in leathern bags, or bottles. The rocky soil of the roads was white, also the little pebbles on it.

Nicodemus, Joseph of Arimathea, Lazarus, the women of Jerusalem, and Mary started on their homeward journey, Lazarus going to Jerusalem, where he had to discharge a seven days' service in the Temple.

Mary did not return to Bethania, but went straight to Galilee by way of Machmas, where she celebrated the Sabbath at the schoolmaster's house. She had Anna Cleophas and one of Elizabeth's relatives from Sapha with her. Sapha was the birthplace of James and John. Mary had brought Elizabeth's rug with her. A servant carried it rolled up in a basket.

When speaking in Juttah to those to whom the Blessed Virgin was showing the rug, Jesus referred to John's eager desire to see Himself. But John had, He said, overcome himself and longed for nothing beyond the fulfillment of his mission, which was that of precursor and preparer, not that of constant companion and fellow laborer. When a little boy he had indeed seen Him. When His

parents were journeying with Him through the desert on
their flight into Egypt, their road led past the spot where
John was, about the distance of an arrow shot. John was
running along a brook among the high bushes. He held
in his hand a little stick upon which was fastened a pen-
non of bark, which he waved to them as he skipped and
danced for joy along the brook, until they had crossed it
and were out of sight. His parents, Mary and Joseph,
Jesus continued, held Him up with the words: "See, John
in the desert!" It was thus the Holy Spirit had led the boy
to salute his Master whom he had already saluted in his
mother's womb. While Jesus was relating the above, the
disciples were shedding tears at the thought of John's
death, and I saw again the indescribably touching scene
to which He was referring. John was naked with the exception of the skin that he wore crossed over one
shoulder and girded around his waist. He felt that his
Saviour was near and that He was athirst. Then the boy
prayed, drove his little stick into the earth, and a gushing
spring spouted up. John ran on some distance ahead and
waited, dancing and waving his little standard at them, to
see Jesus and His parents as they journeyed past the little
current. Then I beheld him hurrying back to a kind of
dell where a great overhanging rock formed a cave. A
stream from that spring found its way into a little cavity
in the dell, which John turned into a well for his own
use. He remained in that cave a long time. The way of
the Holy Family on that journey led across a portion of
Mount Olivet. One half-hour east of Bethlehem they
halted to rest, and then pursued their way, the Dead Sea
to their left, seven hours to the south of the city and two
hours beyond Hebron, where they entered the desert in
which was the boy John. I saw them stepping across the
new rivulet, pausing to rest in a pleasant spot near it, and
refreshing themselves with its waters. On the return
journey of the Holy Family from Egypt, John again saw

Jesus in spirit. He sprang forward exultingly in the direction of his Lord, but he did not then see Him face to
face, as they were separated by a distance of two hours.
Jesus spoke also of John's great self-command. Even
when baptizing Him, he had restrained himself within the
bounds exacted by the solemn occasion, although his
heart was well-nigh broken by intense love and desire.
After the ceremony, he was more intent upon humbling
himself before Him than upon gratifying his love by
looking at Him.

Jesus taught in the synagogue of Hebron on the occasion of a festival celebrated in memory of the expulsion
from the Sanhedrin of the Sadducees who, under Alex-
ander Jannaeus, had been the domineering party. There
were three triumphal arches erected around the synagogue, and to them vine leaves, ears of corn, and all
kinds of floral wreaths were brought. The people formed
a procession through the streets, which were strewn with
flowers, for it was likewise the beginning of the Feast of
the New Moon, that of the sap's rising, and lastly that of
the purification of the four-year-old trees. It was on this
account that so many arches of leaves and flowers were
erected. This Feast of the Expulsion of the Sadducees
(who denied the resurrection) coincided very appro-
priately with that upon which was celebrated the return
of the trees to new life.

In His discourse in the synagogue Jesus spoke very
forcibly against the Sadducees and of the resurrection of
the dead. Some Pharisees from Jerusalem had come
hither for the feast. They did not dispute with Jesus, but
behaved most courteously. He indeed experienced no
contradiction here, for the people were upright and very
well-disposed. He performed some cures both in the
houses and before the synagogue, the cured being mostly
of the working class. There were cripples, consumptives,
paralytics, and simpletons, also others disturbed by cer-

tain temptations.

Juttah and Hebron were connected. Juttah was a kind of suburb joined to Hebron by a row of houses. Formerly they must have been entirely separated, for a turreted wall in ruins, as well as a little valley, ran between the two places. Zachary's house comprised the school of Juttah. It was about a quarter of an hour from the city and was situated on a hill. Around it lay lovely gardens and vineyards, and not far off were other luxuriant vineyards in the midst of which stood a little dwelling. These vineyards likewise belonged to Zachary. The school was adjoining the room in which John was born. I saw all that while Jesus, Mary, and the disciples were examining the rug.

The next time that Jesus taught in the synagogue of Hebron the sacred edifice was thrown open on all sides, and near the entrance, placed in an elevated position, was a teacher's chair by which He stood. All the inhabitants of the city and numbers from the surrounding places were assembled, the sick lying on little beds or sitting on mats around the teacher's chair. The whole place was crowded. The festal arches were still standing and the scene was truly touching. The multitude seemed impressed and edified, and above all not a word of contradiction was heard. After the instruction Jesus cured the sick.

Jesus' discourse on this occasion was full of deep significance. The lessons from Scripture were those referring to the Egyptian darkness, the institution of the Paschal lamb, and the redeeming of the firstborn; there was also something from Jeremias. Jesus gave a marvelously profound explanation of the ransom of the firstborn. I remember that He said: "When sun and moon are darkened, the mother brings the child to the Temple to be redeemed." More than once He made use of the expression, "The obscuring of the sun and of the moon."

He referred to conception, birth, circumcision, and presentation in the Temple as connected with darkness and light. The departure from Egypt, so full of mystery, was applied to the birth of mankind. He spoke of circumcision as an external sign which, like the obligation to ransom the firstborn, would one day be abolished. No one gainsaid Jesus; all His hearers were very quiet and attentive. He spoke likewise of Hebron and of Abraham, and came at last to Zachary and John. He alluded to John's high dignity in terms more detailed and intelligible than ever before, namely, his birth, his life in the desert, his preaching of penance, his baptism, his faithful discharge of his mission as precursor, and lastly of his imprisonment. Then He alluded to the fate of the Prophets and the High Priest Zachary, who had been murdered between the altar and the sanctuary, also the sufferings of Jeremias in the dungeon at Jerusalem, and the persecutions endured by the others. When Jesus spoke of the murder of the first Zachary between the Temple and the altar, the relatives present thought of the sad fate of the Baptist's father, whom Herod had decoyed to Jerusalem and then caused to be put to death in a neighboring house. Jesus nevertheless had made no mention of this last fact. Zachary was buried in a vault near his own house outside of Juttah.

As Jesus was thus speaking in an impressive and very significant manner of John and the death of the Prophets, the silence throughout the synagogue grew more profound. All were deeply affected, many were shedding tears, and even the Pharisees were very much moved. Several of John's relatives and friends at this moment received an interior illumination by which they understood that the Baptist himself was dead, and they fainted away from grief. This gave rise to some excitement in the synagogue. Jesus quieted the disturbance by directing the bystanders to support those that had fainted, as they would soon revive; so they lay a few moments in the arms of their friends, while Jesus went on with His discourse.

To me there was something significant in the words, "Between the Temple and the altar," as recorded of the murder of that first Zachary. They might well be applied to John the Baptist's death since, in the life of Jesus, it also stood between the Temple and the altar, for John died between the Birth of Jesus and His Sacrifice upon the Altar of the Cross. But this signification of the words did not present itself to Jesus' hearers. At the close of the instruction they who had fainted were conducted to their homes. Besides Zachary, John's cousin, Elizabeth had a niece, her sister's daughter, married here in Hebron. She had a family of twelve children, of whom some were daughters already grown. It was these and some others who had been so deeply affected. On leaving the synagogue Jesus went with young Zachary and the disciples to the house of Elizabeth's niece, where He had not yet been. The holy women, however, had visited her several times before their departure. Jesus had engaged to sup with her this day, but it was a very sad meal.

Jesus was in a room with Peter, John, James Cleophas, Heliacim, Sadoch, Zachary, Elizabeth's niece and her husband. John's relatives asked Jesus in a trembling voice: "Lord, shall we see John again?" They were in a retired room, the door locked, so that no one could disturb them. Jesus answered with tears: "No!" and spoke most feelingly, but in consoling terms, of John's death. When they sadly expressed their fear that the body would be ill-treated, Jesus reassured them. He told them no, that the corpse was lying untouched, though the head had been abused and thrown into a sewer; but that too would be preserved and would one day come to light. He told them likewise that in some days Herod would leave Machaerus and the news of John's death would spread abroad; then they could take away the body. Jesus wept with His sorrowful listeners. They afterward partook of a repast which, on account of the retired situation of the apartment, the silence, the gravity, the great ardor and emotion of Jesus, made me think of the Last Supper.

I had on this occasion a vision of Mary's coming to present Jesus in the Temple, which presentation took place on the forty-third day after His birth. The Holy Family, on account of a feast of three days, had to remain with the good people of the little inn outside the Bethlehem gate. Besides the usual offering of doves, Mary brought five little triangular plates of gold, gifts of the Three Kings, and several pieces of fine embroidered stuff as a present for the Temple. The ass that he had pawned to one of his relatives, Joseph now sold to him. I am under the impression that the ass used by Jesus on Palm Sunday sprang from it.

Jesus taught in Juttah also and, accompanied by about ten Levites, went to the houses in the neighborhood, in which He restored many sick to health. Neither lepers, nor raging possessed, nor great sinners male or female, appeared before Him in these parts. That evening He took with the Levites a frugal meal consisting of birds, bread, honey, and fruit.

Joseph of Arimathea and several disciples were come hither in order to invite Jesus to Jerusalem, where numbers of sick were longing for Him. He could, they said, come now without fear of molestation, since Pilate and Herod were in conflict with each other on the subject of the ruined aqueduct, and the Jewish magistrates likewise had their attention fixed upon the point at issue. But Jesus would not go right away, though He promised to do so before His return to Galilee.

John's female relatives celebrated the Sabbath at their own home. They clothed themselves in mourning garments and sat on the ground, a stand full of lights, or lamps, being placed in the center of the apartment.

The Essenians who dwelt near Abraham's tomb came two by two to Jesus. They lived around a mountain in cells cut out of the rock. Upon the mountain was a garden which they owned.

All around Zachary's house were very lovely gardens and remarkably high, thick rosebushes. Coming hither from Jerusalem, one could see it on the hill; about a quarter of an hour farther on and to the right rose a higher hill upon which were his vineyards, and at its foot gushed the spring that Mary had discovered. The Hebron of Abraham was not identical with that in which Jesus now was. The former lay to the south in ruins, separated from the latter by a vale. In Abraham's time when it was still in existence it had broad streets and houses partly hewn out of the rock. Not far from Zachary's house was a place called Jether. I saw Mary and Elizabeth there several times.

The people of Juttah began to suspect from the words of Jesus and the mourning of the Baptist's relatives that John was no longer among the living, and soon the report of his death was whispered around.

Before His departure from Juttah, Jesus visited Zachary's tomb in company with His disciples and the nephews of the murdered man. It was not like ordinary tombs. It was more like the catacombs, consisting of a vault supported on pillars. It was a most honorable burial place for priests and Prophets. It had been determined that John's body should be brought from Machaerus and here buried, therefore the vault was arranged and a funeral couch erected. It was very touching to see Jesus helping to prepare a resting place for His friend. He rendered honor to the remains of Zachary also.

Elizabeth was not buried here, but on a high mountain, in that cave in which John had sojourned when a boy in the desert.

On Jesus' departure from Juttah, He was followed by

an escort of men and women. The latter, after accompanying Him the distance of an hour, took leave, but not till they had knelt and received His blessing. They wanted to kiss His feet, but Jesus would not allow it. Jesus and His disciples were now journeying toward Libna, outside of which they stopped at an inn. The men of the escort now set out for home. Saturnin, Judas Barsabas, and two other disciples who had gone from Galilee to Machaerus, then to Juttah, and lastly had come hither in quest of Jesus, arrived today. With many expressions of grief they related the murder of the Baptist. When Herod and his family, with a numerous escort of soldiers, removed from Machaerus to Hesebon, the news of John's beheading was spread by some deserters. Some of the Centurion Zorobabel's servants who had been wounded at the late disaster in Jerusalem, returning to Capharnaum had also brought the news. Zorobabel had immediately imparted the frightful occurrence to Judas Barsabas, who was in the neighborhood—upon which he, with Saturnin and two other disciples, hastened into the region of Machaerus, where they everywhere received the same account. From Machaerus they had hurried to John's native place in order to take steps for the removal of the body. But hearing that Jesus was at the inn, they had come hither to meet Him. Soon after, accompanied by the sons of Mary Heli, Joseph of Arimathea's nephews, those of Zachary, and the sons of Johanna Chusa and Veronica, they set out for Machaerus, taking Juttah on their route. They took with them an ass laden with all that was necessary for carrying out their design. Machaerus now, with the exception of a few soldiers, was quite deserted.

Jesus tarried awhile in these parts in order not to meet Pilate who, with his wife and a retinue of fifteen persons, was on his way from Jerusalem to Appolonia. He passed through Bethzur and Antipatris. From Appolonia he embarked for Rome, to lodge a complaint against Herod.

Before his departure from Jerusalem, Pilate had held a conference with his officers upon Jesus the Galilean who performed so great miracles and who was then in the vicinity of Jerusalem. Pilate asked: "Is He followed by a crowd? Are they armed?" "No," was the answer. "He goes about with only a few disciples and people of no account whatever, people from the very lowest classes, and sometimes He goes alone. He teaches on the mountains and in the synagogues, cures the sick and gives alms. To hear His instructions, people gather from all quarters, often to the number of several thousands!" "Does He not speak against the Emperor?" asked Pilate. "No. His teachings are all on the improvement of morals. He inculcates the practice of mercy, and impresses upon His hearers to render to the Emperor that which belongs to him, and to God that which is His. But He often makes mention of a Kingdom that He calls His own, and says that it is near at hand." Thereupon Pilate replied: "So long as He does not go around working His miracles with soldiers or an armed crowd, there is nothing to be feared from Him. As soon as He leaves a place in which He has performed miracles and goes to another, He will be forgotten and calumniated. Indeed I hear that the Jewish priests themselves are against Him. No danger is to be apprehended from Him. But if He is once seen going about with armed followers, His roving must come to an end!"

Pilate had already had several encounters with the Jews, who detested him. Once he had ordered the Roman standards to be brought into the city, whereupon the Jews raised a sedition. Another time, on the occasion of a certain feast upon which the Jews were not allowed to bear arms nor to touch money, I saw Pilate's soldiers go into the Temple, break open the box in which were the offerings, and carry off the contents. That was when John was still baptizing at the Jordan near On, and Jesus came out from the desert.

From Libna Jesus went to Bethzur, about ten hours to the north and two hours' distance from Jerusalem. Bethzur was a fortified place. It had citadels, ramparts and moats, which had, however, somewhat fallen to ruin, though not so much as those of Bethulia. Bethzur was certainly as large as Bethoron. The side by which Jesus entered was not steep, while between it and Jerusalem lay a beautiful valley. From the high points of either city, the other could be seen. On the opposite side the ascent was steep and the city built with a view to ward off enemies. The Ark of the Covenant was once at Bethzur for a long time, as was publicly known.

Jesus was very well received at Bethzur. Lazarus and some others of His friends from Jerusalem were already there. The Bethzurites washed Jesus' feet, as also those of the disciples, and with sincere affection offered them an abundant supply of whatever they needed. Jesus lodged at an inn near the synagogue.

The Three Kings, when journeying from Jerusalem to the Crib, passed near Bethzur, took some refreshments at a caravansary, and once more saw the star in this region.

Bethzur must not be confounded with a certain Bethsoron that lay between Bethlehem and Hebron, and near which Philip baptized the servant of Queen Candace. Sometimes this place, namely, Bethsoron, is improperly called Bethzur.

In some houses of Bethzur, Jesus cured without disturbance several old people that were very sick, some of them dropsical. The inhabitants were very well-disposed, and the Elders of the synagogue themselves conducted Jesus to the different houses. He taught also in the school, and I saw Him blessing a great number of children, first the boys and then the girls. He greatly interested Himself with them, and performed some cures among them.

8. ST. JOHN'S REMAINS TAKEN FROM
MACHAERUS AND BURIED AT JUTTAH

When Saturnin, with the disciples, reached Machaerus, they climbed the mountain on which stood Herod's castle. They carried under their arms three strong wooden bars, about a hand in breadth, a leathern cover in two parts, leathern bottles, boxes in the form of bags, rolls of linen cloths, sponges, and other similar things. The disciples best known at the castle asked the guards to be allowed to enter, but on being refused, they retraced their steps, went around the rampart and climbed upon one another's shoulders over three ramparts and two moats to the vicinity of John's prison. It looked as if God helped them, so quickly did they enter, and without disturbance. After that they descended from a round opening above the interior of the dungeons. When the two soldiers on guard at the entrance to John's cell perceived them and drew near with their torches, the disciples went boldly on to meet them, and said: "We are the disciples of the Baptist. We are going to take away the body of our master, whom Herod put to death." The soldiers offered no opposition, but opened the prison door. They were exasperated against Herod on account of John's murder, and were glad to have a share in this good work. Several of their comrades had taken flight during the last few days.

As they entered the prison the torches went out, and I saw the whole place filled with light. I do not know whether all present saw it, but I am inclined to think that they did, since they went about everything as quickly and as dexterously as if it were clear daylight. The disciples first hastened to John's body and prostrated before it in tears. Besides them, I saw in the prison the apparition of a tall, shining lady. She looked very much like the Mother of God at the time of her death. I found out later that it was St. Elizabeth. At first she seemed to me so natural as I watched her rendering all kinds of assistance that more than once I wondered who she could be and how she had gotten in with the disciples.

The corpse was still lying covered with the hairy garment. The disciples quickly set about making the funeral preparations. They spread out cloths upon which they laid the body, and then proceeded to wash it. They had brought with them for that purpose water in leathern bottles, and the soldiers supplied them with basins of a brownish hue. Judas Barsabas, James, and Heliacim took charge of the principal part of these last kind offices to the dead, the others handing what was needed and helping when necessary. I saw the apparition taking part in everything; indeed, she appeared to be the moving spirit of all, uncovering, covering, putting here, turning there, wrapping the winding-sheets—in a word, supplying each one with whatever was wanted at the moment. Her presence seemed to facilitate despatch and order in an incredible manner. I saw them opening the body and removing the intestines, which they put into a leathern pouch. Then they placed all kinds of aromatic herbs and spices around the corpse, and bound it firmly in linen bands. It was amazingly thin, and appeared to be quite dried up.

Meanwhile, some of the other disciples gathered up a quantity of blood that had flowed on the spot upon which the head had fallen, as well as that upon which the body had lain, and put it into the empty bags that had held the herbs and spices. They then laid the body wrapped in its winding-sheet upon the leathern covers, which they fastened on top by means of a rod made for that purpose. The two light wooden bars were run into the leathern straps of the covers, which now formed a kind of box. The bars, though thin and light, showed no signs of bending under their load. The skin that John used to wear was thrown over the whole, and two of the disciples bore away the sacred remains. The others followed with the blood in the leathern bottle and the intestines in the pouch. The two soldiers left Machaerus with them. They guided the disciples through narrow passages back of the ramparts and out through that subterranean way by which John had been brought into the prison. All was done rapidly and with recollection so touching that no words can describe it.

I saw them at first with rapid steps descending the mountain in the dark. Soon, however, I saw them with a torch; two walked between the poles carrying the body on their shoulders, and the others followed. I cannot say how impressive was the sight of this procession proceeding so silently and swiftly through the darkness by the glare of their one torch. They appeared to float on the surface of the ground. How they wept when at the dawn of day they ferried across the Jordan to the place where John had first baptized and they had become his followers. They went around close to the shores of the Dead Sea, always choosing lonely paths and those that led through the desert, until they reached the valley of the shepherds near Bethlehem. Here with the remains they lay concealed in a cave until night, when they journeyed on to Juttah. Before daybreak they reached the neighborhood of Abraham's tomb. They deposited John's body in a cave near the cells of the Essenians, who guarded the precious remains all day.

Toward evening, about the hour when Our Lord also was anointed and laid in the tomb (it being likewise a Friday), I saw the body brought by the Essenians to the vault wherein Zachary and many of the Prophets were reposing, and which Jesus had recently caused to be prepared for its reception.

The Baptist's relatives, male and female, were assembled in the vault with the disciples and the two soldiers who had come with the latter from Machaerus. Several of the Essenians also were present, among them some very aged people in long, white garments. These latter had provided John with the means of subsistence during his first sojourn in the desert. The women were clothed in white, in long mantles and veils. The men wore black mourning mantles, and around their necks hung narrow scarfs fringed at the ends. Many lamps were burning in the vault. The body was extended on a carpet, the winding-sheet removed, and, amid many tears, anointed and embalmed with myrrh and sweet spices. The headless trunk was, for all present, a heartrending sight. They deeply regretted not being able to look upon John's features. The ardent longings of their soul evoked him to their mental gaze such as he had appeared in the past. Each one present contributed a bundle of myrrh or other aromatic herbs. Then the disciples, having reswathed the body, laid it in the compartment hewn out for it above that of his father. The bones of the latter they had re-arranged and wrapped in fresh linens.

The Essenians afterward held a kind of religious service in which they honored John not only as one of their own, but as one of the Prophets promised to them. A portable altar something like a little table was placed between the two rows that they formed on either side, and one of them, with the aid of two assistants, prepared it for the ceremony. All laid little loaves on the altar, in the center of which lay a representation of a Paschal lamb, over which they scattered all kinds of herbs and tiny branches. The altar was covered with a red undercloth and a white upper one. The figure of the lamb shone alternately with a red and white light, perhaps from lamps concealed under it whose glare, passing first through the red and then through the white cover, produced that effect. The priest read from rolls of writing, burned incense, blessed, and sprinkled with water. All sang as in choir. John's disciples and relatives stood around in rows and joined in the singing. The eldest delivered a speech upon the fulfillment of the Prophecies, upon the signification of John's career, and made several allusions touching upon Christ. I remember that he spoke of the death of the Prophets as well as that of the High Priest Zachary, who had been murdered between the Temple and the altar. He said that Zachary, the father of John, had likewise been murdered between the Temple and the altar. His death signified something still higher than that of the ancient High Priest, but John was the true witness in blood between the Temple and the altar. By these last words, he alluded to Christ's life and death.

The ceremony of the lamb had reference to a prophetic vision that John, while still in the desert, had communicated to one of the Essenians. The vision itself referred to the Paschal Lamb, the Lamb of God, to Jesus, the Last Supper, to the Passion, and the consummation of the Sacrifice upon the Cross. I do not think that they perfectly understood all this. They performed the ceremonies in a prophetic, symbolical spirit, as if they had among them at that time many endowed with the gift of prophecy.

When all was over, he who conducted the service distributed among the disciples the little loaves that had lain on the altar, and to each gave one of the little branches that had been stuck on the lamb. The other relatives likewise received branches, but not from those on the lamb. The Essenians ate the bread, after which the tomb was closed.

The holy souls among the Essenians were possessed of great knowledge and prophetic insight upon the coming of the Messiah, also of the interior signification and the reference to Him of the various customs of Judaism. Four generations before the birth of the Blessed Virgin, they had ceased to offer bloody sacrifices, since they knew that the coming of the Lamb of God was near.

Chastity and continence were among them a species of worship celebrated to honor the future Redeemer. In humanity they saw His temple to which He was coming, and they wished to do all in their power to preserve it pure and unsullied. They knew how often the Saviour's coming had been retarded by the sins of mankind, and they sought by their own purity and chastity to satisfy for the sins of others.

All this had in some mysterious way been infused into their Order by some of the Prophets, without their having, however, in Jesus' time, a perfectly clear consciousness of it. They were, as to what concerned their customs and religious observances, the precursors of the future Church. They had contributed much toward the spiritual training and guidance of Mary's ancestors and other holy patriarchs. The education of John in his youth was their last great work.

Some of the most enlightened among them in Jesus' time joined the disciples. Others later on entered the Community, in which, by their own long practice, they gave new impetus to the spirit of renunciation and a well-ordered life and laid the foundation for the Christian life, both eremitical and cloistered. But a great many among them who belonged not to the fruits of the tree, but to the dry wood, isolated themselves in their observances and degenerated into a sect. This sect was afterward imbued with all kinds of heathenish subtleties, and became the mother of many heresies in the early days of the Church.

Jesus had no particular communication with the Essenians, although there was some similarity between His customs and theirs. With a great many of them He had no more to do than with other pious and kindly disposed people. He was intimate with several of the married Essenians who were friends of the Holy Family. As this sect never disputed with Jesus, He never had cause to speak against them, and they are not mentioned in the Gospels, because He had nothing wherewith to censure them as He had in others. He was silent also on the great good found among them since, if He had touched upon it, the Pharisees would have immediately declared that He Himself belonged to that sect.

As it had become known at Machaerus, through the domestics of Herodias, where John's head had been thrown, Johanna Chusa, Veronica, and one of the Baptist's relatives journeyed thither in order to make search for it. But until the vaulted sewer could be opened and drained, the head, which was resting on a stone projecting from the wall, could not be reached. Two months flowed by, and then many of the outbuildings and movables belonging to Herod's court at Machaerus were removed, and the whole castle was fitted up for a garrison and fortified for defense. The sewers were cleaned out and repaired, and new fortifications added to the old. During this work, I saw something very strange. Pits were dug, filled with inflammable matter, and then covered, trees being planted over them to prevent their discovery. They could be set on fire, and their explosion would kill men, overturn and scatter all things far and near like so much sand. Such pits as these were dug to quite a distance all around the walls.

There were many people engaged in carrying away the rubbish, and others gathered up the mud and slime from the sewers to enrich their fields. Among the latter were some women from Juttah and Jerusalem with their servants. They were waiting until the deep, steep sewer in which was the Baptist's holy head, should be cleaned. They prayed by night, fasted by day, and sent up ardent prayers to God that they might be enabled to find that for which they were seeking. The bottom of this sewer, on account of its being dug under the mountain, was very inclined. The whole of the lower end was already emptied and purified. To reach the upper part into which the bones from the kitchen were thrown and where the holy head was lying, the workmen had to clamber up by the stones projecting from either side. A great heap of bones obstructed this part, which was at a considerable distance from the outer entrance.

While the workmen went to take their meal, people who had been paid to do so, introduced the women into the sewer which, as I have said, was cleaned out as far as that heap of bones. They prayed as they advanced that God would allow them to find the holy head, and they climbed the ascent with difficulty. Soon they perceived the head sitting upright on the neck upon one of the projecting stones, as if looking toward them, and near it shone a luster like two flames. Were it not for this light, they might easily have made a mistake, for there were other human heads in the sewer. The head was pitiful to behold: the dark-skinned face was smeared with blood; the tongue, which Herodias had pierced, was protruding from the open mouth; and the yellow hair, by which the executioner and Herodias had seized it, was standing stiff upon it. The women wrapped it in a linen cloth and bore it away with hurried steps.

Scarcely had they accomplished a part of the way when a company of Herod's soldiery, to the number of a thousand, came marching up toward the castle. They had come to replace the couple of hundreds already there on guard. The women concealed themselves in a cave. The danger past, they again set out on their journey through the mountains. On their way they came across a soldier who, having by a fall received a severe wound on the knee, was lying on the road unconscious. Here too they came up with Zachary's nephew and two of the Essenians who had come to meet them. They laid the holy head upon the wounded soldier, who instantly recovered consciousness, arose, and spoke, saying that he had just seen the Baptist, and he had helped him. All were very much touched. They bathed his wounds in oil and wine and took him to an inn, without, however, saying anything to him about John's head. They continued their journey, always choosing the most unfrequented routes, just as had been done when John's body was conveyed to Juttah. The head was delivered to the Essenians near Hebron, and some of their sick, having been touched with it, were cured. It was then washed, embalmed with precious ointments, and with solemn ceremonies laid with the body in the tomb.

9. JESUS IN BETHANIA AND JERUSALEM. CURE OF A MAN SICK FOR THIRTY-EIGHT YEARS

From Bethzur, Jesus proceeded with Lazarus and the disciples to Bethania. They stopped at several places along their route, among them at Emmaus. Jesus taught here and there on the way among the people who were busy tying up the hedges, which were already green.

Martha, Magdalen, and a widow named Salome came to meet them at almost an hour's distance from Bethania. Salome had long dwelt in Bethania with Martha. Through one of Joseph's brothers and like Susanna, she was related to the Holy Family. She was later on present at Jesus' sepulture. They, Martha, Magdalen, and Salome, had been at Lazarus's inn in the desert, whence they returned at dusk to Bethania.

The four Apostles and several disciples whom Jesus had sent to Thabor arrived also on this evening at Bethania. Great was their grief upon hearing now for the first time the details of John's death. Then they related what had happened to themselves. They had taught and cured, according to the instructions received from Jesus, and at one place they had been chased with stones, but without being hit by them. The last place they had visited was Saron near Lydda.

When all in Lazarus's house had retired to rest, Jesus went in the darkness to the Mount of Olives and prayed in a solitary nook. The mount was covered with verdure and groves of noble trees. It was full of retired corners.

Magdalen occupied the little apartments of Mary the Silent's dwelling. She often sat in a very narrow little room that appeared to be formed in a tower. It was a retired corner intended for penitential exercises. She still wept freely. True, she was no longer actually sick, but from contrition and penance, she had become quite pale and reduced. She looked like one crushed by sorrow.

The last two days were days of fasting. They were followed by a feast of joy, which began at the close of the Sabbath and lasted for three days. The real date had fallen earlier, but for some reason the feast had been postponed. It was a feast of thanksgiving for all graces received from the deliverance of the Israelites from Egyptian bondage down to their own time. Its celebration was not confined to Jerusalem, but was observed everywhere. Numbers of the chief priests and the greatest enemies of Jesus had left Jerusalem. Since Pilate had absented himself, they had nothing to fear and a less strict guard to keep.

Next morning Jesus went to Jerusalem and accepted hospitality with Johanna Chusa. Neither Martha nor Magdalen was there.

Toward ten o'clock I saw Jesus in the Temple. He occupied the teacher's chair in the women's porch, where He was reading and expounding the Law. All were amazed at His wisdom. No one raised the least disturbance or made objections to His teaching. Some of the priests present may not have known Him, and those that did were not against Him. His bitter enemies, the Pharisees and Sadducees, were for the most part absent.

About three o'clock, Jesus went with some of the disciples to the Pool of Bethsaida. He entered from without by a door which was closed and no longer used. This was the corner into which the poorest and most abandoned creatures were pushed; and lying in the farthest part and right next the door was a man paralyzed for thirty-eight years. He had been pressed back by the crowd to the farthest extremity of the place, and now lay in a little chamber destined for men.

When Jesus knocked at the closed door, it opened of itself. Passing along through the sick, He made His way to the hall nearest the pool where invalids of all kinds were sitting and lying, and there He taught. The disciples meanwhile distributed among the poor clothes and bread, covers and kerchiefs given them by the women for that purpose. Such attention and loving services were something quite new to these poor sick who were, for the most part, either abandoned to themselves or left to the care of servants. They were greatly touched. Jesus went about them, pausing in several different places to instruct them, and then asking whether they believed that God was able to help them, whether they wished to be cured, whether they were sorry for their sins, whether they would do penance and be baptized. When He named to some of them their sins, they trembled and cried out: "Master, Thou art a Prophet! Thou art certainly John!" John's death was not yet generally known, and in many places the report of his being set at liberty was current. Jesus replied in general terms as to who He really was, and cured several of them. He directed the blind to bathe their eyes in water from the pool with which He had previously mixed a little oil. Then He told them to go quietly home, and not say much about their cure until after the Sabbath. The disciples were at the same time curing in the other porches. All the cured were obliged to wash in the pool.

But when, on account of these cures, some excitement

was beginning to arise, while now one, now another approached the pool to wash, Jesus went with John to that far-off place near the entrance where lay the poor man who had been sick for thirty-eight long years. He had been a gardener, and had formerly been engaged in the care of hedges and the raising of balsam trees. But now, so long sick and helpless, he was reduced to a state of starvation, and lay like a public beggar glad to eat the scraps left by the other sick. As he had been seen here for so many years, he was known to everyone as the incurable paralytic. Jesus spoke to him, and asked him whether or not he wanted to be cured. But he, not thinking that Jesus would cure him, but that He was asking only in a general way why he was lying there, answered that he had no help, no servant or friend to assist him down into the pool when the waters were moved. While he was creeping down, others got before him and occupied the places around the pool to which the steps led. Jesus spoke for a little while to the man, placed his sins before his eyes, excited his heart to sorrow, and told him that he should no longer live in impurity and no longer blaspheme against the Temple, for it was in punishment of such sins that his sickness had come upon him. Then He consoled him by telling him that God receives all and assists all that turn again to Him with contrition. The poor man, who never before had received a word of consolation, who had been allowed to lie moulding and rotting in his misery, who had often bitterly complained that no one offered him any assistance, was now deeply touched at Jesus' words. At last, Jesus said: "Arise! Take up thy bed, and walk!" But these were only the principal words of all that He said. He commanded him to go down to the pool and wash, and then told one of the disciples, who at that moment approached, to take the man to one of the little dwellings erected for the poor by Jesus' friends near the Cenacle on Mount Zion. Joseph of

Arimathea had his stonecutting shops in them.

He who had been so long paralyzed, and whose face was disfigured by skin disease, gathered together his tattered couch and went off cured to wash in the pool. He was so out of himself with joy and in such a hurry that he almost forgot to take away his bed. The Sabbath had now begun, and Jesus passed out unnoticed with John by the door near the place in which the poor man had lain. The disciple who was to announce the sick man went on ahead, for the latter knew where he was to go. When therefore he issued from the buildings around the Pool of Bethsaida, he was met by some Jews who saw that he had been cured. Thinking that he owed the favor to the waters of the pool, they said to him: "Knowest thou not that it is the Sabbath day?" He answered: "He that cured me said to me: 'Arise! Take up thy bed and walk!'" They asked him: "Who is he that said to thee: 'Take up thy bed and walk'?" But the poor man could not say, for he did not know Jesus and had never before seen Him. Jesus had already left the place, and His disciples also.

What the Gospel relates in connection with this miracle, that this man saw Jesus in the Temple and pointed Him out as the One that had cured him; and that Jesus had in consequence a dispute with the Pharisees on the subject of healing on the Sabbath day, took place upon a subsequent feast, but was recorded by John immediately after his account of the cure.[1] I received positive information on this point.

Through those Jews that had reproached the cured man (who had been looked upon by all as incurable) for carrying his bed on the Sabbath day, the report of the miracle was spread in Jerusalem after Jesus had left it. It created great excitement. The other sick who had been cured by Jesus and the disciples at the Pool of Bethsaida attracted little attention, for their cure was attributed to the virtue of the waters. Besides, they did not happen on the Sabbath, and Jesus neither at His entrance nor His departure had been seen by the custodians or superintendents of the pool. With the exception of the sick poor, who lived in the little cells formed in the walls, there were at that time but few persons around the piscina. Those in easy circumstances had already been taken home. In these latter times, in consequence of the movement of the water being rare and mostly at sunrise, only those that had servants could be carried to the pool at the right time; and again, confidence in this manner of curing had greatly decreased. Even the pool itself was neglected, for a part of the wall on one side had gone to ruins. Only people of lively faith frequented it at that time, people such as those that among us go on pilgrimages to holy shrines.

This was the pool in which Nehemias hid the sacred fire. A piece of the wood with which it was covered was afterward thrown aside, and later on was used for a part of Christ's Cross. The pool had developed its miraculous virtue only after it had been made the depository of the sacred fire. In early times, the pious sick who were endowed with the spirit of prophecy used to see an angel descend and agitate the water. Afterward very few, if any, saw that wondrous sight, and lastly the times had become such that if any did see it, they kept it to themselves. Still at all periods, many beheld the waters agitated and bubbling. This pool, after the coming of the Holy Ghost, became the baptismal place of the Apostles. It was with its agitating angel, a mystery typical of holy baptism at the time of the Paschal lamb which, in turn, was a type of the Last Supper and the Redeemer's death.

After this miracle, Jesus went with the disciples into a synagogue near the Temple mount, in which Nicodemus and the other friends were celebrating the Sabbath. Jesus did not teach here. He prayed and listened to the reading of the Holy Scriptures appointed for this Sabbath. They consisted of passages relating to the Departure from Egypt, the Journey through the Red Sea, and the Prophetess Deborah.[2] A canticle celebrating the passage through the Red Sea was sung, and in it were recounted one after another all the benefits that God had showered on the Jews, especially what regarded their worship and Temple. Mention was made of all the priestly vestments and ornaments which God had prescribed on Sinai, also of Solomon and the Queen of Saba. This Sabbath was called Beschallah, and was immediately followed by that feast of three days whose name sounds like Ennorum.[3] It was at one and the same time the commencement, the end, and the feast of thanksgiving for all favors and for all other feasts. In the canticle thanks were given for the innumerable favors that God had shown them from the beginning; namely, for their deliverance from Egypt and the Red Sea, for the Law, the Ark of the Covenant, the Tabernacle, for the priestly vestments, and the Temple, and for their wise King Solomon. They demanded also in that canticle another king as wise as he. United with this feast, which had been instituted by a Prophet long before the existence of either Solomon or the Temple, was a joyous festival founded by Solomon on the occasion of the presents made him by the Queen of Saba, who was struck with admiration at his wisdom. With these gifts, he had given recreation to the priests and the people. Its remembrance was perpetuated by the holiday now going on, in which everyone freely diverted himself. Since this feast could be celebrated anywhere, all the Pharisees and officers of the Temple who could in any way escape availed themselves of the opportunity to visit their friends and recruit their strength for the approaching great feasts of Purim and the Pasch.

Abundant alms were distributed on this feast. Loaves of very fine white bread were baked and given to the poor, as a remembrance of the manna in the desert. This

festival was like the *Amen* of the feasts, the feast of the
beginning and the end.

After the service in the synagogue, Jesus went with
some disciples into the Temple in which were only a few
people. The Levites were coming and going, putting
things in order, and filling the lamps with oil for next
morning. Jesus penetrated into places not open to all,
even into the vestibule of the Sanctuary where stood the
great teacher's chair, in order to see and speak to them.
This He did upon various deep questions, and they
listened for some time. Then came some of the other
Levites and reproached Him with His boldness in daring
to enter those unusual places and at that unseasonable
time. They called Him a contemptible Galilean, etc.
Jesus answered them very gravely, spoke of His rights, of
the house of His Father, and then withdrew. They
derided Him, although He inspired them with secret fear.
Jesus stayed that night in the city.

The next morning Jesus and the Apostles cured a great
many sick in the side buildings of the Cenacle which,
surrounded by a large court, stood upon Mount Sion.
Joseph of Arimathea had rented it for his stonecutting
business. The holy women of Jerusalem were busied
around the sick with all the services that tender charity
would inspire. It was on account of these sufferers that
Joseph of Arimathea, when recently at Hebron, had invited Jesus to Jerusalem. They were for the most part
good, righteous people, acquaintances of the holy women
and friends of Jesus. They had been conveyed by night
into the court of the Cenacle. Jesus spent the whole
morning in performing cures. He taught occasionally,
sometimes by this, sometimes by that group. There were
lame and blind and paralyzed, others with withered and
crippled hands, others with ulcers—men, women, and
children. There were also some men wounded by the
overthrow of the aqueduct. Some had fractured skulls;

others, broken limbs.

They were now busy in the valley of Jerusalem clearing away the rubbish. Some walls falling in had dammed up the water, and laborers were sent into the dyke to dig through the debris. In some places whole trees and large stones were thrown in to stop the course of the waters.

After Jesus had taken a slight repast with the disciples in the Cenacle, at which those that had just been cured were entertained, He and His followers went into the Temple and to the public teacher's chair, near which were kept the rolls of the Law. Jesus demanded the rolls and proceeded to expound the passages appropriate to the day. They referred to the journey through the Red Sea and to Deborah, and again that Psalm treating of the feast was sung. The title is: *"To sing morning or eve."* All were astonished at Jesus' doctrine, and no one dared to contradict Him. Some of the Pharisees alone made bold to ask: "Where didst Thou study? Where didst Thou receive the right to teach? How canst Thou take so great a liberty?" Jesus answered them in terms so grave and severe that they had nothing to reply. Then He left the Temple, and went to Bethania with His disciples and friends.

Jesus' stay in Jerusalem this time was little remarked, since His chief enemies were not there. It was only when from the great teacher's chair He closed the ceremonies of the Sabbath that they paid much attention to Him and again spoke here and there of the Galilean. All Jerusalem was at the time taken up with talk of the fallen aqueduct, the jealousy existing between Herod and Pilate, and the journey of the latter to Rome; even John's death was now discussed but little. Unless some particular excitement arose, the people did not talk much of Jesus. It was there as in other great cities. Occasionally indeed somebody would say: "Jesus the Galilean is now in the city" and another would reply: "If He does not come with several thousand men, He will effect nothing."

While in Bethania, Jesus went to the house of Simon, who no longer appeared in public, for he was sick, his leprosy having begun. A number of red blotches had broken out upon him. Wrapped in a large mantle, he kept himself concealed in a retired apartment. Jesus had an interview with him. Simon looked like one that is anxious not to have his malady noticed, but soon he would be unable to ward off attention. He showed himself as little as possible.

Late that night the disciples returned from Juta, which they had left after the Sabbath. They related to Jesus the circumstances of their bringing away John's body from Machaerus and its burial near his father. The two soldiers from Machaerus had come with the disciples. Lazarus took charge of them, kept them concealed, and provided for their wants.

When Jesus said to the disciples: "Let us retire to some solitude there to rest and mourn, not over John's death, but over the deplorable causes that led to it," I thought, "How will He be able to rest, for the other Apostles and disciples are already gone to Mary in Capharnaum." Crowds from all quarters, even from Syria and Basan, had flocked thither, and the whole country around Corozain was covered with the tents of those that were awaiting Jesus' coming.

1. *Jn.* 5:15 *et seq.*
2. *Ex.* 13:17—15:27; *Jgs.* 4:4, 5:32.
3. Probably "Deborah."

10. JESUS DELIVERS PRISONERS IN TIRZAH

Early next morning, Jesus left Bethania with the six Apostles and about twenty disciples. They shunned all places on the way, and journeyed without stopping eleven hours to the north, until they reached Lebona on the southern slope of Mount Gerizim. St. Joseph before his espousals with Mary had worked here as a carpenter, and he afterward kept up friendly relations with the inhabitants. On a peak of the mountain stood a lonely fortress up to which the road from Lebona led through buildings on one side and old walls on the other. It was on this road that Joseph's workshop stood, and in it Jesus with all His disciples put up. He was, though coming unexpectedly and at a late hour, received with unusual joy and reverence. It was a Levitical family, and up further on the mountain was the synagogue.

From Lebona Jesus and the disciples journeyed with rapid steps the whole of the following day through Samaria in a northwesterly direction toward the Jordan. They traversed Aser-Machmethat, tarried awhile in the inn at Aser, and then went on to the neighborhood of Tirzah, about one hour from the Jordan and two from Abelmahula. The country around was remarkably fine. Here in Tirzah, as in all other places on the way, the feast that I had seen begun in Jerusalem was right joyously commemorated. Gracefully adorned triumphal arches were erected, and public games celebrated. The actors leaped over garlands for a wager, just as our children do nowadays. Great mounds of grain and orchard fruits were heaped up in the open air for distribution among the poor.

Tirzah was built in two parts, and one quarter of the city extended to within half an hour of the Jordan. The whole region was so studded with gardens and orchards that the traveller could not see the city until just within its reach. It was so broken up by gardens and commons that the quarter furthest from the Jordan looked less like a city than like some groups of houses scattered among gardens and walls. The part nearest the Jordan was the better preserved and the more compact. It was built high above a valley and rested on solid piers. A highway ran under it as under a bridge. This road was charming. From it one could see through the valley with its green trees as through a cool grotto far to the other side where the road emerged into the open air.

Tirzah, situated as it was on a height of moderate elevation, commanded a most beautiful view across the Jordan and into the mountain ranges beyond. To the north could be seen Jetebatha, almost hidden by forests; on the right the view extended into Peraea; and across the smooth surface of the Dead Sea arose Machaerus and the country off to the west. Many a glimpse could be had of the Jordan, and here and there in its windings, its waters glistened like long streaks of light as it flowed along between its verdant banks. Westward from Tirzah lay a high mountain range that separated it from Dothan. Abelmahula lay two hours northwestward, in a deep dale more to the south than was that in which Joseph was sold by his brethren. On every side, Tirzah looked down upon numberless gardens and groves of fruit trees, on terraces and espaliers over which were trained balsam shrubs and paradise apples so much used by the Jews at their Feast of Tabernacles. These trees flourished only in very good and sunny positions. Besides those just mentioned, they cultivated also the sugar cane, long, yellow flax like silk, cotton, and a species of grain in whose thick stalk was stored a marrowy pith. The inhabitants were engaged in horticulture and fruit raising. Many were occupied also in preparing flax, cotton, and the sugar cane for market. The street that ran under the city was the grand military and commercial route to Tarichaea and Tiberias. In many places it took the form of a tunnel between hills, as it did here in Tirzah which, as I have said, rested on piers above the road.

In the center of the city, that is, in the center of its ancient surroundings, in a large, deserted-looking space, there stood on a gentle eminence a spacious edifice with massive walls, several courtyards, and round buildings like towers in whose interior were found other courts. It was the old, ruined castle of the Kings of Israel. A part had fallen to decay, but another had been fitted up as a hospital and prison. Some portions were overgrown ruins, on which were laid out gardens of all kinds. On the square before the house was a fountain whose water, by means of a wheel turned by an ass, was raised in leathern bags and poured into a great basin, from which it flowed on all sides through channels into tanks, thus supplying the city in every direction. Every quarter had its reservoir.

At this fountain five disciples from the opposite side of the Jordan joined Jesus and His followers. They were the two youths delivered from slight demoniacal possession, the two men out of whom Jesus had driven the devils into the swine, and a fifth. They had been, in accordance with Jesus' commands, proclaiming their own deliverance and the miracle of the swine in the little cities of the country of the Gerasens and in the Decapolis. They had healed in those places and had announced the approach of the Kingdom of God. They embraced the disciples and washed one another's feet at the fountain. Jesus had come straight from a house outside the city where, with the other disciples, He had passed the night. These five brought Him news that all His disciples whom He had sent into Upper Galilee had returned to Capharnaum, and that an immense multitude of people were encamped in the district around, awaiting His coming.

Jesus now went with the disciples into the castle, sought out the superintendent of the hospital, and requested to be introduced to their quarters. The superintendent complied with His request, and Jesus went through halls and courts until He arrived at the cells and retired corners where lay the sick suffering from diseases of all kinds. He went around among them instructing, healing, and consoling. Some of the disciples were with Him, helping to raise, carry, and lead the sick; others were scattered in the different corridors, performing cures and preparing the way for Jesus. In one of the courts there were several possessed in chains, who yelled and raged when Jesus entered the house. He commanded them to be silent, cured them, and drove the devils out of them. In the most distant part of the hospital were some lepers, and these too He healed. He went alone to them. The cured belonging to Tirzah itself were at once taken away by their friends, not, however, before Jesus had ordered them food and drink. To the poor among them were distributed, besides, the clothing and coverlets that the disciples had brought with them to Tirzah from the inn of Bezech.

Jesus visited also the abode of the sick women. It was a high, round tower with an inner court. In this court, as well as on the outside of the tower, a projecting flight of steps led from one story to another, for in the interior there was no little staircase such as we have. In the exterior apartments were women sick of all kinds of maladies. Jesus cured many. In the apartments nearest the court, from which they were separated by locked doors, women were imprisoned, some for their excesses, some on account of their bold speech, while many others of their number were innocent. In the same building many poor men underwent the rigors of grievous imprisonment, some for debt, others for having joined in a revolt, many also the victims of revenge and enmity, while others were confined merely to get them out of the way. Many of these poor creatures were quite abandoned, left to starve in their prison cells. Jesus heard bitter complaints on this subject from the sick whom He cured and from others. He indeed knew all about it, and it was principally on account of that general misery He had come.

Tirzah counted numerous Pharisees and Sadducees,

and among the latter were many Herodians. The prison was guarded by Roman soldiers and had a Roman superintendent. The lodgings of the guards and overseers were outside the building. Jesus, having applied to the latter for permission, was allowed to visit the part open to strangers. He listened to the prisoners' story of misery and sufferings, directed refreshments to be distributed to them, instructed and consoled them, and forgave the sins of many that confessed to Him. To several of those confined for debt, as well as to many others, He promised release. To others He held out hopes of relief.

From the prison Jesus went to the Roman Commander, who was not a wicked man, and spoke to him gravely and touchingly about the prisoners. He offered to discharge their debts Himself, and to go part security for their innocence and good behavior. He expressed His desire also to converse with those that had for so long a time endured a more rigorous imprisonment. The Commander listened very respectfully to Jesus, but explained to Him that as all those prisoners were Jews who had been put into prison under very particular circumstances, he would have to speak to the Pharisees and to the Jewish authorities of the place before he could grant His request to be allowed access to them. Jesus replied that after He had taught in the synagogue, He would call on him again with the Jewish authorities. Then He returned to the female prisoners, whom He consoled and advised. He received from several the avowal of their misdemeanors and promises of amendment, forgave them their sins, caused alms to be distributed among them, and promised to reconcile them with their friends.

Thus did Jesus from nine o'clock in the morning until nearly four in the afternoon labor in this abode of misery and woe, filling it with joy and consolation on a day upon which in it alone was sorrow to be found, for in the city all was jubilation. It was the first of those holidays

that had been added by Solomon to the Feast of Ennorum, on account of the gifts presented by the Queen of
Saba. Jesus had beheld the Sabbath of this first day celebrated the evening before at Bezech. Today the whole
city, especially the most populous quarters, was alive
with joy. There were triumphal arches, leaping, racing,
and heaps of grain for distribution among the poor. But
around that old castle, at once prison and hospital, all
was still. Jesus alone had thought of its poor inmates, and
He alone had brought them real joy. In the house outside
the city, He took with the disciples a little repast, which
consisted of bread, fruit, and honey. Then He sent some
of His followers to the prison with all kinds of provisions
and refreshments, while He with the rest repaired to the
synagogue.

The report of what Jesus had done in the hospital was
already spread throughout the whole city. Many of those
that He had there cured were returned to the city and
now went to the synagogue; others were assembled outside the sacred edifice, where Jesus and the Apostles
cured many more. In the synagogue were gathered the
Pharisees and Sadducees, and many secret Herodians.
Among the first-named were many of the same sect from
Jerusalem who had come thither for recreation. They
were full of spite and envy at Jesus' doings, which threw
disgrace upon their own. In the school were present also
a great many people from Bezech who had followed
Jesus thither. In His instruction Jesus spoke of the feast
and its signification, which was to afford an opportunity
for recreation, for infusing joy into the hearts of others,
and for doing good. He referred again to one of the Eight
Beatitudes, "Blessed are the merciful." He explained the
parable of the Prodigal Son, which He had already related to the prisoners. Then He spoke of these, as well as
of the sick and their miseries, how forgotten and abandoned they were while others enriched themselves by

seizing upon the funds destined for their support. He inveighed vigorously against the trustees of this establishment, some of whom were among the Pharisees present. They listened in silent rage. In recounting the parable of the Prodigal Son, Jesus made allusion to those that had been imprisoned on account of their misdemeanors, but who were now repentant. This He did in order to reconcile the relatives here present to some of the prisoners. All were very much touched.

Here, too, Jesus related the parable of the compassionate king and the unmerciful servant. He applied it to those that allow the poor prisoner to languish on account of an insignificant debt, while God suffers their own great indebtedness to run on.

The secret Herodians had by their trickery been the cause of the imprisonment of many poor people of this place. To this fact Jesus once vaguely alluded when, in His severe denunciation of the Pharisees, He said: "There are many indeed among you who very likely know how things fell out with John." The Pharisees railed at Jesus. They made use of expressions among themselves, such as these: "He wages war with the help of women, and goes about with them. He will get possession of no great kingdom with such warriors."

Jesus then pressed the head men among the magistrates and Pharisees to go with Him to the Roman superintendent of the prison, and offer to ransom the most miserable and neglected of the inmates. This proposal was made in the hearing of many, consequently the Pharisees could not refuse. When Jesus and His disciples turned off toward the residence of the superintendent, a crowd followed, sounding Jesus' praises. The superintendent was a much better man than the Pharisees, who maliciously ran up the prisoners' debts so high that, for the release of some of them, Jesus had to pay fourfold. But because He had not the money around Him, He gave as a pledge a triangular coin to which hung a parchment ticket upon which He had written some words authorizing the sum to be discharged from Magdalen's property which Lazarus was about to sell. The entire proceeds were destined by Magdalen and Lazarus for the benefit of the poor, for debtors, and the relief of sinners. Magdalum was a more valuable estate than that of Bethania. Each side of the triangular coin was about three inches long, and in the center was an inscription indicating its value. To one end hung a jointed strip of metal, like two or three links of a chain, and to this the writing was fastened.

After the transaction recorded above, the superintendent ordered the poor prisoners to be brought forth. Jesus and the disciples lent their assistance in the execution of his order. Many poor creatures in tatters, half-naked and covered with hair, were dragged forth from dark holes. The Pharisees angrily withdrew. Many of the released were quite weak and sick. They lay weeping at Jesus' feet, while He consoled and exhorted them. He procured for them clothing, baths, food, lodgings, and saw to the formalities necessary to be observed in restoring them to liberty, for they had to remain under the jurisdiction of the prison and hospital a few days until their ransom was paid. A similar occurrence took place among the female prisoners. All were fed, Jesus and the disciples waiting on them, and the parable of the Prodigal Son was afterward related to them.

Thus was this house for once filled with joy. In it appeared to be prefigured the deliverance from Limbo of the Patriarchs to whom John, after his death, had announced the near coming of the Redeemer. Jesus and the disciples spent the night once more in the house outside of Tirzah.

It was this affair here in Tirzah which, when reported to Herod, drew his attention more particularly upon Jesus, and called forth the remark: "Is John risen from the grave?" From this time Herod was desirous of seeing Jesus. He had indeed previously heard of Him from general report and through John, but he had not thought much on the subject. Now, however, his uneasy conscience made him notice what before had passed unremarked. He was at this time living in Hesebon, where he had gathered all his soldiers around him, among them some mercenary Roman troops.

From Tirzah to Capharnaum, whither Jesus now proceeded with His disciples, was a journey of eighteen hours. They did not go up through the valley of the Jordan, but along the base of Mount Gelboa and across the vale of Abez, leaving Thabor on the left. They lodged at the inn on the borders of the lake near Bethulia and journeyed next day to Damna, where Jesus found Mary and several of the holy women who had arrived there before Him. The other six Apostles and some of the disciples had also come to Damna. The two soldiers from Machaerus, whom Lazarus had sent through Samaria, joined Jesus' followers near Azanoth.

11. JESUS IN CAPHARNAUM AND ITS ENVIRONS

There were at this time in Capharnaum no fewer than sixty-four Pharisees assembled from the neighboring districts. On their way thither, they had made inquiries upon the most remarkable of Jesus' cures, and had ordered the widow of Naim with her son and witnesses from that place to be summoned to Capharnaum, as well as the son of Achïas, the Centurion of Giskala. They had also closely interrogated Zorobabel and his son, the Centurion Cornelius and his servant, Jairus and his daughters, several blind and lame that had been cured— in a word, all that had in that part of the country profited by Jesus' healing power. In every case they summoned witnesses, whom they questioned and whose answers they compared.

When, notwithstanding their malice, they were unable to construe what they heard into proofs against the truth of Jesus' miracles, they became still more enraged, and again had recourse to their old story, that He had dealings with the devil. They declared that He went about with women of bad repute, excited the people to sedition, deprived the synagogues of the alms that should flow to them, and profaned the Sabbath, and they boasted that they would now put a stop to His proceedings.

Intimidated by these threats, by the ever-increasing concourse of people, and especially by the beheading of John, the relatives of Jesus were in great trouble. They entreated Him not to go to Capharnaum, but to take up His residence elsewhere, and for this they named many places, such as Naim or Hebron or the cities on the other side of the Jordan. But Jesus silenced them by declaring that He would go to Capharnaum, where He would both teach and cure, for as soon as He stood face to face with the Pharisees, they would cease their boasting.

When the disciples asked Him what they were now to do, Jesus answered that He would tell them, and that He would give to The Twelve to hold the same position to them as He Himself held to the Apostles. When evening came they separated. Jesus went with Mary, the women, and His relatives eastward through Zorobabel's hamlet to Mary's house in the valley of Capharnaum, and the Apostles and disciples departed by other routes. That night Jairus sought Jesus to relate to Him the persecutions he had had to endure. Jesus calmed him. He had been discharged from his office, and now belonged entirely to Jesus.

Capharnaum was full of visitors, sick and well, Jews and Gentiles. The surrounding plains and heights were covered with encampments. In the fields and mountain nooks, camels and asses were grazing; even the valleys and hills on the opposite side of the lake were alive with people waiting for Jesus. There were strangers here from all sides, from Syria, Arabia, Phoenicia, and even from Cyprus.

Jesus visited Zorobabel, Cornelius, and Jairus. The family of the last-named was entirely converted, the daughter much better than formerly, and very modest and pious. Jesus went afterward to Peter's house outside the city, and found it crowded with sick. Heathens, who had never been here before, now presented themselves. The crowd of sick was so great that the disciples had to put up a species of scaffolding in order to afford more room for them. Not only Jesus was everywhere sought for by the sick, but the Apostles and disciples also were called by them. "Art thou one of the Prophet's disciples?" they cried. "Have pity on me! Help me! Take me to Him!" Jesus, the Apostles, and about twenty-four disciples taught and cured the whole morning. There were some possessed present, who cried after Jesus and from whom He drove the demons. No Pharisees were present, but there were among the crowd some spies and some half-disaffected.

After Jesus had performed many cures, He withdrew into a hall to preach, whither He was followed by the cured and others. Some of the Apostles went on healing while the others gathered around Jesus, who again taught on the Beatitudes and related several parables. Among other points, He touched upon prayer which, He said, they should never omit. He related and developed the similitude of the unjust judge who, in order to get rid of the widow ever returning to knock at his door, at last rendered her justice.[1] If the unjust judge was thus forced to comply, will not the Father in Heaven be still more merciful?

Then Jesus taught the multitude how to pray, recited

the seven petitions of the *Our Father,* [2] and explained the first, "Our Father, who art in Heaven." Already on His journeys, He had explained several of the petitions to the disciples; now, however, He took them up as He had done the Beatitudes, and made them the subject of His public instructions. Thus the prayer was all explained by degrees, repeated everywhere, and published on all sides by the disciples. Jesus continued the Eight Beatitudes at the same time. In speaking of prayer, He made use of this similitude: If a child begs his father for bread, will he give him a stone? Or if asked for a fish, will he give a serpent or scorpion?

It was now toward three o'clock. Mary, aided by her sister and other women, also by the sons of Joseph's brethren from Dabereth, Nazareth, and the valley of Zabulon, had prepared in the front part of the house a meal for Jesus and the disciples. During several days they had had, on account of their great labors, no regular hours for meals. The dining room was separated from the hall in which Jesus was teaching near a court crowded with people, who could hear all that was said through the open porticos of the hall. Now when Jesus went on instructing, Mary, taking with her some relatives in order not to go through the crowd alone, approached with the intention of speaking to Him and begging Him to come and partake of some food. But it was impossible for her to make her way through the crowd, and so her request was passed from one to another, until it reached a man standing near Jesus. He was one of the spies of the Pharisees. As Jesus had several times made mention of His Heavenly Father, the spy, not without a secret sneer, said to Him: "Behold Thy Mother and Thy brethren stand without, seeking Thee." But Jesus, looking at him, said: "Who is My Mother, and who are My brethren?" Then grouping The Twelve and placing the disciples near them, He extended His hand over the former with the words: "Behold My Mother!" and then over the latter, saying: "and these are My brethren, who hear the word of God and do it. For whosoever shall do the will of My Father who is in Heaven, he is My brother, My sister, and My Mother."[3] Then He went on with His discourse, but sent His disciples in turn to take what food they needed.

After this, as He was going with the disciples to the synagogue, the sick who could still walk followed Him, imploring His help. He cured them. In the outer porch of the synagogue, although the Sabbath had already begun, a man stepped up to Him, showed Him his hand, crippled and withered, and begged to be helped. Jesus told him to wait awhile. At the same time, He was called by some people who were leading a deaf and dumb possessed who was raging frightfully. Jesus commanded him to lie down quietly at the entrance of the synagogue and there wait. The possessed instantly sat down cross-legged, and bowed his head on his knees, keeping a side-glance fixed on Jesus. With the exception of an occasional slight convulsive shuddering, he remained quiet during the whole instruction.

The Sabbath lesson was about Jethro giving counsel to Moses when the Israelites were encamped around Sinai, of Moses ascending the mount and receiving the Ten Commandments (*Ex.* 18-21), and from the Prophet Isaias, the passages that record his vision of the throne of God and the seraph's purifying his lips with a burning coal (*Is.* 6:1-13). The synagogue was overflowing with people, and a great crowd was standing outside. The doors and windows were all thrown open, and many people were looking in from the adjacent buildings. Numbers of Pharisees and Herodians were present, all filled with rage and bitterness. The recently cured were in the synagogue, as well as all the disciples and relatives of Jesus. The citizens of Capharnaum and the crowds of strangers

were full of reverence and admiration for Jesus, and so
the Pharisees did not dare to attack Him without apparent reason. They had besides come to the synagogue
more out of a desire to support one another in their vain
boasting than to make any serious opposition to Him,
though this latter they were not able to do. They no
longer cared to contradict Him in public, as on such occasions His replies generally put them to shame before
the people. But when Jesus withdrew, they sought by every possible means to turn the people away from Him,
and they set lies afloat against Him.

They knew now that the man with the withered hand
was there, and they wanted to see whether Jesus would
heal him on the Sabbath, that they might accuse Him.
This was especially the desire of those that had just come
from Jerusalem. They were anxious for something to take
home with them and lay before the Sanhedrin. As they
could allege nothing of importance against Him, and
although they well knew His sentiments on the point,
they always returned as if in ignorance to the same question, and to it Jesus with unwearied patience generally
gave the same answer. Several of them now put the que-
ry: "Is it lawful to heal on the Sabbath?" Jesus, knowing
their thoughts, called the man with the withered hand,
placed him in the midst of them, and said: "Is it lawful to
do good on the Sabbath day, or to do evil? To save life,
or to destroy it?" No one answered. Then Jesus repeated
the similitude of which He generally made use on such
occasions: "What man shall there be among you that
hath one sheep: and if the same fall into a pit on the Sabbath day, will he not take hold on it and lift it up! How
much better is a man than a sheep! Therefore it is lawful
to do a good deed on the Sabbath day." He was very
much troubled at the obduracy of these men, and His angry glance penetrated to the bottom of their soul. Taking
the arm of the poor man in His left hand, He stroked it

down with the right, straightened out and separated the crooked fingers, and said: "Stretch out thy hand!" The man stretched out his hand and moved it. It had become as long as the other and was perfectly cured. The whole scene was the work of an instant. The man cast himself with thanks at Jesus' feet and the people broke forth into shouts of jubilation, while the enraged Pharisees withdrew to the entrance of the synagogue to discuss what they had witnessed. Jesus next drove the devil from the possessed whom He had left waiting at the door, and instantly speech and hearing were given him. The people again shouted for joy, and the Pharisees again gave utterance to their slanderous expression: "He has a devil! He drives out one devil by the help of another!" Jesus turned toward them and said: "Who among you can convict Me of sin? If the tree is good, so too is the fruit good; if the tree is evil, so also is the fruit evil, for by the fruit the tree is known. O generation of vipers, how can you speak good things, whereas you are evil! Out of the abundance of the heart the mouth speaketh."

At these words, the Pharisees set up a great cry: "He shall make an end of all this! We have had enough of this!" and one of them carried his insolence so far as to call out: "Dost Thou not know that we can put Thee out?" Jesus and the disciples now left the synagogue, and hurried by different routes, some to Mary's house, some to Peter's near the lake. Jesus took a repast at His Mother's, and then passed the night with The Twelve in Peter's house. The latter, being the more distant of the two, afforded a safer retreat.

The whole of the following day Jesus, the Twelve Apostles, and the disciples spent at Peter's healing the sick. The multitude was waiting for Him and seeking Him in many places, but He remained shut up in the house.

During the day Jesus called before Him the Apostles

and disciples, two and two, as He had sent them, and received from them an account of all that had happened to them during their mission. He solved the doubts and difficulties that had arisen in certain circumstances, and instructed them how they should act in the future. He told them again that He would soon give them a new mission. The six Apostles who had been laboring in Upper Galilee had been well received. They had found the people well disposed and had in consequence baptized many. The others, who had gone to Judea, had not baptized any, and here and there had experienced contradiction.

The crowd around the house becoming greater and greater, Jesus and His followers slipped away secretly. The stars shed their light down upon the little party as they hurried along the bypaths to Peter's barque. They ferried across the lake and landed between Matthew's custom house and Little Corozain. From there they climbed the mountain at whose foot stood the custom house, for Jesus wanted to instruct the disciples in solitude. But the multitude had caught a glimpse of their departure, and the news soon spread through the tents of the encampment. The crowd near Bethsaida soon crossed, some over the lake, others further up over the Jordan bridge, and so Jesus and His party here on the mountain were again surrounded by the immense multitude. The disciples ranged the people in order, and Jesus began again His instructions on the Beatitudes and prayer. He again explained the first petition of the *Our Father*. As the hours flew by, the crowds increased. People came from all the cities around, from Julias, Corozain, and Gergesa, bringing with them the sick and possessed. Numbers were healed by Jesus and the disciples.

The instructions over, the multitude dispersed the next day at the place on which this sermon on the mount had been delivered. Jesus with the Apostles and disciples then retired higher up the mountain to a shady, solitary spot.

Besides The Twelve, there were with Jesus seventy-two disciples. Among them were the two soldiers from Machaerus and some that had not yet been formally received as disciples and had never been on a mission. The sons of Joseph's brother were there.

Jesus then instructed the disciples upon the work in store for them. He told them that they should take with them neither purse nor money nor bread, but only a staff and a pair of sandals; that wherever they were ungraciously received, they should shake the dust from their shoes. He gave them some general directions for their coming duties as Apostles and disciples, called them the salt of the earth, and spoke of the light that must not be placed under a bushel, and of the city seated upon a mountain. Still He did not inform them of the full measure of persecution awaiting them.

The main point, however, of this instruction was that by which Jesus drew a definitive line between the Apostles and the disciples, the former of whom were set over the latter. To them He said that they should send and call the disciples as He Himself sent and called *them,* namely, the Apostles. This they were empowered to do by virtue of their own mission. Among the disciples Jesus likewise formed several classes, setting the eldest and best instructed over the younger and more recently received. He arranged them in the following manner, the Apostles, two by two, headed by Peter and John. The elder disciples formed a circle around them, and back of these the younger, according to the rank He had assigned them. Then He addressed to them words of earnest and touching instruction, and imposed hands upon the Apostles as a ratification of the dignity to which He had raised them; the disciples, He merely blessed. All this was done with the greatest tranquillity. The whole scene was deeply impressive. No one offered the least resistance or showed the least sign of discontent. By this time it was evening, and

Jesus with Andrew, John, Philip, and James the Less, plunged deeper into the mountains, and there spent the night in prayer.

1. *Lk.* 18:1-5.
2. *Matt.* 6; *Lk.* 11.
3. *Mt.* 12:46-50; *Mk.* 3:31; *Lk.* 8:19-21.

12. THE FEEDING OF THE FIVE THOUSAND

When next morning Jesus and the Apostles returned to the mount upon which He had already taught several times on the Eight Beatitudes, He found the multitude assembled. The other Apostles had arranged the sick in sheltered places. Jesus and the Apostles began to heal and to instruct. Many who in those days had now come for the first time to Capharnaum, knelt in a circle to receive Baptism. The water, which had been brought for that purpose in leathern bottles, was sprinkled over them three at a time.

The Mother of Jesus had come with the other women, and she now helped among the sick women and children. She did not exchange words with Jesus, but returned betimes to Capharnaum.

Jesus taught of the Eight Beatitudes and went as far as the sixth. The instruction on prayer begun at Capharnaum He repeated, and explained some of the petitions of the *Our Father*.

Teaching and healing went on till after four o'clock, and all this time the listening crowds had had nothing to eat. They had now followed from the day before, and the scanty provisions they had brought with them were exhausted. Many among them were quite weak and languishing for nourishment. The Apostles, noticing this, approached Jesus with the request that He would close the instruction in order that the people might hunt up lodgings for the night and procure food. Jesus replied: "They need not go away for that. Give them here something to eat!" Philip made answer: "Shall we go and buy two hundred pennyworth of bread, and give them to eat?" This he said with some unwillingness, because he thought Jesus was about to lay upon them the fatigue of gathering up from the environs sufficient bread for all that crowd. Jesus answered: "See how many loaves you have!" and went on with His discourse. There was in the crowd a servant, who had been sent by his master with five loaves and two fishes as a present to the Apostles. Andrew told this to Jesus with the words: "But what is that among so many?" Jesus ordered the loaves and fishes to be brought, and when they were laid on the sod before Him, He continued the explanation of the petition for daily bread. Many of the people were fainting, and the children were crying for bread. Then Jesus, in order to try Philip, asked him: "Where shall we buy bread, that these people may eat?" and Philip answered: "Two hundred pennyworth would not be sufficient for all this crowd." Jesus said: "Let the people be seated, the most famished by fifties, the others in groups of a hundred; and bring Me the baskets of bread that you have at hand." The disciples set before Him a row of shallow baskets woven of broad strips of bark, such as were used for bread. Then they scattered among the people, whom they arranged in fifties and hundreds all down the terraced mountain, which was clothed with grass beautiful and long. Jesus was above, the people seated below Him on the mountainside.

Near the place upon which Jesus taught was a high, mossy bank, in which were several caves. On it Jesus directed a broad napkin to be spread, upon which were deposited the five loaves and two fishes. The loaves lay one upon the other on the napkin. They were long and narrow, about two inches in thickness. The crust was thin and yellow, and the inside, though not perfectly white, was close and fine. They were marked with stripes to make it more easy to break them or cut them with a knife. The fish were of a good arm's length. Their heads were somewhat projecting, not like our fish. Cut up, roasted, and ready for eating, they lay upon large leaves. Another man had brought a couple of honeycombs, and they too were laid on the napkin.

When the disciples numbered the people and seated them in fifties and hundreds as Jesus had directed, He cut the five loaves with a bone knife, and the fish, which had been split down lengthwise, He divided into crosspieces. After that He took one of the loaves in His hands, raised it on high and prayed. He did the same with one of the fish. I do not remember whether He did the same with the honey or not. Three of the disciples were at His side. Jesus now blessed the bread, the fish, and the honey, and began to break the cross-sections into pieces, and these again into smaller portions. Every portion immediately increased to the original size of the loaf, and on its surface appeared, as before, the dividing lines. Jesus then broke the individual pieces into portions sufficiently large to satisfy a man, and gave with each a piece of fish. Saturnin, who was at His side, laid the piece of fish upon the portion of bread, and a young disciple of the Baptist, a shepherd's son, who later on became a Bishop, laid upon each a small quantity of honey. There was no perceptible diminution in the fish, and the honeycomb appeared to increase. Thaddeus laid the portions of bread upon which were the fish and honey in the flat baskets, which were then borne away to those in most need, who sat in the fifties and were served first.

As soon as the empty baskets were brought back, they were exchanged for full ones, and so the work went on for about two hours until all had been fed. They that had a wife and children (and these were separated from the men) found their portion so large that they could abundantly share with them. The people drank of the water that had been conveyed thither in leathern bottles. Most of them used cups formed of bark folded into the shape of a cone, and others had with them hollow gourds.

The whole affair was conducted most expeditiously and with perfect order. The Apostles and disciples were, for the most part, occupied in carrying the baskets here and there and in distributing their contents. But all were silent and filled with amazement at the sight of such a multiplication. The size of the loaves was about two spans, or eighteen inches in length, and a fifth less in breadth. They were divided by ridges into twenty parts, five in length and four in breadth, so that the substance of every one of those parts increased fiftyfold, in order to feed five thousand men. The bread was a good three fingers in thickness. The fish were cut in two lengthwise. Jesus divided each half into numerous portions. It was only the two fish all the time, for it was in substance and not in number that they were most wonderfully increased.

When all had satisfied their hunger, Jesus bade the disciples to go around with the baskets and gather up the scraps, that nothing might be lost. They collected twelve baskets full. A great many of the people asked to take some of the pieces home with them as souvenirs. There were no soldiers present this time, though I was accustomed to see many at all the other great instructions. They had been called to Hesebon, where Herod was then sojourning.

When the people arose from their meal, they gathered everywhere in groups, full of wonder and admiration at this miracle of the Lord. From mouth to mouth ran the word: "This man is genuine! He is the Prophet that was to come into the world! He is the Promised One!"

It was now growing dusk, so Jesus bade the disciples go to their barques and cross before Him to Bethsaida; meanwhile He would take leave of the people and then follow. The disciples obeyed. Taking the baskets of bread they went down to their ships, and some of them crossed over to Bethsaida at once. The Apostles and some of the older disciples remained behind a little longer and then departed on Peter's barque.

Jesus now dismissed the multitude, who were deeply moved. Scarcely had He left the spot upon which He had been teaching when the shout arose: "He has given us bread! He is our King! We will make Him our King!" But Jesus disappeared into the solitude, and there gave Himself up to prayer.

13. JESUS WALKS ON THE SEA

Peter's barque, with the Apostles and several of the disciples, was delayed during the night by contrary winds. They rowed vigorously, but were driven to the south of the proper direction. I saw that every two hours little boats with torches were sent out from either bank. They bore belated passengers to the large ships, and served in the darkness to mark their direction. As, like sentinels, they were relieved every two hours, they were here called night watches. I saw these boats changed four times, while Peter's ship was being driven south of its right course.

Then Jesus walked on the sea in a direction from northeast to southwest. He was shining with light. Rays darted from Him, and one could see His image reversed in the water under His feet. To walk in a direction from Bethsaida-Julias to Tiberias, almost opposite which was Peter's ship, Jesus had to pass between the two night boats that were rowing out into the sea, one from Capharnaum and the other from the opposite bank. The people in these boats, seeing Him walking, raised a long cry of fear and sounded a horn, for they took Him for a phantom. The Apostles on Peter's ship which, in order to find the true course, was guiding itself by the light from one of those boats, glanced in the direction of the sound, and saw Him coming toward them. He appeared to be gliding along more rapidly than in ordinary walking, and wherever He approached, the sea became calm. But a fog rested upon the water, so that He could be seen only at a certain distance. Although they had once before seen Him thus walking, still the unusual and specter-like sight filled them with terror, and they uttered a great cry.

But suddenly they recalled the circumstance of Jesus' first walking on the water, and Peter, once more desirous of showing his faith, cried out again in his ardor: "Lord, if it be Thou, bid me come to Thee!" Jesus replied: "Come!" This time Peter ran a greater distance toward Jesus, but his faith did not yet suffice. He was already close to Him when he again thought of his danger, and on the instant began to sink. He stretched out his hand and cried: "Lord, save me!" He did not, however, sink to so great a depth as the first time. Jesus again addressed to him the words: "O thou of little faith, why dost thou doubt?" When Jesus mounted the ship, all ran to cast themselves at His feet, crying: "Truly, Thou art the Son of God!" Jesus reproved them for their fear and little faith, gave them a severe reprimand, and then instructed them upon the *Our Father*. He ordered them to steer more to the south. They now had a favorable wind and made the journey quickly, taking meanwhile a little rest in the cabin under the rower's stand around the mast. The storm on this occasion was not so violent as that of the preceding, but they had got into the current of the lake, which in the middle was very strong, and they could not get out of it.

Jesus allowed Peter to come to Him on the water in order to humble him, for He knew very well that he was going to sink. Peter was very fiery and strong in believing, and in his zeal he wanted to give a testimony of his faith to Jesus and the disciples. By his sinking, he was preserved from pride. The others had not sufficient confidence to wish to follow his example and, while wondering at Peter's faith, they could see that although it excelled their own it was not yet what it ought to be.

At sunrise Peter's ship put to on the east side of the lake at a little hamlet consisting of only a couple of rows of houses between Magdala and Dalmanutha. The hamlet belonged to the latter. It is this place that is meant when the Gospel says, "into the parts of Dalmanutha."[1]

As soon as they perceived the approach of the ship, the inhabitants began to get all their sick ready, and they came to meet Jesus on the shore. He and the disciples healed in the streets. After that He went to a hill at a short distance beyond Dalmanutha, where all the inhabitants, Jews and pagans, assembled around Him. There He taught upon the Eight Beatitudes and the *Our Father*. He also healed the sick whom they had brought with them.

This little place was near the ferry, and in it the toll was paid. The people in general were occupied with the transportation of iron from the iron city of Ephron unto Basan. This was the point from which they shipped iron to all the other seaports of Galilee. From the mountains they could see over into Ephron.

From this place Jesus embarked with the Apostles for Tarichaea, which was situated from three to four hours south of Tiberias. The city was built on a height, a quarter of an hour from the seashore, down to which, however, were houses scattered here and there. The shore from this point to the efflux of the Jordan was bordered with a wall strong and black, upon which a road extended. It was a recently built city, very beautiful and of pagan architecture, with colonnades in front of the houses. In the marketplace was a beautiful fountain protected by a pillared roof.

Jesus went at once to this fountain and thither flocked the people with their sick, whom He healed. Numbers of women stood veiled with their children at some distance behind the men. Pharisees and Sadducees were standing around Jesus, among them some Herodians, while He discoursed upon the Eight Beatitudes and the *Our Father*. The Pharisees were not slow in bringing forward their accusations which, as ever, turned upon the same points, namely, that He frequented the society of publicans and sinners, that He attracted after Him women of bad repute, that His disciples did not wash their hands before meals, that He cured upon the Sabbath, etc. Jesus cut them short, and called the children to Him. After curing, instructing, and blessing them, He presented them to the Pharisees with the words: "Ye must become like unto these."

Tarichaea was less elevated than Tiberias. Quantities of fish were here salted and dried. Before entering the city, the traveller met large wooden frames upon which the fish lay drying.

The country in these parts was uncommonly fertile. The heights around the city were covered with terraces full of vineyards and every variety of fruit trees. The whole region as far as Thabor and the Baths of Bethulia was, beyond all conception, blooming, teeming with abundance. It was most generally known as the Land of Genesareth.

Toward evening Jesus left Tarichaea and sailed with the disciples across the lake in a northeasterly direction. He taught while on the ship, but only of the *Our Father,* and this time of the fourth petition. When alone with them, Jesus always prepared His disciples for His public, more elevated teachings.

1. *Mk.* 8:10.

14. JESUS TEACHES OF THE BREAD
OF LIFE

Jesus spent the night on the ship, which was anchored on the shore between Matthew's custom office and Bethsaida-Julias. Next morning He discoursed upon the *Our Father* before about a hundred people, and toward midday sailed with the disciples to the region of Capharnaum, where they landed unnoticed and went at once to Peter's. Here Jesus met Lazarus, who had come hither with Veronica's son and some people from Hebron.

When Jesus ascended the height behind Peter's house, over which ran the shortest route from Capharnaum to Bethsaida, the multitude encamped around it followed Him. Several of those present the day before at the multiplication of the loaves, and who had been seeking Him ever since, asked Him: "Rabbi, when camest Thou hither? We have been seeking Thee on both sides of the lake." Jesus, at the same time beginning His sermon, answered them: "Amen, amen, I say to you, you seek Me, not because you have seen miracles, but because you did eat of the loaves, and were filled. Labor not for the meat which perisheth but for that which endureth unto life everlasting, which the Son of Man will give you. For Him hath God the Father sealed." These words stand thus in the Gospel, but they are only the principal points of those that Jesus pronounced on this occasion, for He dwelt largely on the subject. The people whispered to one another: "What does He mean by the Son of Man? We are all children of man!" When upon His admonition that they should do the works of God, they asked what they should do to fulfill those works, He answered: "Believe in Him whom He hath sent!" And then He gave them an instruction upon faith. They asked again what kind of a miracle He would perform that they might believe. Moses gave their fathers bread from Heaven that they might believe in him, namely, the manna. What, they now asked, was Jesus going to give them. To this Jesus answered: "I say to you, Moses gave you not bread from Heaven, but My Father giveth you the true bread from Heaven. For the bread of God is that which cometh down from Heaven and giveth life to the world."

Of this bread Jesus taught in detail, and some of them said to Him: "Lord, give us always this bread!" But others objected: "His Father gives us bread from Heaven! How can that be? His father Joseph is already dead!" Jesus continued to teach on the same subject, dwelling upon it at great length, developing it and explaining in most precise terms. But only a few understood Him. The others fancied themselves wise; they thought they knew all things.

On the following day Jesus, from the hill behind Peter's house, continued the subject of yesterday's discourse. There were about two thousand people present, who exchanged places by turns, some coming forward, others withdrawing, that all might get a chance to hear better. Jesus also changed His position from time to time. He went from one place to another, lovingly and patiently repeating His words of instruction and refuting the same objections. Apart from the crowd were many women, veiled. The Pharisees kept moving to and fro, questioning and whispering their doubts among the people.

Today Jesus spoke out in plain words. He said: "I am the Bread of Life. He that cometh to Me shall not hunger, and he that believeth in Me shall never thirst. All that the Father giveth Me shall come to Me, and him that cometh to Me, I will not cast out. Because I came down from Heaven, not to do My own will, but the will of Him that sent Me. Now this is the will of the Father, who sent Me: that of all that He hath given Me, I should lose nothing, but should raise it up again in the last day. And this is the will of My Father that sent Me: that every one who seeth the Son and believeth in Him, may have life everlasting, and I will raise him up at the last day."

But there were many who did not understand Him, and they said: "How can He say that He has come down from Heaven? He is truly the son of the carpenter Joseph, His Mother and relatives are among us, and we know even the parents of His father Joseph! He has said today that God is His Father, and then He said again that He is the Son of Man!" and they murmured. Jesus said to them: "Murmur not among yourselves. No man can come to Me, except the Father, who hath sent Me, draw him." Again they failed to grasp His meaning, and they asked what the words: "The Father draw him," signified. They took them quite literally. Jesus answered: "It is written in the Prophets, *'And they shall all be taught of God.'* Everyone that hath heard and learned it of the Father cometh to Me!"

Thereupon many of them asked: "Are we not with Him? And have we not yet heard of the Father, learned of the Father?" To which Jesus made answer: "No one hath seen the Father, but He who is of God. He that believeth in Me, hath everlasting life. I am the Bread that cometh down from Heaven, the Bread of Life."

Then they said again among themselves that they knew of no bread that came down from Heaven, excepting the manna. Jesus explained that the manna was not the Bread of Life, for their fathers who had eaten it were dead. But whosoever ate of the Bread that came down from Heaven, should not die. He said that He was the living Bread, and that he who ate thereof should live forever.

All these instructions were accompanied by full explanations and quotations from the Law and the Prophets. But most of the Jews would not comprehend them. They took all literally according to the common, human acceptation, and again asked: "What meaneth these words, that we should eat *Him,* and *eternal life?* Who, then, has eternal life, and who can eat of Him? Henoch and Elias have been taken away from the earth, and they say that they are not dead; nor does anyone know whither Malachias has gone, for no one knows of his death. But apart from these, all other men must die." Jesus replied by asking them whether they knew where Henoch and Elias were and where Malachias was. As for Himself, this knowledge was not concealed from Him. But did they know what Henoch believed, what Elias and Malachias prophesied? And He explained several of their prophecies.

Jesus taught no more that day. The people were in an extraordinary state of excitement; they reflected on His words and disputed their meaning among themselves. Many of the new disciples even, especially those lately received from among John's, doubted and wavered. They had swelled the number of the disciples to seventy, for up to this period Jesus had only thirty-six. The women were now about thirty-four, though the number engaged in the service of the Community at last amounted to seventy. It was increased by all the stewardesses, maidservants, and directresses of the inns.

Jesus again taught the people on the hill outside the city. He said nothing more of the Bread of Life, however, but confined Himself to the Beatitudes and the *Our Father.* The crowd was very great, but because most of the sick were already cured, the thronging and hurrying were less than usual. The carrying of the sick to the scene of action and their subsequent departure always gave rise to much confusion and disturbance, since everyone wanted to be first both in coming and going. All, and especially many of John's disciples, were in great expectation, eager to hear the end of the instruction begun on the previous day.

That evening as Jesus was teaching in the synagogue upon the lesson of the Sabbath, some of His hearers interrupted Him with the question: "How canst Thou call Thyself the Bread of Life come down from Heaven, since everyone knows whence Thou art?" To which Jesus answered by repeating all that He had already said on that subject.

The Pharisees again offered the same objections, and when they appealed to their father Abraham and to Moses, asking how He could call God His Father, Jesus put to them the question: "How can ye call Abraham your father and Moses your Law-giver, since ye do not follow the commandments or the example of either Abraham or Moses?" Then He placed clearly before them their perverse actions and their wicked, hypocritical life. They became confused and enraged.

Now Jesus resumed and continued His instructions on the Bread of Life. He said, "The bread that I will give is My flesh for the life of the world." At these words, murmurs and whispers ran through the crowd: "How can He give us His flesh to eat?" Jesus continued and taught at length as the Gospel records: "Except you eat the flesh of the Son of Man and drink His blood, you shall not have life in you. But he that eateth My flesh and drinketh My blood, hath everlasting life: and I will raise him up in the last day. For My flesh is meat indeed: and My blood is drink indeed. He that eateth My flesh and drinketh My blood, abideth in Me and I in him. As the living Father had sent Me, and I live by the Father, so he that eateth Me, the same also shall live by Me. This is the bread that came down from Heaven. It is not bread like the manna, of which your fathers did eat, and yet died! He that eateth this bread, shall live forever." Jesus then explained many passages from the Prophets, especially from Malachias, and showed their accomplishment in John the Baptist, of whom He spoke at length. They asked when

He would give them that food of which He spoke. He answered distinctly: "In its own time," and then, with a peculiar expression, signified a certain period in weeks. I counted as He spoke, and got: *one year, six weeks, and some days.* The people were very greatly agitated, and the Pharisees took care to incite them still more.

After that Jesus again taught in the synagogue. He explained the sixth and the seventh petitions of the *Our Father,* also the Beatitude, "Blessed are the poor in spirit." He said that they who are learned ought not to be conscious of it, just as the rich ought not to know that they possess riches. Then the Jews murmured again and said: "Of what use would such knowledge or such riches be, if the owner did not know that he possessed either the one or the other?" Jesus answered: "Blessed are the poor in spirit!" adding that they should feel themselves poor and humble before God, from whom all wisdom comes, and apart from whom all wisdom is an abomination.

When the Jews questioned Him again upon His discourse of the preceding day, that on the Bread of Life, on the eating of His flesh and the drinking of His blood, He repeated His former instruction in strong and precise terms. Many of His disciples murmured and said: "This saying is hard, and who can hear it?" Jesus replied that they should not be scandalized, they would witness things still more wonderful, and He predicted to them clearly that they would persecute Him, that even the most faithful among them would abandon Him and take to flight, and that He would fall into the arms of His enemies, who would put Him to death. But, He said, He would not abandon His unfaithful disciples; His Spirit would hover near them. The words, "He would run into the arms of His enemy," were not exactly those used by Jesus. It was rather that He would embrace His enemy, or be embraced by him, but I no longer remember which. It referred to the kiss and perfidy of Judas.

As the Jews were now still more scandalized, Jesus said: "If then you shall see the Son of Man ascend up where He was before? It is the spirit that quickeneth, the flesh profiteth nothing. The words that I have spoken to you are spirit and life. But there are some among you that believe not, therefore did I say to you: No man can come to Me, unless it be given him by My Father."

These words of Jesus were greeted by jeers and murmurs throughout the synagogue. About thirty of the new disciples, principally the narrow-minded followers of John, went over to the Pharisees and began to whisper with them and express their dissatisfaction, but the Apostles and the older disciples gathered more closely around Jesus. He continued to teach, and said aloud: "It is well that those men showed of whose spirit they are the children before they occasioned greater mischief."

As He was leaving the synagogue, the Pharisees and the disloyal disciples who had colleagued with them wanted to detain Him in order to argue with Him and demand explanations on many points. But the Apostles, His disciples, and other friends surrounded Him, so that He escaped their importunities, though amid shouts and confusion. Their speech was such as might be heard from the men of our own day: "Now we have it! Now we need nothing more! He has doubtless proved to every sensible man that He is Himself bereft of reason. We must eat His flesh! We must drink His blood! He is from Heaven! He will ascend into Heaven!"

Jesus went with His followers, though by different routes, to the hill and valley north of the city near the dwellings of Zorobabel and Cornelius. When they reached a certain place, He began to instruct His disciples, and then it was that He asked The Twelve whether they too were going to leave Him. Peter answered for all: "Lord, to whom shall we go? Thou hast the words of eternal life. And we have believed and have known that

Thou art the Christ, the Son of the living God!" Jesus answered among other things: "I also have chosen you twelve, and yet one among you is a devil!"

Mary was present with other women at that last discourse of Jesus on the mountain, as well as that delivered in the synagogue. Of all the mysteries propounded in these discourses, she had long had the interior consciousness; only, just as the Second Person of the Godhead, having taken flesh in her, became Man and her Child, so too was this knowledge hidden, enveloped as it were in the most humble, the most reverential love of her mother-heart for Jesus. Since Jesus had now taught more plainly of these mysteries than ever before, to the scandal of those that willfully shut their eyes to the light, the meditations of Mary were directed to them. I saw her in her chamber that night praying. She had a vision, an interior contemplation of the Angelical Salutation, the Birth, and the Childhood of Jesus, of her own maternity, and of His Sonship. She contemplated her Child as the Son of God, and was so overcome by humility and reverence that she melted into tears. But all these contemplations were again absorbed in the feeling of maternal love for her Divine Son, just as the appearance of bread hides the Living God in the Sacrament.

At the separation of the disciples from Jesus, I saw in two circles the Kingdom of Christ and the kingdom of Satan. I saw the city of Satan and the Babylonian harlot with its prophets and prophetesses, its wonder-workers and apostles, all in great magnificence, more brilliant, richer, and more numerous than was the Kingdom of Jesus. Kings, emperors, and even priests coursed therein with horse and chariot, and for Satan was set a magnificent throne.

But the Kingdom of Christ upon earth I saw poor and insignificant, full of misery and suffering. I saw Mary as the Church, and Christ on the Cross. He, too, was like

the Church, the entrance to which was through the
Wound of His Side.

15. JESUS IN DAN AND ORNITHOPOLIS

As Jesus with the Apostles and disciples was making
the journey from Capharnaum to Cana and Cydessa, I
saw Him in the region of Giskala placing The Twelve in
three separate rows and revealing to each his own
peculiar disposition and character. Peter, Andrew, John,
James the Greater, and Matthew stood in the first row;
Thaddeus, Bartholomew, James the Less, and the disciple
Barsabas, in the second; Thomas, Simon, Philip, and
Judas Iscariot, in the third. Each heard his own thoughts
and hopes revealed to him by Jesus, and all were strongly
affected. Jesus delivered at the same time a lengthy discourse upon the hardships and sufferings that awaited
them, and on this occasion He again made use of the expression: "Among you there is a devil."

The three different rows established no subordination
among the Apostles, one to another. The Twelve were
classed merely according to their disposition and
character. Joses Barsabas stood foremost in the row of
the disciples, and nearest to The Twelve; consequently,
Jesus placed him also in the second row with the Apostles, and revealed to him his hopes and fears. On this
journey Jesus further instructed The Twelve and the disciples exactly how to proceed in the future when healing
the sick and exorcising the possessed, as He Himself did
in such cases. He imparted to them the power and the
courage always to effect, by imposition of hands and
anointing with oil, what He Himself could do. This communication of power took place without the imposition of
hands, though not without a substantial transmission.
They stood around Jesus, and I saw rays darting toward
them of different colors, according to the nature of the

gifts received and the peculiar disposition of each recipient. They exclaimed: "Lord, we feel ourselves endued with strength! Thy words are truth and life!" And now each knew just what he had to do in every case in order to effect a cure. There was no room left for either choice or reflection.

After that Jesus with all His disciples arrived at Elcese, a place distant from Capharnaum one hour and a half. There in the synagogue He delivered the sermon of the Sabbath, in which reference was made to the building of Solomon's Temple. I remember that He addressed the Apostles and disciples as the workmen who were to fell the cedars on the mountain and prepare them for the building. He spoke also of the interior adornment of the Temple. The services over, at which many Pharisees were in attendance, Jesus was invited to dine. The meal was taken at a house of public entertainment. Many people stood around during it, to hear what Jesus was saying, and numbers of the poor were fed. The Pharisees, having remarked that the disciples had not washed their hands before coming to table, asked Jesus why His disciples did not respect the prescriptions of their forefathers, and why they did not observe the customary purifications. Jesus responded to their question by asking why they themselves did not keep the Commandments, why with all their traditions they did not honor their father and mother, and He reproached them with their hypocrisy and their vain adherence to external purification. During this dispute the meal came to an end. Jesus, however, continued to address the crowd that pressed around Him: "Hear ye and understand! Not that which goeth into the mouth defiled a man; but what cometh out of the mouth, this defileth a man. He that has ears to hear, let him hear!" The disciples who had remained behind in the entertainment hall told Jesus that these words of His had greatly scandalized the Pharisees. To which He responded: "Every plant that My Heavenly Father hath not planted, shall be rooted up! Let them alone! They are blind and leaders of the blind. And if the blind lead the blind, both fall into the pit."

When on the following evening Jesus was closing the Sabbath instruction, the Pharisees again reproached Him on account of the irregular mode of the disciples' fasting. But Jesus retorted by charging them with their avarice and want of mercy. Among other things, He said: "The disciples eat after long labor, and then only if others are supplied. But if these latter are hungry, they give them what they have, and God blesses it." Here Jesus recalled the multiplication of the loaves, on which occasion the disciples had given their bread and fish to the hungry multitude, and He asked the Pharisees whether they would have done the same.

From Elcese, Jesus went with the Apostles and disciples through Cedes-Nephtali to Dan, called also Lais, or Leschem. Cedes Nephtali was a stronghold and Levitical city built of black, shining stone. On the way Jesus instructed His followers, His subject always being prayer. He explained the *Our Father*. He told them that in the past they had not prayed worthily, but like Esau had asked for the fat of the earth; but now, like Jacob, they should petition for the dew of Heaven, for spiritual gifts, for the blessing of spiritual illumination, for the Kingdom according to the will of God, and not for one in accordance with their own ideas. He reminded them that even the heathens themselves did not petition for temporal goods alone, but also for those of a spiritual nature.

The city of Dan, situated at the base of a high mountain range, covered a wide extent owing to the fact that every one of its houses was surrounded by a garden. All the inhabitants were engaged in garden tillage. They raised fruits and aromatic plants of all kinds, also calamus, myrrh, balsam, cotton, and many sweet-scented herbs, which formed the staple of their trade with Tyre and Sidon. The pagans of Dan were more mixed up with the Jews than in other cities. Although this region was so delightful and fertile, yet there were many sick in it.

Jesus put up with the disciples at one of His own inns situated in the heart of the city. The Apostles and disciples had established it when on their last mission here. Counting the Apostles, the disciples with Jesus at this time amounted to thirty. They who had already been here and to whom consequently the inhabitants applied, led Jesus around to the different sick. The rest of the disciples scattered among the surrounding places. Peter, John, and James stayed with Jesus, who went about from house to house healing the sick. He cured the dropsical, the melancholy, the possessed, several slightly affected with leprosy, the lame, and especially numbers of blind, and others with swollen cheeks and limbs.

The blindness so prevalent came from the sting of a little insect that infested this country. Jesus pointed out an herb, with whose juice He bade them anoint their eyes in order to prevent the insect from stinging them. He gave to them also a moral application of its meaning. The swellings, which became inflamed and produced gangrene that ended in the death of many thus afflicted, were likewise caused by little insects like mildew that were blown from the trees. They were grayish black, like chimney soot, and were borne like a dense black cloud through the air. The insect bit into the skin and raised a large swelling. Jesus pointed out another insect, which was to be crushed and applied to the bite. He told them in future to make use of it in similar cases. It had fifteen little points on the back, as large as an ant's egg, and it could roll itself up into a ball.

16. THE SYROPHENICIAN

While Jesus was going from house to house in Dan healing the sick, He was perseveringly followed by an aged woman, a pagan, who was crippled on one side. She was from Ornithopolis. She remained humbly at some distance and, from time to time, implored help. But Jesus paid no attention to her, He even appeared to shun her, for He was now healing sick Jews only. A servant accompanied the woman bearing her baggage. She was habited in the garb of a foreigner. Her dress was of striped material, the arms and neck trimmed with lace. On her head she wore a high, pointed cap, over which was tied a colored kerchief, and lastly a veil. She had at home a daughter sick and possessed, and for a long time she had been hoping for aid from Jesus. She was in Dan at the time of the Apostles' mission there, and they now more than once reminded Jesus of her. But He replied that it was not yet time, that He wanted to avoid giving offense, and that He would not help the pagans before the Jews.

In the afternoon Jesus went with Peter, James, and John to the house of one of the Jewish Elders of the city, a man very well disposed, a friend of Lazarus and Nicodemus, and in secret a follower of Jesus. He had contributed largely to the common fund of the holy women and to the support of the inns. He had two sons and three daughters, all of mature age, he himself being an old man far advanced in years. The children were unmarried. The sons wore their long hair parted on top of the head and allowed the beard to grow. Through the daughters' headdress, the hair could be seen similarly parted. They were Nazarites. All were clothed in white. The old father, whose beard was long and white, was led by the sons to meet Jesus, for he could not walk alone. He was shedding tears of reverential joy. The sons washed the feet of Jesus and the Apostles, and presented

them with refreshments, fruit and rolls. Jesus was very
affable and treated the family with great confidence. He
spoke to them of the journeys He was about to make, and
told them that He would not show Himself openly in
Jerusalem at the celebration of the coming Pasch. He did
not remain long in the house, for the people, having
found out His whereabouts, had gathered outside and in
the forecourt. Jesus went out through the court and into
the garden where for several hours He taught and cured
between the terraced walls that supported the gardens.
The pagan woman had waited long at a distance. Jesus
never went near her, and she dared not approach Him.
From time to time, however, she repeated her cry: "Lord!
Thou Son of David, have mercy on me! My daughter is
grievously tormented by an unclean spirit!" The disciples
begged Jesus to help her. But He said: "I was not sent
but to the sheep that are lost of the house of Israel." At
last the woman drew nearer, ventured into the hall, cast
herself down before Jesus, and cried: "Lord, help me!"
Jesus replied: "It is not good to take the bread of the
children and to cast it to the dogs." But she continued to
entreat: "Yea, Lord! For the whelps also eat of the
crumbs that fall from the table of their masters." Then
Jesus said: "O woman, great is thy faith! On account of
these words, help shall be given thee!"

Jesus asked her whether she herself did not want to be
cured, for she was crippled on one side. But she replied
that she was not worthy, and that she asked for her
daughter's cure only. Then He laid one hand on her
head, the other on her side, and said: "Straighten up!
May it be done to thee as thou dost will! The devil has
gone out of thy daughter." The woman stood upright.
She was tall and thin. For some instants, she uttered not
a word, and then with uplifted hands, she cried out: "O
Lord, I see my daughter lying in bed well and in peace!"
She was out of herself with joy. Jesus turned away with

the disciples.

Jesus afterward took a repast at the house of the Nazarites. The Levites of Cades were present, as well as all the Apostles and disciples who had again met together at the inn. It was a grand entertainment, such as had not been given for a long time, and from it abundant alms were distributed to the poor by the disciples. After all was over, Jesus returned to the inn. The Feast of the New Moon was celebrated yesterday and today.

When Jesus on the following morning was healing and teaching under the market porticos, the pagan woman brought to Jesus one of her relatives who had come with her from Ornithopolis. He was paralyzed in the right arm besides being deaf and dumb. The woman begged Jesus to cure him and also to visit her home, that they might there thank Him worthily.

Jesus took the man aside from the crowd, laid His hand on the lame arm, prayed, and stretched out the arm perfectly cured. Then He moistened his ears with a little spittle, told him to raise his cured hand to his tongue, glanced upward, and prayed. The man arose, spoke, and gave thanks. Jesus stepped back with him to the pressing multitude, and the man began to speak wonderful and prophetic words. He cast himself at Jesus' feet and gave Him thanks. Then turning to the Jews and pagans, he uttered menaces against Israel, named some particular places, referred to the miracles of Jesus and the obstinacy of the Jews, and said: "The food that ye, the children of the house, reject, we outcasts shall gather up. We shall live upon it, and give thanks. The fruit of the crumbs that we gather up will be to us what you allow to go to waste of the Bread of Heaven." His words were so wonderful, so inspired, that great agitation arose in the crowd.

Immediately after this, Jesus left the city and climbed with the Apostles and disciples a mountain range to the west of Lesem. They reached a solitary height, where they found a roomy cavern containing seats cut out of the rock. Caves of this kind served as resting places for travellers. Jesus and His followers had been journeying a good two hours, and here passed the night. Jesus instructed the Apostles and disciples on diverse modes of healing and the various ceremonies accompanying them, for they had asked Him why He had ordered the dumb man to put his own hand into his mouth, and why He had taken him aside. Jesus satisfied them on these points, instructed them again upon prayer, and praised the pagan woman who had always implored, not for temporal goods, but for the knowledge of the truth. He prescribed a certain order to be followed by them: They were to go on their missions two and two, they were all to teach the same things, they were to proclaim the last instructions that He had given them. From time to time, they were to meet together in order severally to communicate all that had occurred to them. The Apostles were then to impart to the disciples whatever had happened in the meantime and which ought to be known in common. They should pray together on their journeys, and speak only of the affairs of their mission.

Having resumed their route, they passed the great and very elevated city of Hammoth Dor, after which they climbed steep and toilsome heights until they reached the lofty ridge that commanded a view of the Mediterranean. They now descended the mountain for several hours, passed over a stream that flowed into the sea through the north of Tyre, and put up at an inn on the roadside, between three and four hours from Ornithopolis.

The Syrophenician was a very distinguished lady in her native place. She had passed through these parts on her way home, and had fitted up a very comfortable inn for Jesus. The pagans came out most humbly to meet Jesus and His party, guided them to their destination, and showed them all kinds of attentions with an air at once timid and reverential. They looked upon Jesus as a great Prophet.

Next day Jesus and the disciples ascended a hill in the neighborhood of a little pagan city, and there found a teacher's chair. It had been in existence since the times of the early Prophets, some of whom had often preached from it. The pagans had always held this place in high esteem, and today they had ornamented it by erecting a beautiful awning over the chair.

There were numbers of sick assembled on the hill, but they remained shyly at a distance, until Jesus and the disciples approached and cured many of them. Some had tumors, others were paralyzed, others wasted away, some were melancholy or half-possessed. These last, when cured, appeared as if awaking from sleep. The limbs of some were greatly swollen and inflamed. Jesus laid His hand on the swelling, which was immediately reduced and the inflammation allayed. He directed the disciples to bring a plant that grew there on the naked rock. It had large, succulent, and deeply notched leaves. He blessed one of these leaves, poured on it some water that He carried with Him in a flask, and the disciples bound it, the notched side down, on the part affected.

The healing over, Jesus delivered an instruction on the vocation of the Gentiles. It was more than ordinarily impressive. He explained several passages from the Prophets, and depicted the vanity of their idols. After that He went with the disciples three hours in a north-westwardly direction to Ornithopolis, which was distant from the sea three-quarters of an hour. This city, which was not very large, contained some beautiful buildings. On a height in the eastern environs stood a pagan temple.

Jesus was received with more than ordinary affection. The Syrophenician had prepared everything for the occasion in the most sumptuous and honorable manner, but in

her humility, she left to the few poor Jewish families living in the city the liberty of doing the honors of reception. The whole place resounded with the cure of her
daughter, as well as with that of her own and her deaf
and dumb relative. The last-named, in recounting his
cure, spoke of Jesus in words of inspiration. The inhabitants were ranged outside the houses. The pagans stood
back humbly and closed the procession that went with
green branches to meet Jesus. The Jews, about twenty in
number, among them some very aged men who had to be
led, also the teachers with all the children, headed the
procession. The mothers and daughters followed, veiled.

A house near the school had been prepared for Jesus
and the disciples. It was fitted up by the lady with
beautiful carpets, furniture, and lamps. There the Jews
most humbly washed the feet of Jesus and His disciples
and changed their sandals and clothes, until their own
were shaken, brushed, and cleaned. Jesus then went with
the Elders to the school and taught.

After that, a magnificent entertainment was given in a
public hall, at the expense of the Syrophenician. One
could see in all the preparations, in the dishes, the
viands, and the table furniture generally, that it was a
feast given by the pagans. There were three tables much
higher than those in use among the Jews, with couches
correspondingly high. Some of the viands were very
remarkable, being made up into figures representing
animals, trees, mountains, and pyramids. Some others
were quite deceptive, being in reality very different from
what they appeared; for instance, there were all kinds of
wonderful pastry, birds made out of fish, fish formed of
flesh, and lambs made of spices, fruits, flour, and honey.
There were also some real lambs. At one table, Jesus ate
with the Apostles and the oldest among the Jews; at the
two others, the disciples and the rest of the Jews. The
women and children were seated at a table separated

from the others by a screen. During the meal, the lady
with her daughter and relatives entered to give thanks for
the cures wrought among them, their servants following
with presents in ornamented caskets, which they bore between them on tapestry. The daughter, veiled, stepped
behind Jesus, broke a little vial of precious ointment over
His head, and then modestly returned to her mother. The
servants delivered the gifts (they were those of the
daughter) to the disciples. Jesus returned thanks. The
lady bade Him welcome to her native place, and declared
how happy she should be if she could only show her
good will and, in spite of her unworthiness, repair even
the least of the many injuries that He experienced so
often from her fellow pagans. She spoke humbly and in
few words, remaining all the while at a respectful distance. Jesus ordered the money that formed part of the
gifts, as well as the food, to be distributed in her presence among the poor Jews.

The lady was a widow and very rich. Her husband had
been dead five years. He possessed in his lifetime many
large ships at sea and a great number of servants, besides
much property. He owned whole villages. Not far from
Ornithopolis there was a heathen settlement on a cape
jutting out into the sea, all of which belonged to the lady,
his widow. I think he was a large merchant. His widow
was held in more than ordinary esteem in Ornithopolis,
where the poor Jews lived almost entirely upon her bounty. She was both intelligent and beneficent, and not without a certain degree of illumination in her pagan piety.
Her daughter was twenty-four years old, tall and very
beautiful. She dressed in colors and adorned her neck
with chains, her arms with bracelets. Her wealth brought
around her numerous suitors, and she became possessed
of an evil spirit. She was afflicted with convulsions so
violent that in her frenzy she would spring from her
couch and try to run away; consequently she had to be

guarded and even bound. But when the paroxysm was over, she became again good and virtuous. Her state caused great affliction to herself and her mother, and to both it was a subject of deep humiliation. The poor girl was obliged to live retired, and she had now endured her sufferings for several years. When the mother neared her home, she was met by her daughter who had come out for that purpose, as well as to tell her of her cure, which had taken place at the very instant in which Jesus had promised it. And, oh, her joy and wonder at seeing her once-crippled mother again a tall, graceful woman! And to hear herself distinctly and joyfully greeted by her paralyzed, deaf, and dumb relative! She was filled with gratitude and reverence for Jesus, and helped to prepare everything for His reception.

The gifts that Jesus received consisted of trinkets belonging to the daughter. They had been given to her in her early years by her parents, principally by her father, whose business opened to him communications with distant lands, and whose only and well-beloved child she was. Some were jewels of ancient workmanship, objects wrought of precious metals, such as are ordinarily given to the children of the wealthy. Among them were some things that had formerly belonged to her parents' parents. There were many wonderful-looking little idols of pearls and precious stones set in gold, rare stones of great value, tiny vessels, golden animals, and figures about a finger long, the eyes and mouth formed of gems. There were also odoriferous stones and amber and golden branches that looked like little live trees, laden with colored gems instead of fruit—and very, very many such things! It was a treasure in itself, for some of these objects would now be worth a thousand dollars apiece. Jesus said that He would distribute them to the poor and the needy, and that His Father in Heaven would reward the donors.

On the Sabbath, Jesus visited every one of the Jewish

families, distributed alms, cured, and comforted. Many of these Jews were poor and abandoned. Jesus assembled them in the synagogue where He spoke to them in terms at once deeply touching and consoling, for the poor creatures looked upon themselves as the outcast and unworthy children of Israel. He also prepared many of them for Baptism. About twenty men were baptized in a bathing garden, among them the cured deaf and dumb relatives of the pagan lady.

Jesus visited the Syrophenician also, along with His disciples. She dwelt in a beautiful house surrounded by numerous courts and gardens. Jesus was received with great solemnity. The domestics in festal garments spread carpets under His feet. At the entrance of a beautiful summerhouse, which was supported on pillars, the widow and her daughter came forward veiled to meet Him. They cast themselves at His feet and poured forth their thanks, in which they were joined by their cured relative, once deaf and dumb. In the summerhouse were set forth odd-looking figures in pastry and fruit of all kinds on costly dishes. The vessels were of glass, which looked as if made of many colored threads that appeared to run together and cross one another, as if dissolving one into the other. Among rich Jews I have seen similar vessels, but only in small numbers. Here they seemed to be in abundance. Many such vessels were held in reserve behind curtains in the corners of the hall. They were arranged on shelves up high on the wall. The dishes were set on little tables, some round, others with corners, that could be placed together to form one large table.

Among the refreshments there were very fine dried grapes still hanging on the vine laid on those colored glass dishes, also another kind of dried fruit which arose from the branches as from a little tree. There were reeds with long, cordate leaves and fruit in form like the grape. They were perfectly white, perhaps sugared, and looked like the white part of the cauliflower. The guests snapped them off the stem, and found that they had a sweet, pleasant taste. They were raised not far from the sea, in a swampy place belonging to the Syrophenician.

In a separate part of the hall, the pagan maidens, friends of the daughter, were standing along with the domestics. Jesus went and spoke to them. The lady very earnestly entreated Jesus on behalf of the poor people of Sarepta. She begged Him to visit them as well as others in the neighborhood. She was very intelligent and had a clever way of proposing things. Her words were something to this effect: "Sarepta, whose poor widow had shared her little all with Elias, is itself a poor widow threatened with starvation. Do Thou, the greatest of Prophets, have pity on her! Forgive me, a widow and once poor, to whom Thou hast restored her all, if I make bold to plead also for Sarepta." Jesus promised to do as she wished. She told Him that she wanted to build a synagogue, and asked Him to indicate where it should be. But I do not remember Jesus' reply.

The lady possessed large weaving and dyeing factories. In the little place near the sea and at some distance from her residence, there were great buildings on the top of which were platforms where gray and yellow stuffs were spread out. Among the gifts presented to Jesus were many little dishes and balls of amber, considered in those parts very precious.

Jesus celebrated the close of the Sabbath in the Jewish school, which was very beautifully adorned. In order to console the poor Jews, He taught that the proverb: "Our fathers have eaten sour grapes, and the teeth of the children are on edge," should no longer pass current in Israel. "Everyone that abides by the Word of God announced by Me, that does penance and receives Baptism, no longer bears the sins of his father." The people were extraordinarily rejoiced upon hearing these words.

On the afternoon of the following day, Jesus took leave of the lady who, in union with her daughter and cured relative, presented Him with golden figures a hand in length, and provisions of bread, balsam, fruits, honey in reed baskets, and little flasks. These provisions were destined for His journey and for the poor of Sarepta. Jesus addressed words of advice to the whole family, recommended to them the poor Jews and their own salvation, and departed from the house amid the tears and reverential salutations of all. The lady had always been very enlightened and very earnest in seeking after perfection. Henceforth neither she nor her daughter went any more to the pagan temple. They observed the teachings of Jesus, joined the Jews, and sought by degrees to bring their people after them.

Several times again Jesus repeated His instructions to the disciples upon the order they were to observe and the duties they were to fulfill in their present mission. Thomas, Thaddeus, and James the Less went with some of the disciples (the others remaining with Jesus) down to the tribe of Aser. They were allowed to take nothing with them. Jesus with the nine remaining Apostles, with Saturnin, Judas Barsabas, and another, went northward to Sarepta. Sixteen of the Jews accompanied Jesus the whole of the way, while all the rest and many of the pagans went only a part. He did not enter Sarepta, which was about two and a half hours distant from Ornithopolis, but stopped at a row of houses tolerably far from the city. They occupied the site of the spot upon which the widow of Sarepta was gathering sticks when Elias approached the city. Some poor Jews had settled there. They were still poorer than those of Ornithopolis, who enjoyed the bounty of the Syrophenician. Here too was an inn prepared for Jesus and His followers, and presents for the poor had been sent on in advance—all through the goodness of that lady. The inhabitants, unspeakably happy and deeply impressed, came out with the women and children to meet Jesus and to wash His feet, also those of His followers.

Jesus consoled and taught them. Then He proceeded on His journey a couple of hours to the east, accompanied by the sixteen men from Ornithopolis and some others from Sarepta. The country was rising, and the road uphill. On an eminence near a little pagan city, Jesus delivered an instruction to the inhabitants whom He found there awaiting Him, after which He pressed on farther. Those that had followed Him from Ornithopolis here took leave.

At some distance farther on, Jesus and the disciples ascended in an easterly direction toward Mount Hermon, which forms the culminating peak of the high mountain range that bounds Upper Galilee. He crossed Hermon into an elevated valley and stopped at Rechob to the southwest at the foot of the mountain below Baal-Hermon. This last city was very large and, with its numerous pagan temples, looked down upon Rechob.

17. JESUS IN GESSUR AND NOBE.
CELEBRATION OF THE FEAST OF PURIM

Jesus journeyed seven hours northeastward from Rechob to Gessur, where He stopped with the publicans, many of whom dwelt on the highroad leading to Damascus. Gessur was a beautiful, large city garrisoned by Roman soldiers. Jews and pagans occupied separate quarters, notwithstanding which the communications between them were very intimate. The Jews of Gessur were, on this account, held in low esteem by those of other places.

Many of the Jews and pagans of Gessur had been present at the sermon on the Mount of Beatitudes, and some of their sick were cured by the Apostles who had recently visited the place. There was also a blind man who had been restored to sight at the instruction before the multiplication of the bread. The husband of Mary Suphan was from Gessur, but he was now residing with her at Ainon.

When Absalom was fleeing from David, he took up his abode in Gessur for a time, as his mother Maacha was the daughter of the king of the place, who was named Tholmai.[1]

The Apostle Bartholomew, who had accompanied Jesus hither, was a descendant of that same royal house. His father had for a long time made use of the baths of Bethulia, on which account he had removed to Cana and settled in the valley of Zabulon. It was owing to this that Bartholomew had become an inhabitant of that part of the country. He still had in Gessur a very aged grand-uncle on his mother's side, a pagan and possessed of great property and riches. This old man resided in a large house in the heart of the city. He had himself conducted to the publican quarter in order to see Jesus, who was teaching on a terrace upon which the merchandise passing this way was examined, taxed, and repacked. The old uncle conversed with the Apostles, especially with his nephew Bartholomew, and invited Jesus to his house to dine. All the inhabitants, men and women, Jews and pagans, attended Jesus' instructions. It was a promiscuous audience. Jesus also took a meal with the publicans and many others. There was considerable bustle attending it, for the publicans were putting all their goods in order to make a distribution to the poor.

When Jesus entered the pagan quarter of the city, to visit Bartholomew's uncle, He was received with magnificence according to pagan style. Carpets were spread before Him, and sumptuous refreshments set forth, all in accordance with pagan manners.

The pagans of Gessur adored a many-armed idol,

which supported on its head a bushel measure filled with ears of wheat. Many of them inclined to Judaism, and many others to the doctrines of Jesus. Numbers of them had already been baptized either by John, or by the Apostles at Capharnaum.

The publicans distributed the greater part of their wealth. On the place upon which Jesus had taught, they heaped up great quantities of corn which they afterward measured out to the poor. They likewise bestowed fields and gardens upon poor day laborers and slaves, and repaired all the wrong they had done.

When Jesus was again teaching at the custom house before the pagans and Jews, some strangers arrived, Pharisees, to celebrate here the Sabbath. They reproached Jesus for lodging among the publicans and for having familiar communications with them and the pagans.

Bartholomew's uncle, along with sixteen other aged men, was baptized in a bathing garden, the water from a well of the city being conducted into the garden by a very elevated canal. Joses Barsabas administered the Baptism. The garden had been adorned in festive style, the ceremony was most solemn, and the poor were abundantly supplied with alms, to which the old uncle largely contributed.

Jesus closed the Sabbath by an instruction in the synagogue, took leave of all the people at the custom house, distributed alms to the poor, and went accompanied by a numerous retinue a distance of five hours to the fisher village on the borders of the lake of Phiala. This lake was on a plateau about three hours east of Paneas. He arrived late and lodged with the teacher in a house next the school. The people of the place were for the most part Jews.

Lake Phiala was scarcely one hour long. Its shores were sloping, its waters clear, and its outlet flowed toward a mountain where it disappeared. There were some boats on its surface. The region was covered with fields of grain and beautiful meadows, in the latter of which numbers of asses, camels, and other cattle were grazing; there were also groves of chestnuts. On both sides of the lake lay Jewish fisher villages, each of which had its own school.

Jesus taught in the schools, and went with some of the inhabitants and the Apostles into the homes of the shepherds around the lake. John the Baptist had once sojourned in this region.

From this place, Jesus with John, Bartholomew, and a disciple went three hours southward to Nobe, a city of Decapolis. The inhabitants were pagans and Jews. They dwelt apart, the city being divided into two quarters, each of which had a somewhat different name. All the cities of this part of the country were built of black, glimmering stone. Jesus taught in Nobe and in some of the little places around. John and Bartholomew were with Him, the other Apostles and disciples being scattered throughout the neighboring country.

Jesus prepared the people for Baptism, which was administered by Bartholomew. The water in these places was black and muddy, but it was purified in great, round, stone reservoirs, whence it was allowed to flow into others that were kept covered. The Apostles poured into it some of the water from their drinking vessels, and Jesus blessed the whole. The people, with inclined heads, knelt for Baptism around the stone basin.

The pagans of Nobe received Jesus very solemnly. They went to meet Him carrying green, blooming branches, stretched cordons on either side to keep back the crowd, and spread carpets for Him to walk on. These latter were laid across the streets, and, when Jesus had passed over them, they were raised quickly, carried some distance ahead, and held again in readiness for His approach. This was repeated many times, and as often did Jesus walk over them. The rabbis, who were Pharisees, received Him in the Jewish quarter, where He taught in the synagogue, for it was the Sabbath of the Purim festival. When all was over, there was a banquet given in the public hall. During the entertainment, the Pharisees again disputed on certain points, and twitted Jesus upon His disciples' eating fruit by the wayside and stripping the ears of wheat.

Jesus related the parable of the laborers in the vineyard, also that of the rich glutton and poor Lazarus. He reproached the Pharisees for not having, according to custom, invited the poor to the feast; whereupon they replied that their revenues were too small to allow it. Then Jesus asked whether the present entertainment had been prepared for Him, and when they answered, yes, He laid on the table five large, yellow, three-cornered pieces of money attached to a little chain, saying that they might let the poor have them. Then He directed the disciples to call in many of the poor, who sat down at the table and partook of the viands. Jesus Himself served them, instructing them meantime and distributing to them quantities of food. The money presented by Jesus was perhaps the customary Temple tax usually paid on that day, or merely a gift usual at the time, for the people on this feast interchanged presents of fruits, bread, grain, and garments.

On this feast they read in the synagogue the whole of the history of Esther. They did the same to the sick and aged in their own homes. Jesus also went around reading to the old people the roll of Esther, and healing some of the sick. I saw too festive games and processions of the young maidens and women, who had great privileges on this day. Once they entered the synagogue as if on an embassy, and penetrated even into the upper part. They had chosen one of their number as queen, whom they now escorted in regal robes, and presented to the priests beautiful priestly vestments. They had some games among themselves in a garden. They chose sometimes this one, again that one for queen, and in turn dethroned them. They had also a puppet which they ill-treated and then hanged, while little lads struck with hammers on boards and uttered imprecations. This was meant for a representation of the punishment merited by the wicked Aman.

1. *1 Par.* 3:2.

18. JESUS IN REGABA AND
CAESAREA-PHILIPPI

From Nobe, Jesus went to Gaulon. The road wound westwardly round a high mountain chain for a distance of four hours. Gaulon was inhabited by both Jews and pagans and was distant from the Jordan a couple of hours. Jesus tarried here only a few hours teaching and healing. Continuing His journey, He passed the city of Argos, built at a high elevation on a mountain ridge, and arrived late that night at the stronghold Regaba. He rested with His companions on the grass of a solitary place outside the city, and awaited the other Apostles and disciples, fifteen in number. When these arrived, they all went with their Master to the inn established here for their accommodation. Regaba belonged to the Gergesean district. It was the most northerly of their towns, and one of the best disposed. Gaulon was a frontier town of the tetrarch Philip.

Most of the inhabitants, both Jews and pagans, were already baptized, and their sick had been healed on the Mount of Beatitudes. Jesus spent the whole day in teaching, consoling, and strengthening souls in faith. An immense crowd from the whole country around was here assembled for the Sabbath, and to it was added a caravan from Arabia. This crowd of people brought with them their lame, their blind, their dumb, and other sick. They pressed with such violence that Jesus left the synagogue with the disciples and retired to a mountain. Some of the disciples remained behind and endeavored, as well as they could, to bring the crowd to order. The people followed Jesus to the mountain, where He taught of the *Our Father,* of prayer that should not be made with ostentation and in public places to be seen, and of the granting of prayer. He also healed many of the sick, and then returned to the synagogue in Regaba. During these last days, Jesus had spoken much upon prayer both on His journeys and in the schools. There were some disciples with Him who had not been present at all the explanations of the *Our Father.* They said to Him: "Teach us, also, to pray as Thou hast taught the others!" and He again explained the *Our Father,* and warned them against sanctimonious prayers.

Regaba was situated very high and had a magnificent view over the lake, across Genesareth, and off to Thabor. Still higher than the city, which was not very large, stood upon a rock a square building with great, steep walls, as if hewn from the rocks. It was provided with vaults and chambers, and was a home for soldiers. It was roofed by a platform upon which trees were growing. It was a citadel. From Regaba to the lake the distance was about five hours toward the southwest; to the Mount of Beatitudes, from three to four hours westward; about five hours to Bethsaida-Julias; and from seven to eight hours from the place in which Jesus drove the devil into the swine. To Caesarea-Philippi, it may have been five hours. A road for caravans ran over the high mountain between Regaba and Caesarea.

During these days, Jesus spoke much of the dark future before Him. Men would, He said, persecute Him everywhere and even attempt His life, and once He said that His arrest was near. Since the last excitement at Capharnaum, He had not spoken in public of the Bread of Life, nor of eating His Flesh and drinking His Blood. He had taught of this mystery chiefly in order to try His disciples and to get rid of the bad, whom He wished no longer to retain as His followers.

The elevated surroundings of Regaba were very lovely, though somewhat wild. Off toward the northeast, however, the country was barren and rocky. Excellent fruit, such as they had in Genesareth, did not grow here, but there were quantities of grain, and on the mountains fine pasturelands. Grazing around were great herds of asses and cows. Some of the latter had very broad horns and black snouts which they carried high in the air; others bore their heads lower and their horns forward, while the horns of many others were broken off short. There were also large herds of camels, which at a distance looked quite small. They often slept standing, supported against the trees and rocks. In one quarter, in which trees like beeches were growing, I saw droves of swine. I have never seen either the Jews or the pagans prepare smoked meat, though they dried fish in the sun and salted it. Up here on the mountains there was great scarcity of water, consequently there were cisterns lower down in which the rain was caught, and the water then carried up in leathern bottles.

From Regaba Jesus went with His followers to Caesarea-Philippi, where He arrived about midday. The road thither ran over mountains, and in many places it was very wild. The situation of Caesarea was extraordinarily beautiful. It lay between five hills on one side and a mountain chain on the other. It was surrounded by groves and gardens, and was built in the pagan style of columns and arches. There were perhaps as many as seven palaces, and numbers of pagan temples. Still, the pagans dwelt apart from the Jews. In a little vale outside the city there was a very large pond, in the center of which was a little revolving building. The water welled from it into the pond and thence flowed down to the Jordan. In the pagan quarter of the city, there was a very deep well over which was built a beautiful edifice. It was very deep to look down into. I think it communicated through the mountain with the source that flowed from Lake Phiala. I saw outside the city arches and vaults also through which the water flowed, as if through caves and over bridges.

Jesus was well received. They were on the watch for Him, the caravan having announced His coming. Some of the relatives of the woman whom Jesus had cured of a flow of blood came out as far as the pond to meet Him. He put up near the synagogue at an inn belonging to the Pharisees, and soon was surrounded by a crowd of sick and others. The Apostles healed here and there. Some of the Pharisees of this place were badly disposed toward Jesus. They had formed part of the Commission of Capharnaum.

Jesus cured and taught on a hill outside the city. Strangers from all quarters had brought thither their sick, and these latter were continually crying out: "Lord, command one of Thy disciples to help us!" The Pharisees taunted Jesus, asking Him why He went around with people so mean, why He did not associate with the learned.

Alms consisting of food and clothing were distributed by the disciples. They had been supplied by Enue (she who had been cured of the issue of blood) and her uncle, still a pagan, who dwelt in Caesarea.

The three Apostles and all the disciples who from Ornithopolis had been sent by Jesus to Tyre, Cabul, and the tribe of Aser, met Jesus here at Caesarea as He had appointed. The meeting on such occasions is always very touching. They clasp hands and embrace. The people washed the feet of the newcomers, who immediately took part in the distribution of food and other alms, and the healing of the sick.

Jesus went afterward with all the Apostles and disciples, about sixty in number, to the house of Enue's uncle, where He was received most solemnly according to pagan customs, carpets being spread for Him to walk upon, and green branches and wreaths being carried. The uncle, led by Enue and her daughter, came to meet Jesus, and the women cast themselves down before Him.

It was partly in answer to the prayer of this old man that Jesus had come to Caesarea. He and several other pagans wanted to be baptized, but they had scruples on the subject of circumcision. Jesus never touched upon this point in His public discourse, but He had a private interview with the uncle. In such cases, He never commanded circumcision; though, at the same time, He did not advocate its discontinuance. When pious old pagans, upon receiving Baptism, told Him in confidence of their trouble on this head, Jesus used to console them by telling them that if they did not wish to become Jews, they should remain as they were, but believe and practice what they heard from Him. Such people then lived apart from both Judaism and paganism. They prayed, they gave alms, and became Christians without passing through Judaism. Even to the Apostles, Jesus refrained from expressing Himself on this point, in order not to scandalize them, so that I never remember having heard the Pharisees, who listened so closely to catch Him in His words, ever accuse Him on that head, no, not even at the time of His Passion.

Over the beautifully paved inner court of the old man's house an awning of white stuff was stretched, and through an opening in the center hung a wreath. Besides the trees, the whole court was adorned with garlands of flowers. Baptism was administered under the awning. Before the ceremony, Jesus gave an instruction and spoke in private with the neophytes, who opened their hearts to Him. They exposed to Him their whole life and made their profession of faith in Him. Jesus then absolved them from their sins, and they were baptized by Saturnin in a basin of water which Jesus had previously blessed. The ceremony was followed by a grand entertainment in which all the disciples and the friends of the family took part. The meal was conducted according to pagan customs. The table was higher than those in use among the Jews, and the guests reclined upon long, raised divans, the feet turned out, and one arm resting on a cushion. The edge of the table was indented, and before each of the guests were some small dishes, though the principal viands were on large ones in the center of the table.

Enue, since her cure, was scarcely recognizable, so well and hearty had she become. She and her daughter, who was about twenty-one years old, sat at table beside their uncle. During the entertainment, they arose and withdrew for awhile. When they returned, the mother stood somewhat back while the daughter, wearing a beautiful veil and carrying a little white vase of perfume, went behind Jesus, broke it, and poured the contents over His head. Then with both hands she smoothed it right and left over His hair, and drew the part behind the ears through her hands. After that she gathered up the end of her veil, passed it over His head in order to dry it, and retired. A quantity of food was distributed to the poor outside the house.

This house was not the uncle's former residence. It was one to which he had removed with Enue, in order to avoid intercourse with the pagans and the frequenting of their temples; still it was not in the Jewish quarter. Enue was the daughter of either his brother or sister. She had

had communications with the Jews, one of whom she had married, but he was now deceased. It was, however, from her pagan parents that she inherited all her wealth. On leaving their old home, Enue and her uncle had left behind quantities of corn, clothes, and covers for the poor.

Caesarea-Philippi was four hours east of Lesem, or Lais, whither the Syrophenician had come to Jesus; they were consequently not one and the same city.

During Jesus' stay in Caesarea, the pagans celebrated a feast near the fountain in the city. It had reference to the benefit they derived from the water. Incense was burned on tripods before an idol, around which was gathered a crowd of maidens wearing crowns. The idol was made up of three or four figures sitting back to back, each having its own head, hands, and feet. The arms down to the elbows were fastened to the body, but the hands were outstretched. The fountain on all sides poured out water into basins. On one side it flowed into an enclosed place in which were private halls and bathing cisterns. This was the Jews' bathing place.

When the pagan feast was over, Jesus went thither and prepared several of the Jews, who afterward received Baptism from the disciples. The ceremony concluded, Jesus with several of His disciples returned to the home of Enue and her uncle and took leave of them. Humbly, reverently, and with many tears, these worthy people bade goodbye to Jesus. They had previously sent presents to the place outside the city gate where Jesus continued a while longer His instructions to the poor travellers belonging to the caravan and to others from the city. The presents consisted of bread, corn, garments, and covers, all of which with whatever else they had received, Jesus caused to be distributed among the needy. Many of the devout Jews and the newly baptized followed this example of charity. They measured out corn and distributed linen, covers, mantles and bread to the poor, for whom this was a gala day.

Jesus was afterward constrained by the Pharisees, though in the most polite manner, to enter the synagogue and explain some points to them. The Apostles accompanied their Master, and quite a considerable crowd was present. The Pharisees had devised all kinds of captious questions on the subject of divorce, for there were many complicated matrimonial affairs in this place, and Jesus had already reconciled some parties and set them right. The Pharisees now began to dispute maliciously with Jesus, and call Him to account for all that He exacted of His disciples, for a young man in their party had complained to them of Him. This young man was rich and well-educated, and he had long before pushed himself upon Jesus as His disciple. But Jesus had laid down to him several conditions, namely, that he should leave father and mother, distribute his wealth to the poor, etc. He had again, at Caesarea-Philippi, offered himself to Jesus. But he still wanted to retain his fortune and the right to administer it himself, in consequence of which Jesus had again dismissed him. The Pharisees asked Jesus why He imposed such unheard-of conditions upon people. The young man alleged divers things that Jesus had said and called upon the Apostles to witness to his statements, for they too had heard them. The Apostles became embarrassed. They were not prepared for such an attack, and they knew not what to answer. The Pharisees therefore reproached Jesus with fraternizing with the ignorant only, and ascribed His sending away the young man to the fact that the latter was educated. Jesus replied to them in very severe words, and left them to resume His journey.

On leaving the city, Jesus gave instructions to the Apostles and disciples, and sent them to places at a considerable distance east and northeast. They had before them a long and difficult journey to Damascus, to Arabia, and to cities which they had never yet visited. Jesus Himself with two disciples, leaving Lake Phiala on the left, went to Argob, a city built on a height four hours direct from Caesarea. There He put up with the Levites near the synagogue. Argob was for the most part inhabited by Jews. The few pagans in it were poor and worked for them. Cotton goods were manufactured here, women, children, and men being engaged in spinning and weaving. The place suffered from want of water, which had to be carried up to the city in leathern bottles, and then poured into the cisterns. Jesus taught in a public square, healed some of the sick, and visited in their own homes some old and infirm people, whom He cured and consoled. Almost all the inhabitants had been baptized, and there were no Pharisees among them. A very distant view could be commanded from Argob. They could see far over into Upper Galilee, the Mount of Beatitudes rose before them, and the prospect down into Bethsaida-Julias was remarkably beautiful.

Jesus, with His two disciples, and escorted a part of the way by several people of Argob, started again on His journey. He crossed the mountainous district eastward toward Regaba, and halted at a distance of two hours from that city, at an open cabin belonging to the inn. The caravans, which three times a year passed in this direction, often encamped in this place. Jesus was here met by four of His young disciples, who brought with them a supply of provisions. They had come from Jerusalem, taking Capharnaum in their route.

From the inn Jesus went to the citadel, or stronghold of Regaba, where a great multitude—besides many from the caravan—had gathered. The citadel looked as if hewn out of a rock. Around it stood some rows of houses and a synagogue. Six of the Apostles again joined Jesus here. They had been to neighboring places east of Caesarea, the others having gone to greater distances. These six were Peter, Andrew, John, James the Greater, Philip, and James the Less. There were many Pharisees here. The synagogue was so crowded that even the standing room was occupied. Jesus took His text from Jeremias. He said that now they were eager to see and to hear Him, but the time would come when they would all abandon Him, mock and maltreat Him.

The Pharisees began a violent dispute with Jesus, again bringing forward their charge that He drove out the devil through the power of Beelzebub. Jesus called them children of the father of lies, and told them that God no longer desired bloody sacrifices. I heard Him speaking of the Blood of the Lamb, of the innocent blood that they would soon pour out, and of which the blood of animals was only a symbol. With the Sacrifice of the Lamb, He continued, their religious rites would come to an end. All they that believed in the Sacrifice of the Lamb, would be reconciled to God, but they to whom He was addressing Himself should, as the murderers of the Lamb, be condemned. He warned His disciples in presence of the Pharisees to beware of them. This so enraged these men that Jesus and His disciples had to withdraw and hurry off into the desert. I saw among the listening crowd, some men with cudgels. Jesus had never before attacked His aggressors so boldly. He and His disciples passed the night in the desert and then went to Corozain.

Crowds of people flocked thither, and laid their sick along the road by which Jesus was to come. On His way to the synagogue, He cured the dropsical, the lame, and the blind.

In spite of the violent attacks of the Pharisees, Jesus spoke in prophetic terms of His future Passion. He alluded to their repeated sacrifices and expiations, notwithstanding which they still remained full of sins and abomination. Then He spoke of the goat which at the

Feast of Atonement was driven from Jerusalem into the desert with the sins of the people laid upon it. He said very significantly (and yet they did not understand Him) that the time was drawing near when in the same way they would drive out an innocent Man, One that loved them, One that had done everything for them, One that truly bore their sins. They would drive Him out, He said, and murder Him amid the clash of arms. At these words, a great din and jeering shouts arose among the Pharisees. Jesus left the synagogue and went out into the city. The Pharisees came to Him and demanded an explanation of what He had just said, but He replied that they could not now understand it.

While Jesus was being thus pressed upon, a deaf and dumb man was brought to Him that He might cure him. He was a shepherd of that region, good and pious. His friends brought him to Jesus, whom they implored to lay His hand upon him. Thereupon Jesus commanded that he should be separated from the crowd. His friends obeyed, but the Pharisees followed. Jesus therefore cured him in their presence, that they might see that He healed by virtue of prayer and faith in His Heavenly Father, and not through the devil. Jesus put His fingers into the ears of the mute, moistened His fingers with His own saliva and touched the man's tongue with it. Then sighing, He glanced up to Heaven and said: "Be thou open!" At the same instant, the man could both hear and speak perfectly, and full of joy he gave thanks. But Jesus commanded him to refrain from talking or boasting about his cure.

The crowd becoming greater, for a caravan had just arrived, Jesus and His companions left the city and went two or three hours farther on to Matthew's custom house. But as here too the crowd was on the increase, Jesus, leaving a couple of His disciples behind, embarked with the others and rowed to Bethsaida-Julias, where they landed and remained until night in a solitary place at the foot of the Mount of Beatitudes.

Before daylight they left Bethsaida and rowed again to the east side of the lake, where Jesus delivered a discourse on the mountain ridge beyond Matthew's custom house. There were pagans from Decapolis present, also the people belonging to the caravan. Many sick were brought up the mountain on litters and asses, and Jesus healed them.

Jesus taught of prayer, how and where it should be made, and of perseverance in it. He said: "When a child asks for bread, the father does not give it a stone, nor does he give it a serpent when it asks for a fish, or a scorpion instead of an egg." He remarked as an illustration that He knew pagans who had such confidence in God that they never petitioned for anything, but took with thanks all that was given them. "If servants and strangers have such confidence," said Jesus, "what ought not that of the children of the Father to be?" He spoke also of gratitude for restoration to health, which gratitude should be evinced by amendment of life, and of the punishment incurred by a relapse into sin. The spiritual state of those that relapse is always worse than before their cure. By this time the crowd had become so great that Jesus was again forced to withdraw—not, however, before He had announced a great instruction to be delivered on the following day upon another mountain. This last-named mount was east of the Mount of Beatitudes, and to it flocked the multitude from all sides. The whole region around, mountains and valleys, was covered with encampments, and everywhere resounded the question: "Where is Jesus?" Jesus taught upon the seventh and the eighth Beatitudes, after which, to escape the crowd, He went with the Apostles and disciples on board Peter's ship. They rowed down the lake, but did not land, because the people, having secured boats, were following them.

19. CONCLUSION OF THE SERMON
ON THE MOUNT.
FEEDING OF THE FOUR THOUSAND.
THE PHARISEES DEMAND A SIGN

Next morning Jesus and His followers ascended the high mountain one hour to the northeast of Little Corozain, and beyond that, one upon which the first multiplication of the loaves had taken place. It was in the desert to the right of Corozain, two and a half hours west of Regaba, which was on a still higher elevation. Up where Jesus delivered the instruction there was a large level space, not far from the road by which He had lately travelled from Caesarea-Philippi to Regaba. The place was much used as a camping ground for travellers. The ruins of fortifications were found on it, and a long rocky ledge, upon which the travellers used to spread their provisions at meals. Once upon a time this region was a perfect solitude. Below this plateau were little dells and dales, in which the asses and other beasts of burden could graze. A considerable crowd was already assembled on the plateau, while others were still flocking thither from all quarters.

Here it was that Jesus concluded the Eight Beatitudes and delivered the so-called Sermon on the Mount. His words on this occasion were more than ordinarily forcible and impressive. Crowds of strangers and pagans were present, the whole multitude, exclusive of women and children, numbering about four thousand. Toward evening, Jesus paused in His teaching and said to John: "I have compassion on the multitudes, because they continue with Me now three days, and have nothing to eat; but I will not send them away fasting lest they faint in the way." John replied: "We are far in the desert, and to bring bread this distance would be hard. Shall we gather for them the fruits and berries that are still on the trees around here?" Jesus answered by telling him to ask the other Apostles how many loaves they had. The latter answered: "Seven loaves and seven little fishes." The fishes were, however, an arm in length. Upon receiving this answer, Jesus directed that the empty breadbaskets the people had brought with them, along with the loaves and fishes, should be laid upon the rocky ledge; after which He continued to teach a good half-hour. He spoke very plainly of His being the Messiah, of the persecutions that awaited Him, and of His approaching imprisonment. But on that day, He said, those mountains would quake and that rock (here He pointed to the stone ledge) whereon He had announced the truth they had refused to receive, would split asunder. Then He cried woe to Capharnaum, to Corozain, and to many other places of that region. On the day of His arrest they should all become conscious of having rejected salvation. He spoke of the happiness of this region to which He had broken the Bread of Life, but added that the strangers passing through had carried away with them that happiness. The children of the house threw that Bread under the table, while the stranger, the little whelps, as the Syrophenician had called them, gathered up the crumbs, which were sufficient to vivify and enliven whole towns and districts. Jesus then took leave of the people. He implored them once more to do penance and amend their life, repeated His menaces in the most forcible language, and informed them that this was the last time He would teach in those parts. The people wept. They were full of admiration at His words, although they did not comprehend them all.

After that, Jesus commanded them to take their places on the declivity around the mountain, and, as on the preceding occasion, the Apostles and disciples were directed to range them in order. Jesus divided the bread and fish as before, and the disciples carried the portions round in baskets to the people on both sides of the mount. When all was over, seven baskets of scraps were gathered up and distributed to poor travellers.

During Jesus' discourse, a number of Pharisees had been standing among the crowd. Some of them left and went down into the valley before the close, while others remained long enough to hear Jesus' menaces and to witness the multiplication of the bread. Before the people dispersed, however, these latter descended the mountain, in order to confer with the others as to how they should meet Jesus on His coming down. These Pharisees numbered about twenty. Under the pretext of visiting the synagogues, they constantly followed Jesus in little bands, in order to spy His actions. They had been in Caesarea-Philippi, in Nobah, Regaba, and Corozain. By messengers or by word of mouth, they transmitted to Capharnaum and Jerusalem all they saw and heard.

Jesus took leave of the people, who shed tears and lifted up their voices thanking and praising Him. He broke away from them only with difficulty and went to the lake with the disciples, in order to cross over to the southeastern side into the region of Magdala and Dalmanutha. When about to embark just above Matthew's custom office, the Pharisees approached and, at the foot of the mountain upon which the first multiplication of the loaves had taken place, demanded from Him a sign from Heaven. This they did because He had spoken of frightful tremors of the earth and other signs in nature. He replied to them as is recorded in the Gospel. I heard Him mention also a certain number of weeks at the end of which the sign of Jonas would be given them. This number exactly corresponded with His Crucifixion and Resurrection. Jesus then left them standing there, and went with the Apostles to Peter's ship, which the other disciples had in readiness to receive Him. They rowed out into full sea, and then descended the Jordan current, in which the ship needed only to be steered. They passed the night on board, praying at certain hours, and thus reached the confines of Magdala and Dalmanutha.

Next morning, getting out of the current, they rowed back to the west side of the lake, and then remarked that they had only one loaf with them.

The passage was slow, and Jesus instructed His followers on many points. He spoke of His impending captivity, of His Passion, of the persecution He should endure, and said in terms more significant than ever that He was Christ, the Messiah. They believed His words; but although they could not make them square with their simple, human way of comprehending things, and indulged in their customary views, views derived from their own experience, yet they made a note of them, and ranked them among others of a deeply significant and prophetic nature. He spoke also of His going to Jerusalem and of the persecution that would be attendant on the same. They would, He said, be scandalized on His account, and things would go so far that they would cast stones after Him. Jesus said also that whoever would not renounce all his property and his relatives and follow Him faithfully in His time of persecution, could not be His disciple. He spoke likewise of the journeys He still had to make and of the multiplied labors to be accomplished before His arrest. Many, He said, who had abandoned Him would again return. The disciples asked whether that young man who wanted first to bury his father, would return; whether Jesus would not then receive him, for indeed he appeared to them to deserve it. But Jesus laid open to them that youth's disposition, and showed them how he clung to earthly things. I understood on this occasion that the expression "to bury one's father" was figurative, and meant "to put one's affairs in order." It was this that the young man wanted to do. He wanted to put his affairs in order, and obtain a division of the inheritance between himself and his old father, in order to secure his own share before separating from him. When Jesus spoke of the young man's hankering after temporal goods, Peter exclaimed with animation: "Thank God, I have never had such thoughts since I have followed Thee!" But Jesus rebuked him, saying that he should be silent on that point, until asked to speak.

When Jesus and the disciples arrived at Bethsaida, they went to Andrew's to refresh themselves and there remained undisturbed and without the annoyance of a great crowd since, not knowing whither Jesus had retired, the people had dispersed. There was in Bethsaida an aged man blind from his birth, whom Jesus had hitherto refused to cure. Now, however, he was brought to Him again and when Jesus and the disciples were on the point of returning to the ship, the man cried out to Him for help. Jesus took him by the hand, led him outside the city, and there before His Apostles and disciples, touched his eyes with His tongue and with saliva, laid His hands upon them, and asked whether he saw anything. At these words, the man opened his eyes and stared around, saying: "I see people as large as trees walking about." Jesus laid His hand once more on his eyes, and bade him again look around. Now he saw perfectly. Jesus ordered him to go home and thank God, but not to go about the city boasting of his cure.

Toward evening, Jesus and His Apostles rowed to the opposite shore of the lake and, having landed, took the road up the eastern bank of the Jordan to Bethsaida-Julias. On this journey, the Apostles and disciples who had been despatched from Caesarea-Philippi on their mission toward the east, as they were coming down from the mountains, met Jesus and His party, and all set out together for Bethsaida-Julias.

On the way, Jesus spoke of His approaching arrest and of the dangers that menaced; whereupon the Apostles implored Him not to send them away any more, that they might be near Him in case of need.

An inn had been prepared for them in Bethsaida-Julias. As they drew near to the city, where Jesus' coming had already been announced by the people that had gone thither for the Sabbath, some of the inhabitants came out to meet them. They were received graciously and conducted to the inn for refreshments and washing of the feet. A great number of Gentiles dwelt in Bethsaida, and they now saluted Jesus from a distance.

Jesus taught in the synagogue. There were present many Scribes and Pharisees from Saphet, at which place was a school for the study of science, human and divine.

All were greatly rejoiced at the sudden arrival of Jesus, who visited them now for the first time; the generality of the people were sincere in their desire to see Him, but the Scribes were actuated by vanity. They wished to hear the Teacher whose fame was sounded throughout the whole country, especially at Capharnaum, and to judge of His merits. They were perfectly courteous, though like certain professors cold and proud in their bearing. They disputed with Jesus, putting to Him questions out of the Law and the Prophets. Still there was nothing malicious in their intentions. They were moved rather by curiosity, and impelled by vanity to display their learning before the people.

Jesus read and commented upon the Lesson for the Sabbath, and taught upon the Fourth Commandment: "Thou shalt honor thy father and thy mother, that thy days may be long in the land." To the words, "thy days may be long in the land," He gave a most admirable and profound explanation. "That stream must dry up," He said, "which obstructs its own source." The instruction was followed by a festal entertainment, at which the school children assisted at separate tables. During it, Jesus explained the parable of the workmen in the vineyard.

Julias was a modern city, not yet completed. It was very beautiful, constructed upon the pagan style with numerous arches and columns. It lay along the Jordan. On the east, where it was contiguous with the rising heights, the rear of many of the houses was hewn out of the solid rock.

When Jesus, after having taught once more in the synagogue, was walking outside the city, the inhabitants stopped Him to ask about the true doctrine and what they should do. He answered that they would not follow His instructions, even if He gave them to them. They were, He said, inquisitive. They had already in this region heard His doctrine so often. Did they by these questions, ask another? He had even announced it openly in the synagogue. These people led Jesus to some of their newly constructed buildings, and to a place where lay stores of building materials, wood and stone. They spoke to Him of the beautiful new style of architecture. Jesus embraced the opportunity to relate to them the parables of the house built upon the sand, and of the other built upon a rock. He referred to the cornerstone which the builders would reject, and of the overthrow of their building. On the way He healed several sick people, some lame, others dropsical, and a couple of possessed who were, besides, deprived of reason.

From Bethsaida-Julias, Jesus with The Twelve and about thirty disciples went to the country town Sogane, an hour and a half from Caesarea, where He taught and cured. Some of the inhabitants of Bethsaida-Julias escorted Jesus and His party as far as the point where the Jordan flowed into Lake Merom. The people of Sogane came crowding around Jesus, begging for an instruction. He taught and healed until toward evening, and then with His disciples went back about the distance of an hour to a mount, upon which He spent the greater part of the night in prayer.

20. PETER RECEIVES THE KEYS OF THE KINGDOM OF HEAVEN

On the way to the mount and until Jesus retired to pray, the Apostles and disciples that had last returned from their several missions gave their Master a full account of all that had happened to them, all that they had seen and heard and done. He listened to everything and exhorted them to pray and hold themselves in readiness for what He was going to communicate to them.

When before daybreak they again gathered about Jesus, The Twelve stood around Him in a circle. On His right were first, John, then James the Elder, and thirdly, Peter. The disciples stood outside the circle, the oldest of them nearest. Then Jesus, as if resuming the discourse of the preceding night, asked: "Who do men say that I am?" The Apostles and the oldest of the disciples repeated the various conjectures of the people concerning Him, as they had heard here and there in different places; some, for instance, said that He was the Baptist, others Elias, while others again took Him for Jeremias, who had arisen from the dead. They related all that had become known to them on this subject, and then remained in expectation of Jesus' reply. There was a short pause. Jesus was very grave, and they fixed their eyes upon His countenance with some impatience. At last, He said: "And you, for whom do you take Me?" No one felt impelled to answer. Only Peter, full of faith and zeal, taking one step forward into the circle, with hand raised like one solemnly affirming, exclaimed aloud and boldly, as if the voice and tongue of all: "Thou art Christ, the Son of the living God!" Jesus replied with great earnestness, His voice strong and animated: "Blessed art thou, Simon, son of Jona, because flesh and blood hath not revealed this to thee, but My Father who is in Heaven! And I say to thee: Thou art a rock, and upon this rock I will build My

Church, and the gates of Hell shall not prevail against it. And I will give to thee the keys of the Kingdom of Heaven. And whatsoever thou shalt bind upon earth, it shall be bound also in Heaven; and whatsoever thou shalt loose upon earth, it shall be loosed also in Heaven!" Jesus made this response in a manner both solemn and prophetic. He appeared to be shining with light, and was raised some distance above the ground. Peter, in the same spirit in which he had confessed to the Godhead, received Jesus' words in their full signification. He was deeply impressed by them. But the other Apostles appeared troubled. They glanced from Jesus to Peter as the latter exclaimed with such zeal: "Thou art Christ, the Son of God!" Even John allowed his anxiety to become so manifest that Jesus afterward, when walking along the road with him alone, reproved him gravely for his expression of surprise.

Jesus' words to Peter were spoken just at the moment of sunrise. The whole scene was so much the more grave and solemn, since Jesus had for that purpose retired with His disciples into the mountain and commanded them to pray. Peter alone was sensibly impressed by it. The other Apostles did not fully comprehend, and still formed to themselves earthly ideas. They thought that Jesus intended to bestow upon Peter the office of High Priest in His Kingdom, and James told John, as they walked together, that very probably they themselves would receive places next after Peter.

Jesus now told the Apostles in plain terms that He was the promised Messiah. He applied to Himself all the passages to that effect found in the Prophets, and said that they must now go to Jerusalem for the Feast. They then directed their steps southwestwardly and returned to the Jordan bridge.

Peter, still profoundly impressed by Jesus' words relative to the power of the Keys, drew near to Him on the way to ask for information upon some points not clear to him. He was so full of faith and ardor that he fancied his work was to begin right away, for the conditions, namely, the Passion of Christ and the descent of the Holy Ghost, were as yet unknown to him. He asked therefore whether in this or that case also he could absolve from sin, and made some remarks upon publicans and those guilty of open adultery. Jesus set his mind at ease by telling him that he would later on know all things clearly, that they would be very different from what he expected, and that a new Law would be substituted for the old.

As they proceeded on their journey, Jesus began to enlighten His Apostles upon what was in store for them. They should now go to Jerusalem, eat the Paschal lamb with Lazarus, after which they might expect many labors, much weariness and persecution. He mentioned in general terms many circumstances of His future: namely, His raising of one of their best friends from the dead, which fact was to give rise to such fury among His enemies that He would be obliged to flee; and their going again after another year to the Feast, at which time one of them would betray Him. He told them moreover that He would be maltreated, scourged, mocked, and shamefully put to death; that He must die for the sins of men, but that on the third day He would rise again. He told them all this in detail and proved it from the Prophets. His manner was very grave, but full of love. Peter was so distressed at the thought of Jesus' being maltreated and put to death that, following Him, he spoke to Him in private, disputing with Him and exclaiming against such suffering, such treatment. No, he said, that should not be. He would rather die himself than suffer such a thing to happen! "Far be it from Thee, Lord! This shall not be unto Thee!" he exclaimed. But Jesus turned to him gravely and said with warmth: "Go behind Me, Satan! Thou art a scandal unto Me. Thou savorest not the things that are of God, but the things that are of men!" and then walked on. Peter, struck with fear, began to turn over in his mind why it was that Jesus a short time before had said not from flesh and blood but by a revelation from God he (Peter) had declared Him to be the Christ; but now He called him Satan and, because he had protested against His sufferings, He reproached him with speaking not according to God, but according to human desires and considerations. Comparing Jesus' words of praise with those of His reproof, Peter became more humble and looked upon Him with greater faith and admiration. He was nevertheless very much afflicted, since he became thereby only the more convinced of the reality of the sufferings awaiting Jesus.

The Apostles and disciples proceeded in separate bands, each walking with the Lord by turns. He hurried on quickly, stopping nowhere, shunning the towns and villages as much as possible until nightfall, when they put up at the inn near the Baths of Bethulia. Here Lazarus and some of the disciples from Jerusalem were awaiting Jesus' coming.

Lazarus had already been informed that Jesus and His disciples would eat the Paschal lamb with him, and he had come hither to meet Jesus in order to warn Him, the Apostles, and disciples in respect to this Paschal solemnity. He told them that an insurrection threatened during the Feast. Pilate wanted to levy a new tax upon the Temple in order to erect a statue to the Emperor. He desired likewise certain sacrifices in his honor and that certain high titles of reverence should be publicly decreed him. The Jews were on that account ready for revolt, and a large number of Galileans had risen up against Pilate's proceedings. They were headed by a certain Judas, a Gaulonite, who had numerous adherents and who inveighed hotly against the servitude of his people and the Roman imposts. It would be well, Lazarus said, for Jesus to absent Himself from the Feast, as great disturbances might arise. Jesus, however, replied that His time was not yet come, that nothing would happen to Him. This uprising was but the forerunner of a far greater one that would take place the next year when, as He said, His time would have come. Then would the Son of Man be delivered over into the hands of sinners.

Jesus sent His Apostles and disciples on ahead. They were divided into separate bands and were to journey by different routes. Simon and Thaddeus, Nathanael Chased and Judas Barsabas, He kept with Himself. Some were to go down along the Jordan, while others proceeded westward from Garizim through Ephraim, visiting on their way to the Feast some places at which they had not yet been. Lazarus journeyed with the disciples. Jesus commanded them not to go into the Samaritan cities, and gave them several directions as to their conduct. He Himself went as far as Ginnim, to the estate of Lazarus, where He passed the night.

On the following day He went through Lebona, Korea, and the desert to Bethania.

FROM THE SECOND PASCH
TO THE RETURN
FROM CYPRUS

1. JESUS IN BETHANIA AND JERUSALEM

About three hours from Bethania, but still in the desert, stood a solitary shepherd hut whose occupants depended for the most part on the charity of Lazarus. To this abode, Magdalen with a single companion, Mary Salome, a relative of Joseph, had come to meet Jesus. She had prepared for Him some refreshments. On His approach, she hurried out and embraced His feet. Jesus rested here only a short time and then set out for Lazarus's inn, one hour from Bethania. The two women returned home by another way. Jesus found some of the disciples whom He had sent on their mission already returned and at the inn; others came later, and in Bethania all met again. Jesus did not go through Bethania, but entered Lazarus's dwelling from the rear. On His arrival, all hurried out into the court to meet Him. Lazarus washed His feet, and then they passed up through the gardens. The women saluted Jesus with their veils lowered. A very touching incident attended Jesus' arrival. The four lambs destined for the Paschal solemnity were brought in at the same moment that Jesus entered. They had been separated from the flock, and turned into a little grassy park. The Blessed Virgin, who also was here, and Magdalen had twined little wreaths which were to be hung around their necks. Jesus' coming was just before the commencement of the Sabbath, and He celebrated it with the family in a hall. He was very grave. He read the lesson for the Sabbath, and gave an instruction upon it. During the evening meal, He spoke of the Paschal lamb and of His future Passion.

The insurrection broke out in Jerusalem shortly before the Sabbath began, but yet without violence. Pilate, surrounded by a bodyguard, occupied an elevated position on a wall of the fortress Antonia, and all the people were gathered in the marketplace below. The fortress Antonia was built on a projecting rock at the northwest corner of the Temple. If on leaving Pilate's palace, one turned to the left and went through the arch past the place of flagellation, the fortress would lie on his left. Pilate's new laws, by which a tax was laid upon the Temple, were read to the people. First, the tax was to be used for making an aqueduct to conduct water to the grand marketplace and to the Temple; and secondly, there was question of certain honors, titles, and sacrifices to be offered to the Emperor. Immediately a great tumult arose. Loud cries and mutterings proceeded from the crowd, especially from the quarter occupied by the Galileans. Still the commotion did not reach violence. Pilate addressed some warning words to the people, and gave them time to reflect; whereupon, indignant and murmuring, they dispersed. The Herodians were in secret the prime movers and instigators of the people, yet no one could convict them of such dealings. They kept Judas Gaulonite under their thumb, and he had a whole sect of Galileans as his followers, to whom he constantly inveighed against paying tribute to the Emperor, and stirred up their thirst for liberty under the pretext of zeal for religion. The Herodians were exactly like the Freemasons and other secret societies of our own day. They stirred up the unthinking multitude, who knew not whither their zeal was carrying them until they paid the penalty with their blood.

On the Sabbath Jesus taught in Lazarus's, and then all

went to walk in the gardens. Jesus talked of His Passion and said in plain terms that He was the Christ. His words increased His hearers' reverence and admiration for Him, while Magdalen's love and contrition reached their height. She followed Jesus everywhere, sat at His feet, stood and waited for Him everywhere. She thought of Him alone, saw Him alone, knew only her Redeemer and her own sins. Jesus frequently addressed to her words of consolation. She was very greatly changed. Her countenance and bearing were still noble and distinguished, though her beauty was destroyed by her penance and tears. She sat almost always alone in her narrow penance chamber, and at times performed the lowest services for the poor and sick.

That evening there was a grand entertainment. All the friends from Jerusalem, as well as the holy women from the same place, were present at it. I saw too Heli of Hebron, the widower of one of Elizabeth's sisters, who at the Last Supper filled the office to Jesus of steward and master of the house. He had with him his son, the Levite, who now held possession of John's paternal house, and his five daughters, who were Essenians and unmarried.

Lazarus and his family were the familiar and deeply sympathetic friends of Jesus and His disciples. With their property and goods, they became the powerful helpers and supporters of the Community.

Toward ten o'clock next morning, Jesus went with the Apostles and about thirty disciples across the Mount of Olives and through Ophel to the Temple. All wore the ordinary brown woollen tunic common among the Galileans, added to which Jesus had a broad cincture upon which was an inscription in letters. He attracted no attention, since bands of Galileans similarly clad were to be met in all quarters. The Feast was approaching. Large encampments of huts and tents were ranged around the city, and crowds of people were circulating everywhere.

Jesus taught in the Temple for a whole hour in presence of His disciples and a large number of people. There were several teacher's chairs, from all of which instructions were given. All were so busy with preparations for the Feast, and so taken up with the revolt against Pilate, that no priest of the first grade noticed Jesus, but some malicious, insignificant Pharisees approached Him and asked how He dared show Himself there, and how long this thing was to last, adding that they would soon put a stop to His proceedings. Jesus gave them an answer that put them to shame, and continued His discourse undisturbed, after which He returned to Bethania, and retired in the evening to the Mount of Olives.

On this day a great multitude was again assembled on the marketplace before the fortress Antonia, to speak to Pilate. But he already knew all that they had to say, for he had among them his own spies and soldiers in disguise. The Herodians had roused up Judas the Gaulonite and his Galilean followers, who went fearlessly to Pilate and told him that he should refrain from his design of touching the money belonging to the Temple treasury. As many of them made use of very unbridled language, Pilate ordered his guard to attack them unexpectedly, and about fifty of them were taken prisoner. But at once the rest of the mob rushed to the rescue, freed the prisoners, and then dispersed. About five inoffensive Jews and some Roman soldiers were killed during the affray. This affair served only to increase the general discontent. Herod was in Jerusalem at this time.

On the morning of the following day, Jesus again went to the Temple with all His disciples. His presence had now become known, and waiting for Him in the Temple court through which He had to pass were people with their sick. Already on His way thither, a man suffering from dropsy had been brought to Him in a litter as He ascended the mount. Jesus healed him, and at the Temple some others sick and gouty. In consequence of these cures, He was followed by a numerous crowd. As He drew near the Temple, where they were still busy here and there clearing out and putting in order the places destined for the immolation of the lambs next day, Jesus passed the man whom He had cured at the Pool of Bethsaida, and who was here employed as a day laborer. Jesus turned to him and said: "Behold! Thou hast been cured. Sin no more, that something worse may not befall thee!" This man, who was well-known, had been plied with questions as to who had cured him on the Sabbath day. But he did not know Jesus, whom he here saw again for the first time. Now, however, he made it his business to inform the Pharisees as they passed that this Jesus who on the preceding day had wrought so many cures, was the very one that had cured him at the Pool of Bethsaida. Since the cure of this man had caused great excitement and the Pharisees had been very much tried by what they termed a violation of the Sabbath, they now found in it a new cause of complaint against Jesus. They gathered around His chair and again brought forward the old story of His Sabbath-breaking. There was, however, no special disturbance on that day, although they were very greatly enraged.

Jesus taught two hours in the Temple before a large audience. His subject was the Paschal sacrifice. He said that His Heavenly Father desired no bloody sacrifices from them, but rather a penitent heart, and that the Paschal lamb was merely symbolical of an infinitely higher Sacrifice which would soon be fulfilled. Many of His malicious enemies among the Pharisees came forward, railing at Him and disputing against Him. Among other things they asked in scornful words whether the Prophet would do them the honor to eat the Paschal lamb with them. Jesus answered: "The Son of Man is Himself a Sacrifice for your sins!"

That youth who had said that he would first bury his father, and to whom Jesus had responded: "Let the dead bury the dead!" was also in Jerusalem. He had repeated those words of Jesus to the Pharisees. They now reproached Him with them, and asked Him what He meant by them. How could one dead man bury another? Jesus answered by saying that whoever does not follow His teaching, does not do penance, and does not believe in His mission, has no life in him and is consequently dead; that whoever values goods and riches more than his salvation, whoever follows not His teachings and believes not in Him, has in himself not life, but death. Such were the dispositions of this young man. He had wished to come to terms with his aged father concerning his inheritance and put the latter upon a pension; he had clung to the dead inheritance, and consequently he could have no share in the Kingdom of Jesus and eternal life. It was for this reason that Jesus had told him to let the dead bury the dead while he himself turned to life. Jesus continued to teach in this strain, and reproached them severely for their covetousness. But when He warned His disciples against the leaven of the Pharisees and related the parable of the rich man and poor Lazarus, the Pharisees became so exasperated that they raised a great tumult. Jesus was forced to disappear in the crowd and make His escape, otherwise they would have taken Him prisoner.

The four little lambs destined for the four sets who were to eat the Passover at Lazarus's, and which were daily washed at a fountain and adorned with fresh flowers, were taken on the evening of this day to the Temple at Jerusalem. Each had, fastened to the little wreath around its neck, a ticket with the name and sign of the master of the family to which it belonged. After being washed once more, they were turned into a beautiful grassy enclosure on the Temple mount. All the household of Lazarus performed today their purifications. Lazarus himself brought the water to be used in preparing the unleavened bread, and he also went with a servant into the different rooms. The servant carried a light and Lazarus cleaned out the corners a little. It was a ceremonial performance, after which the servant men and maids swept and cleaned thoroughly. They washed and scoured likewise the vessels and other things that were to be used in preparing the unleavened bread. All this was symbolical of the cleaning out of the old leaven. Simon the Pharisee, of Bethania, had already visited Jesus. Not long ago he appeared to be approaching the state of leprosy, but now he looked more healthy. He was a timorous follower of Jesus. The man healed at the Pool of Bethsaida hurried to Bethania and wherever Jesus permitted Himself to be seen. He told all the Pharisees he met that it was by Jesus he had been cured, consequently they determined to take Jesus into custody and make away with Him.

I saw Jesus several times walking with the disciples and other friends on the Mount of Olives, while Mary, Magdalen, and other women promenaded at some distance. I saw the disciples snapping off ears from the ripe cornfields, and here and there eating fruits and berries. Jesus gave the disciples minute instructions on prayer, warned them against hypocrisy in it, and repeated to them many things that He had before said. He likewise admonished them ever to walk by uninterrupted prayer in the presence of God, His own and their Father.

2. THE PASSOVER IN LAZARUS'S HOUSE

The Paschal lamb at this Passover was not slain in the Temple at so early an hour as at the time of Christ's Crucifixion, when the slaughtering began at half-past twelve o'clock, the same hour at which Jesus Himself was slain upon the Cross. That day was a Friday and, on account of the approaching Sabbath, they began earlier. Today, however, they began about three in the afternoon. The trumpets were sounded, all was in readiness, and the people entered the Temple in separate groups. The rapidity and order with which everything was done were certainly admirable. Though the crowd was great, yet no one obstructed his neighbor's way. Everyone had room to come, to slaughter, and to withdraw. The four lambs for Lazarus's household were slaughtered by the four who were to preside at the tables: namely, Lazarus, Heli of Hebron, Judas Barsabas, and Heliacim, the latter a son of Mary Heli and brother of Mary Cleophas. The lambs were fastened to a wooden spit that had a crosspiece, which gave them the appearance of being crucified. They were roasted upright in a bake oven. The entrails, the heart, and the liver were either replaced in the lamb or fastened to the forepart of the head. Bethphage and Bethania were reckoned as part of Jerusalem, consequently the Pasch could be eaten in either place.

In the evening, when the 15th of Nisan began, the Paschal lamb was eaten. All were girded, new sandals on their feet, and each held a staff in his hand. They began by chanting the Psalms: "Blessed be the Lord God of Israel" and "Blessed be the Lord," while with raised hands they approached the table, two by two, and took their place opposite one another. At the table at which Jesus sat with the Apostles, Heli of Hebron presided; Lazarus was at that of his own family and friends; the disciples were at a third, presided over by Heliacim; and Judas Barsabas did the honors at the fourth. Thirty-six disciples here ate the Pasch.

After the prayer, a cup of wine was presented to the master at each table. He blessed it, sipped, and passed it round, after which he washed his hands. On the table were the Paschal lamb, a dish of unleavened bread, a bowl of brown sauce, another of broth, a third filled with little branches of bitter herbs, and a fourth in which the green herbs were arranged close together in an upright position, thus giving them the appearance of actual growth. The master of each table then carved the Paschal lamb and served it round among the guests, who consumed it very rapidly. They cut off pieces from the closely packed herbs, steeped them in the broth, and ate them. The master then broke one of the unleavened loaves and laid a little piece of it under the tablecloth. All was done very quickly and accompanied by prayers and passages from the Scriptures. The guests stood leaning against the seats. The cup went round once more, the master again washed his hands, and laid a little bunch of bitter herbs on a morsel of bread, which he steeped and ate, all the guests following his example.

The Paschal lamb had to be entirely consumed. The bones were scraped clean with ivory knives, then washed and burned. After some more chanting, the guests reclined at table in due form, to eat and drink. All kinds of elegantly prepared dishes now made their appearance, and mirth and joy prevailed. At Lazarus's house all had beautiful plates from which they ate. At Jesus' last Paschal feast, however, the plates consisted of disks of bread upon which were impressed various figures. They lay in the hollow places scooped out around the table.

The women likewise stood during the Paschal meal, and they too were clothed as for a journey. They sang Psalms, but observed no other ceremonies. They did not carve their lamb themselves, but portions were sent to them from another table. In the side halls of the supper room, a great number of poor ate their Paschal lamb. Lazarus defrayed all the expenses of their meal, and gave them presents besides.

During the supper Jesus taught and explained. He delivered an exceedingly beautiful instruction on the vine, on its cultivation, on the extermination of the bad, the planting of better shoots, and the pruning of the same after every new growth. He then turned to the Apostles and disciples and told them that they were the shoots of which He spoke, that the Son of Man was the true Vine, and that they must remain in Him; that when He would be subjected to the wine press they must continue to publish the knowledge of the true Vine, namely, Himself, and plant all the vineyards with the same. The guests did not separate till very late in the night. All were deeply impressed and joyful.

Judas Barsabas was, with the exception of Andrew, the eldest disciple. He was married, and his family lived in the pastoral state in a row of houses between Machmethat and Iscariot. Heliacim also was married, and lived in the pastoral state on the field of Ginnim. He was much older than Jesus. Jesus seldom sent these disciples into this region.

3. THE RICH GLUTTON AND POOR LAZARUS

The Feast began very early in the Temple, which was opened soon after midnight, the whole place ablaze with lamps. The people came before daybreak with their thank-offerings, consisting of all kinds of birds and animals, which were received and inspected by the priests. Besides these, there were offerings of money, stuffs, corn, oil, etc.

When morning dawned, Jesus, the disciples, Lazarus with his household, and the women, went to the Temple where Jesus remained standing with His own party among the crowd. Many Psalms were sung, the musicians played, sacrifices were offered, and a benediction given which all received on their knees. The people entered in bands, the gates were closed behind them, and after they had sacrificed, they left before another band entered, that no confusion might arise. Numbers, especially strangers, went to the benediction given in the synagogues of the city where there were singing and reading of the Law. Toward noon, about eleven o'clock, there was a pause in the reception of offerings. Many of the people had already dispersed. Some went to the kitchens in the women's porch where the flesh of the victims was prepared for eating, which took place in the dining halls, in which whole families were assembled. The holy women had returned earlier to Bethania.

Up to the moment at which the offerings ceased to be received, Jesus had remained standing with His party; but when the corridors were again thrown open, He went to the great teacher's chair which stood in the Temple in the court before the sanctuary. A numerous crowd assembled around Him, among them many Pharisees, also the man who had been cured at the Pool of Bethsaida. For two whole days he had related what he knew of Jesus, frequently making use of the expression that whoever could do such works as He, must be the Son of God. The Pharisees had, it is true, forbidden him to speak, but to no purpose. As on the day before Jesus had taught very boldly in the Temple, the Pharisees feared that He might bring them into still greater disrepute before the people; and as all their colleagues from the country around, gathered here for the Feast, brought forward complaints and lies against Jesus, they determined to seize the first opportunity to take Him prisoner and pass sentence upon Him. When therefore Jesus began to teach, many of them closed around Him, interrupting His discourse with innumerable objections and reproaches. They asked Him why He did not eat the Paschal lamb with them in the Temple, and whether He had today offered a thanksgiving sacrifice. Jesus referred them to the masters of the feast who had discharged that duty for Him. Then they repeated the old charges, that His disciples observed not the customary usages, that they ate with unwashed hands and stole corn and fruit along the roadside, that He was never seen offering sacrifice, that six days were for labor and the seventh for rest, and yet He had healed that man on the Sabbath, and that He was a Sabbath-breaker. Jesus answered their charges in severe words. Of sacrifice, He said again that the Son of Man was Himself a Sacrifice, and that they dishonored the sacrifice by their covetousness and their slanders against their fellow men. God, Jesus went on to say, did not desire burnt offerings, but contrite hearts; their sacrifices would come to an end, but the Sabbath would continue to exist. It would indeed exist, but for man's utility, for man's salvation. The Sabbath was made for man, and not man for the Sabbath.

Then the Pharisees questioned Jesus on the subject of the parable of poor Lazarus which He had recently related. They asked in ridicule how He knew that story so well, how He knew what Lazarus, Abraham, and the rich man had said. Had He been with the rich man in Hell? Was He not ashamed of Himself to impose such things upon the people? Jesus again took up this parable and taught upon it, reproaching them with their avarice, their cruelty to the poor, their self-satisfied observance of empty forms and customs, along with their total want of charity. He applied the history of the rich glutton entirely to themselves. That history is true. The glutton was well-known until his death, which was a frightful one. I saw again that the rich glutton and poor Lazarus really existed and that by their death they had become well-known throughout the country. But they did not live in Jerusalem, where later on their dwellings so-called were pointed out to pilgrims. They died in Jesus' early years, and they were much spoken of in pious families at that time. The city in which they dwelt was called Aram, or Amthar, and lay in the mountains west of the Sea of Galilee. I no longer know the whole history in detail, but

I still remember this much: The rich man was very wealthy. He lived high, held the first position among his fellows, and was a distinguished Pharisee, very strict in the outward observance of the Law; but he was, on the other hand, extremely severe and merciless toward the poor. I saw him harshly reproving the poor of the place who applied to him, as to their chief magistrate, for help and support. There was a poor, wretched man in the place called Lazarus. He was full of misery and covered with ulcers, but at the same time humble and patient. Hungering for bread, he had himself carried to the house of the rich man, in order to plead the cause of the poor so rudely rebuffed. The rich man was reclining at table carousing, but Lazarus was harshly repulsed as one unclean. He lay at the gate begging for only the crumbs that fell from the rich man's table, but no one gave him to eat. The dogs, more merciful, licked his sores, which means that the heathens were more merciful than the Jews. After that Lazarus died a most beautiful and edifying death. The rich man also died, but his death was frightful. A voice was afterward heard proceeding from his tomb, and the whole country was full of the report of it.

Jesus having ended the parable by the relation of hidden truths unknown to the rest of men, the Pharisees ridiculed Him, asking whether He had been with Lazarus in Abraham's bosom to hear all that talk. As the rich glutton had been a very strict, pharisaical observer of customs, it was especially irritating to the Pharisees to have this parable applied to themselves, also because it was therein implied that they did not listen to Moses and the Prophets. Jesus said to them in plain words that whoever would not hear Him, heard not the Prophets, for they spoke of Him; whoever would not hear Him, heard not Moses, for he spoke of Him; and even if the dead arose, they would not believe their testimony of Him. But the dead should indeed arise and witness to Him (this happened the next year and in that same Temple, at the time of Jesus' death), and yet they, the Pharisees, would not believe. They themselves, He continued, should one day arise, and He would judge them. All that He did, His Father did in Him even to the raising of the dead. Jesus spoke also of John and his testimony, of which, however, He had no need, since His own works bore a still more convincing testimony of His mission, and His Father Himself bore witness to it. But they knew not God. They wanted to be saved by the Scriptures, and yet they kept not the Commandments. However, He would not, as He said, bring a charge against them, for Moses, who had written of Him and whom they would not believe, would do that.

Jesus went on teaching many things in the midst of repeated interruptions. At last the Pharisees became so enraged that they set up a shout, pressed against Him, and sent for the guard of the Temple to take Him into custody. At this moment, it suddenly grew dark and, when the uproar was at its height, Jesus looked up to Heaven and said: "Father, render testimony to Thy Son!" Instantly a dark cloud covered the heavens, a loud noise like a thunderclap resounded, and I heard a piercing voice proclaiming through the edifice: "This is My beloved Son in whom I take My delight!" Jesus' enemies were utterly dumbfounded, and gazed upward in terror. But the disciples, who were standing in a semicircle behind Jesus, began to make a move and closed round Him. Thus escorted, He went without further molestation through the now-opening crowd, out by the western side of the Temple, and out of the city by the corner gate near Lazarus's house. They proceeded a little further northward to Rama.

The disciples had not heard the voice, only the thunder, for their hour was not yet come; but several of the most enraged of the Pharisees heard it. When it was again clear, they made no comment upon what had just taken place, but hurried out and sent people to seize Jesus. But He was not to be found, and the Pharisees were then incensed against themselves for being so taken by surprise as to allow Him to escape.

In His instructions of these days both in the Temple and at Bethania to the disciples and the crowd there assembled, Jesus alluded several times to the obligation of following Him and of bearing the cross after Him. "He that will save his life, shall lose it; and he that will lose his life for My sake shall find it. For what doth it profit a man if he gain the whole world, and suffer the loss of his own soul? Whoever shall be ashamed of Me before this adulterous and sinful generation, of him shall the Son of Man be ashamed when He shall come in the glory of His Father, to render to everyone according to his works." Jesus added that there were some among His hearers who would not see death until they should see the Kingdom of God come in all its power. At these words they mocked Him. I cannot say now what Jesus meant by this. The words of the Gospel always sound to me like the mere headings of the principal doctrines, for Jesus' instructions were much more extended. His discourses that often occupied hours may there be read in a couple of minutes.

Stephen was already in communication with the disciples. On the Feast upon which Jesus healed the man of Bethsaida, he became acquainted with John, and after that he went round a great deal with Lazarus. He was very slender, of an amiable disposition, and a scholar in the Holy Law. He was at this time in Bethania with several other disciples from Jerusalem, and heard Jesus' teachings.

4. JESUS IN ATAROTH AND HADAD-RIMMON

From Rama, Jesus went with the disciples to Thanath-Silo near Sichar. As all the Pharisees were away at the Feast in Jerusalem, Jesus was received very joyfully in Thanath. Only the aged and the infirm, the women and little children remained home from the Feast, also the old shepherds with their herds. In Rama and Thanath I saw the people going processionally through the cornfields, cutting off bunches of grain, and carrying them on a pole into their homes and synagogues. Here and there on the fields and likewise in Thanath-Silo, where He stayed overnight, Jesus taught and made allusion to His approaching end. He called all to Himself to seek consolation, and spoke of the sacrifice most pleasing to God, namely, a contrite heart.

From Thanath-Silo Jesus went to Ataroth, north of the mountain near Meroz, where the Pharisees once brought Him a dead man to be healed. The place was about four hours north of Thanath-Silo. Jesus arrived at Ataroth toward evening. He taught on a hill outside the city, to which a crowd of the aged and the sick, of women and children, followed Him. All the sick, and others that were afraid before the Pharisees, now made their appearance imploring help and consolation. The Pharisees and Sadducees of Ataroth were so exasperated against Jesus that once, when they heard that He was in their neighborhood, they caused the gates of the city to be closed. Jesus taught in very severe terms, though at the same time very lovingly, and warned the poor people against the wickedness of the Pharisees. He continued to speak in plain terms of His mission, of His Heavenly Father, of the persecution that would soon overtake Him, of the resurrection of the dead, of the judgment, and of following Him. He cured many sick: lame, blind, dropsical, sick children, and women afflicted with an issue of blood.

The disciples had prepared for their Master an inn outside Ataroth near a simple-hearted schoolteacher, an aged man, who dwelt there among the gardens. Jesus and His disciples washed their feet, took some refreshments, and repaired to the synagogue in Ataroth to celebrate the Sabbath. There were assembled many who had come hither from the country around, as well as all those that had been cured. An aged Pharisee, a cripple, who had not gone to Jerusalem, presided over the synagogue. He put on great airs, though to the people he was rather an object of ridicule. The Scripture lessons of the day consisted of passages referring to legal impurity contracted by childbirth, to leprosy, to Eliseus's multiplication of the bread of the first fruits and the new corn, and to Naaman's cure.[1]

Jesus had been teaching a long time when He turned to where the women were standing, and called to Him a poor, crippled widow. Her daughters had conducted her into the synagogue and put her into the place she usually occupied. It never entered her mind to ask for help, although she had been sick eighteen years. She was crippled at the waist. When she walked, the upper part of her person was so bent toward the earth that she could almost have walked on her hands. Jesus addressed her as her daughters were leading her to Him: "Woman, be freed from thy infirmity!" and He laid His hand on her back. She rose up straight as a candle, and began to praise God: "Blessed be the Lord God of Israel!" Then she cast herself at Jesus' feet, and all present praised God.

But the deformed old rogue was angry that such a miracle had taken place in Ataroth during the time of his sway. Not daring to expose himself to what might follow from a direct attack upon Jesus, he turned to the people and, with an air of great authority, began to find fault and say: "There are six days upon which we may labor.

Come upon them and be healed, but not upon the Sabbath day!" Jesus responded: "Thou hypocrite! Does not every one of you loose his ox or his ass from the manger on the Sabbath day, and lead it to water? And shall not this woman, a daughter of Abraham, be loosed from the bond in which for eighteen years Satan has bound her?" The crippled Pharisee and his adherents were confounded, while the people praised God and rejoiced at the miracles.

It was truly affecting to behold the daughters and some lads belonging to her family expressing their joy around the cured woman. Yes, all the inhabitants rejoiced, for she was wealthy, beloved and esteemed in the city. It was laughable, though at the same time pitiable, to see the crippled Pharisee, instead of craving relief for himself, raging over the cure of the pious deformed woman. Jesus went on with His instruction upon the Sabbath, and spoke in as severe terms as He had used in the Temple on the occasion of their reproaching Him with the cure of the man at the Pool of Bethsaida. He stayed overnight with the schoolmaster outside of Ataroth, and next day visited the house of the cured woman, who fed numbers of the poor and gave large alms. After that He closed the Sabbath services in the synagogue, and went forward a couple of hours to an inn near Ginnim.

On the following day He and the disciples journeyed about eight hours northward through the vale of Esdrelon and across the brook Cison to Hadad-Rimmon, leaving Endor, Jezrael, and Naim on the right. Rimmon lay, at most, one hour east of Mageddo, not far from Jezrael and Naim, about three hours west of Thabor, and to the southwest about the same distance from Nazareth. It was quite an important and populous city, for a highway both military and commercial ran through it from Tiberias to the seacoast. Jesus put up at an inn outside the city. He taught all along the way and, here and there, cured shepherds and other poor sick. The subject of these instructions was the love of the neighbor. He commanded His hearers to love the Samaritans and all men. He likewise explained the parable of the compassionate Samaritan.

In Hadad-Rimmon Jesus taught chiefly upon the resurrection of the dead and judgment. He healed the sick. A great concourse of people came to His instructions. They had been in Jerusalem, but had reached it only the day after Jesus had left. The Apostles and disciples taught in the surrounding places.

The day after Jesus' departure from Jerusalem, Pilate had forbidden the Galilean zealots to leave the city under pain of death, although they were anxious to do so. Many of them had been arrested as hostages. Shortly after, Pilate set the latter at liberty and gave all of them permission to make their offerings at the Temple and leave the city. He himself toward noon made preparations for his own departure to Caesarea. The Galileans under arrest were no less surprised than delighted at their restoration to freedom. They hurried to the Temple to offer their propitiatory sacrifice, as they had incurred guilt and had not yet offered sacrifice for the same.

It was customary on this day to bring all kinds of gifts to the Temple. Many purchased an animal and brought it to be sacrificed, while others (and these were the most numerous) sold such objects as they could do without and put the proceeds into the box destined for such offerings. The wealthy supplied their poorer neighbors with the means to make their offerings. I saw three different boxes for this purpose, and by each of them instructions were being given, while some of the worshippers were busy with their devotions. Others were out in the place of slaughter with their animals for sacrifice. The Temple was tolerably crowded, yet not to overflowing. I saw in different places little groups of Israelites bowed down in adoration, or standing upright, or prostrate on the ground, their heads enveloped in prayer mantles.

Judas the Gaulonite was standing near one of the alms boxes surrounded by his followers, the Galileans whom Pilate had imprisoned and afterward released. Some of them were mere dupes, others crafty tools of the Herodians. Many of them were from Gaulon, but a still greater number were from Thirza, its environs, and other places infested by Herodians. Now when these people had made the offerings of money and were lost in their devotions, turning neither to the right nor to the left, I saw about ten men stealing upon them from all sides. As they approached, they drew forth from under their mantles three-edged swords about an ell in length, with which they stabbed the nearest of the adorers. Then arose a frightful cry. The defenseless people fled confusedly in all directions, pursued by those that I had seen kneeling and enveloped in their mantles. They were Romans in disguise, and they struck down and stabbed all whom they met. Many of them pressed forward to the alms boxes, and tore out the bags of money; still they did not take all, a good part remained therein. The tumult was so great that a considerable amount of money was thrown about the Temple. The Romans then hurried to the place of slaughter, and stabbed the Galileans there. I saw these Roman soldiers issuing from all corners of the edifice, even jumping in and out of the windows. As when the cry of murder was raised, all that were in the Temple ran in confusion to make their escape, many harmless people belonging to Jerusalem were killed in the tumult, as well as some of the poor people that sold eatables in the forecourt and the recesses of the walls. I saw some Galileans in a dark passage trying to save themselves. They had overpowered some of the Roman soldiers and wrested from them their arms. And now came Judas the Gaulonite into the same passage from the opposite entrance. He too was attempting to make his escape. The other Galileans took him for a Roman and pierced him with their weapons, in spite of his cries that he was Judas, for the confusion was so great, owing to the similarity of clothing between the murderers and their victims, that they indiscriminately attacked everyone they met. The massacre lasted about an hour. The inhabitants, armed with weapons, now began to crowd to the Temple, whereupon the Roman soldiers hurriedly withdrew and shut themselves up in the fortress of Antonia. Pilate had already gone away, the garrison had taken possession of all points in the city capable of being defended, and all avenues of communication were seized and cut off.

I looked down the dizzy height on one side of the Temple into the narrow streets below, and there I beheld frantic women and children running from house to house. They had just received the news of the murder of husbands and fathers, for many of the poor people that dwelt in the neighborhood of the Temple, hucksters and day laborers, had been slain in the mêlée. The confusion in the Temple was frightful, and the people rushed out by every loophole. Elders and superintendents, armed men and Pharisees—all came pouring out. Around were corpses, blood, and scattered coins, while the wounded and dying lay on the ground groaning and weltering in their blood. Soon appeared upon the scene the relatives of those belonging to Jerusalem that had been accidentally murdered, and lamentations, cries of indignation, rage, and anguish arose on all sides. The Pharisees and High Priests were terrified, for the Temple had been frightfully profaned. The priests dared not enter for fear of defilement from contamination with the dead. The Feast was consequently interrupted.

I saw the corpses of the massacred Jerusalemites enveloped in winding-sheets, laid on biers, and borne away by their weeping relatives; those of the others were removed by inferior slaves. Everything else—cattle, eatables, movables of all kinds—had to be left lying in the Temple, because all was now unclean. Everyone retired, excepting the guards and the workmen. The victims counted more in number than those of the overthrow of the building at the construction of the aqueduct. With the exception of the innocent people of Jerusalem, the massacred were, for the most part, adherents of Judas the Gaulonite, who had declaimed so zealously against the imperial tax and the contribution for the aqueduct levied, contrary to the privileges of the Temple, upon the money offered in sacrifice. It was these people who had so boldly inveighed against Pilate's proposals, and who had also slain some Roman soldiers in the fray that had then taken place. Pilate, in attacking them unarmed, avenged the death of his soldiers, as well as wreaked his vengeance upon Herod for the latter's malicious overthrow of the tower. There were among the victims many from Tiberias, Gaulon, Upper Galilee, and Caesarea-Philippi.

1. *Lev.* 12-14; *4 Kgs.* 4:42-5:19.

5. THE TRANSFIGURATION ON MOUNT THABOR.

From the inn near Hadad-Rimmon, Jesus went with some of the disciples eastward to Kisloth Thabor which lay at the foot of Thabor toward the south, about three hours from Rimmon. On the way thither He was joined, from time to time, by the disciples that were returning from their mission. At Kisloth another great multitude of travellers who had come from Jerusalem again gathered around Him. He taught, and then healed the sick. In the afternoon He sent the disciples right and left around the mountain, to teach and to cure. Taking with Him Peter, John, and James the Greater, He proceeded up the mountain by a footpath. They spent nearly two hours in ascent, for Jesus paused frequently at the different caves and places made memorable by the sojourn of the Prophets. There He explained to them manifold mysteries and united with them in prayer. They had no provisions, for Jesus had forbidden them to bring any, saying that they should be satiated to overflowing. The view from the summit of the mountain extended far and wide. On it was a large open place surrounded by a wall and shade trees. The ground was covered with aromatic herbs and sweet-scented flowers. Hidden in a rock was a reservoir, which upon the turning of a spigot poured forth water sparkling and very cold. The Apostles washed Jesus' feet and then their own, and refreshed themselves. Then Jesus withdrew with them into a deep grotto behind a rock which formed, as it were, a door to the cave. It was like the grotto on the Mount of Olives, to which Jesus so often retired to pray, and from it a descent led down into a vault.

Jesus here continued His instructions. He spoke of kneeling to pray, and told them that they should henceforth pray earnestly with hands raised on high. He taught them also the *Our Father,* interspersing the several petitions with verses from the Psalms; and these they recited half-kneeling, half-sitting around Him in a semicircle. Jesus knelt opposite to them, leaning on a projecting rock, and from time to time interrupted the prayer with instructions wonderfully profound and sweet upon the mysteries of Creation and Redemption. His words were extraordinarily loving, like those of one inspired, and the disciples were wholly inebriated by them. In the beginning of His instruction, He had said that He would show them who He was, they should behold Him glorified, that they might not waver in faith when His enemies would mock and maltreat Him, when they should behold Him in death shorn of all glory.

The sun had set and it was dark, but the Apostles had not remarked the fact, so entrancing were Jesus' words and bearing. He became brighter and brighter, and apparitions of angelic spirits hovered around Him. Peter saw them, for he interrupted Jesus with the question: "Master, what does this mean?" Jesus answered: "They serve Me!" Peter, quite out of himself, stretched forth his hands, exclaiming: "Master, are we not here? We will serve Thee in all things!" Jesus began again His instructions, and along with the angelic apparitions flowed alternate streams of delicious perfumes, of celestial delights and contentment over the Apostles. Jesus meantime continued to shine with ever-increasing splendor, until He became as if transparent. The circle around them was so lighted up in the darkness of night that each little plant could be distinguished on the green sod as if in clear daylight. The three Apostles were so penetrated, so ravished that, when the light reached a certain degree, they covered their heads, prostrated on the ground, and there remained lying.

It was about twelve o'clock at night when I beheld this glory at its height. I saw a shining pathway reaching from Heaven to earth, and on it angelic spirits of different choirs, all in constant movement. Some were small, but of perfect form; others were merely faces peeping forth from the glancing light; some were in priestly garb, while others looked like warriors. Each had some special characteristic different from that of the others, and from each radiated some special refreshment, strength, delight, and light. They were in constant action, constant movement.

The Apostles lay, ravished in ecstasy rather than in sleep, prostrate on their faces. Then I saw three shining figures approaching Jesus in the light. Their coming appeared perfectly natural. It was like that of one who steps from the darkness of night into a place brilliantly illuminated. Two of them appeared in a more definite form, a form more like the corporeal. They addressed Jesus and conversed with Him. They were Moses and Elias. The third apparition spoke no word. It was more ethereal, more spiritual. That was Malachias.

I heard Moses and Elias greet Jesus, and I heard Him speaking to them of His Passion and of Redemption. Their being together appeared perfectly simple and natural. Moses and Elias did not look aged nor decrepit as when they left the earth. They were, on the contrary, in the bloom of youth. Moses—taller, graver, and more majestic than Elias—had on his forehead something like two projecting bumps. He was clothed in a long garment. He looked like a resolute man, like one that could govern with strictness, though at the same time he bore the impress of purity, rectitude, and simplicity. He told Jesus how rejoiced he was to see Him who had led himself and his people out of Egypt, and who was now once more about to redeem them. He referred to the numerous types of the Saviour in his own time, and uttered deeply significant words upon the Paschal lamb and the Lamb of God. Elias was quite the opposite of Moses. He appeared to be more refined, more lovable, of a sweeter disposition. But both Elias and Moses were very dissimilar from the apparition of Malachias, for in the former one could trace something human, something earthly in form and countenance; yes, there was even a family likeness between them. Malachias, however, looked quite different. There was in his appearance something supernatural. He looked like an angel, like the personification of strength and repose. He was more tranquil, more spiritual than the others.

Jesus spoke with them of all the sufferings He had endured up to the present, and of all that still awaited Him. He related the history of His Passion in detail, point for point. Elias and Moses frequently expressed their emotion and joy. Their words were full of sympathy and consolation, of reverence for the Saviour, and of the uninterrupted praises of God. They constantly referred to the types of the mysteries of which Jesus was speaking, and praised God for having from all eternity dealt in mercy toward His people. But Malachias kept silence.

The disciples raised their heads, gazed long upon the glory of Jesus, and beheld Moses, Elias, and Malachias. When in describing His Passion Jesus came to His exaltation on the Cross, He extended His arms at the words: "So shall the Son of Man be lifted up!" His face was turned toward the south, He was entirely penetrated with light, and His robe flashed with a bluish white gleam. He, the Prophets, and the three Apostles—all were raised above the earth.

And now the Prophets separated from Jesus, Elias and Moses vanishing toward the east, Malachias westward into the darkness. Then Peter, ravished with joy, exclaimed: "Master, it is good for us to be here! Let us make here three tabernacles: one for Thee, one for Moses, and one for Elias!" Peter meant that they had need of no other Heaven, for where they were was so sweet and blessed. By the tabernacles, he meant places of rest and honor, the dwellings of the saints. He said this in the delirium of his joy, in his state of ecstasy, without knowing what he was saying.

When they had returned to their usual waking state, a cloud of white light descended upon them, like the morning dew floating over the meadows. I saw the heavens open above Jesus and the vision of the Most Holy Trinity, God the Father seated on a throne. He looked like an aged priest, and at His feet were crowds of angels and celestial figures. A stream of light descended upon Jesus, and the Apostles heard above them, like a sweet, gentle sighing, a voice pronouncing the words: "This is My beloved Son in whom I am well pleased. Hear ye Him!"

Fear and trembling fell upon them. Overcome by the sense of their own human weakness and the glory they beheld, they cast themselves face downward on the earth. They trembled in the presence of Jesus, in whose favor they had just heard the testimony of His Heavenly Father.

Jesus went to them, touched them, and said: "Arise, and fear not!" They arose, and beheld Jesus alone. It was now approaching three in the morning. The gray dawn was glimmering in the heavens and the damp vapors were hanging over the country around the foot of the mountain. The Apostles were silent and intimidated. Jesus told them that He had allowed them to behold the Transfiguration of the Son of Man in order to strengthen their faith, that they might not waver when they saw Him delivered for the sins of the world into the hands of evildoers, that they might not be scandalized when they witnessed His humiliation, and that they might at that time strengthen their weaker brethren. He again alluded to the faith of Peter who, enlightened by God, had been the first of His followers to penetrate the mystery of His Divinity, and He spoke of the rock upon which He was going to build His Church. Then they united again in prayer, and by the morning light descended the northwestern side of the mountain.

While going down, Jesus talked of what had taken place, and impressed upon the disciples that they should tell no one of the vision they had seen, until the Son of Man should have risen from the dead. This command struck them. They became more timid in Jesus' presence, more reverential, and since the words: "Hear ye Him!" they thought with sorrow and anguish upon their past doubts and want of faith. But as daylight advanced and they continued their descent, the wonderful impression they had received began to wear off, and they imparted to one another their surprise at the expression: "Until the

Son of Man is risen from the dead." "What does that
mean?" they asked one another, though they did not venture to question Jesus upon it.

They had not yet reached the foot of the mountain
when Jesus was met by people coming to seek Him with
their sick. He healed and consoled. But the people were
struck with awe at the sight of Him, for there was something unusual, something supernatural and glorious in
His appearance. A little lower down the mount He found
assembled a crowd of people, the disciples whom He had
sent out into the environs the day before, and several
Doctors of the Law. These people were returning home
from the Feast. They had met the disciples at their encampment and accompanied them thither, to wait for
Jesus. Jesus saw that they and the disciples were having
some kind of dispute. When they perceived Jesus, they
ran forward to meet and salute Him, but they were
amazed at His extraordinary appearance, for the rays of
His glorification were still around Him. The disciples
guessed from the manner of the three Apostles, who
followed Jesus more gravely, more timidly than usual,
that something wonderful must have happened to Him.
When now Jesus inquired into the subject of dispute, a
man from Amthar—a city on the Galilean mountain
chain, the scene of the history of Lazarus and the rich
glutton—stepped forth from the crowd, threw himself on
his knees before Jesus, and implored Him to help his
only son. The boy was a lunatic and possessed of a dumb
devil, who hurled him sometimes into fire, sometimes
into water, and laid hold of him so roughly that he cried
out with pain. The father had taken him to the disciples
when they were in Amthar, but they had not been able to
help him, and this was now the subject of dispute between them and the Doctors of the Law. Jesus addressed
them: "O unbelieving and perverse generation, how long
shall I be with you? How long shall I suffer you?" and

He commanded the father to bring the boy to Him. The father now led the boy up by the hand. During the journey he had been obliged to carry him like a sheep flung round his neck. The child may have been between nine and ten years old. As soon as he saw Jesus, he began to tear himself frightfully, and the demon cast him to the earth, where he writhed in fearful contortions, foam pouring from his mouth. Jesus ordered him to be quiet, and he lay still. Then He asked the father how long the boy had suffered in this way. He answered: "From early childhood. Ah, if Thou canst, help us! Have mercy on us!" Jesus responded: "If Thou canst believe, for all things are possible to him that believes!" And the father, weeping, exclaimed: "Lord, I do believe! Help Thou my unbelief!"

At these words uttered in a loud voice, the people, who had remained timidly standing at a distance, approached. Jesus raised His hand in a threatening manner toward the boy and said: "Thou dumb and impure spirit, I command thee to go out of him and never again to return into him!" The spirit cried out frightfully through the boy's mouth, convulsed him violently, and went out, leaving him pale and motionless like one dead. They tried in vain to restore consciousness, and many from among the crowd called out: "He is dead! He is really dead!" But Jesus took him by the hand, raised him up well and joyous, and restored him to his father with some words of admonition. The latter thanked Jesus with tears and canticles of praise, and all the lookers-on blessed the majesty of God. This scene took place about a quarter of an hour eastward of that little place near Thabor where Jesus, the year before, had healed the leprous property holder, the one that had sent his little servant boy after Him.

Jesus then proceeded on His way with the disciples. They passed near Cana, crossed the valley of the Baths of Bethulia, and reached the little town of Dothain, three hours from Capharnaum. They took mostly the byways, in order to escape the multitudes returning in troops from Jerusalem. Jesus and His disciples went in bands. Jesus walked sometimes alone, sometimes with this or that band. The Apostles who had been witnesses of His Transfiguration approached their Master on the way, and questioned Him upon the words: "Until the Son of Man is risen from the dead," which were still for them a subject of reflection and discussion. They argued: "The Scribes indeed say that Elias must come again before the Resurrection." Jesus responded: "Elias indeed shall come and restore all things. But I say to you that Elias is already come, and they knew him not but have done unto him whatsoever they had a mind, as it was written of him. So also the Son of Man shall suffer from them." Jesus said several other things, and the Apostles understood that He was speaking of John the Baptist.

When all the disciples were again reunited around Jesus in the inn at Dothain, they asked Him why it was not in their power to free the lunatic boy from the demon. Jesus answered: "Because of your unbelief. For, amen I say to you, if you have faith as a grain of mustard seed, you shall say to this mountain, 'Remove from hence hither,' and it shall remove, and nothing shall be impossible to you. But this kind is not cast out but by prayer and fasting." Then He instructed them upon what was necessary to overcome the demon's resistance. Faith gives to action life and power, while at the same time it derives its own strength from fasting and prayer. He who fasts and prays deprives the demon that he wishes to cast out of his power, which power the exorciser attracts, as it were, into himself.

6. JESUS IN CAPHARNAUM AND ITS ENVIRONS

Jesus went from Dothain by a direct route to Capharnaum, where the feast of the homecoming was solemnly
celebrated. Jesus and the disciples were invited to an entertainment in which some Pharisees also took part.
When about to take their places at table, the disciple
Manahem from Korea presented himself before Jesus,
and with him a young man of good education from
Jericho. Jesus had already rejected the latter, but he
again requested to be received among the disciples. He
had applied to Manahem, because he knew him. He had
large possessions in Samaria, which Jesus had told him
some time before to renounce. Having arranged his
affairs and divided his property among his relatives, he
now returned a second time to Jesus. He had, however,
reserved one estate for his own support, about which he
was extremely solicitous. It was for this reason that Jesus
refused his request, and he went away displeased. The
Pharisees were scandalized, for they were in favor of the
young man. They reproached Jesus, saying that He was
destitute of charity; that He talked of the insupportable
burdens imposed by the Pharisees, and yet He Himself
laid on others burdens equally insupportable. This young
man, they continued, was educated, but Jesus favored
only the ignorant. He refused men the necessaries of life,
and yet sanctioned the violation of long-established
customs. Once again they brought forward their old
charges, Sabbath-breaking, the plucking of corn, the
neglect of hand-washing, etc., but Jesus confounded
them.

While Jesus was staying in Peter's house, some people
from Capharnaum said to Peter outside: "Does not your
Master pay the tribute, the two didrachmas?" Peter
answered: "Yes." And when he went into the house,
Jesus said to him: "What is thy opinion, Simon? The

kings of the earth, of whom do they receive tribute or custom? Of their own children, or of strangers?" Peter answered: "Of strangers" and Jesus replied: "Then the children are free! But that we may not scandalize them, go to the sea and cast in a hook; and that fish which shall first come up, take; and when thou hast opened its mouth, thou shalt find a stater. Take that and give it to them for Me and thee!" Peter went in simple faith to his fishery, let down one of the hooks kept there always ready for use, and with it drew up a very large fish. He felt in its mouth, and found an oblong yellowish coin, with which he paid the tribute for Jesus and himself. The fish was so large that it gave the whole company a plentiful dinner.

After that Jesus asked the disciples upon what subject they had been conversing on the way from Dothain to Capharnaum. They were silent, for they had been questioning who would be the greatest among them. Jesus, however, knew their thoughts, and He said: "Let him that will be the first among you, become the last, the servant of all!"

After dinner Jesus, The Twelve, and the disciples went into Capharnaum where a feast was being celebrated in honor of those that had returned from Jerusalem. The streets and houses were adorned with flowers and garlands. Children and old men, women and scholars, went forth to meet the returned travellers, who marched in crowds through the streets like a procession, and visited the houses of their friends and principal personages of the city. The Pharisees and many others from time to time joined Jesus and the disciples and went around with them.

Jesus visted the homes of the poor and many of His friends, and they presented to Him the children, whom He blessed and to whom He made little presents. On the marketplace, on one side of which stood the old, on the other the new synagogue built by Cornelius, were houses with porticos in front. Here the school children and mothers with their little ones were assembled to salute Jesus. Jesus had been teaching in different places all along the way, and here He blessed and taught the children. He had little tunics distributed among them, the same to the rich as to the poor. They had been prepared by the stewardesses of the Community and brought hither by the holy women of Jerusalem. The children received also fruit, writing tablets, and other gifts. The disciples having asked again who would be the greatest in the Kingdom of Heaven, Jesus called to Him a wealthy lady, the wife of a merchant, who was standing with her four-year-old boy at the door of her house close by. She drew her veil and stepped forward with her boy. Jesus took him from her, and she at once went back. Then Jesus embraced the boy, stood him before Him in the midst of the disciples and the crowds of children standing around, and said: "Whoever becomes not like the children, shall not enter the Kingdom of Heaven! Whoever receives a child in My name, receives Me, yes, rather receives Him that sent Me. And whoever humbleth himself like this little child, he is the greatest in the Kingdom of Heaven."

John interrupted Jesus when He spoke of receiving in His name. The disciples had checked a certain man who, although not among their number, had nevertheless expelled the devil in Jesus' name. Jesus reproved them for so doing and continued His instruction for awhile longer. Then He blessed the boy, who was very lovely, gave him some fruit and a little tunic, beckoned to the mother, and restored her child to her with some prophetic words concerning his future, which were understood only at a later period. The child became a disciple of the Apostles and was named Ignatius. He was afterward a bishop and martyr.

During the whole procession and the teaching of Jesus, a veiled lady had followed in the crowd. She seemed to be out of herself with emotion and joy. With clasped hands she frequently uttered the words half aloud, so that the women standing near her were deeply touched and moved to devotion: "Blessed the womb that bore Thee! Blessed the breasts that gave Thee suck! But far more blessed are they that hear the Word of God and keep it!" She spoke these words with abundant tears and a touching movement of the hands. They came from her inmost heart at every pause that Jesus made, at every striking expression that fell from His lips, and this with extraordinary emotion, love, and admiration. She took an inexpressibly childlike, absorbing interest in the life, the career, the teachings so full of love of the Redeemer. It was Lea, the wife of a malicious Pharisee belonging to Caesarea-Philippi, and sister of the deceased husband of Enue, the woman (also of Caesarea-Philippi) who had been cured of the issue of blood. She it was who, on a former occasion, had exclaimed at one of Jesus' instructions: "Blessed is the womb," etc., and to whom Jesus had replied: "But still more blessed are they that hear the Word of God and keep it!" Since then she had coupled Jesus' response with her own words of admiration. They were constantly on her lips, and had become for her a prayer of love and devotion. She had come hither to visit the holy women, and had made many rich gifts to the Community.

Jesus continued to instruct at the marketplace until the Sabbath began, when He repaired to the synagogue to teach. The Sabbath Lesson was upon the purification of the leprous, and the famine of Samaria that ceased so suddenly according to the prophetic words of Eliseus.

Jesus, the Apostles, and some of the disciples went next to Bethsaida, whither came also many of the other disciples, some from missions, some from their homes. Most of them came from the opposite side of the lake, from Decapolis and Gerasa. They were very much fatigued, and stood in great need of care and attention. They were affectionately received on the shore by their fellow disciples, who embraced them and served them in every way. They were conducted to Andrew's, their feet washed, baths made ready for them, fresh garments supplied, and a meal prepared.

As Jesus was very busily lending a helping hand in their service, Peter entreated Him to desist. "Lord," said he, "art Thou going to serve! Leave that to us." But Jesus replied that He was sent to serve, and that what was done for these disciples was done for His Father. And again His teaching turned upon humility. He that is the least, he that serves all others—he shall be the greatest. But whoever does not serve from a motive of charity, whoever lowers himself to help his neighbor, not in order to comfort a needy brother, but in order to gain distinction at that cost—he is a double-dealer, a server to the eye. He already has his reward, for he serves himself and not his brother. There were on this occasion perhaps seventy disciples present, and there were still some others in and around Jerusalem.

Jesus delivered to the Apostles and disciples a deeply significant and wonderful instruction, in which He said plainly that He was not conceived by man, but by the Holy Ghost. *He spoke with great reverence of His Mother, calling her the purest, the holiest of creatures, a vessel of election, after whom for thousands of years the hearts of the devout had sighed and the tongues of Prophets had prayed.* He explained the testimony of His Heavenly Father at the time of His baptism, but He made no mention of that upon Thabor. He spoke of the present time as happy and holy, since He had come, and declared that the relationship between God and man was once more restored. He referred in most profound words to the Fall of man, his separation from the Heavenly Father, and to the power of Satan and the evil spirits over him. He said that, by His own birth from the purest, the most desired of virgins, the Kingdom and the power of God among men had taken new life, and that by Him and in Him all should again become the children of God. Through Him, both in the order of nature and of grace, was the bond, the bridge between God and man again established, but whoever desired to pass over that bridge must do so with Him and in Him, must leave behind the earthly and the pleasures of this world. He said that the power of the evil spirits over the world and mankind, as well as his share therein, was by Himself brought to naught, and that all the misery arising from that diabolical influence upon nature and mankind could in His name, by interior union with Him through faith and love, be crushed out. Jesus spoke of these things most earnestly and vehemently. The disciples did not comprehend all that He said, and they shuddered when He spoke of His Passion. The three Apostles that had been with Him on Thabor had since then been very grave and meditative.

All this took place during and after the Sabbath. Some of the disciples put up in Capharnaum, some at Peter's outside the city. All expenses were defrayed out of the common stock. It was almost like a Religious Community.

The day after the Sabbath, Jesus went with the disciples northward from Capharnaum toward the mountain from which He had sent them on their first mission. He journeyed about two hours around among the peasants who were cutting corn and among the shepherds, at one time instructing these people, at another the disciples. It was just harvest time.

The corn stood higher than a man. They cut it off at a convenient height, about half an arm long. The ears were longer and thicker than those of our corn and, that the stalks might not sink under their load, the fields were at short intervals provided with hedges of stakes. They had a kind of sickle more like a shepherd's crook than ours.

With the right hand they cut off a handful of stalks, which they held against their breast with the left, and so directed that they fell into their arms. They afterward bound them into little sheaves. It was laborious work, but they performed it very quickly. All that fell to the ground belonged to the poor gleaners who followed in the wake of the reapers.

During the pauses for rest, Jesus instructed the laborers. He questioned them as to how much they sowed, how much they reaped, to whom the corn belonged, what kind was the soil, how they worked it, etc., and around these questions He wove parables relating to sowing, to weeds, to the little grains of wheat, to the judgment, and the consuming of the tares by fire. He taught the disciples also how they should teach, and He gave them another instruction upon teaching. He explained the spiritual signification of the harvest, called them His sowers and reapers, and told them that they must collect the seed-corn for the treasure of a coming harvest, since He would not now be with them long. The disciples became very anxious, and asked if He would not remain with them till Pentecost. Jesus said to them: "What will become of you when I am no longer with you?"

To the shepherds also Jesus introduced His discourse in many ways: "Is this your own flock? Are these sheep of several flocks? How do you guard them? Why do your sheep wander around dispersed?" etc. In this manner He put questions with which He linked His parables of the lost sheep, the good shepherd, etc.

Jesus then went to a valley that lay off toward the west and in a region more elevated than Capharnaum. The mountain of Saphet was on the right. Here He journeyed through valleys and solitary places, teaching now the reapers and shepherds, now the disciples. He enumerated all the duties of a good shepherd and applied them to

Himself, since He was about to give His life for His sheep. He thereby indicated to the disciples how they should treat with such people whom they found in out-of-the-way districts deprived of spiritual assistance, and should sow good seed among them. These journeys of Jesus through solitary places, and His teaching full of peace and love, were deeply touching and impressive.

They returned by a route somewhat more to the northeast and put up at the little city of Lecum, one half-hour from the Jordan, whither the six Apostles had gone on their first mission. Jesus Himself had not yet been there. The inhabitants that had gone to Jerusalem for the Pasch had returned, and there were likewise Scribes and Pharisees in the city. When the disciples visited their acquaintances, the latter related to them the circumstance of the massacre of the Galileans in the Temple, but they made no mention of it to Jesus.

Lecum was a small, well-to-do place, about one half-hour from the Jordan and a couple of hours from the point at which it emptied into the lake. The inhabitants were Jews. Only on the outskirts of the place dwelt a few poor pagans in huts. They had, from time to time, remained behind from the caravans. The raising of cotton formed the chief industry here. They prepared the raw material, and spun and wove covers and various kinds of fabrics. Even the children were thus employed.

The welcome home feast for those that had returned from Jerusalem was being celebrated in Lecum, as it had just been in Capharnaum. The streets were adorned with flowers and garlands of green. Those that had come home visited the houses of their friends, and the schools went out to meet them.

Jesus went into some of the houses to visit the old people, and He cured some sick. On the market square of the place in front of the synagogue, He delivered a long discourse first to the children, whom He caressed and blessed, then to the youths and maidens who, on account of the general festival, were present with their teachers. After they had gone home, He taught successively several groups of men and women, making use of all kinds of similitudes. His subject was marriage, which He treated in very beautiful and deeply significant terms. He began by saying that in human nature much evil is mixed with good, but that by prayer and renunciation the two must be separated and the evil subdued. He who follows his unbridled passions works mischief. Our works follow us and they will at some future day rise up against their author. Our body is an image of the Creator, but Satan aims at destroying that image in us. All that is superfluous brings with it sin and sickness, becomes deformity and abomination. Jesus exhorted His hearers to chastity, moderation, and prayer. Continence, prayer, and discipline have produced holy men and Prophets. Jesus illustrated all this by similitudes referring to the sowing of the grain, to the clearing out of stones and weeds from the field, to its lying fallow, and to the blessing of God upon land justly acquired. In speaking of the married state, He borrowed His similitudes from the planting of the vine and the pruning of the branches. He spoke of noble offspring, of pious families, of improved vineyards, and of races exalted and ennobled. He spoke of the Patriarch Abraham, of his holiness, and the alliance concluded with God in circumcision, and said that his descendants had fallen into disorders by their indulgence of unrestrained passion and their repeated marriages with the heathens. Jesus spoke also of the lord of the vineyard who had sent his son, and He recounted all that had happened to him.

The people were very much moved; many wept and felt impelled to amend their lives. Jesus gave that instruction principally because they had never been taught anything about such mysteries, and also because they lived in a very dissolute way.

Jesus taught also of the essential action of good will in prayer and renunciation, and of man's own cooperation. He said that what they deprived themselves of in food and drink and superfluous comforts, they should place with confidence in the hands of God, imploring Him to allow it to benefit the poor shepherds in the wilderness and others in need. The Father in Heaven would then like a true father of a family hear their prayer, if they like faithful servants shared the abundance He had given them with the poor whom they knew or whom they lovingly sought out. This was real cooperation, and God works with His true servants strong in faith. Here Jesus brought forward the example of a tree (the palm), which by love and desire as it were, but without contact, imparts fertility to its mate.

From Lecum Jesus crossed the Jordan to Bethsaida-Julias, where He taught.

The welcome home feast was being celebrated here likewise. I saw Jesus with the disciples, some of the Scribes and Pharisees, and other distinguished personages of Julias walking about and teaching. Here they told Jesus of the massacre of the Galileans in the Temple. I heard at this time that a hundred persons belonging to Jerusalem and a hundred and fifty of the seditious followers of Judas the Gaulonite had been murdered. These last-named had persuaded many, perhaps forced them by threats, to go with them and offer sacrifice. The hundred Jerusalemites had united with the rebels, although they knew of their unjust determination not to pay the tax to the Emperor, and they were consequently murdered with them.

The country around Julias was extraordinarily charming, fertile, solitary and verdant, full of grazing asses and camels. It was like a zoological garden, the abode of all kinds of birds and animals. Serpentine footpaths wound down to the harbor, and springs were abundant. The noonday sun shone full upon it and flashed on the mirror-like surface of the lake. The highroad to Julias ran nearer to the Jordan, but the country of which I speak was a solitude. Jesus and the disciples recrossed the Jordan and proceeded to Bethsaida and Capharnaum. In the latter place, Jesus taught in the synagogue, for it was the Sabbath. The Scripture assigned for the day were passages from Moses,[1] treating of the annual sacrifice of expiation, of that offered before the tabernacle, of the prohibition to eat the blood of animals, and of the degrees of kindred in which marriage could not be solemnized. Passages were read from Ezechiel, also, upon the sins of the city of Jerusalem.[2]

Jesus and the disciples were invited by one of the Pharisees to dine not far from the dwelling of Cornelius the Centurion. There He found a man afflicted with dropsy, who begged for help. Jesus asked the Pharisees whether it was lawful to heal upon the Sabbath day. They gave Him no answer, so He laid His hand upon the sick man and healed him. As the poor man was retiring with many thanks, Jesus remarked to the Pharisees, as He usually did on such occasions, that not one of them would hesitate to draw out on the Sabbath day his ox or his ass that had fallen into a pit. The Pharisees were scandalized, but they could make no reply.

The Pharisees had invited only their own relatives and friends, and when Jesus perceived that they had taken the best places at table for themselves, He said: "When invited to a wedding, sit not down in the first place, lest perhaps one more honorable than thou be invited also, and the host constrain thee to make room for that one, and thus bring thee to shame. But if one takes the last place and the host says, 'Friend, go up higher,' that brings with it honor. Because everyone that exalteth himself shall be humbled, and he that humbleth himself shall be exalted." Then Jesus addressed the host: "Whoever invites to his feast his relatives, friends, and rich neighbors, who will in turn invite him to theirs, has already received his reward. But whoever invites the poor, the lame, the blind, the infirm, who can make no return to him, he will happily receive his recompense at the Resurrection." To this one of the guests responded: "Yes, blessed indeed will he be that shall sit at the feast in the Kingdom of God!" whereupon Jesus turned to him and related the parable of the great feast.

Jesus had, by means of the disciples, caused many of the poor to be assembled at the Pharisee's. Now He asked the host whether the entertainment had been prepared for Him, and on receiving an answer in the affirmative, He ordered what was left after the guests had finished to be distributed to the poor.

After that Jesus went with the disciples through the Centurion Zorobabel's estate into a beautiful, solitary region between Tiberias and Magdalum. As a numerous crowd followed Him, He took the opportunity to speak of renouncing all things to follow Him. Whoever, He said, wanted to follow Him and be His disciple must love Him more than all his nearest relatives, yes, even more than himself, and must carry his cross after Him. He who wanted to build a tower must first calculate the cost, otherwise he might never finish it, might make himself ridiculous. He who goes to war ought, first of all, to compare the number of his forces with those of his enemy, and if he finds it insufficient, he ought rather to sue for peace. One must renounce all things, in order to become His disciple.

1. *Lev.* 16-19.
2. *Ezech.* 22.

7. JESUS TEACHING ON THE
MOUNTAIN NEAR GABARA

Jesus journeyed on, teaching through the country of Genesareth, and dispatched a large number of the elder disciples to invite the people to an instruction to be given on the mountain beyond Gabara. It was to begin on the following Wednesday and last several days. I heard the day indicated differently, but I knew that the coming Wednesday was meant.

A great many of the disciples rowed across the lake to the country of the Gergeseans, to Dalmanutha, and into the Decapolis. They were commissioned to invite all, for Jesus would not be with them much longer, and they were to bring back as many with them as they could. About forty disciples went on this mission. Jesus kept with Him the Apostles, as well as the disciples that had last returned, all of whom He continued to instruct. He went with them to Tarichaea at the southern extremity of the lake. The journey to Tarichaea could not be made along the lakeshore, for at two hours' distance from that place rose steep cliffs that extended off to the lake. Jesus went around Tarichaea to the west, and crossed over a bridge to a place that seemed to be one of the environs of the city. The bridge spanned the stone dam which extended from Tarichaea to the spot at which the Jordan flowed out of the lake. Near the bridge ran two rows of houses. Before reaching them, Jesus had to pass the abode of the lepers, where He had wrought some cures the preceding year. Being informed of His approach, these cured came out to thank Him, while others, who had come hither since His last visit, now cried to Him for help and He healed them. When arrived at the houses mentioned above, many sick were presented to Him. They had been rowed across the lake from Dalmanutha. Jesus helped them. That dam, along with most of the

houses, was overturned by the earthquake at Jesus' death.
They were abandoned and never rebuilt, since the lakeshore was much changed by the catastrophe. Tiberias
was in reality only half a city, being quite unfinished on
one side.

From all quarters poured immense crowds to the
mountain of Gabara, and ships full of passengers came
over the lake. They brought with them tents and provisions, also sick borne in basket-litters on the backs of
asses. The disciples arranged the multitude, and lent
assistance everywhere.

As Jesus, with the Apostles, was proceeding to Gabara,
He was met by some of the Pharisees, who interrogated
Him as to the meaning of that great movement of the
people, those multitudes hastening to the mountain. The
whole country, they said, was in a state of agitation!
Jesus answered by telling them that they too might, if
they chose, come to hear His discourse next morning,
that He had invited the multitude because He would not
be among them much longer.

The holy women went to the inn at the foot of the mountain in order to provide for the wants of the disciples.

It was toward ten o'clock next day when Jesus appeared upon the mountain. The disciples had put the
people in order and indicated to them how they should in
certain numbers exchange places from time to time, in
order to hear Jesus' discourse, for the multitude was far
greater than could be accommodated within hearing distance of the teacher's chair. The people were under tents,
those from the same district camping together. Each district had its own camp, the entrance to which was
adorned with an arch formed of the fruits peculiar to that
district and surmounted by a crown made of the most
magnificent specimens. Some had grapevines and corn;
others, cotton plants, sugar cane, aromatic herbs, and all
kinds of fruits and berries. Every district had its own dis-

tinctive sign, adorned with flowers and beautifully arranged. The whole produced a very pleasing effect. Numbers of birds, among them pigeons and quails, had taken up their quarters in the camp and were busy picking up the scattered crumbs. They had grown so familiar, so tame, that the people fed them from their hands. A great many Pharisees, Sadducees, and Herodians, Scribes and magistrates of different places were present and had taken possession of the places around Jesus' chair. They had provided themselves with comfortable seats, a kind of stool, or chair, which they had ordered to be brought for their own use.

Jesus collected His disciples close around Him, to the displeasure of the Pharisees who were unwilling to see them preferred to themselves. Jesus began by prayer and calling the people to order. He bade them be attentive, because He was going to teach them what they would not learn from others, but what was at the same time necessary for their salvation. What they could not then comprehend, would be repeated and explained to them later by His disciples whom He would send to them, for He Himself would not be among them much longer. Then loudly and openly He warned the disciples gathered around Him against the Pharisees and false prophets, and instructed the multitude upon prayer and love of the neighbor. The disciples led up the different groups in turn. The Pharisees and others versed in the Law frequently interrupted Jesus with all kinds of contradictory remarks, but He paid no attention to them. He went on with His instruction, speaking very severely against them and warning the people against them until they were greatly incensed. He performed no cures today, but ordered that the weary sick on their beds should be brought up in their turn and placed under awnings near Him, that they too might hear His teaching. He sent word to them to be patient until the close of His instruction. He taught

till evening without intermission, the people taking refreshment by turns. I did not see Jesus eating. He taught
the great multitude so unremittingly that toward evening
His voice became quite shrill and weak. At last, He went
down to the inn on the plain. It had once formed part of
Magdalen's property in Magdalum, and at its sale had
been reserved for the use of the Community.

Lazarus and Martha, Dina and the Suphanite, Maroni
of Naim, Jesus' Mother, and the other Galilean women
were come hither with quantities of provisions, materials
for clothes, and also ready-made clothing. They had prepared a frugal meal for Jesus and the disciples, and all
the rest was distributed to the poor.

Next day Jesus continued His teaching on the mountain. He again spoke of prayer, of the love of the neighbor, of vigilance in good, of confidence in the goodness
of God, and admonished the people not to allow themselves to be confounded by oppressors and calumniators.

The Pharisees today were even more disquieted. They
had gathered in still larger numbers than yesterday, to
dispute with Jesus. They called Him an agitator of the
people, a mischief-maker. They said that He enticed the
people from their labor that they might follow Him
around the country. They had their Sabbath, their
festivals, and their own teaching; there was no need of
His innovations. They repeated for the thousandth time
the old reproaches against Himself and His disciples, and
ended by threatening Him with Herod. They would, they
said, complain to him of Jesus' actions and teaching; he
already had an eye upon Him, and would soon make
short work of His doings. Jesus replied with severity. He
said that He would, undisturbed on Herod's account,
teach and heal until His mission was fulfilled. The
Pharisees were so bold and violent that the people
pressed forward. The confusion became great as they
were pushing and treading on one another's toes, so that

the Pharisees withdrew at last in great disgust.

Jesus nevertheless went on teaching in a very touching and impressive manner. As a great many of those that were on their return journey from Jersusalem, as well as others, had exhausted their provisions, Jesus directed the senior disciples to distribute among them bread, honey, and fish, numerous baskets of which had been brought up from the inn. The holy women had seen to its preparation. Garments, pieces of linen, covers, sandals, and little tunics for the children also were distributed to the needy. The holy women had brought all these things in abundance. They distributed them to the women, and the disciples, to the men.

Meanwhile Jesus continued to instruct the disciples alone, speaking upon the character of the Pharisees and telling them how they should, in the future, comport themselves toward them. After that He descended with them to the inn, where a meal was awaiting them.

During it Lazarus spoke of the massacre of the Galileans in the Temple, of which there was much question among the disciples and the people at large. He told also of the women from Hebron, relatives of the Baptist, and of some from Jerusalem who had gone to Machaerus in search of John's head, as the sewers were being cleared out and the fortress enlarged. Lazarus himself had taken steps in the matter.

Early on the morning of the third day, Lazarus and the holy women returned home, while Jesus and the Apostles went to visit the sick whose huts and tents had been arranged, some in the neighborhood of the inn, and others in the public encampment at the foot of the mount of instruction. They cured all that were there, and did not leave the spot until all were again on their feet. The disciples busied themselves distributing among them what remained of the provisions, clothes, and unmade materials. The cured and their friends filled the air with Psalms

of thanksgiving. At last all took their departure, in order
to reach their homes before the Sabbath.

Jesus next went to Garisima, about one hour to the
north of Sephoris, on a height at the end of the valley.
He sent some of the disciples on ahead to prepare the inn
while He Himself, on account of some sick whom He
wished to visit, took a circuitous route thereto. I saw
Him and His party tarrying awhile in the little place
Capharoth near Jetebatha. The road from Capharnaum
to Jerusalem ran through it. Saul wandered about this
part of the country shortly before his visit to the witch of
Endor and his disastrous battle. It was about five hours
from Capharoth to Garisima, which lay in the midst of
vineyards. It enjoyed the morning and some of the noonday sun, but on the west and north it had nothing but
shade.

The disciples that had been sent on in advance came a
part of the way to meet Jesus, who had an inn just outside the place. They washed one another's feet and, after
partaking of the customary refreshments, Jesus proceeded
to the synagogue, where He taught from Leviticus and
the prophet Ezechiel. He had to endure no contradiction
this time, for His hearers were astonished at His
knowledge of the Law and His wonderful explanations.
The instruction over, He took a repast with His own
followers at the inn. Some of His relatives from the
region of Sephoris were in Garisima, and they ate with
them. Jesus spoke on this occasion of His approaching
end.

Almost a hundred disciples, along with the Apostles,
gathered around Jesus in Garisima for the Sabbath. The
two sons of Cyrinus of Cyprus, who had been baptized at
Dabereth, were also here with other Jews from the same
place. A great multitude of these latter were here encamped. They were returning to Cyprus from the Paschal
festival at Jerusalem and they listened with admiration to

Jesus' teaching on the Sabbath. Jesus' presence was ardently longed for in Cyprus, where there were numbers of Jews, all in a state of spiritual abandonment.

Jesus instructed the disciples in Garisima also, assembling them for this purpose on a hill. Many of them had until now served merely as messengers between the disciples dispersed in various quarters and the friends of Jesus. There were others who had for the most part been detained at home, and who in consequence had missed much of Jesus' teaching, had heard nothing of the way in which they were to conduct themselves on their missions, nor of the application and interpretation of parables. Jesus then, continuing His instruction, explained all things to these disciples in a simple and easy style, and ran quickly through all that He had taught up to the present. After that He went with them from four to six hours northwest from Garisima to the mountains of a very retired region, and there they passed the night. Herds of asses and camels, and flocks of sheep were grazing off in the valleys on the west side of the lofty mountain range that ran through the heart of the country. The valleys here run in a zigzag direction, like the plant known as the common club moss, or wolf's claw. There were a great many palm trees in this wilderness, also a kind of tree whose interlaced branches fell to the earth, and under which one could creep as into a hut. The shepherds of the region used to take shelter under them. Jesus and the disciples spent most of the night in prayer and instruction. Jesus repeated many of the directions He had given when first sending them out upon their earlier missions. I was especially struck on hearing that they were to possess no private purse. That was to be confided to their Superior, one of whom was appointed for every ten. Jesus indicated to them the signs by which they might recognize the places in which they could effect some good, told them to shake the dust from their shoes before those that were ill-disposed, and instructed them as to how they should justify themselves when placed under arrest. They were not to be disturbed as to what they should answer, for words would then be put into their mouth, nor were they to be afraid, since their lives would not be in any danger.

I saw here and there around this region men with long staves and iron hoes. They were guarding the herds against the attacks of wild animals that came up from the seacoast.

Very early the next morning, Jesus sent the disciples and Apostles out on a mission. Upon the latter, as well as upon the eldest disciples, He imposed hands, but the rest He merely blessed. By this ceremony He filled them with new strength and energy. It was not, however, priestly ordination, but only an imparting of grace and vigor to the soul. He addressed to them likewise many words on the value of obedience to Superiors.

Peter and John did not remain with Jesus, but went toward the south, Peter to the country of Joppa, and John more to the east, to Judea. Some went to Upper Galilee, others into the Decapolis. Thomas received his mission to the country of the Gergeseans, whither he went with a troop of disciples, taking a circuitous route to Asach, a city situated on a height between two valleys, about nine hours from Sephoris and one at most to the left from the road. There were a great many Jews in this city, which belonged to the Levites.

Jesus now journeyed in a northwesterly direction. With Him were five Apostles, each of whom had under him ten disciples. I remember having seen on this occasion Judas, James the Less, Thaddeus, Saturnin, Nathanael, Barnabas, Azor, Manson, and the youths from Cyprus. They accomplished on the first day six to eight hours. Several cities lay to the right and left on their road and, from time to time, some of the party would separate from their Master in order to visit them. Jesus passed Tyre on the seacoast to the left. He had indicated to the Apostles and disciples a certain place where, in about thirty days, they were again to join Him. He spent the night like the preceding, under some trees with His companions.

8. JESUS JOURNEYS INTO THE COUNTRY OF ORNITHOPOLIS AND THENCE TAKES SHIP FOR CYPRUS

I saw Jesus with His followers, disciples and others, about fifty in all, journeying through a deep, mountainous ravine. It was a very remarkable-looking mountain. On two sides of it for about an hour in length were dwellings and sheds of light timber, peering into which the passer-by beheld the occupants as if in caves. Sometimes the projecting shed was covered with rushes, moss, or grassy sods. Here and there arose works something like fortifications, to prevent the landslips from the mountain from filling up the road. Here dwelt poor, outcast pagans whose duty it was to keep the road in repair and to free the region from ferocious beasts. They came to Jesus and implored His aid against these animals— long, broad-footed, spotted creatures, like immense lizards. Jesus blessed the country and commanded the animals to retire into a black swamp that was nearby. Wild orange trees grew by the roadside. It was about four hours' distance to Tyre.

Jesus here separated from His companions and, plunging deeper and deeper into the ravine, taught here and there before the caves of its inhabitants. The road led down along the clear and tolerably rapid stream Leontes which, flowing through its deep bed, emptied into the sea a couple of hours north of Tyre. The river was crossed by a high stone bridge, at the opposite end of which was a large inn, where the disciples again met Jesus.

From this place He sent several of His companions into the cities of the Land of Cabul, and Judas Iscariot with some disciples to Cana near Sidon. The disciples had resigned to the care of the Apostles, each to the one set over him as his Superior, whatever money or goods they might happen to have with them. To Judas alone, Jesus gave a sum for himself. Jesus knew his greed for money and would not expose him to the temptation of appropriating that of others. He had remarked his anxiety on the score of money, although Judas loved to boast of his frugality and strict observance of the law of poverty. On receiving the money, he asked Jesus how much he might daily spend. Jesus answered: "He that is conscious of being so strictly temperate, needs neither rule nor direction. He bears in himself his law."

About a hundred persons were at the inn awaiting Jesus. They belonged to that same Jewish tribe whom He had already visited and consoled at Ornithopolis and near Sarepta. Some of them had come hither for the purpose of meeting Him, while others belonged to this district, where they owned a synagogue. They received Him and His followers humbly and joyfully, and washed their feet. They were in their holiday garments of very antique style, wore long beards, and had fur maniples hanging from their arms. They had many singular customs, and something peculiar in their manner of life, like the Essenians. The pagans too of this place were very reverential toward Jesus. They likewise held the Jews in esteem, a circumstance more common throughout this district than in Decapolis. These Jews were descendants from a natural son the Patriarch Judah had had by a servant. This son, fleeing from the persecution of his brothers Her and Onan, had settled here. His family, having intermarried with the pagans of the country, did not go down with the other Israelites into Egypt and at last became quite estranged from the religion and customs of their people.

The pagans with whom these descendants of Judah had intermarried had, when Jacob—after Dina's misfortune—was living near Samaria on Joseph's inheritance, already experienced the greatest desire to enter into marriage relations with Jacob's sons, or at least with his servant men and maids. They crossed the mountains humbly to lay before him their desire to marry amongst his followers, and of their own accord offered to receive circumcision. But Jacob would not listen to their demand. When, then, that persecuted son of Judah sought refuge among them with his family, he was very warmly received by the heathens, and his children soon united with them in marriage. How wonderful the dispensation of God! The rude desire of these Gentiles to unite with the holy race upon whom the Promise rested was not wholly frustrated, and later events brought about the ennobling of these people through the banished scion of Judah.

In spite of the great disorders arising from these mixed marriages, there was still one family among them that preserved itself pure; and it was, for the first time, instructed in the Law by Elias, who often sojourned in this region. Solomon had given himself much trouble to unite these people again with the Jews, but without success. Still there were among them about a hundred pious souls of pure descent from Judah. Elias had succeeded in uniting this separated branch again with Israel; and in the time of Joachim and Anne, teachers came from the country of Hebron in order to keep them to the observance of the Law. The descendants of these teachers were still living among them, and it was through them that the Syrophenician and her people entered into relations with the Jews. They lived in sentiments of deep humility, esteeming themselves unworthy to set foot upon the Promised Land. The Cypriote Cyrinus had, when in Dabereth, spoken of them to Jesus, and the latter took occasion from this fact to discourse long and familiarly with them.

He taught at first in front of the inn, the people standing around under open arbors, or sheds. The inn belonged to the Jews or was hired by them. Afterward He taught in the synagogue, a great many pagans listening to Him from outside. The synagogue was lofty and beautiful. The roof was provided with a platform around which one could walk and command a very extended view of the country.

That evening the Jews tendered Jesus at the inn a festive entertainment, at which they took the opportunity to express to Him in a body their sincere gratitude for His not having despised them, for His coming to them, the lost sheep of Israel, and proclaiming to them salvation. They had kept their genealogical table in good order. They now laid it before Jesus and were deeply moved at finding that they had sprung from the same tribe as Himself. It was a joyful entertainment, and at it all assisted. They spoke much of the Prophets, especially of Elias, whom they named with words of great affection, recounting his Prophecies of the Messias, also those of Malachias, and saying that the time for their fulfillment must now be near. Jesus explained everything to them, and promised to introduce them into the land of Judea. He did, in fact, later on establish them on its southern frontiers between Hebron and Gaza.

Jesus wore in this place a long, white travelling robe. He and His followers were girded and their garments tucked up, as if for a journey. They had no baggage. They carried what was necessary under the outer robe, wrapped round the body above the girdle. Some of them had staves. I never saw Jesus with any regular covering for His head; sometimes He drew over it the scarf that was usually worn around the neck.

There was in this part of the country an ugly kind of spotted animal with membranous wings, which could fly very rapidly. It was like an enormous bat, and it sucked the blood of men and animals during sleep. These animals came from the swamps up on the seashore, and did much damage. Egypt too was once infested with them. They were not real dragons, nor were they so horrible. Dragons were not so numerous, and they lived solitary in the most savage wildernesses. Fruits like nuts were gathered in these parts, some like chestnuts, and berries that hung in clusters.

From the inn, Jesus went to a seaport about three hours distant from Tyre. Alongside of the port there stretched far out into the sea, like an island, a tongue of the mountain, and on it was built the pagan city of Ornithopolis. The few, but devout, Jews of the place seemed to live in dependence upon the heathens. I saw as many as thirty pagan temples scattered here and there. Sometimes it seems to me that the port belonged to Ornithopolis. The Syrophenician owned there so many buildings, factories for weaving and dyeing, so many ships, that I think the whole place must have been at one time subject to her deceased husband or his ancestors. She dwelt now in Ornithopolis itself, though in a kind of suburb. Back of the city arose a high mountain, and behind that lay Sidon. A little river flowed between Ornithopolis and its port. The shore between Tyre and Sidon was, with the exception of the port, but little accessible, being rough and wild. The seaport to which I have alluded was the largest between Sidon and Tyre, and the number of ships crowding its waters made it almost like a little city itself.

The property of the Syrophenician, with its numerous buildings, courts, and gardens, looked like an immense estate. Its factories and plantations were full of workmen and slaves, whose families had their homes there. But just at present, things had come to a standstill; the former activity was not yet resumed. The lady was about to free herself from all such ties, and wished her people to choose a Superior from among themselves.

Ornithopolis was situated about three hours from the little place across the river where Jesus had spent the night, but from the settlement of the poor Jews it was one and a half hours. When Jesus went straight through this place to the port, Ornithopolis lay on His left. The Jewish settlement was toward Sarepta, which received the rays of the rising sun, for on that side the mountains rose in a gentle slope. On the north it was perfectly shady. The situation was very fine. Between Ornithopolis, the Jewish settlement, and the port, there lay so many solitary buildings, so many other little settlements, that looking down upon them from above, one might think that once upon a time they were all united. Jesus had with Him now only James the Less, Barnabas, Mnason, Azor, Cyrinus's two sons, and a Cypriote youth whom those last-named had brought to Jesus. All the other Apostles and disciples were scattered throughout the country on missions. Judas was the last to set out. He went with his little troop to Cana the Greater.

Jesus went with His companions to the home of the Syrophenician who, by her cured relatives, had sent Him an invitation to an entertainment. A number of persons were assembled to meet Him, also the poor and the crippled. Of the latter, Jesus cured many. The dwelling of the Syrophenician with its gardens, courts, and buildings of all kinds was probably as large as Dülmen. Pieces of stuff, yellow, purple, red, and sky blue, were extended on the galleries of many of the buildings. These galleries were broad enough to permit a person's walking on them. The yellow dye was extracted from a plant which was cultivated in the neighborhood. For red and purple, they employed sea snails. I saw great beds in which they were either caught or raised, and there were other places full of slime, like frog's spawn. The cotton plant also was cultivated here, though not indigenous to this part of the country. The soil, in general, was not so fertile as that of Palestine, and around there were a great many ponds and lakes.

Gazing from the shore out upon the sea, one might imagine it to lie higher than the surrounding country, so blue does it rise toward the sky. Here and there on the shore were low trees with large, black trunks and wide-spreading branches. Their dense roots extended so far out on the water that one could walk over them to some distance from the land. The black trunks were, for the most part, hollow, and afforded a shelter for all kinds of noxious insects.

Jesus was received with solemnity. As He was reclining at table, the widow's daughter poured a flask of fragrant ointment over His head. The mother presented Him with pieces of stuff, girdles, and three-cornered golden coins; the daughter, pieces of the same precious metal chained together. He did not tarry with them long, but went with His companions to the seaport, where He was solemnly received by the Jewish inhabitants and by the Cypriote Jews who were gathered there on their way back from the Paschal feast. Jesus taught in the synagogue, around which a great many pagans stood listening from without.

It was by starlight that Jesus, accompanied by all the travellers, went down to the harbor and embarked. The night was clear, and the stars looked larger than they do to us. There was quite a little fleet ready to receive the travellers. One large ship of burden took the baggage, the goods and cattle, and numbers of asses. Ten galleys carrying sail were for the accommodation of the Cypriote Paschal guests, Jesus, and His followers. Five of these galleys were fastened with ropes to the front and sides of the burden ship, which they drew forward after them. The remaining five formed an outer circle to these. Each of these vessels had, like Peter's barque on the Sea of

Galilee, benches for the rowers raised around the mast and below these little cabins. Jesus stood near the mast of the ships that were fastened to the large one and, as they pushed off, He blessed both land and sea. Shoals of fishes swarmed after the flotilla, among them some very large ones with remarkable-looking mouths. They sported around and stretched their heads out of the water, as if hearkening to the instructions given by Jesus during the voyage.

The passage was so unusually rapid, the sea so smooth, and the weather so beautiful that the sailors, both Jews and pagans, cried out: "Oh, what an auspicious voyage! That is owing to Thee, O Prophet!" Jesus was standing near the mast. He commanded them silence and to give glory to the Almighty God alone. Then He spoke of God, one and almighty, and of His works, of the nonexistence of the pagan divinities, of the nearness of the time, yes, even its very presence, in which the highest salvation would be given to earth, and of the vocation of the Gentiles. The whole discourse was addressed to the heathens.

The few women on the ships remained apart by themselves. Many of the passengers were quite seasick during the voyage; they lay around in retired corners and vomited violently. Jesus cured several on board His ship. Then numbers called from the other ships telling Him of their needs, and He cured them from a distance.

I saw them also eating on the ships. They had fire in a metal vessel, and long, twisted strips of something, brown and clear like glue, which they dissolved in hot water. They passed the food around in portions on dishes furnished with a rim and a handle. There were several excavations like plates in each dish destined for different things, such as round cakes, vegetables, etc. The sauce was poured over it.

From Ornithopolis to Cyprus, the sea does not look so broad as below from Joppa. There one sees nothing but water.

Toward evening the ships entered the harbor of Salamis, which was very spacious and secure. It was strongly fortified with bulwarks and high walls, and the two moles that formed it ran far out into the sea. The city itself lay a good half hour inland, though one scarcely remarks the fact since the intervening space is set out with trees and covered with magnificent gardens. The ships in the harbor were numerous. That upon which Jesus was could not go close to the shore which, like a strong, high rampart, rose obliquely; besides this, the ship drew too much water to approach nearer. They cast anchor therefore at some distance. Near the shore were several small boats fastened with ropes. They approached the larger vessels, received their passengers and, by means of the ropes, drew back to the shore. In that upon which Jesus and the disciples sailed to land were some Jews who had come out to welcome and receive Him.

On the shore were numerous others who, having espied the ships in the distance, had come forth from the city in solemn procession. It was customary thus to receive the Jews on their return from the Paschal celebration. Those on the shore were principally old people, women, young girls, and the school children with their teachers. They had fifes, carried flying streamers, green branches, crowns on poles, and chanted songs of joy.

Cyrinus, three elder brothers of Barnabas, and some aged Jews in festive robes received Jesus and His followers, and conducted them to a lovely green terrace at some distance from the harbor. There they found carpets spread, wash basins filled with water, and on tables various dishes with refreshments. Cyrinus and his companions washed the feet of Jesus and His disciples, and presented them to eat.

An old man, the father of Jonas, the new disciple, was now led forward. He fell weeping upon his son's neck, who presented him to Jesus, before whom he bowed low. He had been in ignorance as to what had become of his son, for they with whom he had started on the journey were come back long ago. All present were taken up with caring for the travellers returned. Many pressed through the crowd crying: "Is such a one here? Is such a one there?" and when they found their friends, they embraced them and led them away. The news of the sedition and Pilate's massacre in the Temple, variously exaggerated, had already reached Cyprus, and the people were in great anxiety about their relatives.

The place in which Jesus was received was charming. Toward the west, one saw the immense city with its innumerable cupolas and towering edifices crimsoned by the fiery rays of the sun sinking huge and red below the horizon. Toward the east, the view extended over the sea to the lofty mountain ranges of Syria, which there rose up like clouds against the sky. Salamis stood in the midst of a broad plain, covered with numbers of beautiful high trees, terraces, and pleasure grounds. The soil appeared to me very friable, like dust or sand, but drinking water did not seem to be abundant. The entrance into the harbor was not open. It was guarded by fortified islands, between which were one broad and several smaller roadsteads. The little islands were fortified with semicircular towers, low and broad, through whose open windows could be observed all that was going on outside. The Jewish quarter was in the northern part of the city. When Jesus and His followers left the harbor and went one half-hour toward the city, they turned to the right and, still outside the city, went a considerable distance to the north.

When Jesus and His disciples arrived, the Jews returned from the Pasch were already assembled upon an open, terraced square. One of the ancients, an Elder of the Synagogue, was standing on an elevated point from which he could overlook all below. It reminded one of calling the muster-roll, to see whether all the soldiers were present. The Elder was receiving information upon the details of their journey. He inquired whether any of them had suffered injury by the way, or had any complaints to lodge against a fellow traveller, and requested an account of what had happened in Jerusalem. Jesus and His disciples were not present at this assembly. He was solemnly welcomed by a number of venerable old Jews and from the terrace delivered an exhortation to the assembled crowd, after which they dispersed to their homes.

At the head of the two streets that formed the Jewish quarter stood the magnificent synagogue, the dwellings of the ancients and rabbis, the schools, and at some distance, the hospital for the sick with a reservoir, or pond. The road leading to the city was very firm and solid, covered with fine sand, and shaded by handsome trees. On the highest point of that Jewish place of assembly there was a tree in whose strong, leafy branches one could sit as in an arbor.

Jesus and His followers were escorted by the Elders to a large hall near the synagogue where they spent the night. Here Jesus cured of dropsy some sick who had been carried on litters into the forecourt of the inn. There was in this house a spacious lecture hall, and in it travelling rabbis were lodged. It was very handsome, built in pagan style with a colonnade around it. The interior was one immense room with tiers of seats and teachers' chairs against the walls. On the lower floor and rolled up against the walls were couches, and above them, tucked up and fastened to the wall, were tent covers that could be let down around the beds, thus forming a private alcove. One could from the outside mount to the flat roof of the hall, upon which were placed various kinds of plants in pots.

The father of Jonas, the new disciple, spent the night there, for he did not belong to the city, but Cyrinus and his sons went home.

9. JESUS TEACHES IN SALAMIS

On the morning of the following day, Jesus was accompanied by the Superior, a venerable old man, and some of the teachers to the hospital, a circular building enclosing a garden. In the center of the latter there was a reservoir, or pond, for bathing; but for drinking and cooking purposes, the water was collected in huge casks and purified by means of certain fruits thrown into it. Medicinal herbs were raised around the pond. The third part of the hospital was occupied by invalid females, and it was separated from the rest of the building by doors kept locked. Jesus cured some of the dropsical and gouty male patients, also such as were slightly tainted with leprosy. The newly cured followed Him to the open square upon which, in the meantime, the other Jews had gathered, and where Jesus delivered an instruction first to the men. He took for His subject the gathering of the manna in the wilderness, and said that the time for the true Heavenly Manna of doctrine and conversion of heart had come, and that a new kind of Bread from Heaven was about to be given them.

This instruction over, the men withdrew and the women took their place. A great many pagan women were present, but they remained standing in the background. Jesus instructed the women in general terms, because of the pagans among them. He spoke of the one, Almighty God, of the Father and Creator of Heaven and earth, of the folly of polytheism, and of God's love for mankind.

After that Jesus and His followers went to dine at the Superior's house, whither He had been invited along with several rabbis. It was a very large mansion of pagan architecture with forecourts, open porches, and terraces. All was here prepared for a grand entertainment. Numbers of tables were spread under the colonnade and there were arches erected and adorned with wreaths. It appeared to be a banquet intended principally for Jesus and friends returned from the Paschal solemnity. The Superior conducted Jesus into a side building, in which were his wife and some other women. Several Doctors accompanied them. After the veiled women had with a low inclination saluted Jesus and He had said some gracious words to them, a procession of flower-crowned children appeared, playing on flutes and other instruments, to conduct Jesus to the feast. The table was ornamented with vases and bouquets. It was higher than those in use in Judea, and the other guests reclined less outstretched, closer to one another. They washed their hands. Among the various viands was a lamb. Jesus carved it and distributed it to the guests on little round rolls. It had, however, been cut up and put together again before being placed on the table.

Then the child musicians again made their appearance. Among them were some blind children and some with other defects. They were followed by a troop of gaily dressed little girls from eight to ten years old, among them the daughter, or granddaughter of the host. All were clothed in fine, white material, somewhat glossy. The garments worn in this country were not so ample in make, not so flowing in style as those of Judea. Their hair hung down in three parts, the ends uniting into a curl, or fastened together by some kind of ornament to which hung various little trinkets, fringes, pearls, or red balls like fruit. By this arrangement, their crisp black or reddish-brown tresses were kept from streaming around. Several of the little girls carried a large crown formed of wreaths and various kinds of ornamentation. It was composed of circlets so arranged that each was firm in its own place. To the first and larger one, the second was fastened by clasps, and from the latter rose a glittering tuft, or a small flag. I do not think the wreaths were formed of natural flowers, at least not entirely; for many of the blossoms looked to me like silk, or wool inter-mixed with feathers and various kinds of glittering orna-ments. The little girls placed this great crown like a canopy upon a high pedestal, ornamented in a similar manner, that stood behind Jesus' seat, while others brought aromatic herbs and perfumes in little dishes and alabaster vases, which they set down before Him. A child belonging to the house broke one of the little flasks, poured its contents over His head, and spread it with a linen cloth over His hair, after which the children retired. The little girls went through these ceremonies with per-fect composure and without speaking a word, their downcast eyes never once glancing toward the guests. Jesus very quietly received their attentions and thanked them in a few gentle, gracious words, whereupon the children—without raising their eyes—went back to the women's hall. The women ate all together.

I did not see Jesus and His disciples reclining long at table. Jesus constantly sent food and drink to the tables of the poor by His disciples, who spent most of the time serving others. After some time, Jesus Himself went around from table to table, distributing food, teaching, and explaining.

After the banquet, the Superior and some of the teachers went with Jesus and the disciples out to the aqueduct, which they approached from the west. The city had bad water. I saw some of those stupendous struc-tures, like immense bridges, which contained many great reservoirs, or cisterns. Each quarter of the city had its own waterworks and reservoir. From some they had to pump the water; from others it could be drawn. The

reservoir of the Jews stood apart by itself. They showed
it to Jesus, complained to Him of the scarcity and bad
quality of the water, and wanted Him to improve it. He
spoke of the new reservoir in progress of construction,
said that He wanted Baptism to be given at it, and told
them how it should be arranged.

After that they proceeded to the synagogue, for the
Sabbath was begun. It was an extraordinarily large and
handsome edifice, lit up by numerous lamps and full of
people. Around the outside ran steps and balconies from
which spectators could both see and hear what was going
on inside. All these places were occupied by pagans, and
below they had even crowded into the interior of the synagogue, where they now stood quietly side by side with
the Jews.

The instruction was on passages from the third book of
Moses, treating of sacrifices and various laws, and others
from Ezechiel. It began by some of the Doctors reading
these passages, which Jesus explained and commented
upon so beautifully that all were deeply impressed. He
spoke also of His own mission and its speedy accomplishment. His hearers believed Him to be not only a Prophet,
but still more than a Prophet. He must, they thought, at
least be the one that was to go before the Messiah. Jesus
explained to them that that precursor was John, and
enumerated the signs by which they might recognize the
Messiah—without, however, indicating to them clearly
that He Himself was the Messiah. Nevertheless, they
understood Him, and listened in reverence and respectful
fear. After the instruction all dispersed to their homes,
and Jesus went back with His followers to the house of
the Superior.

On the whole, Jesus was received in Salamis with extraordinary affection. The inhabitants pressed around
Him, all being desirous of showing Him honor, for there
was among them neither sect nor strife. Jesus healed sev-

eral sick persons in their own homes. Jews and heathens lived here on very familiar terms, though in separate quarters. In that of the Jews there were two streets. The house of the sons of Cyrinus was a large, square building. They were engaged in commerce and owned ships. A peculiar style of architecture was predominant in Salamis. I saw numerous turrets and spires, a great deal of latticework, many latticed windows, and all kinds of ornamentation on the edifices. The people presented Jesus and the disciples on their arrival with new sandals and a change of garments. Jesus kept His only till His own were shaken and dusted; then He gave them to the poor.

On the morning of the Sabbath, Jesus taught again in the synagogue on the time of grace and the fulfillment of the Prophecies, and that so eloquently that many of His hearers shed tears. He exhorted to penance and Baptism. This instruction lasted between three and four hours.

Jesus went at the end of it with His disciples and the Doctors to Cyrinus's, whither they had been invited to dine. It stood just between the Jewish and the pagan quarters. Salamis had eight streets, two of which belonged to the Jews. The little party did not go through the latter, but by a route running between the two quarters and at the rear of the houses. In this way they passed the great gates of the city. In the gateways was gathered a crowd of pagans, men, women, and children. They were very respectful and saluted Jesus and His followers timidly from a distance. They had listened to His instruction of the school, and were now come with their friends to the gates.

At the end of the street and half within the walls of the pagan quarter was the magnificent home of Cyrinus, with its courts and side buildings. As soon as the house became visible in the distance, the wife and daughters of Cyrinus were seen approaching with their servants. They saluted Jesus and His disciples. Cyrinus had five daughters, along with nieces and other young relatives. All these children bore with them presents which, after they had bowed low before Jesus, they set down at His feet on carpets which they had previously spread. The gifts consisted of bric-a-brac in all shapes and forms, some of amber, others of coral, notably a little tree of the latter mounted upon a stand. It appeared as if each child wanted to offer the dearest object in her possession, and if she could not get near enough to Jesus Himself, she presented it to one of His companions.

Cyrinus's dwelling was very spacious and built in pagan style, with forecourts and outside flights of steps. On the roof was a well-arranged garden of plants growing in pots. All was adorned in festive style. The table was higher than those in ordinary use, and covered with a red cloth over which was a transparent one of glossy silk, or fine straw plaiting. The couches around the table, too, were more in accordance with pagan customs, shorter than those in use among the Jews. Besides the disciples, the guests numbered about twenty men. The women ate apart, and after dinner all took the customary Sabbath promenade out to the waterworks.

From there Jesus permitted Himself and His disciples to be conducted by Jonas, the new disciple, to the house of his father, which stood surrounded by gardens somewhat distant from the Jewish quarter. It was like a large farmhouse, having something of the cloister in its arrangement. The old man was an Essenian, and with him dwelt, though in a separate part of the house, several old women, widowed relatives, nieces or daughters, who were somewhat differently clothed and wore white veils. The old man was humble and joyous as a child, and allowed himself to be led by his children to meet Jesus. He was at a loss as to what he should give Jesus, for he had no treasures. But he pointed around him, to himself, his sons, his daughters, as if to say: "Lord, all that we have, we ourselves are Thine—and my dearest child, my son is Thine!" He invited Jesus and the disciples to dine with him on the following day.

Jesus then returned to the waterworks and spoke with the Superior about the arrangements for the baptismal well, which was not yet under roof and had no means of letting in water. They had first to beg or buy water from the pagans. It would have to be conveyed thither from the aqueduct which, on the plain, was about one story high with reservoirs on either side. The source of the water was in the mountain range on the west. The new baptismal well had more than four corners, and there were steps leading down into it. Around it were cavities in the form of a tray, which could be filled with water by pressing on a winch. The whole was surrounded by a rampart and nearby, for instructions, was a charming open place covered by an awning.

A great many Jews and heathens were gathered on the spot, and Jesus told them that next day He would instruct those that wanted to receive Baptism. The Jews made frequent allusion to Elias and Eliseus, who likewise had been here.

Jewish women with their children had stationed themselves here and there on the way. Jesus patted the little ones in His vicinity, frequently called the others to Him, and gave to all His blessing. Several pagan teachers, or mothers in yellow veils were standing apart with their little girls and boys. Jesus blessed them from afar.

After that all repaired to the synagogue for the closing exercises of the Sabbath. Jesus again taught upon sacrifice, taking His texts from the third book of Moses (Leviticus) and the Prophet Ezechiel. There was something marvellously sweet and impressive in His words as He showed that the Laws of Moses were now realizing their most elevated signification. He spoke of the offering of a pure heart. He said that sacrifices multiplied a thousand times could no more be of any avail, for one must purify his soul and offer his passions as a holocaust. Without rejecting anything, without condemning or abolishing any of the prescriptions of the Mosaic Law, He explained it according to its real signification, thus making it appear far more beautiful and worthy of reverence. Jesus, at the same time, prepared His hearers for the Baptism and exhorted to penance, for the time was near.

His words and the tone of His voice were like living, deeply penetrating streams of light. He spoke with extraordinary calmness and power, and never very rapidly, excepting sometimes when talking with the Pharisees. At such times, His words were like sharp arrows and His voice less gentle. The tone of His ordinary voice was an agreeable tenor, perfectly pure in sound, without its counterpart in that of any human being. He could, without raising it, be distinctly heard above a great clamor.

The lessons and prayers were chanted in the synagogue on a recitative tone, in the same manner as the choral singing and Mass of the Christians, and sometimes the Jews sang alternately. Jesus read in this way the passages that He explained from Holy Scripture.

After Jesus' instruction, a pious old Doctor of the Law began to address the assembly. He had a long, white beard, was of a meager form and kind, benevolent countenance. He did not belong to Salamis, but was a poor, travelling teacher who journeyed from place to place on the island visiting the sick, consoling the imprisoned, collecting for the poor, instructing the ignorant and little children, comforting widows, and delivering discourses in the synagogues. On this occasion, he appeared to be inspired by the Holy Ghost. He addressed the people in a speech that bore witness to Jesus, such as I never before heard in public from any one of the rabbis. He rehearsed all the benefits of Almighty God to their fathers and themselves, and urged them to gratitude to Him for having permitted that they should live at the coming of such a Prophet, such a Teacher, to whom likewise they owed thanks for having journeyed on their account all the way from the Holy Land. He reminded them of God's mercy to their tribe (they were of the tribe of Issachar), and called upon them to do penance and amend their lives. He said that God would not treat them so severely now as He did when He punished the fabricators and adorers of the golden calf. I do not know the force of his allusion; perhaps many of their tribe had been among the idolaters. He said also marvellous things about Jesus: that he esteemed Him more than a Prophet, though he did not venture to say who He really was, that the fulfillment of the Promises was near, that all should consider themselves happy to hear such instructions from such lips, and to have lived at an epoch of such hope, such consolation for Israel. The people were deeply moved, and many shed tears of joy. All this took place in the presence of Jesus, who was quietly standing on one side among His disciples.

Jesus went afterward with His followers to the house of the Elder, where the conversation became very animated. All present tried to prevail upon Jesus to remain among them. They quoted the words of some of the Prophets relative to persecution and sufferings, which words seemed to apply to the Messiah. They trusted that such might not happen to Jesus, and asked whether He was the precursor of the Messiah. Then Jesus told them about John, and declared to them that He could not remain among them. One of those present, who had been in Palestine when Jesus was there, began to speak of the hatred of the Pharisees against Him, and said some hard things about that sect. But Jesus reproached him for his severity, said a few words in their excuse, and turned the conversation to other subjects.

Next day, in the hospital and at the recently constructed baptismal well, Jesus prepared the people for Baptism. Several in the hospital made known to Him their sins, for which purpose they retired apart wih Him. He caused water for Baptism to be put aside here in basins, and in it the sick were later on baptized by the disciples.

When Jesus arrived at the open square around the baptismal well, He found a great multitude there assembled, among them many heathens, for during the night the people had been pouring in from the surrounding country. Jesus taught under an awning. His discourse turned upon His own mission, upon penance and Baptism, and He explained the *Our Father*.

10. JESUS INVITED TO THE HOUSE OF THE ROMAN COMMANDANT IN SALAMIS

While Jesus was delivering His instruction, a pagan soldier, or constable, made his appearance with a message to the magistrates. It was to this effect, that the Roman Commandant in Salamis wished to speak with the new Teacher and, consequently, invited Him to his house. The soldier delivered his message rather sternly, as if he took it ill that they had not led Jesus to him at once. The magistrates transmitted it to Jesus through the disciples during a pause in the discourse. Jesus replied that He would go, and went on speaking. After His instruction, accompanied by the disciples and Elders, He followed the messenger to the Commandant's. They had to go a distance of half an hour, along the same way by which Jesus had come hither from the port, before reaching the principal gate of Salamis, a beautiful, high archway supported on pillars. As they passed the great walls and large gardens on the way, the pagan people and laborers looked inquisitively after Jesus, and many as He approached shyly hid behind the walls and bushes. On entering Salamis they repaired to a large open square. The houses as they passed along were lined with spectators, standing on the galleries of the courts, behind the lattices, and in the gates. On some of the street corners and under the arches were pagan women and children, ranged three by three in regular order. The women were veiled, and they bowed low to Jesus as He passed. Here and there children, sometimes too the women, stepped forward and presented to Jesus or His companions divers little gifts, such as bunches of aromatic shrubs, little flasks of perfumes, little brown cakes, and objects in the form of stars and other things that exhaled a delicious odor. This appeared to be the custom of the country, a sign of reverential welcome. Jesus lingered a few instants near such groups, cast upon them gracious and earnest glances, and blessed them, though without touching them.

I saw idols standing here and there. They were not like those of Greece and Rome, images in human form, but like those in Sidon, Tyre and Joppa, figures with wings, or scales. I also saw some like dolls.

As they advanced into the city, the crowd following Jesus constantly increased, and people were streaming from all sides toward the open square. In the center of the latter was a beautiful well. Steps led down into it, and through the middle of the basin the water bubbled up. It was protected by a roof supported on pillars, and surrounded by open porches, little trees, and flowers. The entrance to the well was usually closed. The people could get some of its water only by certain privileges, as it was the best in the city and thought possessed of peculiarly wholesome properties.

Opposite this well stood the Commandant's palace with its colonnade. On an open balcony over which was a pillared roof sat the Roman Commandant on a stone seat, watching Jesus' approach. He was dressed in military costume, a white tunic tightly fitting round the body, striped here and there with red. It descended to below the hips and ended in straps, or fringe. The lower limbs were laced. He wore a short red mantle and on his head a hat that looked to me like a shaving dish. He was a strong, robust man with a short beard, black and crisp. Behind him and on the steps of the balcony were standing Roman soldiers.

The pagans were astonished at the marks of respect he showed to Jesus, for when the latter approached, he descended from the balcony, clasped His hand in the end of a linen scarf that he held in his own, and pressed it with the other hand, in which was the other end of the scarf, at the same time bowing low before Him. Then he led Jesus up to the balcony, where he put to Him, most graciously, question after question. He had, he said, heard Him spoken of as a wise Teacher. He himself revered the Jewish Law. If all that was said of Him was true, Jesus did indeed perform great wonders. Who gave Him the power for such things? Was He the promised Comforter, the Messiah of the Jews? The Jews were expecting a king—was He that king? By what means would He get possession of His Kingdom? Had He an army somewhere? Perhaps He was going to collect forces here in Cyprus among the Jews? Would it be long before He would show Himself in all His power? The Commandant put sundry questions of this kind in a tone full of respect and earnestness. His profound sympathy and reverence for Jesus were visible. Jesus answered all in vague and general terms, as He usually did when such questions were put to Him by magistrates. He would, for instance, answer: "Thou sayest it! So they think. The Prophets have thus declared." To the questions relative to His Kingdom, to His army, He answered that His Kingdom was not of this world. The kings of this world had need of warriors, but He gathered the souls of men into the Kingdom of the Almighty Father, the Creator of Heaven and earth. In deeply significant words He touched, in passing, upon many subjects. The Commandant was astounded both at His language and bearing.

He had ordered refreshments to be brought to the well in the open square, and he now invited Jesus and His disciples to follow him thither. They examined the well and partook of the refreshments, which were spread on a stone stand previously covered. There were several brown dishes with sauce of the same color, into which they dipped cakes. They partook also of sticks of confectionery, or strips of cheese, about an arm in length and two inches thick, fruit, and pastry made into figures of stars and flowers. Little jugs of wine were placed around the stand. Others, made of something with colored veining, in shape just like those of Cana only much smaller, were filled with water from the well. The Commandant spoke too with marked disapprobation of Pilate, of the violence he had exercised in the Temple, and of his character in general, also of the demolished aqueduct near Silo.

Jesus held another conversation with the Commandant here at the well. He spoke of water and its different sources, some muddy, others clear, some bitter and salty, others sweet, of the great difference in its effects, of how it was conducted into the well and again distributed in conduits. From such remarks He passed to instructing both pagans and Jews upon the waters of Baptism, the regeneration of mankind by penance and faith, when all would become children of God. It was an admirable instruction with something in it similar to His conversation with the Samaritan at the well. His words made a deep impression upon the Commandant, who was already very well disposed toward the Jews. He wanted to hear Jesus frequently.

In Salamis the separation between Jews and pagans

was not so marked. Here as in Palestine, the more enlightened Jews, and especially the followers of Jesus, ate and drank with the upper class of pagans, although always making use of separate vessels. On their return, Jesus was saluted by many of the heathens, and that still more respectfully than before, owing to the marks of honor shown Him by the Commandant.

Flowers in this country were extremely abundant, and artificial ones were most artistically made of colored wool, silk, and little feathers. I saw the heathen children whom Jesus blessed adorned for the most part with such flowers. The little girls were, like the boys, dressed in very short garments of thin material; the very little ones of the poor had only a cincture around the waist. The young maidens of the wealthier classes wore thin, yellow tunics richly covered with those colored woollen flowers of which I have spoken. Around the shoulders, the ends crossed over the breast, they wore a scarf of thin texture, and on their arms and head, little garlands of artificial flowers. They must have raised silkworms here, for I saw along the walls trees carefully reared whereon those insects were crawling and spinning their cocoons.

11. JESUS AT THE HOME OF JONAS'S FATHER. INSTRUCTION AT THE BAPTISMAL WELL

When Jesus visited the home of the Essenian, the father of Jonas, He was accompanied by His disciples only and some of the Doctors. He was received with the usual courtesies, that is, washing of the feet. The domestic arrangements were here much more simple, more like the country than those of the mansion at which Jesus had first been entertained. The family was large and belonged to the sect of Essenians, to those that married. They lived in great purity, being pious and simple in their manners. The female portion were widows with children already grown, daughters of the old man, with whom they lived. Jonas the disciple was the son of a later marriage, and his mother died in giving him birth. The old man loved him so much the more as he was his only son, and he had been in great anxiety about his being absent for over a year. He had looked upon him as lost, when he received news of him through Cyrinus, whose sons had met Jonas at the Paschal feast and in Dabereth near Thabor. The youth had been travelling for information, as young students often do. He had visited the most remarkable of the Holy Places, the Essenians in Judea, Jacob's tomb near Hebron, and that of Rachel between Jerusalem and Bethlehem. The last-named lay at that time on the direct route between these two places; now, however, it lies somewhat on one side. He had likewise visited all that was most interesting in Bethlehem, as well as Mounts Carmel and Thabor. He had heard of Jesus and had been present at one of the mountain sermons before He went into the country of the Gergeseans. After the Paschal festival, he had gone with the sons of Cyrinus from Dabereth to the last instruction at Gabara. It was then that Jesus received him as a disciple, in which quality he now returned home.

The entertainment was held in a garden in which were long and densely shaded arbors. An elevated green bank, covered with a cloth, served as a table. The couches too consisted of similar grassy banks covered with mats. The meal was made up of various kinds of pastry, broth, vegetables steeped in sauce, lamb's meat, fruit, and little jugs of something, all very simple. The women ate at a separate table, though they seemed more at their ease than other Jewish women. They served at table, their veils lowered, and sitting at some distance, afterward listened to the words of Jesus. On both sides of the garden there were whole rows of arbors formed of dense green foliage. I think they were intended as places for the devotional exercises of the family, which was like a perfect little Essenian Community. They lived by agriculture and cattle-raising, weaving, and spinning.

From this place, Jesus went with the disciples to the newly constructed baptismal well, where He prepared many Jews for Baptism by a discourse in which He exhorted to penance and blessed the baptismal water. Around the central well there were some salver-shaped basins on a level with the surrounding surface. These basins were encircled by little ditches, into which the neophytes descended by a couple of steps. He who baptized stood on the edge of the basin and poured water on the head of the neophytes bowed over the same. The sponsors stood behind and imposed hands on them. By the opening or pressing of a piece of machinery in the central well, the water could be introduced into the basins and ditches. I saw Barnabas, James, and Azor baptizing by three of the basins. Before the ceremony I saw Jesus, from a flat, leathern vessel which they had brought with them from Judea, pouring a little Jordan water taken from His own place of baptism, into the basins, and then blessing the water thus mixed with it. After the Baptism, not only was all this baptismal water poured again into the central well, but the basins were dried with a cloth which was then wrung out into the well. I saw the neophytes with little white mantles around their shoulders.

After that I saw Jesus going in a more westerly direction between gardens and walls, where were awaiting Him several pagans who, prepared by their friend Cyrinus, were likewise desirous of Baptism. He went aside with some of them whom He further instructed, and about thirty of them were baptized in the various bathing gardens around. Water was introduced into the baths for that purpose, which water Jesus blessed.

Besides the two streets belonging to the Jews, there was

in the vicinity of Salamis an entire Jewish city. On one side of Salamis there was a round tower of extraordinary circumference, to which were attached all kinds of dependencies. It was like a citadel. The city possessed many temples, one of which was of uncommon dimensions, and to its terrace one could mount either by an interior or an exterior flight of steps. In the temple were found numerous columns, some so large around that in them were cut steps and little apartments wherein the people could stand on high and look down on the religious ceremonies. A couple of hours from Salamis, I saw another important city.

Westward from the city I saw a caravan of strangers approaching, who encamped under tents. They must have come from the other side of the island; indeed, on account of the direction, I was inclined to think they had come from Rome itself. They had some women with them and a great number of large, heavy oxen with broad horns and low heads. They were bound together, two and two, with long poles over their backs upon which they carried burdens. I think these strangers had come partly on account of the harvest. They brought with them merchandise which they wished to exchange for grain.

Next morning Jesus delivered, on the open square near the baptismal well, a lengthy instruction to both Jews and pagans. He taught of the harvest, the multiplication of the grain, the ingratitude of mankind who receive the greatest wonders of God so indifferently, and predicted for these ingrates the fate of the chaff and weeds, namely, to be cast into the fire. He said also that from one seed-corn a whole harvest was gathered, that all things came forth from one, Almighty God, the Creator of Heaven and earth, the Father and Supporter of all men, who would reward their good works and punish their evil ones. He showed them also how men, instead of turning to God the Father, turn to creatures, to lifeless blocks.

They pass coldly by the wonders of God, while they gaze in astonishment at the specious though paltry works of men, even rendering honor to miserable jugglers and sorcerers. Here Jesus took occasion to speak of the pagan gods, the ridiculous ideas entertained of them, the confusion existing in those ideas, the service rendered them, and all the cruelties related of them. Then He spoke of some of these gods individually, asking such questions as these: "Who is this god? Who is that other? Who was his father?" etc. To these questions He Himself gave the answers, exposing in them the confused genealogies and families of their pagan divinities and the abominations connected with them, all which facts could be found, not in the Kingdom of God, but only in that of the father of lies. Finally He mentioned and analyzed the various and contradictory attributes of these gods.

Although Jesus spoke in so severe and conclusive a manner, still His instruction was so agreeable, so suggestive of good thoughts to His hearers that it could rouse no displeasure. His teaching against paganism was much milder here in Salamis than it was wont to be in Palestine. He spoke too of the vocation of the Gentiles to the Kingdom of God and said that many strangers from the East and from the West would get possession of the thrones intended for the children of the house, since the latter cast salvation far from them.

During a pause in the instruction, Jesus took a mouthful to eat and drink, and the people entertained themselves on what they had just heard. Meanwhile some pagan philosophers drew near to Jesus and questioned Him upon some points not understood by them, also about something that had been transmitted to them by their ancestors as coming from Elias, who had been in these parts. Jesus gave them the desired information, and then began teaching upon Baptism, also of prayer, referring for His text to the harvest and their own daily bread.

Many of the pagans received most salutary impressions from Jesus' instructions and were led to reflections productive of fruit. But others, finding His words not to their liking, took their departure.

And now I saw a great number of Jews baptized at the baptismal well, the waters of which Jesus blessed. Three at a time stood round one basin. The water in the ditches reached as high as the calf of the leg.

12. JESUS GOES TO THE JEWISH CITY

Jesus afterward went with His followers and some of the Doctors to the separate Jewish city, about one half-hour to the north. He was followed by many of His late audience, and He continued to speak with several little groups. The route led over some more elevated places below which lay meadows and gardens. Here and there were rows of trees, and again some solitary ones, high and dense, up which the traveller might climb and find a shady seat. The view extended far around on several little localities and fields of golden wheat. Sometimes the road ran along broad, naked walls of rock, in which whole rows of cells had been hewn out for the field laborers.

Outside the Jewish city stood a fine inn and pleasure garden. Here Jesus' own party entered, while He bade the rest of His escort return to their homes. The disciples washed Jesus' feet, then one another's, let down their garments, and followed their Master into the Jewish city. During the foot-washing, I saw near the inn on one side of the highroad that ran along the city, long, light buildings like sheds, in which were a great number of Jewish women and maid servants busied in selecting, arranging, and carefully preserving the fruits which female slaves, or domestics, carried thither in baskets from the gardens around. The fruits were of all kinds, large and small, also berries. They separated the good from the bad, made all kinds of divisions, and even laid some wrapped in cotton on shelves one over another. Others were engaged in picking and packing cotton. I noticed all the housewives lowering their veils as soon as the men appeared on the highroad. The sheds were divided into several compartments. They looked to me like a general fruitery, where the portion intended for the tithes and that for alms were laid aside. It was a very busy scene.

Jesus went with His party to the dwelling of the rabbis near the synagogue. The eldest rabbi received Him courteously, though with a tinge of stiff reserve in his manner. He offered Him the customary refreshments, and said a few words upon His visit to the island and His far-famed reputation, etc. Jesus' arrival having become known, several invalids implored His help, whereupon, accompanied by the rabbis and the disciples, He visited them in their homes and cured many lame and paralyzed. The latter, with their families, followed Him out of their houses, and proclaimed His praise. But He silenced them and bade them go back. On the streets He was met by mothers and their children, whom He blessed. Some carried sick children to Him, and He cured them.

And so passed the afternoon away till evening, when Jesus accompanied the rabbis to an entertainment in His honor, which entertainment was likewise connected with the beginning of the harvest. The poor and the laboring people were fed at it, a custom which drew from Jesus words of commendation. They were brought from the fields in bands and seated at long tables, like benches of stone, and there served with various viands. Jesus, from time to time, waited on them Himself with the disciples, and instructed them in short sentences and parables. Several of the Jewish Doctors were present at the entertainment; but, on the whole, this company was not so well disposed, not so sincere as the Jews around Jesus' inn near Salamis. There was a tinge of pharisaism about them and, after they had become heated, they gave utterance to some offensive remarks. They asked whether He could not conveniently remain longer in Palestine, what was the real object of His visit to them, whether He intended to stay any time among them, and ended by suggesting that He should create no disturbance in Cyprus. They likewise touched upon diverse points of His doctrine and manner of acting which the Pharisees of Palestine were in the habit of rehearsing. Jesus answered them as He usually did on similar occasions, with more or less severity according to the measure of their own civility. He told them that He had come to exercise the works of mercy as the Father in Heaven willed Him to do. The conversation was very animated. It gave Jesus an opportunity for delivering a stern lecture in which, while commending their goodness to the poor and whatever else was praiseworthy in them, He denounced their hypocrisy. It was already late when Jesus left with His followers. The rabbis bore Him company as far as the city gate.

13. THE PAGAN PRIESTESS MERCURIA. THE PAGAN LITERATI

When Jesus had returned to the inn with the disciples, a pagan came to Him and begged Him to go with him to a certain garden a few steps distant, where a person in distress was waiting to implore His assistance. Jesus went with the disciples to the place indicated. There He saw standing between the walls on the road a pagan lady, who inclined low before Him. He ordered the disciples to fall back a little, and then questioned the woman as to what she wanted. She was a very remarkable person, perfectly destitute of instruction, quite sunk in paganism, and wholly given up to its abominable service. One glance from Jesus had cast her into disquiet, and roused in her the feeling that she was in error, but she was without simple faith, and had a very confused manner of accusing herself. She told Jesus that she had heard of His having helped Magdalen, as also the woman afflicted with the issue, of whom the latter had merely touched the hem of His garment. She begged Jesus to cure and instruct her, but then again, she said perhaps He could not cure her as she was not, like the woman with the issue, physically sick. She confessed that she was married and had three children, but that one, unknown to her husband, had been begotten in adultery. She had also intercourse with the Roman Commandant. When Jesus, on the preceding day, visited the last named, she had watched Him from a window and saw a halo of light around His head, which sight very powerfully impressed her. She at first thought that her emotion sprang from love for Jesus, and the idea caused her anguish so intense that she fell to the ground unconscious. When returned to herself, her whole life, her whole interior passed before her in so frightful a manner that she entirely lost her peace of mind. She then made inquiries about Jesus, and learned from some Jewish women of Magdalen's cure, also that of Enue of Caesarea-Philippi, the woman afflicted with the issue of blood. She now implored Jesus to heal her if He possibly could. Jesus told her that the faith of that afflicted woman was simple; that, in the firm belief that if she could touch only the seam of His garment she would be cured, she had approached Him stealthily and her faith had saved her.

The silly woman again asked Jesus how He could have known that Enue touched Him and that He healed her. She did not comprehend Jesus or His power, although she heartily longed for His assistance. Jesus rebuked her, commanded her to renounce her shameful life, and told her of God the Almighty and of His Commandment: "Thou shalt not commit adultery." He placed before her all the abominations of the debauchery (against which her nature itself revolted) practiced in the impure service of her gods; and He met her with words so earnest and so full of mercy that she retired weeping and penetrated with sorrow. The lady's name was Mercuria. She was tall, and about twenty-five years old. She was enveloped in a white mantle, long and flowing in the back but rather shorter in front, which formed a cap around the head. Her other garments also were white, though with colored borders. The materials in which the heathen women dressed were so soft and clung so closely to the form that the latter could readily be traced by the eye.

The whole morning of the following day was devoted by the disciples to baptizing at the fountain, and I saw Jesus teaching both here and at the waterworks. His instructions were given principally in parables on the harvest, the daily bread, the manna, the Bread of Life that was to be given them, and the one, only God. The laborers were sent to the harvest in groups, and I saw Jesus instructing them as they passed before Him. The people here encamped under tents were also Jews, who had come hither especially on Jesus' account. They had brought their sick with them on beasts of burden, and now today they were placed on litters under awnings and trees in the vicinity of the place of instruction. Jesus cured about twenty lame and palsied.

On reaching the waterworks, He was accosted by several men, learned pagans, who had been present at His instructions of the preceding day. They begged for an explanation upon several points, spoke of their divinities, especially of one goddess that had risen here from the sea, and of another represented in their temple under the form of a fish. This latter was named Derketo. They questioned Him also about a story circulating among the Jews and connected with Elias. It was to this effect, that Elias once saw a cloud rising out of the sea, which cloud was, in reality, a virgin. They would like to know, they said, where she had descended, for from her was to proceed a King. One that was to do good to the whole world. Now, according to calculation, it was time for this to happen. With this story they mixed up another concerning a star that their goddess had let fall upon Tyre, and they asked whether that could be the cloud of which they had spoken.

One of them said that there was a report current of an adventurer in Judea who was making capital of Elias's cloud and the circumstance of the fulfillment of time, in order to proclaim himself king. Jesus gave no intimation that He was the One in question, though He said: "That Man is no adventurer, nor does He proclaim what is false. Many untruths are spread against Him, and thou who now sayest these things, hast joined in calumniating Him. But the time has now come for the Prophecies to be fulfilled." Jesus' interrogator was an evil-minded man, a great tattler. He dreamed not, when talking with Jesus, that he was in the presence of Him whom he was slandering, for he had heard of Jesus only in a general way.

These men were philosophers. They had some intimation of the truth mixed up with faith in their own divinities, which they tried again to explain away by various interpretations. But all the personages and idols which they wanted to explain had, in the course of time, become so mixed up and confused in their minds that even the cloud of Elias and the Mother of God, of whom they knew nothing at all, had to be dragged by them into the general confusion. They called their goddess Derketo the Queen of Heaven. They spoke of her as of one that had brought to earth all that it had of wisdom and pleasure. They said that her followers having ceased to acknowledge her, she prophesied to them all that would befall them in the future; also that she would plunge into the sea and reappear as a fish to be with them forever. All this, they added, had actually come to pass, etc. Her daughter, whom she had conceived in the sacred rites of paganism, was Semiramis, the wise and powerful Queen of Babylon.

How wonderful! While these men were thus speaking, I saw the whole history of these goddesses, as if they had really risen before me and were still alive. I felt impatient to disabuse the philosophers of their gross errors. They appeared to me so astonishingly silly in not seeing them themselves that I kept thinking: "Now, this is so distinct, so clear that I'll explain it all to them!" Then, again, I thought: "How dare you talk about such things! These learned men must know better than you!" and so I tormented myself during that conversation of several hours.

Jesus explained to the philosophers the confusion and absurdity of their idolatrous system. He related to them the history of Creation, of Adam and Eve, of the Fall, of Cain and Abel, of the children of Noe, the building of the Babylonian Tower, the separation of the bad and their gradual falling away into godlessness. He told them that these wicked people, in order to restore their relations with God from whom they had fallen, had invented all kinds of divinities and had by the evil one been seduced into the grossest error; nevertheless, the Promise that the seed of the women should crush the serpent's head was interwoven with all the poetry, customs, and ceremonies of their necromantic art. It was in consequence of this faint idea they had of the Promise that so many personages had from time to time appeared with the vain design of bringing salvation to the world; but they had given to it instead still greater sins and abominations drawn from the impure source from which they themselves had sprung. He told them about the separation of Abraham's family from the rest of mankind; the education of a special race for the guarding of the Promise; the guidance, direction, and purification of the Children of Israel; and He concluded by telling them

about the Prophets, about Elias and his Prophecies, and
that the present time was to be that of their realization.
Jesus' words were so simple, so convincing and impressive that some of the philosophers were greatly enlightened, while others, returning to their mythical accounts, were again entangled in their mazes. Jesus spoke
with the philosophers until nearly one o'clock. Some of
them believed and reformed their lives. These men were
wrapped up in their apparently learned elucidations of all
sorts of foolish and perplexing questions. Jesus had,
however, let a ray of light fall upon their soul, when He
proved to them that to the fallen race of mankind and
their history there always remained a trace, more or less
correct, of God's designs upon men. He showed them
how they, living as they did in a kingdom of darkness
and confusion, had caught at the manifold improprieties
and abominations of idolatry which, in the midst of their
folly, still offered the external glamour of lost truth; but
God, in His mercy toward mankind, formed from a few
of the most innocent a nation from which the fulfillment
of the Promise was to proceed. Then He pointed out to
them that this time of grace was now arrived, that
whosoever would do penance, amend his life, and receive
Baptism, should be born anew and become a child of
God.

Before this interview with the philosophers and immediately after the Baptism, Jesus had sent away Barnabas and some other disciples to Chytrus, a few hours
distant, where the family of Barnabas dwelt. Jesus had
with Him only the disciple Jonas and another disciple
from Dabereth, when He went one half hour westward
from Salamis to a rich, fertile region wherein lay a little
village whose inhabitants were busied with the harvest.
They were chiefly Jews, for their fields lay on this side of
the city. The country was very lovely, and agriculture
was pursued in a manner different from ours. The grain

was raised on very high ridges like ramparts, between which were grazing grounds surrounded by numerous fruit trees, olive trees, and others. They were full of cattle which, though penned up, could graze in the shade, and yet do no harm to the crops. These low meadows were likewise a sort of reservoir for dew and water. I saw a great many black cows without horns; oxen, hump-backed, heavy-footed, and very broad-horned, used as beasts of burden; numerous asses; extraordinarily large sheep with bushy tails; and, apart from the rest, herds of rams, or horned sheep. Houses and sheds lay scattered here and there. The people had a very beautiful school and a place for teaching in the open air, also a Doctor of the Law among them; but on the Sabbath they used to go to the synagogue in Salamis near Jesus' inn.

The road was very beautiful. As soon as ever the harvesters espied Jesus (they had already seen Him in the synagogue and at the Baptism), they left their work and their tools, cast off the piece of bark that they wore on their head as a protection from the sun's rays, and, hurrying in bands down from the high ridges, bowed low before Him. Many of them even prostrated on the ground. Jesus saluted and blessed them, after which they returned to their labor. As Jesus drew near the school, the Doctor, who had been apprised of His coming, went out with some other honorable personages to meet Him. He bade Him welcome, escorted Him to a beautiful well, washed His feet, removed His mantle, which was then shaken and brushed, and presented Him food and drink.

Jesus, with these people and others who had come from Salamis, went from field to field, here and there instructing the reapers in short parables upon sowing, harvesting, the separation of the wheat from the tares, the building of the granary, and the casting of the ill-weeds into the fire. The reapers listened to him in groups, and then returned to their work, while Jesus passed on to another band.

The men used a crooked knife in reaping. They cut off the stalk about a foot below the ear, and handed it to the women standing behind to receive it. The latter tied the ears into bundles and carried them away in baskets. I saw that many of the low ears were left standing, and that poor women came along afterward, cut them and gathered up the fallen ones as their portion. These women wore very short garments. Their waist was wound with linen bands, and their tunic tucked up around the body forming a sack, into which they put the ears they gleaned. Their arms were uncovered, the breast and neck concealed by linen bands, and the head veiled, or simply protected by a chip hat, according as they were married or maidens.

Jesus went on in this way walking and teaching for about a half-hour's distance, and then returned to the well near the school. Here He found a collation set out on a stone table for Himself and companions. It consisted of a thick sauce, honey, I think, in shallow dishes; long sticks of something from which they broke off little scraps and laid them on their bread, little rolls of pastry, fruits, and little jugs of some kind of drink. The well was extremely beautiful. Back of it was a high terrace filled with trees. One had to descend many steps to get to the well cistern, which was cool and shady. The female portion of the Doctor's family dwelt at some distance from the school. They were veiled when they brought the viands for the repast. Jesus gave instructions on the *Our Father*. In the evening, the reapers assembled in the school, where Jesus explained the parables He had related to them in the fields, and taught also of the manna, of the daily bread, and of the Bread from Heaven. He went afterward with the Doctor and others to visit the sick in their huts, and cured several of the lame and dropsical, who lay mostly in little cells built at the back of the houses. He thus visited a lady afflicted with dropsy. Her tiny apartment was only sufficiently large to accommodate her bed. It was open at her feet, thus allowing her to look out upon a little flower garden. The roof was light and could be raised to afford her a glimpse of the sky. Some men and women went with Jesus to the sick lady's hut. They removed the screen, and Jesus thus accosted the invalid: "Woman, dost thou desire to be relieved?" To which she answered humbly: "I desire what is pleasing to the Prophet." Then Jesus said: "Arise! Thy faith has helped thee!" The woman arose, left her little cell, and said: "Lord, now I know Thy power, for many others have tried to help me, but could not do it." She and her relatives offered thanks, and praised the Lord. Many came to see her, wondering at her cure. Jesus returned to the school.

I saw, on that day at Salamis, Mercuria the sinner walking up and down her apartments, a prey to deep sadness and disquietude. She wept, wrung her hands, and, enveloped in her veil, often threw herself on the floor in a corner. Her husband, who appeared to me not very bright, thought like her maids that she had lost her mind. But Mercuria was torn by remorse for her sins; her only thought, her constant dream, was how she could break loose from her bonds and join the holy women in Palestine. She had two daughters of eight and nine years, and a boy of fifteen. Her home was near to the great temple. It was large with massive walls and surrounded by servants' dwellings, pillars, terraces, and gardens. They called upon her to attend the temple, but she declined on the plea of sickness. This temple was an extraordinary building full of columns, chambers, abodes for the pagan priests, and vaults. In it stood a gigantic statue of the goddess, which shone like gold. The body was that of a fish, and the head was horned like a cow. Before it was another figure of less stature, upon whose shoulders the goddess rested her short arms, or claws. The figures stood upon a high pedestal, in which were cavities for the burning of incense and other offerings. The sacrifices in the goddess' honor consisted even of children, especially of cripples. Mercuria's house became subsequently the dwelling of Costa, the father of St. Catherine. Catherine was born and reared in it. Her father descended from a princely race of Mesopotamia. For certain services, he was rewarded with large possessions in Cyprus. He married in Salamis a daughter of the same pagan priestly family to which Mercuria belonged. Even in her childhood, Catherine was full of wisdom, and had interior visions by which she was guided. She could not endure the pagan idols, and thrust them out of sight wherever she could. As a punishment for this, her father once put her in confinement.

The cities in these regions were not like ours, in which the houses stand apart. The buildings of those pagan cities were enormous, with terraces and massive walls in which, again, abodes for poorer people were constructed. Many of the streets were like broad ramparts, and were planted with trees. Under these thoroughfares were found the abodes of numbers of people. Great order reigned in Salamis. Each class of inhabitants had its own street. The school children also I saw for the most part in one particular street, and there were others set apart for the beasts of burden. The philosophers had one large edifice of their own. It was surrounded by courtyards, and I saw them promenading in the street that belonged to them. Wrapped in their mantles, they walked in bands four or five abreast, and spoke in turn. They always kept to one side of the street in going, and to the other in returning. This order was as a general thing observed in all the streets.

The square with the beautiful fountain, in which the Commandant held his interview with Jesus, was much higher than the adjacent streets. To reach it, one had to mount a flight of steps. Around this square were arcades filled with shops. To one side was the marketplace, near which were rows of dense, pyramidal-shaped trees up which one could mount and sit in their bowerlike foliage. The Commandant's palace fronted on this square.

14. JESUS TEACHING IN CHYTRUS

On the following morning, Jesus again went through the harvest fields instructing the laborers. A remarkable fog hung over the country the whole day, so dense that one could scarcely see his neighbor, and the sun glimmered through it like a white speck. The fields ran northeastwardly between the rising heights until they terminated in a point. I saw innumerable partridges, quails, and pigeons with enormous crops. I remember also to have seen a kind of thick, gray, ribbed apple, the pulp streaked with red. It grew on widespreading trees, which were trained on trellises.

Jesus taught in parables of the harvest and the daily bread, and He cured several lame children who lay on sheepskins in a kind of cradle, or trough. When some of the people broke out in loud praise of His teaching, Jesus checked them with words something like these: "Whosoever hath, to him shall be given; and whosoever hath not (that also which he thinketh he hath), shall be taken away from him."[1]

The Jews of this place had doubts upon divers points, upon which Jesus instructed them. They feared to have no part in the Promised Land, they thought that Moses had had no need to cross the Red Sea, and that there was no reason for his wandering so long in the desert since there were other and more direct routes. Jesus met their objections with the reply that they could get possession of the Kingdom of God, and that there was no need, it was true, for so long a sojourn in the desert. He challenged them, since they disapproved such proceedings in Moses, not to wander around themselves in the desert of sin, unbelief, and murmuring, but to take the shortest road by means of penance, Baptism, and faith. The Jews of Cyprus had intermarried freely with the pagans, but in such contracts the latter always became converts to Judaism.

On this walk of instruction through the harvest fields, Jesus and His companions reached the highroad which, running a couple of hours to the west of Salamis, connected the port on the northwestern coast of Cyprus to that on the southeast. Here stood a very large Jewish inn, and at it Jesus and His followers stopped. Not far off stood sheds and an inn with a well for the pagan caravans. The highway was always swarming with travellers. There was no female at the inn; the women dwelt apart by themselves. Jesus had just washed His feet and taken some refreshments when the disciples, who had tarried in Salamis baptizing, arrived. Jesus' companions now numbered twenty. He continued to teach out in the open air the people coming home from their work. They brought to Him some sick laborers who could no longer earn their bread. As they believed in His doctrine, Jesus cured them and bade them resume at once their daily labor.

Toward evening a caravan of Arabs arrived. They had with them, as beasts of burden, oxen yoked in couples. On two poles across their backs, they carried immense bales of goods that rose high above their heads. In narrow parts of the road they went one behind the other, still keeping their burden between them. I saw asses and camels also laden with bales of wool. These Arabs were from the region in which Jethro had dwelt. They were of a browner complexion than the Cypriotes, and had come hither with their goods in ships. In the mining districts through which they passed, they bartered some of their goods for copper and other metals, and they were now pursuing their course southward along the highroad, in order again to embark for home. The beasts bore the heavy metal in long chests, the packages smaller than usual on account of their weight. I think the metal was in bars, or long plates. Some of it was already wrought into various vessels and kettles, which I saw, in packages round and of the form of a cask. The women were exceedingly industrious. During their journey, whether walking or riding, they occupied themselves in spinning, and whenever they encamped, they set to work at weaving covers and scarfs. They could, in consequence, maintain themselves on the journey and renew their own clothing. They used for their work the wool packed on the beasts of burden. While spinning, they fastened the wool to their shoulders, spun the thread with one hand and wound it on the spindle which they turned in the other. When the spindle was full, the thread was wound off upon a bobbin that hung at their girdle.

When these people had unloaded and cared for their beasts, they saluted Jesus and begged to be permitted to hear His doctrine. He commended them for their industry and took occasion from it to ask the question, for whom was all their trouble, for whom all their labor. From this He went on to speak of the Creator and Preserver of all things, of gratitude to God, of God's mercy toward sinners and lost sheep that wander around not knowing their Shepherd. He taught them in mild and loving words. They were touched and rejoiced, and wanted to bestow all kinds of presents upon Him. He blessed their children and left them. With His companions He then directed His steps more to the north toward Chytrus, situated between four and five hours from this place and about six from Salamis. The way now became hilly.

I saw here in the country olive trees and cotton trees,

also a plant from which I think they make a kind of silk. It did not look like our flax, but rather like hemp, and it furnishes a long, soft thread. But most conspicuous of all was a little tree with quantities of beautiful yellow flowers, most charming to behold. Its fruit was almost the same as that of the medlar, or persimmon; it appeared to me to be saffron. To the left, one had a beautiful view of the mountains covered with high forests. Cypresses were numerous, also little resinous bushes of delicious fragrance. Here too among the mountains descended a little stream that in one part formed a waterfall. Still farther on and higher up, there was on one side of the mountain a forest, on the other, the naked soil over which wound a path, and on either side were caves extending into the mountain. Out of these were mined copper and some kind of white metal like silver. I saw the miners boring into them, also from above. The metal must have been smelted on the spot, and that with a certain yellow something of which there was a whole mountain in the neighborhood. The workman kneaded the melted mass into great balls and then allowed them to dry. I heard it said on that occasion that the mountain sometimes caught fire.

After four hours' journey, Jesus reached an inn more than half an hour from Chytrus. All along the road, mines were still to be seen. Here Jesus and His companions halted and the father of Barnabas, along with some other men, received the Lord and extended to Him the usual acts of kindness. Jesus rested here and taught, after which He took a light repast with His companions.

Chytrus lay on a low plain. Jesus approached it from the side upon which were the mines. The population was made up of Jews and pagans. All around the city stood numerous single buildings. It looked like country workshops connected by gardens and fields.

I was very much troubled at the little fruit arising from

Jesus' great fatigue and labor in Cyprus. It was so small that, as the Pilgrim told me, nothing was known of that journey, no mention was made of it in Scripture, not even of Paul and Barnabas's labors there. Then I had a vision concerning it, of which I remember the following details: Jesus gained five hundred and seventy souls, pagans and Jews, in Cyprus. I saw that the sinner Mercuria and her children delayed not to follow Him, and that she brought with her great wealth in property and money. She joined the holy women; and at the first Christian settlements between Ophel and Bethania, made under the deacons, she contributed largely toward the buildings and the support of the brethren. I saw also that in an insurrection against the Christians (Saul not yet being converted) Mercuria was murdered. It was at the time when Saul set out for Damascus. Soon after Jesus' departure from the island, many pagans and Jews with their money and valuables left Cyprus and journeyed to Palestine, and little by little, transferred thither all their wealth. Then arose a great outcry among other members of these families who had not embraced Jesus' doctrine. They looked upon themselves as injured by the departure of their relatives, and they scoffed at Jesus as an impostor. Jews and heathens made common cause together, and considered it a crime even to speak of Him. Many persons were arrested and scourged. The pagan priests persecuted those of their own belief, and forced them to offer sacrifice. The Commandant who had had an interview with Jesus was recalled to Rome and deposed from his office. They even went so far as to send Roman soldiers to take possession of the ports so that no one could leave the island. They did not remain long, but on their departure they took with them some of the inhabitants.

On the way to Chytrus, Jesus instructed the miners in separate bands. Some of the mines were rented by pagans; others, by Jews. The laborers looked very thin, pale, and miserable. Their nude bodies were protected in several places with pieces of brown leather, in which they were encased like turtles in their shells. Jesus took as the subject of His instruction the goldsmith, who purifies the ore in fire. The heathens and Jews were working on different sides of the road, so both could listen at the same time. There were some possessed, or grievously disturbed creatures that had to be bound with cords even when at work, and as Jesus drew near, they began to rage and cry. They published His name, and cried out to know what He wanted with them. Jesus commanded them to be silent, and they became quiet. Some Jewish miners now came forward complaining that the pagans had opened mines under the road in their district, thus encroaching upon their rights, and they begged Him to decide the point between them. Then Jesus directed a hole to be bored near the boundary through the part belonging to the Jews, and the workmen came to the pagan mines. There were found heaps of white, metallic scraps, I think zinc or silver, which had tempted the pagans to overstep their limits. Jesus gave an instruction upon scandal and ill-gotten goods. The pagans were convicted, for the facts witnessed against them. But as the magistrate was not on the spot, nothing could be done, and the pagans withdrew muttering their dissatisfaction.

Chytrus was a very stirring place. The inhabitants, pagans and Jews, lived on easy terms with one another as I more than once saw, though the two sects dwelt in different quarters. The pagans had several temples, and the Jews, two synagogues. Intermarriages were very frequent among them, but in such cases the pagan party always embraced Judaism.

Outside the city Jesus was met by the Jewish Elders and Doctors, also two of the philosophers from Salamis, who having been touched by His doctrine, had followed Him thither in order to hear Him again. After they had given Jesus a reception with the customary attentions, foot-washing and refreshments in the house devoted to such purposes, they petitioned Him for the cure of several sick persons who had been longingly awaiting His coming. Jesus accompanied His escort into the Jewish quarter where, in the street before several of the houses, about twenty invalids were lying, whom He cured. Some among them were lame. They were leaning on crutches, which were like frames resting on three feet. The cured and their relatives proclaimed the praises of Jesus, shouting after Him short passages of encomium taken chiefly from the Psalms, but the disciples told them to keep quiet.

Jesus went next to the house of the Elder of the synagogue where several of the literati were assembled, among them some belonging to the sect of Rechabites. These last-named wore a garb somewhat different from the other Jews, and their manners and customs were peculiarly rigorous. Of these, however, they had already laid aside many. They had a whole street to themselves, and were especially engaged in mining. They belonged to that race that settled in Ephron, in the kingdom of Basan, in whose neighborhood also, mining was carried on. Jesus was invited by the Elder to dinner, which he had ordered to be prepared for Him when the Sabbath was over. But as He had promised to dine with Barnabas's father, He invited all the present guests to accompany Him thither, and begged the Elder to entertain the poor laborers and miners after the synagogue was over with the viands prepared for the dinner.

The synagogue was filled with people, and crowds of pagans were listening on the porches outside. Jesus took His text from the third book of Moses, treating of the sacrifice of the Tabernacle, and from Jeremias, relating to the Promise. He spoke of sacrifices living and dead, answered His hearers' questions upon the difference between them, and taught on the Eight Beatitudes.

There was in the synagogue a pious old rabbi who had been for a long time afflicted with the dropsy, and who as usual had caused himself to be carried thither to his customary place. As the literati were disputing Jesus on various points, he cried aloud: "Silence! Allow me a word!" and when all were still, he called out: "Lord! Thou hast shown mercy to others. Help me, too, and bid me to come to Thee!" Thereupon Jesus said to the man: "If thou dost believe, arise and come to Me!" The sick man instantly arose, exclaiming: "Lord, I do believe!" He was cured. He mounted the steps to where Jesus stood, and thanked Him, while the whole assembly broke forth into shouts of joy and praise. Jesus and His followers left the synagogue and went to Barnabas's dwelling. Then the master of the feast gathered together the poor and the laborers to partake of the dinner that Jesus had left them.

1. *Lk.* 8:18.

15. THE PATERNAL HOME AND FAMILY OF BARNABAS. JESUS TEACHING IN THE ENVIRONS OF CHYTRUS

The father of Barnabas dwelt beyond the western limits of the city in one of the many houses there scattered. Chytrus was surrounded by such dwellings, some of which, standing in clusters, formed villages. The house was quite handsome. On one side it was terraced, the walls brown as if painted in oil or smeared with resin—or was that the natural color? On these terraces were plants and foliage. Besides the terraces the house was surrounded by a colonnade, an open gallery, upon which were beautiful trees. Beyond these were vineyards and an open space full of building wood, all in good order. In it were some trunks of trees extraordinarily thick, and there were all kinds of figures made out of the wood, but all was so well arranged that one could easily walk among them. I think the wood was intended for ship building. I saw too long wagons, but not wider than the wood itself, and provided with heavy iron wheels. They were drawn by oxen yoked far apart. One can see at no great distance from Chytrus a very beautiful forest of lofty trees.

The father of Barnabas was a widower. His sister with her maidservants had a house in the neighborhood; she took care of his household and provided the meals. The pagans that accompanied Jesus, as well as the philosophers from Salamis, did not recline with Him at table, because it was still the Sabbath; but they walked up and down in the open hall, ate from their hand and, standing under the colonnade, listened to Jesus' teaching. The meal consisted of birds and broad, flat fish, besides cakes, honey, and fruit. There were likewise dishes with pieces of meat twisted into a spiral form and garnished with all kinds of herbs. Jesus spoke of sacrifice, of the Promise, and dwelt at length upon the Prophets.

During the dinner, several bands of poor, half-clad children of from four to six years old made their appearance. They had in little loosely woven baskets some kind of edible herbs, which they offered to the guests in exchange for bread or other food. They seemed to prefer that side of the table at which Jesus and His followers were reclining. Jesus stood up, emptied their baskets of the herbs, filled them from the viands on the table, and blessed the little ones. This scene was very lovely, very touching.

Next morning Jesus taught in the rear of Barnabas's house, where there was a plot of beautiful rising ground furnished with a teacher's chair. The path leading to it from the house was through magnificent arbors of grape-vines. A large audience was gathered. Jesus first addressed the miners and other laborers, then the pagans and, lastly, a great crowd of Jews that had married into pagan families. A great many sick pagans had begged Jesus' help and permission to hear His instructions. They were mostly laborers, sick and crippled, who lay on couches near the teacher's chair. Jesus' instruction to the laborers was on the *Our Father* and the refining of ore by fire; that to the pagans, on the wild shoots of trees and grapevines (which had to be cut away), or the one, only God, the children of God, the son of the house and the servant, and the vocation of the Gentiles. Then He turned to the subject of mixed marriages, which were not to be countenanced lightly, though they might be tolerated through condescension. In the latter case, however, they might be allowed only when there was a prospect of converting or perfecting one of the parties, but never merely for the gratification of sensuality. They could be suffered only when both parties were animated by a holy intention. He spoke, nevertheless, more against than for such unions, and declared them happy who had raised pure offspring in the house of the Lord. He touched upon the serious account the Jewish party would have to render, of the responsibility of rearing children in piety, of the necessity of corresponding with grace at the time of its visitation, and of penance and Baptism.

After that Jesus cured the sick and dined with Barnabas. Accompanied by His friends, He next went to the opposite side of the city, where were numbers of beehives placed at an unusually great distance from one another among the large flower gardens. Nearby were a fountain and a little lake. Jesus here taught and related parables, after which all went into the city to the synagogue, where the instruction on sacrifice and the Promise was concluded.

There were at this time some learned Jews travelling through the country. They put all kinds of cunningly contrived questions to Jesus, but He soon solved them. These men seemed to be actuated by some bad design. Their questions referred to mixed marriages, to Moses and the numbers he had caused to be put to death, to Aaron, the golden calf he had ordered to be made, his punishment, etc.

The next day appeared to be either a feast or a fast among the Jews, for there was morning service in the synagogue, that is, prayer and preaching. That over, Jesus left the city by the north side with all His disciples and some pagan youths. His little band was joined by some Jewish Doctors and several Rechabites, so that there were altogether fully one hundred men. They pursued their journey for about an hour to a place which was the principal seat of the bee-raising industry. Far off toward the rising sun stood long rows of white beehives, about the height of a man and woven, I think, of rushes or bark. They had many openings, and were placed one above another. Every group had in front of it a flowery field, and I noticed that balm grew here in abundance. Each field, or garden, was hedged in, and the whole bore the appearance of a city. One could readily recognize the pagan part of it, for here and there standing in niches were puppets with tails, like those of a fish, curving behind them into the air. They had little short paws and faces not altogether human.

The village itself consisted of many little cottages belonging to the bee proprietors, who kept there the vessels and utensils used in their branch of industry. The inn was a large building with all kinds of dependencies. Rows of sheds, or open halls, crossed one another around the courts in which were numerous trestles and long mats. The steward of this establishment provided for the needs of all that were here employed. He was a pagan. The Jews had their own halls and places for prayer. I think the wax and honey were prepared in the house and under the long sheds. It looked like a house for the general gathering in of the produce. I saw here also many of those little trees whose yellow blossoms are so beautiful. The leaves are more yellow than green, and the blossoms fall so thickly on the ground that they form, as it were, a soft carpet. Long mats were spread beneath the trees to catch them. I saw the workmen pressing the flowers to extract from them some kind of coloring matter. The little trees when young were planted in pots, and then transplanted often into the holes of rocks with earth around the roots. There were similar trees in Judea. I saw here also large plants of flax, from which they drew long threads.

Not far from Chytrus, about half an hour to the north, quite a considerable stream issued from the rock, flowed first through the city, and then watered the region by which Jesus had come. In some places it flowed along freely, in others it was bridged over. I think the water supplies of the Salamis aqueducts were obtained from it. It formed at its source a real little lake. In its waters Baptism was yet to be given, and I think there was some allusion made to it. The number of beautiful wildflowers in this region was surprising. All along the roads stood orange trees, fig trees, currant bushes, and grapevines.

Jesus had come here principally to be able to instruct the pagans without interruption, without disturbance from visitors. This He did all the rest of the day in the gardens and arbors of the inn. His hearers stood or lay stretched on the grass, while He instructed them on the *Our Father* and the Eight Beatitudes. When addressing the pagans, He spoke especially of the origin and abominations of their gods, of the vocation of Abraham and his separation from idolaters, and of God's guidance over the children of Israel. He spoke openly and forcibly. There were about a hundred men listening to Him. After the instruction, all took refreshments in the inn, the pagans apart. The repast was made up of bread, long strips of goat cheese, honey, and fruit. The proprietor of the house was a pagan, but very humble and reserved in his manners. That evening, the pagans having retired, Jesus instructed the Jews and they prayed together. All spent the night at the inn.

Chytrus was a far more stirring place than Salamis, where all kinds of business and traffic were confined to the port and a couple of streets. Here, however, there reigned great activity. On the side by which Jesus approached the city, there was a great market where cattle and birds were exposed for sale. Near the heart of the city was another market beautiful to look upon. It was very high and all around it, as well as under its lofty arches, hung many different kinds of colored stuffs and covers. The opposite side of the city was occupied almost entirely by the workers in metal and their foundries. The hammering and pounding were so astonishingly loud that one could not hear his own words, although most of the factories were outside the city. They made all kinds of vessels, especially a kind of oval oven large and light, with a little cover and two handles near the top. In manufacturing them, the metal was first bent into shape, and then put into immense ovens, where the molten mass was blown by means of long tubes into the form of the hollow vessel required. They were yellow outside and white within. All kinds of fruit, as well as honey or syrup, were exported in them. When transported over the sea they were placed on a kind of trestle, and on land they were carried by means of poles run through the handles.

The next day Jesus again taught at the apiary, the number of His hearers having increased to a couple of hundred. In most convincing terms He again explained to the pagans their errors, and represented the existence of their gods as so very pitiful that they had to explain it by all kinds of significations in order to be able even to endure them themselves. And when, continuing His discourse, He exhorted them to renounce their subtleties, their vain imaginations, their continual efforts in behalf of falsehood, and in simplicity of heart to confine their researches to God and His revelations, some of them who had come thither like travelling literati with staves in their hands, became indignant, and turning off murmuring upon their way. Jesus remarked at this conjuncture: "Let them go! It is better that they should do so than remain to make new gods out of what they have just heard." He uttered many prophetic words on the desolation that should one day come upon that beautiful region, its cities and temples, and of the judgment that was to fall on all those countries. He said that when idolatry should have reached its height, then would paganism come to naught, and He dwelt long on the chastisement of the Jews and the destruction of Jerusalem. The pagans took all in better part than did the Jews who, supporting themselves upon their Promises, had always some objections to bring forward. Jesus went through all the Prophets with them, explained the passages relating to the Messiah, and told them that the time for their fulfillment had arrived. The Messiah would arise among the Jews, but they would not own Him. They would mock and deride Him, and when He would assure them He was the One whom they were expecting, they would seize Him and put Him to death. This language was not at all to the taste of many of His hearers, and Jesus reminded them of how they were accustomed to do with their Prophets. He ended by saying that as they had treated the heralds, so too would they act toward the One whom they announced.

The Rechabites spoke with Jesus of Malachias, for whom they entertained great veneration. They told Jesus that they esteemed him an angel of God, that he had come as a child to certain pious people, that he had frequently disappeared for a time, and that no one knew whether he was now really dead or not. They dwelt at length on his prophecies of the Messiah and His new sacrifice, which Jesus explained as relating to the present and the near future.

From the apiary, Jesus went with a large company (which, however, constantly decreased on the road) back again to Barnabas's home, a journey of several hours. The greater number of His party consisted of young men belonging to the Jewish community, and who were about to embark for Jerusalem to celebrate the feast of Pentecost. Nevertheless, they that remained with Jesus formed quite a considerable band. From thirty to forty pagan women and maidens and about ten Jewish girls were assembled at the entrance of the gardens to do Jesus honor. They were playing on flutes and singing canticles of praise; they wore flowery wreaths and strewed green branches in the way. Here and there also they spread mats on the road over which Jesus was to pass, inclined low before Him, and offered Him presents of wreaths, flowers, aromatic shrubs, and little flasks of perfume. Jesus thanked them, and addressed to them some words. They followed Him to the courtyard of Barnabas's house, and set their gifts down in the assembly hall. They had adorned everything with flowers and garlands. This reception, though rural and less noisy, was something similar to that tendered Jesus on Palm Sunday. His escort soon returned to their homes, for it was evening.

I was astonished at the costume of the pagan women. The young girls wore curious-looking caps, like the so-called cuckoo baskets that, when a child, I used to weave of rushes. Some were without ornament; others had a wreath twined around them from which innumerable threads with all kinds of ornamentation fell upon the forehead. The lower edge always consisted of a wreath made of worsted or feather flowers. The veil was worn under the hat, or cap. It was in two parts so that it could be opened in front, or thrown up over the hat; in the latter case, it fell behind as low as the neck. They were girdled very tightly, wore a breastpiece, and around the neck all kinds of ribands and finery. Their lower dress was very full. It consisted of several skirts of thin material one above the other, and each about a span, or nine inches, longer than the one above it, so that the lowest of all was the longest. The arms were not entirely covered. The dress had no sleeves, only long lappets, and little wreaths were fastened round the arms. The material was of different colors: yellow, red, white, blue, some striped and others covered with flowers. Their hair fell around their shoulders like a veil. It was fastened at the ends with a tasselled string, and thus prevented from floating on the breeze. The sandals on their bare feet were bent up into a point at the toe and kept in place by means of laces. The married women's headdress was not so high as that of the young girls. It had a stiff leaf in front that screened the forehead and descended in a point as far as the nose, and thence curved up above the ears, thus exposing them to view with their pearl pendants. It was openworked and wound with braided hair, pearls, and all kinds of ornaments. They wore long mantles that hung very full in the back. The children with them had no other clothing than a band of some kind of stuff, which, passing over one shoulder, crossed the breast, and was tied around the waist, forming a covering for the middle of the body. These women had awaited Jesus fully three hours.

A repast had been prepared at Barnabas's. But the guests did not recline at table. The food was handed to each on a little board, a wooden waiter, such as had been used on the ship. Many old men were assembled here, among them the old Doctor of the Law whom Jesus had cured in the synagogue. Barnabas's father was a solid, square-built old man, and one could easily see that he was accustomed to work in wood. The men of those days looked much more robust than those of the present age.

I next saw Jesus seated in the teacher's chair at the spring outside of Chytrus. He was preparing the neophytes for Baptism, which the disciples conferred, first upon the Jews and then upon the pagans.

Jesus spoke here also with the Jewish Doctors on the subject of circumcision. He said that it should not be imposed upon the converted pagans, unless they themselves desired it. At the same time, the Jews ought not to be expected to allow these converts entrance into the synagogue, for they should avoid scandal. But they should thank God that the pagans, having abandoned their idolatry, were awaiting the hour of salvation. Other mortifications, the circumcision of the heart and of every species of concupiscence, could be imposed upon them. Jesus provided for their instruction and devotions apart from the Jews.

16. JESUS IN THE CITY OF MALLEP

I noticed some men very respectfully closing the well outside of Chytrus, at which the disciples had been baptizing. The crowd that had been present at Jesus' instructions, as well as the newly baptized, were upon the point of separating for their homes. Some were standing around several Jewish travellers that had just arrived. To their questions as to Jesus' whereabouts, they received the answer: "The Prophet taught here from early this morning until noon. But now He is gone with His disciples and about seven philosophers of Salamis, just baptized, to the great village of Mallep." This place was built by the Jews, therefore only Jews lived in it. It was situated on a height toward the base of a mountain chain, and commanded a wondrously beautiful view upon all sides, even as far as the sea. It had five streets, all converging toward the center where, hewn out of the rocky foundation, was a reservoir which received its water supply from the conduit of the well near Chytrus. All around the reservoir were beautiful seats under shady trees, and from it stretched a magnificent view over the whole city and the surrounding country, which was teeming with fruit. Mallep was surrounded by a double entrenchment, the inner one lower than the outer. A great part of it was hewn out of the rock, and beyond it, looking like little valleys, ran ditches all around the city. On the fresh green sward, covered with lovely flowers, stood rows of the most magnificent fruit trees, under which lay the large yellow fruit in the grass, for everything here was now in full harvest. The people were busy drying the fruit that was to be sent to a distance. They manufactured also cloths, carpets, mats, and out of sapwood light, shallow cases in which to dry the fruit.

On Jesus' arrival, He was met at the gate by the Doctors of the synagogue, the school children, and a crowd of people who had come to welcome Him, all adorned as for a feast. The children were singing, playing on musical instruments, and carrying palm branches, the little girls going before the boys. Jesus passed through the children, blessing them as He went, and with His followers, about thirty men, was escorted by the Doctors into a reception hall where the ceremony of washing the feet was performed.

Meanwhile about twenty invalids, some lame, others dropsical, were brought into the street outside the house. Jesus cured them, and directed them to follow Him to the well in the heart of the city. Great was the joy of the relatives as, with the lately cured, they made their way to the place designated, where Jesus gave them an instruction upon daily bread and gratitude toward God.

From here He went to the synagogue and taught upon the petition: "Let Thy Kingdom come." He spoke of the

Kingdom of God in us and of its near approach. He explained to His hearers that it was a spiritual, not an earthly kingdom, and told them how it would fare with them that cast it from them. The pagans who had followed Jesus were standing back of the Jews, for the line of separation was more strictly observed here than in pagan cities.

The instruction over, Jesus assisted at a dinner given by the Doctors, after which they escorted Him to the inn, which they had prepared for Him and His company. A steward had been appointed to see to all things.

On the following day, Jesus taught again in the extraordinarily beautiful synagogue where all the people were assembled. He spoke of the sower, of different kinds of soil, of weeds, and of the grain of mustard seed, which bears fruit so large. He took His similitudes from a shrub that grew in those regions which, from a very small kernel, shoots forth a stalk thick as one's arm and almost as high as a man, and which is very useful. Its fruit was large as an acorn, red and black. Its juice when expressed was used for dyeing. The baptized pagans were not in the synagogue, but outside on the terraces listening to Jesus' words.

When Jesus was afterward taking dinner with the Elders, three blind boys about ten to twelve years old were led in to Him by some other children. The former were playing on flutes and another kind of instrument which they held to the mouth and touched at the same time with the fingers. It was not a fife, and it made a buzzing, humming sound like the Jew's harp. At intervals also they sang in a very agreeable manner. Their eyes were open, and it seemed as if a cataract had obscured the sight. Jesus asked them whether they desired to see the light, in order to walk diligently and piously in the paths of righteousness. They answered most joyously: "Lord, and wilt Thou help us! Help us, Lord, and we

will do whatever Thou commandest!" Then Jesus said:
"Put down your instruments!" and He stood them before
Him, put His thumbs to His mouth, and passed them one
after the other from the corner of the eyes to the temple
above. Then He took up a dish of fruit from the table,
held it before the boys, said: "Do ye see that?" blessed
them, and gave them its contents. They stared around in
joyful amazement, they were intoxicated with delight,
and at last cast themselves weeping at Jesus' feet. The
whole company were deeply touched; joy and wonder
took possession of all. The three boys, full of joy, hurried
with their guides out of the hall and through the streets
to their parents. The whole city was in excitement. The
children returned with their relatives and many others to
the forecourt of the hall, singing songs of joy and playing
upon their instruments, in order thus to express their
thanks. Jesus took occasion from this circumstance to give a
beautiful instruction on gratitude. He said: "Thanksgiving
is a prayer which attracts new favors, so good is the
Heavenly Father."

After dinner, Jesus walked with the disciples and the
pagan philosophers through the beautiful shady meadows
around the city, teaching the pagan men and new disciples.
The elder disciples were themselves instructing separate
groups. That evening Jesus taught again in the synagogue.

Next day He visited the parents of the blind boys
whom He had cured. They were Jews from Arabia, from
the region in which Jethro, Moses's father-in-law, had
dwelt. They had a particular name. They travelled
around a great deal, and had already been baptized near
Capharnaum. They were journeying through that part of
the country at the time, and had heard Jesus' sermon on
the mount. These people, that is, these two families composed of about twenty persons including the women and
children, were tradesmen and manufacturers, who, as
among us the Italians, the Tyrolese, and the inhabitants

of the Black Forest, tarry awhile sometimes here, sometimes there, busying themselves in making clocks, mouse-
traps, figures in plaster of Paris, which they sold to their
neighbors, thus uniting labor and traffic. At this season
they generally visited Mallep for a couple of months.
Outside the city, on the north, they occupied a private
inn in which they had all kinds of tools, weaving ap-
paratus, etc. Their blind boys had, in their wanderings, to
earn something by singing and playing on the flute when
occasion offered. Jesus told the parents that they should
no longer drag the boys around after them, but that they
should remain in Mallep and attend school. He indicated
to them the persons that would receive and instruct their
boys, for He had already arranged all that the day
before. The parents promised to do whatever He
directed.

17. JESUS TEACHING BEFORE THE PAGAN PHILOSOPHERS. HE ATTENDS A JEWISH WEDDING

Jesus walked with the disciples and the seven baptized
philosophers through the charming meadow valley that
led from Mallep to the village of Lanifa and then, gently
rising, turned southward into the mountains. From this
southern side descended a brook, about three feet broad,
which took its rise in the spring near Chytrus. It ran in a
covered bed through the mountains, then through the
village Lanifa and the valley near Mallep whose surrounding moats it fed. But it was not the same water as
that in the elevated fountain in the center of Mallep,
although the street by which Jesus left the city, the fifth
and last of the place, was that of the canal by which the
beautiful reservoir was supplied. Words cannot describe
the charm and quiet of this verdant valley, gently winding
around and entirely shut in by the surrounding heights.

As far as Mallep lay isolated granges on either side of the road, dependent upon the village of Lanifa at the end of the valley. All was perfectly green and covered with the most beautiful flowers and fruits which here grew, some wild, some cultivated. Jesus took the road to the left, on the south side of the brook to Lanifa. He met a band of young people on their way to take ship for Jerusalem, there to celebrate Pentecost. Jesus accosted them with the command to salute Lazarus, but beyond that not to speak of Him. Farther on, He crossed the brook, turned to the north, and descended again into the valley, in order to return to Mallep. On that side He came to another village, which bore the singular name of Leppe.

The harvest was now over, and the people placed together the sheaves destined for the poor.

During the whole journey Jesus taught the pagan philosophers, sometimes walking, sometimes tarrying in some lovely spot. He instructed them upon the absolute corruption of mankind before the Flood, of the preservation of Noe, of the new growth of evil, of the vocation of Abraham, and of God's guidance of his race down to the time in which the promised Consoler was to come forth from it. The heathens asked Jesus for explanations of all kinds, and brought forward many great names of ancient gods and heroes, telling Him of their benevolent deeds. Jesus replied that all men possessed by nature, more or less, human kindness by which they effected many things useful and advantageous for time, but that many vices and abominations arose from such benefits. He showed them the state of degradation, the partial destruction of the nations sunk in idolatry, the ridiculous and fabulous deformity running through the history of their divinities, mixed up with demoniacal divinations and magical delusions which were woven into them as so many truths.

The philosophers made mention also of one of the

most ancient of the wise kings who had come from the mountainous regions beyond India. He was called Dsemschid. With a golden dagger received from God, he had divided off many lands, peopled them, and shed blessing everywhere. They asked Jesus about him and the many wonders which they related of him. Jesus answered that Dsemchid, who had been a leader of the people, was a man naturally wise and intelligent in the things of sense. Upon the dispersion of men at the time of the building of the Tower of Babel, he had put himself at the head of a tribe and taken possession of lands according to certain regulations. He had fallen less deeply into evil, because the race to which he belonged was itself less corrupt. Jesus recalled to them also the fables that had been written in connection with him, and showed them that he was a false companion-picture, a false type of Melchisedech, the priest and king. Jesus told them to fix their attention on the latter and upon the descendants of Abraham, for as the stream of nations moved along, God had sent Melchisedech to the best families that he might guide them, unite them, and make ready for them countries and dwellings, in order to preserve them in their purity and, according to their worthiness or unworthiness, either hasten or retard the fulfillment of the Promise. Who Melchisedech was, He left to themselves to determine; but of him this much was true, he was an ancient type of the then far-off, but now so near grace of the Promise, and the sacrifice of bread and wine which he had offered would be fulfilled and perfected, and would endure till the end of the world.

Jesus' words upon Dsemschid and Melchisedech were so clear, so indisputable, that the philosophers exclaimed in astonishment: "Master, how wise Thou art! It would almost seem as if Thou didst live in that time, as if Thou didst know all these people even better than they knew themselves!" Jesus said to them many more things concerning the Prophets, both the greater and the minor, and He dwelt especially upon Malachias. When the Sabbath began, He went to the synagogue and delivered a discourse upon the passage of Leviticus referring to the jubilee year, also upon something from Jeremias. He said that a man should cultivate his field well, so that his brother, who was to receive it from him, might see in it a proof of his affection.

On the following morning, Jesus continued in the synagogue His discourse on the jubilee year, the cultivation of the field, and the passages from Jeremias. This over, He went with the disciples and, followed by many people, Jews and pagans, to a Jewish bathing garden outside the southern end of the city, the water supply to which was furnished by the Chytrus aqueducts. There was a beautiful cistern in the garden and all around it were the large basins for bathing, pleasant avenues, and long shady bowers. Everything necessary for administering Baptism was already prepared here. Crowds followed Jesus to an open place near the well fitted up for teaching, and among them were seven bridegrooms with their relatives and attendants.

Jesus taught of the Fall, of the perversion of Adam and Eve, of the Promise, of the degeneracy of men into the wild state, of the separation of the less corrupt, of the guard set over marriage, in order to transmit virtues and graces from father to son, and of the sanctification of marriage by the observance of the Divine Law, moderation, and continency. In this way, Jesus' discourse turned upon the bride and bridegroom. To illustrate His meaning, He referred to a certain tree on the island which could be fertilized by trees at a distance—yes, even across the sea, and He uttered the words: "In the same way may hope, confidence in God, desire of salvation, humility and chastity become in some manner the mother for the fulfillment of the Promise." This led Jesus to touch upon the mysterious signification of marriage, in that it typifies the bond of union between the Consoler of Israel and His Church. He called marriage a great mystery. His words on this subject were so beautiful, so elevated, that it seems to me impossible to repeat them. He afterward taught upon penance and Baptism, which expiate and efface the crime of separation, and render all worthy to participate in the alliance of salvation.

Jesus went aside also with some of the aspirants to Baptism, heard their confession, forgave their sins, and imposed upon them certain mortifications and good works. James the Less and Barnabas performed the ceremony of Baptism. The neophytes were principally aged men, a few pagans, and the three boys cured of blindness, who had not been baptized with their parents at Capharnaum.

The Sabbath over, some of the philosophers started the following questions: Whether it was necessary that God should have allowed the frightful deluge to pass over the earth; Why He permitted mankind to await so long the coming of the Redeemer; Could He not have employed other means for the same end, and send One who would restore all things? Jesus answered by explaining that that entered not into the designs of God, that He had created the angels with free will and superior faculties, and yet they had separated from Him through pride and had been precipitated into the kingdom of darkness; that man, with free will, had been placed between the kingdom of darkness and that of light, but by eating the forbidden fruit he had approached nearer to the former; that man was now obliged to coöperate with God in order to receive help from Him and to attract into himself the Kingdom of God, that God might give it to him. Man, by eating the forbidden fruit, had sought to become like unto God; and that he might rise from his fallen state it was necessary that the Father should allow His Divine Son to succor him and reconcile him again to Himself. Man, in his entire being, had become so deformed that the great mercy and wonderful guidance of God were needed, to establish upon earth His Kingdom, which that of darkness had driven from the hearts of men. Jesus added that this Kingdom consisted not in worldly dominion and magnificence, but in the regeneration, the reconciliation of man with the Father, and in the reunion of all the good into one body.[1]

On the following day, Jesus taught again at the place of Baptism. The seven bridal couples were present. Among the bridegrooms two were converted pagans who had received circumcision and espoused Jewish maidens. There were some other pagans inclined toward Judaism, who had sought and obtained permission to assist at the instructions with them.

At first Jesus spoke in general terms upon the duties of the married state, and especially upon those of wives. They should, He said, raise their eyes only to fix them upon those of their husband; at other times they should be kept lowered. He spoke, likewise, of obedience, humility, chastity, industry, and the care of their children. When the women had retired in order to prepare a repast in Leppe, Jesus instructed the men for Baptism. He spoke of Elias and of the great drought that fell upon the whole country, and of the rain cloud which, at the prayer of Elias, had risen out of the sea. (Today there was just such another dense, white cloud of fog resting over the earth. One could not see far around him.) Jesus referred to that drought over the country as to a punishment from God for the idolatry of King Achab. Grace and blessing likewise had withdrawn, and the drought had prevailed even in human hearts. He spoke of Elias's concealment by the torrent of Carith, of his being fed by the bird, of his journeying to Sarepta and his being helped by the widow, of his confounding the idolaters on Carmel, and of the uprising of the cloud by whose rain all things were refreshed. He compared this rain to Baptism, and admonished His hearers to reform their lives and not, like Achab and Jezabel, continue in sin and dryness of heart after the rain of Baptism. Jesus alluded also to Segola, that pious pagan woman of Egypt, who settled at Abila and peformed so many good works that she at last found favor in the sight of God. Then He showed them how the pagans ought to strive to practice virtue that thereby they might attract upon themselves divine grace, for His pagan listeners knew something of Elias and Segola.

After the Baptism of the bridegrooms, Jesus and His followers, along with all the bridal parties and the rabbis, were invited by the Jewish Doctor of the place to an entertainment at the village of Leppe, west of Mallep. The daughter of this Doctor was the bride of a pagan philosopher of Salamis, who had there heard Jesus preach and received circumcision. The way to Leppe ran in a gently undulating course through beautiful walks like those of a garden. Near Leppe ran the highroad to the little port Cerinia, about two miles off. The other road, upon which Jesus spoke with the travelling Arabs, led to the haven of Lapithus more to the west. The pagans of Leppe occupied a row of houses built along the highway, and carried on commerce and other business. The Jews lived apart and had a beautiful synagogue. I saw in the pagan gardens idols like swathed puppets and, in an open square a short distance from the road and surrounded by a hedge, an idol larger than a man and with a head bearing some resemblance to that of an ox. Between the horns was something that looked like a little sheaf. The figure was squatting on its legs, its short hands dangling before it.

The entertainment at Leppe consisted of a simple meal of birds, fish, honey, bread, and fruits. The brides and bridemaids, veiled, sat by themselves at the end of the table. They wore long, striped dresses with wreaths of colored wool and tiny feathers on their heads.

Both during and after the meal, Jesus spoke of the sanctity of marriage. He insisted on the point of each man's having but one wife, for they had here the custom of separating on trifling grounds and marrying again. On this account, He spoke very strenuously, and related the parables of the wedding feast, the vineyard, and the king's son. The groomsmen invited the passersby to share the feast and listen to Jesus' teaching. The three cured boys played on their flutes, while little girls sang and played on various instruments.

It was already dark when Jesus and His disciples returned to Mallep. From the heights along the road, the view was exceedingly beautiful. One could behold the sea, whose surface reflected a most wonderful luster. Great preparations had been made in Mallep for the nuptials of the seven bridal couples. The whole city appeared to be taking part in the feast. One would have said that all the inhabitants constituted one great brotherhood. No poor were to be seen, as they were lodged and provided for in a separate part of the city.

Mallep was built very regularly. It looked like a pancake divided into five equal parts. The five streets that divided the city converged toward the center where was an elevated place ornamented by a fountain, around which were trees and terraces. Four of these quarters, or city wards, were cut through by two cross streets, which ran in a circle around the fountain, the central point of the place. In one of these circular streets was a house in which childless widows and aged women lived together at the expense of the community, kept school, and took care of orphans. There was another house here also for lodging and entertaining poor strangers and travellers. The fifth quarter comprised the public buildings. It was cut into halves by the aqueduct that conducted the water to the fountain. In one half were the public marketplace, several inns, and an asylum for the possessed, who were not permitted here to go at large. Jesus had already cured some of them who had been led to Him with the rest of the sick. In the other half stood the public house used for feasts and weddings, the top of its roof being almost on a level with the fountain near which it was. Its entrance was not facing the fountain, but on the side opposite. From the court in front, a walk about a hundred feet wide and bordered by green trees ran down through the cross streets to the forecourt of the synagogue. It was as long as about two-thirds of one of the five streets. There were other avenues leading thither from the cross streets, but they were open to the people only on feast days and by virtue of special permission.

Now on this day of the marriage festivities, the whole morning was spent in adorning the public feast-house. Meanwhile Jesus and His disciples retired to the inn whither came to Him men and women, some seeking instruction, others advice and consolation, for in consequence of their connection with the heathens, these people often had scruples and anxieties. The young affianced were longer with Jesus than the others. He spoke with the maidens alone and singly. It was something like confession and instruction. He questioned them upon their motives in entering the married state, whether they had reflected upon their posterity and the salvation of the same, which was a fruit springing from the fear of God, chastity, and temperance. Jesus found the young brides not instructed on these points.

In the public avenues, arches were erected, tapestry, wreaths of flowers, and garlands of fruits hung around, and steps and platforms raised, that the spectators might gaze from them down into the pleasure grounds below. In front of the synagogue especially, an open arbor was formed of numerous beautiful little bushes and plants in boxes. Into the courts and bowers around the feast-house, I saw people transporting all things, viands, etc., necessary for the entertainment. Whoever brought from the city something for this end, had a right to take part in the feast. The viands were brought in a kind of long bar-row, which served at the same time as tables. The various dishes, bread, little jugs, etc., stood in them and, from little side openings, could be drawn out by the guests as they reclined before them. The upper surface of the barrow was covered with a cloth, from which they ate. These barrows, or hand-carriages, were woven baskets, long and shallow, provided with a cover and side openings, as I have said, by which to get out the food. The guests reclined on mats and were supported by cushions. All these things were prepared and transported hither from various quarters.

Under the nuptial bower, a tapestried canopy was raised. Jesus and His disciples entered by special invita-tion. As among the bridegrooms some were converted pagans, several pagan philosophers and others of their friends took up the position assigned them not far off. The brides and bridegrooms arrived from different quar-ters. They were preceded by youths and maidens crowned with flowers and playing on musical instruments, accom-panied by the bridemen and bridemaids, and surrounded by their relatives, who escorted them into the nuptial bower. The bridegrooms wore long mantles and white shoes; on their cincture and the hem of their tunic were certain letters, and in their hands they carried a yellow scarf. The brides appeared in very beautiful, long, white woollen dresses embroidered with lines and flowers of gold. Their hair (some of them were golden-haired) was in the back woven into a net with pearls and gold thread and fastened at the ends with a riband. The veil fell over the face and down the back. On the head was a metal band with three points and a high, bent piece in front upon which the veil could be raised. They also wore little crowns of feathers or silk. Several of the veils glistened, as if made of fine silk or similar material. In their hands they carried long, golden flambeaux, like lamps without feet. They grasped them with a scarf, either black or of some other dark color. The brides likewise wore white shoes or sandals.

During the nuptial ceremony, which was performed by the rabbis, I remarked various rites that I cannot recall in order. Rolls of parchment were read—the marriage contract, I think—and prayers. The bridal couple stepped under the canopy; the relatives cast some grains of wheat after them and uttered a blessing. The rabbi pricked both bride and bridegroom on the little finger and let some drops of the blood of each fall into a goblet of wine, which they then drank together. Then the bridegroom handed the goblet to those behind him, and it was put into a basin of water. A little of the blood was allowed to run into the palm of the hand of each. Then each reached the hand, the bride to the groom, the groom to the bride, and the bloodstained spot was rubbed. A fine white thread was then bound around the wound and rings were exchanged. I think that each had two, one for the little finger, the other large enough for the forefinger. After that an embroidered cover, or scarf, was laid over the head of the newly wedded couple. The bride took into her right hand the flambeau with the black scarf, which for a time she had resigned to her bridemaid, and placed it in the right hand of her husband. He then passed it to the left hand and returned it to his bride, who likewise received it in her left hand, and then once more returned it to her bridemaid. There was also a cup of wine blessed, out of which all the relatives sipped. The marriage ceremony over, the bridemaids removed from the brides their headdress, and covered them with a veil.

It was then that I saw that the large net was woven of false hair.

Three rabbis presided at the nuptials, the whole ceremony lasting three hours. Then the brides with their attendant trains went through the embowered walk to the feast house, followed by their husbands amid the good wishes and congratulations of the bystanders. After taking some refreshments, the bridal couples went to the pleasure garden near the aqueduct, there to amuse themselves.

That evening an instruction especially intended for the newly married was given in the synagogue. After the rabbis had spoken, they requested Jesus also to address some words of advice to the young people.

Next day the seven bridal couples, together with all the guests and attended by musicians, went again to the feast house. The disciples of Jesus also were present, but the only part they took in the merrymaking was that of server. The brides and grooms were presented with pastry and fruit on beautiful dishes—gilded apples stuck with gilded flowers and herbs. Then came bands of children singing and playing upon instruments. They were little strangers who made their living in this way; after being rewarded, they withdrew. After that the three little musicians that had been cured by Jesus made their appearance, along with several other choirs from the city, and soon a dance in honor of the occasion was performed. It took place in a long, four-cornered arbor upon a soft and gently swaying floor. It looked as if flexible planks of some kind were laid upon a thick carpet of moss. The dancers stood in four double rows, back to back. Each pair danced, changing hands by means of a scarf, from the first place of the first row to the last of the fourth, all being soon in a serpentine movement. There was no hopping, but a graceful swaying and balancing, as if the body had no bones. The brides, as also all the other women, had their veils raised on the golden hook of their headdress. After the dance all took refreshments which had been placed on stands in each corner of the arbor. Again the music sounded, and all filed out into the garden near the fountain.

Here were exhibited, in the arbors and on the mossy sward, various games of running, leaping, and throwing at a mark. The men played by themselves, as did also the women. Little prizes were awarded and fines imposed, in the shape of money, girdles, small pieces of stuff, scarfs for the neck, etc. Whoever had nothing with which to pay his fine, sent to purchase it from a peddler who, with his goods, had taken his stand not far off. Lastly, all the prizes and fines were handed over to the Elder, who distributed them to the poor among the lookers-on. The brides and maidens played games in circles and in rows. Their dresses were raised to the knees, their lower limbs bound with strips of white, their veils thrown up and wound around the head back to the forehead and ear ornaments. They looked very beautiful and nimble. Each caught hold of her neighbor's girdle with the left hand, and thus formed a ring which they kept constantly revolving. With the right hand they aimed at throwing to one another and catching a yellow apple. Whoever failed to catch in her turn had to stoop, the circle still revolving, to pick it up from the ground. At last, they played in company with the men. They sat in opposite rows and threw into furrows very ripe yellow fruits, which when they met and smashed, gave rise to shouts of laughter. Toward evening, all returned in festal procession. The newly married rode on asses gaily adorned for the occasion, the brides sitting on side-saddles. Musicians led the way and all followed, rejoicing, to the feast house at which an entertainment was awaiting them.

The bridegrooms went to the synagogue and made before the rabbis a vow to observe continence during certain festivals, binding themselves to some penance if they broke it. They promised besides to watch together on Pentecost night and spend it in prayer. From the feast house, the bridal couples were conducted to their future homes. The party that had brought the house as a dowry, stood on the threshold while the relatives led the other thither from the feast house and three times made the rounds of the premises. The wedding gifts were borne in ceremoniously, and the poor received their share.

1. The Church.

18. FEAST OF PENTECOST. JESUS TEACHES ON BAPTISM

Mallep was now astir in preparation for the coming feast: all were busy cleaning, scouring, and bathing. The synagogue and many of the dwellings were adorned with green branches and garlands of flowers, and the ground was strewn with blossoms. The synagogue was fumigated with delicious perfumes, and the rolls of Sacred Scripture were wreathed with flowers.

In the special halls set apart for the purpose in the forecourt of the synagogue, the Whitsuntide loaves were baked, the flour having been previously blessed by the rabbis. Two of them were made from the wheat of that year's harvest. For the others, as also for the large, thin cakes (which were indented, that they might be more easily broken into pieces), the flour had been ordered from Judea. It was ground from the wheat raised in the field upon which Abraham had participated in the sacrifice of Melchisedech. The flour had been transported hither in long boxes. It was called the Seed of Abraham. The baking of these loaves and cakes, in which there was no leaven, had to be finished by four o'clock. There was still another kind of flour there, as well as herbs, all of which received a blessing.

On the morning of this day Jesus gave an instruction at His inn to the baptized pagans and aged Jews. He took for His subjects the Feast of Pentecost, the Law given upon Sinai, and Baptism, all of which He treated in deeply significant terms. He touched upon many passages relating to them in the Prophets. He spoke also of the holy bread blessed at Pentecost, of Melchisedech's sacrifice, and of that foretold by Malachias. He said that the time for the institution of that Sacrifice was drawing near, that when this feast would again come round, a new grace would have been added to Baptism, and that all the baptized who would then believe in the Consoler of Israel, would share in that grace. As difficulties and objections were here raised by some who did not wish to understand His teaching, Jesus chose about fifty whom He knew to be ripe for His instructions, and sent away the others, intending to prepare them later. Taking with Him those that He had selected, He left the city, went to the aqueduct nearby, and there continued His instruction. I saw them on the way sometimes standing still and with many gesticulations putting questions and raising objections; and I saw Jesus, His forefinger raised, frequently explaining something to them. In talking, they gesticulated freely with hands and fingers. As Jesus insisted upon the great grace, upon the salvation that would be conferred upon man by Baptism, and by Baptism alone, after the consummation of the Sacrifice of which He had spoken, some of them asked whether their present Baptism possessed the same efficacy. Jesus answered, yes, if they persevered in faith and accepted that Sacrifice; for even the Patriarchs, who had not received that Baptism, but who had sighed after it and had had a presentiment of it in the Spirit, received grace through both that Sacrifice and that Baptism.

Jesus spoke, too, of the advantages of fervent prayer during this Feast of Pentecost, which devout Jews of all times had observed and upon which they conjured God for the promised Consoler of Israel.

Jesus told them many other deeply significant things which I cannot now rightly repeat. I saw that they sent, from the wedding feast, food to Jesus and His disciples at the inn to which He had returned with them toward the Sabbath.

The heathens from Salamis started for home, and Jesus with the disciples accompanied them part of the way. He warned them not to return again to their worship of idols, and not to engage in business speculations, but as soon as possible to leave their country, for in it the new way would be full of obstacles for them. He directed them to different regions, among which I can recall Jerusalem, the Jewish district between Hebron and Gaza, and that near Jericho. Jesus recommended them to go to Lazarus, John Mark, the nephews of Zachary, and to the parents of Manahem, the disciple whose sight had been restored.

Before the commencement of the Sabbath exercises, the rabbis were solemnly conducted to the synagogue by the school children; the brides, by their female attendants; and the bridegrooms, by the young men. Jesus also went thither with His disciples. Divine service of this day consisted in no special explanation of Scripture, only in singing and alternate reading and praying. The consecrated bread was divided into little pieces in the synagogue. It was regarded as a remedy against sickness and witchcraft. Many of the Jews, among others the seven newly married men, spent the night in the synagogue in prayer. Many of the inhabitants of the city went in bands of ten or twelve out to the gardens and hills of the country around, and there spent the whole night in prayer. They carried a torch on the end of a pole. The disciples and baptized pagans thus passed the night, but Jesus went alone to pray. The women too were gathered together in the houses for the same purpose. On the day of the feast itself, the whole morning was spent in the synagogue, praying, singing, and reading the Holy Scriptures. They made, likewise, a kind of procession. The rabbis, with Jesus at their head and followed by crowds of the people, went processionally through the halls around the synagogue, paused several times at points that look toward different directions of the world, and pronounced a benediction over every region of land and sea. After an intermission of about two hours, they again returned to the synagogue in the afternoon, and the alternate reading and other exercises were resumed. At some of the pauses, Jesus asked: "Do ye understand this?" and then He explained different passages for them. The portions of Holy Scripture read were those from the Departure of the Israelites through the Red Sea to the giving of the Law upon Sinai. During the reading, I saw these events in detail, and of them I can recall the following.

VISION OF THE PASSAGE OF THE RED SEA

The Israelites were encamped on a very low strip of land, about an hour long, on the shore of the Red Sea, which was here very wide. In it were several islands of half an hour in length and from seven to fifteen minutes in breadth. Pharao and his army at first sought the Israelites further up the shore, and found them at last through information given by their scouts. The king thought they would easily fall into his hands, flanked, as they were, by the sea. The Egyptians were very much incensed against them, on account of their carrying off with them their sacred vessels, many of their idols, and the mysteries of their religion. When the Israelites became aware of the approach of the Egyptians, they were terror-stricken. But Moses prayed and bade them trust in God and follow him. At that moment the pillar of cloud arose behind the Israelites, making so dense a veil that the

Egyptians entirely lost sight of them. Then Moses stepped to the shore with his staff (which was forked at the bottom and had a knob on the upper end), prayed, and struck the water. Then appeared before each wing of the army, right and left, as if springing out of the sea, two great luminous pillars, which increased in brilliancy toward the top and terminated in a tongue of flame. At the same time, a strong wind parted the waters along the whole of the army (it was about an hour broad), and Moses proceeded by a gently inclining declivity down to the bed of the sea. The whole army followed, at least fifty men abreast. The ground was, at first setting out, somewhat slippery, but soon it became like the softest meadowland, like a mossy carpet. The pillars of fire lit the way before them, and all was as bright as day. But the most beautiful feature of the whole scene were the islands over which they shed their light. They looked like floating gardens full of the most magnificent fruits and all kinds of animals, which latter the Israelites collected and drove along before them. Without this precaution, they would have been in want of food on the other side of the sea.

The waters were not divided on either side like perpendicular walls, for they flowed off more in the form of terraces. The Hebrews went forward with hurrying, sliding steps, balancing themselves like one speeding downhill. It was toward midnight when they entered the bed of the river. The Ark containing Joseph's relics was carried in the center of the fleeing host. The pillars of light rose up out of the water. They appeared to be constantly rotating, and passed not over the islands, but around them. At a certain height they were lost in a brilliant luster. The waters did not open all at once, but before Moses's steps, leaving a wedge-formed space until the passage was completed. Near the islands, one could see by the light of the pillars the trees and fruits mirrored in the waters.

Another wonderful thing was that the Israelites crossed in three hours, whereas it would have naturally taken nine hours to do so. Higher up the shore, about six to nine hours distant, stood a city which was afterward destroyed by the waters.

About three o'clock, Pharao came down to the shore, but was again repulsed by the fog. Soon, however, he discovered the ford and rolled down into it with his magnificent war chariot, after which hurried his entire army. And now Moses, already on the opposite shore, commanded the waters to return to their original position. Then the fog and the fire uniting to blind and perplex the Egyptians, all perished miserably in the waves. Next morning upon beholding their deliverance, the Israelites chanted the praises of God. On the opposite shore, the two pillars of light united again into one of fire. I cannot do justice to the beauty of this vision.

Next day Jesus went with His disciples into two quarters of the city which He had not yet visited, and to which several persons had sent to invite Him. He cured some invalids, men and women, who lay off by themselves in cells annexed to the courts of the houses, exhorted and consoled many others afflicted with melancholy and whom some secret trouble was consuming. All things were so well regulated in Mallep that every misfortune by which one's honor might be wounded, could be kept secret. Several women asked Jesus how they should act. Their husbands were unfaithful to them, and yet, on account of the public scandal and severe punishment attached to such crimes, they were timid in laying a charge against them. Jesus consoled them and counselled them to patience. He told them to reflect as to whether they would have their husbands warned by Himself or by His disciples, strangers in those parts, that thereby suspicion of having lodged a complaint might not fall upon them and the affair might not become known throughout the country. Many children were brought to Jesus in the different houses, to receive from Him a benediction.

That afternoon, He went to a large house where, in a hall back of the court and separated from one another, numbers of distinguished men lay sick. On the other side of the court lay the women. Among these poor invalids were some melancholy and quite inconsolable, whose tears flowed unceasingly. Jesus cured about twenty of them, prescribed what they should eat and drink, and sent them to the baths. He afterward caused them all to be assembled together and taught first the women, and then the men. This lasted almost till evening, when He went to the synagogue.

19. JESUS DELIVERS A MORE SEVERE LECTURE IN THE SYNAGOGUE

The Scripture lessons of this day treated of God's curse upon those that transgressed His commands, of tithes, of idolatry, of the sanctification of the Sabbath, etc.[1] Jesus' words were so earnest and severe that many of His audience, penetrated with grief, sobbed and wept. The synagogue was open on all sides, and His voice rang out clear and pure like unto no other human voice. He inveighed especially against them that relied upon creatures and looked for help and comfort from human beings. He spoke of the diabolical influence of the adulterer and adulteress over each other, of the malediction of the injured spouses which falls upon the children of such intercourse, but whose guilt rests upon the adulterous parties. The people were so strongly affected that many of them, at the close of the discourse, exclaimed: "Ah, He speaks as if the Day of Judgment were already nigh!" He spoke likewise against pride, against subtle erudition and the close investigation of trifles. By this He alluded to the doings of the great school of Jewish learning here established for such Jews as would afterward add to their store of knowledge by travelling.

After this castigatory discourse many persons sighing for relief and reconciliation with God, sought Jesus at His inn. Among them were learned men and young students belonging to the school of the place seeking advice as to how they should pursue their studies, and others troubled in mind on account of their constant communication with the pagans with whom they carried on trade, though from a kind of necessity as their lands and workshops adjoined. The husbands of the women that had complained of them to Jesus were also among the number, as well as others guilty of similar offenses, but against whom no charge had been laid. They presented themselves individually as sinners before Jesus, cast themselves at His feet, confessed their guilt, and implored pardon. What troubled them especially was the thought that the malediction of their wives might fall upon the illegitimate, though otherwise innocent, children, and they asked whether this curse could not be counteracted or annulled. Jesus answered that it might be annulled by the sincere charity and pardon of the one that had invoked it, joined to the contrition and penance of the guilty party. Besides this, the malediction of which I speak does not extend to the soul, for the Almighty Father has said: "All souls are Mine"; but it affects the body, the flesh, and temporal goods. The flesh is, however, the house, the instrument of the soul, consequently the flesh lying under such a curse causes great distress and embarrassment to the soul already oppressed with the burden of the body received with life. I saw on this occasion that the malediction varies in its baneful effects according to the intention of the one that invokes it and the disposition of the child itself. Many subject to convulsions, many possessed by the demon, owe their condition to this source. The illegitimate children themselves I generally see possessed of remarkable advantages of nature, though of an order earthly and prone to sin. They have in them something in common with those that, in early times, sprang from the union of the sons of God with the daughters of men. They are often beautiful, cunning, very reserved in disposition, agitated by eager desires and, without wishing it to appear, they would like to draw all things to themselves. They bear in their flesh the stamp of their origin, and frequently their soul goes thereby to perdition.

After hearing and exhorting these sinners individually, Jesus bade them send their wives to Him. When they came, He related to each one separately the repentance of her husband, exhorted her to heartfelt forgiveness and entire forgetfulness of the past, and urged her to recall the malediction she had pronounced. If, He told them, they did not act sincerely in this circumstance, the guilt of their husband's relapse would fall upon them. The women wept and thanked and promised everything. Jesus reconciled several of these couples right away that same day. He made them come before Him, interrogated them anew, as is customary at the marriage ceremony, joined their hands together, covered them with a scarf, and blessed them. The wife of one of the faithless husbands solemnly revoked the malediction that she had pronounced upon the illegitimate children. The mother of the poor little ones, who were being raised in the Jewish asylum for children, was a pagan. Standing before Jesus, the injured but now forgiving wife placed her hand crosswise with that of her husband over the children's heads, revoked the malediction, and blessed the children. Jesus imposed upon those guilty of adultery, as penance, alms, fasts, continence, and prayer. He who had sinned with the pagan was completely transformed. He very humbly invited Jesus to dine with him. Jesus accepted and went, accompanied by His disciples. A couple of the

rabbis also were invited and they, as well as the whole
city, marveled at the courtesy, for their host was known
as a frivolous, worldly man who did not trouble himself
much about priests and prophets. He was rich and owned
landed property cultivated by servants. His house was
near that hospital in which Jesus had cured the victims of
melancholy. During the meal two of the little daughters
of the family entered the dining hall, and poured costly
perfume over Jesus' head.

After dinner Jesus and all the people went to the synagogue for the closing exercises of the Sabbath. Jesus
resumed His discourse of the day before, though not in
terms so severe. He told His audience that God would
not abandon them that call upon Him. He ended by dilat-
ing on their attachment to their houses and possessions,
and exhorted them, if they put faith in His teaching, to
forsake the great occasion of sin in which they were living among the pagans, and among those of their own
belief to practice truth in the Promised Land. Judea, He
said, was large enough to harbor and support them,
although at first they might have to live under tents. It
was better to give up all than to lose their soul on account of their idolatry, that is, their worship of their fine
houses and possessions, better to give up all than to sin
through love of their own convenience. That the
Kingdom of God might come to them, it was necessary
that they should go to meet it. They should not put their
trust in their dwellings in a pleasant land, solid and magnificent though they might be, for the hand of God would
fall suddenly upon them, scattering them in all directions,
and overturning their mansions. He knew very well, He
continued, that their virtues were more apparent than
real, that they had no other basis than tepidity and the
love of their own ease. They hankered after the wealth of
the pagans and sought to win it by their usury, traffic,
mining, and marriages, but the day would come when

they would see themselves stripped of all their ill-gotten gains. Jesus warned them likewise against such marriages with the heathens as those in which both parties, indifferent to religion, enter into wedlock merely for the sake of property and money, greater freedom and the gratification of passion. All were deeply moved and impressed by Jesus' words, and many begged leave to be allowed to speak with Him in private.

The whole of the following day and even until late at night, was Jesus engaged visiting the different families in their homes, admonishing, consoling, and pardoning. Two women presented themselves before Him lamenting to Him over their illegitimate children. Jesus sent for their husbands, forgave the guilty parties, and united them once more to their lawful spouses. The children also—without understanding the ceremony, however—were received by the husbands and blessed as their own. It was harder for the wife to admit among her own the illegitimate children of her husband; she had to gain a great victory over herself. But all on this occasion did it so sincerely that they forced, so to say, their husbands to love them more and to bless children of their wives not their own. And so a general reconciliation was brought about, and scandal avoided.

Many sought comfort from Jesus on the score of His energetic admonition to them to emigrate from those pagan lands. Jesus' teaching indeed pleased them and, looking upon themselves as Jews separated from their people, they felt greatly honored by His visit to them, but they did not like the idea of following Him, of leaving their homes. Here they were rich and comfortable, owned a city built by themselves, had a share in a mine, and carried on extensive trade. They enriched themselves by means of the pagans. They were not tormented by the Pharisees, not oppressed by Pilate. They were, as regards this life, in a most agreeable position, but their connec-

tion with the pagans was highly censurable. Pagan property and workshops were in their neighborhood. The
pagan girls liked well to unite in marriage with the Jews,
because they were not treated by them in so slavish a
manner as by those of their own religion, and so they enticed the young Israelites in every way, by presents, attentions, and all kinds of allurements. When converted to
Judaism, it was not from conviction, but from sordid
views, and so insubordination and tepidity easily made
their way into the family. The Jews of Mallep were
besides less simple-hearted and hospitable than those of
Palestine, their social surroundings were more studied
and refined, their Jewish origin not so pure; consequently
they brought forward all kinds of scruples and difficulties
against Jesus' counsel to emigrate to the Holy Land.
Jesus argued that their forefathers owned houses and
lands in Egypt, but that they had willingly and gladly
abandoned them, and He repeated once more His predic-
tion that if they persisted in remaining, misfortune would
fall upon them. The disciples, Barnabas especially, went
around a great deal in the environs teaching and exhorting the people. They were less timid in his presence and
laid before him all their doubts. He always had a crowd
around him.

1. *Lev.* 26 *et Jer.* 17.

20. JESUS VISITS THE MINES NEAR CHYTRUS

From Mallep, Jesus, accompanied by the disciples, the
disciple recently arrived from Naim and the sons of
Cyrinus just come from Salamis (in all about twelve),
went to a village of miners near Chytrus. He took a
roundabout road to it of seven hours. On the way He
paused among the different bands of laborers and spoke
of the path of a good life. Jesus had by the family of

Barnabas and several people of Chytrus been invited to this mining village, because the Jewish miners of the place were celebrating a feast at which they received from their employers various presents besides their share of the harvest. Jesus took a circuitous route to the village, that He might be able to speak to His disciples without interruption and also that He might not arrive too early. During the journey, He permitted the disciple from Naim to deliver the messages and relate the news with which he had been charged; for although Jesus knew all Himself, He was careful not to let it appear, lest such knowledge might be a source of annoyance or anxiety to those around Him.

The disciple had left Jerusalem on the eve of Pentecost just after the money offering in the Temple, and the execution of Pilate's plot. He had gone straight to Naim, thence through Nazareth to Ptolemais, and from the latter place to Cyprus. He told Jesus that His Mother and the other holy women, together with John and some of the disciples, had quietly celebrated the feast of Pentecost at Nazareth; that His Mother and friends sent greetings and entreated Him to stay some time in Cyprus, until minds had grown calm in His regard. The Pharisees, he continued, were already reporting that He had run away. Herod also wanted to summon Him to Machaerus under pretext of conferring with Him upon the subject of the prisoners freed at Thirza, but really to make Him prisoner as he had done John.

The disciple told likewise of Pilate's plot on the eve of Pentecost when the Jews brought their offerings to the Temple. Two friends of Jesus, relatives of Zachary and servers in the Temple, who happened to get mixed up in the tumult, lost their lives. Jesus already knew of the circumstance, and it made Him very sad. The news renewed His grief, as well as that of His disciples. Pilate on the preceding evening left the city, and with some of his troops proceeded westward of the route to Joppa, where he owned a castle. He had demanded the contributions offered to the Temple in honor of the feast, in order to build a very long aqueduct. On all the pillars at the entrances to the Temple he had caused to be placed metal tablets on which were the head of the Emperor and, below, an inscription demanding the tax. The people were roused to indignation at the sight of these pictures, and the Herodians by means of their emissaries stirred up a band of Galileans belonging to the party of Judas the Gaulonite, who had been killed in the last revolt. Herod, who was at Jerusalem in secret, knew all that was transpiring. That evening the mob became perfectly infuriated. They tore down the tables, broke them in pieces, dishonored the portraits, and cast the fragments over the forum in front of the praetorium, crying: "Here is our offering money!" They then dispersed without anyone's especially resenting the act. Next morning, however, when about to leave the Temple, they found the entrances beset by guards demanding the tax imposed by Pilate. When the Jews resisted and tried to force their way out, the disguised soldiers pressed out along with them and stabbed them with short swords. At that moment the alarm became general, and the two Temple servers running to the scene of action lost their lives. The Jews made a brave resistance, and drove the soldiers back into the citadel of Antonia.

On the way Jesus spoke long to His disciples about the inhabitants of Mallep, their hankering after temporal goods, and how distasteful to them was the suggestion to go to Palestine. He referred to the pagan philosophers who were accompanying Him, and told the disciples how they should behave toward them in Palestine when they found them actually in their midst. Jesus did this because they did not appear to accord rightly with the philosophers in the party, and were still somewhat scandalized on their account.

Toward evening they arrived at the mining village, one half hour from Chytrus. It was in the neighborhood of the mines built around a high, rocky ridge, into which the rear of many dwellings ran. Upon this ridge there were gardens and a place suited for instruction, surrounded by shady trees. Steps led up the ridge, the top of which overlooked the village. Jesus on His arrival repaired to a sort of inn where dwelt the overseer who superintended the miners, supplied them with food, and paid them their wages. The people received Jesus with manifestations of joy. All the entrances to the place and the house of the overseer were, on account of the feast, adorned with green arches and garlands of flowers. They led Jesus and His disciples into the house, washed their feet, and presented refreshments to the Lord, who then went with them to the place for teaching upon the rock. Jesus seated Himself, and the crowd reclined around Him. He spoke of the happiness attendant upon poverty and labor, and told them how much happier they were than the opulent Jews of Salamis, that they had fewer temptations to offend God, before whom the virtuous alone are rich. He said also that He had come in order to prove that He did not despise them, and that He loved them. He taught until night in parables on the *Our Father*.

Provisions of all kinds, pieces of stuff for clothing, food and grain were conveyed hither from Chytrus; and on the next day came the father and brother of Barnabas, several distinguished citizens and proprietors of the mines, along with some rabbis from the same place. When the gifts already enumerated had been safely deposited in the public square of the place, where the people were assembled and seated in rows, these visitors entered also. Now began the distribution of gifts: great bowls of grain; large loaves of bread, about two feet square; honey, fruit, jugs of something, pieces of leathern clothing, covers and all kinds of furniture and utensils. The women received pieces of thick stuff like carpet, about one and a half yards square. Jesus and the disciples were present at the distribution, after which Jesus taught again on the rocky height upon which the people had assembled. He took for His subjects the laborers in the vineyard and the good Samaritan, the blessing of poverty and thanksgiving for the same, daily bread and the *Our Father*. After the instruction, the people had a feast under the arbors in the open air at which Jesus, the disciples, and the guests of distinction served. Little boys and girls played on flutes and sang. The meal over, they had some innocent games such as children play; for instance, running, leaping, blindfolding, hiding and seeking, etc. They danced, too, in this way: They stood in long rows, bowed here and there, crossed before one another, and then formed a ring.

In the evening, Jesus went to the mines with about ten boys of from six to eight years old. The children wore only a broad girdle with festive wreaths of woollen or feather flowers around their waist or crossed on their breast. They looked very lovely. In their own childlike way, they showed Jesus all the places in which were the best mines, and related to Him all that they knew. Jesus instructed them in words full of sweetness, and made some useful application of what they told Him. He likewise proposed to them enigmas and related parables. The miners were, despite their rough and dirty labor in the bowels of the earth, very cleanly in their homes and festal garments.

I saw Jesus and the disciples accompanying the disciple from Naim to the port about five hours distant. One group went in front and another followed, while Jesus walked between the two with the disciple and some of the others in their turn. Jesus blessed the disciple on his departure, and his fellow disciples embraced him, after which they returned to the miners' village. The disciple from Naim pursued his journey to the salt regions near Citium. The port was here not so far from the city as was that of Salamis. The sea penetrates far into the land so that the city has the appearance of being built in the midst of the waves. Not far from it rises a very high mountain, and there is a salt mine in the neighborhood. At the quay near the salt mine were only little skiffs and rafts, and a quantity of wood for the building of vessels was floating around.

21. JESUS GOES TO CERYNIA, AND VISITS MNASON'S PARENTS

When Jesus left the miners' village with the disciples, He proceeded in a northwesterly direction across the mountains to the port of Cerynia. They left Mallep to the right, went through a portion of the valley of Lanifa, and passed near the village of Leppe. On the way Jesus rested once on a beautiful shady eminence, and there taught. Toward four in the afternoon they arrived to within about three-quarters of an hour's distance from Cerynia, where they were received by Mnason's family and several other Jews in a garden set apart for prayer and pious reunions. This garden was a retired spot hidden away in a slope of the mountain. Mnason's family dwelt at some distance from the road, and one half-hour from Cerynia. His father was an aged Jew, thin, stooped, and with a long beard, but withal very lively and active. He had two daughters and three sons, one son-in-law, and a daughter-in-law, and all had been living here together for about ten years. Before that they used to travel around buying and selling. They received Jesus with many expressions of joy and humility, washed the travellers' feet in a basin, and presented to them refreshments. This part of the mountain formed a large terrace full of shady walks, and comprised the sacred garden belonging to these people. Jesus taught until near evening, taking for His subjects Baptism, the *Our Father,* and the Beatitudes.

After that Jesus accompanied Mnason's brethren and his father, who was called Moses, to the house, where Mnason presented to Him four children, whom He blessed. Then his mother and sisters came forward veiled, and Jesus addressed to them some words, after which the whole family took a meal together under an arbor in the open air. The table was spread with the best they had: bread, honey, birds, and fruit, the latter still hanging upon little branches. During the meal, Jesus taught. They lodged in a long arbor built of thin, light boards, the exterior entirely overgrown by green foliage. It was furnished with a row of couches.

Mnason's mother was a strong, robust woman. His father was descended from the tribe of Judah, but his ancestors had been carried off in the Babylonian Captivity and had never returned. Moses had travelled much directing caravans, had lived a long time also near the Red Sea, in Arabia; but having become impoverished, had settled in this place with his family. Mnason went to school in Mallep and later on for the sake of his studies travelled to Judea, where he met Jesus. His father with his grown-up children, Mnason being the youngest, lived in lightly built huts. They were not engaged in agriculture; they owned only a few gardens that lay back of their homes, and which were planted out in fruit trees. Having formerly, as caravan director, had much experience in the transportation of goods, the old man had established himself here as a kind of innkeeper, assistant, and commissioner for the commercial caravans that halted before Cerynia. He owned some asses and oxen with which he conveyed small burdens received from the caravans and destined for places remote from the public road. He was like a porter who had now become an innkeeper also for others in the same business as himself. He was poor, but he had managed to maintain in his family strict Jewish discipline. For the rest, commerce did not flow toward Cerynia, but rather to Lapithus, which lay a couple of hours westward on the grand highroad.

Next morning Jesus taught again at the place of instruction before an audience composed of several Jews from the city and the people belonging to a little caravan. These latter were inexpressibly happy to find Jesus here, for they had already heard His instructions at Capharnaum where, too, they had received Baptism. On this occasion, Jesus inveighed against usury and greed of gain which made the Jews eager to enrich themselves off the pagans. He then touched upon Baptism, the *Our Father,* and the Beatitudes. Toward noon they partook of a meal in common, but Jesus did more serving and teaching around the tables than reclining at them Himself.

One of Mnason's married sisters did not make her appearance, because her little daughter had died the day before. She sat closely veiled, lamenting near the corpse. The child could not (I cannot now recall on what account) be buried on that day; but on this, the next day, they were expecting the rabbis from Mallep to conduct the funeral, for it was there they had their graveyard. The child had attained a tolerably good size, although it had always been an invalid. It could neither speak nor walk with facility, but it understood all that was said to it. Mnason, who had visited his home from time to time, had spoken to Jesus about it. Jesus told him that it would soon die, and instructed him how to prepare it for death. Mnason prudently followed Jesus' directions at a time in which the mother was not present. He excited the child to faith in the Messiah, to hearty sorrow for its sins, and to the hope of salvation; he prayed with it, and anointed it with oil that Jesus had blessed. The child died a very good death. I saw it lying on a little bier near the veiled mother, just like a babe in swaddling clothes, its face covered. The casket in which it lay was shaped something like a trough. On its head was a wreath of flowers, and tiny bunches of aromatic herbs were laid closely around it. Its arms and hands also were wrapped in burial bands, but left free from the person. A little white staff rested in its arms. On the top of it was a bouquet made up of a large ear of corn, a vine leaf, a little olive branch, a rose, and foliage peculiar to the country. Several women visited the mother and mourned with her. By the child's side in the coffin they deposited playthings: two little flutes, a little crooked, spiral-shaped horn, a tiny bow spanned with a string, on top of which in a furrow lay a little wand like an arrow. In each arm, besides, the child held a short, gilded staff with a knob on top.

When the rabbis came to conduct the corpse, the coffin was closed with a light lid which, instead of being nailed, was fastened down with a cord. Four men carried it on poles. A lighted lamp in a horn-lantern was borne on a pole and was followed by a crowd of children and grown persons, who all pressed foward with no attention to order. Jesus and the disciples were standing outside the house watching the funeral. Jesus comforted the mother and relatives, and spoke of the Resurrection.

All repaired to Cerynia for the celebration of the Sabbath. The city had three streets facing the sea, the middle one very wide, and these three were intersected by two others. On the opposite side, the land side, it was enclosed by a massive wall, or rampart, in whose exterior were built the houses of the few Jews belonging to the place. Their dwellings were therefore outside the city, but still enclosed by a second wall. In this way, the Jews of Cerynia lived between the two walls of the city, entirely separate from the pagans, who had as many as ten heathen temples, or places dedicated to idols. The Jews of Cerynia were few in number, not very rich, but still possessed of all that was necessary. In one large building they had a school and a synagogue, along with accommodations for both rabbis and teachers. It was high, and had two stories entirely distinct. They had also a beautiful, flowing fountain fed by a stream from another source. The fountain they divided, one part being used for a drinking well, the other being conducted into a delightful garden for bathing purposes.

The Doctors of the Law received Jesus very respectfully at the end of the street and conducted Him first to the school, and then to the synagogue. Here He found seven invalids who had caused themselves to be conveyed thither on litters, that they might listen to His instructions. There were altogether about one hundred men. The Doctors allowed Jesus to teach and conduct the exercises alone. He read from Moses, passages recounting the number of the Children of Israel and their different families, and from the Prophet Osee[1] a grave and severe lecture against idolatry.

In one of these passages was read the circumstance of God's commanding the Prophet to marry an adulteress, the children of which marriage were to receive special names. The Jews questioned Jesus on this passage. He explained it to them. He said that the Prophet, in his whole person and life, had to show forth the condition of God's covenant with the House of Israel, and that the names of the children should be expressive of God's sentence of punishment. Another lesson to be drawn from this passage was, as Jesus said, that acting under the inspiration of God, the good oftentimes united themselves to sinners in order to arrest the transmission of sin. This marriage of Osee with an adulteress and the various names of the children testified to the reiterated mercy of God and the long continuance of crime. Jesus spoke very severely. He exhorted to penance and Baptism, referred to the near approach of the Kingdom of God, predicted the punishment of those that repulsed it, and prophesied the destruction of Jerusalem.

While Jesus was teaching, the sick more than once cried out in the pauses of His discourse: "Lord, we believe in Thy doctrine! Lord, help us!" And when they noticed that He was about to leave the synagogue, they caused themselves to be carried out before Him. They were laid in the forecourt in two rows, and they continued to cry out to Jesus: "Lord, exercise upon us Thy power! Do unto us, Lord, what is pleasing to Thee!" But Jesus did not cure them right away. When, however, the rabbis interceded for the poor invalids, Jesus questioned the latter. "What can I do for you?" He asked. They answered: "Lord, relieve us of our infirmities! Lord, cure us!" "Believe ye that I can do it?" asked Jesus, and all cried out: "Yes, Lord! We do believe that Thou canst do it!" Then Jesus ordered the rabbis to bring the rolls of the Law and to pray with Him over the sick. The rabbis brought the rolls and prayed, after which Jesus commanded the disciples to impose hands upon the sick. They obeyed, laying their hands on the eyes of one, on the breast of another, and so on different parts of the body. Jesus again put the question: "Do ye believe, and do ye wish to be cured?" and again they answered: "Yes, Lord! We believe that Thou canst help us!" Then said Jesus: "Rise! Your faith hath cured you!" and they arose, all seven, thanking Jesus, who ordered them to wash and purify themselves. Some among them had been very much swollen with dropsy. Their sickness was passed, but they were still weak and had to walk with the assistance of a staff.

Several times before in Cyprus, namely at Chytrus, Mallep, and Salamis, I saw Jesus healing in that way, that is, praying with the rabbis and commanding the disciples to impose hands. As these rabbi and Doctors were well-inclined, He caused them to take part like the disciples in this cure, thus to awaken in them confidence. He made use of this new way of curing in order to prepare those that took part in it for the works of the disciples, for there were a great many rabbis among the five hundred and seventy Jews whom Jesus gained in Cyprus.

The cured, along with other Jews from Cerynia, were baptized at the place of instruction near Moses's dwelling. The water used for the purpose had been conveyed thither from a neighboring well, for the house lay rather high and had no spring near it. But to supply the defect, it had a reservoir in the shape of a large, copper basin buried in the earth and surrounded by a little channel lined with stone, which had an outlet into a stone trough. The water in the basin was perfectly pure, for the washing of feet, linen, etc., was all done in the channel. The stone trough was used for watering the cattle and sprinkling the garden beds. The neophytes stood in the channel and were baptized with water from the basin. First, Jesus gave an instruction on penance and purification through Baptism. The men wore long, white garments with maniples and cinctures ornamented with letters. Besides the seven lately cured, there were only eight other Jews baptized. They spoke separately with Jesus, and confessed their sins. Jesus told them to take advantage of the time of grace and to accomplish the Law according to the meaning of the Prophets, and not to be its slaves, for the Law was given to them, and not they to the Law. It was given to them in order to serve as a means to merit grace.

Among the newly baptized were Mnason's brothers and brother-in-law. As to his father, pious though he was, still he was an obstinate Jew and would not hear of being baptized. Mnason had all along tried, but in vain, to prepare him, and Jesus too had spoken to him that day on the same subject. The stubborn old Jew, however, was not to be moved. He shrugged his shoulders, shook his head, and objected with all kinds of plausible reasons in favor of cir-

cumcision, to which he held. Mnason was so troubled at
his father's obstinacy that he shed tears. Jesus consoled
him. He told him that his father was very old and had in
consequence grown obstinate; as for the rest, however, he
had always lived piously, he would weep over his blindness at another time and place, when light would dawn
upon him. Jesus had blessed the baptismal water into
which some from the Jordan was poured. All that remained after the Baptism was carefully scooped out and
buried.

During the Baptism, Jesus went to a lovely garden
back of the hill upon which was the place of instruction.
It was full of fruit trees and fitted up with arbors, and
there awaiting Him were from thirty to forty Jewish
women, closely veiled. They bowed low before Him.
Many of them were in great anxiety and dread lest their
husbands, in order to follow Jesus, would forsake them,
and they be left helpless. They entreated Him therefore
to forbid their husbands' doing such a thing. Jesus replied that if their husbands followed Him, they too
should go to Palestine, where they would find means of
subsistence. He related to them the example of the Holy
Women, and explained to them the character of the
epoch in which they were living. The present was not the
time for a life of comfort and ease, for the day was approaching upon which they ought to go forward to meet
the Kingdom that was drawing near and receive the
Bridegroom. He spoke also of the lost drachma, and of
the five wise and the five foolish virgins. The younger
women begged Jesus to admonish their husbands not to
visit the pagan maidens, since He had in terms so severe
discussed that passage in Osee in which the Prophet
warns against sinning with the heathens. Most of these
young women were, however, tormented with jealousy.
Jesus interrogated them upon their own conduct toward
their husbands, exhorted them to mildness, humility, pa-

tience, and obedience, and warned them against gossiping and making reproaches. After that He closed the Sabbath exercises in the synagogue of Cerynia, and went with His disciples back to Mallep by the shortest route.

1. *Osee* 1:10; 2:21.

22. DEPARTURE FROM CYPRUS

At Mallep, Jesus delivered a long instruction at the fountain. He spoke again of the approach of the Kingdom and of the obligation to go to meet it, of His own departure, and of the short time remaining to Him, of the bitter consummation of His labors, and of the necessity they were under of following Him and laboring with Him. He alluded again to the speedy destruction of Jerusalem and the chastisement that would soon overtake all who rejected the Kingdom of God, who would not do penance and amend their lives instead of clinging to their worldly goods and pleasures. Referring to the country in which they lived, where everything was so pleasant and the conveniences of life so many, Jesus compared it after all to an ornamented tomb whose interior was full of filth and corruption. Then He bade them reflect upon their own interiors, and see what lay concealed under their beautiful exteriors. He touched upon their usury, their avarice, their desire to gain which led them to communicate so freely with the pagans, their violent attachment to earthly possessions, their sanctimoniousness; and He again told them that all the magnificence and worldly conveniences that they saw around them would one day be destroyed, that the time would come in which no Israelite would there be found living. He spoke very significantly of Himself and the fulfillment of the Prophecies, and yet only a few comprehended His words. During this instruction the people presented themselves in bands and by turns, old men, middle-aged men, youths, women, and maidens. All were deeply touched; they wept and sobbed.

Jesus went next with some disciples and others a couple of hours to the east of Mallep, to where the occupants of several farms had begged Him to come, and where He had already gone once before from Mallep. There was, nearby, a shady hill that was used as a place for instruction. The disciple of Naim also had come hither from the port of Citium, to make preparations for his departure from Cyprus.

Jesus here, as at Mallep, delivered a farewell discourse, after which He went around to some huts and cured several invalids who had begged Him to do so. He had already set out on His return journey to Mallep when an old peasant implored Him to go to his house and take pity on his blind son. There were in the house three families of twelve persons, the grandparents, two married sons, and their children. The mother, veiled, brought the blind boy to Jesus in her arms, although it could both speak and walk. Jesus took the child into His arms, with a finger of His right hand anointed its eyes with His own saliva, blessed it, put it down on the ground, and held something before its eyes. The child grasped after it awkwardly, ran at the sound of its mother's voice, then turned to the father, and so from the arms of one to those of the other. The parents led it to Jesus, and weeping thanked Him on their knees. Jesus pressed the child to His bosom and gave it back to the parents with the admonition to lead it to the true light, that its eyes, which now saw, might not be closed in darkness deeper than before. He blessed the other children also, and the whole family. The people shed tears and followed Him with acclamations of praise.

In the house used for such purposes at Mallep, a feast was given, in which all took part. The poor were fed, and presents were given them. Jesus, finally, delivered a grand discourse on the word *"Amen,"* which, He said, was the whole summary of prayer. Whoever pronounces it carelessly, makes void his prayer. Prayer cries to God; binds us to God; opens to us His mercy, and, with the word *"Amen,"* rightly uttered, we take the asked-for gift out of His hands. Jesus spoke most forcibly of the power of the word *"Amen."* He called it the beginning and the end of everything. He spoke almost as if God had by it created the whole world. He uttered an *"Amen"* over all that He had taught them, over His own departure from them, over the accomplishment of His own mission, and ended His discourse by a solemn *"Amen."* Then He blessed His audience, who wept and cried after Him.

Jesus left Mallep with His disciples, Barnabas and Mnason following the next day. They left Chytrus to the right and went straight on across fields, through thickets, and over mountain ridges. Jesus attempted to discharge His indebtedness at the inn with the money brought Him by the disciple from Naim; but when the proprietor refused to receive it, it was distributed to the poor. All those that, either at present or in the future, were from Mallep, Chytrus, or Salamis to follow Jesus into Palestine, were to go by different routes. One party was to cross over from a port northeast of Salamis; and others, who had business at Tyre, were to start from Salamis itself. The baptized pagans went, for the most part, to Gessur.

Arrived at Salamis, Jesus and His followers put up at the school in which, upon His coming to Cyprus, He had sojourned. They entered from the northwest; the aqueduct lay to the right, the Jewish city to the left. I saw them, their garments still girded, sitting in threes by the basin in the forecourt of the school. The basin was surrounded by a little channel, in which they were washing their feet. Every three made use of a long brown towel to dry their feet. Jesus did not always allow His feet to be washed by others; generally each one performed that service for himself. Here their coming had been looked for, and food was at once offered them. Jesus had here a great number of devoted adherents, and in their midst He taught for fully two hours. After that He had a long conference with the Roman Governor, who presented to Him two pagan youths desirous of instruction and Baptism. They confessed their sins with tears, and Jesus pardoned them. Toward evening they were privately baptized by James in the forecourt of the Doctors' dwelling. These youths were to follow the philosophers to Gessur.

Mercuria also sent to beg Jesus to grant her an interview in the garden near the aqueduct. Jesus assented, and followed the servant that had delivered the message to the place designated. Mercuria came forward veiled, holding her two singularly dressed little girls by the hand. They wore only a short tunic down to the knee; the rest of their covering consisted of some kind of fine, transparent material upon which were wreaths of woollen, or feather flowers. Their arms were bare, their feet enveloped in little bands, and their hair loose. They were dressed almost like the angels that we make for representations of the Crib. Jesus spoke long and graciously with Mercuria. She wept bitterly and was very much troubled at the thought of having to leave her son behind her, also because her parents retained at a distance from her her younger sister, who would thus remain in the blindness of paganism. She wept also over her own sins. Jesus consoled her and assured her again of pardon. The two little girls looked at their mother in surprise, and they too began to cry and to cling to her. Jesus blessed the little ones, and went back to the school.

Mnason arrived from Chytrus accompanied by one of his brothers who wished to follow Jesus to Palestine.

After a farewell repast, Jesus and His disciples went to
the place where, by His orders, some of the Roman
Governor's people were awaiting them with asses. These
they mounted. Jesus rode sidewise on a cross seat provided with a support, and by His side rode the Governor.
They passed the aqueducts and, at the rear of the city,
crossed the little river Padius. They took a narrow country road shorter than the ordinary route, which wound in
a curve near the shore. During the whole of that
beautiful night, I saw the Governor generally at Jesus'
side. In front rode a troop of twelve, then came one of
nine, followed by Jesus and the Governor a little apart;
another band of twelve brought up the rear. Besides this
occasion and Palm Sunday, I never saw Jesus otherwise
than on foot. When morning began to break and they
were still three hours from the sea, the Governor, in
order not to attract attention, bade adieu to Jesus. In
parting Jesus presented to him His hand, and gave him
His blessing. The Governor had descended from his ass,
for he wished to embrace Jesus' feet. Then he bowed low
before Him, withdrew a few steps, repeated his obeisance
(it must have been a custom of the place), mounted his
beast, and rode off. The two newly baptized pagans accompanied him. Jesus then rode on till within about an
hour of the place to which He was going, when He and
His party dismounted and sent back the asses with the
servants. They now journeyed on through the salt hills
until they reached a long building where they found some
mariners awaiting them. It was a quiet, solitary spot on
the seashore. There were few trees around the country,
but along the coast an extraordinarily long mound, or
dyke, covered with moss and trees. Facing the sea were
dwelling houses and open buildings belonging to the salt-
works, in which poor Jewish families and some pagans
dwelt. Farther on where the shore was steeper, there was
a little cove down to which a flight of steps led, and here

were anchored three ships in readiness for the travellers. It was easy to land at this spot, and it was from this point that the salt was shipped to the cities along the coast.

Jesus was expected here, and all partook of a repast consisting of fish, honey, bread, and fruit. The water of this place was very bad, and they purified it by putting something into it, I think fruit. They kept it in jugs and leathern bottles. Seven of the Jews belonging to the ships' crew were here baptized, a basin being used for the ceremony.

Jesus went from house to house, consoling the poor occupants, bestowing alms upon them, healing the wounded, and curing the sick, who stretched out their hands pitifully toward Him. First He asked whether they believed that He could cure them; and upon their answering, "Yes, Lord! We do believe!" He restored them to health. He went even to the end of the long dyke, also to the homes of the pagans, who met Him looking timid and shy. Jesus blessed the poor children and gave some instructions.

The disciple from Naim had lately arrived at this place, where he awaited two other disciples. They came in good time, and then all three set out for Palestine to announce Jesus' coming.

Jesus' party counted twenty-seven men, all of whom embarked at evening twilight in three little vessels. That in which Jesus sailed was the smallest, and with Him were four disciples and some rowers. Each of the vessels had in the center, rising around the mast, galleries divided into compartments which served as sleeping places. With the exception of the rowers, who took their stand above, no one of the ship's crew could be seen. I saw Jesus' little vessel sailing out ahead, and I wondered why the others took a different direction. But when it had grown quite dark, I saw them at about half an hour from the shore fast-bound in two places, a torch raised on the mast as a sign of distress. At this sight, Jesus ordered His sailors to row back toward them. They approached one of the ships, threw out to it a rope, sailed round it, and, with it thus in tow, went to the other and did the same. The two were in this way bound to Jesus' vessel, which now they followed. Jesus rebuked the disciples on the two ill-guided vessels for having thought themselves possessed of more knowledge of the way, spoke of self-will, and of the necessity of following Him. The ships had gotten caught in an eddy between two sandbanks.

On the evening of the following day, just before the entrance of the great gulf which the sea forms at the foot of Mount Carmel between Ptolemais and Hepha, I saw Jesus' three vessels rowing back again into deep water, for a little inside the gulf a struggle was going on between a large ship on one side and some smaller ones on the other. The large ship was victorious and several dead bodies were thrown out into the water. As Jesus' vessels drew near the combatants, Jesus raised His hand and blessed them, whereupon they soon separated. They did not see Jesus' vessels, for the latter were awaiting the issue at some distance from the entrance to the gulf. The dispute between the two parties had arisen in Cyprus on the subject of the cargo. The little vessels had here lain in wait for the large one. The combatants hacked away and aimed at one another from the decks with long poles. One would have thought not a soul would escape. The struggle lasted a couple of hours. At last the large ship took the smaller ones prisoner, and moved slowly off with them in tow.

Jesus landed near the mouth of the Cison, east of Hepha, which lies on the coast. He was received on shore by several of the Apostles and disciples, among them Thomas, Simon, Thaddeus, Nathanael Chased, and Heliacim, all of whom were unspeakably delighted to embrace Him and His companions. They went round the gulf for about three hours and a half, and crossed a little

river that flows into the sea near Ptolemais. The long
bridge across this river was like a walled street. It extended to the foot of the height behind which was the
morass of Cendevia. Having climbed this height, they
proceeded to the suburbs of the Levitical city Misael,
which was separated from them by a curve of that same
height. This suburb faced the sea on the west, and on the
south rose Carmel with its beautiful valley. Misael consisted of only one street and one inn, which extended
over the height. Here, near a fountain, Jesus was met by
the people in festal procession, the children singing songs
of welcome. All bore palm branches, on which the dates
were still hanging. Simeon from Sichor-Libnath, the
"City of Waters," was here with his whole family. After
his Baptism, he came to Misael, for his children gave
him no rest until he had again joined the Jews. He had
arranged this reception for Jesus, and all at his own expense. When the procession reached the inn, nine Levites
from Misael came forward to salute Jesus.

23. JESUS GOES FROM MISAEL, THE LEVITICAL CITY, THROUGH THANACH, NAIM, AZANOTH, AND DAMNA TO CAPHARNAUM

To the north of the suburb and on a declivity halfway
up the height lay the beautiful pleasure garden of Misael,
commanding a magnificent view of the gulf. Higher up
on the hill one could see the pond, or morass, of Cendevia and Libnath, the "City of Waters," which was an
hour and a half distant. It was nearer the sea, which here
makes a bend into the land, than Misael, which was a
couple of hours from the sea. Debbaseth was five hours
to the east of the Cison, and Nazareth about seven. Jesus
walked in the garden with His disciples and related the
parable of a fisherman that went out to sea to fish, and
took five hundred and seventy fishes. He told them that

an experienced fisherman would put into pure water the good fish found in bad, that like Elias he would purify the springs and wells, that he would remove good fish from bad water, where the fish of prey would devour them, and that he would make for them new spawning ponds in better water. Jesus introduced into the parable also the accident that had happened on the sandbank to those that, out of self-will, had not followed the master of the vessels. The Cypriotes who had followed Jesus could not restrain their tears when they heard Him speak of the laborious task of transporting fish from bad to good water. Jesus mentioned clearly and precisely the number "five hundred and seventy good fish" that had been saved, and said that that was indeed enough to pay for the labor.

He spoke of Cyprus to the Levites, who rejoiced that Jews from that country were coming hither. Many were coming also from Ptolemais, and would pass this way. There was question of measures to be taken. Jesus spoke of the danger that threatened them there, whereupon the Levites asked anxiously whether the heathens of their country would ever become so powerful as to prove dangerous. Jesus answered by an allusion to the judgment that was to fall upon the whole country, the danger that threatened Himself, and the chastisement that would overtake Jerusalem. His hearers were unable to comprehend how He could again return to Jerusalem. But He said that He had still much to do before the consummation of His labors.

The Syrophenician from Ornithopolis sent hither by some of the disciples little golden bars and plates of the same metal chained together. She was desirous to send one of her ships to Cyprus, in order to facilitate Mercuria's flight from the island.

On an invitation from the Levites, Jesus accompanied them to Misael, a very ancient city, surrounded by walls and towers, in the latter of which dwelt some pagans. Elizabeth had for a long time sojourned here with her father, who exercised the functions of a Levite, and Zachary too was once at Misael. Elizabeth was born in an isolated country house two hours from Misael in the plain of Esdrelon. The property belonged to her parents, and she afterward inherited it. In her fifth year she entered the Temple. When she left it, she returned for a time to Misael and, after another period spent at the house in which she was born, she went to Zachary's home in Judea. Jesus spoke of her and of John. He insisted in terms so significant upon John's office of precursor of the Messiah that it was easy to guess who He Himself was.

While in the city, Jesus went with the Levites, to visit and cure the sick of several families. Some of the invalids were children, and several of the adults were lame. They held out to Jesus their hands enveloped in linen bands. Jesus visited Simeon also in his own house, and then proceeded to the synagogue, where He closed the Sabbath exercises. Here the women stood in a kind of high tribune not far from the chair of the teacher. Jesus' teaching turned upon sacrifice for sin and upon Samson. He rehearsed the principal deeds of the latter, and spoke of him as of a saint whose life was prophetic. Samson, Jesus said, did not lose all his strength, for he had retained sufficient to do penance. His overturning of the heathen temple upon himself was owing to a special inspiration from God.

Judas, who loved to execute business commissions, and Thomas, whose family owned rafts in the port and who was well-known here, went with several disciples to Hepha to make arrangements for the expected Cypriotes.

Jesus meanwhile, with about ten of His disciples, among them Saturnin, went on to the Levitical city of Thanach, where He was received by the Elders of the synagogue. The Pharisees here, though not open enemies of Jesus, yet were cunning and on the watch to catch Him in His speech. I saw that by their own equivocal language. They said that He would undoubtedly visit their sick, and asked Him whether He would extend that same charity to a man who had been in Capharnaum, and who was now in a very suffering state. They thought that Jesus would refuse to see the latter, who had shown himself one of His bitterest opponents in Capharnaum. His present sickness, a very singular one indeed, they supposed to be a punishment for his conduct on that occasion. He hiccoughed and vomited continually, the upper part of his body was constantly convulsed, and he was visibly pining away. He was a man between thirty and forty, and had a wife and children. When Jesus went to see him, He asked him whether he believed that He could help him. The poor man, quite dejected and ashamed of his former conduct, answered: "Yes, Lord! I do believe!" Then Jesus laid one hand on his head and the other on his breast, prayed over him, and commanded him to rise and take some nourishment. The man arose, and with tears thanked Jesus, as did likewise his wife and children. Jesus addressed some gracious and comforting words to them, but made not the slightest allusion to the man's proceedings against Himself. That evening when the Pharisees beheld the cured man appear in the synagogue, they completely renounced all desire to contradict Jesus in His speech. He taught of the accomplishment of the Prophecies; of John the Baptist, the Precursor of the Messiah, and of the Messiah Himself. His words were so significant that His hearers might readily conclude that He was alluding to Himself.

From Thanach, Jesus went to a carpenter shop, in which Joseph had first worked after his flight from Bethlehem. It was a building wherein fully a dozen people were engaged in the manufacture of wooden articles.

They dwelt in little homes around the enclosure. The shop in which Joseph had worked was now occupied by the descendants of his master. They no longer worked at the business themselves, but employed poor people for that purpose. The goods, which consisted of thin planks, rods, grated screens, and lattice-work, were principally exported on ships. The report was still current in this place that the Prophet's father had once labored here, but they no longer knew distinctly whether it was Joseph of Nazareth or not. I thought at the time: "If these people, after so short a lapse of time, know so little about these things, it is certainly not surprising that we too should know so little." Jesus delivered an instruction in the yard adjoining the workshop, taking for His subjects the love of labor and the thirst for gain.

From Thanach, Jesus went to Sion, a horrible old place two hours west of Thabor. With its ancient citadel and synagogue, near which some Pharisees dwelt, it lay somewhat high. Below and far behind some ramparts on the banks of the Cison, was a group of houses whose locality was not very healthful. The ramparts were so high that one could not see over them. The occupants of these houses appeared to be dependents upon those above them, by whom they were oppressed and tormented. Jesus, in His instruction given in the synagogue, inveighed against the Pharisees who imposed upon others grievous burdens that they would not themselves touch, against the oppression of the neighbor, and the thirst after power. He spoke also of the Messiah who, He said, would be very different from what they expected. Jesus had gone to Sion in order to console the poor, oppressed people. He visited their low, narrow, and obscure quarter of the city, and cured several poor sick in their huts, most of them gouty and paralyzed. The Pharisees banished all the sick to this miserable place, in which they could scarcely get a breath of fresh air. Jesus and the disciples gave the poor creatures presents of linen and strips of other materials.

Jesus and the disciples went from this place to Naim in about an hour and a half. Several disciples and the youth of Naim whom Jesus had raised from the dead came to meet Him near the well outside the city, so that Jesus had with Him now about twelve disciples, though no Apostles. The disciples belonging to Jerusalem had come hither from the Holy City with some of the holy women, while others, having celebrated the Feast of Pentecost with Mary at Nazareth, awaited at Naim on their return journey the coming of Jesus. He put up at an inn prepared for Him at Naim in one of the houses belonging to the widow, whom He went to see shortly after His arrival. The female portion of the family came out veiled to meet Him in the portico of the inner court, and cast themselves at His feet. Jesus saluted them graciously, and accompanied them into the reception hall. There were five women present besides the widow herself; namely, Martha, Magdalen, Veronica, Johanna Chusa, and the Suphanite. They, the holy women, sat apart at the end of the hall, on a kind of raised trestle like a long, low sofa. They sat cross-legged on cushions and rugs. The seat they occupied was raised high enough to show the feet upon which it rested. The women were silent until Jesus addressed them, and then each spoke in her turn. They related what was going on at Jerusalem, and told Jesus of the snares Herod had laid for Him. They became so animated in their recital that Jesus raised His finger and reproached them with their worldly solicitude and their judgments of others. Then He told them all about Cyprus, of those whom He had won to the truth, and spoke in words of love of the Roman Governor in Salamis. When the women expressed it as their opinion that it would be well if he too left the island, Jesus replied: "No. He must stay there and render service to many souls until My own work shall be accomplished. Then another will succeed him, and he too will prove himself a friend of the Community."

Magdalen and the Suphanite were nothing like as beautiful as they used to be. They were pale and thin, and their eyes red from weeping. Martha was very energetic, and in business affairs very talkative. Johanna Chusa was a tall, pale, vigorous woman, grave in manner, but at the same time active. Veronica had in her deportment something very like St. Catherine; she was frank, resolute, and courageous. When the holy women were thus gathered together, they used to work industriously, sewing and preparing for the Community all sorts of things, which were distributed among their private inns, or laid away in the storerooms. From these latter the Apostles and disciples supplied their own needs, as well as those of the poor. When there was no special work of this kind to be done, the holy women spent their time in sewing for poor synagogues. They generally had with them their maid-servants, who preceded or followed them on their journeys, and carried the various materials, sometimes in leathern pouches, sometimes attached to their girdle under their mantle. These maids wore tightly fitting bodices and short tunics. When the holy women were to remain some time at any place, their maids returned and awaited their coming at some of the inns along the route. Veronica's maid was with her a long time. She was in her service even after Jesus' death.

When on the Sabbath Jesus repaired to the synagogue, He did not go to the teacher's chair, but stood with His disciples in the place in which travelling teachers were accustomed to stand. But after bidding Him welcome and the prayers being said, the rabbis constrained Him to take His place before the open rolls of Scripture and to read therefrom. The Sabbath Lesson treated of the Levites, the murmuring of the people, the quails sent by

God, and the punishment that befell Miriam;[1] and from the Prophet Zacharias, some passages referring to the vocation of the Gentiles and to the Messiah.[2] Jesus' words were severe. He said that the heathens would occupy in the Messiah's Kingdom the places of the obdurate Jews. Of the Messiah, He said that they would not recognize Him as such, for He would be totally different from what they expected. Among the Pharisees were three more insolent than the others; they had been on the commission at Capharnaum. The cure of the Pharisee at Thanach had vexed them exceedingly, and they said that Jesus had effected it merely that the Pharisees of that place might connive at His doings. They recommended Him to be quiet and not to disturb the Sabbath with His cures. It would be just as well for Him, they said, to go back whence He came and to forbear creating any excitement. Jesus replied that He would fulfill the duties of His mission, journeying and teaching until His hour had arrived. The Pharisees gave no entertainment to Jesus in Naim. They were full of spite against Him, because His doctrine and charity drew after Him all the poor, the miserable and the simplehearted, whom their own severity alienated.

The season about this time in Naim was indescribably delightful. Jesus took the Sabbath day's journey with the disciples, to whom He unfolded, in very earnest and confidential words, His own future. He exhorted them to remain true and faithful, for great sufferings and persecutions were in store for Him. They should not, He said, be scandalized at Him. He would not forsake them, neither must they abandon Him, although the treatment He would receive would put their faith to the proof. The disciples were touched to tears. They went to the garden of Maroni, the widow, where too came the holy women. Jesus told them about the reconciliation that had taken place among the married couples in Mallep, and dwelt especially upon that between the couple with whom He had once taken a meal, and who had resolved to remove to Palestine. He spoke of Mercuria also, saying that she would first join the Syrophenician, who was likewise making preparations to leave Ornithopolis. They would first go to Gessur and thence proceed further on. Already many people had left Cyprus, and a certain number would soon land at Joppa.

When Jesus left the garden with the disciples, in order to close the Sabbath in the synagogue, He found on His way several sick persons who had caused themselves to be carried there in litters. They stretched out their hands to Him, imploring His help, and He cured them. And so He reached the synagogue whither also some others had had themselves conveyed on their beds. There was one man among them ill of the gout and terribly swollen, and there were others whom on His last journey Jesus had refused to cure because their faith was not pure. He had allowed them to continue in their sufferings that they might be brought at last to implore their cure more humbly. And now came the Pharisees, greatly incensed at Jesus' curing these invalids, for they had spread the report that He was unable to do so. They set up a great hue and cry at what they called His desecration of the Sabbath. But Jesus went on with the cures until seven had been effected.

Jesus answered the infuriated Pharisees sharply, asking them whether it was forbidden to do good on the Sabbath; whether they did not nourish themselves, take care of themselves, on the Sabbath day; whether the curing of these sick was not in itself a sanctification of the Sabbath day; whether they ought not on the Sabbath day to console the afflicted; whether they should on the Sabbath day retain possession of goods unjustly acquired; whether, on the Sabbath day, they should leave in their affliction the widows, the orphans, and the poor whom they had oppressed and tormented during the whole week; and He upbraided them soundly for their hypocrisy and their oppression of the poor. He told them openly that, under the pretext of providing for the synagogue, which already had a superfluity of all that was necessary, they extorted the means of the poor, and in that same synagogue made the Law for them a heavy burden; but not content with that, they would now cut them off from the grace of God on the Sabbath, prevent their receiving health on the Sabbath, while they themselves on the Sabbath feasted and drank upon what they had pitilessly wrung from them. By these words Jesus silenced the Pharisees, and all entered the synagogue. The Pharisees laid before Jesus the rolls of Scripture and invited Him to teach. This they did craftily in the hope of being able to convict Him of error and bring a charge against Him. When, then, Jesus alluded to the era of the Messiah and said that numbers of pagans would come over to the people of God at that time, they asked Him mockingly whether He had not gone Himself to Cyprus, in order to bring the pagans back with Him. Jesus spoke likewise of the tithes, of imposing burdens on others and not carrying them one's self, and of the oppression of orphans and widows, for from Pentecost till the Feast of Tabernacles the tithes were brought to the Temple. But in places remote from Jerusalem, as this was, the Levites collected them. And here it was that abuses crept in, for the Pharisees extorted the tithes from the people and converted them to their own use. It was against this that Jesus inveighed. The Pharisees were highly exasperated and on leaving the synagogue gave vent to their spleen.

From Naim Jesus went with some of the disciples up the height this side of the Cison. Proceeding in a northeasterly direction, they arrived at Rimmon where there was a school under the charge of some Levites. These now came to the school to meet Jesus, who gave an instruction to the youths and little boys on an open square in front of the schoolhouse. Thither also flocked many of the people who had already listened to Jesus' teachings at Naim. He explained to the children the general duties imposed by the Mosaic Law, but did not enlarge before them upon the dangers of the present time, as He was accustomed to do before His more elderly audiences. Rimmon consisted of a long row of houses on a slope of the mountain. The inhabitants were mostly gardeners and vinedressers who disposed of their fruits at Naim and worked also in the gardens of that place. From Rimmon, Jesus ascended the eastern side of Thabor. He was accompanied a good part of the way by the Levites who had been collecting the tithe offerings in Rimmon. After a journey of about three hours, He reached Beth-Lechem, a place in ruins east of the city of Dabereth. It comprised only one row of houses occupied by poor peasants, whom Jesus visited in their homes, encouraging them in their miseries and healing their sick.

Leaving Beth-Lechem, He journeyed on for about four hours through the valley in which was the well of Capharnaum, and toward dusk arrived at Azanoth where He had a private inn. Here He found some friends from Capharnaum awaiting Him: Jairus and his daughter; the blind man of Capharnaum to whom He had restored sight; the female relatives of Enue, the woman healed of the bloody flux; and Lea, the woman who had cried out to Him, "Blessed is the womb that bore Thee!" The women, their veils down, fell on their knees before Jesus, and He blessed them. They shed tears of joy upon beholding Him again. Jairus's daughter was well and full of life, and withal quite changed, for she was now devout and modest. Jesus taught until far into the night. On the following day He went to Damma, where He had outside the city a private inn over which a relative of Joseph's family presided. Lazarus and two disciples belonging to

Jerusalem were here waiting for Him. Indeed, Lazarus had already been eight days in those parts attending to the real estate in land and houses of the Magdalum property, for only the household goods and similar effects belonging to Magdalen had as yet been disposed of. Jesus embraced Lazarus, a favor He was accustomed to extend only to him and the elder Apostles and disciples; to the others, He merely extended His hands. Jesus spoke of the Cypriotes, those that had accompanied Him and those that were to follow later, and made some remarks as to how they should be supported. I heard on this occasion that James the Less and Thaddeus were to proceed to Gessur, in order to receive and accompany the seven pagan philosophers who were to arrive there. Jesus treated Lazarus with marked confidence. On this occasion they walked alone together for a long time. Lazarus was a tall man, grave and gentle and very self-possessed in manner. Moderate in all things, even his familiar intercourse with others was stamped with a something that wore an air of distinction. His hair was black and he bore some resemblance to Joseph, though his features were sterner and more marked. Joseph's hair was yellow, and there was something uncommonly tender, gentle, and obliging in his whole deportment.

From Damma Jesus with Lazarus, the disciples, the steward of the inn along with his son who was soon to be admitted to the number of the disciples, went almost two hours eastward to the village belonging to the Centurion Zorobabel of Capharnaum. It was situated on the southern side of a rocky hill which shut in the valley of Capharnaum on the south, and upon which lay the Centurion's gardens and vineyards. Here Jesus instructed the servants and field laborers. He took for His text the Messiah and the near coming of His Kingdom, announced to them the signs enumerated by the Prophets and showed how they had all been fulfilled, warned and

implored them to amend their lives, and assured them
that the Messiah would not appear under the form expected by the Jews, consequently only the small number
of the humble and contrite would recognize Him. He told
them too that the Messiah would make known His
doctrines by the lips of more than one, as He had formerly spoken through the mouth of many Prophets. Some
melancholy and possessed mutes were brought to Jesus.
He laid His finger moistened with spittle under their
tongues, and commanded Satan to depart, whereupon I
saw some of them fall unconscious and then rise up
cured, while others fell into convulsions for a short time,
after which they too were restored to perfect health. All
praised God and gave thanks for their cure. After that,
Jesus, taking a solitary route, went to His Mother's in the
valley east of Capharnaum, a distance of about three-
quarters of an hour.

The holy women were already with the Blessed Virgin,
they having come from Naim by the direct road. They
did not leave the house to receive Jesus, neither did Mary
hurry out to meet her Son. After He had washed and let
down His robe, Jesus entered the large apartment, in
which several little alcoves were cut off by curtains.
Mary, her head veiled and humbly inclined, stretched out
to Him her hand when He had first proffered His, and
He graciously, though gravely, saluted her. The other
women stood veiled, forming a semicircle in the rear. I
have indeed seen Jesus when alone with Mary, in order
to console and strengthen her, press her to His breast
while conversing with her. But Mary herself, since His
going forth to teach, treated Him as one would treat a
saint, a Prophet; or as a mother might treat her son were
he a Pope, a Bishop, or a King. Still, there was something much more noble, more holy in Mary's demeanor,
though marked at the same time with indescribable
simplicity. She never embraced Him now, but only ex-

tended her hand when He offered His.

Some time after, I saw Jesus and Mary eating together alone. A little, low table stood between them. Jesus reclined at one side, and Mary sat at the other. On it was a fish, some bread, honey, cakes, and two little jugs. The other holy women were in the little curtained alcoves in groups of two or three, or in a side hall serving the repast of the disciples, among whom they had several relatives. Jesus told His Mother about Cyprus and the souls He had there gained. She expressed her joy quietly, but asked few questions. Her words were chiefly those of maternal solicitude touching the dangers that awaited Him. Jesus replied gently that He would fulfill His mission until the hour came for His return to His Father.

1. *Num.* 8-12.
2. *Zach.* 2:10; 4:8.

24. ARRIVAL OF THE APOSTLES AND DISCIPLES IN CAPHARNAUM

Not long after Jesus' return to Capharnaum, there were gathered around Him almost thirty disciples. Some were come from Judea with the news of the arrival at Joppa of ships bringing two hundred Cypriote Jews, who were there to be received by Barnabas, Mnason, and his brother. John, who was still at Hebron with the relatives of Zachary, was charged with providing suitable quarters for these emigrants. The Essenians also occupied themselves with the same cares. For a time the Cypriotes were lodged in the grottos until proper destinations could be assigned them. Lazarus and the Syrophenician provided settlements near Ramoth-Gilead for the Jewish emigrants from the region of Ornithopolis. The disciples lately come to Capharnaum put up, some at Peter's outside the city, some in Bethsaida, and some at the school in the city itself. James the Less and Thaddeus came from Gessur with three of the pagan philosophers—fine, handsome young men who had received circumcision. Andrew and Simon came also with several other disciples, and the welcome they received was most touching. Jesus, according to His wont, presented the newly converted to His Mother. There was a tacit understanding, an interior agreement between Jesus and Mary, that she should take the disciples into her heart, into her prayers, into her benedictions and, to a certain degree, into her very being, as her own children and the brothers of Jesus, that she should be their spiritual Mother as she was His Mother by nature. Mary did this with singular earnestness, while Jesus on such occasions treated her with great solemnity. There was in this ceremony of adoption something so holy, something so interior, that I am unable to express. Mary was the vine, the ear, the spike of Jesus' Flesh and Blood.

The disciples related where they had been and all that had happened to them. In some places stones had been thrown after them, but without striking them; from others they were obliged to flee, but everywhere they were wonderfully protected. They had, too, met good people, had cured, baptized, and taught. Jesus had commanded them to go to the lost sheep of Israel only. They had likewise sought out the Jews in the pagan cities, though without meddling with the heathens excepting with such as were servants to the Jews. In Gazora, northeast of Jabes Galaad, Andrew and the disciples that accompanied him had redeemed Jewish slaves from bondage, sacrificing to this purpose all that they possessed. They asked Jesus whether they had done rightly, to which He answered in the affirmative. Jesus did not hearken to all that some of them had to say. Many of them, while eagerly and with a certain warmth of manner relating their missionary labors, Jesus interrupted with words something like these:

"I know that already." To others who spoke simply and humbly, He listened for a length of time, and called upon the silent to relate what had happened to them. When they whom He had interrupted asked why He would not hear their account, Jesus answered by showing them the difference between their own and their brethren's speech. Frequently also He interrupted their narratives with parables; for instance, that of the tares sown among the good seed and which, after it had grown up, was to be burnt at the time of harvest. He said that all that had been sown would not come up. He spoke of several that had fallen away from the disciples, and exhorted those present not to place too great security in their good works, for they would still have to undergo great temptations. He recounted the parable of the lord going afar to take possession of a foreign kingdom. He gave over to his servants remaining behind a certain number of talents for which later on he required an account. This parable referred to Jesus' own journey to Cyprus and to the account He was now exacting from the disciples of their activity during His absence. As He spoke, He frequently turned first to one, then to another whose thoughts He divined, with the words: "Why art thou thinking useless thoughts?" or, "Do not think in that way!" or, "Thy thoughts are now taking a wrong direction. Think in this way, and not in that!" He read the thoughts of His hearers and reproved them accordingly.

When the hour sounded the commencement of the Sabbath, Jesus went with the disciples to the synagogue, where He found the Pharisees already standing around the lecture hall. But Jesus walked straight up to it, and they at once made room for Him. The instruction was on Rahab and the scouts sent by Josue to Jericho.[1] The Pharisees were furious at what they called Jesus' audacity, and they said to one another: "Let Him go on now with His talk. This evening, or when the Sabbath is over, we shall hold a council and soon find means to close His lips." Jesus, knowing their malice, remarked that they were spies of a very peculiar kind, for they came not to find out the truth but to betray Him and His followers. His language against them was very severe, and He spoke likewise of the destruction of Jerusalem, and the judgment in store for those of the people that would not do penance and recognize the reign of the Messiah. He introduced into His discourse also the parable of the king whose son was slain in the vineyard by the unfaithful servants. The Pharisees dared not interrupt Him. All the holy women were present in the synagogue, where they had places set apart for them.

That afternoon Jesus, at the earnest request of the parents of some sick children, went with several of the disciples to about twenty houses of Capharnaum, both of the rich and of the poor, and cured a great many children, boys and girls from three to eight years old. The malady must have been a sort of epidemic, for they were all affected in pretty much the same way. The little sufferers' color was quite yellow, their throat, cheeks, and hands swollen. Their condition was similar to that attendant on many other sicknesses, scarlet fever, for instance. Jesus did not cure them all in the same way. On some He laid His hand on the parts affected, others He anointed with spittle, and over others He breathed. Many of them rose up at once. Jesus blessed them and gave them over to their parents with some words of admonition. For others, He commanded prayer and a certain kind of nursing. This was for the greater good of both children and parents. The marketplace of Capharnaum was on an eminence, and to it four streets ran. Jesus visited this part of the city and entered the home of Ignatius, whom He cured. The boy was a very lovely child of about four years. His parents were wealthy. They were engaged in the sale of brass or bronze vessels, for I saw many such standing in long corridors. For a couple of days the parents of Ignatius had begged Jesus to visit them, for He had just cured the child of their neighbor, the carpet merchant. The market was surrounded by arcades, in which the goods of the various dealers were exposed for sale. In the center played a fountain, and at either end rose two large edifices. The Pharisees were full of wrath at these cures. Three of them went into the courtyard before Peter's house, in the porticos of which lay sick who had been transported thither, and whom Jesus was now healing. They forced their way through the crowd till they stood before Him. Then they addressed Him, suggesting that He should leave off curing, excite no disturbance on the Sabbath, and expressed their desire to enter into an argument with Him. But Jesus turned away from them saying that He had nothing to do with them, that He could not cure them, since they were incurable.

At the closing Sabbath exercises that evening, Jesus again taught in the synagogue. He spoke of the murmuring of the Israelites on the news brought by the scouts sent to view the Promised Land, of the curse that fell upon them, in consequence of which they perished in the wilderness, and only their children were permitted to see the Land of Promise. He laid special stress upon malediction and benediction, of which He spoke in very energetic terms. Then He went on to speak of those that falsify the things pertaining to the Kingdom of God, of those that would never enter into it, of the non-recognition of the Messiah, and of the chastisement that menaced Jerusalem and the whole country. And now two of the Pharisees, mounting the teacher's stand, began to comment upon some passages in the day's Lesson, in which it was recorded that God had commanded Moses in the wilderness to cause a certain man to be stoned by all the people for having gathered sticks on the Sabbath day. This fact the Pharisees cited as an argument against the cures wrought on the Sabbath. Jesus responded by asking whether the health of the poor and necessitous was like wood destined for the fire; whether hypocrisy, lifeless and inflexible, had not in it much more of the nature of wood; and the looking out for scandal in the healing of the poor, the uncharitable faultfinding of those that had beams in their own eyes, was not a gathering of sticks—not, however, to prepare food for themselves, but to cast them as stumbling blocks in the path of truth, to use them as fuel for distilling the poison of discord and persecution. Is it not permitted to receive on the Sabbath that for which we pray on the Sabbath, and also to give it to others on that same day if we have it? Then Jesus explained the passages in the Law that referred to manual labor. He said that it was prohibited on the Sabbath only to leave man free for the performance of spiritual exercises. How could the Sabbath prevent the cure of the sick, since such cures sanctified the Sabbath? In this way Jesus refuted the Pharisees and so confounded them that they had nothing more to say. Some few of His hearers were moved by His words. They reflected in silence upon what they had heard, while others put their heads together, saying: "Yes! It is He! He is the Messiah! No mere man, no Prophet could teach in that way!" Significant looks were exchanged throughout the crowd generally, for the people rejoiced over the Pharisees' humiliation; some, however, obdurate at heart, joined with the latter in taking scandal.

After about fifteen of the disciples had assembled in Capharnaum, Jesus took them with Him to the mountain near Bethsaida, where He had taught about the eating of His Flesh and the drinking of His Blood. On this occasion, His instruction turned upon their own mission and labors, and the fruit they were to bring forth. The holy women were present. In this instruction Jesus related the parable of the workmen in the vineyard. He praised and encouraged the disciples and blessed them in a body, His hands outstretched above thier heads, and they were again filled with strength and courage.

On the evening of that day, Peter, James the Greater, and Matthew, together with some of the ancient disciples of John, went to salute Jesus at His Mother's. Peter shed tears of joy. During the meal they took together Jesus again related the parable of the fisher, the five hundred and seventy fishes and their transportation into good water, the same upon which He had taught in Misael, also in Capharnaum before the holy women and the disciples. In the same manner, all the other parables were often repeated and explained in various ways by Him. The next day He went with the Apostles and disciples down to the ships. Peter's large barque and that of Jesus were bound together at some distance from the shore. They allowed them to float on the water without oar or rudder, for Jesus wanted to converse with the disciples undisturbed by the crowd. It was a beautiful day. They had stretched the sails overhead for shade, and they did not return till evening. Peter was very eager to talk, and he related with a certain complacency how much good they had effected. Jesus turned to him, and bade him to be silent. Peter, who so loved his Lord, immediately held his peace, and saw with regret that he had again been too ardent. Judas was vehemently desirous of praise, though he had not the candor to let it appear. He was on his guard more, however, that he might not be put to shame than that he might not sin.

When I consider the life of Jesus and His travelling about with His Apostles and disciples, the certain conviction often forces itself upon me that, if He came now amongst us, He would encounter difficulties still greater than in His own day. How freely could He and His followers then go around teaching and healing! Apart from the Pharisees, thoroughly hardened and vainglorious as they were, no one put obstacles in His way. Even the Pharisees themselves knew not on what ground they stood with Him. They did indeed know that the time of the Promise had come in which the Prophecies were to be fulfilled, and they saw in Him something irresistible, something holy and wonderful. How often have I seen them seated consulting the Prophets and the ancient commentaries upon them! But never would they yield assent to what they read, for they expected a Messiah very different from Jesus. They thought that He would be their friend, one of their own sect, and still they did not venture to decide upon Jesus. Even many of the disciples thought that He must certainly possess some secret power, a connection with some nation or king. They fancied that He would one day mount the throne of Jerusalem, the holy king of a holy people, that then they themselves would hold desirable positions in His Kingdom and would also become holy and wise. Jesus allowed them to indulge these thoughts for awhile. Others looked upon the affair in a more spiritual sense, though not going so far as to the humiliation of the Crucifixion. But very few acted through childlike, holy love and the inspiration of the Holy Spirit.

When at last all the Apostles were returned from their missions, the latest arrivals being Thomas, John, and Bartholomew, Jesus went with them to Cana, whither came also the seventy disciples and the holy women from Capharnaum. On an eminence in the center of the city there was a teacher's chair, from which Jesus taught, taking for His subject His own mission and its accomplishment. He said that He had not come into this world to enjoy the comforts and pleasures of life, and that it was foolish to demand of Him anything else than the fulfillment of His Father's will. He said in terms more signficant than ever that He Himself was the One so long expected, but that He would be received by only a few, and that when His work was done, He would return to His Father. He spoke warningly and entreatingly, begging His hearers most earnestly not to reject salvation and the moment of grace. He again pointed out the accomplishment of the Prophecies. His teaching was so wonderful, so impressive, that the people of Cana said one to another: "He is more than a Prophet! No one has ever before spoken this way in Israel!"

In the house of the father of the Bride of Cana, an entertainment was given, at which the poor of the place were fed and presents bestowed upon them. Jesus and the Apostles served. At the close of the feast, Jesus related the parable of the wise and the foolish virgins, explained it to His hearers, and spoke much of the near coming of the Bridegroom. It was a kind of memorial feast of the marriage at Cana, for now as then all the Apostles, disciples, and friends were again assembled together. The house was garlanded with flowers, and the water urns of the first miracle were again in use. Children, bearing wreaths and pyramids of flowers, entered the festive hall playing on musical instruments. Bartholomew, Nathanael Chased, and some of the disciples had made some beautiful mottos relative to the spiritual nuptials of the soul with God.

From Cana Jesus went with all the Apostles and disciples to the mount of instruction near Gabara. They walked slowly in bands, and frequently paused around Jesus to hear His words. He was very affectionate to them and often addressed them with the words: "My beloved children!" He commanded them to relate their experience, to tell how things had gone with them. The Apostles spoke first. They had on the preceding days recounted some of their experience, though not all. Now each was to hear what the others had done and all that had happened to them. Jesus said to them so sweetly: "My dear little children, now will be seen who has loved

Me and in Me My Heavenly Father; who has published the word of salvation and wrought cures in order to do My will, not his own, or not for the sake of vain renown." Thereupon they began to relate their experience: first, an Apostle, and after him, the disciple that had accompanied him. This took place principally upon a hill which was about two hours from the mount of instruction and the same distance from Cana. People used to ascend it for sake of the view, which around these parts was somewhat limited.

Peter began eagerly to tell of the different kinds of possessed that had fallen in his way, his manner of treating them, and how Satan had retired before him when commanded in the Name of Jesus. In his enthusiasm, he had again forgotten the reproof received on board the ship. Once more, he was all fire and zeal. He said that in the land of the Gergeseans, he had encountered a couple of possessed whom several others were unable to free from the demon. Here he named the unsuccessful disciples, among whom were the two Gergeseans themselves once possessed. But he, Peter, had easily expelled the devils; they had instantly submitted to him. Jesus silenced him by a look. Then raising His eyes to Heaven, while all looked on in breathless expectation, He said: "I have seen Satan falling from Heaven like lightning." And at the same moment, I saw a lurid light whirling and shooting through the air. Jesus reproved Peter for his too great warmth, as well as all the others that had, either in thought or word, yielded to a spirit of boasting. They should, He said, act and work in His Name and by Him, in humility and faith, never harboring the thought that one could do more than another. He said: "Behold, I have given you power to tread upon serpents and scorpions and upon all the might of the enemy, and nothing shall hurt you. But yet rejoice not in this, that spirits are subject to you, but rejoice in this, that your names are written in Heaven." Several times He addressed them kindly and lovingly in the words: "Beloved little children," and listened to the account given by many of them. Thomas and Nathanael received a reprimand for some negligence of which they had been guilty, but it was given with great love and sincerity.

While standing on the hill, Jesus appeared to be penetrated with joy, grave and celestial, and He held His hands raised to Heaven. I saw Him surrounded with splendor that fell upon Him like a transparent cloud of light. He was perfectly enraptured and, in a transport of joy, He exclaimed: "I confess to Thee, O Father, Lord of Heaven and earth, because Thou hast hidden these things from the wise and prudent, and hast revealed them to little ones. Yea, Father, for so it hath seemed good in Thy sight. All things are delivered to Me by My Father, and no one knoweth who the Son is but the Father, and who the Father is but the Son, and to whom the Son will reveal it!" And then turning to the disciples, He said: "Blessed are the eyes that see the things which you see! For I say to you that many Prophets and kings have desired to see the things that you see, and have not seen them; and to hear the things that you hear, and have not heard them."

Having arrived at the mount beyond Gabara, Jesus delivered an instruction in detail upon all that the Apostles had related to Him. He imparted to them the knowledge of many things of which they as yet knew not, and showed them wherein they had erred or acted with too little resolution. He enlightened them upon the different kinds of possession and taught them how the demon should be expelled. He spoke of all that was in store for them, of His own mission and its near accomplishment, and told them that He would shortly allow them to return to their homes to rest awhile, after which they were again to labor, to teach, and spread abroad the Kingdom of God. He thanked them for their diligence and obedience, and then returned with them to Capharnaum whither they arrived as night closed in. There were many others on the mountain besides the Apostles and disciples.

On the following Sabbath Jesus taught in the synagogue of Capharnaum upon Samuel's resignation of the judicial office. His words were grave and forcible. The Pharisees felt themselves attacked on all sides, but as they could detect nothing false in Jesus' doctrine of which to accuse Him, they reproached Him with the trifling imperfections they had discovered in the actions of His disciples. They said that His disciples did not observe the fast rigorously, that they even stripped the ears of corn on the Sabbath, and gathered fruit by the roadside and ate it, that they were rough and unclean in their clothing, that they entered the synagogues in garments covered with the dust of travel and without being decently let down, and that they were not particular about washing before meals. Thereupon Jesus delivered a discourse full of severe censure against the Pharisees, in which He depicted their conduct and actions, called them a race of vipers, who imposed upon others burdens that they would by no means take upon themselves. He alluded to their Sabbath promenades, their oppression of the poor, their dishonesty with regard to the tithes, their hypocrisy. They blamed, He went on to say, the mote in their neighbor's eye, while unmindful of the beam in their own, and He ended by declaring that He would continue His journeys, His teaching, and His healing, until the time for His departure from this earth. While Jesus was delivering this severe lecture a young man from among the Pharisees, rising suddenly and approaching nearer to Him, lifted his hands to Heaven and cried out in a loud voice: "Surely, this is the Son of God, the Holy One of Israel! He is more than a Prophet!" and thus he continued to sound Jesus' praises in an inspired strain. This incident created great excitement throughout the synagogue. Two old Pharisees grasped the young man by the arm and dragged him out, he proclaiming all the while the praise of Jesus, who meantime went on with His discourse. When outside the synagogue, the young man loudly and vehemently declared to those that he found there that he had separated from the Pharisees. When Jesus left the synagogue, he cast himself at His feet and earnestly implored to be admitted among His disciples. Jesus assented on condition that he would leave father and mother, give all that he had to the poor, take up his cross, and follow Him. Then some of the disciples, among whom was Mnason, took the young man off with them.

That evening Jesus closed the Sabbath exercises in the synagogue. He had repaired thither with the Apostles and disciples some time before the usual hour, that all might hear what He had to say to His followers and thereby understand that He had no need to teach in secret. In this instruction, He warned them against the Pharisees and false Prophets, commanded them to be vigilant, explained the parable of the good and watchful servants and contrasted it with that of the slothful. As Peter during the discourse asked whether His words were meant for all His hearers or only for the disciples, Jesus now addressed Himself to him. He spoke to him as if he were the master of the house, the overseer of the servants. He extolled the good householder, and at the same time condemned severely the negligent one that fulfilled not his duty.

Jesus continued to teach until the Pharisees came to close the Sabbath, and when He wanted to give place to them, they very courteously addressed Him with, "Rabbi, do Thou explain the Lesson," and laid the roll of Scriptures before Him. Thereupon Jesus taught, in a manner most impressive, upon Samuel's abdication of the judicial office. He quoted the words used by him on that occasion: "I am old and gray-headed";[3] and explained them in such a way that the Pharisees could plainly see that

He was applying them to Himself. He said something to this effect: "Ye have had Me a long time among you, and ye are tired of Me! Ye are constantly renewing your accusations, but I am always the same."

Samuel's questions to the people, "Have I committed this or that injustice against you? Have I taken any man's oxen or ass? Have I oppressed anyone?" Jesus cited as those of God and the Sent of God, and the explanation that He gave of them pointed most clearly to those Doctors and Pharisees who could not venture to put similar questions to the people. The clamoring of the Israelites after a king by whom, like the heathen nations, they wanted to be ruled, and their rejection of Judges, signified, Jesus said, their perverse expectation of a worldly kingdom, of a king and a Messiah surrounded by magnificence, with whom they could pass their lives in splendor and enjoyment; a Messiah who, instead of expiating their sins and disorders by His own labors, sufferings, penance, and satisfaction, would envelop them together with their filth and vices in his own rich mantle of royalty, and even reward them for their crimes.

That Samuel did not cease to pray for the nation and that by his prayer he caused thunder and lightning in the sky above them, Jesus explained as an effect of God's compassion for the good; and He assured them that the Sent of God, whom instead of receiving they would reject, would likewise implore His Father's mercy for them until the end. The rain and thunder granted to prayer, Jesus explained as the signs and wonders that were to attend upon the Sent of God to rouse and convert the good. They and their king, as Samuel had said, would find favor with God if they walked before Him who would not reject them. Then Jesus declared to them that the righteous would receive justice and the grace of knowledge, but against the wicked, Samuel would rise up in judgment. Jesus afterward referred to David and his anointing as king in opposition to Saul, to the separation of the good from the bad, and to the destruction of Saul and his family.

The Pharisees took care not to contradict Jesus in the synagogue, that they might not (as was always the case on such occasions) be put to shame before the people. They had, however, resolved beforehand to attack Him at the entertainment to which they had invited Him along with the Apostles and a part of the disciples. It was given in an open hall of the house belonging to the Ruler of the synagogue, and there were at least twenty Pharisees present. Before taking their places at table, one of them put a large wash basin before Jesus, asking whether He did not want to wash, and he went on talking of the holy old customs and commandments of the Israelites, and called upon Jesus and His followers to observe them. But Jesus repulsed him. He told him that He saw through his trick, and wanted no water from him. When at table, they began to dispute with Him upon the discourse He had delivered that day. But He convicted and confounded them in such a manner that many of them became perfectly furious, and several others were so frightened and touched that during the disputation, which they carried on walking up and down, twelve of them withdrew from their obstinate colleagues. Thus was the number of Jesus' enemies decreased.

One of the young men of Nazareth who had so often, but vainly, petitioned to be received among the disciples, here presented himself again before Jesus with the question: "Master, what must I do to possess eternal life?" Thereupon followed the scene recorded in the Gospel,[4] and Jesus recounted the story of the compassionate Samaritan. Meanwhile the Pharisees reproached Jesus for not receiving the young man among His disciples. It was, they said, because the youth was well educated, and Jesus knew that He could not silence him so easily as He could the others. They again accused the disciples of irregular conduct, of uncleanliness, of stripping the wheat ears on the Sabbath, of gathering fruit on the wayside, of eating out of time, of ill breeding, and of many other similar things. They reproached Peter in particular with being a wrangler and quarreller like his father. Jesus defended the disciples. They might indeed be joyful, He said, as long as the Bridegroom was with them. After these words He withdrew, passing through the beautiful cemetery near the synagogue that lay in the direction of Jairus's house, and thence by the land route to Bethsaida. He prayed alone until after midnight, when He retired to His Mother's. The Pharisees had hired the rabble to throw stones after the disciples, but God protected them. They knew not where Jesus had gone.

The Jews that had emigrated from Cyprus to Palestine lived at first in caves, but by degrees their settlement became a city, which received the name of Eleutheropolis. It was situated west of Hebron and not far from the well of Samson. More than once the Jews sought to destroy the little colony, but after every attack of the kind, the inhabitants again returned. The caves lay under the city, so that in times of persecution, the inhabitants could take refuge in them. In the first attack, which was made at the time of the stoning of St. Stephen, when the colony between Ophel and Bethania was destroyed, Mercuria lost her life. The people of this colony often went to the Cenacle and to the church at the Pool of Bethsaida, to carry thither their offerings and contributions, and at the destruction of Ophel they fled to Eleutheropolis. Joses Barsabas, son of Mary Cleophas and her second husband Sabas, became the first Bishop of that city, and there during a persecution he was crucified on a tree.

1. *Num.* 13, 14; *Jos.* 2.
2. *Num.* 15:32-36.
3. *1 Kgs.* 12:2, etc.
4. *Lk.* 10:25-37.

25. JESUS INSTRUCTS THE NEW DISCIPLES UPON PRAYER AND THE EIGHT BEATITUDES

Early the next day Jesus left Mary's house with the latest received and not yet well-instructed disciples, and crossing the road between Capharnaum and Bethsaida, went to that mount of instruction from which He had once despatched the Apostles on their respective missions.[1] It was about three hours from Capharnaum. On the way, He encountered Mnason and some other disciples along with the converted Pharisee from Thanach near Naim. The last-named had been very much touched by the cure of a Pharisee at Thanach, and still more deeply impressed by Jesus' last discourse on the mountain beyond Gabara. On the Mount of the Apostolic Mission, there was a well-arranged and shaded place for holding instructions. At the foot of the mountain was a long hut in which ten poor paralytics belonging to the surrounding country lay, their limbs fearfully contorted. They were cared for by the shepherds of the district. Jesus cured and instructed them.

Here in the solitude of the mountain, the disciples entreated Jesus to teach them again how to pray. He did so, repeating to them the *Our Father,* dwelling at length on each separate petition, and explaining it with the same examples that He had used on a former occasion: that, for instance, of the man seeking bread and persistently knocking at his friend's door until he got what he wanted; that of the child asking an egg of its father, who would surely not give it a scorpion; and, in fine, all the other illustrations He had already brought forward to show the effects of persevering prayer and the paternal relations that existed between God and man. He taught all His disciples in the same way, going over and over the same instruction with touching patience and unwearying pains, that they might be able in turn to repeat everywhere on their missions exactly the same things. He conducted these instructions to the disciples just as one would do among children, questioning them separately upon the explanations He had given, setting them right, and again explaining what they had not understood. Finally, He went over the whole prayer and gave the interpretation of the word *Amen,* as He had formerly done in Cyprus, saying that this word contains everything in itself, that it is the beginning and the end of prayer. Some other people and a couple of Pharisees from Bethsaida-Julias arrived while Jesus was speaking, and they too heard a part of His instruction. One of the latter invited Him to dine at his house in Bethsaida-Julias, which invitation Jesus accepted.

When He and the disciples started for Bethsaida, they directed their steps to the south of the Jordan bridge. On their way they came, this side of Bethsaida, to an inn where His Mother, the widow of Naim, Lea, and two other women were waiting to take leave of Him, because He was now going to teach on the other side of the Jordan. Mary was very much afflicted. She had a private interview with Jesus, in which she shed abundant tears and begged Him not to go to Jerusalem for the Feast of the Dedication of the Temple. She spoke so supplicatingly and in so loving a manner that I felt she must surely divine the holy destiny of her Son. Jesus supported her on His breast and consoled her gently and lovingly. He told her that He must fulfill the mission for which His Father had sent Him and for which also she had become His Mother, and that she must continue strong and courageous, in order to strengthen and edify the others. Then He saluted the other women, gave them His blessing, and they returned to Capharnaum, while He and the disciples went on to Bethsaida-Julias where He was received by the Pharisees. Besides those belonging to the city, there were present some others from Paneas, for it was a kind of feast day commemorative of the burning of a bad book written by the Sadducees. The Pharisees brought forward their old complaints against Jesus. When about to take His place at table, one of them pulled Him by the arm, saying that he was astonished that a man who could teach so well as He, should be so little mindful of holy observances as to eat without washing. Jesus responded that the Pharisees purified the outside of the cup and platter, but that within they were full of wickedness. To this the Pharisee replied by asking how He knew the state of his interior. Jesus answered that God, who formed the exterior, made also the interior, and that His eye could scan it clearly. The disciples drew Jesus to one side and begged Him not to speak with too much warmth, for they might possibly be put out, but He reproved them for their cowardice.

That evening Jesus taught in the synagogue, but did not work any cures, for the Pharisees had intimidated the people. They were very proud, and had here a kind of high school.

From Bethsaida-Julias, Jesus took a northeasterly direction toward the mountain upon which the multiplication of the loaves had taken place. It was about an hour and a half from Bethsaida. There He found assembled all the Apostles and disciples with many people from Capharnaum, Caesarea-Philippi, and other places. He taught upon the Eighth Beatitude, "Blessed are ye when men hate and persecute you for the Son of Man's sake," also upon the passage "Woe to the rich, to them that are filled with the goods of this world, for in them they already have their reward; but as for you, rejoice that it is still in store for you." He spoke likewise of the salt of the earth, of the city on the mountain, of the light on the candlestick, of the fulfilling of the Law, of the hiding of good works, of prayer made in the privacy of one's chamber, and of fasting. Of the last-mentioned, Jesus said that it should be practiced joyously with anointing of the head, and not be turned into a sanctimonious parade of piety. He went on to the laying up of treasure in Heaven, freedom from worldly solicitude, the impossibility of a man's serving two masters, the narrow gate, the broad road, the bad tree with its bad fruit, the wise man that built on a solid foundation, and the fool that built upon sand. This discourse lasted over three hours. During it the audience went down once to the foot of the mountain to get something to eat. Jesus continued His instruction to the Apostles and disciples, exhorting them upon all those points on which He had spoken when sending them out upon former missions. He animated them to believe, to have confidence, and to persevere. On the next day, the number of His hearers having increased to several thousands, Jesus taught again on the mountain. On account of the caravans that traversed these parts, there were people present from all sections of the country, also many sick and possessed. The Pharisees in attendance had not come to dispute, although they received some rather severe thrusts during the discourse. Jesus' miracles were too manifest and the people too enthusiastic over Him, to allow them a word. The people had food with them, and they seated themselves on the ground to partake of it. Among the cured was a blind man from Jericho, who had also been lame. One of the disciples had cured him of lameness, but had not restored his sight. He was a cousin of Manahem. The latter led him to Jesus, who restored his sight.

The new disciples, whom during these last days He had with admirable patience taught like children by question and answer, Jesus now sent out two and two with the words: "I send ye like sheep among wolves." One of Joseph of Arimathea's nephews arrived here from Jerusalem with the news that Lazarus was sick.

Jesus kept with Himself only the Apostles Peter, James, John, Matthew, and some of the disciples, with whom He went to Matthew's custom office and thence by sea to Dalmanutha. I saw Him afterward in the city of Edrai where He taught on the Sabbath, then in the Levitical city of Bosra, and finally in Nobah.

In Nobah, outside the pagan quarter of the city, dwelt a colony of sincere Rechabites. On their return from the Babylonian Captivity they found their city in the possession of the pagans, but they retook it and again re-established themselves in it. They cherished an extraordinary hatred against the Pharisees and Sadducees, whom they shunned as much as possible. They were engaged in cattle raising, and led a very strict life. They drank no wine, excepting on certain feast days, and tenaciously held to the letter of the Scripture. Jesus admonished them on this point, and gave them an instruction on the spirit of the letter. They were very humble, and took in good part all that He said. Many were baptized, among them some pagans, and a great number of possessed were delivered from the Evil One. There was a whole hospital full of these poor creatures at Nobah. Peter, James, and John cured and taught also. Jesus met no opposition in this place, and He effected a wonderful amount of good. He put up at the inn near the synagogue. Nobah was a free city which, although belonging to the Decapolis, ruled itself.

From Nobah, Jesus journeyed five hours southwestwardly to the exceedingly lovely pastoral village called the "Field of Jacob's Peace." It received this name from the fact that it was here, when returning to Palestine and pursued by Laban, he had encamped for the first time. The mountain range of Galaad[2] takes its rise here. The shepherds of this place were the descendants of that Eleazar, Abraham's servant, who had brought Rebecca for his master's son Isaac. Among them also were some of the posterity of those people whom Melchisedech had freed from the tyranny of Semiramis and established in these regions. They had afterward intermarried with the descendants of Eleazar. There were three beautiful wells in this place. They lay at the foot of a lovely hill all around which, as if built in a verdant rampart, were cool shepherd dwellings. At a distance one might have taken them for a mountain terrace. The oldest and most honorable among the herd owners dwelt on the hill, upon which there was likewise a place for instruction. Far around were enclosed pasture grounds for camels, asses, and sheep, each species having its own, and near the fountains were reservoirs for watering them. The shepherds dwelt in the neighborhood of the fountains, under tents that rested on solid foundations. There were long rows of mulberry trees, but the most beautiful sight of all was a long walk with palings on either side upon which ran a vine, often to the distance of two hundred paces, laden with fruit something like gourds. This walk led from the hill to Selcha and formed, as it were, one continuous arbor. Some days before, the inhabitants had celebrated a feast commemorative of the deliverance of their forefathers from the slavery of Semiramis. They attended the synagogue at Selcha, and it was from there too that teachers came to instruct them. This little village was held in respect throughout the country around, and was looked upon as a monument to Jacob's memory. Hospitality was here exercised freely. For a trifle, the Arab caravans and all other strangers were lodged and cared for by the shepherds.

Toward midday, Jesus with three of the Apostles arrived at one of the fountains, where the eldest of the shepherds washed His feet and offered Him fruit, honey, and bread. Jesus' coming had been expected, consequently many sick had been carried to the large house on the hill. Jesus cured them. Nearly four hundred shepherds, along with women and children, had assembled to greet Him. The women's dresses were shorter than those worn in Palestine generally. Jesus gave them an instruction on the hill, speaking to them with the greatest simplicity and confidence. He reminded them of the caravan of the Three Kings which, two and thirty years before, had rested in this place. Then He spoke of the star that was to rise out of Jacob and of which Balaam had prophesied, of the newborn Child of whom the Magi had been in search, of John, his teaching and his testimony, and concluded by saying that the promised Messiah, the Consoler, the Saviour, was then in the midst of the Israelites, but that they would not recognize Him. Jesus related to them also the parables of the good shepherd, the seed sown in the earth, and the harvest, for in this region there was a harvest of fruit as well as of wheat, the ears of which were extraordinarily large. He told them also of the shepherds near Bethlehem, of their finding the Child even before the Kings, and of the announcement made to them of it by the angels. The people fell in love with Jesus, and many of them wanted to leave all and follow Him, just for the pleasure of listening to Him always. But He advised them to remain at home and practice what He had taught them. From Selcha, which was almost an hour north of this place, messengers arrived with an invitation to Jesus to visit their city. He did so with the disciples. He was solemnly received at the city gate by the teachers and children in procession, and He taught in the synagogue, taking for the subject of His discourse the testimony rendered by John. Many of His hearers were baptized and cured. The children received His blessing.

From Selcha Jesus went with His followers for about an hour and a half along the so-called Way of David which, following the windings of the valley, led down to the Jordan. This road was deep, a kind of hollow, in

which water sometimes flowed. It ran through the
solitudes of the mountains, and at several points along it
were to be found places provided with troughs and stores
of fodder for the camels, also rings for fastening them.
When journeying through this country, Abraham saw a
supernatural light on this road and had a vision, and
when David, upon the advice of Jonathan, sought safety
for his parents in the region of Maspha[3], he lay concealed here with three hundred men, from which circumstance it received the name of "David's Way." David
here received from God a prophetic vision in which he
saw the caravan of the Three Kings and heard, as if from
the heavens open above him, melodious chanting
proclaiming the praises of the promised Consoler of
Israel. Malachias also, being obliged to flee after a battle,
followed a mysterious light that led him to this region
where, too, he lay hid for a time; and the Three Holy
Kings, giving rein to their camels upon leaving the confines of Selcha and entering this road, descended by it
singing sweet hymns of thanksgiving. They then proceeded along the shore until they reached the point opposite Korea, where they crossed the Jordan and arrived
at Jerusalem through the desert beyond Anathot. They
entered the Holy City by the same gate through which
Mary had passed when she went up from Bethlehem for
her purification.

From "David's Way," Jesus turned to the little place
called Thantia, where He went immediately to the synagogue and taught, His subjects being Balaam, the Star
of Jacob, some passages from Micheas, and Bethlehem
Ephrata.[4] He next went to visit many sick in their own
homes. He healed them along with several others whom
the disciples had not been able to cure. There was no
organized care of the sick and the poor in Thantia. The
disciples had indeed endeavored to establish something of
the kind, but it was Jesus Himself who effected the de-

sired change. A great many of the people received Baptism from the disciples.

Both the people and the rabbis of Thantia were pious. They were in the habit of making pilgrimages to the "Way of David," and there, in fasting and prayer, crying to Heaven for the coming of the Messiah. They indulged the hope of there having visions and apparitions of the Messiah who, they thought, would even come to them along that way. While Jesus was preaching, they said more than once to one another: "He speaks as if He were the Messiah Himself! But no, that is not possible!" As they were under the impression that the Messiah was to come invisibly like an angel into Israel, they thought that Jesus might possibly be His herald and precursor. Jesus told them that they would perhaps recognize the Messiah when it would be too late. I saw that many from Thantia, both before and after the Crucifixion, joined the Community. From Thantia Jesus journeyed four hours eastward to the ruined citadel of Datheman. Near it was the mountain that had been chosen by Jephte's daughter upon which to mourn with her twelve young companions. Upon it were prophets and hermits, something like the Essenians. It was on this same mountain that Balaam was tarrying in solitude and meditation when summoned by the Moabite king to appear before him.[5] He was of noble origin, his family very wealthy. From early youth, he had been filled with the spirit of prophecy, and he belonged to that nation that was ever on the lookout for the promised star, among whom were the ancestors of the Three Holy Kings. Though a reprobate, Balaam was no sorcerer. He served the true God only, like the enlightened of other nations, but in an imperfect manner, mingling many errors with the truth. He was very young when he retired into the solitude of the mountains, and upon this one in particular he dwelt a long time. I think he had around him some other prophets, or pupils. When he returned from the Moabite king, Balac, he wished to take up his abode upon this mountain, but was prevented by divine interposition. By his scandalous counsel to the Moabites[6], he fell from grace, and now he wandered in despair around the desert in which at last he miserably perished.

The people of this region believed firmly in the sacred character of "David's Way." They told Jesus that they would not dwell in the country beyond the Jordan where they could not dare make mention of all that had formerly been seen, all that had taken place on the "Way of David."

1. See "The Mission of the Apostles and Disciples," p. 95.
2. *Gen.* 31:25, etc.
3. *1 Kgs.* 22:3.
4. *Num.* 22:2, 25:10; *Mich.* 5:7, 6:9.
5. *Num.* 22:5.
6. *Num.* 31:16.

THE RAISING OF LAZARUS.
JESUS IN THE LAND OF
THE THREE HOLY KINGS

1. JESUS IN BETHABARA AND JERICHO.
ZACHEUS THE PUBLICAN

When Jesus and the Apostles approached Bethabara on the Jordan, they found already assembled there an innumerable crowd of people. The whole country was full, and they were encamping under sheds and trees. Numbers of mothers with crowds of children of every age, even infants in the arms, were coming in procession. As they proceeded up the broad street to meet Jesus, the disciples who led the way wanted, on account of His great fatigue (for He had already blessed a great many), to repulse the women and children, and that even a little rudely. But Jesus checked them, and bade them bring the crowd to order. On one side of the street stood in five long rows children of all ages, one behind the other, the boys and girls apart, the latter being by far the more numerous. The mothers with infants in their arms were placed behind the fifth row. On the other side of the street stood the rest of the people, who passed in turn from the last rank to the first. Jesus now went down along the first row of children, laying His hand on their head and blessing them. He laid His hand on the head of some, on the breast of others; some He clasped to His breast, and some He held up as models to the others. He instructed them, exhorted them, encouraged them, and blessed them. When He had thus passed down one row of children, He crossed to the opposite side of the street and came up among the grown people, exhorting and instructing them, and even placing before them the example of some of the children. Then He went down the next row of children and came up, as before, among the grown people whose front ranks had been replaced by those from behind. And so it went on, until even the infants in the last row had received a loving caress and blessing. All the children blessed by Jesus received an interior grace, and later on became Christians. Jesus must have blessed fully a thousand children on this occasion, for the concourse continued during several days. He labored constantly, ever grave, mild, and gentle, with a certain secret sadness in His manner very touching to see. He taught now along the streets, now in some house into which they had pulled Him by His robe. He related many parables, by which He instructed both the wise and the simple, and impressed upon the former the obligation of thankfully returning to God all that they had received from Him, as He Himself did.

Of the holy women, Veronica, Martha, Magdalen, and Mary Salome were gone on to Jerusalem. I saw Mary Salome with her sons, John and James the Less, coming to Jesus and requesting that they should be allowed to sit, one at His right and the other at His left. Messengers had been sent thither by the Pharisees in Jerusalem, but many of them, being converted, remained; while others, returning in a rage to Jerusalem, repented on the way and later on became Jesus' followers.

Jesus left Bethabara with the Apostles, and on His way He was entreated to visit a house in which lay ten lepers. The Apostles, dreading contact with the leprous, went on ahead in a southerly direction, with the intention of waiting for Jesus under a tree. The lepers, enveloped in their mantles and full of sores, lay in a retired part of the house. Jesus commanded them to do something, and it seems to me that He touched one of them and then left them. The lepers one after another were taken by two people to a little pool near the house, and washed in the bathing tubs, after which they were able to present themselves to the priests as cured.

Jesus next went through another building that had a four-cornered courtyard. On either side of the latter was a covered archway, in one of which lay men, sick and crippled, and in the other, afflicted women. The beds were laid in rows of hollow places, scooped out in the ground to receive them. Another covered way on the same line cut through the middle of the house and led to a space in which the cooking and washing were done. Between this middle walk and those in which the sick lay, were grass plots. Jesus again cured several here. As He proceeded on His way, I saw following Him one of the lately healed lepers proclaiming His praise. Jesus looked around, and the man fell on his face giving thanks. Further on the route, Jesus blessed many children who had been brought by their mothers to meet Him.

The road travelled by Jesus and the Apostles on leaving Bethabara ran on the right past Machaerus and the city of Madian. They again approached the Jordan, made a circuit of Bethabara, and went by roundabout ways through a desert region toward Jericho. As they proceeded on their journey, the disciples who had been sent out on missions returned to Jesus one after another and related to Him all that they had done. He instructed them in parables, but I remember only these words of His discourse: "They who say that they are chaste, but who eat and drink only what pleases their appetite, are like those that try to extinguish a fire with dry wood." Another parable referred to the future of the Twelve Apostles. Jesus said: "Now ye cling to Me, because ye fare well"; but they did not understand that by these words He meant the peace and beautiful instructions that they then enjoyed. "In the time of need," He continued, "ye will act otherwise. Even they whom I carry about with Me like a mantle of love, will cast that mantle off and flee." These words referred to John in the garden of Gethsemani. In a little town near the Jordan, I saw a woman entreating Jesus to cure her daughter, who was covered with ulcers. Jesus told her that He would send one of the disciples to her. But she wanted Him to go Himself, which, however, He did not do. When He was drawing near to Jericho, the woman again approached and begged His aid. She urged that she had now renounced all that He had commanded her. Jesus, however, still repulsed her. Her child was the fruit of sin, and Jesus reproached her with a fault (it appeared to be but a small one) to which she had already clung for several years. He told her that she should not come again to Him until she had freed herself from it. Then I saw the woman hurrying past the Apostles and disciples toward Jericho.

Having almost reached the city, four Pharisees sent by their colleagues of Jerusalem came and warned Him not to enter lest Herod would put Him to death. This they did, however, not because they cared for Him, but because having heard of His numerous miracles, they were afraid of Him. Jesus replied that they should say to Herod, the fox, these words only: "Behold, I cast out devils and do cures today and tomorrow, and the third day I am consummated.[1]" Two of these Pharisees were converted and followed Jesus, but the other two returned in a rage to Jerusalem.

Then came to Jesus two brothers belonging to Jericho. They could not agree on the subject of their patrimony; one wanted to remain, the other desired to go away. One of them proposed that Jesus, so renowned everywhere, should divide the patrimony between them, and they had in consequence come to meet Him. But He refused, saying that it was not His business. And when even John remarked to Him that it was a good work, and Peter seconded the word, Jesus replied that He was not come to distribute earthly goods, but only heavenly ones. After which He took occasion to deliver a long exhortation before the rapidly increasing crowd. But the disciples as yet did not always understand Him rightly. They had not yet received the Holy Ghost and so they went on expecting an earthly kingdom.

Jesus was again met by crowds of women with their children, for whom they implored a blessing. The disciples, disturbed by the recent menaces of the Pharisees and desirous of shunning such excitement, tried to drive the women back, for they were entrusted with the duty of keeping order. But Jesus commanded them to allow the children to come forward. They needed His blessing, He said, in order that they too might become His disciples. Then He blessed many of the infants at the breast and the children of ten and eleven years. Some He did not bless, but later on these again presented themselves.

Just outside the city, which was surrounded by gardens, pleasure grounds, and villas, Jesus and His followers encountered a dense crowd composed of people from all parts of the country around. They had assembled with their sick, who were lying on litters under sheds and tents. They had been waiting for Jesus, and now they beset Him and His disciples on all sides. Zacheus, one of the chief publicans, who dwelt outside the city, had stationed himself on the road by which Jesus had to pass. As he was short in stature, he climbed a fig tree[2] in order to be able to see Jesus better in the crowd. Jesus looked up into the tree and said: "Zacheus, make haste and come down, for this day I must abide in thy house." Zacheus hurried down, bowed humbly to Jesus, and very much touched returned home to make preparations for receiving his honored Guest. When Jesus said that He must that day enter into Zacheus's house, He meant into his heart, for on that day He went into Jericho itself, and not into the house of Zacheus. On arriving at the city gate, Jesus found none of the people assembled to welcome Him, for through dread of the Pharisees they were remaining quietly in their homes. The crowd, gathered at some distance from the city, were all strangers come to implore Jesus' assistance in their various needs. He cured a blind man and a deaf mute, but some others He sent away. He blessed the children, especially the babes at the breast, and told the Apostles that men must in this way be accustomed to devote their children from earliest youth to Him, and that all thus blessed would follow Him. Among those sent away was a woman afflicted with a flow of blood. She had come some days before with the firm resolve to implore Jesus for her cure. I heard Jesus saying to the disciples that whoever does not persevere in prayer, is not in earnest and has no faith.

As the Sabbath now began, Jesus went with His Apostles and disciples to the synagogue of the city and afterward to the inn. He and the Apostles dined in the open refectory, the disciples in the archway. The meal consisted of little rolls, honey, and fruit. They ate standing, Jesus meantime teaching and relating parables. Every three of the Apostles drank from one cup, but Jesus had one to Himself. The woman that had already been twice repulsed came again to Jesus imploring help for her daughter, but with no better success than before, because she was not sincere. She had been questioning among the Pharisees of Jericho about what was said of Jesus in Jerusalem.

Zacheus also here presented himself to Jesus. The new disciples had already taken it ill outside the city that Jesus had accosted the ill-famed publican and even wanted to abide with him, for Zacheus in particular was a subject of scandal to them. Some were related to him, and they were ashamed of his remaining a publican so long and up to the present unconverted. Zacheus drew near the hall in which the disciples were dining, but no one wanted to have anything to do with him, no one invited him to eat. Then Jesus stepped out into the hall, beckoned Zacheus in, and offered him food and drink.

On the following day, when Jesus went again to the synagogue and told the Pharisees to give place to Him as He intended to read and explain the Sabbath Lesson, they raised a great contention, but they did not prevail. He inveighed against avarice, and cured an invalid who had been carried on a litter to the door of the synagogue. The Sabbath over, Jesus went with His Apostles to Zacheus's dwelling outside of Jericho. None of the disciples accompanied Him. The woman so desirous of help for her daughter again followed Jesus on the road out to Zacheus's. He laid His hand on her to free her from her own bad disposition, and told her to return home, for her child was cured. During the meal, which consisted of honey, fruit, and a lamb, Zacheus served at table, but whenever Jesus spoke, he listened devoutly. Jesus related the parable of the fig tree in the vineyard which for three years bore no fruit, and for which the vinedresser implored one more year of indulgence. When uttering this parable, Jesus addressed the Apostles as the vineyard; of Himself He spoke as the owner; and of Zacheus as the fig tree. It was now three years since the relatives of the last-named had abandoned their dishonorable calling and followed Jesus, while he all this time had still carried on the same business, on which account he was looked upon with special contempt by the disciples. But Jesus had cast upon him a look of mercy when He called him down from the tree. Jesus spoke also of the sterile trees that produce many leaves, but no fruit. The leaves, He said, are exterior works. They make a great rustling, but soon pass away leaving no seed of good. But the fruits are that interior, efficacious reality in faith and action, with their capability of reproduction, and the prolongation of the tree's life stored away in the kernel. It seems to me that Jesus, in calling Zacheus down from the tree, did the same as to engage him to renounce the noise and bustle of the crowd, for Zacheus was like the ripe fruit which now detached itself from the tree that for three years had stood unfruitful in the vineyard. Jesus spoke, likewise, of the faithful servants who watched for the coming of their lord, and who suffered no noise that could prevent them from hearing his knock.

It appeared as if Jesus was now in Jericho for the last time, and as if He wished to pour out upon it the fullness of His love. He sent the Apostles and disciples two by two out into the districts around into which He Himself would go no more. In Jericho itself, He went from house to house, taught in the synagogue and on the streets, and everywhere to a great concourse of people. Sinners and publicans encompassed Him on all sides, and on the roads by which He had to pass lay the sick, sighing and imploring help. He taught and cured without intermission, and was so earnest, so gentle, and so tranquil. The disciples, on the contrary, were anxious and dissatisfied on account of Jesus' so unconcernedly exposing Himself to the snares that the enraged Pharisees, of whom almost a hundred were gathered here from different parts of the country, sought to prepare for Him. They sent messengers to Jerusalem to consult as to how they could take Him into custody. The Apostles too were in a certain dread, as if they thought that Jesus laid Himself open to danger and treated with the people rather rashly. Once I saw Jesus surrounded by a great crowd seeking His help, and among them were some sick that had caused themselves to be carried to Him. The disciples meanwhile kept at a distance. The palsied woman with the issue of blood whom He had already sent away more than once had caused herself to be carried to the bath of purification, or expiation, with which was connected the forgiveness of sin. She crept afterward to Jesus and touched the hem of His robe. He instantly stood still, looked after her, and healed her. The woman arose, thanked her Benefactor, and returned cured to her home in the city. Jesus then taught upon persevering and repeated prayer. He said that one should never desist from his entreaties. I was thinking meantime of the great charity of the good people who had brought the woman so long a distance, carrying her here and there after the Lord, and begging the disciples to inform them whither He was going next, that they might procure for her a good place. Owing to the nature of her sickness, which was regarded as unclean, she could not rest anywhere and everywhere. She had to solicit her cure for eight days long.

Before Jesus' departure from Jericho, messengers from Bethania brought to the disciples the news of how earnestly Martha and Magdalen were longing for His coming, as Lazarus was very sick. Jesus, however, did not go to Bethania, but to a little village north of Jericho. Here too, a crowd had assembled, and numbers of sick, blind, and crippled were awaiting His arrival. Two blind men, each with two guides, were sitting by the roadside, and when Jesus passed by they cried out after Him, begging to be cured. The people tried to silence them with threats, but they followed Jesus, crying after Him: "Ah, Thou Son of David! Have mercy on us!" Then Jesus turned, commanded them to be led to Him, and touched their eyes. They saw and followed Him. A great tumult arose on account of the cure of these blind men, as well as of those to whom Jesus had restored sight on His entrance into Jericho. The Pharisees instituted an inquiry into the case, and interrogated the father of one of the cured as well as himself. The disciples meantime were very desirous that Jesus should go to Lazarus's, in Bethania, for there they would be in greater peace and less molested. They were in truth a little discontented, but Jesus went on curing numbers. Words cannot express how gentle and forbearing He was under such imputations, attacks, and persecutions, and how sweetly and gravely He smiled when the disciples wanted to divert Him from His purpose. He next went in the direction of Samaria. Not far from one of the little villages along the highroad, about a hundred paces to one side, there stood a tent in which ten lepers were lying in beds. As Jesus was passing, the lepers came out and cried to Him for help. Jesus stood still, but the disciples went on. The lepers, entirely enveloped in their mantles, approached— some quickly, others slowly, as their strength permitted— and stood in a circle around Jesus. He touched each one separately, directed them to present themselves to the priests, and went on His way. One of the lepers, a Samaritan and the most active of the ten, went along the same road with two of the disciples, but the others took different routes. These were not cured all at once; although able to walk, they were not made perfectly clean till about an hour afterward.

Soon after this last encounter, a father from a shepherd village a quarter of an hour to the right of the road came to meet Jesus and begged Him to go back with him to the village, for his little daughter was lying dead. Jesus went with him at once, and on the way was overtaken by the cured Samaritan who, touched by his perfect cure, had hurried back to thank his Benefactor. He cast himself at the feet of Jesus, who said: "Were not ten made clean? And where are the nine? Is not one found among them to return and give glory to God, but only this stranger? Arise, go thy way! Thy faith hath made thee whole!" This man later on became a disciple. Peter, John, and James the Greater were with Jesus at this time. The little girl, who was about seven years old, was already four days dead. Jesus laid one hand on her head, the other on her breast, and raising His eyes to Heaven prayed, whereupon the child rose up alive. Then Jesus told the Apostles that even so should they do in His name. The child's father had strong faith, and full of confidence he had awaited Jesus' coming. His wife wanted him to send word to Jesus, but he was full of hope and waited until He came. Soon after, he gave up his business to another and, when his wife died after Jesus' death, he became a disciple and acquired a distinguished name. The little girl restored to life likewise became very pious.

Jesus next visited the shepherd huts that lay scattered far around, and cured many of the sick in them. He went from hut to hut all along the mountainous country in the direction of Hebron. I saw Him alone with Peter in one of these abodes, in which a marriage was being celebrated. The bridal couple returned from the nuptial ceremony, which was performed in the school, escorted by their friends and walking under a kind of canopy. A band of little girls adorned with wreaths of colored wool led the way playing on lutes, and gaily dressed boys with similar instruments brought up the rear of the procession. A priest from Jericho was present. When the party entered the house, they were both surprised and delighted to see Jesus, who bade them not to interrupt the wedding festivities lest some might be vexed at it. The guests then drank out of little glasses. The bride retired with the women, and the children played and danced before her. Then I saw the bridegroom and the bride go to Jesus in a room set apart, where He again joined their hands with His own right and blessed their clasped hands, and gave them an instruction upon the indissolubility of marriage and the merit of continency. After that He reclined at table with Peter and the priest, while the bridegroom waited upon them. The priest, however, was angry that the most honorable places had been given to the stranger guests, Jesus and His Apostles, and so he soon withdrew from the entertainment. I saw too that he hunted up some of the Pharisees, who later on unexpectedly attacked the Lord and called Him to account. In the heat of their discussion, one of them pulled His mantle from His shoulder, but Jesus remained calm. As they could neither harm Him nor gain a victory over Him, they withdrew.

Jesus, with more than ordinary love and kindness, tarried awhile in this shepherd dwelling. The bride's parents and some others of the old shepherds who presented themselves before Him, belonged to those that had visited Him at the Crib on the night of His birth. They began at once, in touching terms, to tell all about that night and to honor Jesus, and the younger ones related what they had heard about it from their deceased parents. They brought to Jesus some aged sick who, on account of the feebleness of old age, could no longer walk, also some sick children, and Jesus cured them all. He told the young married couple to go, after His death, to His Apostles, to be baptized and instructed, and to become His followers. During the whole journey, I never saw Jesus so bright and cheerful as He was among these simple people. I saw that all who had honored Him in His childhood received the grace to become Christians.

From this place, Jesus took a more southerly direction into the mountainous district toward Juttah. The wedding guests formed His escort. He had with Him now six Apostles, including Andrew. On the way He cured a number of sick children who were very much swollen and unable to walk. The people of this region were not very good. When Jesus reached a little village among the mountains, He went straight to the synagogue to teach. The priests forbade it, and went to call assistance, but they were obliged to resign the teacher's chair to Jesus, to whom the people listened with joy. The disciples were eager for Jesus now to turn His steps to Nazareth, His native city, since He was always making allusion to His approaching end. But He was desirous that the good among the people here should profit by the time remaining to Him, and so He did not go to Nazareth. He taught upon the words: "No man can serve two masters." He said also that He was come to bring the sword upon earth, that is to say, the separation from all that is bad. It was thus He explained this word to the disciples.

1. *Lk*. 13:32.
2. *Ficus Sycomorus*, Pharaoh's Fig, very common in Palestine.

2. JESUS ON THE WAY TO BETHANIA. THE RAISING OF LAZARUS

As Jesus was tarrying in a little place near Samaria where too the Blessed Virgin and Mary Cleophas were come to spend the Sabbath, they received the news of Lazarus's death. After this event, which happened in Bethania, his sisters left that place and went to their country house near Ginaea, with the intention of there meeting Jesus and the Blessed Virgin. The remains of Lazarus were embalmed and swathed in linen bands, according to the Jewish custom, and then laid in a coffin of woven rods with a convex cover. All the Apostles were again united around Jesus. They went in several bands to Ginaea, where Jesus taught in the synagogue and, after the closing exercises of the Sabbath, went out to Lazarus's country house. There they found the Blessed Virgin, who had gone on before. Magdalen came to meet Jesus and to tell Him of her brother's death, adding the words: "Lord, if Thou hadst been here, my brother had not died!" Jesus replied that his time was not yet come and that it was well that he had died. Still He told the two sisters to allow all the effects of their brother to remain at Bethania, for that He Himself would go there shortly.

The holy women, therefore, set out for Bethania, while
Jesus and the Apostles returned to Ginaea, from which
they went to the inn one hour distant from Bethania.
Here another messenger came to Him bearing the earnest
request of the sisters that He should repair to Bethania,
but He still delayed to go. He rebuked the disciples for
their murmuring and impatience at His delaying so long
to go to Bethania. He was always like one who could not
give an account of His views and actions to them,
because they did not understand Him. In His instructions
to them He was always more desirous of discovering to
them their own thoughts and, on account of their earthly-
mindedness, of arousing in them distrust of self than of
informing them of the reasons of things that they could
not comprehend. He still taught upon the laborers in the
vineyard, and when the mother of James and John heard
Him speak of the near fulfillment of His mission, she
thought it only proper that His own relatives should have
honorable posts in His Kingdom. She consequently approached Him with a petition to that effect, but He
sternly rebuked her.

At last Jesus turned His steps to Bethania, continuing
all along the way His instructions to the Apostles.
Lazarus's estate stood partly within the walls surrounding
the environs of the city, and partly—that is, a portion of
the garden and courtyard—outside those walls, which
were now going to ruin.

Lazarus was eight days dead. They had kept him four
days in the hope that Jesus would come and raise him to
life. His sisters, as I have said, went to the country house
near Ginaea, to meet Jesus; but when they found that He
was still resolved not to go back with them, they had
returned to Bethania and buried their brother. Their
friends, men and women from the city and from
Jerusalem, were now gathered around them, lamenting
the dead as was the custom. It seems to me that it was

toward evening when Mary Zebedeus went in to Martha, who was sitting among the women, and said to her softly that the Lord was coming. Martha arose and went out with her into the garden back of the house. There in an arbor was Magdalen sitting alone. Martha told her that Jesus was near, for through love for Magdalen, she wanted her to be the first to meet the Lord. But I did not see Magdalen go to Jesus, for when He was alone with the Apostles and disciples He did not allow women easy access to Him. It was already growing dusk when Magdalen went back to the women and took Martha's place, who then went out to meet Jesus. He was standing with the Apostles and some others on the confines of their garden before an open arbor. Martha spoke to Jesus and then turned back to Magdalen, who also by this time had come up. She threw herself at Jesus' feet, saying: "If Thou hadst been here, he would not have died!" All present were in tears. Jesus too mourned and wept, and delivered a discourse of great length upon death. Many of the audience, which was constantly increasing outside the bower, whispered to one another and murmured their dissatisfaction at Jesus' not having kept Lazarus alive.

It seems to me that it was very early in the morning when Jesus went with the Apostles to the tomb. Mary, Lazarus's sisters, and others, in all about seven women, were likewise there, as also a crowd of people which was constantly on the increase. Indeed the throng presented somewhat the appearance of a tumult, as upon the day of Christ's Crucifixion. They proceeded along a road upon either side of which was a thick, green hedge, then passed through a gate, after which about a quarter of an hour's distance brought them to the walled-in cemetery of Bethania. From the gate of the cemetery, a road led right and left around a hill through which ran a vault. The latter was divided by railings into compartments, and the opening at the end was closed by a grate. One could, from the entrance, see through the whole length of the vault and the green branches of the trees waving outside the opposite end. Light was admitted from openings above.

Lazarus's tomb was the first on the right of the entrance to the vault, down into which some steps led. It was a four-cornered, oblong cave, about three feet in depth, and covered with a flat stone. In it lay the corpse in a lightly woven coffin, and around it in the tomb there was room for one to walk. Jesus with some of the Apostles went down into the vault, while the holy women, Magdalen, and Martha remained standing in the doorway. But the crowd pressed around so that many people climbed up on the roof of the vault and the cemetery walls in order to see. Jesus commanded the Apostles to raise the stone from the grave. They did so, rested it against the wall, and then removed a light cover or door that closed the tomb below that stone. It was at this point of the proceedings that Martha said: "Lord, by this time he stinketh, for he is now of four days." After that they took the lightly woven cover from the coffin, and disclosed the corpse lying in its winding sheet. At that instant Jesus raised His eyes to Heaven, prayed aloud, and called out in a strong voice: "Lazarus, come forth!" At this cry, the corpse arose to a sitting posture. The crowd now pressed with so much violence that Jesus ordered them to be driven outside the walls of the cemetery. The Apostles, who were standing in the tomb by the coffin, removed the handkerchief from Lazarus's face, unbound his hands and feet, and drew off the winding sheet. Lazarus, as if waking from lethargy, rose from the coffin and stepped out of the grave, tottering and looking like a phantom. The Apostles threw a mantle around him. Like one walking in sleep, he approached the door, passed the Lord and went out to where his sisters and the other women had stepped back in fright as before a ghost.

Without daring to touch him, they fell prostrate on the ground. At the same instant, Jesus stepped after him out of the vault and seized him by both hands, His whole manner full of loving earnestness.

And now all moved on toward Lazarus's house. The throng was great. But a certain fear prevailed among the people; consequently the procession formed by Lazarus and his friends was not impeded in its movements by the crowd that followed. Lazarus moved along more like one floating than walking, and he still had all the appearance of a corpse. Jesus walked by his side, and the rest of the party followed sobbing and weeping around them in silent, frightened amazement. They reached the old gate, and went along the road bordered by verdant hedges to the avenue of trees from which they had started. The Lord entered it with Lazarus and His followers, while the crowd thronged outside, clamoring and shouting.

At this moment Lazarus threw himself prostrate on the earth before Jesus, like one about to be received into a Religious Order. Jesus spoke some words, and then they went on to the house, about a hundred paces distant.

Jesus, the Apostles, and Lazarus were alone in the dining hall. The Apostles formed a circle around Jesus and Lazarus, who was kneeling before the Lord. Jesus laid His right hand on his head and breathed upon him seven times. The Lord's breath was luminous. I saw a dark vapor withdrawing as it were from Lazarus, and the devil under the form of a black winged figure, impotent and wrathful, clearing the circle backward and mounting on high. By this ceremony, Jesus consecrated Lazarus to His service, purified him from all connection with the world and sin, and strengthened him with the gifts of the Holy Ghost. He made him a long address in which He told him that He had raised him to life that he might serve Him, and that he would have to endure great persecution on the part of the Jews.

Up to this time, Lazarus was in his grave clothes, but now he retired to lay them aside and put on his own garments. It was at this moment that his sisters and friends embraced him for the first time, for before this there was something so corpselike about him that it inspired terror. I saw meanwhile that Lazarus's soul, during the time of its separation from his body, was in a place peaceful and painless, lighted by only a glimmering twilight, and that while there he related to the just, Joseph, Joachim, Anne, Zachary, John, etc., how things were going with the Redeemer on earth.

By the Saviour's breathing upon him, Lazarus received the seven gifts of the Holy Ghost and was perfectly freed from connection with earthly things. He received those gifts before the Apostles, for he had by his death become acquainted with great mysteries, had gazed upon another world. He had actually been dead, and he was now born again. He could therefore receive those gifts. Lazarus comprises in himself a deep significance and a profound mystery.

And now a meal was ready, and all reclined at table upon which were many dishes and little jugs. A man served. After the meal the women entered, but remained at the lower end of the hall, to hear the teachings of Jesus. Lazarus was sitting next Him. There was a frightful noise around the house, for many had come out from Jerusalem, even the guards, and were now besetting the house. But Jesus sent the Apostles out, to drive off both people and guards. Jesus continued His instruction till after lamplight, and told the disciples that He was going next morning with two Apostles to Jerusalem. When they placed before Him the danger attending such a step, He replied that He would not be recognized, that He would not go openly. I saw them afterward taking a little sleep, leaning around against the wall.

Before daybreak Jesus, accompanied by John and Matthew, who had girded up their garments somewhat differently from their usual custom, started from Bethania for Jerusalem. They went around the city and, taking by-roads, reached the house in which later on the Last Supper was celebrated. There they remained quietly the whole day and the next night, Jesus instructing and confirming His friends of the city. I saw Mary Marcus and Veronica in the house, and fully a dozen men. Nicodemus, to whom the house belonged, but who had gladly resigned it for the use of Jesus' friends, was not there. He had on that very day gone to Bethania to see Lazarus.

I saw also a gathering of Pharisees and High Priests who had come together to discuss Jesus and Lazarus. Among other things I heard them say that they feared Jesus would raise all the dead, and then what confusion would ensue!

At noon on that day, a great tumult arose in Bethania. If Jesus had been there, they would have stoned Him. Lazarus was obliged to hide, and the Apostles, to slip away in different directions. All the other friends of Jesus in Bethania were likewise forced to lie in concealment. Minds became calm, however, when people took into consideration that they had no right to take action against Lazarus.

Jesus passed the whole night till early next morning in the house on Mount Sion. Before day He left Jerusalem with Matthew and John and fled across the Jordan, not by the route He had formerly taken on the side of Bethabara, but by another off to the northeast. It may have been toward noon when He reached the opposite shore of the Jordan. That evening the Apostles from Bethania joined Him, and they spent the night under a great tree.

In the morning they started for a little village in the neighborhood, and on their way found a blind man lying on the roadside. He was in charge of two boys, who were not, however, related to him. He was a shepherd from the region of Jericho. He had heard from the Apostles that the Lord was coming that way, and he was now crying out to Him for a cure. Jesus laid His hand on his head, and the man received his sight. Then he cast off his old rags and, in his undergarment, followed Jesus to the village, where in a hall Jesus taught of following Him. He said that they who wanted to do so must, as the blind man did his rags, leave all, to follow Him with full use of their sight. A mantle was given to the man cured of blindness. He wanted to join Jesus at once, but he was put off till he should prove his constancy. Jesus taught here until nearly evening. There were about eight Apostles with Him.

After that, as He drew near a little city, Jesus was hungry. I could not help smiling at the thought of His being hungry, for Jesus' hunger was very different from that of others. He was hungering after souls. From the last place that He had visited, some people who had not the right dispositions went with Him. On the roadside stood a fig tree that bore no fruit. Jesus went up to the tree and cursed it. It withered on the instant, its leaves turning yellow, and the trunk becoming crooked. Jesus taught in the school upon the sterile fig tree. There were some malevolent Doctors and Pharisees who invited Jesus to take His departure. A little stream spanned by a bridge ran by this place[1] into the Jordan. The school was built on an eminence. Jesus and His party spent the night at an inn.

1. Betharan, perhaps.

3. JESUS BEGINS HIS JOURNEY INTO THE LAND OF THE THREE HOLY KINGS

Next day when Jesus and His companions left that last place, they took a northeasterly direction through the land of the tribe of Gad. I heard Jesus saying whither He was now about to journey. He told the Apostles and disciples that they should separate from Him, designated to them where they should and where they should not teach, and where they should again join Him. He was now, He said, about to make an extraordinary journey. He would spend the next Sabbath in Great Corozain, then go to Bethsaida, and from there to the south into the region of Machaerus and Madian. Thence He would proceed to where Agar had exposed Ismael,[1] and Jacob had set up the stone.[2] Then He would journey to the east around the Dead Sea and on to the place upon which Melchisedech had offered sacrifice before Abraham. On this site there stands today a chapel, in which Divine Service is sometimes celebrated. It is built of red stone, and overgrown with moss. Jesus declared His intention of going likewise to Heliopolis in Egypt, where He had once dwelt in childhood. There were some good people there who as children had played with Him, and who had not entirely forgotten Him. They were constantly asking what had become of Him, but they could not believe that He of whom they heard so much was the Child of their remembrance. He will return from the other side through Hebron and the valley of Josaphat, pass the place at which He had been baptized by John, and through the desert in which He had been tempted. He announced that His absence would be for about three months, and that His followers would be sure to find Him at the end of that time at Jacob's Well near Sichar, though they might meet Him before that, when He would be returning through Judea. He gave them minute instructions in a long discourse, above all as to how they should during His absence conduct themselves in their missionary duties. I remember these words, that wherever they were not well received, they should shake the dust from their shoes. Matthew returned home for awhile. He was a married man. His wife was a very virtuous person and, since Matthew's vocation, they had lived in perfect continency. He was to teach in his own home, and quietly put up with the contempt of his former associates.

In Great Corozain, Jesus taught on the Sabbath in the synagogue. Peter, Andrew, and Philip were with Him. Toward noon a man from Capharnaum, who had been waiting for Jesus, approached Him. His son, he said, was sick unto death, and He implored the Lord to go with him and cure him. But Jesus commanded him to return home, for his son was already restored to health. There were many others gathered around Jesus, some belonging to the city, and others from a distance. Some were sick and looking for a cure, others were in search of consolation. He satisfied some at once, but to others He held out the promise of future assistance.

On the evening of that Sabbath, Jesus took leave of the inhabitants outside the synagogue, and proceeded with several of the Apostles up to where the Jordan empties into the sea, in order to cross to the other side. The ferry was higher up, and that made the journey much longer. Here they crossed on a kind of raft formed of beams laid one over another like a grating. In the center, on a raised platform, was a coop, or little half-tub into which the water could not penetrate, and there the baggage of the passengers was deposited. The raft was propelled by means of long poles. The shore of the Jordan was not very high in this place, and it seems to me there were some little islands lying around in this part of the river. I saw the Lord and the three Apostles travelling by moonlight. Outside of Bethsaida, as was customary at the entrance to the cities of Palestine, stood a long shed under which travellers used to ungird their garments and brush off the dust of travel before entering the city; generally some people were to be found there to wash their feet. This was the case on the arrival of the Lord and the Apostles, after which they repaired to Andrew's, where they partook of a meal of honey, rolls, and grapes. Andrew was married, and his house was by no means a small one. It had a courtyard, was surrounded by walls, and was situated at one side of the city. Peter and Philip accompanied the Lord, but Andrew went on ahead. There were in all twelve men present at the meal, and at the end of it, six women came in to hear Jesus' teaching. Next day, as He was leaving Bethsaida with the three Apostles, He paused for awhile in a house outside the city in which were all kinds of goods and chattels peculiar to fishing. A great many men were assembled there, and Jesus gave them an instruction. Setting out at last, He journeyed up the shore of the Jordan, crossed the bridge far above the ferry just mentioned, and proceeded through eastern Galilee to the land of Basan.

I saw in a region beyond the Jordan, a district covered with white sand and tiny white pebbles, several disciples in an open shepherd shed awaiting the Lord's coming. They had brought with them three youths, tall and slim. While awaiting Jesus, the disciples had gathered yellow and green berries as large as figs, also little yellow apples that grew some on bushes, others on trees, from which they broke them off with chopping sticks. The road by which Jesus and the three Apostles came appeared to be not much frequented, for it was overgrown with long grass, and extended under an avenue of spreading fruit trees whose branches interlaced overhead. The Apostles broke off some of the fruit and put it into their pockets, but Jesus took none. He had travelled all night through mountainous districts. The disciples who had been awaiting His coming now went forward to meet Him. They pressed around Him with words of salutation, but without offering their hands. In front of the shed lay a long, broad, four-cornered log, around which Jesus and the others threw themselves in a reclining posture as at table, and before each was placed a portion of the fruit just gathered. They had brought with them also little jugs containing some kind of beverage. Off in the distance lay a city and behind it rose a mountain chain. I think this region was in the land of the Amorrhites. From this place the road again took a downward direction. I saw Jesus and His companions journeying the whole day and, in the evening, arriving at a little scattered village. On the roadside stood an inn. The travellers entered and were soon surrounded by a crowd of inquisitive people. They had not heard much of Jesus, but they were for the most part good and simple-hearted. Jesus related to them the parable of the good shepherd, and then travelled on a short distance to another inn, at which He and His followers ate and slept. The Lord told the latter that He intended to go alone with the three youths through Chaldea and the land of Ur, Abraham's birthplace, and thence through Arabia to Egypt. The disciples should scatter here throughout the district and instruct the inhabitants; as for Himself, He added, He would teach wherever He went. In fine He again told them that, at the end of three months, they would meet at the Well of Jacob near Sichar. I saw Simeon, Cleophas, and Saturnin among the disciples.

At dawn of day Jesus bade farewell to the Apostles and disciples, to each of whom He extended His hand. They were very much troubled at His taking with Him only the three youths. These youths were from sixteen to eighteen years old and very different from the Jews. They were more slender and active, and wore long garments. They were like children to Jesus, whom they waited on most affectionately. Whenever they came to water, they washed His feet. They ran off on the road here and there, and came back with little rods, flowers, fruits, and berries. Jesus instructed them most lovingly and explained to them in parables all that had happened up to that time.

The parents of these youths belonged to the family of Mensor. They had come to Palestine with the caravan of the Three Kings and, at the departure of the same for home, had remained behind among the shepherds in the Valley of the Shepherds. They became Jews, married the daughters of the shepherds, and came into possession of meadow lands between Samaria and Jericho. The youngest of the youths was named Eremenzear and later on was called Hermas. He was the boy whom Jesus, at the prayer of his mother, had cured in the region of Sichar, after His interview with the Samaritan at Jacob's Well. The next one was Sela, or Silas; and the eldest, Eliud, received in Baptism the name of Siricius. They were called, also, the secret disciples, and at a later period they were associated with Thomas, John, and Paul. Eremenzear wrote an account of this journey.

On this journey, Jesus wore a brownish tunic, knitted or woven, that fell around Him in folds long and full; over that He had a long garment of fine white wool with wide sleeves. It was fastened at the waist by a broad girdle of the same material as the scarf that He wound around His head when sleeping. Jesus was taller than the Apostles. Walking or standing, His fair, grave face rose above them. His step was firm, His bearing erect. He was neither thin nor stout, but nobly formed with an appearance of perfect health. His shoulders were broad, and His chest well developed. Exercise and travelling had strengthened His muscles, although they presented no sign of hard labor.

The road taken by Jesus and the youths after parting from the Apostles was a constantly ascending one in a direction toward the East, over a white, sandy soil and through cedars and date trees. Opposite arose the mountains of Galaad. Jesus wanted to spend the coming Sabbath in the last Jewish city met in this direction. I think it was called Cedar. Jesus and the youths ate on the way

the fruits of the trees and berries. The youths carried
pouches filled with little rolls, jugs containing some kind
of drink, and staves. The Lord sometimes broke off a
staff for Himself from a tree in passing, and again cast it
aside. His feet, otherwise bare, were protected by sandals. In the evening they went to some solitary house occupied by rude, simple people, and there slept for the
night. Jesus nowhere made Himself known, although He
everywhere taught in beautiful parables of all kinds, but
principally in those relating to the good shepherd. The
people questioned Him about Jesus of Nazareth, but He
did not tell that it was Himself. He in turn put questions
to them concerning their work, their business affairs, so
that they concluded He was a travelling shepherd looking
around after good pasture lands, as was often the case in
Jewish countries. I did not see Him effect any cure nor
work any miracle in these parts. Next morning He journeyed on. He may now have still been some miles from
Cedar, which was built on rising ground, the mountain
chain behind it. Abraham's fatherland was in this direction, but far off toward the northeast; the land of the
Three Kings was toward the southeast.

Some of the disciples had returned to their homes,
while others had scattered around the country teaching.
Zacheus of Jericho accompanied them awhile, after
which he returned home, gave up his business, sold all
that he had, bestowed the proceeds upon the poor, and
went with his wife (with whom he henceforth lived in
continency) to another place. The Lord told the disciples
that nine weeks would pass before they should join Him
again.

The excitement in Jerusalem on account of Lazarus
was very great. Jesus absented Himself during it, that
people might lose sight of Him, while the conviction of
the truth of this miracle disposed many to conversion.
When Jesus returned He was very thin. There is no written

account of this journey, since no Apostle accompanied the Lord on it; perhaps too the Apostles did not even know of all the places in which He had been. As well as I remember, I then saw this road for the first time.

Jesus journeyed on with His three young companions to the southeast, taking byways most frequently, and spending the night, like the preceding one among the shepherds, in a solitary house. The people of these parts were good and artless. They gazed at Jesus in wonder, and loved Him at once. He related to them many of the parables He was accustomed to use in Judea, and to them they listened with delight. But He neither healed nor blessed. When they asked Him about Jesus of Nazareth, He answered by telling them about those that had quitted all to follow Him, and then passed to parables that explained what He had said. The people thought He was a shepherd looking around for herds or meadows.

1. Bersabee, to the south of Palestine.
2. *Gen.* 46:1, 4; 26:23, 24.

4. JESUS IN CEDAR

Jesus and the youths reached Cedar before the Sabbath. They had not travelled by the highroad, but by roundabout ways. As it was too late to enter the city, they passed the night at a large public inn at which other wayfarers had sought shelter. There were open sheds with sleeping accommodations in the enclosure, and the whole was surrounded by a courtyard. A man, the one that superintended the establishment, unlocked the inn, after which he returned to the city. Next morning, he came out again to the inn, and then received a small sum for his services. The travellers went their several ways, but the superintendent took Jesus and His companions back with him to his own house in the city. Cedar was situated at the foot of a mountain, in a valley through which flowed a river. It consisted of an old and a new city separated by the little river which flowed from the east and off toward Palestine. The shore was very steep, and the river was spanned by two arches very solidly built. On this side the place was poor and insignificant, and inhabited principally by Jewish shepherds who likewise engaged in the manufacture of light huts, shepherd and stable utensils. On the opposite side, Cedar presented a more opulent appearance. There were no Jews there, but only heathens. The Jewish costume was somewhat modified here, for some of the people wore a pointed cap. In the city this side of the river, there was a synagogue, and upon a square surrounded by grass plots and walks of clean white sand, played a fountain. This was the most beautiful spot in the city.

The Lord and the boys went with their host to the synagogue, and quietly celebrated the Sabbath. At the end of the prayers, Jesus asked whether He might venture to relate something to them, and when the good people showed their willingness to listen, He recounted the parable of the Prodigal Son. They listened attentively, admired Him greatly, but knew not who He was. He called Himself a shepherd seeking the lost lambs in order to lead them into good pasture. They regarded Him as a Prophet and, during the rest of the day, conducted Him to their houses where too He taught. The next day He gave an instruction at the fountain. The men and women sat at His feet, and He pressed the children to His breast. He told them about Zacheus climbing up the fig tree, of his leaving all and following Him; of him who in the Temple had said: "I thank God that I am not like the publican"; and lastly, of that other who, striking his breast, said: "Lord, be merciful to me, a poor sinner!" The inhabitants of Cedar became very fond of Jesus and thought no harm of Him. They begged Him to stay with them till the next Sabbath and then teach again in their school, and when they asked Him about Jesus of Nazareth, He related to them many things of Him and His doctrine.

On leaving this place, Jesus and His travelling companions proceeded eastward from Cedar into a country of beautiful meadowlands and palm trees, and thence to Edon. On the way, He visited a house that stood off by itself, and in which both the father and mother of the family had long been bedridden with incurable maladies. Several children were going and coming around the house. All were good. Here also they asked Him about Jesus of Nazareth, of whom they had heard divers reports. Jesus answered them in a beautiful parable of a king and his son, in which he spoke of the One of whom they inquired. He told them that He would be persecuted, and that He would return to His Father's Kingdom, which He would share with all those that had followed Him. As Jesus spoke I had a vision of His Passion, His Ascension, His throne surrounded by all the angels and set next His Father's, meaning His dominion over the world; and, lastly, I saw the reward portioned out to His followers. I saw likewise the vision of His Kingdom and the whole parable that He was relating to the people, and I saw too that He impressed upon their hearts a lasting picture of it. When He asked them whether they believed all He had told them and whether they would follow the good King, and they had protested their belief and their willingness, He promised the two old people that God would reward them by curing them and allowing them to follow Him to Edon. And all on a sudden, they were restored to health and, to the astonishment of the beholders, were indeed able to follow Jesus to Edon. The man's name was Benjamin, and he was a direct descendant from Ruth. I think that Titus was either a son or a relative of this couple so suddenly cured. He was at that time between fourteen to sixteen years old. He went to Cedar and to every other place in this region in which Jesus taught, in order to hear Him and to listen to others talking about Him. Marcus, whose birthplace was nearer Judea, was acquainted with this family, and so too was Silas.

Jesus and the three youths, on leaving that house, went on to Edon through lovely fields and meadows shaded by palm trees. Jesus carried a shepherd's crook in His right hand. In the public feast house, on a large, open square to the left of the entrance to the city, a marriage was being celebrated. The house contained a large hall, at the end of which was the kitchen. All around it were sleeping apartments, in each of which there were three beds that could be separated from one another by an ornamented screen. Although it was clear daylight, a lamp was burning in the hall. The guests, male and female, as also the bride and bridegroom, adorned with flowery wreaths, were all assembled in the same apartment. Boys were singing and playing upon flutes and other instruments. These pious people were awaiting Jesus, whom they looked upon as a Prophet. They had heard of His teaching and parables in Cedar and the surrounding district, and had in consequence invited Him to their wedding. They received Him joyfully and reverently, washed His feet and those of His young companions, and dried them with their own garments. They took from Jesus His staff, placed it in a corner, and prepared for Him a table. On it were some little rolls, a honeycomb almost a foot in length, and some red berries from the top of which they detached before eating a little circle of black leaves tipped with white. There were, too, little earthen jugs and cups on the table and some small dishes. The last mentioned looked like glazed earthenware, out of which with little spoons they put something into their drink. The guests reclined at table upon small leaning benches, and to Jesus was given the seat between the bridegroom and the bride. The women sat at the lower end. Jesus blessed the food and drink, of which all then partook.

During the meal, Jesus taught. He told the guests about that Man in Judea who, at the marriage of Cana in Galilee, had changed water into wine. When the couple whom the guests had known so long as sick, but who had been restored to health, made their appearance, the amazement was great. They related all that the Lord had told them of the King and His Kingdom, declared their belief in it, and said that they were as certain of having a share in that same Kingdom as they were now conscious of the fact of having been cured. Jesus repeated to them the parable and told them in plain words that there was still a wall between them and the dominions of that King, but that they could force their way through it if they would overcome themselves. It was morning before the party retired to bed. The Lord and the young boys slept back of the dining hall. Before He lay down, however, He went aside and, kneeling, prayed with uplifted hands to His Heavenly Father. I saw streams of light issuing from His mouth, and another stream of light, or an angelic form, descending toward Him. This often happened even in full daylight when at any time Jesus retired to a solitary place to pray. I knew this about Him even in my childhood, and when I saw Him praying thus alone, I tried to imitate Him. I saw the Blessed Virgin, up to the conception of the Saviour, generally standing in prayer, her hands crossed on her breast, and her eyes lowered; but after the most holy Incarnation, she generally knelt, her face raised to Heaven, and her hands uplifted.

Next morning, on account of the great concourse of people, Jesus taught in the open air. He settled many matrimonial affairs, for the people of this place had lost the true conception of the Law on that head. They wanted to espouse two blood relatives in succession, and

they questioned Jesus on the matter. He explained to
them that it was not allowed by the Mosaic Law, and
they promised to refrain from such unions. It was told
Jesus also that in one of the neighboring places, a certain
man was on the point of marrying for the sixth time, his
five deceased wives being sisters of the present affianced.
Jesus said that He would visit that place. He returned to
Cedar for the Sabbath, and taught the whole day in the
school. He gave decisions upon many questions and
doubts concerning the Law and marriage and reconciled
some married couples that were at variance.

5. JESUS GOES TO SICHAR-CEDAR AND
TEACHES UPON THE MYSTERY
OF MARRIAGE

From Cedar, Jesus, with a numerous escort, wended
His way northward, the country everywhere presenting a
more level aspect. I saw them reach a shepherd village
outside of which were open sheds, long rows of trees with
interlacing branches, and huts formed of green boughs
and leaves. Under one of the sheds, all partook of figs,
grapes, and dates. They were still there, the night being
mild and lovely, when the stars shone out in the sky and
the dewdrops glittered brightly below.

When the rest of the party dispersed to their homes,
Jesus with the three youths went around the district
teaching, and arrived toward evening of the following day
at the little city of Sichar-Cedar, built on the declivity of
a mountain range. Some people came out to meet Him.
They conducted Him to the public house of the city,
which was something like that of Cana in Galilee, and
there He found a crowd assembled. Some young married
people had lost their parents by a sudden death, and they
were now entertaining at this house all those who had
followed the remains to the grave. In front of the house

was a courtyard enclosed by a railing, and in it an arbor of skillfully woven foliage. In each of the four corners stood a stone cistern full of water out of which grew creeping plants. They were trained up on palings and then allowed to run on arches to the center of the yard, where a carved column of marble supported the verdant roof thus formed. The plants, like reeds or sedges, retained their freshness a long time. This decoration, as well as all the garlands that adorned the house, was of extraordinary beauty. In a hall just off the courtyard, Jesus' feet and those of His companions were washed, and the customary refreshments presented. Then they went to another apartment, in which a meal was in readiness. Jesus insisted upon serving at table. He handed to all the guests bread, fruit, and large pieces of honeycomb, and poured from jugs into the drinking cup of each three kinds of beverage: one was a green juice; another, some kind of yellow drink; and the third, a perfectly white fluid. Jesus taught all the time. Sichar-Cedar was the place of which Jesus had been told at the wedding feast that so many were living there in unlawful marriage relations.

Only the husband of the mourning married couple was present at the funereal feast. He was named Eliud. He had been at the marriage feast at Edon, and on his return home found that both his parents-in-law had departed this life. They had died suddenly, overcome by grief at the discovery that their daughter, Eliud's wife, was an adulteress. Eliud himself had no intimation of the fact, nor consequently of the cause of the sudden death of his parents-in-law. When the meal spoken of above was over, Jesus allowed Himself to be conducted by Eliud to his home. The youths did not go with Him. Jesus spoke to the wife in private. She was in great sorrow. She sank at His feet in tears, and confessed her sin. When Jesus left her, Eliud conducted Him to His sleeping chamber. I saw the Lord saying some grave and touching words to him and, when Eliud left Him, He prayed awhile and then went to rest. Early next morning Eliud, with a wash-basin and a green branch, went in to Jesus, who was still lying on the bed supported on His arm. He arose; Eliud washed His feet and dried them in his own garments. Then the Lord told him to conduct Him to his chamber, for that He wanted in turn to wash his feet. Eliud would not hear of this. But Jesus told him gravely that if he would not yield, He would instantly leave his house, that it must be, that if he wanted to follow Him he must not refuse to obey. On hearing these words, Eliud led Jesus to his bedchamber and brought Him a basin of water. Jesus grasped him by the hands, gazed lovingly into his eyes, said a few words on the subject of foot washing, and then informed him that his wife was an adulteress, but penitent, and that he must pardon her. At this information Eliud fell prostrate on the ground, writhing and weeping in an excess of mental agony. Jesus turned away from him and prayed. After a little while, the first bitter struggle being over, Jesus went to him, raised him from the ground, spoke words of consolation to him, and washed his feet. When Eliud had become calm, Jesus commanded him to call his wife. He did so, and she entered the room closely veiled. Jesus took her hand, laid it in that of Eliud, blessed them both, consoled them, and raised the wife's veil. Then He dismissed them with directions to send their children to Him, whom when they came He blessed and led back to their parents. From this time forward Eliud and his wife remained faithful to each other, and both made a vow of continency. On that same day, Jesus visited many other homes in order to lead their occupants from the error of their ways. I saw Him going from house to house, conversing with the people upon their various affairs and thus winning their confidence.

On the mountain near this place, Sichar-Cedar, there were whole rows of beehives. The declivity of the mountain was terraced, and on the terraces resting against the mountain stood numerous square, flat-roofed beehives about seven feet in height, the upper part ornamented with knobs. They were placed in several rows, one above the other. They were not rounded in the back, but pointed like a roof, and they could be opened from top to bottom on the shelf side. The whole apiary was enclosed by a fine trellis of woven reeds. Between these stacks of hives there were steps leading up to the terraces, and to the railings on either side, bushes bearing white blossoms and berries were trained. One could mount from terrace to terrace, upon each of which were similar arrangements for bees.

When Jesus was asked by the people whence He had come He invariably answered in parables, to which they gave simple-hearted credence. Under the bower of the public house He delivered an instruction, in which He related the parable of the king's son who came to discharge all the debts of his subjects. His hearers took the parable in its literal sense and rejoiced greatly over what it promised. Jesus then turned to the parable of the debtor who, after having obtained a delay for the payment of his own great debt, insisted upon bringing before the judge the man that owed him a trifle. He told them also that His Father had given Him a vineyard which had to be cultivated and pruned, and that He was looking for laborers to replace the useless, lazy servants whom He was going to chase away, and who were mete images of the branches they had neglected to prune. Then He explained to them the cutting away of the vinestock, spoke of the quantity of useless wood and foliage, and of the small number of grapes. To this He compared the hurtful elements that had, through sin, entered into man. These, He said, should be cut off and destroyed by the exercise of mortification in order that fruit might be produced. This led to some words on marriage and its precepts, as well as upon the modesty and propriety to be observed in it, after which He returned to the vine and told the people that they too ought to cultivate it. They replied quite innocently that the country was not adapted to vine culture. But Jesus responded that they ought to plant it on that side of the mountain occupied by the apiary, for that was an excellent exposure for it, and then He related a parable treating of bees. The people expressed their readiness to labor in His vineyard, if He would allow them. But He told them that He had to go and discharge the debts, that He had to see that the true vine was put into the wine press, in order to produce a lifegiving wine, and to teach others how to cultivate and prepare the same. The simple-hearted people were troubled at the thought of His going away, and implored Him to remain with them. But He consoled them by saying that if they believed Him, He would send them one who would make them laborers in His vineyard. I saw that the inhabitants of this little place were afterward baptized by Thaddeus, and that all emigrated during a persecution.

Jesus recalled none of the Prophecies, performed no miracles in this place. In spite of their moral disorders, these people were simple and childlike. Married couples living apart were again united by Jesus, and He explained to the man who, after having married five sisters was now about to espouse the sixth, that such unions were unlawful.

Jesus gave another instruction upon marriage. He illustrated His subject by deeply significant similitudes taken from the cultivation of the vine, the care of the vineyard, and the pruning away of the superfluous branches. I was particularly impressed by His remarkable and clearly convincing words to this effect, that wherever discord reigned in the married state and wherever marriage failed to produce good, pure fruit, the fault lay principally on the wife's side. It is for her to endure and to suffer, it is for her to form, to preserve, the fruit of marriage. By her spiritual labors and victories over self, she can perfect her own soul and the fruit of her womb, she can eradicate whatever evil there may be in it, since her whole conduct, all her actions, redound to the blessing or the ruination of her offspring. In marriage there should be no question of sensual gratification, but only of penance and mortification, of constant fear, of constant warfare against sin and sinful desires, and this warfare is best carried on by prayer and self-conquest. Such struggles against self, such victories over self on the mother's part, secure similar victories to her children. All this instruction was given by the Lord in words as wonderful for their significance as for their simplicity. He said many other things, clear and precise, on the same subject. I was so impressed by the truth of what He said and its great necessity that the thought rushed impetuously to my mind: Why is not all this put in writing! Why is there no disciple present who could write it all down, that people far and wide might know it? For in the whole of this vision I was, as it were, present among Jesus' audience, and I followed Him here and there. As I was so earnestly revolving that thought, my Heavenly Bridegroom turned and addressed me in words to this effect: "I rouse charity, I cultivate the vineyard wherever it will best produce fruit. Were these things written down, they would suffer the fate of so many other writings, they would fall into oblivion, or be misinterpreted, or utterly condemned. The words that I have just spoken, as well as innumerable others that have never been written, will become more productive in effects than what has been preserved in writing. It is not the written Law that is obeyed; but they that believe, hope, and love, have everything written in their heart." The way in which Jesus taught all this, the constant use of parables by which He illustrated from the nature of the vine all that He said of marriage and, on the other hand, the borrowing from marriage apt illustrations of the cultivation of the vine—all was inexpressibly beautiful and convincing. The people questioned the Lord most simply, and He gave them answers that showed still more clearly how perfectly His similitudes explained His doctrine.

At noon the nuptial ceremony between a poor young couple took place in front of the synagogue, and at it Jesus assisted. Both were good and innocent, consequently the Lord was very kind to them. The bridal procession to the synagogue was headed by little boys of six years with wreaths on their heads and flutes in their hands, white-robed maidens carrying little baskets of flowers which they strewed on the ground, and youths playing on harps, triangles, and other musical instruments now little known. The bridegroom was dressed almost like a priest. Both he and the bride were attended by assistants who, during the ceremony, laid their hands on their shoulders. The marriage was performed by a Jewish priest, in a hall whose roof had been opened just above the bridal party. It was near the synagogue. When the stars began to appear in the sky, the Sabbath exercises were celebrated in the synagogue, after which a fast that lasted until the next evening was begun. When that was over, the wedding festivities were held in the public house used on such occasions, during which Jesus related many parables, such as that of the Prodigal Son and the mansions in His Father's house. The bridegroom had no house of his own. He was to make his home in that belonging to the mother of his bride. Jesus told him that, until he should receive a mansion in His Father's house, he should take up his abode under a tent in the vineyard which He Himself was going to lay out on the mount of the bees. Then He again taught on marriage, upon which

He dwelt for a long time. If married people, He said, would live together modestly and chastely, if they would recognize their state as one of penance, then would they lead their children in the way of salvation, then would their state become not a means of diverting souls from their end, but one that would reap a harvest for those mansions in His Father's house. In this instruction, Jesus called Himself the Spouse of a bride in whom all those that should be gathered, would be born again. He alluded to the marriage feast of Cana, and told of the changing of water into wine. He always spoke of Himself in the third person, as of that Man in Judea whom He knew so well, who would be so bitterly persecuted, and who would finally be put to death.

The people heard all this in simple, childlike faith, and the parables were for them real facts. The bridegroom appeared to be a school teacher, for Jesus told him how he should teach by his own example. Jesus made allusion also to Ismael, for Cedar and the country around were peopled by his descendants. They were, for the most part, shepherds, and esteemed themselves inferior to the people of Judea, of whom they spoke as of a very great nation, a chosen race. They still clung to the ancient manner of living. The owner of numerous herds lived in a large house surrounded by a moat, and in the midst of the pasture grounds by which it was encompassed stood the houses of the under-shepherds. To the well, which belonged to the head proprietor, only his own herds had a right to go, though those of his neighbors enjoyed the same privilege if there existed an agreement to that effect. Such patriarchal settlements were scattered thickly here and there, though otherwise the place was of little importance.

Moved thereto by Jesus' words, the people determined to build for the newly married pair a light habitation on the bee mount where, later on, the vineyard was to be laid out. Every friend in the place constructed for the tent a light wicker wall which was then covered with skins, and afterward coated with something of a viscid nature. When a piece of the work was finished, it was transported to the site for which it was destined. Each one did what was in his power, some more, some less, and they shared with one another whatever was needed. The Lord told them how all was to be done, and they listened in wonder at His knowing so much about such things. He had taught them at the marriage feast that the old and the poor should take the upper places. Jesus went with the people to the little hill in front of the bee mountain, in order to choose there the best site for the vineyard. The back of the tent was to rest against the rising ground of the vineyard. As the Feast of the New Moon just now began, all returned with Jesus to the public house. He knew that, when He said that they should build a house for the newly married pair, many had thought and said to one another: "Perhaps He has no house of His own, no place of abode. Will He, perhaps, take up His residence with these people?" Therefore it was that Jesus now told them that He was not going to stay among them, that He had no abiding place on this earth, that His Kingdom was yet to come, that He had to plant His Father's vineyard, and water it with His Blood upon Mount Calvary. They could not now comprehend His words, He said, but they would do so after He had watered the vineyard. Then He would come back to them from a dark country. He would send His messengers to call them, and then they would leave this place and follow Him. But when He should come again for the third time, He would lead into His Father's Kingdom all those who had faithfully labored in the vineyard. Their sojourning here was not to be long, therefore the house they were building was to be a light one, rather a tent that could be easily removed. Jesus next gave a long instruction upon mutual charity. They should, He said, cast their anchor in the heart of their neighbor, that the storms of the world might not separate and destroy them. He spoke again in parables of the vineyard, saying that He would remain only long enough to lay out the vineyard for the newly married pair and teach them to plant the vines, then He would depart in order to cultivate that belonging to His Father. Jesus taught all these things in language so simple, and yet so nicely adapted to the point in question, that His hearers became more and more convinced of its truth, retaining at the same time their simplicity. He taught them to recognize in all nature, in life itself, a law hidden and holy, though now disfigured by sin. The instruction lasted till late into the night, and when Jesus wanted to take leave of them, the people detained Him. They clasped Him in their arms, exclaiming: "Explain it all to us again, that we may understand it better." But He replied that they should practice what He had preached to them, and He promised to send them one who would make it all clear to them. During this assembly they partook of a slight repast, at which all drank out of the same cup.

The young man for whom the Lord had caused the house to be built was named Salathiel, and the bride's name was a word that signified "pretty," or "brunette."[1] With the greater part of the inhabitants of the place, they were baptized by Thaddeus. The Evangelist Mark also was in this region for awhile. Thirty-five years after Christ's Ascension, Salathiel with his wife and three grown-up sons removed to Ephesus. I saw him there in company with the goldsmith Demetrius, who had once raised an insurrection against Paul, but who was afterward converted. Demetrius gave him a long account of Paul, and narrated the history of his conversion. Paul was not then at Ephesus. Salathiel, his three sons, and Demetrius went to join him, while the wife of the first-named remained behind at Ephesus in a house to which many from her own country came and resided with her. Almost all the Jews left Ephesus at this time. Salathiel and his three sons, Demetrius, Silas, and a man named Caius were all in the same ship with Paul when he suffered shipwreck near the island of Malta, and they went with him to the island. From his prison in Rome, Paul assigned to each of the three sons of Salathiel the place in which he was to labor.

When Jesus went with the men to the bee mount, in order to show them how to plant the vines, the site for the tent house was already marked off and an espalier erected. The men told Jesus that grapes raised in those parts were always bitter, to which Jesus responded that that was because they belonged to a poor species. They were of a bad stock, they were allowed to run wild without pruning; consequently they had the appearance only of grapes, without their sweetness. But, He added, those that He was now about to plant would be sweet. The instruction turned again upon marriage which, Jesus said, could produce pure, sweet fruit only when it was guarded by self-command, mortification, and moderation united to pain and labor.

From the young plants that He had ordered to be brought to the spot, Jesus chose five, which He laid in the ground that He had Himself previously loosened, and He showed the men how to bind them to the espalier in the form of a cross. All that He said while thus engaged of the nature and training of the vine referred to the mystery of marriage and the sanctification of its fruit. When Jesus continued this instruction in the synagogue, He spoke of the obligation of continency in order to conception and, as a proof of the same, brought forward the depth of corruption into which men had fallen in this particular. Man, He said, might in this respect learn a lesson from the elephant. (There were a few of these

animals in that region). At the close of the instruction
Jesus repeated that He must now soon leave them, in
order to plant and water the vine on Mount Calvary, but
He would send some to teach them all things and to lead
them into His Father's vineyard. When at the same time
He spoke of the Kingdom and the mansions of His
Father, the people asked Him why He had brought
nothing with Him from that Kingdom and why He went
about so poorly clad. Jesus answered that that Kingdom
was reserved for such as followed Him, and that no one
would receive it without deserving it. He was, He said, a
stranger seeking for faithful servants whom He might call
into the vineyard. He had therefore built the bridegroom's house so lightly because the earth was not to be
a permanent abode for his posterity and they were not to
cling to it. Why should a solid habitation be constructed
for the body, since it is itself only a fragile vessel? It
should indeed be cared for and purified as the house of
the soul, as a sacred temple, but it should not be
polluted, or to the prejudice of the soul either over-
burdened or treated too delicately. From such discourse
Jesus turned again to the house of His Father, to the
Messiah, and all the signs by which He might be recognized. Among the latter He mentioned the fact that He
was to be born of an illustrious race, though of simple,
pious parents, and added that, according to the signs of
the time, He must have already come. They should, Jesus
said, attach themselves to Him and observe His teachings.

Jesus next taught on the love of the neighbor and good
example. Turning to the bridegroom Salathiel, He told
him to allow his house to stand open, to have perfect
confidence in what He had said to him, and to live
piously; if he did so, God would guard his house for him
and nothing would be stolen from him. Salathiel had
received for his new house far more than was actually

needed, for Jesus had inveighed against selfishness. They must, He said, be willing to sacrifice for God and the neighbor. The communication between Jesus and these people became more and more intimate and, in order to rescue them from the ignorance into which they had fallen, He taught under manifold similitudes upon the chastity, modesty, and self-conquest that should grace the married state. The similitudes referred to the sowing and the harvest. He went also to visit two parties who were about to marry notwithstanding their relationship to each other in prohibited degrees. One couple were blood relatives. Jesus summoned them into His presence and told them that their design sprang from the desire of temporal goods, and that it was not lawful. They were terrified on finding that He knew their thoughts, for no one had said anything to Him about it; so they relinquished their intention. Here they washed one another's feet, and the bride wiped Jesus' feet with the end of her veil, or the upper part of her mantle. Both the man and the woman recognized Jesus by His teaching as more than a Prophet. They were converted and followed Him. Jesus next went out to a house in the country, in which lived a stepmother who wanted to marry her stepson, though the latter as yet did not clearly comprehend her design. Jesus made known to the son the danger in which he was, and bade him flee from the place and go labor at Salathiel's, which he obediently did. The Lord washed his feet also. The stepmother, whom Jesus gravely rebuked for her guilt, was greatly exasperated. She did no penance and went to perdition.

The people of this region must have had, through their ancestors, some special relations with the Ark of the Covenant. They asked Jesus what had become of the Holy Mystery contained in the Ark. He answered that mankind had received so much of It, that It had now passed into them, and that from the fact that it was no longer to be found, they might conclude that the Messiah was born. Many people of this country believed that the Messiah was put to death among the Holy Innocents.

JESUS RAISES A DEAD MAN TO LIFE

About one hour to the east of Sichar stood the dwelling of a rich herd proprietor. The house was surrounded by a moat. The owner had died suddenly in a field not far from his house, and his wife and children were in great affliction. The remains were ready for interment, and the family had sent messengers into the city to beg the Lord and some others to come to the funeral. Jesus went, accompanied by His three disciples, Salathiel and his wife, and several others—about thirty in all. The corpse, ready for the grave, was placed in a broad avenue of trees before the house. The man had been struck dead in punishment of his sins, for he had seized upon part of the possessions of some shepherds who, owing to his oppressive treatment, were obliged to leave that section of the country. Shortly after the commission of this sin, he had fallen dead upon the very ground that he had unjustly appropriated. Standing in front of the corpse, Jesus spoke of the deceased. He asked of what advantage was it to him now that he had once pampered and served his body, that house which his soul had now to leave. He had, on account of that body, run his soul into debt which he neither had and which he never could discharge. The wife of the deceased was plunged in grief. She had constantly repeated before Jesus' coming: "If the Jewish King from Nazareth were here, He could raise him from the dead!" In reply to these words, Jesus said: "Yes, the Jewish King can do it. But men will persecute Him on that account. They will kill Him who gives life, and they will refuse to acknowledge Him!" To which those around responded: "If He were among us, we would acknowledge Him!"

Jesus resolved to put them to the test. He spoke of faith, and promised that the Jewish King would help them, provided they believed and practiced all that He taught. Then He separated the family of the deceased along with Salathiel and his wife from the rest of the assistants, whom He directed to withdraw, while He spoke with the wife, the daughter, and the son of the dead man. Even before the others had gone out, the wife had addressed these words to Jesus: "Lord, Thou speakest as if Thou Thyself wert the King of the Jews!" But Jesus had motioned her to be silent. When now those others, whom He knew to be weaker in faith, had retired, Jesus told the family that if they would believe in His doctrine, if they would follow Him, and if they would keep silence upon the matter, He would raise the dead man to life, for his soul was not yet judged, it was still tarrying in the field, the scene of its injustice as well as of its separation from the body. The family promised with all their heart both obedience and silence, and Jesus went with them to the field in which the man had died. I saw the state in which the soul of the deceased was. I saw it in a circle, in a sphere above the spot upon which he had died. Before it passed pictures of all its transgressions with their temporal consequences, and the sight consumed it with sorrow. I saw too all the punishments it was to undergo, and it was vouchsafed a view of the satisfactory Passion of Jesus. Torn with grief, it was about to enter upon its punishment, when Jesus prayed, and called it back into the body by pronouncing the name Nazor, the name of the deceased. Then turning to the assistants, He said: "When we return, we shall find Nazor sitting up and alive!" I saw the soul at Jesus' call floating toward the body, becoming smaller, and disappearing through the mouth, at which moment Nazor rose to a sitting posture in his coffin. I always see the human soul reposing above the heart from which numerous threads run to the head.

When Jesus and His companions returned to the house they found Nazor, still enveloped in his funereal bands and his hands bound, sitting up in the coffin. His wife unbound his hands and loosened the bands. He stepped forth from the coffin, cast himself at Jesus' feet, and tried to embrace His knees. But the Lord drew back and told him that he should purify himself, should wash, and remain concealed in his chamber, that he should not speak of his resurrection until He Himself had left that region. The wife then led her husband into a retired corner of the dwelling, where he washed and clothed himself. Jesus, Salathiel and his wife, and the three disciples took some food and remained at the house. The coffin was placed in the vault. The Lord taught until after nightfall. On the following morning He washed the feet of the resuscitated Nazor and exhorted him for the future to think more of his soul than of his body, and to restore the ill-gotten property. After that He called the children to Him, spoke of God's mercy which their father had experienced, and exhorted them to the fear of God; then He blessed them and led them to their parents. The mother, also, Jesus conducted to the father. He presented her to him as to one returned from afar, in order that they might live together in a stricter and more God fearing manner.

Jesus on that day taught many things relating to marriage, in similitudes. He addressed Himself especially to the newly married couple. To Salathiel He said: "Thou hast allowed thy heart to be moved by the beauty of thy wife! But think how great the beauty of the soul must be, since God sends His Son upon earth to save souls by the sacrifice of His Body! Whoever serves the body, serves not the soul. Beauty inflames concupiscence, and concupiscence corrupts the soul. Incontinence is like a creeping plant that chokes and destroys the wheat and the vines." These last words turned the instruction again upon the subject of vine and wheat culture, and Jesus warned His hearers to keep far from their fields and vineyards two running weeds which He designated by name. At last He announced to them that on the coming Sabbath He would teach in the school at Cedar, and on that occasion they would hear what they must do to become His followers and share in His Kingdom. He told them, moreover, that He would then depart from that region and journey eastward to Arabia. When they asked Him why He was going among those heathens, those star-worshippers, He answered that He had friends among them who had followed a star in order to greet Him at His birth. These He wanted to search after, that He might invite them also into the vineyard and the Kingdom of His Father, and put them on the straight road to it.

An extraordinarily great multitude assembled in Cedar to meet Jesus, who now began publicly to heal crowds of sick. Sometimes while passing among those that had been brought hither by their friends, He merely pronounced the words: "Arise! Follow Me!"—and they rose up cured. The wonder and admiration produced by these miracles reached such a pitch of enthusiasm that had not Jesus Himself suppressed it, the whole country would have risen in one sudden transport of joy.

Salathiel and his wife were among the assembly at Cedar. Jesus once more spoke to them of the duties of the married state, and gave them detailed instructions upon the way in which they should live together in order to become a good vine (that is, one that would produce pure and excellent fruit, such as would become disciples of His Apostles, saints, and martyrs). He inculcated the observance of modesty and purity, bade them in all their actions aim at purity of intention, exhorted them to prayer and renunciation, and rigorously commanded perfect continence after the period of conception. He spoke of the mutual confidence that ought to exist between husband and wife, and of the obedience of the latter to the former. The husband should not keep silence when the wife asks him questions. He ought to respect her and be indulgent toward her, since she is the weaker vessel. He should not mistrust her if he sees her talking with others, neither should she be jealous upon beholding him doing the same; still each should be careful not to give to the other cause for vexation. They should suffer no third party to come in between them, and should settle their little differences themselves. He told the wife that she should become a pious Abigail, and pointed out to them a region suitable for the cultivation of wheat. They must, He said, raise a hedge around their vineyard, which hedge was to consist of the admonitions He had just given them.

Before leaving Cedar, Jesus gave in the synagogue another very long instruction, in which He again explained the connection existing between all the points upon which up to that time he had here taught separately. He spoke in simple, childlike allegories of the mysteries of Original Sin, the vicious propagation of the human race, their ever-increasing corruption, the dispositions of God's grace and His guidance of the chosen people from generation to generation down to the Blessed Virgin, the mystery of the Incarnation and the regeneration of fallen man from death to eternal life through the Son of the Virgin. Here He introduced the parable of the grain of wheat which had to be buried in the ground before it could spring forth into new fruit, but He was not understood by His hearers. He told them that they should follow Him not for a short time only, but on a long journey that would end only at the Judgment. He spoke of the resurrection of the dead and of the last

Judgment, and He bade them *watch!* Then He related the parable of the slothful servants. Judgment comes like a thief in the night; death strikes at every hour. They, the Ismaelites, were typified by the servants, and they ought to be faithful. Melchisedech, He said, was a type of Himself. His sacrifice consisted of bread and wine, but in Him they would be changed into flesh and blood. At last Jesus told them in plain terms that He was the Redeemer. At this revelation, many became timid and fearful, while others grew more ardent and enthusiastic in their adherence to Him. He enforced upon them in particular love for one another, compassion, sympathy in joy and sorrow such as the members of the body feel for one another.

The pagans from the pagan quarter of Cedar were present at this instruction, to which they listened from a distance. They had been very hostile toward the Jews, but from this time many approached them and questioned them in a friendly manner about Jesus' doctrine and miracles.

1. "Bräunchen," or "Feinchen."

6. JESUS REACHES THE FIRST TENT CITY OF THE STAR WORSHIPPERS

When Jesus with the three youths left Cedar, Nazor, the Ruler of the synagogue, who traced his origin up to Tobias, Salathiel, Eliud, and the youth Titus accompanied Him a good part of the way. They crossed the river and passed through the pagan quarter of the city, in which just at that time a pagan feast was being celebrated and sacrifice was being offered in front of the temple. The road ran first eastward and then to the south through a plain that lay between two high mountain ridges, sometimes over heaths, again over yellow or white sand, and sometimes over white pebbles. At last they reached a large, open tract of country covered with verdure, in which stood a great tent among the palm trees, and around it many smaller ones. Here Jesus blessed and took leave of His escort, and then continued His journey awhile longer toward the tent city of the star worshippers. The day was on its decline when He arrived at a beautiful well in a hollow. It was surrounded by a low embankment, and near it was a drinking ladle. The Lord drank, and then sat down by the well. The youths washed His feet and He, in turn, rendered them the same service. All was done with childlike simplicity, and the sight was extremely touching. The plain was covered with palm trees, meadows, and at a considerable distance apart there were groups of tents. A tower, or terraced pyramid of pretty good size, still not higher than an ordinary church, arose in the center of the district. Here and there some people made their appearance and from a distance gazed at Jesus in surprise not unmingled with awe, but no one approached Him.

Not far from the well stood the largest of the tent houses. It was surmounted by several spires, and consisted of many stories and apartments connected together by partitions, some grated, others merely of canvas. The upper part was covered with skins. Altogether it was very artistically made and very beautiful. From this tent castle five men came forth bearing branches, and turned their steps in the direction of Jesus. Each carried in his hand a branch of a different kind of fruit: One had little yellow leaves and fruit, another was covered with red berries, a third was a palm branch, one bore a vine branch full of leaves, and the fifth carried a cluster of grapes. From the waist to the knees they wore a kind of woollen tunic slit at the sides, and on the upper part of the body a jacket wide and full, made of some kind of transparent, woollen stuff, with sleeves that reached about halfway to the elbow. They were of fair complexion, had a short, black beard, and long, curling hair. On their head was a sort of spiral cap from which depended many lappets around their temples. They approached Jesus and His companions with a friendly air, saluted them and, while presenting to them the branches they held in their hands, invited them to accompany them back to the tent. The vine branch was presented to Jesus, the one who acted as guide carrying a similar one. On entering the tent Jesus and His companions were made to sit upon cushions trimmed with tassels, and fruit was presented to them. Jesus uttered only a few words. The guests were then led through a tent corridor lined with sleeping chambers containing couch beds, and furnished with high cushions, to that part of the tent in which was the dining hall. In the center of the hall rose the pillar that supported the tent; and around it were twined garlands of leaves and fruits, vine branches, apples, and clusters of grapes—all so natural in appearance that I cannot say whether they really were natural or only painted. Here the attendants drew out a little oval table about as high as a footstool. It was formed of light leaves that could be opened quickly and its feet separated into two supports. They spread under it a colored carpet upon which were representations of men like themselves, and placed upon it cups and other table furniture. The tent was hung with tapestry, so that no part of the canvas itself could be seen.

When Jesus and the young disciples stretched themselves on the carpet around the table, the men in attendance brought cakes, scooped out in the middle, all kinds of fruits, and honey. The attendants themselves sat on low, round folding stools, their legs crossed. Between their feet they stood a little disk supported on a long leg, and on the disk they laid their plate. They served their guests themselves turnabout, the servants remaining outside the tent with everything that was necessary. I saw them going to another tent and bringing thence birds, which had been roasted on a spit in the kitchen. This last-named apartment consisted merely of a mud hut in which was an opening in the roof to let out the smoke from the fire on the hearth. The birds were served up in quite a remarkable manner. They were (but I know not how it was done) covered with their feathers, and looked just as if they were alive. The meal over, the guests were escorted by five men to their sleeping rooms, and there the latter were quite amazed at seeing Jesus washing the youths' feet, which service they rendered Him in return. Jesus explained to them its signification, and they resolved to practice in future the same act of courtesy.

NOCTURNAL CELEBRATION OF THE STAR WORSHIPPERS

When the five men took leave of Jesus and His young companions, they all left the tent together. They wore mantles longer behind than before, with a broad flap hanging from the back of the neck. They proceeded to a temple which was built in the shape of a large four-cornered pyramid, not of stone but of very light materials such as wood and skins. There was a flight of outside steps from base to summit. It was built in a hollow that rose in terraces and was surrounded by steps and parapets. The circular enclosure was cut through by entrances to the different parts of the temple, and the entrances themselves were screened by light, ornamental hedges. Several hundred people were already assembled in the enclosure. The married women were standing back of the men; the young girls, back of them; and last of all, the children. On the steps of the pyramidal temple were illuminated globes that flashed and twinkled just like the stars of heaven, but I do not know how that was effected. They were regularly arranged, in imitation of certain constellations. The temple was full of people. In the center of the building rose a high column from which beams extended to the walls and up into the summit of the pyramid, bearing the lights by which the exterior globes were lighted. The light inside the temple was very extraordinary. It was like twilight, or rather moonlight. One seemed to be gazing up into a sky full of stars. The moon likewise could be seen, and far up in the very center of all blazed the sun. It was a most skillfully executed arrangement, and so natural that it produced upon the beholder an impression of awe, especially when he beheld by the dim light of the lower part of the temple the three idols that were placed around that central column. One was like a human being with a bird's head and a great, crooked beak. I saw the people offering to it in sacrifice all kinds of eatables. They crammed into its enormous bill birds and similar things which fell down into its body and out again. Another of these idols had a head almost like that of an ox, and was seated like a human being in a squatting posture. They laid birds in its arms, which were outstretched as if to receive an infant. In it was a fire into which, through the holes made for that purpose, the worshippers cast the flesh of animals that had been slaughtered and cut up on the sacrificial table in front of it. The smoke escaped through a pipe sunk in the earth and communicating with the outer air. No flames were to be seen in the temple, but the horrible idols shone with a reddish glare in the dim light. During the ceremony, the multitude around the pyramid chanted in a very remarkable manner. Sometimes a single voice was heard, and then again a powerful chorus, the strains suddenly changing from plaintive to exultant; and when the moon and different stars shone out, they sent up shouts of enthusiastic welcome. I think this idolatrous celebration lasted till sunrise.

Before taking leave of these people on the following

morning, Jesus gave them a few words of instruction. To their questions as to who He was and whither He was journeying, He answered by telling them about His Father's Kingdom. He was, He said, seeking friends that had saluted Him at His birth. After that He was going down to Egypt, to hunt up some companions of His childhood and to call them to follow Him, as He was soon to return to His Father. He spoke to them on the subject of their idolatrous worship for which they put themselves to so much trouble and slaughtered so many sacrifices. They should adore the Father, the Creator of all things, and instead of sacrificing victims to idols which they themselves had made, they should bestow those gifts upon their poor brethren. The abodes of the women were back of and entirely separate from the tents of the men, each of whom had many wives. They wore long garments, jewels in their ears, and headdresses in the form of a high cap. Jesus commended the separation of the women from the men. It was well, He said, for the former to stand in the background, but against a multiplicity of wives He inveighed strenuously. They should have but one wife, He said, whom they should treat as one that owed submission, though not as a slave. During this instruction, Jesus appeared to them so lovable, so much like a supernatural being, that they implored Him to remain with them. They wanted to bring a wise, old priest to converse with Him, but Jesus would not allow it. Then they produced some ancient manuscripts which they consulted. They were not rolls of parchment, but thick leaves, which looked as if made of bark, and upon which the writing was deeply imprinted. These leaves were very like thick leather. The pagans insisted upon the Lord's remaining and instructing them, but He refused, saying that they should follow Him when He had returned to His Father, and that He would not neglect to call them at the right time.

When about to leave, Jesus wrote for them with a sharp metallic rod on the stone floor of their tent the initials of five members of His race. It looked to me like only the letters, four or five of them, entwined together, and among them I recognized an *M*. They were deeply engraven on the stone. The pagans gazed in wonder at the inscription, for which they at once conceived great reverence. Later on they converted the stone upon which it was traced into an altar. I see it now at Rome enclosed in one of the corners of St. Peter's church, nor will the enemies of the Church be able to carry it off!

Jesus would not allow any of these pagans to accompany Him when He departed. He directed His steps southward with His young disciples through the widely scattered tents and passed the tower of the idols. He remarked to the youths how affectionately He had been received by these pagans for whom He had done nothing, and how maliciously the obstinate, ungrateful Jews had persecuted Him, although He had loaded them with benefits. Jesus and His young companions hurried on rapidly the whole of that day. It seems to me that He still had a journey of some days, about fifty miles, before reaching the country of the Kings.

JESUS ENCOUNTERS A PASTORAL TRIBE

Shortly before the commencement of the Sabbath I saw Jesus in the neighborhood of some shepherd tents, where He and His young companions sat down by a fountain and washed one another's feet. Then He began to celebrate the Sabbath, praying with the youths and instructing them in order that even here in a strange land, the Jews' reproaches that He did not sanctify the Sabbath day might not be verified. He slept that night with the three youths in the open air by the well. There were no permanent dwellings in this place, and no women among the shepherds. They had only one temporary inn, or caravansary, near their distant pasture grounds. Next morning, the shepherds gathered around Jesus and listened to His words. He asked them whether they had not heard of some people who, three and thirty years before, had been guided by a star to Judea, to salute the newborn King of the Jews. They cried out: "Yes! Yes!" and He went on to tell them that He was now travelling in search of those men. The shepherds exhibited a childlike joy and love for Jesus. On a lovely spot surrounded by palm trees, they made for Him a beautiful high seat or throne, up to which led steps covered with sod. They worked so very quickly, cutting and raising the sods with long stone, or bone knives, that the seat was soon finished. The Lord seated Himself upon it, and taught in most beautiful parables. The shepherds, about forty in number, listened like little children and afterward prayed with Jesus.

That evening the shepherds took down one of their tents, and uniting it to another, formed thereby one large hall, in which they prepared for the whole party an entertainment consisting of fruit, a kind of thick pap rolled into balls, and camel's milk. When Jesus blessed the food He was about to take, they asked Him why He did so, and when He explained the reason, they begged Him to bless all the rest of the food, which He did. They wanted Him also to leave behind Him some blessed food; and when they brought Him for that purpose things soft and very perishable, He called for fruits that would not decay. They brought them, and He blessed some white balls made of rice. He told them always to mix a little of the blessed provisions with their other food, which then would never spoil, and the blessing would never be taken away.

The Kings already knew through dreams that Jesus was coming to see them.

A WONDERFUL GLOBE

I saw the Lord again teaching from the mossy throne. He taught about the creation of the world, the Fall of Man, and the promise of Redemption. Jesus asked whether they preserved the tradition of any promise. But they knew only a few things connected with Abraham and David, and those were mixed up with fables. They were so simple, just like children in school. Whoever knew anything in answer to a question, said it right out. When Jesus saw how innocent and ignorant they were, He wrought a great miracle in their behalf. I cannot recall exactly what He said, but He appeared to catch with His right hand at a sunbeam from which He drew a ball like a little luminous globe, and let it hang from the palm of the same hand by a ray of light. It seemed to be large enough to contain all things, and all things could be seen in it. The good people and the disciples beheld in it everything just as the Lord related it to them, and they all stood in awe around Him. I saw the Most Holy Trinity in the globe, and when I saw the Son in it, I did not see Jesus any longer upon earth, only an angel hovering by the globe. Once Jesus took the globe upon His hand, and again it seemed as if His hand itself was the globe, in which innumerable pictures unfolded, one from another. I heard something about the number three hundred and sixty-five, as if relating to the days of the year, connected with which also there was something in the pictures formed in the globe.

Jesus taught the shepherds a short prayer, in which occurred words like those of the *Our Father,* and He gave them three intentions for which they should alternately recite it. The first was to thank for creation; the second, for Redemption; and the third, I think, was for the Last Judgment. The whole history of the Creation, the Fall, and the Redemption was unfolded in successive pictures in this globe, along with the means given to man to participate therein. I saw all things in the globe connected by rays of light with the Most Holy Trinity, out of whom all things proceeded, but from whom many separated miserably. The Lord gave to the shepherds an idea of Creation by the globe which sprang forth from His hand; an idea of the connection of the fallen world with the Godhead and its Redemption, by the suspension of the globe from His hand by a thread; and when He held it in His hand, He gave them some idea of Judgment. He taught them likewise about the year and the days that compose it inasmuch as they are figures of this history of Creation, and then He showed by what prayers and good works they ought to sanctify the different seasons.

When the Lord concluded His instruction, the luminous globe with its varied pictures disappeared as it had come. The poor people, quite overcome by the sense of their own profound misery and the godlike dignity of their Guest, showed signs of deep affliction and cast themselves, along with the three youths, prostrate on the ground, weeping and adoring. Jesus too became very sad and prostrated on the grassy mound upon which He had been sitting. The youths attempted to raise Him; and when at last He arose of Himself, the shepherds rose also, and standing around Him timidly ventured to ask Him the cause of His sadness. Jesus answered that He was mourning with those who mourned. He then took one of the hyacinths that grew wild in that region (but which were far larger and more beautiful than those we have), and asked them whether they knew the properties of that flower. When the sky is troubled, He said, it wilts, it pines as it were, and its color grows pale, and so too a cloud had passed over His own sun. He told them many other remarkable things about these flowers and their signification. I heard Him also calling them by an exceedingly strange name which, I was told, corresponded to our name for it, the hyacinth.

ABOLITION OF IDOL WORSHIP

Although Jesus knew full well, He questioned the shepherds upon the kind of worship they practiced. He was like a good teacher who becomes a child with his children. Thereupon the good people brought to Him their gods in the shape of all kinds of animals, sheep, camels, asses—all very skillful imitations of the animals themselves. They appeared to be made of metal, and were covered with skins; and, what was truly laughable, all the idols represented female animals. They were provided with long bags, in imitation of udders, to which were attached reed nipples. These bags they filled with milk, milked them at their feasts, drank, and then danced and leaped about. Everyone selected from his herd the most beautiful, the most excellent cattle, which he raised with care and looked upon as sacred. It was after these holy models that the poor idolaters made their gods, and it was with their milk that they filled the udders. When they celebrated religious services, they brought all their idols together into one tent decorated for the occasion, and then began great carousing as at a kermess. The women and children also were in attendance, and milking and eating, drinking, singing, dancing, and adoring of the idols went on vigorously. It was not the Sabbath they were celebrating, but the day after.

While the pagans were relating all this to Jesus and showing Him their idols, I saw the whole thing taking shape and being enacted before my eyes. The Lord explained to them what a miserable shadow of true religious service theirs was and, after some more words to that effect, ended by telling them that He Himself was the Chosen from the herd. He was the Lamb from whom flowed all the milk that was to nourish the soul unto salvation. Then He commanded them to abolish their zoolatry, to drive the living animals back among the herds, and the metal of which the idols were composed to be given to the poor. They should, He said, erect altars, burn upon them incense to the Almighty Creator, the Heavenly Father, and give thanks to Him. They should moreover pray for the coming of the Redeemer, and divide their goods with their poor brethren, for not far off in the desert lived people so poor that they had not even tents to shelter them. Whatever parts of their slaughtered cattle they could not eat, ought to be burned as a sacrifice, also the bread that was over and not intended for the poor. The ashes should be sprinkled upon unproductive ground, which Jesus pointed out to them, in order to attract upon it a blessing. As He prescribed these different points He explained the reasons for observing them. Then He alluded again to the Kings that had visited Him. The people said, yes, they had heard that thirty-three years before, those Kings had journeyed afar in search of the Saviour and in the hope of finding along with Him everything that could be conducive to happiness and salvation. The Kings, they added, had returned to their country and changed something in their religious worship, but that was all they had ever heard about them.

Jesus next went around with these shepherds among their herds and huts, teaching them all kinds of things, even about the different herbs growing there. He promised to send someone to them soon to instruct them. He assured them that He had come on earth not merely for the Jews alone, as they in their humility thought, but for every single human being that sighed for His coming. From the little that they knew of Abraham, this poor shepherd tribe had conceived great esteem for sobriety. The three youths were impressed in a special manner by the late miracle of the luminous globe. Their relations toward the Lord were very different from those of the Apostles. They served Him in dependence, silence, and childlike simplicity. Unlike the Apostles, they never had anything to reply to their Master. The Apostles, however, held an office, whereas these youths were like poor, dependent scholars.

JESUS CONTINUES HIS JOURNEY
TO THE
TENT CITY OF THE KINGS

When Jesus left the shepherds and pursued His journey to the land of the Three Kings, about twelve of them bore Him company. They appeared to have some kind of a tax to pay for which they were taking with them birds in baskets. This journey was a very lonely one, for on the whole length of the route they did not meet one dwelling house. The road was, however, distinctly marked out, and there was no chance of the traveller's losing his way in the desert. Trees lined the roadside bearing edible fruits the size of figs, and here and there were found berries. At certain points, marking one day's journey, resting places were formed. They consisted of a covered well surrounded by trees, whose tops were drawn together in a large hoop, their pendent branches thus forming an arbor. These resting places were furnished with conveniences for making a fire and passing the night. During the great noonday heat, Jesus and the youths rested at one of these wells and refreshed themselves with some fruit. Each time they thus paused on their journey, Jesus and the youths washed one another's feet. The Lord never permitted any of the others to touch Him. The youths, drawn by His goodness, at times treated Jesus with childlike confidence, but again, when they thought of His miracles, His divinity, they cast timid and frightened glances toward Him and looked at one another. I saw too that Jesus often appeared to vanish before them, although He did not fail to direct their attention to all that they met on their way and instruct them upon the same.

They journeyed a part of the night. When they paused to rest, the youths struck fire by revolving two pieces of wood together. They had also a lantern at the end of a pole. It was open on top, and its little flame shed around a reddish glare. I do not know of what it consisted. I saw during the night wild animals running furtively about. The road ran sometimes over high mountains, not steep but gently rising. In one field I saw many rows of nut trees, and people filling sacks with the nuts that had fallen. It looked something like a gleaning. There were other trees whose leaves were gone but the fruit was still remaining, peach trees with slender trunks planted on rising ground, and another that looked almost like our laurel. Some of the resting places for travellers were under large juniper bushes whose branches were as thick as the arm of a good-sized man. They were closely grown together overhead, but thinned out below, so as to afford a delightful shelter. The greater part of the journey, however, was through a desert of white sand interspersed with places covered, some with small white pebbles, others with little polished ones like birds' eggs; and there were large beds of black stones, like the remains of fractured pipkins, or pieces of hollow pottery. Some of these fragments were provided with holes like regular rings, or handles, and the people in the country around used to come in search of them in order to utilize them as bowls and other vessels. The last mountain the travellers crossed was covered with gray stones only. They found on descending its opposite side a dense hedgerow, behind which flowed a rapid stream around a piece of cultivated land. By the shore lay a ferryboat formed of the trunks of trees woven together with osiers. On this they crossed the stream, and then directed their steps to a row of huts built of sticks woven together and overlaid with moss. They had pointed roofs, and all around the central apartment were sleeping places furnished with mossy seats and couches. The occupants were modestly clothed and wore blankets around them like mantles. At some distance I saw tent buildings, much larger and stronger than any I had hitherto seen. They were raised on a stone foundation, and had several stories reached by outside steps. Between the first and the second hut was a well, by which Jesus seated Himself. The youths washed His feet, and then He was conducted to a house set apart for strangers. The people here were very good. They who had accompanied Jesus now left Him for their homes, taking with them provisions for the way.

This region of moss cabins was of very considerable extent, and numberless dwellings such as described lay around among the meadows, fields, and gardens. The large tent palaces could not be seen from here, for they were still at quite a distance; but they were plainly visible from the descent of the mountain. The whole country was extraordinarily fruitful and charming. On the hills were numerous clusters of balsam trees, which when notched distilled a precious juice. The natives caught it in those stone vessels which looked something like iron pots, and which they found in the desert. I saw also magnificent wheat fields, the stalks as thick as reeds, vines, and roses, flowers as large and round as a child's head; and others remarkable for their great size. There were also little purling brooks clear and rapid, overarched by carefully trimmed hedges whose tops were bound together to form a bower. The flowers of these hedges were gathered with care, and those that fell into the water were caught in nets, spread here and there for that purpose, and thus preserved. At the places at which the blossoms were fished out there were gates in the hedges, which were usually kept closed. The people brought and showed to the Lord all the fruits they had.

When Jesus spoke to them of those men who had

followed the star, they told Him that on their return from Judea to the place from which they had first noticed the star, they built on the spot a lofty temple in the form of a pyramid. Around it they erected a city of tents in which they dwelt together, although before that they had lived widely apart. They had received the assurance that the Messiah would eventually visit them, and that upon His departure they too would leave the place. Mensor, the eldest, was still alive and well; Theokeno, the second, borne down by the weakness of old age, could no longer walk. Seir, the third, had died some years previously, and his remains, perfectly preserved, lay in a tomb built in pyramidal form. On the anniversary of his death, his friends visited it, opened it, and performed certain ceremonies over the remains, near which fire was kept constantly burning. They enquired of Jesus after those of the caravan that had remained behind in Palestine, and sent messengers to the tent city, a couple of hours distant, to inform Mensor that they thought they had among them an envoy of that King of the Jews so desired by him and his people.

When the hour for the Sabbath approached, Jesus asked for one of the unoccupied cabins to be placed at the service of Himself and His disciples, and as there were here no lamps of Jewish style, they made one for themselves and celebrated their holy exercises.

7. JESUS CEREMONIOUSLY ESCORTED BY MENSOR TO HIS TENT CASTLE

When the Kings received the news of Jesus' arrival, they made great preparations for His reception. Trees were bound together so as to form covered walks, and triumphal arches erected. These latter were adorned with flowers, fruits, ornaments of all kinds, and hung with tapestry. Seven men in white, gold-embroidered mantles, long and training, and with turbans on their heads ornamented with gold and high tufts of feathers, were despatched to the pastoral region to meet Jesus and bear to Him a welcome. Jesus delivered in their presence an instruction in which He spoke of right-minded pagans who, though ignorant, were devout of heart.

The dwelling place of the Kings was so commodious and so rich in ornamentation that words cannot describe it. It was more like a delightful pleasure garden than a real tent city. The principal tent looked like a large castle. It consisted of several stories raised upon a stone foundation. The lowest was formed of railings through which the eye could penetrate, and the upper ones contained the various apartments, while all around the immense building ran covered galleries and flights of steps. Similar tent castles stood around, all connected together by walks paved with colored stones ornamented with representations of stars, flowers, and similar devices. These walks, so clean and beautiful, were bordered on either side by grass plots and gardens whose beds, regularly laid out, were full of flowers, slender trees with fine leaves, such as the myrtle and dwarf laurel, and all kinds of berries and aromatic plants. In the center of the city, upon a grassy mound such as described, rose a very high and beautiful fountain of many jets. It was surmounted by a roof supported on an open colonnade around which were placed benches and other seats. The streams from the jets shot far around the central column. Back of this stood the temple, with its surrounding colonnades, containing the vaults of the Kings, among which was the tomb of King Seir. This temple was open on one side, but closed on the others by the doors leading to the vaults. It was in shape a four-cornered pyramid, but the roof was not so flat as those that I saw on the early part of the Lord's journey. Spiral steps with railings ran up around the pyramid, whose summit was executed in openwork. I noticed also a tent house in one side of which youths were being educated; and on the other, but entirely separate, girls were instructed in various branches. The dwellings of the females were all together and outside of this enclosure. They lived entirely separate from the men. Words cannot say with what elegance the whole city was laid out, and with what care it was preserved in its beauty, freshness, and neatness. The buildings presented an airy appearance characterized by simplicity of taste. Beautiful gardens with seats for resting were everywhere to be met. I saw an immense cage, more like a large house than a cage, filled from top to bottom with birds; further on, I saw tents and huts in which dwelt smiths and other workmen. I saw also stables and immense meadows full of herds of camels, asses, great sheep with fine wool, also cows with small heads and large horns, very different from those of our country.

I saw no mountain in this region, only gently rising hills, not much higher than our pagan sepulchral mounds. Down through these hills, through pipes inserted for that purpose, borings were made in search of gold. If the boring tube were brought up with gold on its point, the mine was opened in the side of the hill and the gold dug out. It was then smelted in the neighborhood of the mine in furnaces heated not with wood, but with lumps of something brown and clear, which too was dug out of the earth.

Mensor, who was under the persuasion that it was only an envoy from Jesus who had arrived, set all in motion to give him as solemn a reception as if it were the King of the Jews Himself who had come. He deliberated with the other chiefs and priests, and prescribed the various details of His reception. Festal garments and presents were prepared, and the roads by which He was to come magnificently decorated. All was carried forward with joyous earnestness. Mensor, mounted on a richly caparisoned camel which was laden on both sides with

small chests, and attended by a retinue of twenty distinguished personages, some of whom had formed part of
the caravan to Bethlehem, set out to meet Jesus who,
with the three youths and seven messengers, was on His
way to the tent castle. Mensor's party chanted, as they
went along, a solemn, plaintive melody such as they had
nightly sung during their journey to Bethlehem. Mensor,
the eldest of the Kings, he of the brownish complexion,
wore a high, round cap ornamented with some kind of a
white puffed border, and a white training mantle embroidered in gold. As a mark of honor, a standard floated
at the head of the procession. It looked like a horse's tail
fastened to a pole, the top of which was indented with
points. The way led through an avenue across lovely
meadows carpeted here and there with patches of tender
white moss that glanced like dense fungus in the rays of
the sun. At last, the procession reached a well covered by
a verdant temple of artistically cut foliage. Here Mensor
dismounted from his camel and awaited the Lord, who
was seen approaching. One of the seven delegated to
escort Jesus ran on before and announced His coming.
The chests borne by the camels were now opened, and
magnificent garments embroidered in gold, golden cups,
plates, and dishes of fruit were taken out and deposited
upon the carpet that was spread near the well. Mensor,
bowed with age, supported by two of his retinue and attended by his train-bearer, went to meet Jesus. His whole
demeanor was marked by humility. He carried in his
right hand a long staff ornamented with gold and ter-
minating in a scepter-shaped point. At a glance from
Jesus he experienced, as formerly at the Crib, an interior
monition similar to that which had drawn him, first of
the three, down upon his knees. Reaching his staff to
Jesus, he now prostrated again before Him, but Jesus
raised him from the ground. Then the old man ordered
the gifts to be brought forward and presented to Jesus,

who handed them to the disciples, and they were replaced
upon the camel. Jesus did indeed accept the splendid garments, though He would not consent to wear them. The
camel likewise was presented to Him by the old man, but
Jesus thanked without accepting.

They now entered the bower. Mensor presented to the
Lord fresh water into which he had poured some kind of
juice from a small flask, and fruit on little dishes. In a
manner inexpressibly humble, childlike, and friendly,
Mensor questioned Jesus about the King of the Jews, for
he still looked upon Him as an envoy, though he could
not explain to himself his inward emotion. His companions conversed with the youths and wept for joy when
they heard from Eremenzear that he was the son of one
of those followers of the Kings that had remained behind
and settled near Bethlehem. He was a descendant of
Abraham by his second wife, Ketura. Mensor wanted
Jesus to ride upon his camel when they were again starting for the tent castle, but Jesus insisted on walking, He
and the young disciples heading the procession. In about
an hour they reached the vast circular enclosure wherein
stood Mensor's dwelling and its dependencies, and
around which, in lieu of walls, was stretched white tent
cloth. Under the triumphal arch before the entrance,
Jesus and the disciples were met by a troop of maidens in
festive attire. They came forward, two by two, carrying
baskets of flowers which they strewed over the way by
which He had to pass until it was entirely covered with
them. The path led through an avenue of shade trees
whose top branches were bound together. The maidens
wore under their upper garment which fell around them
in the form of a mantle, wide white pantalets; on their
feet, pointed sandals; around their heads, bands of some
kind of white stuff; and on their arms and breast and
around their necks were wreaths of flowers, wool, and
glistening feathers. They were clothed very modestly,

though they wore no veils. The shady avenue ended at a covered bridge which led across the moat, or brook, into the large garden around which the brook ran. In front of the bridge was erected a highly ornamented triumphal arch, under which Jesus was received by five priests in white mantles with long trains. Their robes were richly adorned with lace, and from the right arm of each hung a maniple to the ground. They wore on their head a scalloped crown in the front of which was a little shield in the form of a heart, and from which rose a point. Two of them bore a fire-pan of gold, upon which they sprinkled frankincense from a golden vessel shaped like a boat. They would not allow the trains of their mantles to be held up in Jesus' presence, but tucked them up in a loop behind.

Jesus received all these honors quietly, as He afterward did those of Palm Sunday.

The magnificent garden was watered by many little streams and laid off in triangular flowerbeds by paths beautifully paved with ornamental stones. Through the center of it ran an embowered walk, likewise paved with colored stones in figures, to a second covered bridge. The trees and garden bushes were trained in all kinds of figures. I saw some cut to represent men and animals. The outside row was formed of high trees, but the inner ones were smaller, more delicate, and there were many shady resting places.

The second bridge once crossed, the way led to the middle of a large, circular place that formed the center of the surrounding enclosure. There on a mound entirely surrounded by water stood, over a well, an open edifice, like a little temple. The roof, formed of skins, was raised upon slender pillars. The whole island was one lovely garden, and opposite to it rose the large royal tent.

When Jesus crossed the second bridge, He was received by youths playing on flutes and tambourines. They dwelt near the bridge in low, four-cornered tents which stretched right and left in arches. They must have been a kind of bodyguard, for they carried short swords and stood on guard. They wore caps garnished with something like a feather horn, and they had many kinds of ornaments hanging around them, among them the representation of a large half-moon, in which was a face regularly cut out. The procession halted before the little island of the well. The King dismounted from his camel and led Jesus and the disciples to the fountain, which consisted of a wellspring with many circles of jets one above another, all made of shining metal. When a faucet was turned, the streams of water spouted far around and ran down the mound in channels, through the green hedges, and into the surrounding brook. All around the fountain were seats. The disciples washed Jesus' feet, and He theirs. A covered tent avenue ran over the bridge from the fountain to the other side of the great, circular place and up to Mensor and Theokeno's tent castle. On one side of the tent castle stood, in the spacious enclosure around the fountain island, the temple, a four-cornered pyramid. It was not so high as the tent castle and was surrounded by a colonnade, in which was found the entrance to the vaults of the deceased Kings. Around the temple pyramid ran a flight of spiral steps up to the grated summit. Between the temple and the fountain island, the sacred fire was preserved in a pit covered by a metallic dome upon which was a figure with a little flag in its hand. The fire was kept constantly burning. It was a white flame that did not rise above the mouth of the pit. The priests frequently put into it pieces of something that they dug out of the ground.

The tent castle of the Kings was several stories high. The lowest, that is, the one next above the solid foundation, was merely grated, so that one could see quite through it. It was full of little bushes and plants, and served as a garden for Theokeno, who could no longer walk. Covered steps and galleries ran around the tent castle from the ground up to the top. Here and there were openings like windows, though not symmetrically placed. The roof of the tent had several gables, all ornamented with flags, stars, and moons.

After a short time spent at the fountain, Jesus was escorted through the covered tent avenue to the castle and into the large octagonal hall. In the center rose a supporting column all around which, one above another, were little circular cavities in which various objects could be placed. The walls were hung with colored tapestry upon which were representations of flowers, and figures of boys holding drinking cups, and the floor was carpeted. Jesus requested Mensor to conduct Him at once to Theokeno, whose rooms were in the trellised basement near the little garden. He was resting on a cushioned couch, and he took part in the meal that was served up in dishes of surpassing beauty. The viands were prepared very elegantly. Herbs, fine and delicate, were arranged on the plates to represent little gardens. The cups were of gold. Among the fruits was one particularly remarkable. It was yellow, ribbed, very large, and crowned by a tuft of leaves. The honeycombs were especially fine. Jesus ate only some bread and fruit, and drank from a cup that had never before been used. This was the first time that I saw Him eating with pagans. I saw Him teaching here whole days at a time, and but seldom taking a mouthful.

He taught during that meal and, at last, told His hosts that He was not an envoy of the Messiah, but the Messiah Himself. On hearing this, they fell prostrate on the ground in tears. Mensor especially wept with emotion. He could not contain himself for love and reverence, and was unable to conceive how Jesus could have condescended to come to him. But Jesus told him that He had come for the heathens as well as for the Jews, that

He was come for all who believed in Him. Then they asked Him whether it was not time for them to abandon their country and follow Him at once to Galilee, for, as they assured Him, they were ready to do so. But Jesus replied that His Kingdom was not of this world, and that they would be scandalized, that they would waver in faith if they should see how He would be scorned and maltreated by the Jews. These words they could not comprehend, and they inquired how it could be that things could go so well with the bad while the good had to suffer so much. Jesus then explained to them that they who enjoy on earth have to render an account hereafter, and that this life is one of penance.

The Kings had some knowledge of Abraham and David; and when Jesus spoke of His ancestors, they produced some old books and searched in them, to see whether they too could not claim descent from the same race. The books were in the form of tablets opening out in a zigzag form, like sample patterns. These pagans were so childlike, so desirous of doing all that they were told. They knew that circumcision had been prescribed to Abraham, and they asked the Lord whether they too should obey this part of the Law. Jesus answered that it was no longer necessary, that they had already circumcised their evil inclinations, and that they would do so still more. Then they told Him that they knew something of Melchisedech and his sacrifice of bread and wine, and said that they too had a sacrifice of the same kind, namely, a sacrifice of little leaves and some kind of a green liquor. When they offered it they spoke some words like these: "Whoever eats me and is devout, shall have all kinds of felicity." Jesus told them that Melchisedech's sacrifice was a type of the Most Holy Sacrifice, and that He Himself was the Victim. Thus, though plunged in darkness, these pagans had preserved many forms of truth.

Either the night that preceded Jesus' coming or that which followed, I cannot now say which, all the paths and avenues to a great distance around the tent castle were brilliantly illuminated. Transparent globes with lights in them were raised on poles, and every globe was surmounted by a little crown that glistened like a star.

8. JESUS IN THE TEMPLE OF THE KINGS. FEAST OF THE APPARITION OF THE STAR.

The Lord's first visit to the temple of the Kings took place by day, and He was escorted to it from the tent castle by the priests in solemn procession. They now wore high caps. From one shoulder depended ribbons with numbers of silver shields, and from the opposite arm hung the long maniple. The whole way to the temple was hung with drapery, and the priests walked barefoot. Here and there in the neighborhood of the temple, women were sitting, anxious to see the Lord. They had little parasols, little canopies on poles, to shade them from the sun. When Jesus passed in the distance, they arose and bowed low to the ground. In the center of the temple rose a pillar from which chevrons extended to the four walls, and from the highest point was suspended a wheel covered with stars and globes, which was used during the religious ceremonies.

The priests showed Jesus a representation of the Crib which, after their return from Bethlehem, they had caused to be made. It was exactly like that which they had seen in the star, entirely of gold, and surrounded by a plate of the same metal in the form of a star. The little child, likewise of gold, was sitting in a crib like that of Bethlehem, on a red cover. Its hands were crossed on its breast up to which from the feet it was swathed. Even the straw of the manger was represented. Behind the child's head was a little white crown, but I do not now know of what it was made. Besides this crib there was no other image in the temple. A long roll, or tablet, was hanging on the wall. It was the sacred writings, and the letters were principally formed of symbolical figures. Between the pillar and the crib stood a little altar with openings in the sides, and they sprinkled water around with a little brush, as we do holy water. I saw also a consecrated branch, with which they performed all kinds of ceremonies, some little round loaves, a chalice, and a plate of the flesh of victims sacrificed. As they were showing all these things to Jesus, He enlightened them on the truth and refuted the reasons they advanced for their use.

They took Him also to the tombs of King Seir and his family, which lay in the vaults in the covered way that surrounded the pyramidal temple. They looked like couches cut in the wall. The bodies lay in long, white garments, and beautiful covers hung down from their resting places. I saw their half-covered faces and their hands bare and white as snow; but I know not whether it was only their bones or whether they were still covered with dried skin, for I saw that the hands were deeply furrowed. This sepulchral vault was quite habitable, and there was a stool in each of the tombs. The priests brought in fire and burnt incense. All shed tears, especially the aged King Mensor, who wept like a child. Jesus approached the remains and spoke of the dead. Theokeno, speaking to Jesus of Seir, told Him that a dove was frequently seen to alight on the branch which, according to their custom, they stuck on the door of his tomb, and he asked what it meant. Jesus in reply asked him what was Seir's belief. To this Theokeno answered: "Lord, his faith was like unto mine. After we began to honor the King of the Jews, Seir up to his death desired that all he thought and did, all that was to befall him, might ever be in accordance with the will of that King."

Thereupon Jesus informed him that the dove on the branch signified that Seir had been baptized with the baptism of desire.

Jesus drew for them on a plate the figure of the lamb resting on the Book with the Seven Seals, a little standard over its shoulder, and He bade them make one on that model and place it on the column opposite the crib.

Since their return from Bethlehem, the Kings had every year celebrated a memorial feast of three days in honor of that upon which, fifteen years before the Birth of Christ, they had for the first time seen the star containing the picture of the Virgin who held in one hand a scepter, and in the other a balance with an ear of wheat in one dish and a cluster of grapes in the other. The three days were in honor of Jesus, Mary, and Joseph. They reverenced St. Joseph in a special manner, because he had received them so kindly and graciously. It was now time for this annual festival, but in their humility in presence of the Lord, they wanted to omit the usual religious ceremonies, and begged Him to give them an instruction instead. But Jesus told them that they must celebrate their feast, lest the people in their ignorance of what had just taken place might be scandalized at the omission. I saw many things connected with their religion. They had three images in the form of animals standing around outside the temple: one was a dragon with huge jaws; another a dog with a great head; and the third was a bird with legs and neck long, almost like a stork, only that it had a peaked bill. I do not think that these images were adored as gods. They served only as symbols of certain virtues whose practice they inculcated. The dragon represented the bad, the dark principle in man's nature, which he must labor to destroy; the dog, which had reference to some star, signified fidelity, gratitude, and vigilance; and the bird typified filial love. The images embodied besides all kinds of deep, profound mysteries, but I cannot now recall them. I know well however that no idolatry, no abomination was connected with them. They were embodiments of great wisdom and humility, of deep meditation upon the wonderful things of God. They were not made of gold, but of something darker, like those fragments that were used for smelting the ore, or perhaps what remained after that process. Below the figure of the dragon I read five letters, A A S C C or A S C A S, I do not remember exactly which. The dog's name was Sur, but that of the bird I have forgotten.

The four priests delivered discourses in four different places around the temple before the men, the women, the maidens, and the youths. I saw them open the dragon's jaws and I heard them say at the same time: "If, hateful and frightful as he is, he were now alive and about to devour us, who alone could help us but the Almighty God?"—and they gave to God some special name that I cannot now recall. Then they caused the wheel to be taken down from its place, put it on the altar in a track formed to receive it, and one of the priests made it revolve. There were several circles one inside the other all hung with hollow golden balls, which glittered and tinkled at every revolution, thus announcing the course of the constellations. This revolving of the wheel was accompanied by singing, the refrain being to this effect: "What would become of the world if God should cease to direct the movement of the stars?" This was followed by the offering of sacrifice before the golden Christ Child in the crib, and the burning of incense. Jesus commanded them to do away with those animals for the future, and to teach mercy, love of the neighbor, and the Redemption of the human race; as for the rest, they should admire God in His creatures, give Him thanks, and adore Him alone. On the evening of the first of these three festivals, the Sabbath began for Jesus; therefore, He withdrew with

the three youths into a retired apartment of the tent castle
to celebrate it. They had with them white garments
almost like grave clothes. These they put on, along with a
girdle, ornamented with letters and straps, which they
crossed like a stole over the breast. On a table covered
with red and white stood a lamp with seven burners.
When in prayer, Jesus stood between two of the youths,
the third behind Him. No pagan was present at Jesus'
celebration of the Sabbath.

During the whole of the Sabbath, the pagans were
gathered together in the enclosure around their temple,
men, women, youths, and maidens—all had their respective tiers of seats. After Jesus had finished His celebration of the Sabbath, He went out to the pagans and then
I witnessed a wonderful scene. In the center of the
women's circle stood the image of the dragon. The
women were very differently clothed according to their
rank. The poorest wore under their long mantles only a
short garment, very simple; but the more distinguished
were arrayed like her whom I now saw step in front of
the dragon. She was a robust-looking woman of about
thirty. Under the long mantle, which she laid aside when
seated, she wore a stiff, plaited tunic and a jacket very
closely fitting around the neck and breast, and ornamented with glittering jewels and tiny chains. From the
shoulder to the elbow hung lappets like open half-sleeves,
and the rest of the arms, like the lower limbs, was
covered with lace and bracelets. On her head she wore a
close-fitting cap that reached down to the eyes, partly
concealed the cheeks and chin, and which was formed
entirely of rows of curled feathers. Above the middle of
the head, bent from the forehead back, arose a kind of
roll or pad through which could be seen the hair, braided
and ornamented. A great many long ornamental chains
were pendent from the ears down to the breast.

Before the priest began his instruction, the woman, attended by many others, went in front of the dragon, cast herself down and kissed the earth. She performed this action with marked enthusiasm and devotion. At this moment Jesus stepped into the middle of the circle and asked why she did that. She answered that the dragon awoke her every morning before day when she arose, turned toward the quarter in which the image stood, prostrated before her couch, and adored it. Jesus next asked: "Why dost thou cast thyself down before Satan? Thy faith has been taken possession of by Satan. It is true indeed that thou wilt be awakened, but not by Satan. It is an angel that will awake thee. Behold whom thou adorest!" At the same moment, there stood by the woman, and in sight of all present, a spirit in the form of a figure lank and reddish, with a sharp, hideous countenance. The woman shrank back in fright. Jesus, pointing to the spirit, said: "This is he that has been accustomed to awake thee, but every human being has also a good angel. Prostrate before him and follow his advice!" At these words of Jesus, all perceived a beautiful luminous figure hovering near the woman. Tremblingly she prostrated before him. So long as Satan stood beside the woman, the good angel remained behind her, but when he disappeared, the angel came forward. The woman, deeply affected, now returned to her place. She was called Cuppes. She was afterward baptized Serena by Thomas, under which name she was later on martyred and venerated as a saint.

In His instruction to the youths and maidens who were assembled in the vicinity of the bird, Jesus warned them to observe due measure in their love of both human beings and the lower animals, for there were some among them that almost adored their parents, and others that showed more affection for animals than for their fellow men.

On the last day of the festival, Jesus desired to deliver a discourse in the temple to the priests and Kings and all the people. That the aged King Theokeno also might be among His hearers, Jesus went to him with Mensor, and commanded him to rise and accompany Him. He took him by the hand and Theokeno, nothing doubting, rose up at once able to walk. Jesus led him to the temple and from that time forward he retained the use of his limbs. Jesus ordered the doors of the pyramidal temple to be opened, that all the people outside could both see and hear Him. He taught sometimes outside among the men and women, the youths, the maidens, and the children, relating to them many of the parables that He had formerly recounted to the Jews. His auditors were privileged to interrupt Him in order to ask questions, for He had commanded them to do so. Sometimes also He called upon a certain one to say aloud before all the others the doubts that troubled him, for He knew the thoughts of everyone. Among the questions they asked was this: Why He raised no dead to life, cured no sick, as the King of the Jews had done? Jesus answered that He did not perform such miracles among pagans, but that He would send some men who would work many wonders among them, and that through the bath of Baptism they should become clean. They should, He said, until that time take His words on faith.

Jesus then gave an instruction to the priests and kings alone. He told them that whatever in their doctrine bore an appearance of truth, was a mere lie: it had only the semblance, the empty form of truth, and the demon himself gave it that form. As soon as the good angel withdraws, Satan steps forward, corrupts worship, and takes it under his own guardianship. Heretofore, Jesus continued, they had honored all those objects to which they could attach some idea of strength, and of that worship they had omitted many things after their return from Bethlehem. Now, however, He told them they should do away with those figures of animals, should melt them down:

and He indicated to them the people to whom their value should be given. All their worship, all their knowledge, He said, valued nothing. They should inculcate love and mercy without the aid of those images, and thank the Father in Heaven that He had so mercifully called them to the knowledge of Himself. Jesus promised them that He would send one who would more fully instruct them, and He directed them to remove the wheel with its starry representations. It was as large as a carriage wheel of moderate size and had seven concentric rims, on the uppermost and the lowest of which were fastened globes from which streamed rays. The central point consisted of a larger globe, which represented the earth. On the circumference of the wheel were twelve stars, in which were as many different pictures, splendid and glittering. I saw among them one of a virgin with rays of light flashing from her eyes and playing around her mouth, while on her forehead sparkled precious stones; and another of an animal with something in its mouth that emitted sparks. But I could not see all distinctly, because the wheel was constantly revolving. The figures were not all visible at the same time, for at intervals some were hidden.

Jesus desired to leave them some bread and wine blessed by Himself. The priests had, in obedience to His directions, prepared some very fine white bread like little cakes, and a small jug of some kind of red liquor. Jesus specified the shape of the vessel in which all was to be preserved. It was like a large mortar. It had two ears, a cover with a knob, and was divided into two compartments. The bread was deposited in the upper one; and in the lower one, in which there was a small door, the little jug of liquor was placed. The outside shone like quicksilver, but the inside was yellow. Jesus placed the bread and the wine on the little altar, prayed, and blessed, while the priests and the two Kings knelt before Him, their hands crossed on their breast. Jesus prayed over them, laid His hands on their shoulders, and instructed them how they should renew the bread, which He cut for them crosswise, giving them the words and the ceremony of benediction. This bread and wine were to be for them a symbol of Holy Communion. The Kings had some knowledge of Melchisedech, and they questioned Jesus concerning his sacrifice. When He blessed the bread for them, He gave them some idea of His Passion and of the Last Supper. They should, He told them, make use of the bread and wine for the first time on the anniversary of their adoration at the Crib, and after that three times in the year, or every three months, I cannot recall it exactly.

Next day Jesus again taught in the temple wherein all were gathered. He went in and out, leaving one crowd to go to another. He allowed the women and children also to come and speak to Him, and He instructed the mothers how to rear their children and teach them to pray. This was the first time that I saw many children gathered together here. The boys wore only a short tunic, and the little girls, mantles. The children of the converted lady were present. She was a person of distinction and her spouse, a tall man, was near King Mensor. She had fully ten children with her. Jesus blessed them, laying His hand not on the head as He did to the children of Judea, but on the shoulder.

He instructed the people upon His mission and His approaching end, and told them that His journey into their country was unknown to the Jews. He had, He said, brought with Him as companions youths that would take no scandal at what they saw and heard, and who were docile to all His words. The Jews would have taken His life, had He not made His escape. But apart from all that, He was desirous of visiting them because they had visited Him, had believed in Him, hoped in Him, and loved Him. He admonished them to thank God for not allowing them to be entirely blinded by idolatry and for giving them the true belief in Himself and the grace to keep His Commandments. If I do not mistake, He spoke to them also of the time of His return to His Heavenly Father, when He would send to them His disciples. He told them too that He was going down into Egypt where as a child He had been with His Mother, for there were some people there who had known Him in His childhood. He would, however, remain quite unknown, as there were Jews there who would willingly seize Him and deliver Him to His enemies, but His time was not yet come.

The pagans could not understand the human foresight of Jesus. In their childlike simplicity, they mentally asked themselves: "How could they do such things to Him, since He is truly God!" Jesus answered their thoughts by telling them that He was man also, that the Father had sent Him to lead back all the scattered, that as a man, He could suffer and be persecuted by men when His hour would have come, and because He was a man, He could be thus intimate with them.

He warned them again to renounce all kinds of idolatry and to love one another. In speaking of His own Passion, He touched upon true compassion. They should, He said, desist from their excessive care of sick animals, and turn their love toward their fellow beings both as regards body and soul; and if there were in their neighborhood none that stood in need of assistance, they should seek at a distance for such as did, and pray for all their destitute brethren. He told them also that what they did for the needy, they did for Him, and He made them understand that they were not to treat the lower animals with cruelty. They had entire tents filled with sick animals of all kinds, which they even provided with little beds. They were especially fond of dogs, of which I saw many large ones with enormous heads.

ARRIVAL OF THE LEADER OF A
STRANGE TRIBE

Jesus had already taught these pagans for some time, when I saw approaching a caravan on camels. It paused and remained standing at some distance while an old man, a stranger and the leader of the tribe, dismounted and drew near. He was attended by an aged servant whom he very highly respected, and both stood still at a little distance from the assembly. No one noticed them until the Lord's discourse was ended and He, with the disciples, had retired to the tent to take some refreshment. Then the stranger was received by Mensor, and shown to a tent. He afterward went with his old servant to the priests and told them that he could not believe Jesus to be the promised King of the Jews, because He treated with them so familiarly. The Jews had as he well knew, he continued, an Ark wherein was their God, and to it no one dare approach, consequently this Man could not be their God. The old servant also gave utterance to some erroneous conceptions of Mary; still both he and his master were good people. This King too had seen the wonderful star, but he had not followed it. He spoke much of his gods, whom he held in high esteem, and told how gracious they were to him, and that they brought him all kinds of good luck. He related also an incident that happened during a war which he had lately waged, and in which his gods had helped him and his old servant had brought him a certain piece of news. This King was of lighter complexion than Mensor, his clothing was shorter, and the turban round his head not so large. He was very much attached to his idols, one of which he always carried about with him on a camel. It was a figure with many arms, and with holes in its body in which could be placed the sacrifices offered it. He had some women in his caravan, which consisted of about thirty persons. As for himself, he was a very simple-minded man. He looked upon his old servant as an oracle, indeed he honored him even as a prophet. The latter had induced his master to make this journey, that he might show him, as he said, the Greatest of all the gods, but Jesus did not appear to answer his expectations. What the Lord said of compassion and beneficence pleased him greatly, for he was himself very charitable. He declared that he looked upon it as the greatest crime to neglect human beings for the sake of the lower animals. A meal was afterward prepared for the stranger, but at which Jesus was not present. I did not see Him even conversing with him. The King's name sounded like Acicus. The old servant was an astrologer. He was clothed like a prophet in a long robe with a girdle that had many knots around it. His turban had numerous white cords and knots pendent from it. They looked as if made of cotton, and he wore a long beard. The royal stranger and his followers were of fairer complexion than the natives of these parts, among whom they were going to sojourn for some time. The women and their other followers they had left behind near the women's tents. They had come a two days' journey. I did not see Jesus conversing with them, but I heard Him say that they would come to the knowledge of the truth, and He praised the King's compassion for men. I heard names that sounded like Ormusd and Zorosdat. The husband of Cuppes was a son of Mensor's brother. He had, when a youth, accompanied his uncle to Bethlehem. He and Cuppes were of a yellowish-brown complexion, and both were descendants of Job.

Jesus still taught after nightfall in and around the temple. The whole place was brilliantly illuminated, the temple itself a blaze of light. The inhabitants of the whole region were gathered together, old and young, men and women. Upon the first command of Jesus, they had removed the idols. But I now saw something in the temple that I had not before noticed. Up in the roof, I saw a whole firmament of shining stars, and in between were reflected little gardens and brooks and bushes, which were placed up high in the temple and illumined with lights. It was a most wonderful contrivance, and I cannot imagine how it was done.

9. JESUS LEAVES THE TENT CITY OF THE KINGS, AND GOES TO VISIT AZARIAS, THE NEPHEW OF MENSOR, IN THE SETTLEMENT OF ATOM

Jesus left the tent city of the Kings before daybreak when the lamps were still burning. They had arranged for Him a festive escort such as had welcomed Him, but He declined the attention and would not even accept a camel. The disciples took with them only some bread and some kind of liquor in flasks. The aged Mensor earnestly entreated Jesus to remain longer with them. He laid the crown that he wore on his turban at Jesus' feet, and offered Him all that he possessed. His treasures were deposited under a grating in the floor of his tent, as in a cellar. They lay there in bars, lumps, and little heaps of grains. Mensor wept like a child. The tears rolled like pearls down his brownish-yellow cheeks. His ancestor Job had the same complexion. It was a very delicate, shining brown, not so dark as that of the people near the Ganges. All wept and sobbed on parting.

Jesus left the city by the side upon which stood the temple, and passed the magnificent tent of the converted Cuppes, who ran forward with her children to meet Him. Jesus drew the children to Himself and spoke to the mother, who cast herself prostrate at His feet in tears. Mensor, the priests, and many others escorted Jesus, walking at His side two and two in turn. Jesus and the disciples carried staves. When Mensor and the priests reached home, it was already dark. Lamps were burning everywhere and all the people were gathered in and around the temple, kneeling in prayer or prostrate on the ground. Mensor announced to them that everyone who was not willing to live according to the Law of Jesus, and who did not believe in His doctrine, should leave his dominions. There were people here of a complexion still darker than Mensor. His tent city, with its temple and the burial place of the Kings, was the metropolis of the star worshippers, but at some hours' distance in the surrounding district there were other tent settlements.

Jesus journeyed eastward. He took up His first night quarters in a shepherd village belonging to Mensor's tribe and at about twelve hours from his tent castle. He slept with His disciples in a circular tent, whose sleeping places were separated from one another by movable screens.

Next morning Jesus left before the inhabitants were awake. I saw Him arrive at a stream that was too wide to ford, in consequence of which He turned His steps northward along its banks until He came to a spot that could be easily crossed. Toward evening He arrived at some huts, built either of moss or earth, near which was an uncovered well surrounded by a rampart. Here He and His companions washed their feet and, without a reception from anyone, turned into a hut made of leafy branches and there slept during the night. This hut was round with a pointed roof. It was open on all sides and appeared to be formed of twisted branches and moss; around it was a closely woven hedge to keep off wild animals. This region was very fruitful. I saw most beautiful fields bordered by rows of thick, shady trees, and at the corners where the trees met were dwellings, not tents like Mensor's, but round huts woven of branches. The inhabitants of this region were of a sunburnt complexion; their skin was not so rich a brown as Mensor's. They were clad very much like the first star worshippers whom Jesus had met on this journey. The women wore wide pantalets and over them a mantle. The people appeared to be engaged in weaving. From tree to tree, far apart from each other, were stretched pieces of stuff and thread, and many were busy working upon them at the same time. The whole length of the fields, the trees were trimmed in ornamental form, and seats were arranged up in the branches.

At the first dawn of morning, when the stars were still to be seen in the sky, several people went to the hut, but when they saw Jesus and the disciples still upon their couches, they drew back full of awe and prostrated on the ground. They had toward morning received through a courier from Mensor the news of Jesus' coming, but they did not know that He was already among them. Jesus arose, girded His white undergarment, threw on the mantle which the disciples used to carry in a bundle on their journeys, and after He had prayed with the youths and they had washed His feet, He stepped out of the hut to where the people were lying prostrate on their faces, and bade them not to be frightened at Him. Then He went with them to their temple, a great, oblong building with a flat roof upon which one could walk. It had two railings on the roof, and by them I saw some people gazing at the sky through tubes. In front of the temple was the closed fountain, esteemed sacred by the natives, and a pan of coals. The latter was raised a little above the ground, so that one could see under it. All around the temple were places for the people, separated from one another by bars. The priests that I saw wore long, white garments, trimmed from top to bottom with many-colored laces, and a broad girdle with a long end upon which were glittering stones and an inscription in letters. From their shoulders hung strips of leather, to which little shields were attached. When Jesus reached the temple, He called one of the priests down from the roof where he was observing the stars. The lord of this pastoral settlement, a paternal nephew of Mensor, came forth from the temple to greet Jesus and hand to Him the peace branch. Jesus took it and passed it to Eremenzear, who handed it to Silas who, in turn, gave it to Eliud. Eremenzear again received it and bore it into the temple, followed by Jesus and the rest of the party. Here they found a little round altar upon which stood a cup without a handle, something like a mortar. In it was a yellowish pap, into which Eremenzear stuck the branch. This latter was either dried or artificial. It had leaves on both sides, and it seems to me that Jesus said it would become green. The images in the temple were enveloped as with a covering, or mask of very light, stiff material. A teacher's chair had been erected in the enclosure of the temple, and there Jesus taught. He questioned His hearers, as if they were children, upon all that He said. The women stood far in the background. The people were very childlike and accepted everything willingly. Jesus spent the greater part of the day in teaching, and that night accepted hospitality from the lord of the settlement, whose dwelling consisted of several stories. It was a circular edifice with outside steps running around it. Above the door was fastened an oval shield of yellow metal, upon which were inscribed the words, "Azarias of Atom." Azarias had not been able to live upon good terms with Mensor, and hence the latter had divided with him the pasture grounds; but after Jesus' visit, he changed for the better. The interior of his dwelling was very beautiful, fitted up with fine colored carpets and tapestry, and communicating by a covered tent corridor with the apartments of his wife.

When the Sabbath began, Jesus withdrew with His disciples in order to celebrate it as He had done in the tent city of the Kings.

THE WONDERFUL CURE OF TWO SICK WOMEN

While Jesus was celebrating the Sabbath with the disciples in the open hut in which He had passed the first night, I saw the sick wife of Azarias seeking her cure before an idol. The lady had many children, and I saw in her apartments several other women, maidservants perhaps. Back from the fireplace and in a corner between the apartments stood a slab, or table, supported on columns. On it was a beautiful pedestal pierced on all sides with holes and covered with a little ornamental roof of leaves and foliage. The pedestal supported an idol in the form of a sitting dog with a thick, flat head. It was resting upon some written pages which were fastened together with cords in the form of a book, one of its forepaws raised over it as if drawing attention to it. Above this idol arose another, a scandalous-looking figure with many arms. I saw priests bringing in fire from the pan near the temple and pouring it under the hollow figure of the sitting dog, whose eyes began to sparkle, and from his mouth and nose immediately issued fire and smoke. Two women conducted Azarias's wife (who was afflicted with an issue of blood) up to the idol and placed her upon cushions and rugs before it. Azarias himself was present. The priests prayed, burnt incense, and offered sacrifice before the idol, but all to no purpose. Flames shot forth from it, and in the dense black smoke issued horrible doglike figures that disappeared in the air. The sick woman became perfectly miserable. She sank down faint and exhausted like one in a dying state, saying "These idols cannot help me! They are wicked spirits! They cannot longer remain here, they are fleeing from the Prophet, the King of the Jews, who is amongst us. We have seen His star and have followed Him! The Prophet alone can help me!" After uttering these words, she fell back immovable and, to all appearances, lifeless.

The bystanders were filled with terror. They had been under the impression that Jesus was only an envoy of the King of the Jews. They went immediately to the retired hut in which He and the disciples were celebrating the Sabbath, and respectfully begged Him to go to the sick woman. They told Him that she had cried out that He alone could help her, and they informed Him likewise of the impotence of their idols.

Jesus was still in His sabbatic robes, the disciples also, when they went to the sick woman, who was lying like one at the point of death. In earnest, vehement words, Jesus inveighed against idols and their worship. They were, He said, the servants of Satan, and all in them was bad. He reproached Azarias for this, that after his return from Bethlehem, whither as a youth he had accompanied the Kings, he had again sunk so deep into the abominations of idolatry. He concluded by saying that if they would believe in His doctrine, would obey the Commandments of God, and would allow themselves to be baptized, He would in three years send His Apostle to them, and He would now help the lady. Then He questioned the latter, and she answered: "Yes, I do believe in Thee!" All the bystanders gave Him the same assurance.

The screens had been removed from around the tent, and a crowd of people were standing by. Jesus asked for a basin of water, but bade them not to bring it from their sacred fountain. He wanted only ordinary water, nor would He use their holy water sprinkler. They had to bring Him a fresh branch with fine, narrow leaves. They had likewise to cover their idols, which they did with fine, white tapestry embroidered in gold. Jesus placed the water on the altar. The three disciples stood around Him, one at either side, right and left, and the third behind Him. One of them handed Him a metal box from the wallet that they always carried with them. Several such boxes of oil and cotton were placed one above the other.

In that which the disciple handed to Jesus, there was a fine, white powder, which appeared to me to be salt. Jesus sprinkled some of it on the water, and bent low over it. He prayed, blessed it with His hand, dipped the branch into it, sprinkled the water over all around Him, and extended His hand to the woman with the command to arise. She obeyed instantly, and rose up cured. She threw herself on her knees and wanted to embrace His feet, but He would not suffer her to touch Him.

This cure effected, Jesus proclaimed to the crowd that there was another lady present who was much more indisposed than the first and who, notwithstanding, did not ask His help. She adored not an idol, but a man. This lady, by name Ratimiris, was married. Her malady consisted in this, that at the sight, the name, or even the thought of a certain youth, she fell into a sort of fever and became ill into death. The youth, meanwhile, was perfectly ignorant of her state.[1] Ratimiris, at the call of Jesus, stepped forward greatly confused. Jesus took her aside, laid before her all the circumstances both of her sickness and her sins, all which she freely acknowledged. The youth was one of the temple servers, and whenever she brought her offerings, which he was charged to receive, she fell into that sad state. After Jesus had spoken awhile with her alone, He led her again before the people, and asked her whether she believed in Him and whether she would be baptized when He would send His Apostle hither. When she, deeply repentant, answered that she did believe and that she would be baptized, Jesus drove the devil out of her. The evil one departed in the form of a spiral column of black vapor.

The youth's name was Caisar, and there was something of John in his appearance. He was pure and chaste, a descendant of Ketura and a relative of Eremenzear, who also was from this place. It was for this reason that on their reception, Jesus had given to him the peace branch first.

Caisar spoke with the disciples, for he had long had secret presentiments of salvation. He told them several dreams he had had, among others one in which he dreamed that he had carried a great many people through water. The disciples thought that it signified perhaps that he would convert many. I saw that he accompanied Jesus on His departure. Three years after Christ's Ascension, when Thomas baptized in these parts, he returned with Thaddeus. Later on he was sent by Thomas to the Bishop of a certain place where, though innocent, he was, to the great joy of his soul, crucified as a robber and criminal.

Jesus taught here until day dawned and the burning lamps went out. He commanded the people to destroy their images of the devil, and reproached them for adoring woman under a diabolical figure, and yet treating their women worse than dogs, which animals they held sacred. Toward morning Jesus retired again into the solitary house in order to celebrate the Sabbath.

I was told why Jesus kept this journey so secret. I remember that He said to His Apostles and disciples that He would go away for a little while only, in order that the public might lose sight of Him, but they knew nothing of the journey. He had taken with Him those innocent boys because they would not be scandalized at His intercourse with the heathens, and would not remark things too closely. He had likewise strictly forbidden them to speak of the journey, on which account one of them said in all simplicity: "The blind man whom Thou didst forbid to speak of his cure, did not remain silent, and yet Thou didst not punish him!" Jesus replied: "That happened for the glory of God, but this would bear fruits of scandal." I think the Jews, and even the Apostles themselves, would have been somewhat scandalized had they known that Jesus had been among the pagans.

When the Sabbath was over, the Lord called all together again and instructed them. He blessed some water for them and directed them to prepare for Him a chalice like that used by Mensor. Here too as in the former place, He blessed for them bread and the red liquor. In the cup into which Eremenzear upon his arrival had stuck the branch in order to keep it fresh, there was a yellowish-green substance, something like pap, which consisted of the pulp of a plant from which the juice had been expressed. This juice the natives drank as something holy. I saw Jesus the whole night between Saturday and Sunday teaching in front of the temple. He Himself helped to smash the idols, and He told the pagans how they should distribute the value of the metal. I saw Him also, as in Mensor's land, imposing hands upon the shoulders of the priests, teaching them how to divide the blessed bread, and here as there preparing the beverage. The vessel used here, however, was larger.

Azarias later on became a priest and martyr. The two women also whom Jesus cured here, were afterward martyred like Cuppes. The Lord spoke against a multiplicity of wives, and gave instructions on the married state. The wife of Azarias, as well as Ratimiris, wanted Jesus to baptize them right away. He replied that He could indeed do so, but that it would be inopportune. He must first return to the Father and send the Consoler, after which His Apostles would come and baptize them. They should, He said, live in the desire of Baptism and submission to His will, and such dispositions would, to those that might die in the interim, serve as Baptism. Ratimiris was in fact baptized under the name of Emily by Thomas when, three years after Christ's Ascension, he visited this country accompanied by Thaddeus and Caisar. They came in a direction more from the south than did Jesus, and it was then that the Kings and their people were baptized.

1. Sister Emmerich laughed much at this woman, and was wholly unable to comprehend her weakness. (Pilgrim's note to First Edition).

10. JESUS GOES TO SIKDOR, MOZIAN, AND UR

From Atom, Jesus went first toward the south, then eastwardly through a very fertile region cut up by rivers and canals and planted with fruit trees of various kinds, especially peaches, which grew in long rows. I heard the names Euphrates, Tigris, Chaldar, and I think Ur, the land of Abraham, and that place at which Thaddeus suffered martyrdom were not far distant. Toward evening, Jesus reached a row of flat-roofed houses occupied by Chaldeans. I heard Sikdor as the name of the place in which were established two schools, one for the priests of the country and the other for young girls. The people were not so fully clothed as those of the royal tent city. They wore only blankets over their cinctures, but they were good, and so lowly minded that they thought the Jews alone were the chosen for salvation. They had on a hill a pyramid surrounded by galleries, seats, and immense tubes pointed on high through which they observed the stars. They also predicted future events from the course of animals, and interpreted dreams. Their temple with its forecourt and fountain was oval in form, and occupied the center of the place. It contained numerous metal statues of exquisite workmanship. The principal object of note was a triangular column upon which rested three idols. The first had many feet and arms, the former not in human shape, but like the paws of animals. In its hands it held a globe, a circle, a large ribbed apple on a stem, and bunches of herbs. The face of the figure was like a sun, and its name was Mytor, or Mitras. The second was a unicorn, and it was called Asphas, or Aspax. This animal was represented in the act of using its horn in a struggle against a wild beast that was standing on the third side of the column. It had the head of an owl, a hooked beak, four legs with talons, two wings, and a tail, which last appendage ended like that of a scorpion.

Above these two animals, namely, the unicorn and the wild beast, and projecting from one of the sharp edges of the column, stood another figure, which represented the mother of all the gods. Her name was Woman, or Alpha. She was the most powerful of all their divinities, and whoever desired to obtain anything from the supreme god was obliged to plead for it through her. They called her, likewise, the Granary. Out of the figure issued a large sheaf of wheat, apparently growing, which she clasped with both hands. The head was bowed, and on the neck, bent low between the shoulders, rested a vessel of wine. Above the figure hung a crown, and above the crown were inscribed on the column two letters, or symbols, that looked to me like an O or a W. The lesson taught by these images was that the wheat was to become bread and that the wine was to inebriate all mankind.

There was besides in the temple a brazen altar, and what was my astonishment to see upon it, under a revolving dome, a little circular garden railed in with gold wire like a bird cage, and above it the image of a young virgin! In the center of the garden and roofed in by a little temple was a fountain with several sealed basins one above the other. In front of the fountain rose a green vine with a cluster of red grapes, which drooped over a press whose form reminded me of a cross. From the upper end of a tall stem projected a funnel-shaped, self-opening, leathern pouch with two movable arms, through which the juice of the grapes put into it could be pressed out and allowed to flow down below upon the stem. The little garden was about five or six feet in diameter. It was planted with delicate green bushes and little trees, which like the vine and its grapes looked perfectly natural. They owed this symbol to their star gazing, and they had many others that bespoke their presentiments of the Blessed Mother of God. They sacrificed animals, but had a special horror of blood, which they always allowed to run off into the earth. They had likewise their sacred fire and water, their chalice of vegetable juice, and their little loaves, like the people of Atom. Jesus reproved them for their idolatry and for mixing up heavenly predictions and prognostics with Satanic errors. Their symbols, He said, had in them indeed some notions of truth, but they were discordant and filled with Satan. He explained to them the symbol of the garden enclosed. He told them that He Himself was the vine whose sap, whose blood, was to quicken the world, that He Himself was the grain of wheat which was to be buried in the earth thence to rise again. Jesus spoke here much more freely, much more significantly than among the Jews, for these people were humble. He comforted them by telling them that He had come for all mankind, and He commanded them to break up their idols and give their value to the poor. They showed signs of deep feeling when He was about leaving them, and threw themselves at His feet across the path in order to prevent His departure.

Some time after, I saw Jesus with the four disciples resting under a great tree that was surrounded by a hedge. It was in front of a house, from which they had been supplied with the bread and honey that they were eating. They journeyed on the whole of the night. I saw them on a plain walking sometimes over white stones, sometimes over meadows carpeted with white blossoms. On their way, they came across numbers of slender peach trees. At times the Lord paused, pointed around, and said something to the disciples. The country was intersected by numerous streams and canals. As a general thing, Jesus journeyed with extraordinary rapidity. He some-times travelled twenty hours without interruption. His way back to Judea described a very great curve. I am al-ways under the impression that Eremenzear wrote some details of this journey, though only a few fragments of his account escaped the fire that destroyed the rest.

On the evening of the second day of their departure from Sikdor, I saw Jesus and the disciples drawing near to a city outside of which rose a hill covered with circular gardens. Most of them had a fountain in the center and were planted with fine ornamental trees and shrubbery. The way taken by the Lord ran toward the south; Babylon lay to the north. It seemed as if one would have to descend a mountainous country to reach Babylon, which lay far below. The city was built on the river Tigris, which flowed through it. Jesus entered quietly and without pausing at the gates. It was evening, but few of the inhabitants were to be seen, and no one troubled himself about Him. Soon, however, I saw several men in long garments, like those worn by Abraham, and with scarfs wound round their head, coming to meet Him and inclining low before Him. One of them extended toward Him a short, crooked staff. It was made of reed, something like that afterward presented to Christ in derision, and was called the staff of peace. The others, two by two, held across the street a strip of carpet upon which Jesus walked. When He stepped from the first to the second, the former was raised and spread before the latter to be again in readiness for use, and so on. In this way they reached a courtyard, over whose grated entrance with its idols waved a standard upon which was represented the figure of a man holding a crooked staff like that presented to Jesus. The standard was the standard of peace. They led the Lord through a building from whose gallery floated another standard. It appeared to be the temple, for all around the interior stood veiled idols and in the center was another veiled in the same way, the veil being gathered above it to form a crown. The Lord did not pause here, but proceeded through a corridor, on either side of which were sleeping apartments. At last He and His attendants reached a little enclosed garden planted with delicate bushes and aromatic shrubs, its walks paved in ornamental figures with different kinds of colored stone. In the center rose a fountain under a little temple open on all sides, and here the Lord and the disciples sat down. In answer to Jesus' request, the idolaters brought some water in a basin. The Lord first blessed it, as if to annul the pagan benediction, and then the disciples washed His feet and He theirs, after which they poured what remained into the fountain. The pagans then conducted the Lord into an open hall adjoining, in which a meal had been prepared: large yellow, ribbed apples and other kinds of fruit; honeycombs; bread in the form of thin cakes, like waffles; and something else in little, square morsels. The table upon which they were spread was very low. The guests ate standing. Jesus' coming had been announced to these people by the priests of the neighboring city. They had in consequence expected Him the whole day and at last received Him with so much solemnity. Abraham also had received a staff of welcome such as had been presented to Jesus.

The name of this city was Mozin, or Mozian. It was a sacerdotal city, but sunk deep in idolatry. Jesus did not enter the temple. I saw Him teaching a crowd of people on a graded hill surrounded by a wall. It was in front of the temple and near a fountain. He reproved them severely for having fallen into idolatry even more deeply than their neighbors, showed them the abominations of their worship, and told them that they had abandoned the Law. I heard Him referring to the destruction of the Temple in the time of their forefathers, and speaking of Nabuchodonosor and Daniel. He said that they should separate, the believing from the spiritually blind, for there were some good souls among them, and to these He indicated whither they should go. Many of the others were stiff-necked. There was one point that they would not understand, and that was the necessity for abolishing polygamy. The women dwelt in a street to themselves at the extreme end of the city, to which, however, there was communication by shaded walks. They seemed to be held in great contempt, and after a certain age the young girls dared not appear in public. No woman of this place saw Jesus. Only the boys were present with the men.

Jesus used severe words toward these people. They were, He said, so blinded, so obstinate, that when the Apostle that He was going to send would make his appearance, he would find them unprepared for Baptism. Jesus would not remain longer with them. As He was leaving the city, a procession of young girls met Him at the gate, chanting hymns of praise in His honor. They wore white pantalets, had garlands around their arms and necks, and flowers in their hands.

From Mozian, Jesus went with His companions across a large field to a village of pastoral tents. He sat down near the fountain, the disciples washed His feet, and some men of the place approached with the branch of welcome and gave Him a glad reception. They were clad in long garments, more like Abraham than any others I had yet seen, and they possessed an astronomical pyramid. I saw no idols. These people appeared to be pure star worshippers and to belong to that race of whom some had accompanied the Kings to Bethlehem. They appeared to me to be only a little band of shepherds, of whom the Superior alone had a permanent dwelling. Jesus ate bread and fruit in his house standing, and drank out of a special vessel. He afterward taught at the well. When He was leaving them, the people threw themselves across His path and entreated Him to remain with them.

On departing from this place, Jesus travelled throughout the whole of that night and the following day. Once I saw Him with the disciples taking a little rest by a fountain under a large shade tree. It was a public resting place for travellers, and there Jesus ate some bread and took a drink. The city to which He was going was thirty hours to the south of Mozian, but still on the Tigris. It was called Ur, or Urhi. Jesus reached it on that evening before the commencement of the Sabbath. Abraham was from this region. Jesus went to a well outside the city which was surrounded by large shade trees and stone benches. Here the disciples washed the Lord's feet and then their own, lowered their girded garments, and entered the city, whose architecture struck me as different from any other I had seen in these parts. The men and women did not appear to live so much apart. There were many towers provided with galleries and tubes for observing the stars, and to them led steps both inside and outside. The people knew from the stars of the Lord's coming, consequently they had expected Him and taken every stranger for Him. When, therefore, Jesus' entrance into the city was noticed by some, they hurried to a large flat-roofed house which stood in a large open space, in order to give notice of His arrival. From this house, which appeared to be a school and from which waved a flag, there now issued several men in long garments of one single color, and proceeded to meet Jesus. They were girded with cinctures whose ends hung long and loose, and they wore round caps bordered by a roll of wool, or little feathers, whose strips met on top and formed a plume. The hair could be seen through them. The men prostrated before Jesus, and then led Him and His companions back to the school, which consisted of one immense hall. To it flocked crowds of people. Jesus taught for a short time from an elevated seat at the top of a flight of steps, after which He was conducted to another house in which a meal had been prepared. But Jesus took only a few mouthfuls standing, and then went alone with the disciples into a retired apartment where they celebrated the Sabbath. Next day He taught near a fountain on an open place upon which was a stone seat used for teaching. All the women of the place were present, and so enveloped in their narrow garments that they could scarcely walk. Their caps were like cowls, from which hung two lappets. Jesus spoke of Abraham, and made some severe remarks on the fact of their being sunk in idolatry. There were idolatrous temples here, but the idols were veiled. The Lord did not go into any of them. Thomas did not baptize these people at his first visit to them.

When Jesus left Ur, the people accompanied Him, strewing branches in His way. He journeyed toward the west for a long time, over a beautiful plain which toward the end became sandy, and lastly was covered with underwood. About noon they reached a well by which they sat down to rest. The remainder of the journey was made through a wood and over cultivated land, until toward evening they arrived at a great, round building encircled by a courtyard and moat. All around stood heavy-looking houses with flat roofs. That of the great building was covered with verdure and even trees, while in the massive wall of the courtyard were the abodes of some poor people. At the fountain in the courtyard Jesus and the disciples washed their feet, as usual. And now, from the round house came forth two men in long garments profusely trimmed with laces and ribands, and wearing feather caps on their heads. The elder of the two carried a green branch and a little bunch of berries, which he presented to Jesus, who with the disciples followed him into the building. In the center of the house was a hall, lighted from the roof, whose fireplace was reached by steps. From this circular apartment, they proceeded around through irregularly shaped rooms opening one into the other, and whose end wall, concave in form, was hung with tapestry, behind which all sorts of utensils were kept. The floor was level, and like the walls covered with thick carpets. In one of these apartments, Jesus and His companions took a frugal repast and drank something from vessels never before used. What the beverage was, I do not know.

After the meal, the master of the house took Jesus all around and showed Him everything. The whole castle was filled with beautifully wrought idols. There were figures of all sizes, large and small, some with a head like that of an ox, others like that of a dog, and a serpent's body. One of them had many arms and heads, and into its jaws could be put all kinds of things. There were also some figures of swathed infants. Under the trees in the courtyard, stood idols in the form of animals, for instance, birds looking upward, and other animals standing around. These people sacrificed animals, but they had a horror of blood, which they always allowed to run off into the earth. They had, also, the custom of distributing bread, of which the more distinguished among them received a larger portion.

Jesus taught at the fountain in the courtyard, and strongly inveighed against their diabolical worship, though His words were not taken in good part. I saw that their chief was particularly obstinate in his errors. He was irritated at Jesus, and even contradicted Him. Thereupon I heard Jesus telling the people that, as a proof of the truth of His words, on the night of the anniversary of the star's appearing to the Kings, the idols would fall to pieces, those that represented oxen would bellow, the dogs would bark, and the birds would scream. They listened to His predictions disdainfully and incredulously. This was what Jesus had told all whom He had visited on this journey. In all places at which He stopped on His way into the land of the heathens, He predicted that this would happen. On the holy night of Christmas, I had a vision of this whole journey from the pagan city near Kedar to the tent city of the Three Kings, and thence to this last pagan castle; and everywhere I saw the idols going to pieces, and heard bellowing and barking and screaming from those that represented animals. The Kings I saw at prayer in their temple. Numerous lights burned around the little crib, and it seems to me there was now the figure of an ass standing by it. They, it is true, no longer revered their idols; but those in the form of animals bellowed as a sign that Jesus was really the One to whom the star had led them, a fact still doubted perhaps by some weak in faith.

11. JESUS GOES TO EGYPT, TEACHES IN HELIOPOLIS, AND RETURNS TO JUDEA THROUGH THE DESERT

From the castle of the idols, Jesus' route now lay toward the west. He travelled quickly with His four companions, pausing nowhere, but ever hurrying on. First, they crossed a sandy desert, toiled slowly up a steep mountain ridge, pursued their way over a country covered with vegetation, then through low bushes like juniper bushes, whose branches, meeting overhead, formed a covered walk. After that they came to a stony region overrun with ivy, thence through meadows and woods until they reached a river, not rapid, but deep, over which they crossed on a raft of beams. It was still night when they arrived at a city built either on both sides of the river, or on one of its branches, or on a canal. It was the first Egyptian city on their route. Here, unobserved by anyone, Jesus and His companions retired under the porch of a temple, where were some sleeping places for travellers. The city appeared to me very much gone to ruin. I saw great, thick walls, massive stone houses, and many poor people. I had an interior perception that Jesus had journeyed hither by the same side of the desert by which the Children of Israel had come.

Next morning, as Jesus and the disciples were leaving the city, children ran after them crying out: "There go holy people!" The inhabitants were very much excited, inasmuch as great disturbances had happened the night before. Many of the idols had fallen from their places, and the children had been dreaming and uttering prophetic words about certain "holy people" that had entered the city.

Jesus and the disciples departed hurriedly, and plunged into the deep ravines that traversed the sandy region. That evening I saw them, not far from a city, resting and taking food at the source of a brook, the disciples having washed Jesus' feet. Nearby on a great round stone was stretched the figure of a dog in a lying posture. It had a human head, the expression of the face quite friendly. It wore a cap, like that worn by the people of the country, a band with hanging lappets notched at the ends. The figure was as large as a cow. Under a tree outside the city stood an idol whose head was like that of an ox. It had holes pierced in its body and several arms. Five streets led from the gate into the great city, and Jesus took the first to the right. It ran along the city wall, which was like a rampart on top of which were gardens, and a carriage way. In the lower part of the walls were dwellings shut in by light doors of wickerwork. Jesus and His disciples passed through the city by night without speaking to anyone, or being remarked by anyone. Here too, there were several idolatrous temples, and many massive buildings gone to ruins in whose walls people lived.

At a good distance from this city, the way led over an immense stone bridge across the broadest river (*the Nile*) that I saw on this journey. It flowed from south to north, and divided into many branches that ran in different directions. The country was low and level, and off in the distance I saw some very high buildings in form like the temples of the star worshippers, though built of stone and much higher. The soil was exceedingly fruitful, but only along the river.

About one hour's distance from that city in which
Jesus as a child had dwelt with His Mother (*Heliopolis*),
He took the same road by which, with Mary and Joseph,
He had entered it. It was situated on the first arm of the
Nile, which flows in the direction of Judea. I saw here
and there on the way people clipping the hedges,
transporting rafters, and laboring in deep ditches. It was
nearly evening when Jesus approached the city. Both He
and the disciples had let down their garments, something
that I had never seen them do before reaching their destination. Some of the laborers, as Jesus came in sight,
broke off branches from the trees, hurried forward to
meet Him, cast themselves down before Him, and presented them to Him. After He had taken them in His
hand, they stuck them down into the ground along the
roadside. I know not how they recognized Jesus. Perhaps
they knew by His garments that He was a Jew. They had
been waiting and hoping for His coming that He would
free them. I saw others, however, who appeared indignant, and who ran back to the city. About twenty men
surrounded Jesus as He went to the city, before which
stood many trees.

Before entering, Jesus paused near a tree that was
lying over on one side in such a way that its roots were
being torn out of the earth, and around them was a large
puddle of black water. This puddle was enclosed by a
high iron grating, the bars of which were so close that
one could not put his hand through. In this place an idol
had sunk at the time of Mary and Joseph's flight with the
Child Jesus into Egypt, on which occasion the tree, too,
had been uprooted. The people conducted Jesus into the
city. Before it lay a large, four-cornered, perfectly flat
stone, on which, among other names, was inscribed one
that bore reference to the city and that ended in the sylla-
ble *polis*. Inside the city, I saw a very large temple sur-

rounded by two courts, several high columns tapering toward the top and ornamented with numerous figures, and a great many huge dogs with human heads, all in a recumbent posture. The city showed evident signs of decay. The people led Jesus under the projection of a thick wall opposite the temple, and called to several of the citizens of the neighborhood. Then came together many Jews, young and old, among the latter some very aged men with long beards. Among the women there was one, tall and advanced in years, who pleased me especially. All welcomed Jesus respectfully, for they had been friends of the Holy Family at the time of their sojourn here. In the back of the projecting wall was a space, now ornamented in festal style, in which St. Joseph had prepared an abode for the Holy Family. The men who had in their childhood lived in this neighborhood with Jesus, introduced Him to it. The apartment was lighted by hanging lamps.

That evening Jesus was escorted by a very aged Jew to the school, which was very ably conducted. The women took their stand back on a grated gallery, where they had a lamp to themselves. Jesus prayed and taught, for they reverently yielded precedence to Him. On the following day, I saw Him again teaching in the synagogue.

The inhabitants of this city wore white bands around their heads, their tunics were short, and only a part of their shoulders and breast was covered. The edifices were extraordinarily broad and massive, built of immense blocks of stone upon which numerous figures were carved. I saw also great figures that bore prodigious stones, some upon their neck, others on their head. The people of this country practiced the most extravagant idolatry. Everywhere were to be met idols in the form of oxen, recumbent dogs with human heads, and other animals held in peculiar veneration in special places.

When Jesus, escorted by many of the inhabitants, left

Heliopolis, He took with Him a young man belonging to the city, and who now made His fifth disciple. His name was Deodatus, and that of his mother was Mira. She was that tall old lady who had, on the first evening of Jesus' arrival, been among those that welcomed Him under the portico. During Mary's sojourn in Heliopolis, Mira was childless; but on the prayer of the Blessed Virgin, this son was afterward given her. He was tall and slender, and appeared to be about eighteen years old. When His escort had returned to the city, I saw Jesus journeying through the desert with His five disciples. He took a direction more to the east than that taken by the Holy Family on their flight into Egypt. The city in which Jesus had just been was called Eliopolis (*Heliopolis*). The E and the L were joined back to back, something that I had never before seen, on which account I thought there was an X in the word.[1]

Toward evening, Jesus and His disciples reached a little city in the wilderness inhabited by three different kinds of people: Jews, who dwelt in solid houses; Arabs, who lived in huts built of branches covered with skins; and still another kind. These people had drifted hither when Antiochus ravaged Jerusalem and expelled many of its inhabitants. I saw the whole affair. A pious old priest[2] slew a Jew who had gone forward to sacrifice to the idol, overturned the altar, called all good people together and, like a hero, maintained the Law and testament of God. It was during this persecution that these good people had fled hither. I saw also the place at which they first lived. The Arabs, having joined them, were likewise expelled with them. At a still later period they, the Arabs, fell again into idolatry. As usual the Lord went to the fountain, where He was welcomed by some of the people and conducted to one of their houses. There He taught, for they had no school. Jesus told them that the time was at hand when He should return to the Father, that the Jews

would maltreat Him, and He spoke as He had everywhere done on this journey. They could scarcely believe
what they heard, and they wanted very much to retain
Him with them.

When He left this place, two new disciples followed
Him, the descendants of Mathathias. The travellers now
plunged deeper into the wilderness and hurried onward
day and night with but short intervals of rest. I saw them
in a lovely spot of beautiful balsam hedges taking some
rest at that fountain which had gushed forth for the Holy
Family on their flight into Egypt, and with whose waters
Mary had refreshed herself and bathed her Child. The
road by which Jesus had returned from Egypt here
crossed the circuitous byway that Mary had taken on her
flight thither. Mary had come by an indirect route on the
west side of the desert, but Jesus had taken the eastern
one which was more direct. On His journey from Arabia
to Egypt, Jesus could descry on His right Mount Sinai
lying off in the distance.

When Jesus reached Bersabee, He taught in the synagogue. He formally declared His identity, and spoke of
His approaching end. From this place also He took with
Him on His departure some young men. It was about
four day's journey from Bersabee to Jacob's Well near
Sichar, the spot appointed for Jesus and the Apostles to
meet again. Before the beginning of the Sabbath Jesus
reached a place in the vale of Mambre where He celebrated the Sabbath in the synagogue and taught. He
likewise visited the homes of the inhabitants and healed
their sick. From this place to Jacob's Well it may have
been twenty hours at most. Jesus now travelled more by
night, in order that the news of His return to Judea might
not be the occasion of some sudden rising among the
people. He took the route through the shepherd valleys
near Jericho to Jacob's Well, at which He arrived during
the evening twilight. He had now sixteen companions,

since some other youths had followed Him from the vale of Mambre. In the neighborhood of the well was an inn where, in a locked place, was stored all that was necessary to contribute to the traveller's comfort when he stopped to rest. A man had the care of opening both the inn and the well. The country stretching out from Jericho to Samaria was one of indescribable loveliness. Almost the whole road was bordered by trees, the fields and meadows were green, and the brooks flowed sweetly along. Jacob's Well was surrounded by beautiful grass plots and shade trees. The Apostles Peter, Andrew, John, James, and Philip were here awaiting Jesus. They wept for joy at seeing Him again, and washed His and the disciples' feet.

Jesus was very grave. He spoke of the approach of His Passion, of the ingratitude of the Jews, and of the judgment in store for them. It was now only three months before His Passion. I have always seen that the feast of Easter falls at the right time when it happens late in the season. Jesus went with His sixteen new disciples to visit the parents of Eliud, Silas, and Eremenzear, who dwelt in a shepherd village not far off. The Apostles, however, betook themselves to Sichar for the Sabbath.

1. Sister Emmerich saw ⅂L.
2. Mathathias. See *1 Mach.* 2:23-25.

12. JESUS IN SICHEM, EPHRON, AND JERICHO

As Jesus was journeying with the new disciples from the shepherd village, where He remained only a few hours, to Sichem, I frequently saw Him standing still and giving them animated instructions. He ordered Eliud, Silas, and Eremenzear to disclose to no one where they had gone with Him nor what had befallen them on that journey, and He told them some of the reasons for silence on those subjects. I saw Eremenzear holding the sleeve of Jesus' robe and begging to be allowed to write down something about it. Jesus replied that he might do so after His death, but ordered him at the same time to leave the writing with John. I cannot help thinking that a part of that writing is still in existence somewhere.

Peter and John came forward to meet the Lord on His way, and outside the gate of the city were waiting six of the other Apostles. They conducted Him and the disciples to a house, the master of which, though he had never before seen Jesus, gave Him a cordial reception. Jesus, however, appeared not to wish to make Himself publicly known, but rather to be confounded with the Apostles. The feet of the newly arrived were washed, and when the Sabbath began, the lamps were lighted. Jesus and His companions put on long, white garments and girdles, and after prayers went to the school, which was built on a little eminence. After that they partook of a meal prepared by their host, at which some Jews with long beards were present. The eldest of them was clothed as a priest of superior rank, and was led by attendants. Neither in the school nor at table did Jesus make Himself known. The host had a false look, and it seemed to me that he was a Pharisee.

The meal over, Jesus demanded that the synagogue should be opened for Him. He had, He said, listened to their teaching, but now He too would teach. He spoke of signs and miracles, which are of no avail when in spite of them people forget their own sinfulness and want of love for God. Preaching was for them more necessary than miracles. Even before the meal the Apostles had besought Jesus to express Himself more clearly, for they did not yet understand Him. He was always talking of His approaching end, they said, but He might before it go once more to Nazareth, there to show forth His power and by miracles proclaim His mission. At this juncture also Jesus replied that miracles were useless if people were not converted by Him, if after witnessing them, they remained what they were before. What, He demanded, had He gained by signs and miracles, by the feeding of the five thousand, by the raising of Lazarus, since even they themselves were hankering after more. Peter and John were of one mind with their Master, but the others were dissatisfied. On the way to Sichem, Jesus had explained to Eliud, Silas, and Eremenzear why He had wrought no signs and wonders on His last journey. It was, He said, because the Apostles and disciples should confirm His doctrine by miracles, of which they would perform even more than He Himself had done. Jesus was displeased at the Apostles' wanting to find out from the three youths where He had been and what He had done. They were very much vexed at the youths' silence on being questioned. Jesus announced to them that He was going to Jerusalem and would preach in the Temple.

I saw that the Jews of Sichem sent messengers to report in Jerusalem that Jesus had again appeared, for the Pharisees of Sichem were among the most dissatisfied. They threatened to seize Jesus and deliver Him at Jerusalem. But Jesus replied that His time had not yet come, that He would Himself go to Jerusalem, and that not for their benefit, but for that of His own followers had He spoken.

Jesus now dismissed the Apostles and disciples to different places, keeping with Himself only the three that were in the secret of His last journey. With them He started for Ephron, in order to meet the holy women at a rented inn near Jericho. He had previously announced to them His return by the parents of the three disciples. On the journey from Sichem to Ephron, it was very foggy, and quantities of rain fell. Jesus did not confine Himself to the straight route. He went to different localities, different towns and houses, consoling the inhabitants, healing the sick, and exhorting all to follow Him. The Apostles and disciples likewise did not take the direct road to the places to which they were sent, but turned off into the farms and houses lying along their way in order to announce Jesus' coming. It was as if all who sighed after salvation were to be again stirred up, as if the sheep that had strayed in the forest because their Shepherd had gone away were, now that He had come back, to be gathered again by the shepherd servants into one herd. When, toward evening, Jesus with the three disciples arrived at Ephron, He went into the houses, cured the sick, and called upon all to follow Him to the school. This place had a large synagogue, consisting of two halls, one above and the other below. A crowd of people, men and women, some from Ephron and some from neighboring places, flocked to the instruction. The synagogue was crowded. Jesus directed a chair to be placed in the center of the hall whence He taught first the men and then the women. The latter were standing back, but the men gave place to them. Jesus taught upon the necessity of following Him, upon His approaching end, and upon the chastisement that would fall on all that would not believe. Murmuring arose in the crowd, for there were many wicked souls among them.

From Ephron Jesus despatched the three trusty disciples to meet the holy women who, to the number of ten, had reached the rented inn near Jericho. They were the Blessed Virgin, Magdalen, Martha, and two others, Peter's wife and stepdaughter, Andrew's wife, and Zacheus's wife and daughter. The last-mentioned was married to a very deserving disciple named Annadias, a shepherd and a relative of Silas's mother. Peter, Andrew, and John met Jesus on the road, and with them He went on to Jericho. The Blessed Virgin, Magdalen, Martha, and others awaited His coming near a certain well. It was two hours before sundown when He came up with them. The women cast themselves on their knees before Him and kissed His hand. Mary also kissed His hand, and when she arose, Jesus kissed hers. Magdalen stood somewhat back. At the well, the disciples washed Jesus' feet, also those of the Apostles, after which all partook of a repast. The women ate alone and, when their meal was over, took their places at the lower end of the dining hall to listen to Jesus' words. He did not remain at the inn, but went with the three Apostles to Jericho, where the rest of the Apostles and disciples along with numerous sick were assembled. The women followed Him. I saw Him going into many of the houses and curing the sick, after which He Himself unlocked the school and ordered a chair to be placed in the center of the hall. The holy women were present in a retired part. They had a lamp to themselves. Mary was with them. After the instruction, the holy women went back to their inn and on the following morning returned to their homes. Crowds were gathered at Jericho, for Jesus' coming had been announced by the disciples. During His teaching and healing on the following day, the pressing and murmuring of the Pharisees were very great, and they sent messengers to Jerusalem to report. Jesus next went to the place of Baptism on the Jordan where were lying numbers of sick in expectation of His coming. They had heard of His reappearance and had begged His aid. There were little huts and tents around, under which they could descend into the water. I saw too the basin in the little island in which He had been baptized. Sometimes it was full, but again, the water was allowed to run off. They came from all parts for this water, from Samaria, Judea, Galilee, and even from Syria. They loaded asses with large leathern sacks of it. The sacks hung on either side of the beast, and were kept together over the animal's back by hoops. Jesus cured numbers. Only John, Andrew, and James the

Less were with Him.

No Baptisms took place at this time, only ablutions and healing. Even the baptism of John had in it more of a sacramental character than the ablutions on this occasion. The last time that Jesus was in Jericho, many persons were healed at a bath in the city, but it was not Baptism. There was at this part of the Jordan a bathing place much resorted to, which John had merely enlarged. In the middle of the well on the island in which Jesus was baptized, the pole on which He had leaned was still standing. Jesus cured many without application of water, though He poured it over the heads of the leprous, and the disciples wiped them dry.

Baptism proper came into use only after Pentecost. Jesus never baptized. The Mother of God was baptized alone at the Pool of Bethsaida by John after Pentecost. Before the ceremony he celebrated Holy Mass, that is, he consecrated and recited some prayers as they were accustomed to do at that time.

When the crowd became too great, Jesus went with the three Apostles to Bethel, where the Patriarch Jacob saw on a hill the ladder reaching from earth to Heaven. It was already dark when they arrived and approached a house wherein trusty friends were awaiting them: Lazarus and his sisters, Nicodemus, and John Marc, who had come hither from Jerusalem secretly. The master of the house had a wife and four children. The house was surrounded by a courtyard in which was a fountain. Attended by two of his children, the master opened the door to the guests, whom he conducted at once to the fountain and washed their feet. As Jesus was sitting on the edge of the fountain, Magdalen came forth from the house and poured over His hair a little flat flask of perfume. She did it standing at His back, as she had often done before. I wondered at her boldness. Jesus pressed to His Heart Lazarus, who was still pale and haggard. His hair was very black. A meal was spread, consisting of fruit, rolls, honeycomb, and green herbs, the usual fare in Judea. There were little cups on the table. Jesus cured the sick who were lying in a building belonging to the house. The women ate alone and afterward ranged in the lower part of the hall to hear Jesus' preaching.

Next morning Lazarus returned to Jerusalem with his companions, while Jesus with the three Apostles went by a very circuitous route to the house of a son of Andrew's half-brother, whose daughter lay ill. They reached the well belonging to the house about noon. The master of the house, a robust man engaged in the manufacture of wicker screens, washed their feet and led them to his home. He had a great many children, some of them still quite small. Two grown sons from sixteen to eighteen years of age were not at home but at the fishery on the Sea of Galilee, in Andrew's dwelling place. Andrew had sent messengers to tell them that Jesus had returned, and to come to meet Him at a certain place.

After a repast, the man led Jesus and the Apostles to his sick daughter, a girl about twelve years old. For a long time she had been lying upon her bed perfectly pale and motionless. She had the greensickness, and she was also a simpleton. Jesus commanded her to arise. Then with Andrew He led her by the hand to the well, where He poured water over her head. After that, at the Lord's command, she took a bath under a tent, and returned to the house cured. She was a tall child. When Jesus with the Apostles left the place, the father escorted Him a part of the way. Before the hour of the Sabbath, Jesus reached a little city. He took up His quarters at an inn in the city wall, and then went at once with His followers to celebrate the Sabbath in the synagogue.

Next morning He went again to the synagogue, where He prayed and delivered a short instruction. I saw a great crowd around Him. They brought to Him numbers of sick of divers kinds, and He healed them. I saw that all the people of this place honored Jesus and pressed around Him. The concourse was great. The Apostles also cured and blessed; even the priests led the sick forward.

I saw Jesus cure in this place a leper who had often been carried and set down on the road He was to travel, but whom He had always passed by. They had, just before Jesus' coming, brought the poor creature from a distant quarter of the city, where he dwelt in a little abode built in the wall. They brought him to Jesus sitting on a couch in a kind of litter shut in by hangings. No one went near the sick man excepting Jesus, who raised the curtain, touched the invalid, and directed that he should be taken to the bath near the city wall. When this order was executed, the scales of leprosy fell from him. He had been afflicted by a double leprosy, for that of impurity was added to the ordinary disease. The Lord healed likewise many women of a flux of blood. When He was healing in the court outside the synagogue, the crowd was so great that the people tore down the barriers and climbed upon the roof.

On leaving this place, Jesus journeyed on with the three Apostles and reached a strong castle (*Alexandrium?*) surrounded by moats, or ponds with discharging channels attached. It seemed that there were baths here, and I saw all kinds of vaults and massive walls. When Jesus manifested His intention to enter this castle, the Apostles made objections to His doing so. He might, they said, rouse indignation and give occasion for scandal. Jesus rejoined that if they did not want to accompany Him, they should suffer Him to enter alone, and so He went in. It contained all sorts of people, some of whom appeared to be prisoners, others sick and infirm. Guards were standing at the gates, for the inmates dared not go out alone. Several always went together and attended by a guard. They were obliged to work in the country around the castle, clearing the fields and digging trenches. When Jesus with the Apostles attempted to pass through the gate, the guards stopped them, but at a word from Him, they respectfully allowed Him to enter. The inmates assembled around Him in the courtyard, where He spoke with them and separated several from the rest. From the city, which was not far off, Jesus summoned two men who appeared to be officers of the law, for they had little metallic badges hanging on straps from their shoulders. Jesus spoke with them, and it looked as if He were giving bail for those that He had separated from the rest of the inmates. Later on, I saw Him leaving the castle with five and twenty of those people, and with them and the Apostles travelling up the Jordan the whole night. This hurried march brought Him to a little city in which He restored to their wives and children several of the prisoners lately freed. Others crossed the Jordan higher up, and then turned to the east. They were from the country of Kedar where Jesus had taught so long before His journey to the star worshippers. Jesus sent the Apostles away on this road. When journeying through the valleys near Tiberias and past the well of Jacob, the three *silent* disciples and the other companions of His visit to the heathens joined Jesus. They continued their journey a part of the night, rested only a few hours under a shed, and toward evening of the next day arrived in Capharnaum. Here a young man called Sela, or Selam, was presented to Jesus. He was a cousin of the bridegroom of Kedar to whom Jesus had given the house and vineyard on the occasion of His journey to the star worshippers. It was the bridegroom who had sent Sela to Jesus, and he had been in Andrew's house awaiting His coming. He threw himself on his knees before Jesus, who imposed hands upon his shoulders and admitted him to the number of His disciples. Jesus made use of him at once, sending him to the superintendent of the school to demand the key and the roll of Scriptures that had been found in the Temple during the seven years that it had stood dilapidated and deprived of divine service. The last time Jesus taught here, He had made use of the same roll of Scriptures, which were from Isaias. When the youth returned, Jesus and His companions went into the school and lighted the lamps. Jesus directed a space to be cleared and a pulpit with a flight of steps to be placed in it. A great crowd was gathered, and Jesus taught a long time from the roll of Scriptures. The excitement in Capharnaum was very great. The people assembled on the streets, and I heard the cry: "There is Joseph's Son again!"

Jesus left Capharnaum before daylight next morning, and I saw Him going into Nazareth with the disciples and several of the Apostles who had joined Him. I saw on this occasion that Anne's house had passed into other hands. Jesus went also to Joseph's old home, now closed and unoccupied. Thence He proceeded straight to the synagogue. His appearance was the signal for great excitement among the people, who ran out in crowds. One possessed, who had a dumb devil, suddenly began to shout after Him: "There is Joseph's Son! There is the rebel! Seize Him! Imprison Him!" Jesus commanded him to be silent. The man obeyed, but Jesus did not drive the devil out of him.

In the school Jesus ordered room to be made and a teacher's chair to be set for Him. On this journey He acted with perfect freedom and taught openly as one having a right to do so, which proceeding greatly incensed the Jews against Him. He visited likewise many of the houses in the neighborhood of Joseph's old home, and healed and blessed the children; whereupon the Jews who during the instruction had been tolerably quiet, became extremely indignant. Jesus soon left the city, telling the Apostles to meet Him on the mount of the multiplication of the loaves, whither He went accompanied by the disciples only.

When they reached the mountain, it was already night, and fires were kindled on its summit. Jesus stood in the center, the Apostles ranged around Him, the disciples forming an outer circle. A considerable crowd had gathered. Jesus taught the whole night and until almost morning. He indicated to the Apostles, pointing with His finger here and there, whither they should go on their mission of healing and teaching. It looked as if He were giving them orders as to their journeys and labors for the time just about to follow. They and many of the disciples took leave of Him here, and at morning dawn He turned His steps southward.

On this journey Jesus was implored by a father and mother to go into their house and cure their daughter who was a lunatic, pale and sick. He commanded her to arise, and she was cured.

One hour's distance from Thanath-Silo all the Apostles, bearing green branches, came to meet Jesus. They prostrated before Him and He took one of the branches in His hand. Then they washed His feet. I think this ceremony took place because they were all again reunited, and because Jesus once more appeared openly as their Master and was about to preach again everywhere. Accompanied by the Apostles and disciples He went to the city, where the Blessed Virgin, Magdalen, Martha, and the other holy women, except Peter's wife and stepdaughter and Andrew's wife, who were still at Bethsaida, received Him outside an inn. Mary had come from the region of Jericho and had here awaited Jesus. The other women also had come hither by different routes. They prepared a meal of which fifty guests partook, after which Jesus, having ordered the key to be brought, repaired to the school. The holy women and a great many people listened to His instruction.

13. JESUS GOES TO BETHANIA

Next morning Jesus cured many sick of the city, although He passed before a number of houses without performing any cures. He healed also at the inn. After that He dismissed the Apostles, sending some to Capharnuam, and others to the place of the multiplication of the loaves. The holy women went to Bethania. Jesus Himself took the same direction, and celebrated the Sabbath at an inn with all the disciples whom He had brought back with Him from His great journey. They hung a lamp in the middle of the hall, laid a red cover on the table and over it a white one, put on their white Sabbath garments, and ranged round Jesus in the order observed at prayer. He prayed from a roll of writings. The whole party numbered about twenty. The Sabbath lamp burned the whole day, and Jesus alternately prayed and instructed the disciples in their duties. There was present a new disciple named Silvanus, whom Jesus had received in the last city. He was already thirty years old and of the tribe of Aaron. Jesus had known him from early youth, and looked upon him as His future disciple at the children's feast given by holy Mother Anne when, as a boy of twelve, He returned from His teaching in the Temple. It was at the same feast that He had chosen the future bridegroom of Cana.

On the way to Bethania, Jesus, to continue His instructions for the benefit of the new disciples, explained to them the *Our Father,* spoke to them of fidelity in His service, and told them that He would now teach awhile in Jerusalem, after which He would soon return to His Heavenly Father. He told them also that one would abandon Him, for treason was already in his heart. All these new disciples remained faithful. On this journey, Jesus healed several lepers who had been brought out on the road. One hour from Bethania, they entered the inn at which Jesus had taught so long before Lazarus's resurrection and to which Magdalen had come forth to meet Him. The Blessed Virgin also was at the inn with other women, likewise five of the Apostles: Judas, Thomas, Simon, James the Less, Thaddeus, John Marc, and some others. Lazarus was not there. The Apostles came out a part of the way to meet the Lord at a well, where they saluted Him and washed His feet, after which He gave an instruction which was followed by a meal. The women then went on to Bethania while Jesus remained at the inn with the rest of the party. Next day, instead of going straight to Bethania, He made a circuit around the adjacent country with the three silent disciples. The rest of the Apostles and disciples separated into two bands, headed respectively by Thaddeus and James, and went around curing the sick. I saw them effecting cures in many different ways: by the imposition of hands, by breathing upon or leaning over the sick person, or in the case of children, by taking them on their knees, resting them on their breast and breathing upon them.

On this journey, Jesus cured a man possessed by the devil. The parents of the young man ran after Jesus just as He was entering a little village of scattered houses. He followed them into the court of their house, where He found their possessed son who, at the Lord's approach, became furious, leaping about and dashing against the walls. His friends wanted to bind him, but they could not do it, as he grew more and more rabid, flinging right and left those that approached him. Thereupon Jesus commanded all present to withdraw and leave Him alone with the possessed. When they obeyed, Jesus called to the possessed to come to Him. But he, heeding not the call, began to put out his tongue and to make horrible grimaces at Jesus. Jesus called him again. He came not, but, with his head twisted over his shoulder, he looked at Him. Then Jesus raised His eyes to Heaven and prayed.

When He again commanded the possessed to come to Him, he did so and cast himself full length at His feet. Jesus passed over him twice first one foot and then the other, as if treading him underfoot, and I saw rising from the open mouth of the possessed a black spiral vapor which disappeared in the air. In this rising exhalation, I remarked three knots, the last of which was the darkest and strongest. These three knots were connected together by one strong thread and many finer ones. I can compare the whole thing to nothing better than to three censers one above the other, whose clouds of smoke, issuing from different openings, at last united with one another.

The possessed now lay like one dead at Jesus' feet. Jesus made over him the Sign of the Cross and commanded him to rise. The poor creature stood up. Jesus led him to his parents at the gate of the courtyard, and said to them: "I give you back your son cured, but I shall demand him again of you. Sin no more against him." They had sinned against him, and it was on that account that he had fallen into so miserable a condition.

Jesus now went to Bethania. The man just delivered and many others went thither also, some before Jesus, others after Him. Many of those that had been cured by the Apostles were likewise present in the city, and a great tumult arose when the cured everywhere proclaimed their happiness. I saw some priests go to meet Jesus and conduct Him into the synagogue, where they laid before Him a book of Moses from which they desired Him to teach. There were many people in the school, and the holy women were in the place allotted to females.

They went afterward to the house of Simon of Bethania, the healed leper, where the women had prepared a repast in the rented hall. Lazarus was not there. Jesus and the three silent disciples spent the night at the inn near the synagogue, the Apostles and other disciples at that outside Bethania; Mary and the other women stayed with Martha and Magdalen. The house in which Lazarus formerly dwelt was toward the Jerusalem side of the city. It was like a castle, surrounded by moats and bridges.

Next morning Jesus again taught in the school where among the many disciples present were Saturnin, Nathanael Chased, and Zacheus. Many sick had been brought to Bethania. In the house of Simon, the healed leper, a meal was again prepared, at which Jesus distributed all the viands to the poor and invited them to partake with the other guests. This gave rise to the report among the Pharisees and in Jerusalem that Jesus was a spendthrift who lavished upon the mob all that He could lay hands on.

While Jesus was teaching in the school, the crowds of sick, all men, were ranged in a double row of tents from the school to Simon's house. There were no lepers among them, for they showed themselves only in retired places. When Jesus approached the tents, three disciples followed Him like Levites, two on either side, but a little behind Him, and the third directly behind Him. There was no crowd. Jesus went up along one row of tents and down by the other, curing in various ways. He merely passed by some of the sick, and exhorted others without curing them. He told them that they should change their manner of life. Some He took by the hand and commanded to rise, while others He merely touched. One man affected with the dropsy, He stroked over the head and body with His hand, and the swelling immediately went down. The water poured from his whole person in a stream of perspiration. Many of the cured threw themselves prostrate at Jesus' feet. His companions raised them and led them away. When the Lord returned to the school, He caused the cured to be seated near Him, and then He taught.

I saw Jesus sending out the disciples two by two from Bethania into the country to teach and to heal. Some He told to return to Bethania, and others to Bethphage. He Himself with the three silent disciples journeyed a couple of hours southward from Bethania to a little village where He healed the sick. Here I saw Him going into the house of a man whom He had once cured of dumbness, but who having sinned again, had now become paralyzed. His hands and fingers were quite distorted. Jesus addressed to him some words of exhortation and touched him. The man arose. He healed likewise several girls who were lying pale and sick. Sometimes they lay unconscious as if dead, and again they alternately wept and laughed heartily. They were lunatics.

When, before the Sabbath, Jesus again returned to Bethania and went to the school, I heard the Jews boasting against Him that He could not yet do what God had done for the Children of Israel when He rained down manna for them in the desert. They were indignant against Jesus. Jesus passed the night this time not in Bethania, but outside in the disciples' inn.

While at this inn, three men came to Him from Jerusalem: Obed, the son of the old man Simeon, a Temple servant and a disciple in secret; the second, a relative of Veronica; and the third, a relative of Johanna Chusa. This last-mentioned became, later on, Bishop of Kedar. For a time also he lived as a hermit near the date trees that, on her flight into Egypt, had bent down their fruit to Mary that she might partake of it. These disciples asked why He had so long abandoned them, why He had in other places done so much of which they knew nothing. In His answer to these questions, Jesus spoke of tapestry and other precious things which looked new and beautiful to one that had not seen them for some time. He said also that if the sower sowed his seed all at once and in one place, the whole might be destroyed by a hailstorm, so the instructions and cures that were scattered far and wide would not soon be forgotten. Jesus' answers were something like the above.

These disciples brought the news that the High Priest and Pharisees were going to station spies in the places round Jerusalem in order to seize Him as soon as He appeared. Hearing this, Jesus took with Him only His two latest disciples, Selam of Kedar and Silvanus, and travelled the whole night with them to Lazarus's estate near Ginea, where Lazarus himself was then stopping. Two days previously he was in the little city between Bethania and Bethlehem, in the neighborhood of which the Three Kings had rested on their journey to the latter place; but on receiving a message from Jesus, he had left and gone to his estate. Jesus knew very well that the three disciples would bring Him this news from Jerusalem and that He Himself would leave Bethania, therefore it was that He had already passed two nights not in Bethania, but in the disciples' inn outside.

Jesus arrived before dawn (it was still dark) at Lazarus's estate and knocked at the gate of the courtyard. It was opened by Lazarus himself who, with a light, conducted Him into a large hall where were assembled Nicodemus, Joseph of Arimathea, John Marc, and Jairus, the younger brother of Obed.

I saw Jesus afterward with the two disciples again in Bethabara and Ephron, where He celebrated the Sabbath. Andrew, Judas, Thomas, James the Less, Thaddeus, Zacheus, and seven other disciples were present, having come hither from Bethania to meet Jesus. When Judas was about leaving Bethania, I saw the Blessed Virgin earnestly exhorting him to be more moderate, to watch over himself, and not interfere in affairs as he did.

In Ephron, Jesus healed the blind, the lame, the deaf and dumb, who had been brought thither for that purpose. He delivered one possessed also from the power of the devil.

On leaving Ephron, He went to a place north of

Jericho where there was an asylum for the sick and the poor. Here He restored sight to an old blind man whom once before, when engaged in healing, He had sent away, although at the same time He had restored sight to two others by anointing their eyes with salve made of clay mixed with spittle. He now cured this man by His word alone. The village was situated on His way.

From this last place Jesus returned to Lazarus's estate, and thence went with Lazarus to Bethania, whither the holy women came to meet Him.

ESSENTIAL CATHOLIC READING

At your bookdealer or direct from the Publisher.

ESSENTIAL CATHOLIC READING

At your bookdealer or direct from the Publisher.

ESSENTIAL CATHOLIC READING

At your bookdealer or direct from the Publisher.

ESSENTIAL CATHOLIC READING

At your bookdealer or direct from the Publisher.

ESSENTIAL CATHOLIC READING

Confession of a Roman Catholic . . . . Paul Whitcomb
The Catholic Church Has the Answer . . . . Paul Whitcomb
The Sinner's Guide . . . . Ven. Louis of Granada
True Devotion to Mary . . . . St. Louis De Montfort
Life of St. Anthony Mary Claret . . . . Fanchón Royer
Autobiography of St. Anthony Mary Claret . . . St. A. M. Claret
I Wait for You . . . . Sr. Josefa Menendez
Words of Love . . . Srs. Menendez, Betrone, Mary of the Trinity
Little Lives of the Great Saints . . . . John O'Kane Murray
The Rhine Flows into the Tiber . . . . Fr. Ralph Wiltgen
Prayer — The Key to Salvation. . . . . Fr. Michael Müller
Sermons on Our Lady . . . . St. Francis de Sales
The Victories of the Martyrs . . . . St. Alphonsus Liguori
Canons and Decrees of the Council of Trent. . . . . Schroeder
St. Dominic's Family . . . . Sr. Mary Jean Dorcy
Sermons for Every Sunday . . . . St. Alphonsus Liguori
What Faith Really Means . . . . Fr. Henry Graham
A Catechism of Modernism. . . . . Fr. J. B. Lemius
What Catholics Believe . . . . Fr. Lawrence Lovasik
Alexandrina — The Agony and the Glory . . . . Francis Johnston
Blessed Margaret of Castello. . . . . Fr. William Bonniwell
The Ways of Mental Prayer . . . . Dom Vitalis Lehodey
Who Is Teresa Neumann? . . . . Fr. Charles Carty
Summa of the Christian Life. 3 Vols. . . Ven. Louis of Granada
Fr. Paul of Moll — A Flemish Benedictine . . . . van Speybrouck
St. Francis of Paola. . . . . Simi and Segreti
Communion Under Both Kinds . . . . Michael Davies
Abortion: Yes or No?. Dr. John Grady
The Story of the Church . . . . Johnson, Hannan, Dominica
Religious Liberty . . . . Michael Davies
Hell Quizzes. . . . . Radio Replies Press
Indulgence Quizzes. . . . . Radio Replies Press
Purgatory Quizzes. Radio Replies Press
Virgin and Statue Worship Quizzes. . . . . . . Radio Replies Press
The Holy Eucharist . . . . St. Alphonsus
The Way of Salvation and of Perfection . . . . St. Alphonsus
The True Spouse of Jesus Christ. . . . . St. Alphonsus
Dignities and Duties of the Priest . . . . St. Alphonsus
Textual Concordance of The Holy Scriptures. . . . . Fr. Williams
Douay-Rheims Bible. . . . . Leatherbound

At your bookdealer or direct from the Publisher.

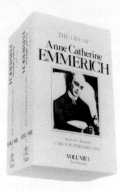